Art in the Anthropocene

Critical Climate Change

Series Editors: Tom Cohen and Claire Colebrook

The era of climate change involves the mutation of systems beyond 20th century anthropomorphic models and has stood, until recently, outside representation or address. Understood in a broad and critical sense, climate change concerns material agencies that impact on biomass and energy, erased borders and microbial invention, geological and nanographic time, and extinction events. The possibility of extinction has always been a latent figure in the textual production and archives; but the current sense of depletion, decay, mutation and exhaustion calls for new modes of address, new styles of publishing and authoring, and new formats and speeds of distribution. As the pressures and re-alignments of this re-arrangement occur, so must the critical languages and conceptual templates, political premises and definitions of "life." There is a particular need to publish in a timely fashion experimental monographs that redefine the boundaries of disciplinary fields, rhetorical invasions, the interface of conceptual and scientific languages, and geomorphic and geopolitical interventions. Critical Climate Change is oriented, in this general manner, toward the epistemo-political mutations that correspond to the temporalities of terrestrial mutation.

Art in the Anthropocene

Encounters Among Aesthetics, Politics, Environments and Epistemologies

Edited by Heather Davis and Etienne Turpin

OPEN HUMANITIES PRESS

London

2015

First edition published by Open Humanities Press 2015
Freely available online at
http://openhumanitiespress.org/books/art-in-the-anthropocene

Copyright © 2015 Heather Davis and Etienne Turpin,
chapters by respective Authors.

This is an open access book, licensed under Creative Commons By Attribution Non-Commercial No-Derivatives license. Under this license, authors allow anyone to download, display, print, distribute, and/or copy their work so long as: the authors and source are cited, the work is not altered or transformed, and the purpose is non-commercial. No permission is required from the authors or the publisher in these cases. Statutory fair use and other rights are in no way affected by the above. Read more about the license at: creativecommons.org/licenses/by-nc-nd/3.0.

Cover art, figures, and other media included with this book may be under different copyright restrictions. Please see the Permissions section at the back of this book for more information.

Cover Art Details: Mary Mattingly, House and Universe, 2013.
© Mary Mattingly.

ISBN-978-1-78542-005-4

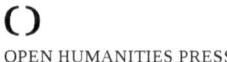
OPEN HUMANITIES PRESS

Open Humanities Press is an international, scholar-led open-access publishing collective whose mission is to make leading works of contemporary critical thought freely available worldwide. More at http://openhumanitiespress.org.

Contents

001	**Acknowledgements**
003	**Art & Death: Lives Between the Fifth Assessment & the Sixth Extinction** introduction by Heather Davis & Etienne Turpin
031	**Edenic Apocalypse:** **Singapore's End-of-Time Botanical Tourism** project by Natasha Myers
043	**Diplomacy in the Face of Gaia** Bruno Latour in conversation with Heather Davis
057	**Becoming Aerosolar:** **From Solar Sculptures to Cloud Cities** project by Tomás Saraceno, Sasha Engelmann & Bronislaw Szerszynski
063	**In the Planetarium:** **The Modern Museum on the Anthropocenic Stage** essay by Vincent Normand
079	**Physical Geology / The Library** project by Ilana Halperin
085	**The Existence of the World Is Always Unexpected** Jean-Luc Nancy in conversation with John Paul Ricco translated by Jeffrey Malecki
093	**Cloud Writing:** **Describing Soft Architectures of Change in the Anthropocene** essay by Ada Smailbegović
109	**The Cerumen Strata:** **From Figures to Configurations** project by Richard Streitmatter-Tran & Vi Le
117	**Geochemistry & Other Planetary Perspectives** essay by Ursula Biemann

131	**Images Do Not Show:** **The Desire to See in the Anthropocene** essay by Irmgard Emmelhainz
143	**The Fates of Negativity** Anselm Franke in conversation with Etienne Turpin
155	**Design Specs in the Anthropocene:** **Imagining the Force of 30,000 Years of Geologic Change** project by Jamie Kruse & Elizabeth Ellsworth (smudge studio)
167	**The Marfa Stratum:** **Contribution to a Theory of Sites** essay by Fabien Giraud & Ida Soulard
181	**On the Building, Crashing, and Thinking of** **Technologies & Selfhood** Peter Galison in conversation with Etienne Turpin
191	**We're Tigers** project by Ho Tzu Nyen
199	**Technologies of Uncertainty in the Search for MH370** essay by Lindsay Bremner
213	**Last Clouds** project by Karolina Sobecka
223	**Islands & Other Invisible Territories** essay by Laurent Gutierrez & Valérie Portefaix (MAP Office)
233	**Plants that Evolve (in some way or another)** project by Mixrice (Cho Jieun & Yang Chulmo)
241	**Indigenizing the Anthropocene** essay by Zoe Todd
255	**Anthropocene, Capitalocene, Chthulhocene** Donna Haraway in conversation with Martha Kenney

271	**Ecologicity, Vision, and the Neurological System** essay by Amanda Boetzkes
283	**My Mother's Garden:** **Aesthetics, Indigenous Renewal, and Creativity** essay by Laura Hall
293	**A History According to Cattle** project by Terike Haapoja & Laura Gustafsson
299	**PostNatural Histories** Richard W. Pell in conversation with Emily Kutil & Etienne Turpin
317	**Dear Climate** project by Una Chaudhuri, Fritz Ertl, Oliver Kellhammer & Marina Zurkow
327	**The Anthropocene:** **A Process-State at the Edge of Geohistory?** essay by Peter Sloterdijk, translated by Anna-Sophie Springer
341	**Public Smog** project by Amy Balkin
347	**Life & Death in the Anthropocene:** **A Short History of Plastic** essay by Heather Davis
359	**Ecosystems of Excess** project by Pinar Yoldas
371	**The Last Political Scene** Sylvère Lotringer in conversation with Heather Davis & Etienne Turpin
379	**#MISANTHROPOCENE:** **24 Theses** poem by Joshua Clover & Juliana Spahr
385	**Contributors**
401	**Permissions**

Acknowledgements

We would like to begin by thanking all the contributors to this volume for their patience and perseverance; the book is a machine for provocation because of your generosity, solidarity, and commitment. We are also grateful to Oscar Santos and Human Resources Los Angeles for hosting an early discussion of the book with Sylvère Lotringer. A very special thank you to Lucas A.J. Freeman for tireless interview transcription and editing, to Jeffrey Malecki for translation support and disturbingly thorough copy editing, to Erik Bordeleau for ad hoc translation support, and to Anna-Sophie Springer for advice, support, and translation in this collection. Thanks also to Mary Mattingly for sharing artwork for the cover, and to the Institute for Figuring for images of their beautiful crochet coral reef project. We also owe a debt of gratitude to Sara Dean for her patient and precise design of this book. This project has benefited tremendously from the advice and mentorship of our editors in the Critical Climate Change series, Claire Colebrook and Tom Cohen, as well as our allies at the Open Humanities Press, Sigi Jottkandt and David Ottina, to whom we are especially grateful for the chance to bring this collection together, and to make it available as an open-access publication.

Heather Davis owes an enormous debt of gratitude to all those who listened and provided advice on this project as it has unfolded, especially to Michael Nardone for his patience, love, and support throughout. I would also like to thank Elizabeth Grosz, Dehlia Hannah, Nicole Starosielski, Margaret Wertheim, and Ada Smailbegović for their friendship and intellectual generosity. This project would not have been possible without the financial support of the FQRSC. I am especially grateful to Michael Bérubé and the Institute for the Arts and Humanities for continued support.

Etienne Turpin would like to thank the many contributors to this volume who are also dear friends and collaborators, as well as the many friends, mentors, and colleagues who have shaped his views on the Anthropocene, including Nabil Ahmed, Lauren B. Allen, Brock Baker, George Beccaloni, Pierre Belanger, Andrew Berry, Lori Brown, Melissa Cate Christ, Nigel Clark, Sonja Dahl, Seth Denizen, Stefania Druga, Anna Feigenbaum, Matthias Glaubrecht, Jason Groves, Nasrin Himada, Stuart Kendall, Eduardo Kohn, Sanford Kwinter, Adrian Lahoud, Dian Ina Mahendra, Miho Mazereeuw, Kiel Moe, Rudolf Mrazek, Hammad Nasar, Dietmar Offenhuber, Godofredo Pereira, Karen Pinkus, Rick Prelinger, Simon Price, Robert Prys-Jones, Farid Rakun, Alessandra Renzi, Laura Rozek, Megan Shaw Prelinger, AbdouMaliq Simone, Kyle Steinfeld, Paulo Tavares, Jane Wolff, and Joanna Zylinska. A special thanks again to Sigi Jottkandt and David Ottina for their continued friendship and support. I would also like to thank my University of Wollongong senior colleagues Pascal Perez, Katina Michael, Lesley Head, as well as my research collaborators at the SMART Infrastructure Facility, especially Matthew Berryman, Robert Ogie, and

Rohan Wickramasuriya. A special thanks to Tomas Holderness for countless hours of conversation and collaboration, and my ongoing gratitude goes out to our incredible research team at PetaJakarta.org, without whom this work would not have been possible, especially Sara Dean, Yantri Dewi, Fitria Sudirman, Alifa Rachmadia Putri, Ariel Shepherd, Mohammad Kamil, Tatyana Kusumo, Olivia Dun, and Frank Sedlar. Finally, terimah kasih banyak to my colleagues in Indonesia from Universitas Indonesia, BPBD DKI Jakarta, Jakarta Timur, and Lembaga Ilmu Pengetahuan Indonesia, for their continued support, advice, humour, and hospitality.

Art & Death:
Lives Between the Fifth Assessment
& the Sixth Extinction

Heather Davis & Etienne Turpin

In the 1930s Henri Cartier-Bresson remarked indignantly, "The world is going to pieces and people like [Ansel] Adams and [Edward] Weston are photographing rocks!"[1] With his condemnation of the inorganic as an unworthy subject for photography, we understand Cartier-Bresson to be arguing for a more socially engaged art practice, one that would recognize the political economic realities of the Depression and the ways in which this decisively human context is precisely what allows art to share meaning and transform values. It is a strangely contemporary question: in the face of exploitation, brutality, and impoverishment, shouldn't art address human suffering and struggle? Such a perspective—albeit one contested by Adams even then—assumes a difference in kind between the shameful reality of human exploits and their stony substrate. It is remarkable that in less than a century we should find the terms of this debate uncannily entangled: what does it mean for art to encounter the Anthropocene? If art is now a practice condemned to a *homolithic earth*—that is, to a world "going to pieces" as the literal sediment of human activity—how can aesthetic practices address the social and political spheres that are being set in stone? Becoming-geological undoes aesthetic sensibilities and ungrounds political commitments. As such, this collection brings together a multitude of disciplinary conversations concerned with art and aesthetics that are emerging around the Anthropocene thesis, drawing together artists, curators, scientists, theorists, and activists to address the geological reformation of the human species.

Necessarily, this volume exceeds itself and its editors in every respect, reaching urgently beyond its paginated form toward environmental concerns, aesthetic predilections, epistemological limits, and ethical aporiae. We certainly didn't set out to contain the discourse of the Anthropocene, nor is it our intention to exhaust the potential lines of flight it provokes; the book is an intellectually dissipative structure, operating as a conceptual centrifuge for further speculation and future action. It is not from some desire to add another conjunctive term to the growing literature on the Anthropocene that we turn to art; rather, art, as the vehicle of *aesthesis*, is central to thinking with and feeling through the Anthropocene. And we believe the inherent relation between the two occurs at a number of strata and across various scales. First, we argue that the Anthropocene is primarily a sensorial phenomenon: the experience of living in an increasingly diminished and toxic world. Second, the way we have come to understand the Anthropocene has frequently been framed through modes of the visual, that is, through data visualization, satellite imagery, climate models, and other legacies of the "whole earth."[2] Third, art provides a polyarchic site of experimentation for "living in a damaged world,"[3] as Anna Tsing has called it, and a non-moral form of address that offers a range of discursive, visual, and sensual strategies that are not confined by the regimes of scientific objectivity, political moralism, or psychological depression.[4] To approach the panoply of complex issues that are aggregated within and adjacent to the Anthropocene, as well as their interconnections and intra-actions, it is necessary to engage with and encounter art.[5] But before going further, we'd like to get some formalities out of the way regarding the Anthropocene thesis.

As you've probably heard by now, the International Commission on Stratigraphy and the International Union of Geological Sciences are currently debating the relevant scientific merits of the so-called Anthropocene Epoch, which would allow the organization to recognize a diachronic rift separating the epoch of the Holocene—since the last Ice Age receded almost twelve millennia ago—from our current "human epoch."[6] The term was first popularized by the Dutch chemist Paul J. Crutzen in a 2002 paper he published in *Nature*, after which references to the Anthropocene began to appear within scientific publications regarding hydrospheric, biospheric, and pedospheric research.[7] As both an acknowledgement of this creeping informal nomenclature and an attempt to reify it with the requisite scientific standardization, in 2007, the British stratigrapher Jan Zalasiewicz, then serving as chairman of the Geological Society of London's Stratigraphy Commission, asked his colleagues to review the merits of these yet-to-be-substantiated (at least from the point of view of stratigraphic science) epochal claims. Since then, the Anthropocene thesis has made its way into a number of other scientific studies, as well as nearly every corner of the social sciences, humanities, and arts.

To determine whether or not the Anthropocene satisfies the necessary criteria for a new geological epoch, stratigraphers and geologists are considering various anthropogenic effects, including, but certainly not limited to: the rise of agriculture and attendant deforestation; the extraction of coal, oil, and gas, and their atmospheric consequences; the combustion of carbon-based fuels and emissions; coral reef loss; ocean acidification; soil degradation; a rate of life-form extinction occurring at thousands of times higher than throughout most of the last half-billion years; and, perhaps most surprisingly, a rate of human propagation—a completely unabated explosion in population growth—which, according to the renowned biologist E.O. Wilson, is "more bacterial than primate."[8]

Even from this abbreviated list of possible considerations, evidence suggests a dramatic human impact; however, from the point of view of geology, the obvious problem is that, unlike all other geological epochs (and the even longer eras within which they accumulate), the Anthropocene is still in the making. Because we cannot know precisely how the stratifications that register our anthropogenic effects will stack up, the stratigraphic assemblage of the Anthropocene is produced through a process of speculative geology, operating according to an intensive physical intertext of geohistories, present concerns, and future imaginaries. Not least among its intellectual virtues, this speculative dimension helps call attention to—and occasionally overturn—certain bad habits of thinking that allow humans to conceive of objects, whether micro- or hyper-, aesthetic or mundane, as distinct from the processes of their emergence and decay.[9]

Of course, speculative considerations regarding the legibility of anthropogenic change also stir up the disputatious matter of when the period can be said to have begun.[10] Three dominant positions now shape the geological debate. In the estimation of paleoclimatologist William Ruddiman, the eight-thousand-year-old invention of agriculture and its attendant deforestation led to an increase in atmospheric carbon dioxide; this suggests that humans have been a primary geological force on the planet since nearly the beginning of the Holocene, making the Anthropocene nearly co-extensive with the last eleven and a half thousand years, since the most recent ice age. Crutzen has suggested his own date for the beginning of the epoch, putting the invention of the steam engine in the late-eighteenth century at the beginning of an uninterrupted rise in carbon dioxide emissions that can be read in ice-core samples. This date might be more precisely located in 1789, the year that witnessed the invention of the steam engine by James Watt—the technology that enabled human forces to exceed the modest limits of muscle- (whether human or animal), wind-, and water-power—as well as the publication of Immanuel Kant's essay, "What is Enlightenment?" This date is thus especially peculiar, since, for Crutzen, the moment at which human and natural history become inseparable coincides with the most decisive event of their (philosophical) separation, Kant's alleged "Copernican Revolution."[11] Finally, a decisive mark for the beginning of this new epoch could be located in the irradiated soil that is immediately apparent in the sedimentary records following the bombing of Hiroshima and Nagasaki,[12] and at the test sites on appropriated Indigenous territories. Not only did the end of WWII mark the proliferation of these radionuclides, but it also designated the dramatic postwar spike in population growth, consumption, and technological development referred to as the "Great Acceleration."[13] This potential starting point would also highlight the recent explosive growth of the global human population, which now exceeds seven billion.[14]

In his remarkable essay reflecting on nuclear catastrophe from Hiroshima to Fukushima, the philosopher Jean-Luc Nancy makes an appeal to remain "exposed," that is, to endure our encounter with catastrophic loss by allowing ourselves to sense it. If we move too quickly, even catastrophes, like everything else under capitalism, become little more than general equivalents of exchange. "We are being exposed to a catastrophe of meaning," Nancy asserts, adding, "Let's not hurry to hide this exposure under pink, blue, red, or black silks. Let us remain exposed, and let us think about what is happening [*ce qui nous arrive*] to us: Let us think that it is we who are arriving, or are leaving."[15] The Anthropocene invites these considerations of arrival and departure, ones that are variously taken up throughout the book. The broad areas of concern that form the subtitle of this book are too common among the contributions, and too entangled within each contribution, to be parcelled out sectionally; we thus decided to leave the book as a collection of forces, vectors, concerns, and perspectives that can be engaged and read in multiple orders. While the collection itself is not divided thematically, we nevertheless want to provide a few lines of entry—lines that have animated our own thinking, writing, and activism—to the volume that follows. In order to embrace this abundance without reducing it to generalities, the remainder of the introduction proceeds according to four especially intense trajectories of the Anthropocene. We begin with "Extrapolations Beyond Geology," examining how the proposal for an era of the *anthropos* has both disrupted and enticed other intellectual orbits well beyond stratigraphy and geology; in "Aesthesis and Perception," we address the role of sensation in constituting experience, as well as the potential for sharing sensation across genres, disciplines, and species; we then move to "Spatial Politics to Contested Territories" in order to narrate some of the critical transformations within the field of aesthetics that have occurred over the last half century, as tools for data visualization, forensics, and territorial analysis have shaped art in both concept and practice; finally, in "Numeracy and the Survival of Worlds," we consider the role of numeracy as a requisite epistemic guide for temporal knowledges dealing in difficult-to-conceive sequences of time, such as the Anthropocene. We conclude this introduction by asking what imaginaries might be possible under the sign of the Anthropocene, and how they could be constructed to refuse both false hope and the apocalyptic foreclosure of possible futures. We also want to acknowledge that whatever the outcome of the International Stratigraphic Commission in considering the merits of the Anthropocene thesis, the cultural, aesthetic, and theoretical implications of this discourse are neither isomorphic, nor easily dismissed. What follows, then, might be considered a propositional itinerary, accompanied by some preliminary heuristics, for encountering art in the Anthropocene.

Extrapolations Beyond Geology

> This is exactly what I fear with the Anthropocene thesis; it proposes a "future perfect continuous" tense, which puts theorists into a very agreeable position.
>
> — Isabelle Stengers[16]

Beyond the stratigraphic discussion, the Anthropocene can be felt as a call to re-imagine the human through biology and geology.[17] It is a call, in other words, to place our industrialized present—a present that consumes time itself—within a temporal frame that is at once evolutionary and geologic. As a charismatic mega-concept (and one that seems to herald its own extinction through its enunciation), it emphasizes the need, as Donna Haraway says, "for a word to highlight the urgency of human impact on this planet, such that the effects of our species are literally written into the rocks."[18] The Anthropocene is a term that beckons environmental justice thinking, asking what worlds we are intentionally and inadvertently creating, and what worlds we are foreclosing while living within an increasingly diminished present. It has become a concept that speaks not just to the hallmarks of our time, such as climate change and the so-called Sixth Extinction, but creates a need to think through the interconnections and interactions of these events in conjunction with political economic logics and their attendant debts to the future.[19] This is because, despite its emergence from a relatively unknown corner of the geological sciences, the Anthropocene is a collective assemblage of scientific enunciation that is also an inherently political concept, albeit one that many critics have suggested remains inadequate for describing the present situation.

As many contributors to this volume make clear, the devastation that characterizes the Anthropocene is not simply the result of activities undertaken by the species *Homo sapiens*; instead, these effects derive from a *particular* nexus of epistemic, technological, social, and political economic coalescences figured in the contemporary reality of petrocapitalism. This petrocapitalism represents the heightened hierarchical relations of humans, the continued violence of white supremacy, colonialism, patriarchy, heterosexism, and ableism, all of which exacerbate and subtend the violence that has been inflicted upon the non-human world. The dissatisfaction with the term Anthropocene, due to its etymological obfuscation of these forms of specific and historical violence, has lead to a proliferation of alternative terms, with "Capitalocene" the most widely circulated alternate designation for our contemporary epoch.[20] The Capitalocene, as articulated by Donna Haraway, points directly to a voracious political economic system that knows no bounds, one where human lives, the lives of other creatures, and the beauty and wealth of the earth itself are figured as mere resources and externalities. "Profit above all else," the logical extension of the surplus value accumulated through colonialism and slavery, has proven to be the most destructive force the world has ever seen. In the Judeo-Christian tradition, it is the law that is written in stone; in the Anthropocene, it is the violence of a lawless, murderous order called capitalism. If the Anthropocene calls us to imagine humanity written into the rock of the Earth itself, capitalism is the instrument of this brutal inscription, for it is not the products of *humanity* that will come to be stratified, but the externalities of Monsanto and Dupont, the radiation of nuclear bombs, and the oil spills of Exxon Mobile, as Haraway makes clear in this volume. In other words, figuring the Anthropocene as a "species question" hides the most significant problem of our present situation: the asymmetrical power relations that have resulted in the massive transformation of the Earth through industrialized agriculture, resource extraction, energy production, and petrochemicals. Nevertheless, using the Anthropocene to simply restate one's political commitments more emphatically, without addressing the pressing questions of population growth, technological interdependencies, and the contingent obligations of human settlement patterns, is an exercise in ideological futility; finding new approaches to posing problems is the work of both making art and making theory in the Anthropocene.[21]

To emphasize the historical specificity of the Anthropocene, Jean-Luc Nancy and Peter Sloterdijk both propose the term "Technosphere" in order to emphasize the significance of the Industrial Revolution in Europe, and to name technological processes as well as the attendant belief in a teleological orientation to technology. This, of course, is not detached from particular people and particular epistemologies named by Sloterdijk's alternate designation, the "Eurocene."[22] Indeed, a word like Eurocene might open up spaces for thinking more coherently about the colonial implications of the Anthropocene, which are made even more explicit by the term "Plantationocene."[23] In a recent article published in *Nature*, Simon Lewis and Mark Maslin argue that the Anthropocene should be dated to 1610 (the "Orbis Spike"), as the Columbian Exchange "led to the largest population replacement in the past 13,000 years, the first global trade networks linking Europe, China, Africa, and the Americas, and the resultant mixing of previously separate biotas."[24] This biological evidence for the Anthropocene also highlights how these systems of globalization and trade were dependent on genocide and slavery. The Anthropocene, by this dating, is thus the era of colonial genocide.

In this collection, Laura Hall and Zoe Todd both insist on an ethical relationality with Indigenous Peoples and philosophies to begin the process of decolonization, one that would help us move away from the conditions that created the Anthropocene, and perhaps from the notion of the Anthropocene itself. Hall writes: "As vitally important as it is to take on the human and ecological challenges facing our species as a result of environmental degradation, perspectives that do not seek to understand the Creation stories and truths of Indigenous Peoples globally—and which pin evolutionary nihilism equally on all groups involved throughout time and history—exacerbate existing ecologically damaging colonial relationships."[25] Todd argues forcefully in her essay that the increasing prominence of the Anthropocene is tantamount to a colonizing move, as a space marked by white supremacy—or what Sara Ahmed has called "white men as buildings"—that serves to erase other ways of being and other kinds of knowledge, epistemologies that are often drawn on implicitly without proper citation or acknowledgement. Rather, the move toward an ethical relationality that Todd highlights would bring attention to the processes of engagement, and require the time and commitment to the deep, difficult work of decolonization, coupled with what Deborah Bird Rose, drawing from the Indigenous epistemologies of the Victoria River District of the Northern Territory in Australia, calls "taking care of country."[26] Todd writes:

> Rather than engage with the Anthropocene as a teleological fact implicating all humans as equally culpable for the current socio-economic, ecological, and political state of the world, I argue that we should turn to examining how other peoples are describing our "ecological imagination." To tackle the intertwined and complex environmental crises in which the world finds itself, a turn towards the reciprocity and relationships that [Dwayne] Donald addresses in his writings and talks must be seriously considered, as locally informed responses to *in situ* challenges around the globe cannot be constructed using one philosophical, epistemological, or ontological lens.[27]

In a move to think through the entangled relations that might better describe our present moment, Haraway also proposes the "Chthulucene," "after the diverse earth-wide tentacular powers and forces and collected things with names like Naga, Gaia, Tangaro (burst from water-full Papa), Terra, Haniyasu-hime, Spider Woman, Pachamama, Oya, Gorgo, Raven, A'akuluujjusi, and many many more."[28] These compose "a litter of the tentacular dreadful [ones] without gender," the ones "who become with each other in and from the slimy mud and brine, in tangled temporalities that evade binaries like modern and traditional."[29] This move helps to make explicit that the Anthropocene is not merely descriptive; it is a social imaginary that has exceeded its intended categorization and whose parameters delimit ways of thinking about the world well beyond the confines of geo-scientific debate. Although the names Eurocene, Technocene, Capitalocene, and Plantationocene are necessary political interventions to draw attention to the origins of our current planetary situation, do we really want the epoch to be named as such for the next 10,000 years?[30] Isn't there a necessity to think *with* geology and biology, with the power of imagining all that might take place, rather than condemning our descendants to live in a world perpetually marked by the events of a few hundred years? As Bruno Latour suggests in this volume, perhaps the best way to fight capitalism is not to grant it this kind of enduring power, but to instead take a deflationary approach. As Latour remarks, "Let's limit the numbers of things that you can attribute to capitalism and let's distribute them and see what's actually happening. […] I mean: don't overdo it, don't exaggerate what you grant, even if you are fighting it."[31] This task demands of us a social imaginary that takes us far beyond our increasingly shortsighted present, into geological and biological futures.

The most obvious point of departure in popular discussions of such futures within the mainstream media is the environmental crisis.[32] The most substantial summary of this crisis, to date, has come in the form of Fifth Assessment Report of the Intergovernmental Panel on Climate Change; this report and its predecessors—one from each of the main Working Groups and the Synthesis Report—are comprised of the findings from thousands of scientific studies related to the climate of the Earth System, as well as an edited and collated summary.[33] Meanwhile, there is a growing awareness that the Earth System has entered a mass-extinction event, similar to the previous five documented great extinctions that have occurred on the planet.[34] The Anthropocene can be understood as the geological record of these two events, or the registering of their facticity—this is its profound "environmental" question. Yet, environmental discourses and sentiments are mobilized within petrocapitalism according to a multitude of agendas; the "environment" can never be assumed as a universal sign. Natasha Myers explores the sanitized environment as a cynical form of spectacle in the context of Singapore's "Gardens by the Bay," asking what other environmental imaginaries are possible.[35] The public perception of environmental risk and its aesthetic of smog is addressed in the work of Amy Balkin, who intervenes in both the generalized apathy and bureaucratic lethargy that suffuse contemporary environmental discourse.[36] Pinar Yoldas adds to this discussion of the Anthropocene environment an excessive projection of bio-futures, imagining extreme forms-of-life that will inherent and thrive on the wasted Earth.[37] With regard to the mode of address and public discourse, Marina Zurkow, Oliver Kellhammer, Fritz Ertl, and Una Chaudhuri's project "Dear Climate" attempts to reposition the paste-up aesthetic and intervene in the false solemnity plaguing neoliberal discussions of climate change.[38] Between two largely inconceivable events—the realization of irreversible climate change and the horizon of a mass extermination—the environmental crisis beckons art practice to re-imagine futures beyond the cynical recklessness of the myopic capitalist horizon.

The generalized instability co-produced by climate change, mass extinction, and the resource wars that characterize the Anthropocene has also begun to register within discourses of governance and bureaucracy. These discussions range from the call for a planetary form of "Earth System governance" to condemnations of the cynical view of human action and organization underpinning the contemporary fetishization of "resilience" to the extremities of the Anthropocene.[39] Inevitably, questions of governance in this context require a consideration of various systems of systems—the illegible and often invisible infrastructure that coordinates much of modern human survival—a concern we return to in more detail below. It is clear that much of what passes for governance is no longer a matter of democratic representation. Instead, as Maurizio Lazzarato has presciently observed, "For neoliberals, the state, although continuing to intervene, must 'assist' capital alone, assuring, on the one hand, the distribution of revenue to the advantage of business, creditors, and the wealthiest of the population, and, on the other hand, the privatization of all welfare-state services. [...] The state is no longer able to represent the general interest; on the contrary, it is radically subordinated to financial logic, functioning as a component part of its mechanisms."[40] Through these axiomatics of state capitalism "governance" is enacted, ruthlessly appropriating every mechanism available that might expedite accumulation for further investment and expulsion.[41] And remarkably, it is this vast, interconnected, and highly coordinated extermination of difference in the name of the "general equivalence" of profit that retains the name "civilization."[42]

Civilizational collapse, then, is no longer a matter of fanaticism or apocalypse, but a casual *fait accompli*.[43] Indeed, there are even studies to tell us what our remains, following various catastrophic events, might look like to some other entities that would find our ruined planet worthy of study.[44] The psychotechnical effects coincident with such implosive planetary scenarios, whether realized or indefinitely deferred by an infinite cascade of contained catastrophes, are completely unprecedented. As Baudrillard makes explicit, there is simply no reason to assume that the psychosocial faculties of the human species are capable of enduring the aggregated outcomes of human activity. To keep pace with the flood of reports attempting to document the collapse, it often seems as if psychological, affective, and environmental crises are all racing to outstrip one another in the spectacle of what Sylvère Lotringer calls, in this volume, the "last political scene."[45] Sleepless, anxious, and hyper-mediated: it looks to some like our affluent zones are beginning to suffer from collapse fatigue—and yet the implications of our actions are only just beginning to reveal themselves.[46] Among this scene and its spinoff 'cenes, the cumulative effects of human activity are producing a "homolith" that needs to be addressed not simply through staid political, economic, and rational approaches, but through the aesthetic, creative, and imaginative acts that define contemporary art practice.

Aesthesis & Perception

> Once the science of synthesis [...] is underway, what happens to artistic renditions of the natural world?
>
> —Esther Leslie[47]

The Anthropocene can be framed as the global condition of being born into a world that no longer exists, as Bill McKibben has recently claimed.[48] We are all "being overtaken by processes that are unmaking the world that any of us ever knew," Deborah Bird Rose asserts.[49] This overtaking is primarily an aesthetic event. Our sensorial and perceptive systems are being refashioned at rates that we can barely keep up with, as the world around us changes so rapidly. We daily experience what used to be a sublime moment; anthropogenic mountains are now so ordinary that we don't even notice them. Nicholas Mirzoeff has argued that Impressionism and other artistic genres might be usefully re-read through the lens of our de-sensitization to the world around us. He writes, "[t]he aesthetics of the Anthropocene emerged as an unintended supplement to imperial aesthetics—it comes to seem natural, right, then beautiful—and thereby anaesthetized the perception of modern industrial pollution."[50] His insight could be equally applied to the ever more colourful sunsets caused by particulate matter in the atmosphere, or to the aestheticized presentation of environmental destruction or explosive urbanization in the photographs of Edward Burtynksy and Vincent Laforet, respectively. Whether framing Anthropocene aesthetics through the arts or our sensory experience of an increasingly unpredictable world, "The Anthropocene is so built in to our senses that it determines our perceptions, hence it is aesthetic."[51] The fact that we have become so anaesthetized to these realities necessitates a reconsideration of the historical avant-garde. Beyond the modernist valorization of the principle of shock in art, our current climate demands a different kind of aesthetic and sensorial attention. In *Regarding the Pain of Others*, Susan Sontag presciently warned: "Shock can become familiar. Shock can wear off."[52] There is no shock that could be greater than that of realizing the scope and scale of the human transformation of the world.

Amanda Boetzkes, drawing upon Inuit observations that "the world has tilted on its axis," also argues for the re-ordering of our biological perception under the Anthropocene: "It appears that Husserl's idea of the earth as 'original ark' is now obsolete; we now have to recalibrate our sensorial systems to adjust to contradiction, catastrophe, and ecological volatility born of human activities that override and neutralize long-standing histories of local knowledge. The Anthropocene has altered the terms and parameters of perception itself."[53] These terms and parameters of perception are not limited to humans: as we are shaping the world around us, significant among these shifts are the effects our companion plants and animals, be they fruit flies, chickens, or trees. Not only have we greatly reduced the amount of diversity of domestic plants and animals, but, as Richard Pell points out in a wide-reaching conversation with Emily Kutil, these organisms have been shaped by human intention.[54] The Museum for Postnatural History documents the ways in which we have bred plants and animals to have certain kinds of characteristics, the cumulative effects of which have re-shaped the collective perceptions and sensations of organisms on the earth—it is not just the number of species that are being reduced, but entire ways of feeling, thinking, acting, and being.[55]

One problem is that we are adapting so quickly to these new terms and conditions, both by shielding ourselves through various technological apparatuses (for those who can afford to do so) and through ingenious survival strategies, that it is often difficult to remark on these new perceptual and sensorial realities. In response to the obvious demands that new ecological conditions are making on people, such as the increased movement of climate refugees from Sub-Saharan Africa and Southeast Asia, or Northern peoples who are literally watching their ways of life vapourize, the arts can become a way of attuning to new realities. In her contribution to this collection, Ursula Biemann attends most carefully to these fraught naturecultures, not least in her work *Egyptian Chemistry*, which examines the "specific material-mental configuration" of metachemistry along the Nile that opens up new connections, times, and perceptions within the mediatized spaces of the Anthropocene.[56] Similarly, Mixrice follows the transplantation of a thousand-year-old tree from its original location to an apartment complex where it acts as decoration, tracking to the strange allegiances that are formed among those who are called upon to protect the trees. As Ada Smailbegović evokes in her lyrical essay on "cloud writing," poetry—the craft of "attending to," through thick, layered, and repetitive description—opens different modes of perception through a detailed awareness of time and movement. Time is central to the conceptualization of the Anthropocene, for it forces evolutionary and geological considerations into Western thought. As Smailbegović argues, "many of the temporalities that are relevant for developing a politics of time in the Anthropocene—such as minute and incrementally accumulating processes of change, or the long duration of geological time, or even the temporal rhythms relevant to particular non-humans—may not be directly available to the human sensorium."[57] Indeed, this is what so many of the artistic interventions in this book attempt to fathom: the various times that pass through ours, the ways in which time can bend and elongate, and how time is written into our bodies, composing the relations we have to all the other things around us. Time, as Richard Streitmatter-Tran and Vi Le make clear in their contribution about the Cerumen Strata, is the accumulation of a lifetime of passing through environments that offer certain kinds of affordances, which then influence the collective perceptions and sensations of the organisms of the Earth. Attuning ourselves, through poetry, art, and description, to pay attention to other times; developing techniques to begin to think through the limits of our temporal frameworks, and then thinking beyond them—these are crucial practices; in fact, they are matters of survival.[58]

If we are to learn to adapt in this world, we will need to do so with all the other creatures; seeing from their perspective is central to re-organizing our knowledge and perceptions. The ability to think the human *species* implied by the terminology of the Anthropocene within a particular *Umwelt* (a concept proposed by Jakob von Uexküll) affords us the possibility of opening up and onto the life worlds of other species. To think of ourselves as biological organisms first, as one type among the worlds of other critters, allows for more open and curious relations to the other beings with whom we co-compose the world.[59] This kind of meta-species thinking—exposing the interconnections, while allowing other animals to come to the fore—unfolds in Terike Haapoja and Laura Gustafsson's "A History According to Cattle" and Ho Tzu Nyen's "We're Tigers". In the former, Haapoja and Gustafsson re-frame history from the point of view of cows, inviting the viewer to see not only the life-form of a biological organism, but its forms of life, its culture, and its ways of creating lineage and history.[60] Meanwhile, the latter portrays the importance of tigers in Malay culture, blurring the distinction between the human and the tiger, and thereby displaying on a visceral level how the human is completely entangled with the (unseen) other. Indeed, this is why "the Javanese do not, after sundown, utter the word *macan* (tiger) for fear of invoking its presence."[61] To acknowledge this predatory dimension of nature, to recognize both danger and fear, is no less critical to a multispecies perspective than is welcoming among our human worlds the multitude of worlds composed by our companions.

From Spatial Politics to Contested Territories

> You can't write poems about trees when the woods are full of policemen.
>
> —Bertolt Brecht[62]

Throughout the twentieth century, the relationship between art, land use, and politics has been highly fraught. Within the context of art and art theory over the last five or six decades, we can detect a significant transition in North American and European visual culture: as the concept and practice of art has moved increasingly to consider the material configuration of the world, thereby bringing the gallery into everyday life, the scale, range, and granularity of artistic inquiry have all undergone notable mutations. In *Evictions: Art and Spatial Politics*, Rosalyn Deutsche attempts to bring the political struggles of urban life under neoliberalism more fully into the register of art discourse, notably in her reading of Krzysztof Wodiczko's work. She writes: "To challenge the image of the homeless person as a disruption of the normal urban order, it is crucial to recognize that this 'intrusive' figure points to the city's true character. Conflict is not something that befalls an originally, or potentially, harmonious urban space. Urban space is the product of conflict."[63] As art discourse encountered urban struggles and transformed its terms of engagement, there was also a need to address the various other trajectories of animating art practice; to understand these forces and the transitions they fostered, it is necessary to follow closely the curatorial practice and theoretical writing of Lucy Lippard. Her curatorial work, in the "number shows" of the late 1960s and early 1970s, already began to break away from the confines of urban space to explore zones of interactivity between human settlements, resource areas, conceptual frames, and feminist practices. Land art, public art, earth art, and sculpture in the expanded field all began to move away from gallery- or studio-based work following larger trends in conceptualism and minimalism, questioning the relationship between the organic and inorganic, and the territories that such divisions both relied on and made possible.[64] This work spans a range of strategies and movements too numerous to detail here, from crude, large-scale installations that merely re-presented the formalism of modernist sculpture to the embedded propositions of Helen and Newton Harrison, and from pointed and humorous critiques such as those of Ant Farm to Robert Smithson's "Abstract Geology," which engaged with the entanglements of materiality and intellection; these practices and their attendant provocations can thus be read on a longer arc of artist-led inquiry that arrives in the present with post-conceptual art projects like the Center for Land Use Interpretation, and also includes many of the artists in this volume (not least of which is Mary Mattingly, whose work appears on the cover). What is particularly interesting in this movement from the studio to the landfill is that the role of art becomes equally contentious *and* exploratory; its position is opened up to inquiry in ways that remain inconclusive and open-ended, but nevertheless political and partisan. This ability to sustain contradiction while interrogating the very modes of its production is especially valuable when engaging the scale and scope of the Anthropocene.

In this volume, Vincent Normand's essay "In the Planetarium" follows a course through the modern museum to examine how its spatial logics echo and reinforce what he calls the "ontological template" established by the scientific, political, and aesthetic project of modernity. Critical to Normand's argument is an understanding of the space of art—the museum—as "an imminent entity in the anthropological matrix of modernity, inseparable from its dynamic lines of transfer between subjects and objects, purification and hybridization."[65] It is Normand's ambition to contest the very terms of this territory by returning again to the spatial configurations that produced its normative topology. Ida Soulard and Fabien Giraud also address the space of reason within the configuration of modern art practice and the legacies of Donald Judd.[66] For Soulard and Giraud, the concepts of site and site-specificity both require reformatting in the wake of the Anthropocene thesis; such reconfigurations of spatial reasoning enable new modes of navigation and new vehicles for inquiry. Both of these pieces thus bring the question of memory into the logic of spatial configuration. The contested territory of the Anthropocene is not only an expanded field; it is a positioning with regards to time rendered elastic through the conceptual tools of epistemic archaeology, which extracts other, non-dominant lineages and genealogies.[67]

In the twenty-first century, the spatial enframing of the Earth as "resource" is also complicated by the proliferation and ubiquity of communication technologies.[68] Not only does the mining of rare earth metals and minerals significantly impact the surface of the Earth, but the role these technologies play in systems of surveillance, control, and social mediation, as well as the obsolete detritus produced by such systems, both on Earth and in orbit, demand scrutiny. Trevor Paglen's stunning landscape photography of military black sites helps to illustrate how these shadow worlds of advanced technology anchor and animate many realities we take for granted; increasingly, we realize that it is precisely through mediated systems, information and communications technologies, and their planetary-scale infrastructures that the project of "governance" is manifest in the Anthropocene.[69] The pressures of political economic structures and the machinations of corporate actors have long disturbed any presumed autonomy of art or the "art world," as the remarkable cartographic work of Paglen's predecessor Mark Lombardi demonstrates so well. But, what is most critical to a minor genealogy of art in the Anthropocene is a definitive recognition that what we are here calling "art" is produced according to an "internal" logic of lineages and referents, but also by way of innumerable external social pressures, technical innovations, and geopolitical transformations that also shape the spatial tactics and operative strategies of contemporary art practice.

The dynamic interaction between "art" and its outside is especially evident among the shifting formats of dissemination for art production—Smithson's so-called "printed matter."[70] Moving away from banal academic standards, art historians, and art critics, the transformation of art publishing—beginning with artist books and artist-led publishing ventures in the 1960s and 1970s—changed art practice and its media, but also fed back into cultural discourse and helped enable projects like Zone Books, which further intervened from a new hybrid perspective in the fields of aesthetics and art theory. Through these collective assemblages of enunciation, the conceptual terrain of art at the end of the twentieth century moved increasingly away from deconstruction and psychoanalysis toward an open field of naturecultures, infrastructure assemblages, and other newly contested territories. Publications like *Zone 1/2: The Contemporary City,* edited by Michel Feher and Sanford Kwinter, and *Zone 6: Incorporations,* edited by Jonathan Crary and Sanford Kwinter, opened the door to a more lithe, materialist mode of spatial inquiry that relied on design, theory, and erratic, polyvalent research practices, thereby eliding the rigid categories of "art," "design," and "research."[71] More recently, the work of Eyal Weizman and the Forensis group has pushed questions of spatial politics beyond the mere physical traces of conflict, moving into the shifting conceptual terrain of evidence production, forensic aesthetics, and remote-sensing and satellite imagery within the context of various modes of violence.[72] Finally, collections such as *Sensible Politics: The Visual Culture of Nongovernmental Activism*, edited by Meg McLagan and Yates McKee, have convincingly brought together questions of visual culture in the context of activist practice and political struggle.[73] What is notable among these respective endeavours is that they challenge the inherited spatial politics of art practice in order to further break apart categories and disciplines, looking more attentively for what works than for what it means—including appropriated technical tools, programs, platforms, and software that have dramatically influenced approaches to art-as-research and exhibition-led inquiry.

And yet, the widespread availability of imagery from remote-sensing satellites, the accessibility of GPS-enabled devices, and the proliferation of open-source GIS software have not arrived in the artist's toolbox for free.[74] Paul Edwards has carefully described the transfer of technologies from the military to the world of civilian and commercial operations, noting how these passages are never fully defined in advance[75]; the same technological apparatuses that were created for the purposes of war have also been essential to international collaboration in the context of climate change.[76] Still, the transfer of tools and technologies into civilian life and artistic practice requires a deeper understanding of the commercial and military substratum of contemporary capitalism, as argued by Heather Davis in her essay on plastic in this volume. Joshua Clover and Juliana Spahr also make explicit that a #misanthropocene insurgency requires the rearrangement of the material infrastructure of the world along disruptive, aesthetic lines: "This is how to set an oil well on fire. Rub and lean against it. Spread your front legs and swing your neck at it. The power of a blow depends on the weight of your skull and the arc of your swing. Then sparks."[77]

Numeracy and the Survival of Worlds

> One two three four five six seven eight nine
> What I use in the battle for the mind.
>
> —Chuck D[78]

Within the global political economy, numeracy has become an increasingly valuable form of knowledge. We don't only mean the vicissitudes of the stock market, the parameters of predatory algorithms, or the veracity of the latest polls within our failing democracies; in fact, these representations don't matter so much in the Anthropocene. Instead, we mean the seemingly endless flow of numbers within the hyper-mediated spectacle of terminal capitalism: 400 PPM of atmospheric CO_2. Seven billion people. "One in eight birds, one in four mammals, one in five invertebrates, one in three amphibians, and half of all turtles facing extinction."[79] Consuming 400+ years of planetary biomass per day as fossil fuel. The future, too, is also increasingly represented as a long string of numbers: a global temperature rise of plus or minus two degrees Celsius, or plus or minus three degrees Celsius, or plus or minus six degrees Celsius, by 2100. Or 2050. An ice-free Arctic in the next ten years, maybe as soon as 2020. We also mean historical numbers as the means to anticipate the future of the Earth System: "The long-term sea level that corresponds to current CO_2 concentration is about twenty-three metres above today's levels, and the temperatures will be six degrees Celsius or more higher. These estimates are based on real long-term climate records, not on models."[80] And: "This planet has not experienced an ice-free Arctic for at least the last three million years."[81]

In their recent book, *To Our Friends*, The Invisible Committee condemns these numbers, along with the hubris of the Anthropocene, writing:

> At the apex of his insanity, Man has even proclaimed himself a "geological force," going so far as to give the name of his species to a phase of the life of the planet: he's taken to speaking of an "anthropocene." For the last time, he assigns himself the main role, even if it's to accuse himself of having trashed everything—the seas and the skies, the ground and what's underground— even if it's to confess his guilt for the unprecedented extinction of plant and animal species.[82]

They continue emphatically: "But what's remarkable is that he continues relating in the same disastrous manner to the disaster produced by his own disastrous relationship with the world. He *calculates* the rate at which the ice pack is disappearing. He *measures* the extermination of the non-human forms of life."[83] And, even more to the point, "He talks about it scientifically with numbers and averages. He thinks he's saying something when he establishes that the temperature will rise by so many degrees and the precipitation will decrease by so many inches or millimeters. He even speaks of 'biodiversity.' He observes the rarefaction of life on earth *from space*."[84] But who is this *Man*? Can we be so sure that the scientific study of climate change is a mode of excluding the "sensible experiences" of the birds, insects, and plants that *confirm*, at least to these authors, that changes are *really* happening?

Science is, at least in this depiction, a dissociated and all-too-abstract realm, ignorant of the smell of the soil and the taste of the breeze; but will attacks on mere caricatures emancipate the misplaced assumptions of technoscientific culture? Science is maybe nothing more than the formalization of communities of sense experience, however expensive or technically sophisticated are the extensions of sense that make these experimental experiences shareable.[85] From this perspective, it is not the construction of communities of shared calculation, measurement, and visualization that requires redress, but the modes of interaction among other communities of sense, both human and non-human.[86] As Lindsay Bremner makes clear in this volume, the technologies of uncertainty that characterize contemporary technoscientific culture are caught up in what Karin Knorr Cetina has called a "synthetic situation." For Bremner, what is vital to understand about the failed search for the missing Malaysian Airways Flight MH370 is that it reveals the limit condition of contemporary human knowledge. Gloria Meynen identifies this "problem [as] based in multiple translations: the world simply cannot be incorporated."[87] Laurent Gutierrez and Valérie Portefaix of MAP Office also consider the role of invisible territories in shaping knowledge and sensation through a series of projects documented in this collection. Meanwhile, Karolina Sobecka traces the contours of a Borgesian paradox at the heart of scientific observation: perhaps we only really "see" what we are paying close attention to, yet we are frequently subject to inattentional blindness. How do we address these subjective, affective structures of perception that pattern and animate scientific objectivity? In our conversation with Peter Galison, we also discuss the technologies of the self that reformat the very concept of subjectivity, the very possibility of knowing oneself. To dismiss these technoscientific modes of co-producing selfhood, an agenda put forward by Martin Heidegger, forecloses any attempt to think through the implications of the massive technological transformations that characterize the macro and micro scales of the Anthropocene. Thus, like Smudge Studio, who propose a new series of specifications for design in the Anthropocene, we are interested in another line of engagement, one that doesn't so easily dismiss science, protocols, or numbers, which are signs that can also enable a common language of mutual aid; with all due respect to our invisible comrades, then, we don't want to give up our numbers so quickly.[88]

On the contrary, Shiv Visvanathan postulates that numeracy is a critical element of contemporary social emancipation.[89] In his remarkable essay on the scientist and engineer S.V. Seshadri, "Between Cosmology and System: The Heuristics of a Dissenting Imagination," Visvanathan explores the relationship between energy and justice in the context of postcolonial India. His observations are especially valuable when trying to grasp the scale of the Anthropocene: "numeracy is the ability to see discrete entities in a connected whole or continuum. Those lacking in numeracy usually present two kinds of deficiencies. The first is the inability to see discreteness in continuity. The second is to see only discreteness and not to perceive the continuum at all. Both deficiencies can create survival problems in a developing society."[90] Yet, he continues: "One must emphasize that innumeracy is not just a lack of arithmetic skill. It is a tacit knowledge, the awareness of a resource limitation."[91] Visvanathan describes "a feel for quantity and its allocation" as an absolute, essential survival skill "linked to time in a significant way. 'Time is an essential constituent of numeracy, in fact time is the prime numeraire.' This problem of time, science, and development constitutes one of the fundamental issues of exploitation."[92] In this sense, not only is the epistemological element of numeracy critical for understanding resource depletion and its consequences, and not only does it allow for more considered and emancipatory social relationships, it is also a means to transform the very work of science, "to create a science that thought with its hands, a science that was more sexual and sensual, a science that was sensitive to suffering."[93] Such an approach to numeracy unfolds as an ecology of knowledge practices, not technocratic administration; in this view, understanding numbers has a close affinity with struggle and a sensitivity to suffering.

Numeracy is thus a way of encountering epistemological diversity, not a reductive means to foreclose it. As Boaventura de Sousa Santos, João Arriscado Nunes, and Maria Paula Meneses write in their introduction to *Another Knowledge is Possible: Beyond Northern Epistemologies*, "The ecology of knowledges is an invitation to the promotion of non-relativistic dialogues among knowledges, granting 'equality of opportunities' to the different kinds of knowledge engaged in ever broader epistemic disputes aimed both at maximizing their respective contributions to build a more democratic and just society and at decolonizing knowledge and power."[94]

In this context, then, "Epistemological diversity is neither the simple reflection or epiphenomenon of ontological diversity or heterogeneity nor a range of culturally specific ways of expressing a fundamentally unified world. There is no essential or definitive way of describing, ordering, and classifying processes, entities, and relationships in the world. The very action of knowing, as pragmatist philosophers have repeatedly reminded us, is an intervention in the world, which places us within it as active contributors to its making."[95] So it is that we might, in the end, agree with The Invisible Committee, who go on to propose that, instead of denigrating calculative reason and its multifarious numeracies, it might be of some value as a mode of engagement: "Obsessed as we are with a political idea of revolution, we have neglected its technical dimension. *A revolutionary perspective no longer focuses on an institutional reorganization of society, but on the technical configurations of worlds.*"[96] They continue:

> In other words: we need to resume a meticulous effort of investigation. We need to go look in every sector, in all the territories we inhabit, for those who possess strategic technical knowledge. Only on this basis will the passion for experimenting towards another life be liberated, a largely technical passion that is the obverse, as it were, of everyone's state of technological dependence. This process of knowledge accumulation, of establishing collusions in every domain, is a prerequisite for a serious and massive return of the revolutionary question.[97]

Once the *posture* of the revolutionary is overcome by the movements of her body in coordination with other bodies, times, and relationships, it is no longer a question of blaming numbers, scientists, or technical systems. In fact, among all the competing scientific models attempting to describe the numeracy of the present and its probable trajectory—that is, the recognition of the limitations of continuity—we can even discover one call for open revolt.[98] In her discussion of Brad Werner's presentation to the American Geophysical Union in 2012, "Is Earth Fucked? Dynamical Futility of Global Environmental Management and Possibilities for Sustainability via Direct Action Activism," Naomi Klein notes that among the various scenarios run in his model of complex system interaction, only one factor made enough of a difference to allow human life to continue given the direction of contemporary capitalism. Klein writes, "Werner termed it 'resistance'—movements of 'people or groups of people' who 'adopt a certain set of dynamics that [do] not fit within the capitalist culture.' According to the abstract for his presentation, this includes 'environmental direct action, resistance taken from outside the dominant culture, as in protests, blockades and sabotage by Indigenous Peoples, workers, anarchists and other activist groups.'"[99] Similarly, in her "Minoritarian Manifesto for Re-occupying the Strata," Kathryn Yusoff lists ten demands, the tenth of which asks us to "Rethink the revolutionary subject in the context of the earth."[100] This task—of reimagining revolutionary subjectivization in the context of our geological reformation—is perhaps the most compelling and necessary of our current era. What world does this scientifically supported numeracy of revolt encounter among allied epistemologies and diverse insurrectionaries; and, perhaps most importantly, what worlds does it imagine?

Futures Worth Imagining

There are still songs to sing beyond mankind.

—Paul Celan

William S. Burroughs observed something vital to understanding the politics of the Anthropocene: "A government is never more dangerous than when embarking on a self-defeating or downright suicidal course."[101] The homogenizing trajectory of the global political economy and its modes of state capitalism smells of a moralizing, hypocritical, and cop-ridden planet, where "[t]here are already great islands where the stench announces this ending,"[102] where the cumulus excrement of humanity has irreversibly despoiled the earth. But *who* announces the end? The *anthropos*? Or the police and the bureaucrats? Who tells us how to feel it, or think it, or obey it? *We prefer not to be told*—trying to inhabit a suicidal system assumes a sad defeat from the outset; it is an approach lacking in both numeracy and imagination. But there is a ditch on both sides of this road to nowhere. The violence of hope—of just *wishing* for an outcome other than the one we know to be imminent—has its counterpart in that other ditch, the malicious stupidity of those feigning puppets of Rupert Murdoch and friends who claim to need a little more clarification, more "facts," as they *buy time* to pillage the last of the welfare state and terrify their audiences with threats of refugee invasions and terrorist sleeper cells.[103] If we are going to stop hoping for the best, let's stop worrying about the worst while we're at it. Nothing instills panic in a self-defeating government like the confidence to walk away, to make something else—without being macho or naïve about it: "They will never let you experiment in peace."[104] Still, we're tired of pretending it will all be *okay*. Our works of art are building other infrastructures, and we can't say if we'll be coming back.[105] What most characterizes the Anthropocene is that it is an era of *intensity*, and the worlds we are making through our art practices, science, and research are not made to measure. We made this book together because we wanted to think with these intensities with others. Illana Halperin makes this clear: we've been full of geology all along and we couldn't have it any other way, even if we wanted to.[106] What is different in the repetition of *this* crisis—the same crisis we've been hearing about since Walter Benjamin described its creeping, fascist *pathos*[107] —is that it appears to *implicate all of us*.[108]

The cunning of the Anthropocene *as a sign* is that it smuggles in a series of implications and assumptions about the *anthropos* and the *kairos* it names.[109] While the many critical discussions regarding the sign have contested the patriarchal, colonial, and Eurocentric strands woven into this scientific nomenclature,[110] McKenzie Wark has recently pointed out its achievement *as a sign*: "Rather than 'interrogate' Crutzen's Anthropocene—and where did *that* metaphor come from?—perhaps it is better to see it as what it is: a brilliant hack. The Anthropocene introduces the labor point of view—in the broadest possible sense—into *geology*. Perhaps the challenge is then to find analogous but different ways to hack other specialized domains of knowledge, to orient them to the situation and the tasks at hand."[111] Deleuze adds to the concept of the hack a critique of method: "There is no more a method for learning than there is a method for finding treasures, but a violent training, a *paideia*, which affects the entire individual."[112] Because culture "is an involuntary adventure," both learning and thought "take time."[113] Learning to think-with and become-with the uncanny sign of the Anthropocene isn't some fatalistic exercise, "even though the thing one is fighting is abominable,"[114] but a comportment to the fragility of encounters, shared but separated, incommensurate but not lamentable for being so. The Anthropocene does not mean we are merely "all in it together"; we are in it inasmuch as it is in us, this geological reformation, through our shared separation. As Irmgard Emmelheinz makes abundantly clear in her contribution to this collection, images do not show a way home; art is not a palliative mode of reconciliation. Quoting Jean-Luc Godard and Anne-Marie Miéville, "The human species has blown up and dispersed in the stars. We can neither deal with the past nor with the present, and the future takes us more and more away from the concept of home. We are not free, as we like to think, but lost."[115] We like to think that the credulous pseudonym *Homo sapiens*—that perpetrator also known as *anthropos* by the social scientists—is merely a place-holder, an empty if ambitious sign whose substantive articulation is both held in abeyance *and* articulated by the work of the work of art: art's *labour* is both a sensing and a spacing of the shared separation of the Anthropocene. Whatever we humans are, we are now *in* the Anthropocene—sensing and spacing this *kairos* through our aesthetic apprehensions, political commitments, epistemic comportments, and environmental bonds inasmuch as we share in the separations it affords and overturns.[116] It is best not to approach such an immense reality head on, but to come more slowly and from the back, following a queer line, as John Paul Ricco does in *The Decision Between Us*:

> Separation is the spacing of existence, and is, by definition, never solitary but always shared. It is that which affirms that for anything to exist, there must be more than one thing, each one separated from each other one, together partaking in the spacing between that is opened up by separation. Existence, therefore, is relational and shared, and hence is always to be understood as coexistence. Not the coming together of solitary and autonomous beings, but existence as sharing or partaking in separation as the *there is* of existence—the spacing (*there*) of being (*is*) together. If separation is the spacing of existence, and if existence is always relational and shared, then sharing in separation is the praxis of coexistence—of being-together. [117]

Being-together as a sharing in separation, as a praxis of coexistence, is necessarily and precisely beyond both measure and nomenclature.[118] Such a measureless existence affords us a perspective—one decidedly less fatalistic than we are now so accustomed to—regarding intensities and aesthetics in the Anthropocene. We can't say where it goes; in bringing together these essays, projects, and interviews, the measure of our work will be the measurelessness of the worlds which take little bits of this book elsewhere as they continue to resist, struggle, and become-together something more powerful than universals and more sensitive than identities. As Raqs Media Collective has written so beautifully:

> Without a recalibration of the senses, at the level of our global species-being, without at least half a conversation to understand, and then attenuate and nuance our desires and needs, we cannot conceive of another mode of production, another set of social relations, another ethic of husbandry between ourselves and the earth.
>
> That is why we send pictures from deserts and write words on water, that is why we make earthworks that stand on the landscape of the mind. That is why we listen to the whispers of an eccentric planet. So that it can listen to us in turn, and keep wanting us, and our children, and their children, around.
>
> The world is all, that is the case.[119]

Notes

1. Quoted in Lucy R. Lippard, *Undermining: A Wild Ride Through Land Use, Politics, and Art in the Changing West* (New York and London: The New Press, 2014), 9.

2. See Anselm Franke in this volume; see also *The Whole Earth: California and the Disappearance of the Outside* (Berlin: Sternberg Press & HKW, 2013), the exhibition catalog for *The Whole Earth* (26 April–7 July 2013), curated by Diedrich Diederichsen and Anselm Franke at the Haus der Kulturen der Welt, Berlin.

3. "Anthropocene: Arts of Living on a Damaged Planet," was a conference organized by Anna Tsing that took place at the University of California, Santa Cruz, 8–10 May 2014.

4. On the sensory elements of climate science, see McKenzie Wark, "Climate Science as Sensory Infrastructure," in *The White Review*, www.thewhitereview.org/features/climate-science-as-sensory-infrastructure.

5. On the concept of intra-action, see Karen Barad, "Intra-actions," interview with Adam Kleinman, *Mousse* 34 (2012): 76–81.

6. For an excellent summary of the debate, and one of the first popular scientific descriptions of the Anthropocene, see Elizabeth Kolbert, "Enter the Age of Man," *National Geographic* 219, no. 3 (March 2011): 60–85.

7. For a much earlier version of this position, see Antonio Stoppani, "Excepts from *Corso di Geologia*," ed. Etienne Turpin and Valeria Federighi, trans. Valeria Federighi, *Scapegoat: Architecture | Landscape | Political Economy*, Issue 05: Excess (Summer/Fall 2013): 346–354.

8. Quoted in Kolbert, "Enter the Age of Man."

9. On the powers of speculative fiction for organizing thought, see Hans Vaihinger, *The Philosophy of "As If": A System of the Theoretical, Practical, and Religious Fictions of Mankind* (London and New York: Routledge, 2009 [1924]).

10. For a history of geological thought and its broader cultural implications, see the magisterial work of Martin Rudwick, especially *Earth's Deep History: How It Was Discovered and Why It Matters* (Chicago and London: University of Chicago Press, 2014), *Worlds Before Adam: The Reconstruction of Geohistory in the Age of Reform* (Chicago and London: University of Chicago Press, 2008), and *Bursting the Limits of Time: The Reconstruction of Geohistory in the Age of Revolution* (Chicago and London: University of Chicago Press, 2005).

11. For a prescient analysis of Kant's separation of the noumenal and phenomenal registers, and the consequences of this philosophical parsing, see Iain Hamilton Grant, "Prospects for Post-Copernican Dogmatism: The Antinomies of Transcendental Naturalism," *Collapse* V, ed. Damian Veal (Urbanomic, 2009): 415–454; for an analysis of the problematic division between natural and human history, as well as the political limits of universalism lurking within the Anthropocene discussion, see Dipesh Chakrabarty, "The Climate of History: Four Theses," *Critical Inquiry* 35 (Winter 2009): 197–222.

12. Simon L. Lewis and Mark A. Maslin, "Defining the Anthropocene," *Nature* 519 (12 March 2015): 176.

13. Kolbert, "Enter the Age of Man."

14. There is also a growing literature regarding human population expansion and its limits; see, among others, Stephen Emmott, *10 Billion* (London: Penguin Books, 2010), and Danny Dorling, *Population 10 Billion* (London: Constable, 2013).

15. Jean-Luc Nancy, *After Fukushima: The Equivalence of Catastrophes*, trans. Charlotte Mandell (New York: Fordham University Press, 2015), 8.

16 Interview with Isabelle Stengers, by Heather Davis and Etienne Turpin, "Matters of Cosmopolitics," in *Architecture in the Anthropocene: Encounters Among Design, Deep Time, Science and Philosophy*, ed. Etienne Turpin (Ann Arbor: Open Humanities Press), 178.

17 For an especially influential reading of this interrelation, see Manuel DeLanda, *A Thousand Years of Nonlinear History* (New York: Zone, 1997).

18 See the conversation between Donna Haraway and Martha Kenney in this volume.

19 On the force of debt as a political economic axiomatic of state capitalism, see the remarkable assessment made by Lazzarato in *Governing by Debt* (Los Angeles: Semiotext(e), 2015).

20 See Haraway and Kenney in this volume; see also, Jason Moore, "The Capitalocene," June 2014, www.jasonwmoore.com/uploads/The_Capitalocene_Part_I_June_2014.pdf; and, Andreas Malm, "The Origins of Fossil Capital: From Water to Steam in the British Cotton Industry," *Historical Materialism* 21, no. 1 (2013): 15–68.

21 On reimagining the canon of critical theory beyond the usual suspects, see McKenzie Wark, *Molecular Red: Theory for the Anthropocene* (New York and London: Verso, 2015).

22 The designation of the Eurocene was made even more pointed in a recent paper presented at the "After Extinction" conference at the University of Wisconsin, Milwaukee (30 April–2 May, 2015) by Nicholas Mirzoeff, when he claimed that the proper name of the Anthropocene should be the "white supremacy-scene."

23 "In a recorded conversation for *Ethnos* at the University of Aarhus in October, 2014, the participants collectively generated the name Plantationocene for the devastating transformation of diverse kinds of human-tended farms, pastures, and forests into extractive and enclosed plantations, relying on slave labor and other forms of exploited, alienated, and usually spatially transported labor." Donna Haraway, "Anthropocene, Capitalocene, Plantationocene, Chthulucene: Making Kin," *Environmental Humanities* 6 (2015): 162.

24 Lewis and Maslin, "Defining the Anthropocene," 174.

25 See Laura Hall in this volume.

26 Deborah Bird Rose, "Anthropocene Noir," *Arena Journal* 41/42 (2013): 216.

27 See Zoe Todd in this volume.

28 Haraway, "Anthropocene, Capitalocene, Plantationocene, Chthulucene," 160.

29 Again, see the conversation between Haraway and Kenney in this volume.

30 Thanks to Christian Schwägerl for this important point.

31 See Bruno Latour in conversation with Heather Davis in this volume.

32 For an introduction to this discussion, see *The Anthropocene and the Global Environmental Crisis: Rethinking Modernity in a New Epoch*, ed. Clive Hamilton, François Gemenne, Christophe Bonneuil (New York and London: Routledge, 2015).

33 For an overview of the history of the IPCC and the undertaking of planetary climate science, see Paul N. Edwards, *A Vast Machine: Computer Models, Climate Data, and the Politics of Global Warming* (Cambridge and London: MIT Press, 2010).

34 See Richard Leakey and Roger Lewin, *The Sixth Extinction: Patterns of Life and the Future of Humankind* (New York: Doubleday, 1995); Terry Glavin, *The Sixth Extinction: Journeys Among the Lost and Left Behind* (New York: Thomas Dunne Books, 2006); and Elizabeth Kolbert, *The Sixth Extinction: An Unnatural History* (New York: Henry Holt and Company, 2014).

35 See Natasha Myers in this volume.

36 See Amy Balkin in this volume.
37 See Pinar Yoldas in this volume.
38 See Zurkow, Kellhammer, Ertl and Chaudhuri in this volume.
39 See Frank Biermann, *Earth System Governance: World Politics in the Anthropocene* (Cambridge, MA: MIT Press, 2014), and Brad Evans and Julian Reid, *Resilient Life: The Art of Living Dangerously* (Cambridge: Polity, 2014).
40 Maurizio Lazzarato, *Governing by Debt*, 229–30.
41 On the role of complexity and logistics within capitalist axiomatics, see, respectively, Saskia Sassen, *Expulsions: Brutality and Complexity in the Global Economy* (Cambridge and London: Harvard University Press, 2014), and Deborah Cowen, *The Deadly Life of Logistics: Mapping Violence in Global Trade* (Minneapolis: University of Minnesota Press, 2014).
42 On the concept and consequences of equivalence, see Jean-Luc Nancy, *After Fukushima.*
43 Roy Scranton, "Learning How to Die in the Anthropocene," *The New York Times*, 10 November 2013, www.opinionator.blogs.nytimes.com/2013/11/10/learning-how-to-die-in-the-anthropocene.
44 See, among other studies, Jan Zalasiewicz, *The Earth After Us: What Legacy Will Humans Leave in the Rocks?* (New York: Oxford University Press, 2009); Alan Weisman, *The World Without Us* (New York: Picador, 2007); and more generally, Jared Diamond, *Collapse: How Societies Choose to Survive or Fail* (London: Penguin, 2005).
45 See the conversation with Sylvère Lotringer in this volume.
46 Jonathan Crary, *24/7: Late Capitalism and the Ends of Sleep* (London and New York: Verso, 2014).
47 Esther Leslie, *Synthetic Worlds: Nature, Art and the Chemical Industry* (London: Reaktion Books, 2005), 11.
48 Bill McKibben, *Eaarth: Making a Life on a Tough New Planet* (New York: Henry Holt & Company, 2010).
49 Bird Rose, "Anthropocene Noir," 208.
50 Nicholas Mirzoeff, "Visualizing the Anthropocene," *Public Culture* 26, no. 2 (2014): 220.
51 Ibid., 223.
52 Susan Sontag, *Regarding the Pain of Others* (London: Penguin Books, 2003).
53 See Amanda Boetzkes in this volume; for a further discussion of the epistemological consequences of this shift, see Daniel Falb, "Epistemologies of Art in the Anthropocene," in *Art in the Periphery of the Center*, ed. Christophe Behnke, Cornelia Kastelan, Valérie Knoll, and Ulf Wuggenig (Berlin: Sternberg, 2015), 302–317.
54 See Richard Pell and Emily Kutil in this volume.
55 On these questions of extinction, see Thom van Dooren, *Flight Ways: Life and Loss at the Edge of Extinction* (New York: Columbia University Press, 2014), and Thom van Dooren, "The Last Snail: Loss, Hope, and Care for the Future," in *Land & Animal & Nonanimal*, ed. Anna-Sophie Springer and Etienne Turpin (Berlin: K. Verlag & HKW, 2015), 1–14.
56 See Ursula Biemann in this volume.
57 See Ada Smailbegović in this volume.
58 See Yates McKee, "Of Survival," *Impasses of the Post-Global: Theory in the Era of Climate Change, Vol. 2*, ed. Henry Sussman (Ann Arbor: Open Humanities Press, 2012), 76–105.

59 For another elaboration of the non-human within the trajectory of anthropological research, see Eduardo Kohn, *How Forests Think: Toward an Anthropology beyond the Human* (Berkeley and Los Angeles: University of California Press, 2013); Eduardo Viveiros de Castro, *Cannibal Metaphysics: For a Post-structural Anthropology*, ed. and trans. Peter Skafish (Minneapolis: Univocal, 2014); and Philippe Descola, *Beyond Nature and Culture*, trans. Janet Lloyd (Chicago and London: University of Chicago Press, 2013).

60 See Haapoja and Gustafsson in this volume.

61 See Ho in this volume; see also Brian Massumi, *What Animals Teach Us About Politics* (Durham and London: Duke University Press, 2014).

62 On the geopoetics of the Anthropocene, see Don MacKay, "Ediacaran and Anthropocene: Poetry as a Reader of Deep Time," *Prairie Fire* 29, no. 4 (Winter 2008/2009): 4–15.

63 Rosalyn Deutsche, *Evictions: Art and Spatial Politics* (Cambridge, MA: MIT Press, 1996), 278.

64 For a discussion of the non-human forces of the Earth, and their refusal to be anthropogenically managed, see Nigel Clark, *Inhuman Nature: Sociable Life on a Dynamic Planet* (London: SAGE, 2011).

65 See Vincent Normand in this volume; see also Jonathan Crary, *Suspensions of Perception: Attention, Spectacle and Modern Culture* (Cambridge and London: MIT Press, 2001); and Jonathan Crary, *Techniques of the Observer: On Vision and Modernity in the Nineteenth Century* (Cambridge and London: MIT Press, 1992).

66 See Ida Soulard and Fabien Giraud in this volume; see also Levi Bryant, Nick Srnicek, and Graham Harman, eds., *The Speculative Turn: Continental Materialism and Realism* (Melbourne: re.press, 2011); Robin MacKay and Armen Avenessian, eds., *#Accelerate: The Accelerationist Reader* (Falmouth: Urbanomic, 2014); and Svenja Bromberg, "The Anti-Political Aesthetics of Objects and Worlds Beyond," *Mute Magazine* (25 July 2013), www.metamute.org/editorial/articles/anti-political-aesthetics-objects-and-worlds-beyond.

67 Geoffrey C. Bowker, *Memory Practices in the Sciences* (Cambridge, MA: MIT Press, 2008).

68 On media in the Anthropocene, see especially Jussi Parikka, *A Geology of Media* (Minneapolis: University of Minnesota Press, 2015), and Jussi Parikka, *The Anthrobscene* (Minneapolis: University of Minnesota Press, 2015).

69 On "materialized effort" and the legibility of politics, see AbdouMaliq Simone, *City Life from Jakarta to Dakar: Movements at the Crossroads* (London and New York: Routledge, 2010).

70 *Robert Smithson: The Collected Writings*, ed. by Jack Flam (Berkeley: University of California Press, 1996).

71 On the strategic underpinning of this enterprise, see Sanford Kwinter, *Far From Equilibrium: Essays on Technology and Design Culture* (Barcelona and New York: Actar, 2008).

72 See especially Eyal Weizman, *Hollow Land: Israel's Architecture of Occupation* (London and New York: Verso, 2007); and E. Weizman, S. Schuppli, S. Sheikh, F. Sebregondi, T. Keenan, A. Franke, eds., *Forensis: The Architecture of Public Truth* (Berlin: Forensic Architecture and Sternberg Press, 2014).

73 Meg McLagan and Yates McKee, eds., *Sensible Politics: The Visual Culture of Nongovernmental Activism* (New York: Zone, 2012).

74 Laura Kurgan, *Up Close at a Distance: Mapping, Technology, Politics* (New York: Zone Books, 2013).

75 See Paul N. Edwards, *The Closed World: Computers and the Politics of Discourse in Cold War America* (Cambridge, MA: MIT Press, 1996).

76 On one remarkable example of such a collaboration—*The International Geophysical Year*, which lasted from 1 July 1957–31 December 1958, and included over 60,000 scientists from sixty-six nations—see Walter Sullivan, *Assault on the Unknown: The International Geophysical Year* (New York: McGraw-Hill, 1961).

77 See Joshua Clover and Juliana Spahr in this volume.

78 "Shut 'em Down," Public Enemy, *The Enemy Strikes Black* (1991) [Album].

79 Rachel Nuwer, "Extinction Rates Are Biased And Much Worse Than You Thought," www.smithsonianmag.com/smart-news/extinction-rates-are-biased-and-much-worse-than-you-thought-24290026.

80 From a briefing document provided to the U.N. Conference of the Parties in Copenhagen (2009), quoted in Eric Zuesse, "Global Warming Is Rapidly Accelerating," 31 December 2013, www.huffingtonpost.com/eric-zuesse/global-warming-is-rapidly_b_4499119.html.

81 Evolutionary biologist Guy McPherson, quoted in Dahr Jamail, "Are We Falling Off the Climate Precipice? Scientists Consider Extinction," 22 December 2013, www.informationclearinghouse.info/article37194.htm.

82 The Invisible Committee, *To Our Friends* (Los Angeles: Semiotext(e), 2015), 32.

83 Ibid.

84 Ibid., 32–33.

85 This modest conception of scientific inquiry has a strong affinity with McKenzie Wark's persuasive reading of Alexander Bogdanov's vision of science; see Wark, *Molecular Red*, 3–61.

86 On experimental cultures in science, see the conversation with Peter Galison in this volume; see also Peter Galison, *Image and Logic: A Material Culture of Microphysics* (Chicago and London: University of Chicago Press, 1997), and Peter Galison, *How Experiments End* (Chicago and London: University of Chicago Press, 1987).

87 Gloria Meynen, "Think Small," *Grain, Vapor, Ray: Textures of the Anthropocene*, ed. Katrin Klingan, Ashkan Sepahvand, Christoph Rosol, and Bernd M. Scherer (Cambridge, MA: MIT Press, 2015), 64.

88 See smudge studio (Jamie Kruse & Elizabeth Ellsworth) in this volume.

89 This discussion of numeracy is completely indebted to the work of Visvanathan. See especially Shiv Visvanathan, "Between Cosmology and System: The Heuristics of Dissenting Imagination," in *Another Knowledge is Possible: Beyond Northern Epistemologies*, ed. Boaventura de Sousa Santos (London and New York: Verso, 2008), 182–218; and Shiv Visvanathan, "From the Annals of the Laboratory State," *Alternatives* 12 (1987): 37–59; a special thanks to Nabil Ahmed for sharing these works at an early stage of research for this book.

90 Visvanathan, "Between Cosmology and System," 213.

91 Ibid., 214.

92 Ibid.

93 Ibid., 190.

94 Boaventura de Sousa Santos, João Arriscado Nunes, and Maria Paula Meneses, "Opening Up the Canon of Knowledge and Recognition of Difference," in *Another Knowledge Is Possible: Beyond Northern Epistemologies*, ed. Boaventura de Sousa Santos (London and New York: Verso, 2008), xx.

95 Ibid., xxxi. On pragmatism, rationality, and art, see Giraud and Soulard in this volume.

96 The Invisible Committee, *To Our Friends*, 95.

97 Ibid., 96.

98 Naomi Klein, "How Science Is Telling Us All to Revolt," *New Statesman*, 29 October 2013, www.newstatesman.com/2013/10/science-says-revolt; see also Naomi Klein, *This Changes Everything: Capitalism vs. The Climate* (New York: Simon & Schuster, 2014).

99 Ibid.

100 Kathryn Yusoff, "Project Anthropocene: A Minoritarian Manifesto for Reoccupying the Strata," www.geocritique.org/project-anthropocene-minoritarian-manifesto-reoccupying-strata-kathryn-yusoff.

101 William S. Burroughs, "The Limits of Control," in *The Adding Machine: Selected Essays* (New York: Arcade Publishing, 1986), 121.

102 Michel Serres, *Malfeasance: Appropriation Through Pollution?* trans. Anne-Marie Feenberg-Dibon (Stanford: Stanford University Press, 2011), 70.

103 "The violence of hope" is a concept borrowed from Kent Brintnall, who elaborated on this trajectory during his presentation "Movement Politics: Acephalic, Apocalyptic, Apophatic" at The Annual Meeting of the American Comparative Literature Association (Seattle, March 2015).

104 Gilles Deleuze and Félix Guattari, *A Thousand Plateaus: Capitalism and Schizophrenia*, trans. Brian Massumi (Minneapolis: University of Minnesota Press, 1987).

105 See Tomás Saraceno, Sasha Engelmann, and Bruno Szerszyski in this volume; see also Keller Easterling, *Extrastatecraft: The Power of Infrastructure Space* (London and New York: Verso, 2014), and Etienne Turpin, "Aerosolar Infrastructure: Polities Above and Beyond Territory," in *Tomás Saraceno: Becoming Aersoloar* (Vienna: Österreichische Galerie Belvedere, 2015).

106 See Illana Halperin in this volume.

107 On the aestheticization of politics as a vital element of fascist regimes, see Walter Benjamin, "The Work of Art in the Age of Its Technological Reproducibility," in *Selected Writings: Volume 3, 1935–1938*, ed. Howard Eiland and Michael Jennings (Cambridge, MA: Belknap Press, 2002), 121.

108 For an overview of the new metaphors substituted for the anthropos, see Wark, *Molecular Red*, 223.

109 Ibid.

110 For an exceptional overview of the distinction between, on the one hand, the Anthropocene Epoch and its boundary marker as determined by the principles of stratigraphy and, on the other, the Anthropocene as a concept used in other disciplines to define human impact on the Earth System, see Mark A. Maslin and Simon L. Lewis, "Anthropocene: Earth System, Geological, Philosophical and Political Paradigm Shifts," *The Anthropocene Review* (2015): 1–9.

111 Ibid.; on the labour point of view, see especially ibid., 3–61.

112 Gilles Deleuze, *Difference and Repetition*, trans. Paul Patton (New York: Columbia University Press, 1994), 165.

113 Ibid.

114 Michel Foucault, "Preface" to Gilles Deleuze and Félix Guattari *Anti-Oedipus: Capitalism and Schizophrenia*, trans. Robert Hurley, Mark Seem, and Helen R. Lane (Minneapolis: University of Minnesota Press, 1983), xiii.

115 See Emmelheinz in this volume.

116 On the ethical questions provoked by the Anthropocene thesis, see especially Joanna Zylinska, *Minimal Ethics for the Anthropocene* (London: Open Humanities Press, 2014); Katherine Gibson, Deborah Bird Rose, and Ruth Fincher, eds. *Manifesto for Living in the Anthropocene* (Brooklyn: Punctum, 2015); and Alexandra Pirici and Raluca Voinea, "Manifesto for the Gynecene," www.infinitexpansion.net/gynecene.

117 John Paul Ricco, *The Decision Between Us: Art and Ethics in a Time of Scenes* (Chicago and London: University of Chicago Press, 2014), 1; for more on shared spaces of unbecoming and their various logics, see also John Paul Ricco, *The Logic of the Lure* (Chicago and London: University of Chicago Press, 2002); and Jean-Luc Nancy and John Paul Ricco in this volume.

118 See the conversation between Nancy and Ricco in this volume; see also Jean-Luc Nancy and Aurélien Barrau, *What's These Worlds Coming To?* trans. Travis Holloway and Flor Machain (New York: Fordham University Press, 2015); and Jean-Luc Nancy, *The Sense of the World*, trans. Jeffrey S. Librett (Minneapolis: University of Minnesota Press, 1997).

119 Raqs Media Collective, "Three and a Half Conversations with an Eccentric Planet," *Third Text* 27, no. 1 (January 2013): 114.

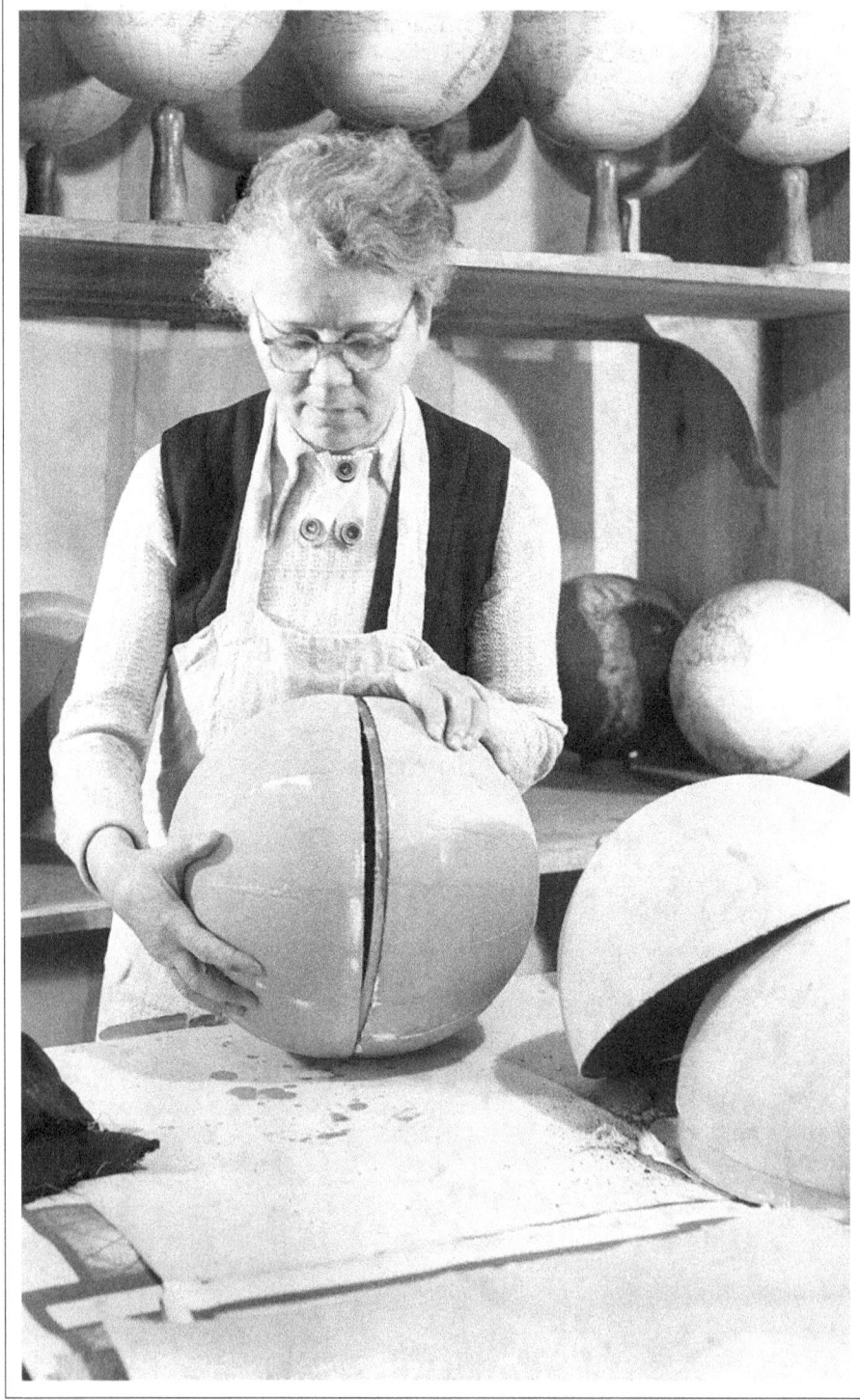

Edenic Apocalypse:
Singapore's End-of-Time Botanical Tourism

Natasha Myers

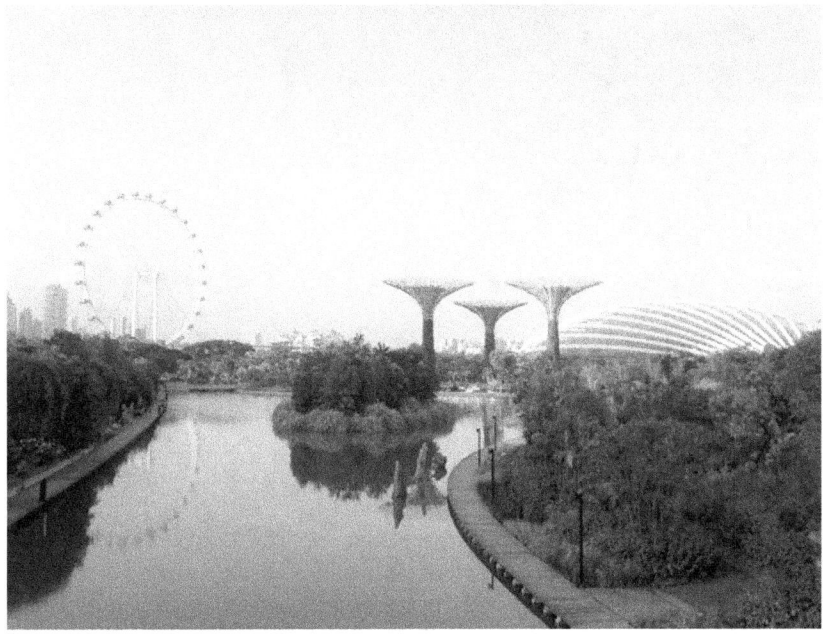

Fig. 01

Singapore is synonymous with excess and artifice. An island city-state just south of the Malaysian peninsula, Singapore is a dense urban garden built on drained and reclaimed swampland. Since the 1950s, Singapore has positioned itself as a "Garden City" and a leader in "green" economic policies. Indeed, the island's verdant vegetation has long been figured as a source of economic and aesthetic value to lure foreign investment. Here, lush canopies reach over roadways, and tree trunks are thick with epiphytic growth. Orchid blossoms even adorn airport baggage carousels. Now figured as a "City in a Garden," Singapore's extensive botanical gardens and numerous "green" tourist sites are major attractions for both locals and visitors. In place of its endemic swampland species, showy invasives are actively propagated. And, as more land is reclaimed from the sea to accommodate rapid developed, concrete now contours 87% of the island's once-natural shoreline. Artifice is Singapore's nature.

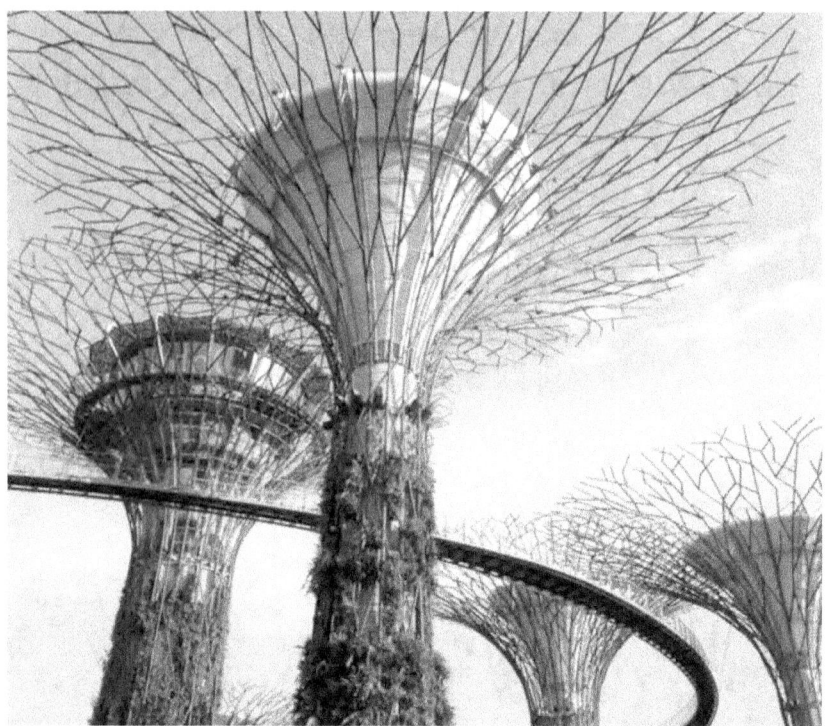

Fig. 02 Nature is everywhere luxuriously simulated at "The Gardens By the Bay," Singapore's billion-dollar infrastructure for botanical tourism. Open to the public in 2012, this award-winning feat of environmental architecture sits on fifty-four hectares of reclaimed land on the south shores of the island. Clusters of vertical gardens, modeled on tree forms, punctuate the landscape. These "Supertrees," some fifty metres tall, are integral elements of the Garden's "sustainable" infrastructure: they gather solar energy and vent heat and gases from electricity-generating incinerators that burn the city's waste biomass. Connected by aerial walkways, the largest Supertree houses an air-bound restaurant. The Gardens also feature two of the world's largest climate-controlled conservatories, massive infrastructures whose soaring curves and smooth organic forms resemble apparitions from some science-fiction fantasy. These engineered climates make possible the imperialist impulse to collect up and host diverse worldly natures here in Singapore's searing heat.

Fig. 03 Singapore's extreme neoliberal vision for unfettered economic growth is barely tamed by discourses of sustainability. Dreams of "green" development are propelling many cities' massive infrastructure projects. Indeed, where some might hope to amplify the inherent contradiction between economic growth and sustainability, in Singapore this distinction is erased. Here more sustainability means more growth; and this manifests as a kind of growth with unsustainable effects.

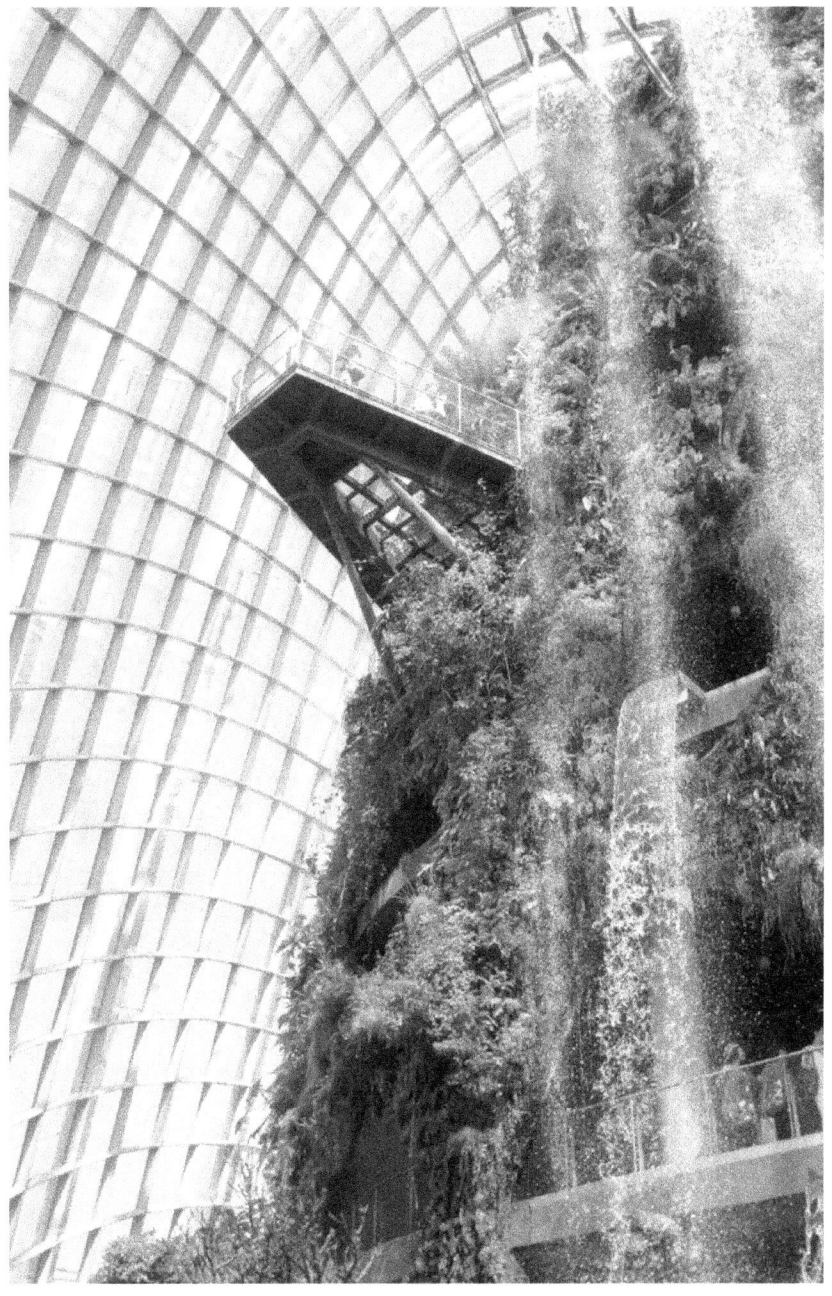

Fig. 03

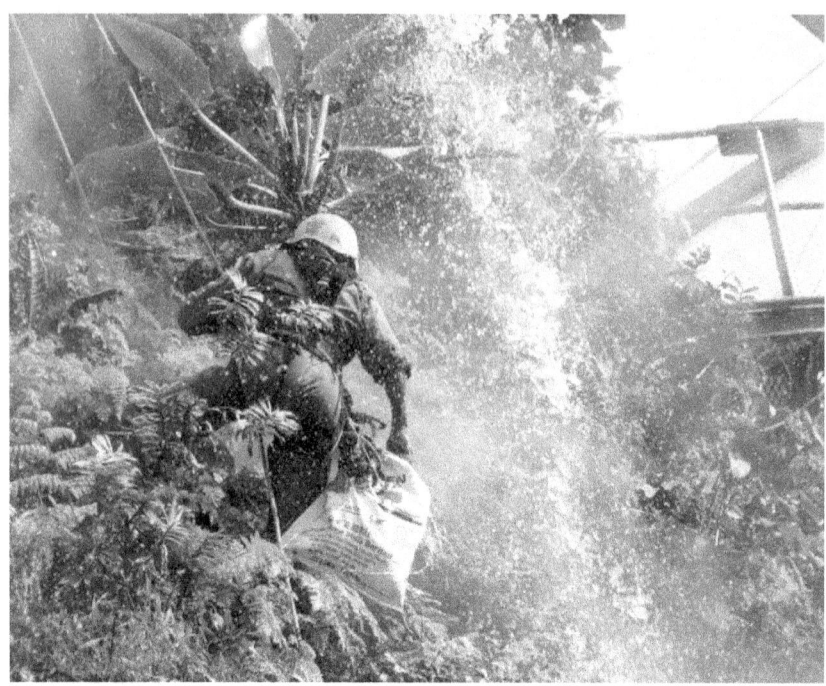

Fig. 04 I enter The Cloud Forest, an ecological simulation of epic proportions. Moist, cooling air licks at my skin, which is still radiating heat from the sun on this 34°C day. A forty-two metre mountain covered in lush vegetation sweeps my gaze upward. The spectacle is overwhelming. I can barely take it all in. That is until my eyes lock in on a body tethered to a long rope and swinging through the mist. A man reaches out and pulls himself across this lush wall, plucking errant leaves and shoots and stuffing them into a sack. His brown skin marks him as one of the many migrants whose intensive and precarious physical labours have built this very structure and daily keep this lush garden flourishing. This is a living infrastructure that itself thrives on the energetic, material, and affective labours of marginalized people. I paid S$28 for entry, a fee waived for local residents with the correct identity cards. Many others live and work in this city without such ready access.

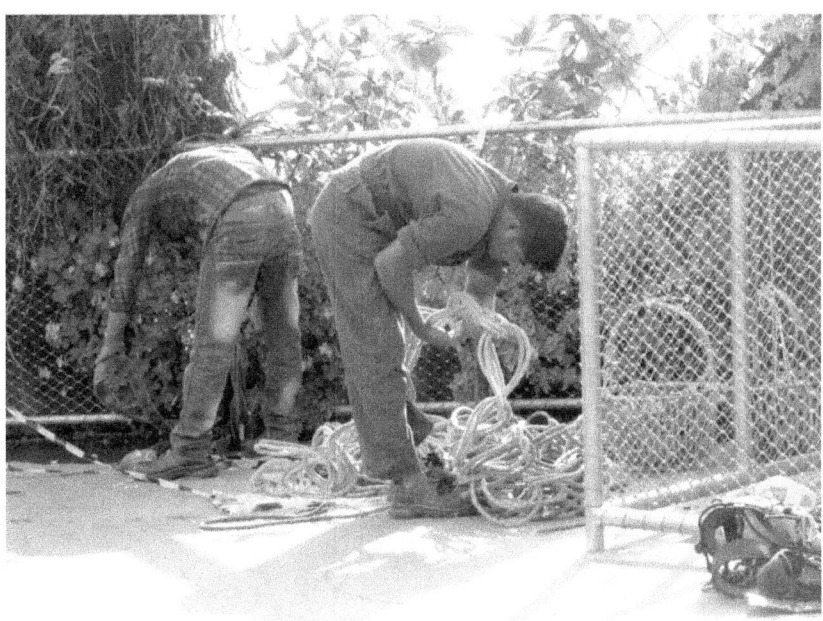

This is a city fully under construction. It is being built up on the backs of a massive migrant labour force from Bangladesh, Sri Lanka, India and surrounding regions. Singapore's "total foreign workforce," including construction workers and domestic labourers totaled over 1.3 million at the end of 2013, approximately 24% of the city-state's total population. The "unskilled" laborers who work in construction make up nearly a quarter of all foreign workers in Singapore. Life is precarious for those who risk life and limb on construction sites with high injury and fatality rates. Their low wages prevent them from participating in the life of this city of affluence and opulence, which caters predominantly to foreign "talent" and investors. This is a city in which it costs S$90,000 for a 10-year permit to drive a car.

Fig. 05

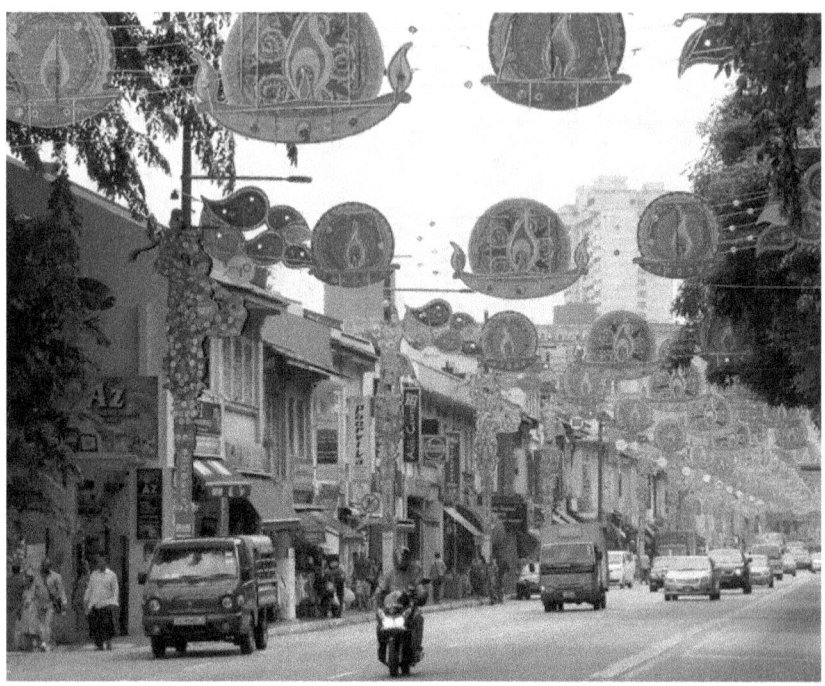

Fig. 06   On any given Sunday evening in Singapore's "Little India," throngs of South Asian men flood into the streets to savour their limited time off work. There they gather in groups on street corners or patches of grass. Some wander through the streets hand-in-hand. Tensions have been flaring of late. A riot took over Little India's streets in December 2013. Singapore's government was quick to dismiss this event as the escalation of a minor dispute. Critical news outlets around the world took this opportunity to publish exposés on exploitation, condemning labourers' poor working and living conditions and reading the riot as an expression of profound discontent.

Fig. 07   The Garden's conservatories masquerade as cooling stations for overheated tourists. And yet they also offer respite from Singapore's choking haze, smoke from forest fires that are rapidly consuming Borneo—that epicenter of earth's biodiversity that is now being terra-formed into a giant palm oil plantation. What visitors don't initially realize is that the Cloud Forest is actually a climate change demonstration site. Interspersed through the exuberant expanse of vegetation and vaulted beams, the themes of collapse and extinction are present but muted by awe-inspiring aerial walkways and simulated clouds. Visitors are guided to the "Lost World" at the top of the mountain. There a display mixes rare and endangered plants with Indigenous sculptures of animalized humans. The Lost World is where it becomes clear that the Garden's efforts to make life thrive here do nothing to mitigate the forces that are letting life die everywhere else.

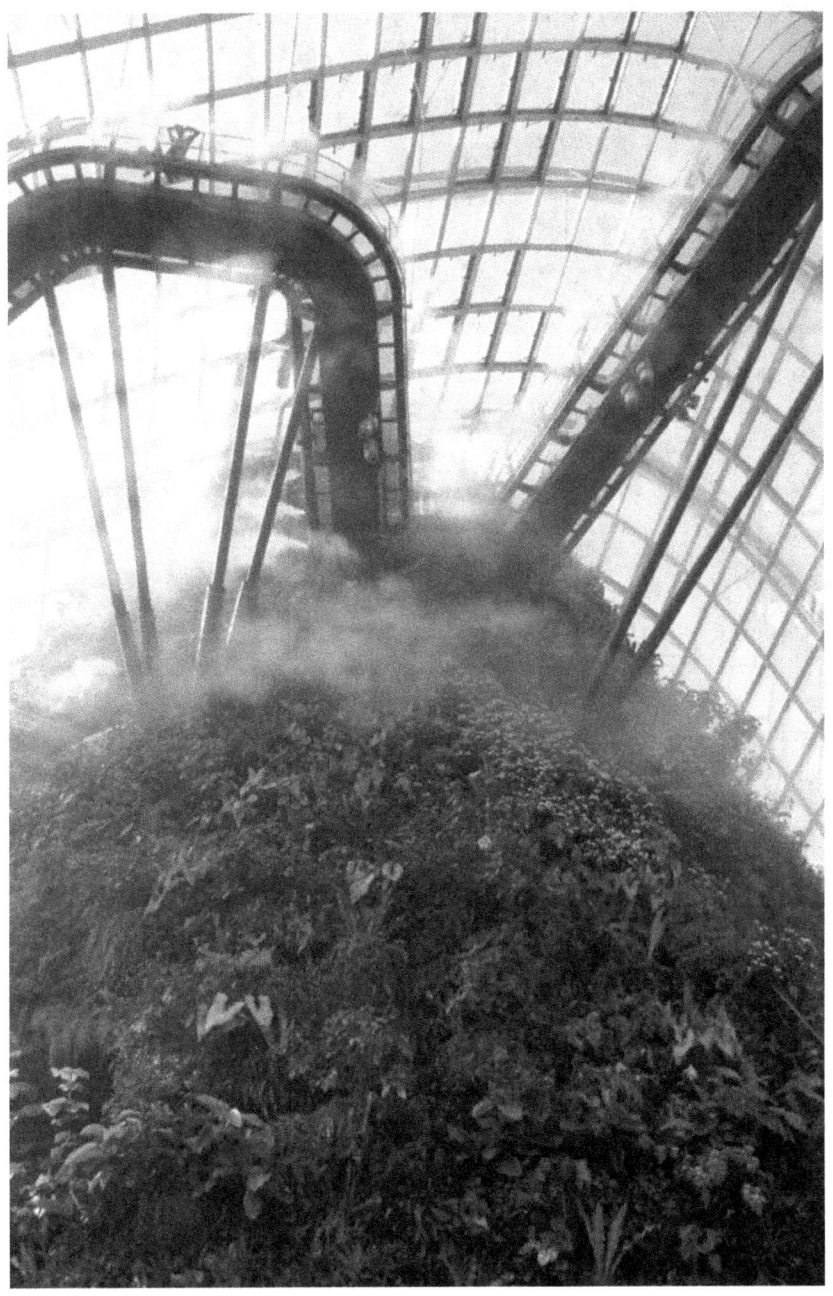

Fig. 07

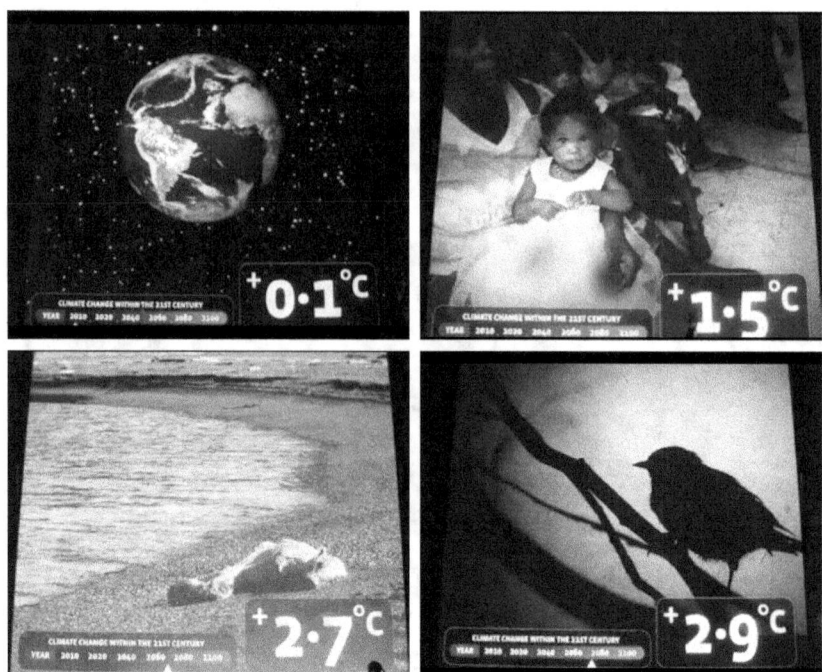

Fig. 08 It is on the lower levels of the Cloud Forest conservatories that the garden's pleasures are fractured and interrupted. There lush displays give way to dire scientific visualizations of a warming planet. The "exit through the gift shop" draws visitors through "Earth Check," a dramatic climate-change data-visualization room pulsing with animated graphic displays projected on black walls. From there, visitors pass into a massive theatre. It is here that they must confront simultaneously the beauty and allure of botanical spectacle and terrifying visions of total collapse. An immense double channel video projection loops incessantly, splashing light and colour across twenty metre screens on the rear wall and floor. The video charts in vivid images, voice-overs, and an urgent soundtrack the devastating year-by-year projections of the rise in global temperature.

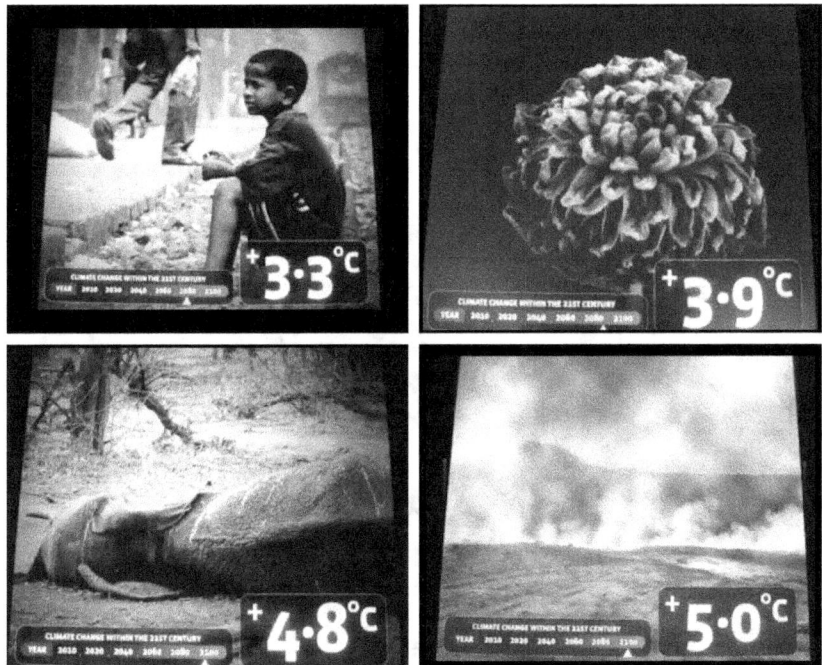

Reaching the end, the film suddenly spirals backward as a voice urges viewers to reconsider all they have just seen: "Yet this is only one possible future. If we act quickly we can prevent all this from happening. Adapt our technology. Adapt our farm practices. Adapt our policies. Adapt our lifestyles."

Fig. 09

Watch how each rise in temperature is likely to affect plants and animals in different parts of the world:

> "+ 0.7 Degrees: Hot, dry areas get hotter and dryer. There are more wildfires.
>
> +1.1 Degrees: Small mountain glaciers disappear. Threatening water supplies for 15 million people.
>
> +1.5 Degrees: Malnutrition, malaria, and other diseases continue to increase.
>
> +1.8 Degrees: All coral reefs are bleached.
>
> +2.7 Degrees: The last polar bear dies.
>
> +2.9 Degrees: Half of all species are doomed to extinction.
>
> +3.9 Degrees: 1 in every 5 plants is critically endangered or extinct.
>
> +4.3 Degrees: 50 % decrease in fresh water availability.
>
> +5.0 Degrees: And so we reach 2100, it is 5 degrees warmer, the earth is a dry rock dying in space."

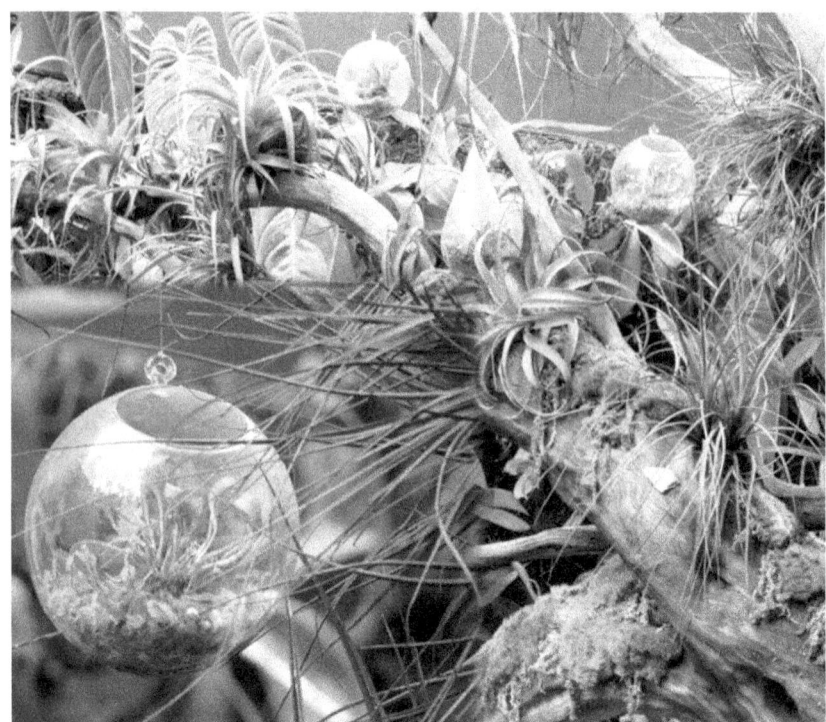

Fig. 10   And yet one cannot erase these images of colossal habitat and species extinction. Visitors shuffling out of the theatre leave with a not-so-subtle message: "It's over folks." The end-of-times are nigh. Indeed, we exit the theatre through an exhibit of an already extinct ecology, one populated by "relic plants" that just barely remember their prehistoric ancestors. It is here that visitors confront most palpably the death and extinction that underwrites all the life made to thrive in these gardens.

Fig. 11   Gardens by the Bay has engineered an ambivalent affective ecology, one that simultaneously elates with the allure of vital simulations, and throws visitors into what Donna Haraway calls the "slew of despond." Indeed, the anxieties of the Anthropocene are better rendered as the affects of what Haraway is now calling the Capitalocene. It is in this simulation of an already lost world that we can see how capital continues to profit from the very extinctions that it drives, here in the guise of entertainment for climate-change education.

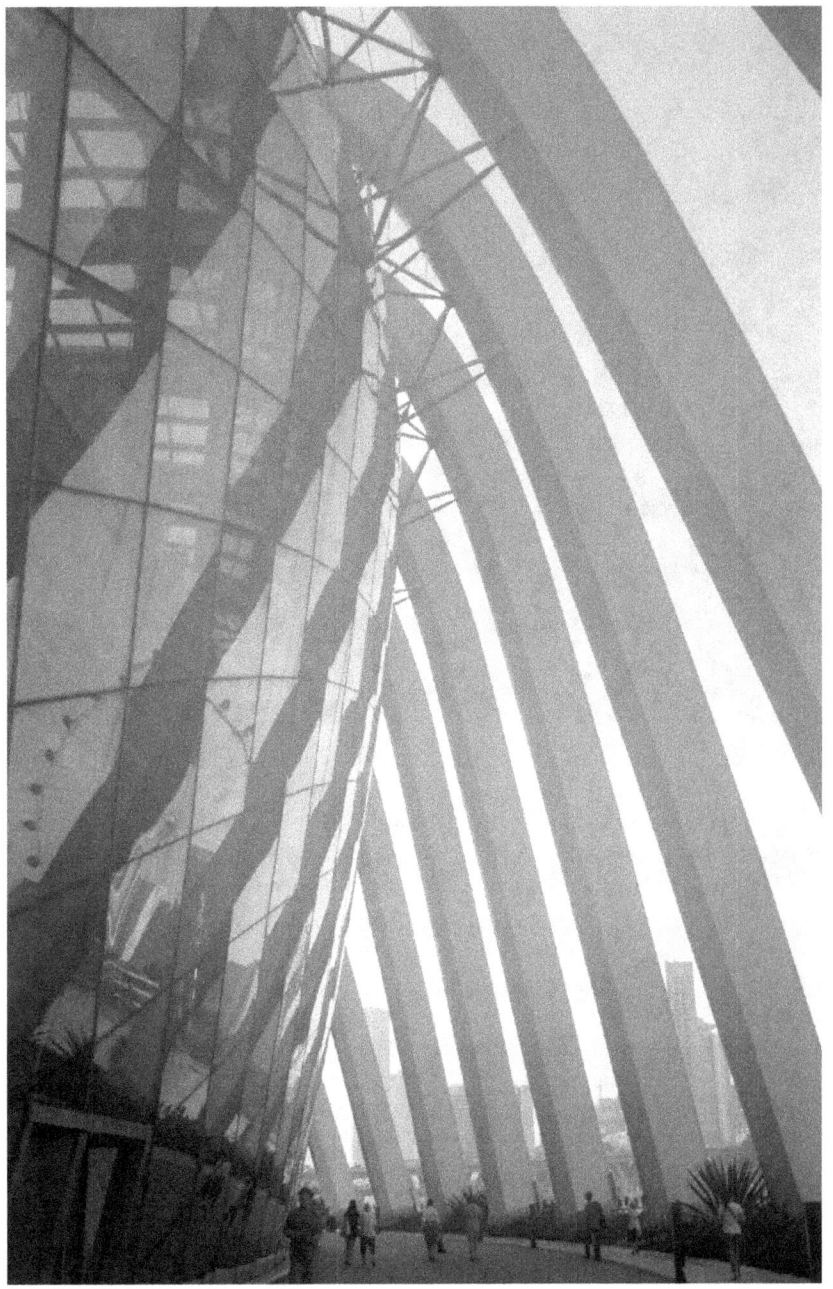

Fig. 11

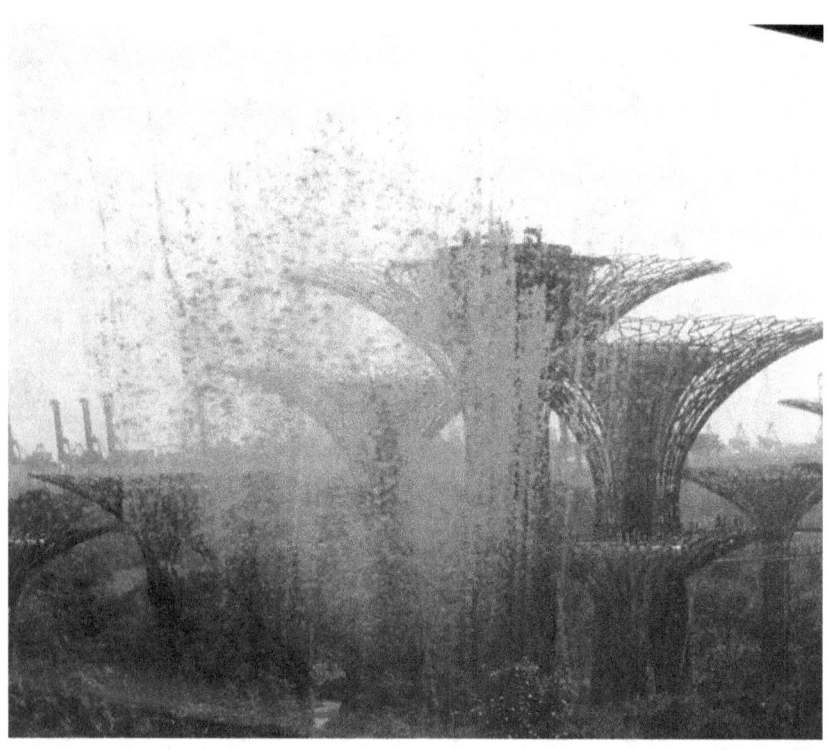

Fig. 12 While touring this perfectly maintained space, I am drawn to one pane of glass that reveals what happens when this space is not so meticulously maintained by so many labouring hands. This grungy smear blocks the view of what should be such a photogenic landscape, one that includes not only the Garden's Supertrees, but also an imposing sweep of port-land cranes, such potent markers of Singapore's booming economy. It is at this moment that the massive and impressive edifices of the conservatories suddenly appear more like fragile, thin envelopes enclosing a precariously simulated Eden. At the same time it becomes clear that it is the very conception and construction of this Earth Ship—the excessive extraction of plant species, metals, and materials—that is accelerating the destruction. I realize then that this is not just a garden of leisure and spectacle. It is both a living memorial to an already vanishing world, and a thriving fantasy of the earth's immanent undoing. It is the very materialization of this fantasy that is bringing on the end-of-times. Perhaps the only response is to write against this dream: to conjure another possible future. The question then becomes how to work athwart the apocalyptic future that this garden dreams so furtively? What other fantasies can be conjured?

Diplomacy in the Face of Gaia
Bruno Latour in conversation with Heather Davis

A March 2014 article in *The Guardian* predicted that industrialized civilization will collapse due to anthropogenic climate change within the next hundred years. The piece has gone viral, but the message does not come as breaking news for Bruno Latour.[1] For decades Latour has been making the argument that modernization has been on a warpath, and has most recently called for a revitalization of politics under the threat and promise of Gaia in the 2013 Gifford Lectures. Originally trained as an anthropologist, Latour has spent his career analyzing the practices of science in order to re-situate the epistemological assumptions of objectivity that subtend the subject-object divide. What he has shown is the utter inconsistency of such an orientation by elaborating the multiple actants within a given network that assert ontological plurality. These epistemic concerns are not benign or neutral, as they cannot be disentangled from politics, or from our very sense of being.

At least since the *Politics of Nature: How to Bring the Sciences into Democracy* (2004), Latour has been insisting upon the necessity for the modernization project to cede to what he calls "ecologization," or the understanding of our interconnected dependence upon the non-human world in which we are embedded and of which we are composed. His most recent work, *An Inquiry into Modes of Existence: An Anthropology of the Moderns* (AIME, 2013), can be seen as an extension and elaboration of *We Have Never Been Modern* (1991), flipping the argument on its head in order to take stock of our modern values in order to begin the difficult work of composing a people capable of facing Gaia.[2] This project could not come sooner, as the effects of climate change are beginning to be felt acutely across the globe, and are only predicted to get much worse. I had the opportunity to sit down with Bruno Latour in the AIME office in Paris to discuss these ideas; what follows is an edited transcript from our conversation in February 2014.

Heather Davis I want to begin with a statement you made in an interview for the Anthropocene Project at the Haus de Kulturen der Welt (HKW) in Berlin. You claim that one of the things that the Anthropocene provokes is the necessity to understand the interrelationship of science and politics, and that because of this set of ecological catastrophes we no longer have the luxury of believing in a clear division between these two domains. Do you think we are seeing, as a result of this collapse, a broader epistemic shift in the sciences towards alternate world-making devices, such as narration and storytelling?

Bruno Latour I think it's wishful thinking on the part of the people from the humanities that the sciences have changed that much. But it is a useful kind of wishful thinking because it is a way to move the argument out of the standard situation where you have people like us in science studies saying that science and politics have always been intermingled and most scientists, the vast majority, still saying we should separate them as much as possible. There is a change of mind of *some* scientists involved in ecology and climate on this question because they realize their usual defensive position—that is, maintaining science as separated as possible from politics—simply does not wash anymore. I am not sure they welcome the alternative that we propose, but at least they are listening to it in a way that is different from the previous characterizations of science studies as either dangerous or friendly relativism. So, in that sense there is a change, which I think is discernable among many scientists who are themselves attacked by other scientists in the name of science. The usual defense of "well, we are just doing science" is moot.

A second important thing is that the statements we now make about the world, about Gaia, are now framed as a warning. It is very, very difficult now to maintain the old idea of a division between statement of fact and statement of value when you say that "there is now 440 parts per million of CO_2 in the atmosphere." Even if you say it as coldly as possible, it sends a message that you should do something. So, the division between fact and value, which is the traditional way of handling these questions, is weakened.

Third, because of the very logic of the Anthropocene, you are inserted into the phenomena you study in a way that is unexpected and still unfathomed. The idea of a science that emerges from the dispassionate study of external phenomena is now much more difficult to sustain. The very distinction between the social and natural sciences breaks down because the argument that you are not supposed to be involved in what you study can no longer be maintained. A chemist working on CO_2 is fully integrated into a feedback mechanism, whatever he or she does, in a way that resembles an economist involved in policy, or a sociologist involved in statistics. So that's the third reason why the distinction between science and politics, and the old constitution of separating the two, seems in great need of an alternative. Now, I believe we have an alternative, but to say that it has been enthusiastically embraced by scientists would clearly be wishful thinking.

HD Do you believe the alternative is in the mode of diplomacy or the mode of narrativity?

BL Well, that is what I want to distinguish. Narrativity is another problem which is linked, but it's a much more puzzling philosophical question that is far less acceptable for the scientists, even those I've just mentioned, although it is of course very interesting for the humanities. But, when you consider that science is not about an abstract idea of "Data," but about data that have been obtained through a long process involving lots of instruments and carried out by the whole institution of science with agents throughout the world, then you can trace your way back to the origin of the scientific revolution, where the distinction was made between storytelling and data production. From that standpoint, it might be possible to imagine other things: entangled narratives or quali-quantitative data sets, there are lots of ways of approaching these questions. But, I think this argument would be more difficult to accept for the scientists. They are ready to move from the scientific-political question, but are they ready to move to the question of narrative? It is difficult because these words, like rhetoric, are difficult to implement positively. You can do that with Donna Haraway, but it's very hard to do that with my friend the CO_2 scientist from Paris VII, even when he is completely ready to abandon the idea of science and politics as separate domains and to talk about the "geopolitics of CO_2." I don't think you can move in the direction of narrative, even though when you add geopolitics, policy, alternative futures, and alternative cosmologies, you might nudge scientists in this direction.

There is a very important aspect of this discussion for the literary people, which is the source of my interest in collaborating with the novelist Richard Powers. The question is: are data a subset of narratives, or an opposition to narratives, or are narratives inside data? It is a question that you can approach from many different angles, such as the scientific, or quantitative study of literature. The literary study of science is of course something that interests me a lot, and that is not very surprising because there are lots of scientific traditions that feel perfectly at ease with this, especially natural history. In a way, it's one of the reasons why sciences of climate, let's say the Gaia sciences, are so strange to the eyes of other scientists and physicists—because they look a lot like natural history. [Alexander von] Humboldt would have understood them without difficulty. But, if it is close to natural history, then it is close to natural philosophy; this is actually very surprising for scientists and has become the cause of many of the worries of the physicists and mathematicians who are against the science of "climate responsibility" (a term itself that hovers on the distinction between fact and value). Those scientists are often against climate science because they say we cannot have made all the progress in basic science to end up back in natural history, where we were at the time of Humboldt and the European discovery expeditions. They are completely puzzled when they see that Charles D. Keeling got his data from the Hawaii Center by being there everyday for thirty years, or even fifty years.[3] So, when it doesn't look like big science, and it doesn't look like basic science, and it doesn't look like fundamental science, what then? It's the science of care, and it's as surprising for physicists and mathematicians as it is in women's studies. What does care do? What is care? With an instrument you do the same exercise every day; that doesn't look like particle physics. That is one reason why people—and I don't mean the people who are paid by the oil industry and coal industries, I'm not talking about those guys—are surprised, disappointed, worried that after the twentieth-century achievements of big science and basic science, science has "regressed" to model building (which they often see as an inferior science), to natural history, and to care. So that is one reason why there is skepticism. But, of course, in the history of science, many, many natural sciences have been, first of all, powerful narratives and very humble piecemeal constructions. As Simon Schaffer always says: if the philosophy of science had started with agriculture and not with physics it would be very different; that sort of prejudice under the division of labour between the humanities and the sciences has allowed these questions to be forgotten, but it is important to re-make the link.

HD You have shown in much of your work, most notably in *We Have Never Been Modern*, that within the epistemological assumptions of objectivity there is a tremendous effort exerted to assert the inanimacy of natural objects and animals, even while the liveliness of the world appears in the language of scientific documents. There is a revealing tension between trying to de-animate "facts" while at the same time relying upon the animism of the world.

BL Yes, the de-animation argument... I have never seen a scientist who would easily get into it, even though I've made it for a long time. There is a limit here. You have to go to semiotics, which I think is impossible for a practicing scientist. You have to consider the text like semioticians do; no matter how literate, or cultivated, or open scientists are, that move is very, very difficult. That's really a skill you learn when you are coming from the humanities. So, if I show them that their scientific paper on volcanoes or CO_2 is full of agents, actants, beings-transformed, etc., and that it might only be in the last line that all this is said to be just a set of causes and effects, you can show them that and they will agree, but it won't sink in. This is what we learn from having done PhDs in exegesis, literature, the humanities, etc.: narrative is hard to approach through literature for scientists. To me, it's much better to encourage this shift when you go into the detail of an experimental setting. You can help scientists attune to many of the features that they usually do unconsciously, or unwittingly, in their prose. We have a case that interests us a lot here about ants. Because ants and ANT (Actor Network Theory) are very related, we are always interested in ants. If you look at research about ants, many people would say that ants are not directed by any sort of superior entity—the organicist version—and that it is only "individual" ants that do the acting. But, we in the humanities are trained to be attentive to the dozens of cases where, in the texts of the same scientists who say we have abandoned the idea of a super organism, in fact, ants appear as a character, an actant, they are doing the job of a society, of a big organism, precisely what was not supposed to be there. There it works when you can show scientists that the semiotic aspect of a narration is actually carrying them where they don't want to go. They say, "I don't want to have a second degree with a society and a superior organism." Then I'll say "Look, here, twenty-five times in the text you wrote that a society, or a nest, or the colony is actually acting. Is this not a nice contradiction?" But they protest that it is only a matter of language and writing. And, I reply, "Yes, exactly!" So, you can do this, but it's a micro-negotiation.

Of course, there is a third level—complete metaphysics—which is inaccessible to humanities people and to scientists—the question of whether the world itself is narrated. I don't mean narrated by a human, but has itself an articulation that makes it accessible to words. And that would be more of a basic metaphysics. But that's not something you can put into the public because it's an esoteric argument. My argument would be that the world *is* articulated, so that narration is just one of the many ways to frame it. There is in the world, in the pulsation of the world itself, something that lends itself to articulation by speech. So, there are different levels to the argument.

To answer your question, what's interesting in the Anthropocene is that we pose all of those questions for scientists, as well as for those on the side of politics, the humanities, and art. Because of the Anthropocene situation there are lots of connections that were superficial before, where people would say "yes, it's nice to have a link between artists and scientists, they are creative," but now these are more directly connected. We had a meeting last year, last October in Toulouse, where we had the artists Tomás Saraceno and Adam Lowe, plus a musician, a graphic novelist, a physicist, a modeler, an oceanographer, philosophers, sociologists, etc., where we were all trying to understand how to handle the Anthropocene in our respective languages.[4] And it was clearly not at all the sort of discussion I organized maybe thirty years ago in San Diego, where you would have had artists capturing some sort of aesthetic aspect of science. Here, we are talking about the common articulation of the Anthropocene. That has changed. So in that sense, you're right, there's a narrativity, and an urgency also, shared by people who are completely different in their approach. I do think the conversation has changed, so that is why this experiment around the Anthropocene is so exciting.

HD One of the things I've been curious about in your work is how you are thinking about Gaia in relationship to the Anthropocene, particularly because they are each loaded with very specific ideological constructions—one from the realm of the deities, and the other from scientific discourse—that don't necessarily cohere. In your work, what do these two conceptualizations of the present environmental catastrophe do? Do you see a tension in using them together?

BL First, in terms of the history of concepts, they're not within the same timeframe. I mean Gaia exists before the Anthropocene; that is, in a deeper history, rather than being contemporary. In terms of agency, Gaia, if we follow Lovelock's argument, used to be indifferent to us. It's very complicated, even for Lovelock it's complicated. The traditional version, I mean the 1970s version of Gaia, is indifferent to humans. Now, of course, the Anthropocene makes the loop so tight that it might no longer be true that Gaia is indifferent, we certainly act on it or her in some profound ways. For me, I'm using these two concepts philosophically because I'm not an earth scientist, even though I read a lot of this work. Gaia is the localization of nature, that's what's so interesting and completely disturbing for scientists and natural scientists—it doesn't apply to Venus, it doesn't apply to the moon (well, that's not completely true). And, it's a restricted conception of nature, so there is what I call the infra-lunar aspect to Gaia. Then there are the highly complex dynamics of Gaia, for which there are lots of metaphors, none of which are very good: one organic, one cybernetic. But there are a lot of studies now on the weakness of those metaphors. I use Gaia as the name of a mystery or problem surrounding the question of composition of all these agents that are connected in some way, which I try to articulate, not to my satisfaction, in the Gifford Lectures. I hope I will do better in the published essays. But what is so interesting in Gaia is quite independent from the human race. Gaia was interesting 10,000 years ago; even two millennia ago, Gaia was still interesting.

Now the Anthropocene is a kind of fabulous acceleration of one of the many connections inside Gaia around the question of the human. If Gaia is local, the Anthropocene is even more local: it is local in time. It is the result of one species, and it's impossible not to be anthropocentric about it. So, it's about one species, and one small time span. That is what interests Dipesh Chakrabarty so much—it's simultaneously a deepening of history, because it now moves CO_2, plate tectonics, pollution, etc., but in an extraordinary restriction, because it is basically describing a period of only 200 years, or even sixty, which provides a very different view of history. I think it is very important to maintain the distinction between the two, even though you can consider that the Anthropocene is an acceleration, a sudden acceleration, a tipping point of Gaia's history. Because of the Anthropocene, the destiny of Gaia is connected to ours in a way that's not predictable, which would not have been predicted by Lovelock twenty years ago. There is this argument from James Hansen, a scientist and activist from NASA who retired recently, who put forward a scenario that because of us the earth could become like Mars: that is, a dead planet. It's one of the scenarios; in that sense, Gaia is linked to us in a way whereby it or she cannot be indifferent to us.

HD But in a mode of bleak optimism, I think it's important to remember all of the previous mass extinction events on the planet: although the current extinction is happening at an amazing rate, life will go on.[5]

BL But the Mars scenario is really a dead planet. This is why it is a bleak optimism, because in most Lovelock scenarios we disappear along with many other species, but life goes on. But, the point of view of bleak optimism is actually a view from nowhere. I don't think we require a scenario of disappearance. I think that's a mistake, because futures are multiple and there are many ways in which humans will cope. The question is what politics anticipate the catastrophe sufficiently so that these futures stay open. And that is, of course, one of the reasons why so many people, like Isabelle Stengers, are worried about the word Anthropocene—because its political acumen will make it disappear very quickly. I take it as a very, very mobilizing term. But I hear what other critics say: the Anthropocene can be highly demobilizing because of its re-naturalization of the human, which is also the idea that many geologists have. So we are back to another kind of reductionism, except now we, the humans, are the geological force. The human as geological force can also be read as another dialectic revamped; it could be the dialectics of nature. I mean, you read Engels and you just modify a little bit the expansion and the intensity and you have exactly the same story; so it's a dangerous term.

And then there is the third immense danger, which Clive Hamilton has studied: geo-engineering, or a sort of optimistic version of the Anthropocene.[6] There are people who welcome the Anthropocene and say, "great, we are finally at the scale of the phenomenon that we want to obtain." What the father of the H-bomb, Edward Teller, wanted to do was to create great works of infrastructure by building dams and cavity seas to re-engineer the Earth. There is even a little bit of that perspective in Sloterdijk. So, there are a lot of ways of welcoming the Anthropocene, just as there are a lot of ways of re-naturalizing the Anthropocene. For me, the critique that's the most troubling to consider is that the human is already unified under the sign of the Anthropocene. Of course, politically that's absurd. There is no human able to play the role of the *anthropos*. So, in that sense, I am not completely sure that the Anthropocene concept will last. I can see why it is interesting now, but the moment of interest might be short-lived because there are many reasons why it's counterproductive.

HD I completely agree with your hesitations. It is also a concept that has picked up speed very quickly in theoretical and art circles, and has become a capturing device, or a collecting term. It's a very seductive concept, which I think is both its strength and weakness.

BL It has a couple of advantages. One is that you don't have to say anything about science studies anymore. At the time of the Anthropocene, you don't have to show again that science and politics are related, so that speeds things up. But to re-present this question at the time of the Anthropocene, nothing is simplified, because all the apparatuses of Man—Man dominating Nature—come back, except it takes a slightly dystopian version, which can be shifted a little bit and it becomes utopian again. Then we say: "Oh great, we're so strong that we can re-make the planet"; we've become the engineers of the planet. I don't think it's a concept that's going to last, but while it's here we should use it because it is a connector, and it brings together artists, scientists, and philosophers. That's why we're commissioning this monument to the Anthropocene by Tomás Saraceno in Toulouse; once it's built, I will forget about the Anthropocene. We will use other terms.

HD I want to return to the question of politics because I think that the strength of your most recent book, *An Inquiry into Modes of Existence: An Anthropology of the Moderns*, is to unravel all of the primary institutions that you identify—law, religion, politics, economy—in order to recompose a modality where we can begin to rebuild the political systems that are necessary to confront what is coming towards us. But clearly, not all of us are going to be affected by the force of climate change equally.

BL That is why the *anthropos* is not the right agent of history.

HD Exactly, but isn't the proposition about the people of OWAAB (Out of Which We Are All Born) that you discuss in the Gifford Lectures—that is, of a people ready to face Gaia—caught in the same problem as the *anthropos*?[7] Don't we need to account for environmental justice?

BL   There is the obvious geopolitical question, which is raised by everybody working on this issue, and that is the complete inequality of the impact of ecology. All of the negative impacts are intensified for the people who are not responsible. That is basically true. All the people who are not responsible, or the least responsible, or are only now becoming responsible, are the ones most affected. For example, even the Chinese, who, because they are no longer poor, share some responsibility, feel an impact infinitely greater in terms of living conditions than those in the US. So, that's a geopolitical question to which I have nothing in particular to say, because it's obvious. The question is: how do you do politics in a way that leads to a different type of work. How do you re-present the issue? How do you break down the national state system of negotiation so that you can actually build what Carl Schmidt called leagues, or lines, which are different from nations? So that is very interesting, but it's another topic for debate.

The project of AIME was conceived before the concept of Gaia became a symbolic figure for a new politics. I had read Lovelock, of course, many, many years ago, but the project of AIME is twenty-seven years old. From the beginning it was inspired by ecological politics and the environmental movement. But there is preliminary work to be done on what a collective is before you can turn your interests to what is required by Gaia. Of course, the AIME project is only a horizon, a horizon of a possible sovereign—or sovereignty as I developed it in the Gifford Lectures—something that weighs on you in a way that was not the way nature was before. So it's a very complicated new role that I think we have to politicize in terms of political philosophy, but this is very difficult to do. What is the request of Gaia? That's where the fact that Gaia is the name of a goddess is especially interesting. So a whole elaboration of what Gaia is becomes necessary.

But in AIME, the solution is simpler. Whatever you describe as ecology, the responsibility largely weighs on those who have invented what we call modernization. This is hard to contest when modernization is now everywhere, including India, China, and Brazil. So, my argument is quite simple. It is to ask what has happened as modernization. It's pretty important that we have an idea of what that means, especially because then you can open a negotiation with the other collectives whose responsibility is very minimal, but whose ways of life and organizing their polity and their cosmos are very important as a resource for us. You cannot enter the world of Eduardo Viveiros de Castro's American Indians without having done this preparatory work because otherwise it will remain a dispute about modernizing or not modernizing.[8] So my attempt in AIME is preparatory to meeting Gaia. It is to say, when the former modern will finally understand what we have done and also what we are worth—not only flagellating ourselves—we might be able to build other connections with all of the other ways of being, including those in the modern's own collective. Because there are many other ways of being which have never been modern, even inside. Then the question of turning to Gaia becomes interesting. That is what the whole project is about; we will publish another version of the book that just goes through all the crossings.[9] There is one table entirely of the aims of AIME throughout the whole book, and it's quite amusing because then you see the preparatory work required to meet Gaia. The book attempts to change the view of technology in a way that is not the way of mastery, which then allows you to modify the ways which law and religion are understood, and then you can begin to negotiate with other techniques. But it's also a slightly bizarre project because it asks, in a time of urgency, to think slowly about what we have done. That's what we'll do in Montreal in March with our meeting with Eduardo Kohn and others. We will simulate the negotiation. If we, the Westerners, present ourselves with AIME's terms, how does it change our connection with other collectives? How can we read the literature differently so that it's not just about beliefs? And, of course, this is completely fanciful...

HD ...completely fanciful but deadly serious. Throughout the book I was thinking about the question of the diplomat and diplomacy. This position seems necessary, in terms of composing a new kind of collectivity, but I was also hesitant about how the figure of the diplomat seems already to presume two, or more, opposing sides. And the diplomat itself is—you highlight this—slippery, not quite trustworthy...

BL ...it is someone who betrays.

HD Yes. Diplomacy is an incredibly useful mode of connection, and it is always a kind of betrayal. Were you thinking of the diplomat as a betrayal of the moderns? The diplomat itself seems to be such a modern idea.

BL No, but betrayal is part of diplomacy because the diplomat betrays those who have sent him or her precisely because he or she modifies their values. He or she sees that the official attachment is not the one to be ready to die for. So, betrayal is a necessity; it introduces a margin and a space to manoeuvre. But the reason why diplomacy is the metanarrative of the project is because it's not science. It's a diplomatic project about how to compose—in all senses of the word composition. So, to say that there is a horizon of diplomacy is to say we have to state our agreement or disagreement. We are scientific peers, learning what it is to be together. And that's one of the problems for AIME because the project is not a scientific project, the inquiry is more like an inquest, even though inquest is a legal term. We present AIME, and then it's judged by my peers, which is ridiculous because the thing will explode immediately. That's what the Americans are doing when they discuss the book, they just say: "This guy has not read Hannah Arendt and yet he speaks about politics... he doesn't even cite Heidegger." Of course, it's not a scientific project! It's a diplomatic project where the diplomatic figure is actually part of one mode, which is the mode of [PRE] or preposition.[10] Some people say that it is only philosophy, but it's a philosophy à la Isabelle Stengers and Donna Haraway; it's a philosophy of composition. It's a diplomatic philosophy. It's not a neo-realist or neo-rationalist definition of philosophy. It's still uncertain, but the position is that we won't be able to face Gaia if we are modern. I mean there is no place for moderns and for Gaia; one of us has to cede.

It's perfectly possible that with geo-engineering and re-modernization we might actually go one step further and delay the catastrophe to the next century; this is completely possible. But let's say we succeed in establishing that modernization has to be re-modernized—this is Ulrich Beck's argument—it has to be deeply modified. How do we do that? Well, we do that by putting on the table the values we think we are beholden to for the first time. Then we can open the negotiations because we don't mistake our values for our metaphysics, so to speak. This enables us to defend science without defending epistemology, to defend politics without defending Hobbes, and so forth. So that gives a margin of maneouvre. When we have re-opened this connection with the collective we can say that what we used to call ecology or ecologization can now be a synonym for civilization, or a new form of globalization, but in a very, very different form than just an extension of modernism. That's what I call composition. Of course, it's absurdly big. But the advantage of thinking big here is that you simultaneously see all the problems. And, for the few people who are interested in the project, this is what interests them—that you simultaneously, for once, make an inventory of values.

HD Near the end of the book, in the chapter on economy, you discuss the way in which the world itself emits values, how the world emits morality. You write, "And just as no one, once the instrument has been calibrated, would think of asking the geologist if radioactivity is 'all in his head,' 'in his heart,' or 'in the rocks,' no one will doubt any longer that the world *emits morality* toward anyone who possesses an instrument sensitive enough to register it".[11] This idea isn't disconnected from previous thinkers, such as Jakob von Uexküll, for whom values are necessary for organisms to differentiate between the things in their environment and to adapt to them. But, for me, morality is such a loaded term, tied to a history of good and evil, which Nietzsche's philosophical project was dedicated to eliminating. Why return to morality?

BL Value is in the world. That is a general principle for all the modes, it starts with [REP], which is Whitehead's argument.[12] Value has been withdrawn from the world as a modernist operation, which is very bizarre—even for the moderns in practice—and, of course, very bizarre for all other collectives. Value is a property of the world. I use morality because there is morality in all of the modes—there is an inner fiction. The difference between good and bad is what defines the mode. And law has a different definition of morality than religion, etc.

But there is one mode that is very difficult to disentangle, and that is the economy, which is a big problem. As long as we cannot disentangle economy, economies, and economics, it's very difficult to move out of the modernist situation because it's very difficult to encounter the other agencies. This problem does not occur in biology, chemistry, or physics, where very few people encounter the world. Even though the naturalist, scientific reductionist worldview weighs heavily, its weight is nothing compared to that of the economy. So the real enemy is the economy. Not because it's a bad science—it's an interesting science—but because it makes so many assumptions about what it is to be political, what it is to be legal, what it is to be in the world, and so forth. So morality is one way of re-visiting the question of the optimum, which has been placed at the centre of the economy. It's one way of revisiting scruples. Morality in this scheme of things, even though it's the last one on the list, has a somewhat grandiose position—although it's simultaneously a local one—because there is morality all over the place, in many different modes. I'm very interested in the morality of law and religion. I thought it was useful to re-emphasize that when we arrive in this domain of economy, the first absolutely essential question is morality, not under any sort of final definition which would be a calculation—that's the behavioural definition, the calculation of pleasure and pain, invented at the beginning of the nineteenth century—but as worry, doubts, scruples. I try every time to find a very traditional definition, and to give it a little twist. So the scruple about ends and means is very traditional, but it was unfairly limited to humans.

I have to say that the whole part on the economy is the one that is in the most need of re-drafting, because I went at it too bluntly. I tried to be subtler in the other chapters, but here I approach it fighting, in part because the enemy is so strong. The question of science is, in fact, a piece of cake compared to the economy, because we are more deeply entrenched in second nature than in first nature. When I was in Karlsruhe last week, I showed my students a Greenpeace campaign that said, "If the world was a bank, it would already have been saved." This is a magnificent motto.

So, ethics is a beautiful way to organize philosophy, but the aim here is very small, which is to say, if you want to re-populate the economy, you have to re-populate the passionate interests, or everything difficult to access from economic theory or an anthropology of economy. To re-populate organizational theory is extremely difficult because organizational theory is very difficult to foreground. How do you allocate resources to take an economic turn—the place where the numbers of people interested in it would be maximum, and where the people mobilized is minimum. That's the part where morality has to take over, so to speak.

But your question is important. The argument is actually that morality is a sum of all the other modes, because every one of them carries this difference between good and bad which does not wait for the mode of morality to arise. The great difficulty with the project in general is that many terms are multi-modal, and yet specialized by the way they have been elaborated into history. The reading has to be transversal. We are now imagining other ways to do this, to get into the writing. What Christophe Leclercq, the project manager for AIME, did recently was publish all the crossings in one column on the AIME website, so you can see all the interconnections, which gives another idea of the project.[13]

HD In your Royal Academy Lecture in the Humanities and Social Sciences called "The Affects of Capitalism," you make a strong argument for how the economy, under a capitalist framework, now occupies the position of a modern transcendent principle.[14] Can you say more about the relationship between capitalism and economy?

BL I'm getting at this question from the scientific studies of economics, of economics as a science, and not from the fight against capitalism on the left. I'm deeply suspicious of the massive agency that is attributed to capitalism, which is a bit like Gaia. So, I think that this Greenpeace slogan "If the world was a bank it would already have been saved" is very true, but true because of a philosophical investment made in capitalism by both the enemy and by the proponent. My line has been deflationary. Let's limit the numbers of things that you can attribute to capitalism and let's distribute them and see what's actually happening. This is what the French sociologist Gabriel Tarde did, and I published a little book on Tarde in relation to that.[15] I take this approach out of an irritation towards leftism, but also an irritation regarding the empirical realm. I mean, how do you study capitalism if it's too big, if it's too powerful, if it's too integrated, if it's too coherent? When there are so many things attributed to capitalism, there is also the danger of paralysis. This is dangerous when you link it to geo-engineering, Gaia, and the Anthropocene because there is an irreversible trajectory built around the link between capitalism and geo-engineering as an answer to the crisis as a Plan B (one I hope might be reversible). Hacking, cutting into pieces, distributing, banalizing, and limiting capitalism is, for me, the same sort of thing I did with science. I mean: don't overdo it, don't exaggerate what you grant, even if you are fighting it. With science, it's clearer; people who fight against the expansion of objectivity and the danger of techno-science, even though they think it's a critique of science, say nothing about science itself. Science is linked to networks and small things. My bourgeois, provincial, French attitude is that when something is networked, you can do something to it and something against it; but you cannot do anything against what is assumed to be overpowering, immense, definitive, and gigantic.

Notes

1. Nafeez Ahmed, "Nasa-funded Study: Industrial Civilisation Headed for 'Irreversible Collapse'?" *The Guardian,* 14 March 2014, www.theguardian.com/environment/earth-insight/2014/mar/14/nasa-civilisation-irreversible-collapse-study-scientists.
2. Bruno Latour, *An Inquiry into Modes of Existence: An Anthropology of the Moderns* (Cambridge, MA: Harvard University Press, 2013). The digital platform includes notes, bibliography, index, glossary, and supplementary documentation at www.modesofexistence.org.
3. Charles D. Keeling was a chemist whose research measuring CO_2 levels at the Mauna Loa Observatory led to the discovery of anthropogenic climate change. See Charles D. Keeling, "Rewards and Penalties of Monitoring the Earth," *Annual Review of Energy and the Environment* 23 (November 1998): 25–82.
4. "What Aesthetic for the Sciences of Gaia?" Festival La Novela, Toulouse, France, 9 October 2013.
5. Elizabeth Kolbert, *The Sixth Extinction: An Unnatural History* (New York: Henry Holt and Co., 2014).
6. Clive Hamilton, *Earthmasters: The Dawn of the Age of Climate Engineering* (New Haven: Yale University Press, 2013).
7. Bruno Latour, *Facing Gaia: Six Lectures on the Political Theology of Nature*, 2013 Gifford Lectures on Natural Religion, http://www.bruno-latour.fr/node/486.
8. Eduardo Viveiros de Castro, *From the Enemy's Point of View: Humanity and Divinity in an Amazonian Society* (Chicago: University of Chicago Press, 1992).
9. See www.modesofexistence.org/crossings.
10. [PRE] is defined as that which "is necessary in the inquiry since it allows us to go back to the interpretive keys which allow us to prepare for what comes after: in the [NET] mode, which describes networks, it allows for the definition of the minimal metalanguage necessary for the deployment of modes." See Latour, *An Inquiry into Modes of Existence*.
11. Latour, *An Inquiry into Modes of Existence*, 456; emphasis in original.
12. [REP] is the abbreviation for reproduction, "a particular mode of existence that does not overlap in any way with the notions of world, nature or the physical, but which brings out existents' capacity to provide for their subsistence by running the risk of reprise and reproduction. Even though this mode has been shaped by the question of forces and living beings, it bears on all societies and thus on institutions, corporate bodies etc., too." See Latour, *An Inquiry into Modes of Existence*.
13. See www.modesofexistence.org/questions-common-to-each-of-the-crossings.
14. This lecture is online at www.youtube.com/watch?v=8i-ZKfShovs&ntz=1.
15. Bruno Latour and Vincent Antonin Lepinay, *The Science of Passionate Interests: An Introduction to Gabriel Tarde's Economic Anthropology* (Chicago: Prickly Paradigm Press, 2009).

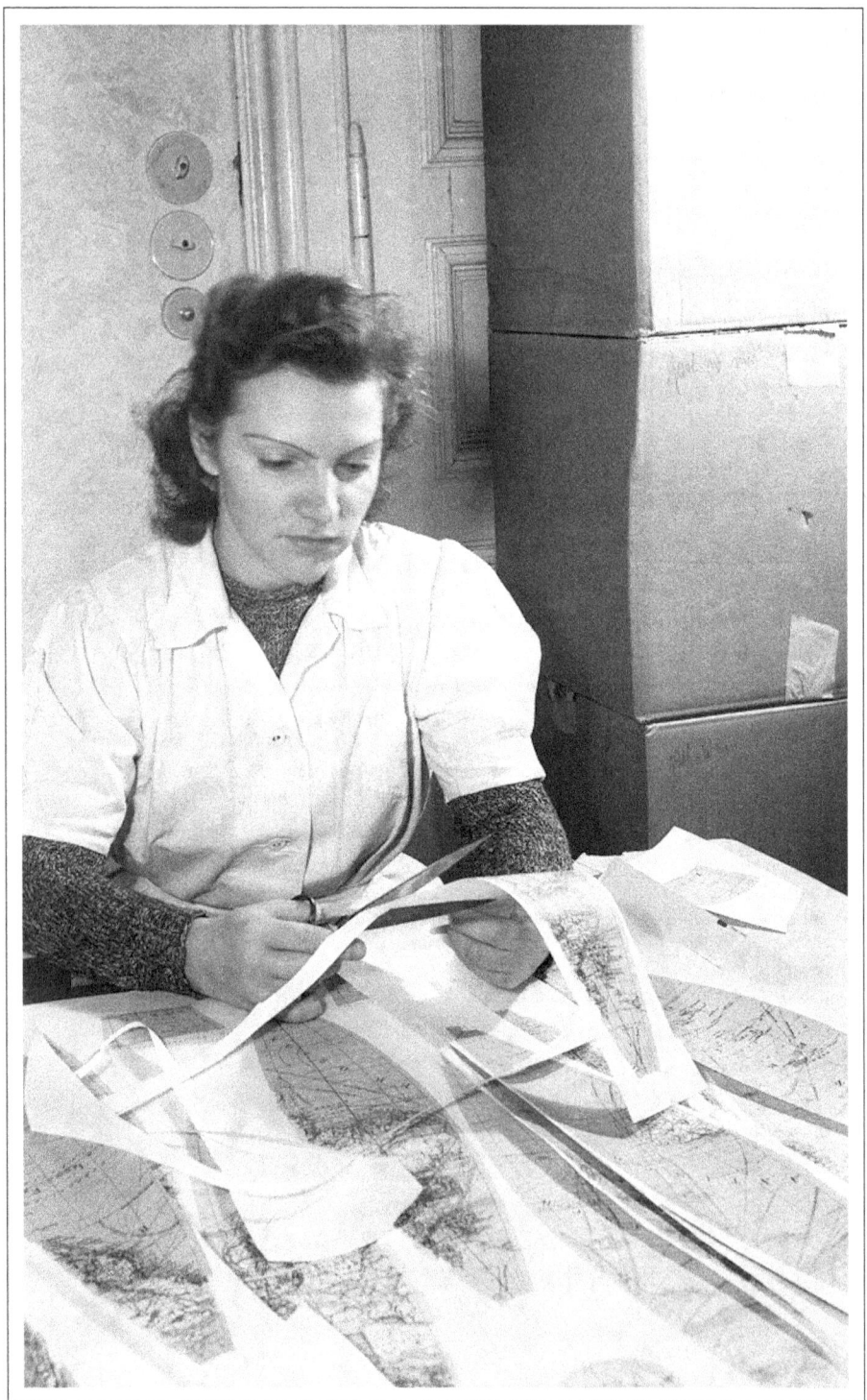

Becoming Aerosolar:
From Solar Sculptures to Cloud Cities

Tomás Saraceno, Sasha Engelmann & Bronislaw Szerszynski

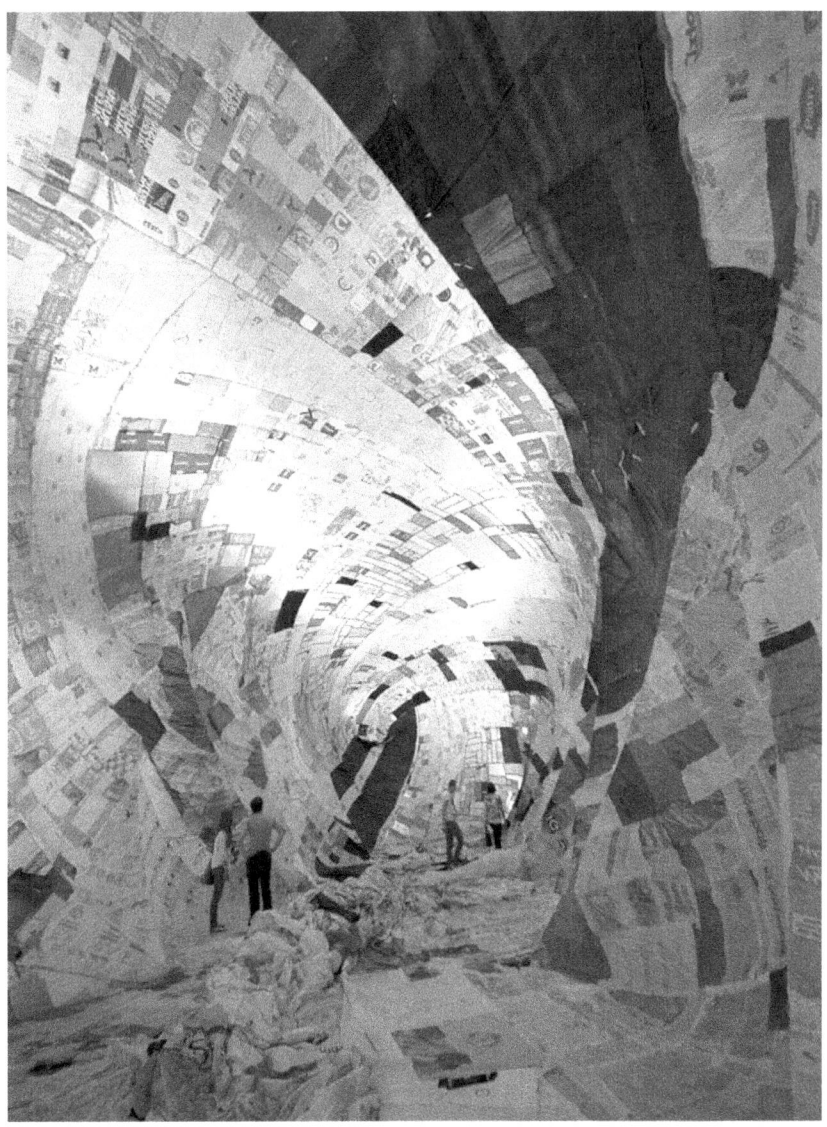

Museo Aero Solar, presented by Tomás Saraceno for the "*Anthropocene Monument,*" 2014, at Les Abattoirs, Toulouse, France, curated by Bruno Latour, Olivier Michelon, and Bronislaw Szerszynski; photo courtesy Tomás Saraceno, 2014.

Fig. 01

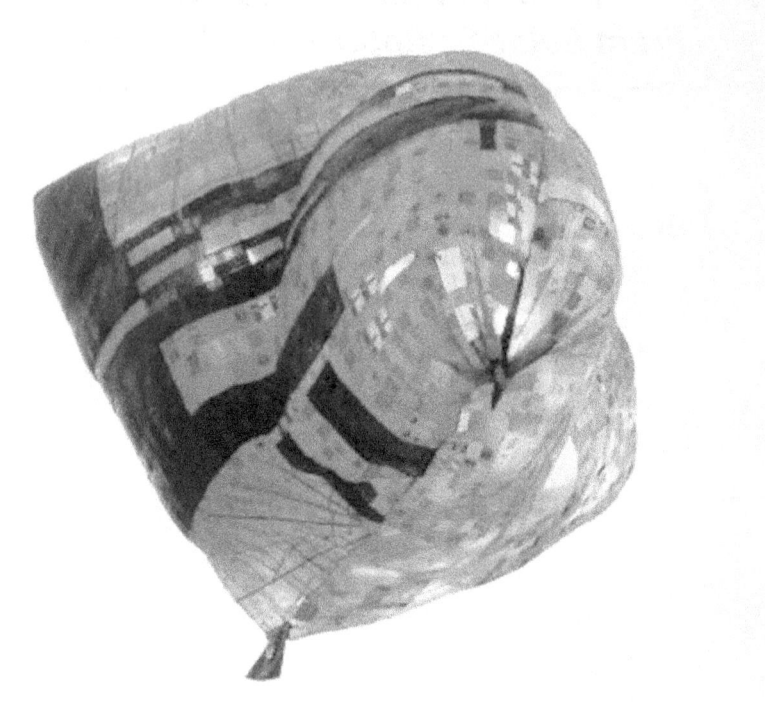

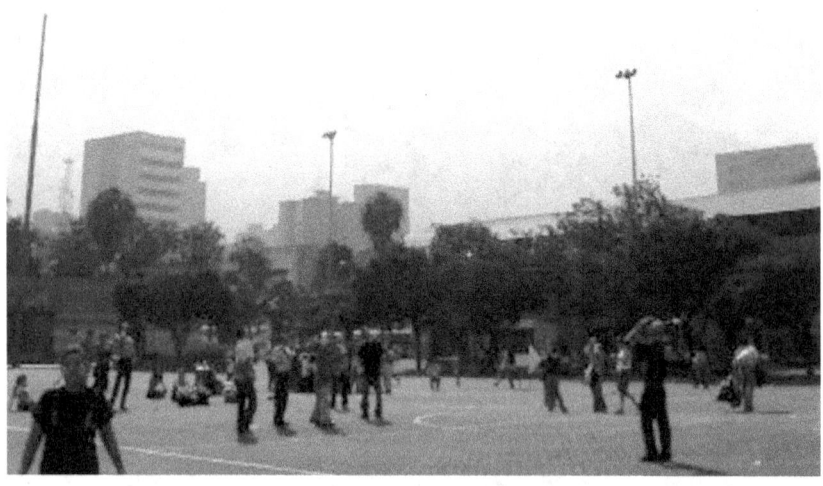

Fig. 02   *Museo Aero Solar* at Medellín, Colombia, 2009. *Museo Aero Solar* is a flying museum, a solar sculpture completely made up of reused plastic bags, with new sections being added each time it travels the world, thus changing techniques and shapes, and growing in size every time it sets sail in the air. *Museo Aero Solar* stands for a different conception of space and energy, both anomalous and forceful at the same time. The core of the Museo resides in the inventiveness of local inhabitants, not in its image: among collective action and art, do-it-together technology and experiment, it is a voyage both backwards and forward in time; photo courtesy Alberto Pesavento, 2009.

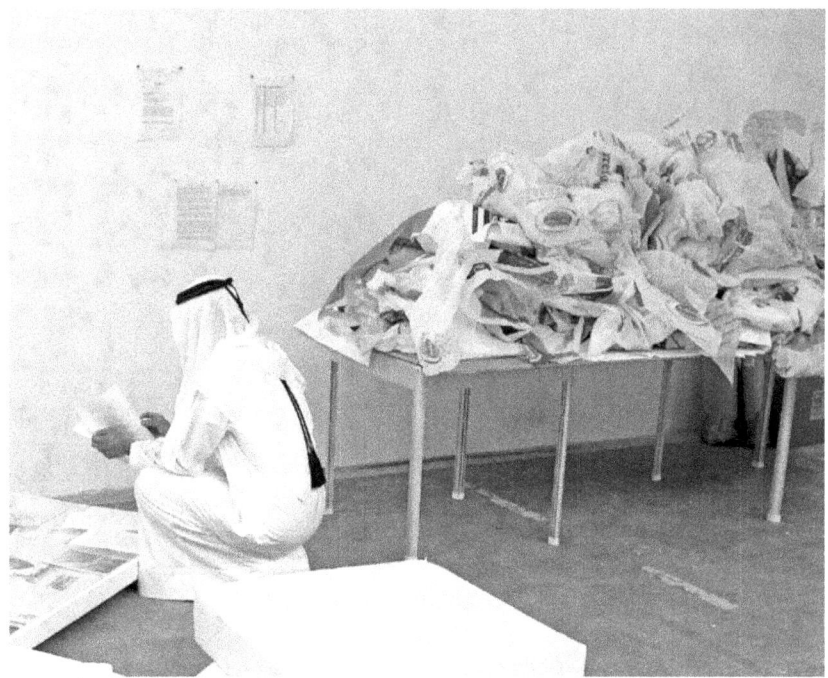

Museo Aero Solar at Sharjah, United Arabs Emirates, 2007; photo courtesy of Tomás Saraceno, 2007.   Fig. 03

To become aerosolar is to imagine a metabolic and thermodynamic transformation of human societies' relation with both the Earth and the Sun.[1] It is an invitation to think of new ways to move and sense the circulation of energy. And, it is a scalable process to re-pattern atmospheric dwelling and politics through an open-source ecology of practices, models, data—and a sensitivity to the more-than-human world.

Nikolai Kardashev predicted that as societies advanced, they would become more adept at harnessing the energy of their nearest star. Studies of past transitions in society's energetic relation with the sun suggest two possibilities for sustaining large populations: "solar societies" that monopolize land area, capturing sunlight through agriculture and domesticated animals, and increasingly through biofuels and solar panels; or "fossil-fuel societies" that break the dependency on land surface by mining ancient hydrocarbons. Becoming aerosolar would realize a third, alternative future in which civilization is truly solar-powered, but also liberated from Earth's surface to become airborne. This is the promise of a future *solar-cene.*

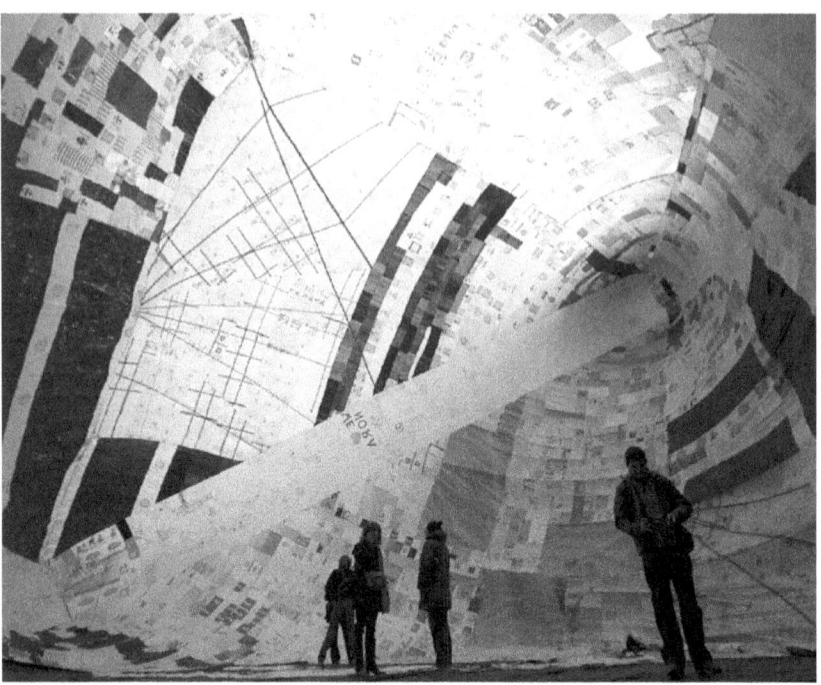

Fig. 04   *Museo Aero Solar* at Lyon, France; photo courtesy of Tomás Saraceno, 2007.

To become aerosolar is to gain buoyancy when air inside an envelope is heated, expands, and generates lift. Large aerosolar structures can become buoyant through the temperature differential created by the metabolism of living bodies in their interiors; smaller ones achieve buoyancy by capturing the short waves of sunlight during the day and infrared radiation from the Earth at night. They do not use helium, hydrogen, solar panels, or batteries; there is no burner, except for the sun or living beings inside.

Some flying solar sculptures can provide platforms for artistic practice and citizen science, redistributing access to the air above us. Such sculptures can reveal the internal shape of the atmosphere through their movement; circle the globe on jet streams; monitor atmospheric chemistry, convection, and fluid dynamics; and expand the critical zones of our sensing of the Earth System. In the spirit of groups like OpenStreetMap and Grassroots Mapping, solar lighter-than-air vehicles can also take high-definition images of Earth's surface and combine this aerial cartography with continuous sensing of the dynamics of the Earth's atmosphere. In this way, they link aerography and alternative cartographies, advancing beyond traditional techniques of mapping the "shape" of the Earth, while promoting free and democratic access to aero-stratigraphic data.

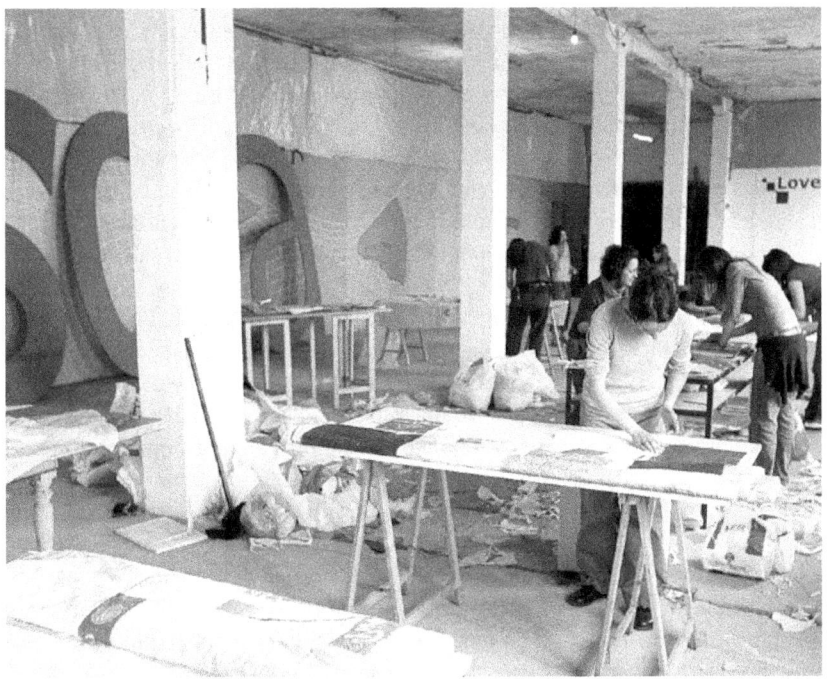

Museo Aero Solar at Isola Art Center neighbourhood in Milan, Italy, 2007; photo courtesy of Tomás Saraceno, 2007.

Fig. 05

One of these solar, lighter-than-air sculptures is Museo Aero Solar, which is both a solar museum and a "monument" to the Anthropocene.[2] Working together, people melt the edges of reused plastic bags in an act that embodies an ethos of care and generosity, transforming waste plastic from the iconic material of the "bad" Anthropocene into a shared aerial canvas for a possible "good" Anthropocene. The Museo is launched at dawn: as the sun warms the membrane, energy is pulled into the air inside. As the pressure differential increases, the Museo inflates and rises, flying to a new place where it will be recovered and launched again.

Launching a solar sculpture like Museo Aero Solar requires a sensitivity to the elements, especially as they are influenced by the sun. To watch the object inflate is to sense molecules vibrating against the inner membrane. It is to understand that during the daytime, the lower atmosphere is unstable, causing vertical masses of air to rise. Bodies of air alter the refractivity of the atmosphere, bending radio and GPS signals.

But the Museo also heralds a new way of life, suggesting that we as living beings could inhabit and move through the volume of the atmosphere. It makes us realize that our bodies are just like the Museo: membranes and passages permeated by air. And if we, too, lift from the surface, we move with the airy masses, sensing stillness in motion. Solar, lighter-than-air sculptures could provide new nomadic ways of dwelling on the Earth, as macroscopic forms of aeroplankton set themselves adrift on the winds, containing diverse and hybrid forms of life. New, shifting assemblies would appear in the air—cumulo-cities, cirrus-cities, stratocumulo-cities—as aerosolar structures cohere one day and dissipate another, according to the interacting dynamics of atmospherics, economics, politics, and culture.

However, activating the potential of an aerosolar society would require us not only to cultivate a new, thermodynamic imagination, but also to challenge the existing, politically demarcated volumes partitioning the atmosphere. The current "rules of the air" favour a fossil-fuel-based economy of heavier-than-air transport. We are petitioning international bodies to change these rules: just as steamboats give way to sail boats on international waters, so should planes give way to lighter-than-air solar vehicles.

In the words of the great aerial voyager Alberto Santos-Dumont: "We were off, going at the speed of the air current in which we now lived and moved. Indeed for us, there was no more wind [...] infinitely gentle is this unfelt movement forward and upward."[3]

Notes

1   This article is an experiment in thinking and writing together. Tomás Saraceno is an artist who has been working for the last fifteen years on the ideas of Cloud Cities/Air Port Cities and started Museo Aero Solar in conversation with Isola Art Center. Bronislaw Szerszynski's research draws on the social sciences, humanities, arts, and natural sciences in order to locate contemporary changes in the relationship between humans, environment, and technology in the longer perspective of human and planetary history. Sasha Engelmann's research concerns the political and aesthetic dimensions of air and atmosphere. We would like to thank Derek McCormack, Etienne Turpin and Nigel Clark, who, through many conversations, have helped us deepen these ideas. Becoming Aerosolar is intended as a future entry in Wikipedia: we welcome you to edit, contribute to, and appropriate this text so that it reflects a wider authorship.

2   Museo Aero Solar was presented in the exhibition "Anthropocene Monument," curated by Bruno Latour, Bronislaw Szerszynski, and Olivier Michelon at Les Abattoirs, Toulouse, 3 October 2014–4 January 2015.

3   Alberto Santos-Dumont, quoted in Paul Hoffman, *Wings of Madness: Alberto Santos-Dumont and the Invention of Flight* (New York: Theia, 2003), 41.

In the Planetarium: The Modern Museum on the Anthropocenic Stage

Vincent Normand

Importing the concept of the Anthropocene into art theory and aesthetics implies negotiating with a simple yet acute contradiction. The Anthropocene indifferently encircles both human affairs and the materiality of the planet, thus constituting a tool of "figuration" which makes visible inherited epistemological separations by radically destabilizing them. At the same time, the Anthropocene is a universalizing and unifying machine ceaselessly invoking the largest possible frames, in which art's manifold horizon of representations can easily fade into the background.

This contradiction echoes another one, relative to the historical constitution of the space of art as an allegedly autonomous sphere of experience, whose negativity and transgressive ethos were founded on the economy of the limit which defined the symbolic and epistemic frameworks of modernity, while also producing a field of reflexivity that allowed it to stand at a critical distance from them. Moreover, if most of the modernist and postmodernist discussions of the situation of art in the twentieth century have focused on this question of autonomy (either as an event to be brought forward, purified and achieved, or as a condition to be critically deconstructed), surprisingly, the material and concrete history of the gradual entry of art into a regime of exceptionality and extra-territoriality (its epistemological and symbolical "insularization" throughout modernity) remains to be written.

The claim of this essay is that such a history can be initiated through a modeling of the ontological template against which modernity established its scientific, political, and aesthetic project. In the cosmography drawn up by this ontological template, the modern institution of art played a paradoxical role—one that the concept of Anthropocene helps to both circumscribe and make legible. By addressing the series of continuities transversing Earth systems and humans' activity of "world-making," the Anthropocene opens a space of ontological and epistemic insecurity that demands a history of the limits and borders that, throughout modernity, have shaped, organized, and secured the geometry of the "compeareance"[1] between the subject and the world, where the space of art has been a fundamental constituent. "Back to Earth," or so goes the Anthropocenic narrative: nothing seems more pressing than to invent new ways of thinking what Donna Haraway calls "naturecultures," and to understand them historically. This materialist imperative for art history thus requires a double move: an archaeology of the grand narratives in which a series of "great divides" historically emerged (between nature and culture, reason and unreason, subjects and objects, etc.) in order to find a vantage point from which to address their structures; and a practice of art's inscription in these structural divides in order to situate its role in their conceptualization and possible transformation.

The genre of exhibition occupies a central place in this history. The exhibition has been shaped throughout modernity by both the scientific positivity of the museological institution and by the negativity of modernist aesthetic experience. As such, the exhibition can be mobilized as a genre hinging together several modern ontological designations. If the task is to model the role of the space of art in the historical constitution of the modern ontological template, then one of the great implicit yet integrated structures for art throughout modernity must be turned into the object of study. This object is the modern museum, whose exhibition model has become an in-built backdrop for our relation to art, whose symbolic and epistemic workings lie at the nexus of many modern imperatives, and whose role on the "Anthropocenic stage" needs to be ungrounded.

The Naturalist Rift and the Space of Reason

The first consequence of the concept of the Anthropocene is the transfer, at a geologic level, of the qualification of nature as an anthropogenic entity, thus triggering a significant shift in its modern ontological status. If nature was previously conceived as the mere background to human experience, on the Anthropocenic stage nature only ever partially enters the sphere of human constructions. As such, the Anthropocene disorganizes what one might call, borrowing anthropologist Philippe Descola's system of four ontologies,[2] the "naturalist rift," or the dichotomy between nature and culture that characterizes Western modernity's cosmography—the cleft crossing through the modern world on the sides of which subjects and objects have been historically distributed. This naturalist dualism found its modern form via the ontological tipping point of the seventeenth-century mechanist revolution in science, which gradually configured the *épistémè* as the background against which the rationalization of the domain of the subject and that of the object unfolded. Hence, the Anthropocene, from the objective position of geology, unsettles the very geometry of the limits that defined modernity as a project of Reason, in which the epistemic identification of objective truths and the ontological delineation of subjectivity historically took place.

It has often been noted that Paul Crutzen, the Dutch chemist who coined the term Anthropocene, also proposed to link its origin to the invention, in 1784, of the steam engine—that instrument with which humans began to powerfully dig into the earth in search of underground suns and ancestral forests, seeking to transform their energy via calorific machines. An archetype of the paradigmatic shift in the relation between humans and their environment triggered by the industrial revolution and the emergence of capitalism, its apparition must be put in parallel with a contemporary mental reorientation, epitomized by the "Copernican revolution" proposed by Immanuel Kant in 1787. This revolution—articulated by a radical separation between the figure of Man and the background provided by a unified concept of Nature—enacted the absolute discontinuity between the "historical subject" and the objective world. It emancipated the subject from the ancient hierarchical "closed world" to organize her entry into a democratic "boundless universe," giving to the figure of Man its ontological state of exception and its role of "globe-constructor" or world-maker. As such, this Copernican reorientation of the subject outlines the central aspirations of the modern Western project of Reason: the symmetrization of "subject" and "world," orientating thought towards the dismantling, stratum by stratum, of the world of appearances; the systematic transformation of implicit background conditions in explicit themes of reflection; the extraction of the modern subject from Nature; and the attribution of transcendence to subjectivity via the rationalization of its space of projection—the autonomous theatre of thought, or the space of Reason.

The Anthropocene makes explicit the systemic and material continuity between human gestures and the milieux in which they operate. In other words, it reveals, in its co-extensivity with modernity, that the age of extraction of *anthropos* from Nature has been, simultaneously, the age of constitution of *anthropos* as a geological stratum. In this respect, the Anthropocene makes the modern gesture of separation between Nature and the historical subject a process inseparable from the erosion of the ground on which it was enacted. It figures the movement whereby the historical becoming of Man encounters against that which it was positing its movement, revealing the human figure and the backdrop of Nature in their mutual ontological instability. By revealing the unstable relation between the "background" and "figure," the Anthropocene introduces a new precariousness in the ontological template that bolstered the constitution of the modern space of Reason.

By making explicit that the social construction of reality has been enacted through the ecological destruction of the planet, the Anthropocenic stage organizes a collision of humans with the Earth. As such, the Anthropocene introduces a strange chronotope to scientific discourse, by collapsing the distinction between "deep" cosmological time and "shallow" anthropological time: as Deleuze and Guattari foresaw,[3] once the window that separated us from the unlimited Nature "outside" is broken, geology becomes a moral science (and vice versa). In many respects, by registering that modern instruments of knowledge and the appropriation of Nature have not merely contributed to an analytic image of it, but also helped produce it synthetically, the Anthropocene ratifies to some extent the symmetrical anthropology initiated by Bruno Latour in the 1990s. Latour affirms that the Moderns "see double." In what he sets out as the "Constitution of the Moderns,"[4] there exists a fundamental dissociation in the world rendered by modern knowledge, a gradual divorce between the *theory* the Moderns produced of themselves (a master narrative of *purification*, of the isolation of objective meanings in Nature, of a radical discontinuity between Nature and Culture, and between subjects and objects) and what the Moderns did in *practice* (a story of *hybridization*, of ceaseless associations between Nature and technique, of incessant combinations between objective reality and subjectivity in the construction of "networks" and "quasi-objects"). By working to understand Natural laws, the Moderns can be said to have engineered Nature. This dissociation characterizes what could be defined as the "schizophrenia" of the Moderns: by negating the official existence of hybrids, they repressed—and ultimately stirred up—their proliferation in the technologically mediated "mess" of networks. The Anthropocene makes explicit this "binocular" rendition of the world that defines modern epistemology. By simultaneously revealing the theoretical discontinuities that constitute modern knowledge and the networks of material continuities that underlie its activity, the Anthropocene figures the twofold economy and chiastic nature of modernity's ontological template.

Although the Latourian model allows one to locate "houses" of purification in the Modern Constitution (in which scientific and political divisions are theoretically performed, and subjects and objects purified), as well as the consequent identification of cases of "hybridity" that the Moderns did not allow to be represented as "real" in their Constitution (the insane, the primitive, cases of technological "mediality" between subjects and objects), the space it assigns to the institution of art (and its site of exhibition, the museum) is defined only as a site for the deposit of the "remains" of modern great divides (values to be respected, traditions, feelings, madness, etc.). As such, the institution of art is not liable to the dynamics of division drawn by the polarities of purification and hybridization, thereby ostracizing the space of art (in its institutional-museological contours or in its aesthetic definition) to the side of the imaginary or mere "fiction." In this regard, Latour's model remains to be completed with a materialist approach to art history, such as that advanced by Jonathan Crary.[5] For Crary, the process of modernization produced an unprecedented mass of knowledge that simultaneously created hybrids, mixtures, and associations between vision and technology (under the form of new disciplinary technologies of capture and control of the attention of the human subject), the conditions of possibility for a purification of the aesthetic field, and the constitution of a new "frontier" around the visual arts (via a true emancipation of vision within Modernist art theory and experimentation). Following Crary, any consistent account of modern culture must confront the ways Modernism, far from being a mere reaction, redemption, or transcendence of the process of scientific purification and economic rationalization, is inseparable from its operations.

The space of art must therefore be defined as an immanent entity in the anthropological matrix of modernity, inseparable from its dynamic lines of transfer between subjects and objects, and purification and hybridization. In such a materialist articulation, it becomes possible to argue that the space of art—and especially the space of its exhibition—historically provided the great divides crossing the ontological template of the Moderns with a specific scenography, and to inscribe this space—both in its institutional outline and in its aesthetic definition—as an additional "house" in the Latourian model.

Clinic: Anatomy of the Border

If Walter Benjamin, in *The Arcades Project*, did not see any difference between the optical experience of a museum, a botanical garden, and a casino, it is because the identity of the modern museum is inscribed in a series of technological, epistemological, and anthropological determinations shared by many modern technologies of the gaze and cultural practices that, together, define modernity as a reformation of vision. Indeed, the modern museum can be said to have provided the Kantian "Copernican revolution" of the subject with an instrumental framework.

The modern museum's birth can be traced to the Reign of Terror in Paris in 1793, with the parallel opening of the Muséum central des arts de la République in the Louvre and the Muséum nationale d'histoire naturelle in the Jardin des Plantes. As curator Anselm Franke has suggested, the museum is defined by the "dialectical reversal" it imprints on the "life" of objects.[6] Working as a global isolator, it de-animates previously animated entities by uprooting them from their "milieu," and re-animates "dead" objects by over-determining their signification and projecting them in a restricted field of attention. As such, the museum performs a withdrawal that regulates and purifies the relation of the Cartesian subject with the contents of a world consequently defined as the outside. Its interior can indeed be considered as the interface between the two domains Descartes set apart, *res cogitans* and *res extensa*, the observer and the world. The museum is the site where an ordered projection of the world, of "extended substance," is made available for inspection by the mind. But the crucial aspect of the museum (as well as of other modern machines of exhibition such as the zoological garden) is its relation to the surrounding undifferentiated environment: it objectifies specimens in the world, intensifying their visibility without sacrificing their vitality. The process of objectification radically differentiates the museum from the cosmological model of the humanist cabinets of curiosities. It is a tool of epistemological conviction that "occults" the world of the object by making its original milieu absent, while inscribing the object in the "denaturalized" space of the institution and its logico-spatial order. As such, objectification can be modeled as a *denaturalizing cut* that endows the exhibited object with what Latour calls a "graph," a mode of inscription mobilizing meanings and referents that make the object "speak." The modern museum can thus be defined as an apparatus laying out a "silent" space criss-crossed by denaturalizing cuts, the space of an exchange put to death, de-animated, and instantly reanimated in a set of new continuities by way of synthetic mediations (elements modulating the phenomenological experience of objects: scenography, display cabinets, zenithal or focused lighting, para-texts, etc.).

In this respect, the modern museum incorporates an operation and a state of isolation that define the activity of the laboratories of scientific modernity: vivisection and quarantine.[7] As a space dedicated to the production of limits, the modern museum opens a space of visibility analogous to the one Michel Foucault, in his history of madness and the archeology of medical perception,[8] identified in the

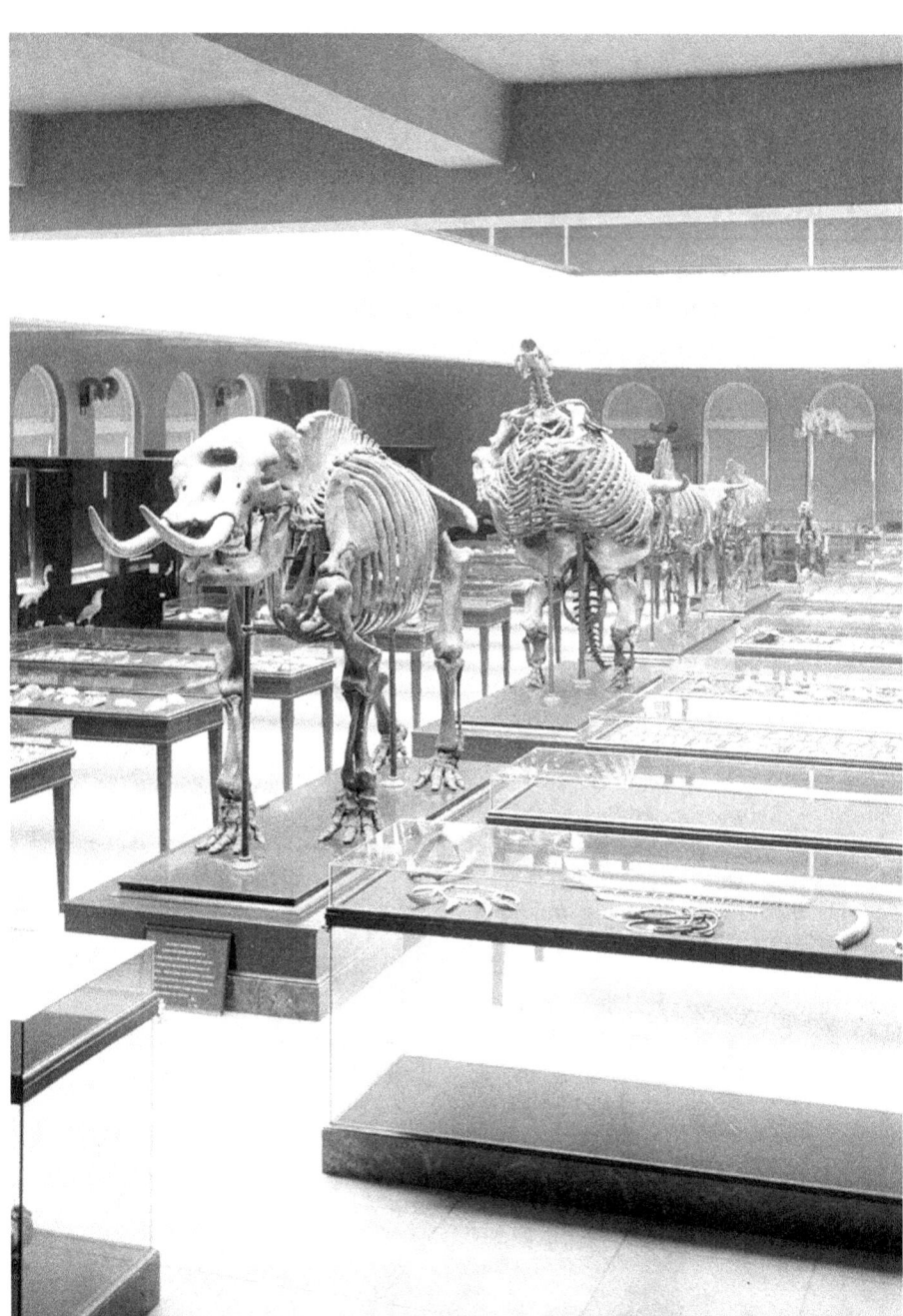

Fig. 01 *Interior view of the Los Angeles County Museum of Natural History showing displays of prehistoric skeletons*, photograph, 1920. Los Angeles, California Historical Society Collection.

clinic. Foucault elevated the clinical gesture to the rank of anthropological truth by demonstrating that the "anatomico-clinical" method of auscultation of symptoms on bodies came to constitute the implicit lattice of the modern experience of knowledge at large. The key to understanding the space of visibility opened by the clinic is the twofold and paradoxical economy of the limit by which it becomes a space of production, multiplication, and projection of dynamic boundaries. As Foucault suggests, the inscription of a limit between reason and non-reason in social space consists in a gesture of caesura that lets tumble, on both sides of its sharp-cutting edge, entities suddenly made mute and deaf to each other (the sane and the insane), thus requiring the synthetic mediation of an institution of scientific veridiction to make them speak again: the clinic. In an ever-deepening instrumental continuity, the institution administers the border by which it has produced itself. The epistemic model of the clinical gesture is thus essentially double in nature: the separation is eclipsed by the positivity of the institution the moment it imprints itself in social space.

The clinic can be enlarged as the model of modern knowledge in that it mirrors the dialectical articulation of the visible and the utterable by which modern science has purified the category of the object. The process of "border production" of objectivizing procedures—the "outlining" and "slicing" of things into epistemic categories that constitute the modern cosmography of taxonomies and atlases—and the articulation of these borders in the language of scientific positivity can be said to consist primarily in clinical gestures. As Lorraine Daston and Peter Galison have argued, the modern notion of objectivity, differentiated from other epistemic ideals in the making of scientific images such as "truth-to-nature" or "trained judgment," cannot be separated from the objectivizing gaze.[9] Objectivity can then be considered a tool of veridiction that not only bolsters the process of objectivization of things in Nature, but culminates in a regime of visibility where the very act of seeing finds its vanishing point in the subjectivity of the observer. Objectivity also defines the "triangle of truth" assembled by the clinical gestures of scientific modernity: it projects limits and borders that *denaturalize* objects in the world and also cross through the interior of the subject and modern scientific culture. The "sleight of hand" of modern knowledge can thus be identified in the specific way rationalist boundaries and objective limits constantly *naturalize* themselves, by multiplying at all scales of knowledge, universalizing their language, and hence appearing as facts obscuring their existence as mere instruments of epistemic appraisal: the logic of the limit enacts the *denaturalization* of the objects it examines while *naturalizing* the borders it imprints between them onto a new ontological ground.

In the denaturalized space of the museum, the vanishing point of this naturalization is the spectator. The scenography of a gallery space such as a museum of natural history transports the logic of the clinic to the scale of Nature. By imprinting denaturalizing cuts around its objects while naturalizing these cuts with synthetic mediations, the dialectical reversal triggered by the process of objectification in the museum is configured by the twofold economy of clinical gestures: if the experience of the modern museum is virtually an experience of the limit, then the actuality of its operations lies in the "graft" of this limit to the eye of the observer. The modern museum simultaneously institutes and bridges the rift that structures modern cosmography: it is the institution that is allowed, in the purification complex of the Latourian Modern Constitution, to represent hybrids (mixtures of nature and technique); it is the site where the modern limit between persons and things is rehearsed in the form of a chain of mediality between spectator and artifact. Hence, the mode of existence of an objectified specimen in a museum leads its observer to *literally* "see double" by constantly facing the unlimited recurrence of the limit, in a fundamentally schizophrenic fashion. In this configuration, the mode of encounter assembled by the museum between the object and the subject consists in the negotiation with an ever-deepening chasm, an inscrutable breach on either side of which, in a ceaseless retreat, subjects and objects are constantly re-distributed.

This chasm, equally and symmetrically inscribed in the objective world and the subjectivity of the spectator, allows for the inscription of the museum in the heart of the modern diagram of power and knowledge, and at the core of its ontological template. By providing the modern line of transfer between subjects and objects with a specific scenography, as well as with an epistemic and phenomenological pivot, the modern museum yields and authorizes modes of mediality between entities that the Modern Constitution works at purifying. It is the very rule of the twofold economy of the limit of which it is the product: deepening objective limits in the world means, in mirror, delineating a subject, intensifying the continuity of modes of subjectivation with operations of objectification, amplifying the association of the human sensorium with technology. It can thus be said of the exhibition model built by the modern museum that it lies at the nexus of two rationalist imperatives: the call for things to comply with the human cognitive apparatus, and the demand for human cognition to comply with technology. Simultaneously purifying the space of compearance between subjects and objects and populating it with a technological field of relations, the museum is inscribed in the line of transfer between the polarities of the Latourian Modern Constitution, purification and hybridization on the one hand, Nature and Culture on the other. As such, it is one of the key sites where a modern politics of vision is constituted: there, a technology of alignment of subjectivity with operations of objectification assembles new procedures of individuation.

Salon: Topology of the Limit

The nine *Salons* Denis Diderot wrote between 1759 and 1781 are commonly referred to both as the origin of art criticism and as a document registering the institutionalization of exhibitions that heralded the public art museum. In his well-known essay "Absorption and Theatricality: Painting and the Beholder," Michael Fried identified Diderot's *Salons* as the place of birth for a new attention paid to the pictorial arts, and of the "invention" of modern painting as such, recognizing in Diderot's critic of theatricality his own Modernist thesis: whenever a theatrical self-consciousness arises in the viewer, the technical features and symbolic frames of the representation are made visible, revealing the "hybridity" of the perceptual experience and threatening its autonomy, thus calling for a "purification" of the medium in order to safeguard the absorption of the viewer's attention in the aesthetic field. In the model we propose here, theatricality can be understood in a radically different way, that is, as the very *medium* of "aesthetic consciousness" and of the narrative of autonomy of art, the vehicle of its entry into a regime of exceptionality and negativity, whereby the structures from which it has been historically isolated by modernist theory (the systemic conditions of modernity and its economy of the limit) are put to a test, woven further, and turned into a sovereign experience. As art historian Juliane Rebentisch suggests in her study of the debates on theatricality that surrounded the appearance of minimalism,[10] the implicit critique of the autonomy of art that Michael Fried identified in what he coined as "literal art" is a tendency toward boundary-crossing that should be redefined as an intensification (rather than a transgression) of the modernist effects of "theatricalization," which provided aesthetic subjectivity with its sovereignty and autonomy. In this model, Diderot's *Salons* appear as a fascinating expression of the modern politics of vision, allowing for the definition of the aesthetic experience provided by the art museum as an intrinsic entity of the ontological template of modernity.

Theatre is for Diderot the one object where aesthetic and ethical aspects intersect. In a vertiginous exegesis titled *L'oeil révolté* ("*The revolted eye*"),[11] the literary historian Stéphane Lojkine argues that Diderot's *Salons* consist of a discursive and visual apparatus that mirrors the exhibition and defines them as the site where the philosopher elaborated a modern "politics of sight." According to Lojkine the *Salons* circumscribe a space where a new attention is paid to the geometry of the relation between the figures displayed in the pictorial space and the viewer anchored in the exhibition space. Diderot settles this relation in terms of a scenic apparatus: an abstract topology modeled after the theatre. As Lojkine demonstrates, a virtual wall appears to separate beholder and image, just as the invisible "fourth wall" implicitly separates the public from the stage in a theatre. In his successive *Salons*, Diderot imagines a viewer seeing paintings as if gazing through a semi-transparent partition wall—a suppressed and repressed separation—as the virtuality of an optic interdiction. His descriptions materialize this interdiction: for Diderot, the screen of representation is explicitly referred to as a theatre stage, into which the spectators' gaze virtually irrupts, and where the represented figures, much like actors in a theatre, are blind to the viewer's presence. The artworks celebrated by Diderot are precisely those whose composition pertains to the theatrical model without exposing it as a reflexive space. By negating the gaze of the beholder, the canvas elides the mechanics of desire it triggers in the viewer. In Diderot's *Salons*, the fourth wall of representation works as a one-way mirror behind which the figure is studied, unwittingly, by a spectator who is both investigator and witness.

This new geometry of attention allows Lojkine to describe the aesthetic relation between viewer and painting in the *Salons* as a space of "scopic crystallization,"

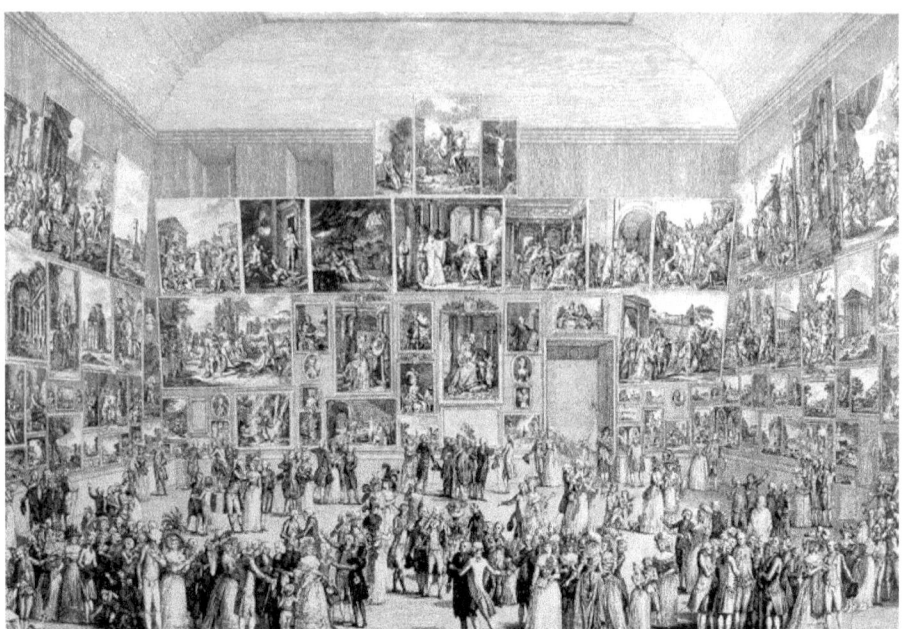

Fig. 02   Pietro Antonio Martini, *Exposition au Salon de 1787*, etching, 1787. Paris, Bibliothèque nationale de France.

a "vague" dynamic space connecting the eye of the viewer with the figures. In a marine painting by Claude Joseph Vernet, Diderot describes the "spectacle of waters" as a space within which the eye plays an "optic *fort-da*"[12]: here, a navigation occurs between the restricted scenic space of representation and that of the public, in an indefinite set of reflections where sight crystallizes. This "fort-da" of scopic crystallization carries the crucial feature of the new aesthetic relation that emerges between the subjectivity of the viewer and the object of the representation, or the figure. This feature is what Lojkine calls the "revolt" of the eye. The fourth wall constitutes the aesthetic relation as an intermittent separation that the mind posits and revokes, establishes in order to revolt against it. The scenic apparatus carries the foundation of a revolt against itself because one cannot see the figures without transgressing the invisible frontiers that enclose their space of visibility.

Diderot's revolt of the eye models the chain of mediality that the art museum, from its earliest exhibitions, started to assemble: the circuit of the aesthetic relation is, for the eye, an experience of the crossing of a geometric limit, reaching out beyond the perceptual experience itself, in an effect of "theatricalization" that Rebentisch defines as "the specific aesthetic destabilization of the subject's hermeneutic access to the aesthetic object."[13] In this articulation between the geometry of the figures and what can be seen by the viewer, another modern "triangulation" appears, not that of the clinic, but that of theatricality, based on a limit that is accomplished when exceeded in a scopic fort-da. The real revolt here is not only that of the eye, but that of the image, which is ceaselessly revolving, carrying the spectator outside the margins of social space and perceptual experience and then circling around to fold her gaze back to its parterre. In Diderot's *Salons*, aesthetic experience can be understood as a space characterized by a manifest solidarity between the eruption of art's objective limits and the vector of subjectivity exceeding them.

In his homage to Georges Bataille titled "A Preface to Transgression" (from 1963, the same year as *Birth of the Clinic*), Foucault defined with great precision the way modern thought bound together limit and excess. According to Foucault, modernity does not restore the subject to a fully circumscribed and positive world, but to a world ceaselessly unfolded and "unknotted" in the experience of the limit, a world done and undone in the excess that transgresses it:

> Transgression is an action which involves the limit, that narrow zone of a line where it displays the flash of its passage, but perhaps also its entire trajectory, even its origin; it is likely that transgression has its entire space in the line it crosses. The play of limits and transgression seems to be regulated by a simple obstinacy: transgression incessantly crosses and re-crosses a line which closes up behind it in a wave of extremely short duration, and thus it is made to return once more right to the horizon of the un-crossable. [...] The limit opens violently onto the limitless, finds itself suddenly carried away by the content it had rejected and fulfilled by this alien plenitude which invades it to the core of its being.[14]

Transgression gives density to the limit it crosses. The experience of crossing the limit is one of a sudden reimport in the "infra-thin" space of transgression of that which the limit kept apart. In Diderot's theatrical model, the aesthetic experience assembled by the museum is precisely where this relation to the limit is interiorized and transformed into a sovereign experience. In this model of the modern economy of the limit, the negativity of aesthetic experience can be understood as a site where the interiority of the subject is virtually oriented outside its bounds in a "vectorial" experience that crosses the rational apparatus of the museum, producing openings outside the positive world of the Moderns, while constantly weaving its space of projection further. As such, the negativity attached to the space of art in the modern cosmography is precisely that which encodes it within the modern limit regime.

Aesthetics did not pierce openings outside the ontological designations of modernity, but has always been an immanent entity of their constitution. As such, it demands to be inscribed at the core of the anthropological matrix of the Moderns. The experience of the limit which characterizes the aesthetic experience framed by the art museum brings about both a geometric purification and rationalization of the modern politics of vision (its rigorous projection in a "theatre of sight"), and an ever-complexifying hybridization of perceptual experience (by way of a scopic crystallization that is nothing more than a case of mediality where a technologically mediated image absorbs the viewer's attention). Here again, the museum, both as a

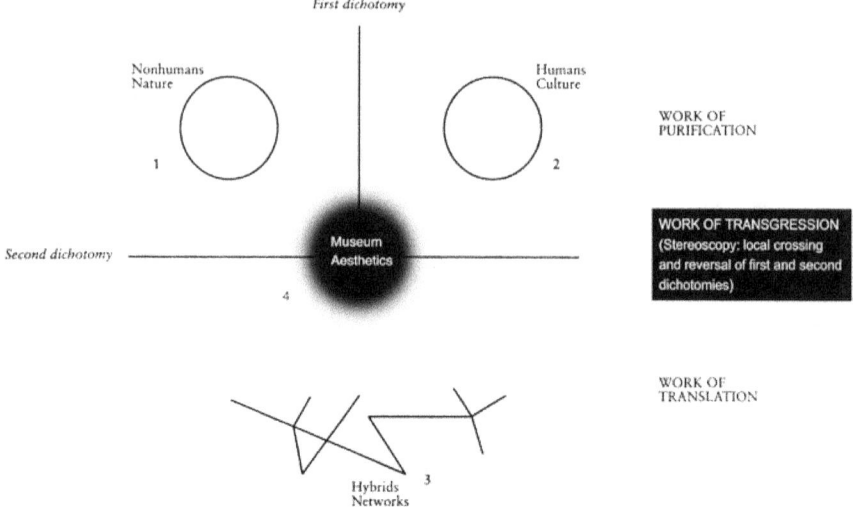

Fig. 03   *Model of the Inscription of the Space of Art in the "Modern Constitution,"* after Bruno Latour, *We Have Never Been Modern*, translated by Catherine Porter (Cambridge, MA: Harvard University Press, 1993), 11.

machine of purification and as a site of hybridization of experience, is determined by the twofold economy of the modern limit regime. The aesthetic experience inaugurated by the art museum thus appears as a crucial node in the ontological template of modernity given by the Latourian Modern Constitution. As a sphere of figuration where hybrids enter the space of purification and where subjects and objects mobilize each other, the space of art—by way of its implicit economy of transgression, its negativity—can be modeled as a nodal point organizing the recurrent and systemic reversal of modern dichotomies. All at once, by connecting subjects and objects, and through the pathway of purification and hybridization, the space of art articulates the lines of transfer that cleave the modern world.

The Genre of Exhibition: A Stereoscopic Facies[15]

The space of art lies at the hinge of the modern ontological designations that bolstered the extraction of *anthropos* from the background of Nature. The space of art, both in its institutional contours (the modern museum) and in the negativity of aesthetic experience, historically provided modern ontological boundaries with a specific scenography, in which they turned into the medium of an independent, extra-territorial, and sovereign experience, endowing modernism with its transgressive ethos. As such, the space of art is fully embedded in the epistemic structures and dynamics of what has come to be known as the Anthropocene: it is a site of invention of intensive tipping points in the lines of transfer that weave the modern space of Reason.

In this model, it is possible to perceive that the extra-territorial character of the space of art historically appeared within the framework of the modern activity of discovery, acquisition, division, and symmetrization of conceptual realms. Its inscription as an intrinsic entity of an anthropological model of modern great divides allows one to read the modernist (read: Greenbergian and Friedian) stance as a constricted, almost trivial effort to purify the very vehicle of hybridity, and postmodernist and deconstructivist perspectives as mournful attempts at hybridizing a reified and caricatured purification model. This inscription also allows one to refute the dead ends inherent to these stances, and to read art in its dynamic and continuous tension with a considerably enlarged epistemological and political horizon, in which images, figures, and formal expressions can be considered in light of their historical continuity and complex articulation with the normative and systemic conditions of modernity. Localizing the space of art at the centre of the Modern Constitution allows us to perceive it as a space where, throughout modernity, the schizophrenic ontological template of modernity has been turned into a "stereoscopic" outlook on its infrastructure, where everything the Moderns repressed as mere fiction and which in return haunted the ontological foundations of their Constitution (cases of mediality between persons and things, entanglements between matter and signs), came back and irrupted in their Republic.

The qualification of the space of art as the site of a stereoscopy projected back onto the schizophrenic ontological template of modernity shows that initiating a materialist history of art—one that confronts the state of ontological insecurity introduced by the concept of Anthropocene—demands that we take the modern economy of the limit at face value. It requires simultaneously an archaeology of historically, epistemologically, and technologically integrated structures of production of representations, and the inscription of artistic gestures within the grand narratives these structures configured. And this work requires a model, not in a normative sense, but as an instrument of description belonging to the logic of discovery, allowing us to see at a glance, or at least alternatively, the realms that the illustrious "seeing double" of the Moderns historically separated, and that the Anthropocene aligns, in order to gain conceptual traction on them. It requires an "optic" making palpable, intelligible, and appropriable the ontological ruptures and epistemological discontinuities that we have inherited from modernity, in order to organize new continuities between their systemic conditions and their singular expressions, between "backgrounds" and "figures."

Jonathan Crary, undoubtedly inspired by the optical apparatuses punctuating Walter Benjamin's *Berlin Childhood around 1900* and *One-Way Street*, made the stereoscope both the trigger and the technical expression of the reformation that vision underwent in the middle of the nineteenth century.[16] The stereoscope, which installed the viewer in front a mirror directing her eyes toward two different images, cleaved sight in two, and signalled the eradication of the subjective "point of view" that had historically configured the relation of the observer to the object of her vision. With the stereoscope, the relation of observer to image is not a relation to an object extrinsically quantified relative to its position in space, but to two dissimilar images whose position simulates the intrinsic anatomical structure of the observer's body. Accompanying the technological reconfiguration of vision that constitutes the prehistory of cinema, the stereoscope suggests a technique of beholding that makes literal and explicit the alignment of subjectivity with the modern process of rationalization, by inscribing its splintering logic directly into the viewer's perception.

It is not as a disciplinary device, but as a machine explicating the systemic conditions of representation and as a structure mediating the subject with these conditions, that the optical model of the stereoscope embodies the twofold gesture of a materialist art history engaged with both background conditions and singular figures. A stereoscopic view of art in the space of Reason would mean bringing the modern "seeing double" to a space where the domains it historically separated are not aligned or reconciled, but where is invented between them non-normative mediations, or stereoscopic fusions. This stereoscopy would consist of coming, quite literally, face to face with the modern ontological designations and their conventional dichotomies, being installed on the ridge of their logic of partition, in the nexus of the dialectical constitution of the worldviews they assemble, in order to unground background structures of figuration, and to reinscribe figures (expressions, images, formal articulations, artworks, etc.) in narrative frameworks from which, on account of these structures, they have been historically isolated and insulated.

Considering the position of the space of art within the broader geography of modern ontological divides, the genre of exhibition seems uniquely suited to engage with such a stereoscopy. It is first through the scenography provided by the modern museum that the space of art posited itself at the hinge of the ontological designations of modernity. From the scenography of natural history museums to that of the first Salons, the genre of exhibition has been shaped throughout modernity by both the clinical positivity of the scientific fact that scripts the museological apparatus (and the truth effect it produces) and by the negativity of modernism's transgressive ethos (and its theatre of boundary-crossings). In other words, the implicit scripts and codes of the genre of exhibition are to be found in the historical articulation of "Clinic" and "Salon," of the science of showing and the knowledge of seeing. The exhibition can thus be seen to consist of a genre and an optical tool entirely situated in the space of mediation between the entities the ongoing process of modernization decodes, dismantles, and sets apart. As such, the genre of exhibition can be conceived of as a space where subjects and objects can be projected in a dialogic situation, in which they can engage in a process of reciprocal (stereoscopic) figuration that can itself be explored as dynamic and historically contingent: a space where ontological certainties are disembowelled by contingency.

"World" and "Earth" are the terms the Anthropocene subjects to a stereoscopic fusion: they are terms that, when conflated entirely, lead either to neo-primitivism or to radical eliminativism, and hence require an optical apparatus or an epistemological scaffolding allowing one to perceive and conceptualize them at once without mistaking one for the other. A materialist art history or curatorial practice being true to the requirements of this stereoscopic fusion would thus not consist in pulling down the separations built by modernity's purification models (including the borders that delimited art's regime of exceptionality), but to develop a "boundary practice" embracing and making explicit the dynamic aspect of the limits they projected, by making visible both the emancipatory power of autonomization and sovereignty of the activity of production of figures, and their debt toward the systemic conditions that form their background. Thinking art in the universalizing frameworks of the Anthropocene without sacrificing its political horizon could thus mean refusing to bridge, undo, or blur the divides from which the space of art emerged, and model vehicles for seeing from both of the sides of the limit they inscribe in us.

Notes

1. The term is borrowed from Jean-Luc Nancy and Jean-Christophe Bailly, who use the French *comparution*, which refers to the act of appearing in court after been summoned. The Scottish common-law term "compearance" appears to be the best translation. Jean-Luc Nancy and Jean-Christophe Bailly, *La comparution (politique à venir)* (Paris: Christian Bourgois, 1991).

2. Philippe Descola distinguishes between four ontologies characterizing different types of societies: animism (where non-human entities can be the terms of a relation), totemism (where differences within the non-human realm are signs of human variety), analogism (where differences between human and non-human interiorities are systematically translated as differences between human and non-human physicalities), and naturalism (western modernity's ontology, the only one to posit a limit between the self and others, introducing the idea of Nature that implicitly underlies a worldview based on the dichotomy between Nature and Culture). Philippe Descola, *Beyond Nature and Culture*, trans. Janet Lloyd (Chicago: University of Chicago Press, 2013).

3. See Gilles Deleuze and Félix Guattari, "10,000 B.C.: The Geology of Morals (Who Does the Earth Think It Is?)," chapter three of *A Thousand Plateaus: Capitalism and Schizophrenia, Vol. 2*, trans. Brian Massumi (Minneapolis: University of Minnesota Press, 1987), 39–74.

4. Bruno Latour, *We Have Never Been Modern*, trans. Catherine Porter (Cambridge, MA.: Harvard University Press, 1993).

5. Jonathan Crary, *Suspensions of Perceptions: Attention, Spectacle and Modern Culture* (Cambridge, MA.: MIT Press, 2001).

6. Anselm Franke, "Much Trouble in the Transportation of Souls, or: The Sudden Disorganization of Boundaries," in *Animism*, ed. Anselm Franke (Berlin: Sternberg Press, 2010), 11.

7. See Shiv Visvanathan, "From the Annals of the Laboratory State," *Alternatives* 12 (1987): 37–59.

8. Michel Foucault, *Madness and Civilization: A History of Insanity in the Age of Reason*, trans. Richard Howard (New York: Random House, 1965 [1961]), and *The Birth of the Clinic: An Archaeology of Medical Perception*, trans. Alan Sheridan (New York: Routledge, 1991 [1963]).

9. Lorraine Daston and Peter Galison, *Objectivity* (New York: Zone Books, 2007).

10. Juliane Rebentisch, *The Aesthetics of Installation Art*, trans. Daniel Dendrickson and Gerrit Jackson (Berlin: Sternberg Press, 2012).

11. Stéphane Lojkine, *L'Œil révolté: les Salons de Diderot* (Paris: Actes Sud, Editions Jacqueline Chambon, 2007).

12. In Denis Diderot, *Salon de 1767*, 1767. Although Vernet's marine remains unidentified, it is described extensively in the segment of the Salon titled "La Promenade Vernet."

13. Rebentisch, *The Aesthetics of Installation Art*, 36.

14. First published as "Hommage à Georges Bataille," *Critique* 195–196 (1963): 751–770.

15. In medicine, "facies" designates the appearance or facial expression of an individual that is typical of a particular disease or condition; in geology, the character of a rock expressed by its formation, composition, and fossil content; and in ecology, the characteristic set of dominant species in a habitat.

16. Jonathan Crary, *Techniques of the Observer* (Cambridge, MA: MIT Press, 1992).

Physical Geology / The Library
Ilana Halperin

"The Eldfell Agate," formed in 1973, Neil McLean, National Museums Scotland. Fig. 01

Boiled milk in a 100°C sulphur spring in the crater of an active volcano; stood with a friend on both sides of the Mid-Atlantic Ridge; talked with geologists inside a lava tube inhabited by life-affirming bacteria; formed sculptures in caves and hot springs; spent time with geology collections formed inside the body; and held the Allende Meteorite, the oldest known object in the solar system, between my two hands. Corporeal mineralogy. We are autobiographical trace fossils.

In 2003, I spent my thirtieth birthday with a volcano born the same year. To mark this event, I visited the Eldfell volcano on the Icelandic island of Heimaey, celebrating our simultaneous appearance in 1973. In 2012, I went back to the island. Standing on the volcano, I thought about how Eldfell and I are now almost forty. I wondered about returning to Eldfell when we both turn fifty, sixty... How, while we both share our lifetimes now, that will only continue for a certain amount of time, and then Eldfell will go from a

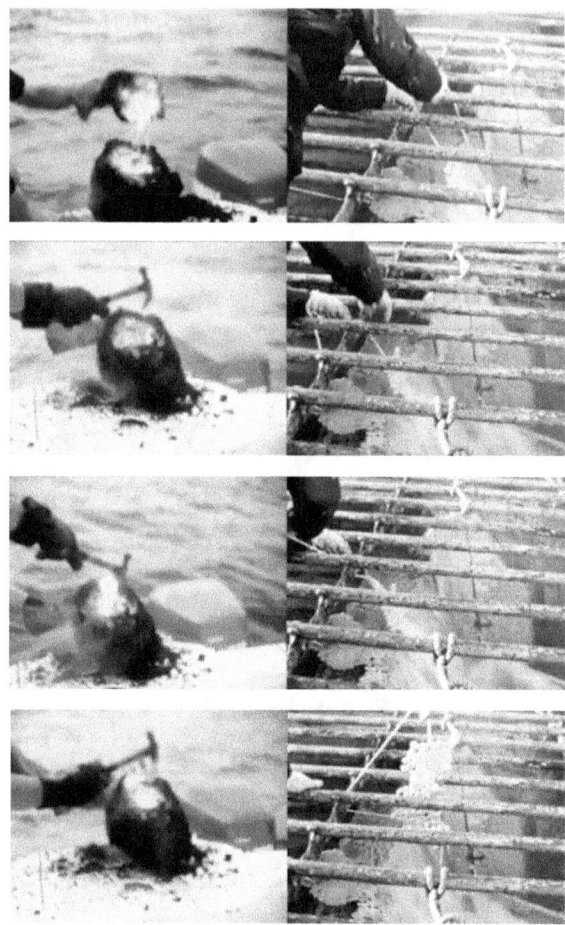

Fig. 02 *Physical Geology (new landmass/fast time)*, 2009. *Physical Geology (geothermal)*, 2011. Stills from Super 8 film diptych, Ilana Halperin. These stills are part of an ongoing series of Super 8 films entitled *Geological Home Movies*. Left hand images are from *Physical Geology (new landmass/fast time)*, a film on the rupturing of slow geologic time by the fast lava flows of volcanic eruption, filmed on location in Hawaii at the "lava entry ocean point." Right hand images are from *Physical Geology (geothermal)*, a new film which charts the formation of geothermally occurring sculptures in Iceland over three weeks in the deep arctic winter, filmed on location at the geothermal power plant which feeds the Blue Lagoon, Iceland.

human time scale—thirty years old, forty years old—to a geological time scale—150 years old—1,000 years old, 800 hundred million years old.

I spoke with a volcanologist about volcanology as a science. Ultimately, a volcano's life is much longer than yours or mine, so to learn about a volcano, study it, get to know it, you must accept that you may never see its full range

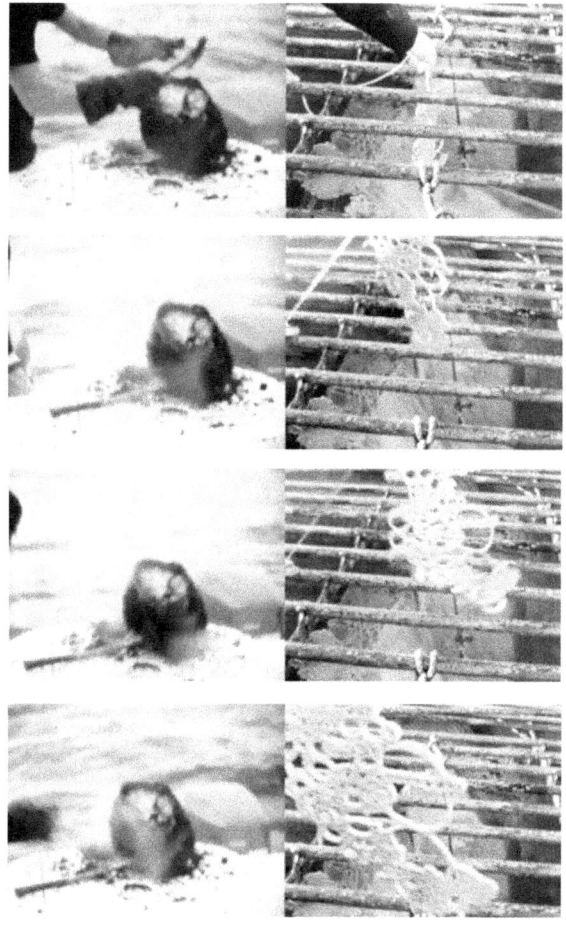

of behaviours firsthand. A calm volcano might have a violent eruption 400 years from the day you first meet, and even multiple generations of volcanologists may still only cover 300 years in the long life of an active mountain. So, part of the process is the tradition of passing along everything you know about your volcano to the next volcanologist who will be there when you are gone. Inbuilt into the story of each person who gets to know a volcano is the story of that same person's obsolescence. A volcano perpetually erases what we know of its own history.

One evening in Edinburgh, Sara Barnes approached me and said: "I have been thinking about your work lately, I came across something that I think you might be very interested in—it's a collection of body stones." "Body stones?" "Body stones—gall stones, kidney stones—they are all made of geology." Out of this conversation grew a totally unexpected line of enquiry, the idea that we as humans are also geological agents—we form geology.

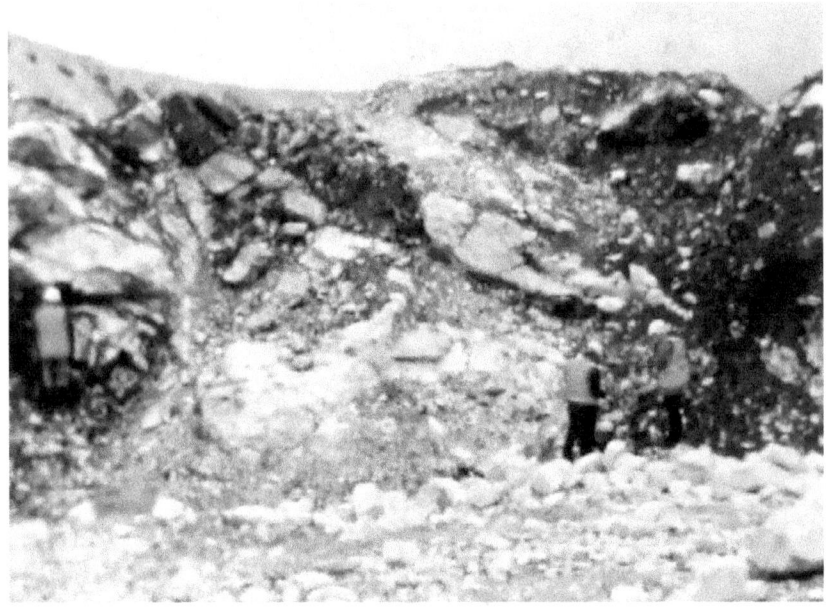

Fig. 03 *The Library*, 2013. Still from Super 8 film, Ilana Halperin. The Library was shot over the course of one year in three locations: en route to the Icelandic island of Heimaey, the site of the Eldfell volcanic eruption in 1973; at the Ledmore Marble quarry in Northern Scotland; and near Inverness during a mineral prospecting field session in a disused mica mine first opened during the Second World War. Each site and story correlates with an artwork featured in the exhibition *The Library* at National Museum of Scotland, 2013.

We are like volcanoes, producing new landmasses on a micro scale. We are closer relations to Eyjafjallajökull than previously thought.

Our bodies follow an example set by much earlier life forms. I had a conversation with Rachel Walcott, Head of Earth Systems at National Museums Scotland, about what constitutes life in the world of geology. She told me about a piece of Galena, the natural form of lead. Microbes feasting on its mineral body have left a trace fossil of activity across its surface, forming miniature canyons and valleys through the course of their meal. The boundary between the biological and geological begins to blur.

What is the relationship between a body stone and a volcanic rock? What constitutes the geological record when we form geology and geology forms life? In northern Scotland there is a marble quarry. Around 535 million years ago, the marble in Ledmore mostly began as stromatolites, the first traces of organic life on earth. The stromatolites died, were crushed, compressed and cooked by new rock finding its way through fissures in the dolostone (a near relation of limestone). And marble occurred. Though stromatolites

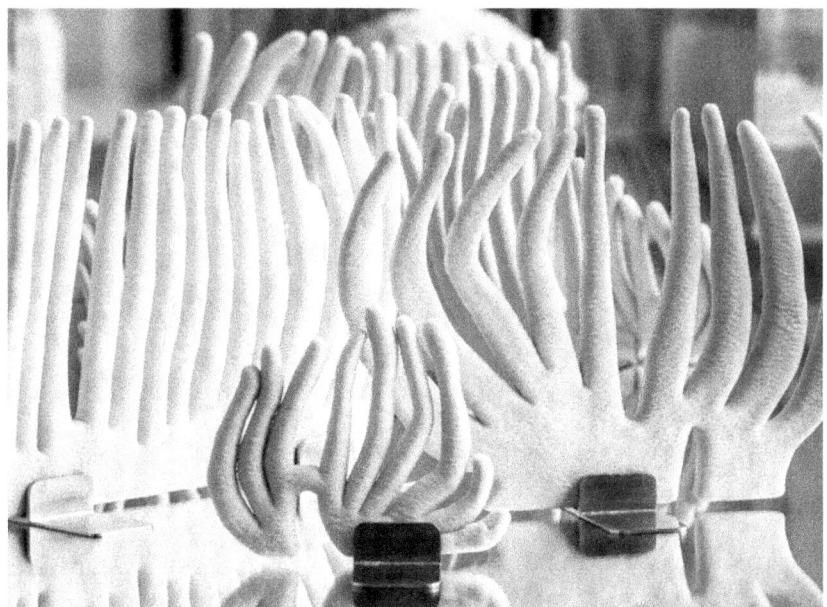

"The Mineral Body," Neil McLean, from *The Library*, National Museums Scotland, 2013. Wood encrusted in limestone, formed from December 2012 to March 2013. In a small thermal town in the mountains of the Auvergne in France, seven generations ago Eric Papon's family founded the Fontaines Pétrifiantes in Saint Nectaire to create limestone sculptures made via the same process that forms stalactites in a cave. In a normal limestone cave it takes one hundred years for a stalactite to grow one centimetre, in the Fontaines Pétrifiantes one centimetre grows in one year. Through an elaborate process, carbonate rich waterfalls are directed over 25-metre-high "casting ladders" located inside a volcanic mountain. Eric places objects on the rungs of each ladder. Quickly objects become covered in a new layer of calcium carbonate—limestone. The limestone sculptures in "The Mineral Body" were formed over the course of four months in the Fontaines Pétrifiantes.

Fig. 04

and coral are found on different branches of the phylogenetic tree, both eventually become stone. We will too, or our bones will. Bones and coral are material cousins, composed of calcium carbonate.

Returning to corporeal mineralogy, I spent time with two collections of body stones, both in the Berliner Medizinhistorisches Museum der Charité. One is a historical collection of stones from the 1700s, excavated by Johann Gottlieb Walter and Friedrich August Walter, a father-and-son team of body mineralogists. The second collection is contemporary and belongs to Navena Widulin, the medical museum's préparateur.

Encountering Navena Widulin's collection on display in her laboratory, you would think you were looking at shelves of precious gems and minerals. She began her collection of body stones in the mid-1990s. Now surgeons and

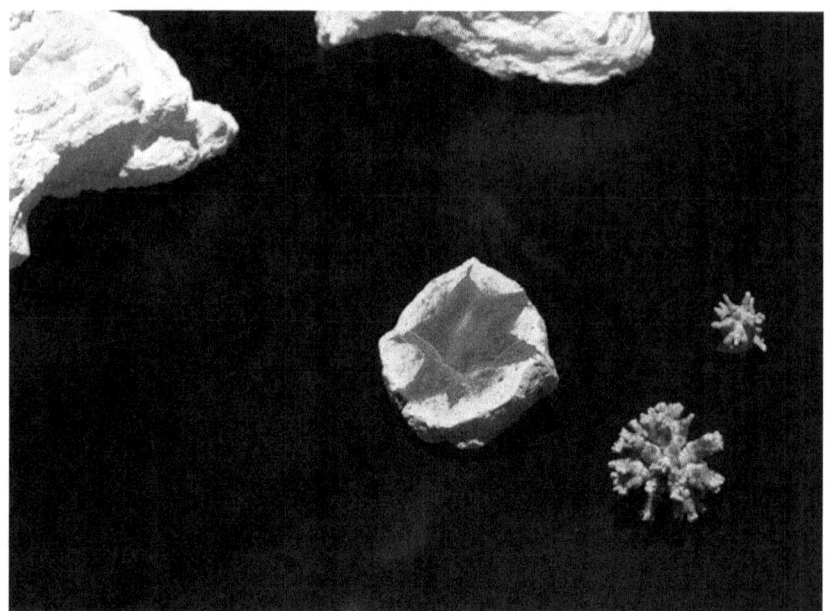

Fig. 05   "Body Stones and Other New Landmass," Thomas Bruns. An installation view of the exhibition *Steine*, curated by Sara Barnes and Andrew Patrizio at the Berliner Medizinhistorisches Museum der Charité in 2012, including a Red Star Agate from Museum für Naturkunde in Berlin, two Morning Star bladder stones from the Berliner Medizinhistorisches Museum der Charité, and silica mineral deposits formed in the Blue Lagoon in Iceland.

pathologists throughout Germany send her stones in the post whenever they extract one from someone living or dead. In the body, each stone is a biological entity: once out of the body it belongs to the realm of geology.

A body stone is a new territory, a miniature planet traveling through an interior universe. New landmass. We should name stones as we name stars, each one in memory of someone close.

The earth is 4.5 billion years old, give or take a few million years. When I was 30 I found a crystal shard on the slopes of Eldfell. Upon returning to the volcano, marking almost a decade more of life, I happened upon agates which had emerged from the "new lava" in 1973. Though twelve months is not long in the context of geological time, within daily human life a lot can happen in a year. A person can form, and we can form geology.

The geological record is a series of ossified biological moments, from calcium carbonate sculptures formed in caves, to marble made from the first moments of organic life, to a chunk of Galena more animal than mineral. These sedimentary layers are each somewhere in between.

The Existence of the World
Is Always Unexpected

Jean-Luc Nancy in conversation with John Paul Ricco
translated by Jeffrey Malecki

In a recent article in *The New York Times* titled "Learning How to Die in the Anthropocene,"[1] Roy Scranton argues that the current geological, technological, and climatic global situation has shifted the classic philosophical problem from how to die as individuals to how to die as a civilization. Scranton served in the United States Army from 2002 to 2006 and was stationed in Iraq following the US invasion in 2003. A couple of years later, when Hurricane Katrina hit New Orleans, Scranton realized that he was witnessing "the same chaos and urban collapse I'd seen in Baghdad, the same failure of planning and the same tide of anarchy." It is precisely this inextricable interdependence—and therefore the always potentially catastrophic destructive effects—of the natural and technological that Jean-Luc Nancy refers to as "eco-technology." For, as Nancy is keen to remind us, "nature always contains and offers the prime matter for technology, whereas technology alters, transforms, and converts natural resources towards its own ends."[2] With "this eco-technology that our ecologies and economies have already become," we are confronted with the geopolitical logic of globalization today. What is new about the eco-technical logic currently operating is that the reciprocal relations between the economic and ecological wed technology and nihilism at an unprecedented worldwide scale, one that may prove to encompass the human species. But proof for whom in that case?

As Nancy goes on to argue, "whereas until now one used to describe ends (values, ideals, and senses) as being destitute, today ends are multiplying indefinitely at the same time as they are showing themselves more and more to be substitutable and of equal value."[3] It is based upon this understanding of *the equivalency of ends* constructed by the eco-technical, that Nancy has provided ways in which to think about the connections between the Iraq invasion and Hurricane Katrina as at once military, geopolitical, technological, natural catastrophes, and environmental disasters. Which is not to cast them as equivalent catastrophes, but rather to understand them as events entirely caught up in the catastrophic logic of general equivalence in which every moment has become economized, as every single thing has been monetized. In response to this, Nancy has put forth the notion of the "condition of an ever-renewed present," which he goes on to define as "not an immobile present but a present within historical mobility, a living sense of each moment, each life, each *hic et nunc* [here and now]. A sense that is characterized by exposure to its own infinity, to its incompleteness"—and thus, we might add, to its in-equivalence to every other moment and thing.[4]

So perhaps it is not only a matter, as Roy Scranton argues, of learning to see each day as the death of what came before, but in doing so, of seeing that day as the birth of the present in and as its own—ever-renewed—finitude.

Meaning: no longer the projection of a future or as part of the project of future ends. Instead, as Nancy has recently argued, "what would be decisive, then, would be to think in the present and to think the present."[5] That is, of the present not as absolute and final presence, but as appearing near, proximate, close to, and in rapport with. As he goes on to explain, if one wants to speak of "end" it is necessary to say that the present has its end in itself, in both senses of goal and cessation. The finitude of each singularity is thus incommensurable to every other, and therein exists the equality of all singularities—their in-equivalence. It is in this way that Nancy calls for an adoration of—or esteem for—the inestimable singularity of living beings and things, and the equality that lies in their in-equivalence to any general schema, measure, principle, or horizon. This is a matter of attending to the inestimable worth of things as opposed to the appropriation of each and every priceless experience.[6] Therefore Nancy closes his recent book *After Fukushima: The Equivalence of Catastrophes*, with the following claim: "To demand equality for tomorrow is first of all to assert it today, and by the same gesture to reject the catastrophic equivalence. It is to assert common equality, common incommensurability: a communism of nonequivalence."[7] For Nancy, the proliferation of so many common ordinary things today is not only the obvious evidence of capitalist production and accumulation, but also the fact that (as quoted above) "ends are multiplying indefinitely," and precisely for this reason offer "more and more motives and reasons to discern what is incomparable and nonequivalent among 'us.'"[8]

Therefore, as Maurice Blanchot contended in 1959, when philosophy lays claim to its end "it is to a measureless end," such that "measurelessness is the measure of all philosophical wisdom,"[9] so too in our reading and engagement with the work of Jean-Luc Nancy today do we come to realize that when philosophy (or more modestly, thought) confronts the prospect of the end of humanity, that *the incommensurable remains the measure of eco-technical wisdom*. Furthermore, given the ways in which Nancy has enabled us to understand art as "the privileged domain for an interrogation of finality,"[10] aesthetic praxis is one of the principle means by which we confront the problematic of ends. It is in this way that his comments below will prove indispensible to ongoing considerations of the interconnections between art, aesthetics, politics, and environments in what has come to be called the Anthropocene.[11]

John Paul Ricco For at least the past twenty years now—from the publication of your book *Le sens du monde* (1993, English translation *The Sense of the World*, 1997) to *La création du monde ou la mondialisation* (2002), and, most recently, *Dans quels mondes vivons-nous?* (with Aurélien Barrau, 2011) and *L'équivalence des catastrophes (après Fukushima)* (2012)—a significant portion of your work has been concerned with the possibility of making, forming, or configuring a world in the current context of global capitalism, conflicts in the name of religion, and ecological devastation, to name just a few of the major forces and currents that have come to define our contemporary globality.[12] You have formulated this division and these alternatives by drawing out the distinctions between *globalisation* (globalization) and *mondialisation* (world-forming). Is the Anthropocene thesis just another worldview or picture (*cosmotheoros*)? More precisely perhaps, is it a picturing of the world through which humans take humanity out of (the picture of) the world? Or, does this thesis provide us with an opportunity or an occasion to think and decide on making or configuring a world—*mondialisation*—in the midst of, yet other than, globalization?

Jean-Luc Nancy Maybe I should start by preventing a potential misunderstanding. In your question, you mention "the possibility of making, forming or configuring a world in the context of global capitalism, etc." The phrase "in the context of" is a bit improper. It's possible that I've contributed to this ambiguity, especially in my texts from a dozen years ago, because I was still able to believe, then, that it was possible to transform capitalism from within. I was dependant on this aspect of Marx, who thought capitalism was responsible for a "historical mission" to develop productive forces. I haven't changed too much, but now I lean towards the view (also from Marx) that capitalism may come to transform itself by collapsing under the weight of financialization or from the effects of ecological devastation. But what would such a "transformation" mean? It would only have significance if it effectively displaced the general pattern of production and "growth," which is nothing but a more organic name for the primacy of production. Human life becomes dependent upon products when it is thought of as production, and away from the unproductive, or a life in tune with the cosmos, with existence, and with the incommensurable (life otherwise maintained by reproduction and not the production of its conditions).

This outrageously brief and simple sketch at least gives an idea of something that would be less a transformation of capitalism than a civilizational shift. Another regime of sense (or value) must replace the regime of production and general equivalence—just as this regime replaced one of reproduction (the domination of agriculture, weak or lacking development and growth, etc.; wealth that is accumulated and/or spent instead of invested, reinvested, and multiplied). Nietzsche was very aware of this necessity: *Umwertung der Werten*, the reevaluation of all values, the reversal of the very meaning of existence. So, "in the context of" (and further, "in the midst of, yet other than…") is a very problematic formula. Certainly a transformation takes place within a given milieu (ensemble, context), and the modern world was born "in" a world that didn't yet exist. But the important thing lies on the side of this "in" that is both inside and outside at the same time…

I'm hardly able to comment on the "Anthropocene thesis" because I'm not familiar with the work that has been developed in the name of this neologism. However, I find it quite understandable that a new era in world history is being proposed beginning with the age of industrial development in Europe. A new temporal rhythm was introduced at that time, with its own character—the construction and implementation of nearly all the data of the earth, its matter, energy, space—which introduced a difference that merits the analogy with the great physical, chemical, and biological transformations of past epochs. We can wonder perhaps if Technocene isn't a more appropriate term, because the human appeared well before the Anthropocene, but that's not a very interesting discussion.

What's undeniable is that humanity at large, and with it other living species and the mineral kingdom, entered conditions of existence totally at odds with what came before. Until then, natural constraints—climate, soil conditions, the size of seas and rivers—sometimes prevailed, and sometimes played a major role in determining the modes of existence of human groups. Now, these constraints have largely been replaced by the effects of human technical activities which have passed through several remarkable stages (steam, electricity, oil, the atom, semi-conductors—before arriving today at other stages such as nanotechnology and genetic modification). Where once we were able to aim for a mastery of nature directed at human well-being, we now find ourselves faced with an inverted mastery by human technique over the entirety of individual and social conditions of existence, and also over the group of conditions called "natural" (relating to the animal and the cosmos). The focus, therefore, disappears in favour of a set of entangled and often contradictory goals, which are rather faint representations of progress guided by this or that model of "civilization." Of course, an "image of the world" is no longer possible, other than one that is itself hyper-complex, even confused or excessively reticulated. It's not a coincidence that contemporary physics no longer assumes a unique object—the "universe"—subject to an observation protocol, but instead must imagine one or several "multiverses" that have necessitated a reconsideration of the status of "scientific" knowledge.

In a very clear way, our own history requires us to entirely rethink the idea of the "world" (similar to how the great discoveries of the fifteenth and sixteenth centuries forced us to remodel the image of the world, as much European as Chinese, Aztec, or African, etc.). I use the term "idea" [*l'idée*] and not "image" [*l'image*] precisely because from here on we are beyond the representation of a form (image, conception, structure).

JPR In the image of humanity's erasing of the human from geological time that in part accompanies the assertion of the Anthropocene (a form of "species death," or what Elizabeth Kolbert refers to as the "sixth extinction"), and following upon the death of God, and the eco-technological rewriting of the concept of nature, does something like "world" still remain as an "ethos" or "habitus"?

JLN Yes, without a doubt. We have—or we live—another type of ethos (home, sojourn, abode and/or customs, behaviour). We are accustomed to speeds, intensities, quantities of population or energy that have no equivalent in our past—but we inhabit them, we engage with them raw, we cultivate their own possibilities. Perhaps this ethos comes across as suicidal. It's interesting to consider for a moment the possibility that the human species and the entire anthropomorphic transformation of the earth and its surroundings will end at some time, as will the galaxies and stars. There isn't any "point of view" to think this, but it would only mean that there is no longer anything to see or say, or signify, that this "sense" as we more or less understand it is only an episode from an immense *hors-sense* (outside/beyond-sense).

But even this compels us to think about it. It has a "place" if I can say that we are thinking it [*Cela n'a "lieu" si je peux dire que si nous le pensons*]. And, it perhaps reveals to humans something of supreme importance: a sense of the fortitude of meaning. I like the word "fortuitous," even if the substantives "fortitude" or "fortuity" are rare and clunky, because fortuitous goes further than "contingent" or "risky." Or better yet, *inopiné* [unexpected, sudden], a French word meaning "that of which we don't have an opinion or judgment, that which we haven't yet imagined." In other words, that which arrives beyond all possibility of speech: the unforeseen, but with an extra nuance of irruption, of emergence, and rearrangement of the expected order of things. "Contingency," for its part, is a term too associated with "necessity" and immediately appears to indicate a lack of necessity, an accident with respect to substance.

Not only is that which happens to us unexpected, but maybe the unexpected—without-an-organizing-discourse—is also the regime of the existence of the world, of humans, and all beings...

JPR Is there a way to address climate change and environmental devastation without enacting what you have described in *The Sense of the World* as "philosophical melancholy," or what Derrida referred to as an "apocalyptic tone" in philosophy?

JLN I no longer know what I was referring to there. But in any case, yes, I think there's no reason to sink into melancholy or "apocalyptic" proclamations. Certainly, we must know that total catastrophe is possible. But if it takes place, it will be like the death of each individual—the end as opening onto an empty and dazzling infinity. The striking and obscure fact of an existence. The difference, for the end of the world, is that there won't be any witnesses to mourn or greet the final glare. But this is very difficult to imagine—that there wouldn't be anyone. So instead we have to think something along the lines of *Mad Max* or *The Road*, but where the survivors would also be thinkers.

JPR I want to raise the issue of what you have framed as "the problematic of ends." Following on the previous remark, is there a way to speak in terms of "the end of the world" (as one of the chapters of *The Sense of the World* is titled) without becoming preoccupied with "ends"? Within the context of our discussion of the Anthropocene, this question might take us back to Derrida's lecture "The Ends of Man," from 1968, as well as the eponymous Cerisy colloquium on Derrida that you and Philippe Lacoue-Labarthe organized in 1981. In drawing these possible lines of connection, one might ask how the Anthropocene thesis is, or is not, yet another figuration of the "kingdom of ends." In turn, can you speak about how for you "art" is a name for one of the principal ways in which humanity has confronted the absence of ends?

JLN The "ends" today are clearly endless. This should make us realize that all teleology is the result of being hung up on a representation of the present-future, and of necessity. But if we are in the *unexpected*, we must disengage ourselves from these patterns. The kingdom of ends is the kingdom without end, not in the sense of meaningless absurdity, but as thought removed from goals, from orientation. When we love, when we drink, when we write, when we sing, we are not directed by goals: we expose ourselves to the finitude of love, of drunkenness, of text, of song.

So to the end of your question, I answer yes, "art" is above all the name of that which remains clear of ends and goals. "Art"—provided we do not confuse it with decoration, the aesthetic, the museum, or the art market, nor with subjectivity, "commitment," etc.—means: *technique (ars) without an end or goal.*

But the best way not to venerate art, seeing in it the only access to the "without-end," is to consider the existence of people—"the people" [*les gens*], everyone, or at least the vast majority of humans, those living: people live, have children, devote themselves to their families or certain causes or groups, or even withdraw into themselves and still live for this, they don't commit suicide; sometimes they revolt, often even, but rarely are the rebellious suicidal—even if there are a few. I mean that it's difficult to avoid a sense, somehow implicit but strong, distinct and tenacious, that the "value" of life is both evident and obscure. We can't attribute this persistence, even obstinacy, to a more or less dazed resignation. People are not asleep or unconscious, as they are often represented in texts claiming to speak for everyone but in fact only address the preoccupations of a handful of intellectuals.

I'm not saying we have to accept the state of the world as it is: I'm saying that we have to mediate the most common experience, that of living "above all," or almost above all, because it means something other than blindness or ignorance. Everyone is ready to ask "Why go on? What's the purpose of life?" [à *quoi bon vivre?*], but almost no one commits suicide afterwards. Suicide is not opting for non-being: it is a strong and violent act of refusal or recusal, an act that implies that I should have the power to live, and that to live in this way I'm compelled to throw my suicide in the face of others.

The meaning of "sense" as devoid of purpose, accomplishment—in the sense of fulfilment of purpose and fullness reached—is the most commonly shared sense among us (and perhaps all living things).

JPR In your recent book *L'équivalence des catastrophes (après Fukushima)*, you do not posit that all disasters ("natural" or "man-made") are equivalent, but argue rather that what the globalized world now suffers from is the catastrophe of general equivalence (for Marx: money, market value), and the rendering equal of everything to everything else. Can you briefly elaborate on this argument, and further, explain the contrast that you make between "general equivalence" and what you theorize as a "communism of inequivalence"?

JLN The idea of general equivalence simply comes from Marx: all "value" is calculable in terms of exchange value, of which money is the real form. This value allows all exchange (buying, selling, investing, making profits) and supersedes all use values. A car has a use value, but its price often has nothing to do with its use, which is itself determined by a number of factors: work, the city, distances, the state of public transport, etc.—each of which refers to the uses themselves always subject to the calculation of exchange: how much will I make, for example, if I build a rental building or even if I buy a cargo ship to trade in scarce resources?

But money as the value of all values has meant the increasing erosion of sacred or glorious values (which in turn succumb to equivalence: the art market, the high-end leisure market, luxury in general...). We do have a vague sense of one exceptional value, which is impossible to calculate: we speak of human "dignity." But we've hardly done anything to give it its proper place.

On the other hand, we have come to conceive of dignity in terms of equality—on the condition that we stop measuring equality using money and comfort. Of course, we must demand a strict equality of access to what constitutes a "worthy" life. But we must also understand that there can also be inequivalences that don't prevent dignity from being common to everyone. My car is not worth as much as my wealthy cousin's, but we are equal according to the common finitude of our existences. And this equality—called "communism"—is not realized through money. It's up to us to create it. In some respects, religion has led the way; all the great religions contain the seeds of this thought. But they are also machines of power and domination, and thus also of inequality.

JPR What role or function or place does art (as praxis and technique) have in this "communism of inequivalence"?

JLN I think this is answered in my previous responses—but I'll add this: great art arises when a great thought emerges. Nascent capitalism along with humanism generated extraordinary art (painting, music, poetry). There won't be another great period of art until there's a new spiritual force, equal to that of capital.

JPR I am struck by the way in which, in much of your work, you describe the world as "patent." How are we to hear and understand the various semantic meanings of this word, and why do you think it is a particularly appropriate and important way to think about the world today?

JLN "Patent" is a rarely used word in French, and also somewhat precious... so I ask you to forgive me. It comes from Spinoza: *veritas se ipsam patefacit*, truth is manifest in itself. Which is to say that there is always a forceful and clear manifestation of truth. So, too, that which is evident is true. What I said above about people's lives is evidence of this. At the same time, it's obvious that the sky is empty—well, full of other galaxies, but lacking any divine presence. But this is not evidence of a void: it is evidence of a world that makes perfect sense in itself—to itself, if I can say that. I just said "evidence," which is much more common than "patency." But evidence is a banal and overused word, often confused with visible proof. If it's sunny, it's evident that the sun is shining. But it's not evident in this way that the being that I am "has" a sense of its existence. And without a doubt, it doesn't "have" it, it "is" it. I am my own sense that I certainly don't possess, neither as knowledge nor as intuition. But I am because I exist. It's patent.

There is also something patent in a proverb like "As long as there is life, there is hope." Even if "hope" is a term that requires further discussion. Or in the title of that excellent film by Kiarostami, *Et la vie continue*.[13]

There is a logic, or perhaps rather an analytic, of patency that remains to be deployed. Wittgenstein said: "The creation of the world is the actual world." This both means that we cannot find a specific "creation" by a "creator," and also that the existence of the world reveals itself in a patent way—obvious, undoubted, powerful—and at the same time always unexpected.

Notes

1 Roy Scranton, "Learning How to Die in the Anthropocene," *The New York Times*, 10 November 2013.

2 Aurélien Barrau and Jean-Luc Nancy, *What's These Worlds Coming To?* trans. Travis Holloway and Flor Méchain (New York: Fordham University Press, 2015), 43.

3 Ibid., 45.

4 Jean-Luc Nancy, *After Fukushima: The Equivalence of Catastrophes*, trans. Charlotte Mandell (New York: Fordham University Press, 2015), 59.

5 Ibid., 37.

6 The appropriation of the priceless is represented in contemporary commercial media, for example, by those advertisements for MasterCard. For while we are told that "there are some things money can't buy, for everything else there is MasterCard," these assuring words only come at the end of the recited calculation of each purchase made during an especially memorable and unique (i.e. "priceless") experience with someone. There is an elision here, such that we are clearly meant to be left with the impression that MasterCard = priceless.

7 Nancy, *After Fukushima*, 41.

8 Ibid., 50.

9 Maurice Blanchot, *Friendship*, trans. Elizabeth Rottenberg (Stanford: Stanford University Press, 1997), 91–92.

10 Barrau and Nancy, *What's These Worlds Coming To?* 45.

11 This interview was conducted via email in July and August 2014. John Paul Ricco and the editors of this volume wish to thank Jean-Luc Nancy for the generosity he extended in responding to these questions.

12 See Aurélien Barrau and Jean-Luc Nancy, *What's These Worlds Coming To?*; Jean-Luc Nancy, *The Sense of the World*, trans. Jeffrey S. Librett (Minneapolis: University of Minnesota Press, 1997); Jean-Luc Nancy, *The Creation of the World, or Globalization*, trans. François Raffoul and David Pettigrew (Albany: State University of New York Press, 2007); and Nancy, *After Fukushima*.

13 Abbas Kiarostami, *Life, and Nothing More...* (1992).

Cloud Writing:
Describing Soft Architectures of Change in the Anthropocene

Ada Smailbegović

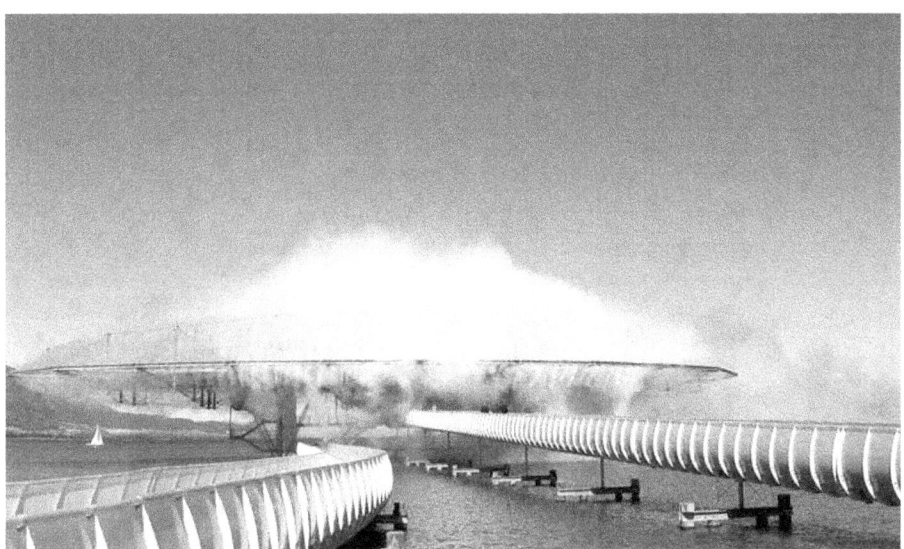

The Blur Building, front view, Yverdon-les-Bains, Switzerland; copyright Diller + Scofidio.　　　　　　Fig. 01

> If, as wavists, we believe that change is not determinate, and if we can record the present in enough detail, within a series of closed temporal frames, then kinds of change will perceptibly emerge from the detail of sensing.
>
> —The Perfume Recordist, "Notes on Perfume"

The Isthmus Between Clouds and Architecture

Description of Change One

> At this instant the sky is bright blue. In the foreground, halfway up the frame, a low-lying cumulus cloud is forming above the surface of the lake. A white volume begins to change and spread outward. At its middle the mass of the cloud is wide and vibrant so that it appears to form a bright solid. Moving and unmoving blocks of sky become visible. A steel structure appears as an orbit of vertical columns and a tensile spun canopy resting on the surface of an elevated saucer. The vapour begins rising again from the left corner of the frame, filling and filling the space until no discernment is possible between the shape of the cloud and the sky.

Description of Change Two

> At this instant the sky is bright blue. In the foreground, halfway up the frame, a low-lying cumulus cloud is forming above the surface of the lake. A white volume begins to change and spread outward. At its middle the mass of the cloud is wide and vibrant so that it appears to form a bright solid. The woolpack begins unraveling at the edges, the wind rending it into fine wisps that involute in the way that smoke strands bend, thicken for an instant and then move outwards until they are morselled to nothing and consumed. Moving and unmoving blocks of sky become visible. A steel structure appears as an orbit of vertical columns and a tensile spun canopy resting on the surface of an elevated saucer. The vapour begins rising again from the left corner of the frame, filling and filling the space until no discernment is possible between the shape of the cloud and the sky. Darker clouds appear, overhung by straggling clouds that sail over them passing quickly, driven by the lower winds. Then the sky is spread over with one continuous cloud, streaked by silver lines of water running between the ridges of the vapour.

Description of Change Three

> At this instant the sky is bright blue. In the foreground, halfway up the frame, a low-lying cumulus cloud is forming above the surface of the lake. A white volume begins to change and spread outward. At its middle the mass of the cloud is wide and vibrant so that it appears to form a bright solid: solid but not crisp, white like the white of egg, and bloated-looking. The woolpack begins unraveling at the edges, the wind rending it into fine wisps that involute in the way that smoke strands bend, thicken for an instant and then move outwards until they are morselled to nothing and consumed. A shallow valley forms in the middle with widening slopes, which begin to form a shape of the letter V. Moving and unmoving blocks of sky become visible. At once the clouds seem to cleave asunder. A steel structure appears as an orbit of vertical columns and a tensile spun canopy resting on the surface of an elevated saucer. The sky is flat, unmarked by distances, a white thin cloud, chalky and milk-coloured, with a remarkable oyster-shell molding. The

vapour begins rising again from the left corner of the frame, filling and filling the space until no discernment is possible between the shape of the cloud and the sky. Darker clouds appear, overhung by straggling clouds that sail over them, passing quickly driven by the lower winds. Then the sky is spread over with one continuous cloud, streaked by silver lines of water running between the ridges of the vapour.

These numbered sections are experiments in description, composed in an attempt to depict the vapourous dynamics of the architecture of the Blur Building, designed by Elizabeth Diller and Ricardo Scofidio as a temporary installation for the Swiss National Expo held in Yverdon-les-Bains, Switzerland, in 2002. [Fig. 01] The architects used water and air as primary construction materials, drawing up the lake water available at the site and atomizing it into a fine mist by passing it through "a dense array of high-pressure water nozzles."[1] The result is a cloud building, composed of innumerable tiny droplets of vapour suspended above a steel pavilion elevated over the surface of Neuchâtel Lake. The steel structure of the Blur Building is minimal, acting primarily as a "soft pneumatic skin" that houses the water nozzles, a viewing platform that elevates the visitors above the cloud, and "an angel bar" that serves many different kinds of bottled water. The minimalism of the sparse structural elements is emphasized by a proclivity for the rapid transformation of form, exhibited by the building's vapourous composition. As such, the Blur Building acts as an architectural construction that emphasizes transience by operating within a non-monumental temporality that is responsive to the vicissitudes of the weather.

As a temporary construction, the Blur Building was dismantled following the Expo, and so these descriptions were created not through direct observation, but instead come from viewing the vapour dynamics that constituted the building in a video recording on display as part of the MoMA's *Applied Design* exhibition (2 March 2013 – 20 January 2014). The procedural imperative for creating these descriptions comes from a text titled "Notes on Perfume," which accompanied the audio-olfactory performance of *The Perfume Recordist* by Lisa Robertson and Stacy Doris.[2] Writing collaboratively through the persona of "The Perfume Recordist," the two poets theorize a procedure for documenting the luminous and changing detail of the present: "If, as wavists, we believe that change is not determinate, and if we can record the present in enough detail, within a series of closed temporal frames, then kinds of change will perceptibly emerge from the detail of sensing."[3] This passage, which appears as the epigraph to this essay, elaborates a methodology according to which description can act as a technology of amplification, flooding the delineated frame of the present with luminous grain of detail, in turn rendering perceptible a more variegated sense of the kinds of change that dynamically constitute the present, thereby opening the unfurling edge of this present toward the future in indeterminate ways. In other words, through this amplification in the "detail of sensing," differentiated rhythms of change become evident, as "kinds of change" sift themselves into minute and heterogeneous temporalities of changing shapes and qualities.

Upon first attempts at observation, the shape of the Blur Building seemed uniform, white, and "blob-like," once the initial wisps of vapour had thickened into a cloud-like volume. But what at first seemed like an exercise in mesmerizing pulses of repetition opened itself out to an increasing resolution of detail: the variance in the brightness of the nearly solid vapour mass, the differentiated shapes of the fraying edges of the vapour unfurling into the blue of the sky—were they like curling wisps of smoke or like tearing cloth? Other vocabularies seemed necessary to articulate this detail. To facilitate this, my process of repeated observation and description opened out to a longer history of weather description, drawing on the modalities of description employed by two literary figures of the late eighteenth and early nineteenth century: Dorothy Wordsworth, who wrote extensively in the form of journal entries that kept a careful and often ecstatic daily record of the weather, and the Victorian poet Gerard Manley Hopkins, who likewise kept a weather journal filled with luminous detail. With the help of these anachronistic atmospheric vocabularies, the vapour of the Blur Building and the surrounding clouds acquired the sheen of egg-white, the texture of wool, the inner marbling of an oyster shell. In other words, different rhythms and textures of change, evident in the weather journals composed by Hopkins and Wordsworth, infused themselves into my increasingly detailed descriptive accounts of the vapour dynamics of the Blur Building. This process of layering several finite and idiosyncratically dispersed historical frames parallels Robertson's own methodological impulse to draw on descriptive practices of natural history, and in particular early meteorological description, tracking their passage through eighteenth-century and Romantic poetry; or, as Laurel Peacock suggests, in "Lisa Robertson's Feminist Poetic Landscapes," Robertson uses "scraps of antique discourses [to] fashion a new garment," and through this "construct[s] more livable poetic habitats."[4] In this way, Robertson's work offers an "inventive *ecopoiesis*," which "reads the earth's climate as a diary," always seeking "to engage it as a temporal phenomenon [...], a soft, viable architecture lining the movement of days and weeks and years."[5] As such, Robertson's poetics of description, with its attunement to the temporalities of meteorological variation and change, offers a way to attend to the changes in climate and other human-induced planetary transformations that have recently been framed as the period of the Anthropocene.

Temporalities of the Anthropocene:
Starfish Time + Egg Time + Larval Time

The Anthropocene is a way of framing time; it offers a means for characterizing a new epoch defined by human impact on the geological, atmospheric, and ecological processes occurring on Earth. Understanding the Anthropocene not merely as an abstract taxonomic category but as a felt temporality requires a careful attunement to the variegated kinds of change that compose this temporal frame in the unfolding moment of the present. Such an attunement to the particulate differences that compose change is difficult because many of them occur at rhythms of transformation that are below the threshold of temporal sensitivity available to human perception.

Imagine, for instance, a sea floor covered with starfish. To a human observer, this may appear to be a scene of near stillness, as the cold purple and red shapes of the starfish seem only slightly more animate than the rocks beneath them. Viewing this scene with the aid of time-lapse photography, however, reveals that the starfish are rapidly moving across the sea floor according to the parameters of their own *Umwelt*.[6] Some of them, like the morning sun star (*Solaster dawsoni*), inch rapidly across the seafloor to attack other starfish, such as leather stars (*Dermasterias imbricata*), which move more slowly and are thus too sluggish to evade the morning sun star. The lens of a camera—capable of capturing increments of change at a different number of frames per second than the human eye—floods the stillness of such an underwater scene with innumerable details, revealing contracting arrays of orange dots and spines moving with hydraulic slowness as individual tube feet attach and detach from the rocky substrate. Such a mediated series of images brings the rhythms of *starfish time* into contact with the temporal pace of the human perceptual world.

The temporal dimension of the human *Umwelt*, as the above example illustrates, is tuned into a limited set of rhythms and durations. Therefore, many of the temporalities that are relevant for developing a politics of time in the Anthropocene—such as minute and incrementally accumulating processes of change, or the long duration of geological time, or even temporal rhythms relevant to particular non-human organisms as they encounter anthropogenic environmental change—may not be directly available to the human sensorium. It is not just the different rhythms of non-human temporality that are difficult to sense, but temporality as a compound entity of other variables, such as increasing temperature, which is literally speeding up the time of certain biological processes, such as egg hatching or pupation. This *egg time* or *larval time* is a factor of temperature measured in units called degree-days, so that certain developmental processes require a kind of accumulation of heat that can occur over the course of a week if the temperatures are warm, or may take longer if the weather is cool. Shifts in this form of physiological time will have drastic effects on biological species as a result of rising temperatures associated with climate change, with "changes in, say, larval hatching times [that] can cause cascade-like changes in entire ecosystems, when these larvae act as food for other animals."[7] In other words, while many processes of change associated with the Anthropocene occur at temporal scales well below or beyond the human range of perception, they are also subject to sudden or irreversible change, because when complex systems are perturbed, the pressures they are undergoing may be offset or stabilized for a time until, by slowly accumulating, they reach a critical threshold at which rapid and irreversible change occurs.

I would like to stress the significance of developing a different descriptive procedure for thinking the temporalities of the Anthropocene, one that does not simply use the future as a focalizing point from which to retroactively view the past and the present, thus pre-emptively binding these times together into a predetermined, inevitable teleological end. One strategy I explore in this essay for creating an alternate perspective on Anthropocene temporality involves developing a poetics of description as a mode of affective and aesthetic amplification, which can delineate the fluctuating details of change occurring in the present in order to open out towards a less teleological sense of the future. This future will undoubtedly be marked by anthropogenic change, yet we may still be responsive to it in such a way that will allow various non-human agents to shape possibilities for change, indeterminacy, and differentiation among organic and inorganic processes that constitute the planet. In other words, the central question that I am asking is how poetics and the methodologies of description that it opens up for registering and indexing change in the present can offer a higher perceptual resolution of the variegated temporalities that make up the epoch of the Anthropocene. This mode of descriptive poetic amplification of differentiated temporalities of change carries political significance for our understanding of the forces shaping the current ecological crisis because it carries the potential for displacing other conceptualizations of Anthropocene time which threaten to retroactively collapse the present into the past and the future, thereby foreclosing the political potential of the current moment. A more variegated sense of temporality offers the possibility of registering a wider range of rhythms and durations that do not fit neatly on either side of the dichotomy between fixity and change.

The understanding that nature is undergoing continuous change certainly precedes the formulation of the Anthropocene. Such views of nature as changeable have arisen a number of times within the Western philosophical and scientific tradition, starting with ancient thinkers such as Heraclitus and Lucretius, and becoming particularly prominent in the natural sciences of the nineteenth century through the work of evolutionary thinkers such as Jean-Baptiste Lamarck and Charles Darwin, as well as in the conceptualization of geological change elaborated by Charles Lyell. However, in the essay "The Climate of History: Four Theses," Dipesh Chakrabarty explains that even when historians did assume that geological changes were constantly transforming the surface of the Earth, such change was considered so gradual in comparison to the transformations induced by humans that it was not relevant to the anthropocentric scale that history, as a discipline, took into consideration. Chakrabarty notes that "man's environment did change but changed so slowly as to make the history of man's relation to his environment almost timeless and thus not a subject of historiography at all."[8] In other words, nature, for much of human history, has effectively served as an "apparently timeless backdrop for human actions."[9] Chakrabarty argues that the Anthropocene and attendant "anthropogenic explanations of climate change spell the collapse of [this] age-old humanist distinction between natural history and human history."[10] In this regard, it is the acceleration of rhythms of change, as a result of anthropogenic activity, that has brought into relief the processes occurring at geological time scales and made these the concern of history, as well as politics.

Feminist thinkers, in particular, have drawn on the traditions of natural history that have struggled to convey the sense of nature as changing, as well as on the philosophical traditions that have intertwined with them, to develop a non-essentialist understanding of nature and the biological body as a site of indeterminacy.[11] For example, in *The Nick of Time*, Elizabeth Grosz writes that "the natural world prefigures, contains, and opens up social and cultural existence to endless becoming; in turn, cultural transformation provides further impetus for biological becoming."[12] Grosz, whose work draws on Darwin's evolutionary theory, as well as Henri Bergson's philosophy of time and Luce Irigaray's feminist philosophy, locates the potential for change within nature and biological life, so that all instantiations of culture, sociality, and politics are, in fact, elaborations of the ongoing transformation and complexity of nature. In what follows, I attempt to triangulate these understandings of the relationship between nature and change in the discourses of natural history with both feminist philosophy and poetics of description. It is within this triangulation where poetics becomes a chiasmic site, which trafficks among these disciplinary methodologies and discourses, that I hope to develop a descriptive methodology which can amplify and distinguish the manifold rhythms of Anthropocene temporality.

Robertson's book *The Weather* operates as such a chiasmic site of description, forging connections between natural history, feminist thought, and experimental poetics to develop a way of diachronically indexing change through the differentiated grammar of its sentences. *The Weather* was composed as part of a site-specific, six-month research residency at Cambridge, during which Robertson "embarked on an intense yet eccentric research in the rhetorical structure of English meteorological description."[13] Speaking in an interview in *The Capilano Review* about the composition process she used in writing *The Weather*, Robertson situates her interest in mixing these descriptive practices in relation to the moment when scientific and literary modes of description still converged with one another: "It was a discourse that was happening before science and literature were differentiated, strictly speaking, and so it was like the last gasps of a more integrated practice of description, where natural history had very minimal and totally erasable boundaries in relation to literary description."[14] In seeking a historical connection between the descriptive practices of poetics and natural history, Robertson situates herself in a longer tradition of twentieth- and twenty-first-century avant-garde poetics whose practitioners, including Gertrude Stein, Lyn Hejinian, Clark Coolidge, and Christian Bök, have forged intersections between literary and scientific practices.[15] In composing *The Weather*, Robertson became particularly interested in how different practices of description depicted meteorological phenomena, which are continuously undergoing change: "clouds [in particular] presented a specific formal difficulty to description and nomenclature […] since [their] appearance as a thing was so ephemeral."[16] This interest led Robertson to research, among other things, BBC shipping forecasts, William Wordsworth's *The Prelude*, John Constable's cloud sketches, as well as the work of the nineteenth-century British amateur meteorologist Luke Howard, who, in his *Essay on the Modifications of Clouds*, devised a system for the taxonomic nomenclature of clouds, by carefully observing how clouds in the sky were diachronically changing from one form to another.

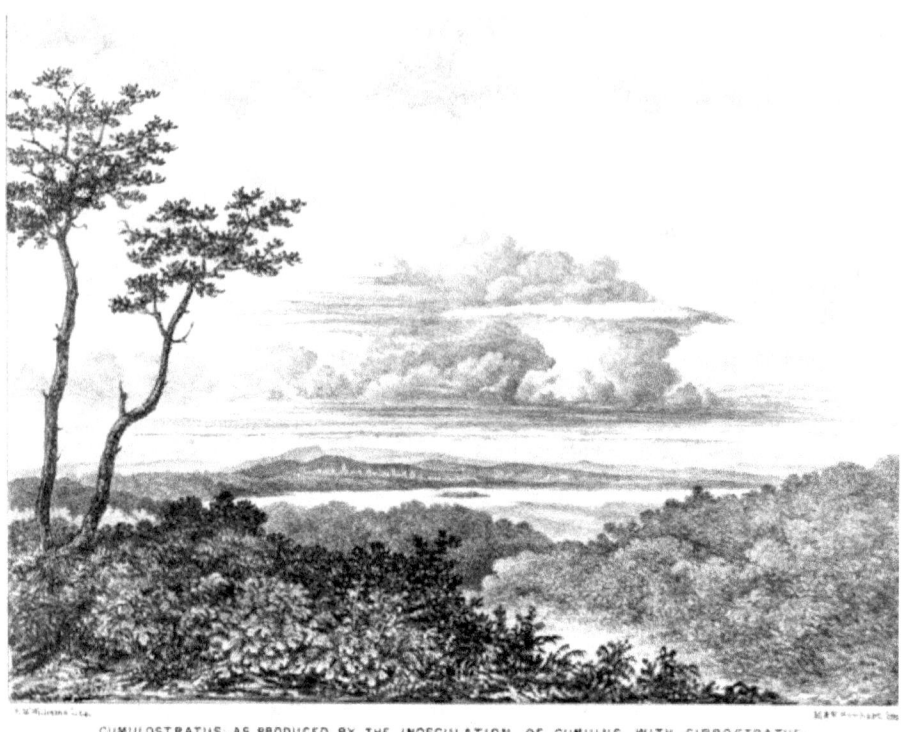

CUMULOSTRATUS, AS PRODUCED BY THE INOSCULATION OF CUMULUS WITH CIRROSTRATUS
CIRRI ABOVE, PASSING TO CIRROCUMULUS

Fig. 02   A plate from Luke Howard's *Essay on the Modifications of Clouds*, depicting the formation of Cumulo-stratus clouds. London: John Churchill & Sons, New Burlington Street, 1865.

Cloud Writing: Luke Howard's Soft Taxonomy

Howard was concerned that the transience and mutability of clouds made their all too soft edges incongruous with the scientific project of taxonomic classification. The secret of Howard's taxonomy lay in its capacity to avoid the typically ossifying, atemporal effects of classification, and attend, instead, to the mutability of clouds. Thus, in addition to the three primary cloud types, Cirrus, Cumulus, and Stratus, Howard developed the taxonomic categories of Cirro-cumulus, Cirro-stratus, Cumulo-stratus, and Cumulo-cirro-stratus or Nimbus. These transitional categories offer a way of attending to the qualities of clouds as activities that possess patterned modes of behaviour, causing them to transition from one of these morphological forms to another with some regularity. [Fig. 02] Howard's attempt to formulate a taxonomy whose categories would be responsive to differentiated modes of activity is attuned to the difficulties of depicting natural phenomena that are continuously in flux.

Howard's focus on the temporal dynamics of cloud taxonomy allows him to remain attentive to the continuously shifting boundaries of clouds: their movement between existing as discrete entities and the sense that cloud edges always remain pliable and soft, casting them towards other clouds and the infinite possibilities of mixing and dissolution. While Howard is very careful to devise a form of taxonomy that is "soft" enough to respond to the malleable and transient qualities of clouds, he is also insistent that there are regularities in the behaviour of clouds and that the whole project of devising a taxonomy of various atmospheric vapours is not a futile one. "If Clouds were the mere result of the condensation of Vapour in the masses of atmosphere [...and] if their variations were produced by the movements of the atmosphere alone," Howard conjectures, then the study of them would "be deemed a useless pursuit of shadows," as their forms, in this case, would be merely "the sport of winds" and would hence be ever varying and indefinable.[17] Instead, Howard argues that the various modifications of clouds are a result of specific causes which govern the movement of the atmosphere, and that through a careful observation of "the countenance of the sky and of its connexion with the present and ensuing phenomena," one can come to understand how these causes will operate and how the different varieties of clouds will transition from one form to another.[18] Howard bemoans that the experience produced through the labours of "frequent observation" is "usually consigned only to the memory of the possessor, in a confused mass of simple aphorisms" and that, as these single observations lose "connexion with the rest of the Chain" of weather events that accompany them synchronously in space or sequentially in time, they often serve only to mislead the meteorologist who is trying to discern regularities in cloud phenomena.[19]

\ Cirrus: ○ Cumulus: — Stratus: \○ Cirro-cumulus: ╰ Cirro-stratus: ○⌒ Cumulo-stratus: \○⌒ Cirro-cumulo-stratus, or Nimbus.

Cloud-writing typographic marks from Luke Howard's *Essay on the Modifications of Clouds* (London: John Churchill & Sons, New Burlington Street, 1865). Fig. 03

As a result, Howard believed that the secrets of effective meteorological observation come to reside "only in the mind before which their relations have passed, though perhaps imperceptibly, in review."[20] It was his desire in devising a taxonomy of clouds to expose and make available to others the transient flow of relations that constitutes the changes in weather phenomena. For this purpose Howard devised a form of cloud-writing, suggesting the use of concrete, nearly hieroglyphic marks as indicators of specific cloud types, which would help convey the sequence of transitions and relations between weather phenomena. [Fig. 03]

Howard suggests that such marks be inserted into "a column headed *Clouds*" in meteorological registers and that "modifications which appear together be placed side by side, and those which succeed to each other" in the sequential order within the column.[21] Such a mode of cloud writing would create diachronic and synchronic fields of relations, which would allow the reader of the meteorological register to gauge the coincidence of cloud types and envision the temporal flux through which different cloud types would metamorphose from one modification to another.

Howard's careful recording of the changing skies presents a conceptual and observational space in which to examine how phenomena can possess both the regularity of differentiated patterns, while also having the capacity for open-ended future transformation. Due to their highly changeable qualities, clouds occupy the uncertain position between existing as discrete entities and operating as modes of activity.[22] Staring at the blue horizon of the sky, one may be able to point to a discrete, fluffy cumulus cloud sailing by and exclaim "here is a cloud," but the next minute that cloud may have fused its vapourous, fuzzy edges with another cloud it encountered on the way, forming an amalgam or a mixture that can no longer be parsed into discrete entities. In other words, Howard's cloud taxonomy offers a way for thinking about the formation of "soft entities" that are pliable and caught in a processual flow of transformation, and yet, at the same time, are not entirely diffuse, but instead possess a capacity for differentiated rhythms of coalescence and change.[23] As such, Howard's observations of clouds and his formulation of "cloud writing" can act as a conceptual laboratory in which to develop modes of description that would remain attuned to the changing details of the Anthropocene, with its variegated temporal rhythms of speed and slowness of non-human materiality that do not collapse into sharp contrasts between fixity and change.

Movement of Qualities: Descriptions of Change in the Anthropocene

I propose that Robertson's book *The Weather* can be read as a form of "cloud-writing," similarly setting up fields of synchronic and diachronic relations in order to produce descriptions of change that attempt to convey the activity of the changing sky in another medium—in this case poetic language, with its own distinct capacities for lively dynamism. This difficulty of recording a continuously changing sky is addressed by Robertson in such a way that the patterns of repetition and change within descriptive passages of the poem relay the effects of flux:

> The tint twice over. Days heap upon us. Where is Kathleen. The tint twice. The clouds darker than the plain part and darker at the top than the bottom. The clouds lighter than the plain part and darker at the top than the bottom. The lights of the clouds lighter. The others smaller. The same as the last. The same as the last. The tint twice in the openings and once in the clouds. Days heap upon us. The tint twice over. Days heap upon us. With others smaller. With others smaller.[24]

This is the concluding section of the poem "Tuesday," and it repeats many of the syntactical patterns that have already occurred earlier in the poem. For instance, the most explicitly descriptive sentence—"the clouds darker than the plain part and darker at the top than the bottom"—directly precedes a nearly identical syntactic iteration of itself with the substitution of the adjective "lighter" in lieu of the initial "darker" in the first part of the sentence. Both of these sentences have occurred earlier on in the poem, with the sentence beginning with the "darker clouds" repeating in succession, followed by the three iterations of the sentence beginning with the "lighter clouds." These minute differences and repetitions recreate the states of temporary suspension that Howard described in his natural historical accounts of the sky, along with the subtle changes in the patterns of light and dark that infuse the clouds with colour and brightness. And yet, even the instances of complete syntactic repetition interject temporality into this description of the landscape of the sky. And this temporality functions in a variegated manner to produce differentiated speeds and rhythms of change.

This manner of tracking minute shifts or micro-dynamics of change and, in turn, developing a complex language of description capable of tracking the shifting qualities of the sky in all of their luminous and delineated detail, resembles the attunement to the details of the changing weather evident in the early weather journals of Wordsworth and Hopkins. It is this attention to the details of the changing sky that allows Hopkins, for instance, to note that the vapourous film of a cloud is pealing off as if with a texture of "tearing cloth," and then an instant later folding "like the corner of a handkerchief" and beginning to coil "as a ribbon or a carpenter's shaving may be made to do."[25] Or, for Wordsworth to note the changing appearance of the sea in her *Alfoxden Journal* as "perfectly calm blue, streaked with deeper color by the clouds, and tongues or points of sand" on 23 January 1798, and then again as "the blue-grey sea, shaded with immense masses of cloud, not streaked" on 26 January.[26] These descriptions possess a level of detail and procedural diligence of repeated observations and recording of the subtle, incremental changes occurring in the same landscape over the course of days or years.[27]

Robertson divides *The Weather* into seven discrete prose pieces—each titled for a day of the week and interleaved with short pieces in verse titled "Residence at C," ending with a longer verse section titled "Porchverse." This serves to draw conceptually on the daily patterns of weather description that tune perceptual attention to the minute variations of the changing skies. While Robertson's text is not based on direct observation of meteorological phenomena, each of the discrete daily sections formally relays the micro-dynamics of change through grammatical variation. In other words, varying rhythms of activity are produced in each section of the book through the diachronic dimension of the syntax and its capacity to convey differentiated rhythms and causal relations. In a sense, then, the act of reading *The Weather* is akin to asking about the particularities of the weather on a given day—"Sunday," for instance—and relies on a mixture of deixis and a hesitant enumeration of qualities. This sense of hesitancy within the description occurs because the qualities are extracted from the specificity of materials—their sheen, texture, or their capacity to fold and wrinkle—and then used as attributes for abstract concepts: "All the soft coercions. Maybe black and shiny, wrinkled. A sky marbled with failures."[28] In this way coercion becomes soft and also, perhaps, black, shiny, and wrinkled. In the case of failure, the dynamics of this movement of qualities are more complex, with the sky acquiring the contrasting colouration encased within the veins running through a slab of marble. At the same time, the active and fluid quality of water vapour that composes clouds ricochets back and inserts a different temporality into the hardness of marble, pointing to the gradual process of metamorphism that brings marble into existence, as well as the manner in which the veins and swirls of coloured marble are a result of this process, acting on various mineral impurities, such as clay, silt, sand, and iron oxides, which were originally present as grains or layers in the limestone.

A similar transposition of hard and soft qualities index different temporal rhythms of coalescence in Robertson's poetic essay "Soft Architecture: A Manifesto," published in her book *Occasional Work and Seven Walks from the Office for Soft Architecture*. In this case, the material landscape that is infused with transience is not the changing sky, but the textures of architectural surfaces: "Yet our city is persistently soft. [...] So the camp is a permanent transience, the buildings or shelters like tents—tents of steel, chipboard, stucco, glass, cement, paper, and various claddings—tents rising and falling in the glittering rhythm which is null rhythm, which is the flux of modern careers."[29] In Robertson's description, the expected soft, fabric materiality of tents is replaced by hard materials, producing unexpected "tents of steel," glass, and cement. Hence the evident transience of tent-like structures inserts itself surreptitiously and comes to occupy architectural structures seemingly built of more permanent, harder, less variable materials. In this transaction Robertson renders even cement "soft" by shifting the perceptual temporality of flux as it acts within and transforms materials. What becomes evident, as a result, is that even materials that appear static and hard are continuously shifting, although perhaps at slower rhythms or rates of change than other more malleable forms of matter.

Just as Doris and Robertson take on the persona of "the Perfume Recordist," in "Soft Architecture: A Manifesto," Robertson herself adopts the performative identity of The Office for Soft Architecture (OSA), appropriating the concept of soft architecture from architectural theory as a way of enacting site-specific work of documenting changes in textures of urban environments, in this case the city of Vancouver. In architectural discourse, "soft" signals both a concern with the malleability of a material and its ability to respond to changing circumstances and needs. In the second issue of the journal *Bracket: Architecture, Environment, Digital Culture*, editors Neeraj Bhatia and Lola Sheppard outline the conceptual history of the term "soft" in architectural discourse, locating its origins in the work of 1960s architects such as Cedric Price, Buckminster Fuller, and the architectural collective Archigram. In one sense, the term *soft* signifies the quality of a material that yields "to touch or pressure, [by being] smooth, pliable, malleable or plastic," while from another perspective, it may extend to temporal properties that characterize a particular structure or a system, making it more adaptable to transformations occurring in complex and changing environments.[30] As a structure composed of soft, vapourous materials that are continuously changing in response to the meteorological environment around them, the Blur Building is an exemplary case of soft architecture.[31] The softness of its shape, which arises from the difficulty of discerning the discreetness of its edges as they come into contact with the vapourous bodies of the atmosphere that surrounds them, literally *blurs* the distinctions between "natural" and "human-produced weather" phenomena, transforming the Blur Building into a micro-model of Anthropocene weather.

In the context of the Anthropocene, the shifting edges of the Blur Building open up the present, even the seeming hardness and fixity of human-built architectural structures, to ongoing change, indicating that what appears as the given reality of the contemporary moment is open to an indeterminate set of futures.[32] As an architectural form composed of different materially instantiated temporalities, the Blur Building offers a material model for the transposition of qualities that also takes place within the grammatical and figurative textures of poetic description. Acting as a kind of material-semiotic isthmus, the Blur Building transposes both the material and figurative dimensions of the vapourous materiality of clouds onto the more typical materials used in contemporary architectural construction in a way that parallels Robertson's metaphoric infusion of soft, tent-like, fabric materialities into the glass and cement buildings of a contemporary architectural landscape. My analysis of the poetics of description in the Anthropocene continuously skirts this edge between the material and the metaphorical in the hope that poetics can act as a kind of chiasmic site that moves between the material and the semiotic without abandoning either of these dimensions.[33] In an essay "7.5 Minute Talk for Eva Hesse (Sans II)," published in her book *Nilling*, Robertson offers a lithe proposition regarding how such movement between metaphor and material may occur: "But the metaphorical space can't be inhabitable without welcoming meaning's propensity to move across materials: Metaphorical meaning does not identify itself with a position; it moves in a fluctuation, serially, to indicate modes of materiality."[34] The descriptions of the Blur Building with which I opened attempt this movement of meaning "across materials," carrying the sheen of egg-white, the texture of wool, the inner marbling of an oyster shell into the luminosity or a "tint" that shifts as a thread through the assembling and reassembling clouds. The capacity of poetic description to carry different isolated textures and durations across materials can produce a kind of amplification of detail in a manner that indexes minute temporalities of change, while also creating broad temporal inversions or transpositions across materials. This allows poetic description to defamiliarize the anthropocentric perspective of time in favour of an Anthropocene politics of temporality that is responsive to the variegated rhythms of non-human and human matter.

Notes

1. Elizabeth Diller and Ricardo Scofidio, *Blur: The Making of Nothing* (New York: Harry N. Abrams, 2002), 44. See also: *Blur Building,* Yverdon-les-Bains, Switzerland. 1998–2003, film, MoMA Number: 556.2006.a–d.

2. The project consists of several iterations, one of which was a performance that took place as part of the Positions Colloquium organized by the Kootenay School of Writing in Vancouver in August 2008. The citations below come from an accompanying manuscript: Lisa Robertson and Stacy Doris, "Notes on Perfume," from *The Perfume Recordist* (unpublished).

3. Robertson and Doris, *The Perfume Recordist.*

4. Laurel Peacock, "Lisa Robertson's Feminist Poetic Landscapes," *Open Letter* 14, no. 5 (2011): 89.

5. Erin Gray, "'Words Are Fleshy Ducts': Lisa Robertson and the Runnel Theory of Poetry," *Open Letter* 14, no. 5 (2011): 73, 76, emphasis in the original. For additional critical context placing Robertson's work in an ecopoietic tradition, see Adam Dickinson, "The Weather of Weeds: Lisa Robertson's Rhizome Poetics," *Rhizomes* 15 (Winter 2007).

6. The term *Umwelt* was developed by the ethologist Jakob von Uexküll to characterize the perceptual world of an organism within which only certain, salient aspects of its environment are available to perception.

7. Jan Zalasiewicz, Mark Williams, Will Steffen, and Paul Crutzen, "The New World of the Anthropocene," *Environmental Science & Technology* 44 (2010): 2229.

8. Dipesh Chakrabarty, "The Climate of History: Four Theses," *Critical Inquiry* 35 (Winter 2009): 204.

9. Ibid., 205.

10. Ibid., 201.

11. The link between histories of feminist thought and the discourse of the Anthropocene was the topic of a recent academic conference, "Anthropocene Feminism," held at the Center for 21st Century Studies at University of Wisconsin-Milwaukee, April 2014.

12. Elizabeth Grosz, *The Nick of Time: Politics, Evolution, and the Untimely* (Durham and London: Duke University Press, 2004), 1–2.

13. Lisa Robertson, *The Weather* (Vancouver: New Star Books, 2001).

14. Lisa Robertson, "The Animal, The Pronoun: An Interview," interview by Ted Byrne, *The Capilano Review* 3, no. 15 (Fall 2011): 16.

15. In *The Language of Inquiry*, Lyn Hejinian traces the impulse towards description in avant-garde poetics by situating poetry as a field of inquiry in relation to other knowledge practices, reaching all the way back to the empiricist regimentation of observation and description that arose as a result of the invention of the scientific method. See Lyn Hejinian, *The Language of Inquiry* (Berkeley and Los Angeles: University of California Press, 2000). For further critical engagement with the relationship between poetics and the discursive practices of natural history, see Lytle Shaw, *Fieldworks: From Place to Site in Postwar Poetics* (Tuscaloosa: The University of Alabama Press, 2013).

16. Lisa Robertson, "The Weather: A Report on Sincerity," *Chicago Review* 51, no. 4 / 52, no. 1 (Spring 2006): 32.

17. Luke Howard, *Essay on the Modifications of Clouds* (London: John Churchill & Sons, New Burlington Street, 1865), 1.

18. Ibid.

19. Ibid., 2.

20 Ibid., 3.

21 Ibid., 14.

22 In this regard, Howard's understanding of the co-instantiation of processes of differentiation and change serves as an antidote to the trajectory of Object Oriented Ontology (OOO), which tends to suggest that the pre-existence of discrete objects is necessary for any differentiation to occur. While Graham Harman's version of OOO posits a necessary relationship between the existence of discrete and persistent objects and the capacity for differentiation and change, Howard's thinking about the co-occurrence of these processes, without the preceding existence of discrete entities, offers a compelling alternative. See Graham Harman, "On Vicarious Causation," *Collapse II* (March 2007): 187–221.

23 For a contemporary theoretical complement to Howard's empirical discoveries, see Gilbert Simondon's writing on individuation and change in *L'individuation psychique et collective*: A la lumière des notions de forme, information, potentiel et métastabilité (Paris: Editions Aubier, 1989).

24 Robertson, *The Weather*, 22.

25 Gerard Manley Hopkins, *A Hopkins Reader*, ed. John Pick (New York and London: Oxford University Press, 1953), 46.

26 Dorothy Wordsworth, *Journals of Dorothy Wordsworth, Vol. 1*, ed. Ernest de Selincourt (New York: The Macmillan Company, 1941), 3–4.

27 For a critical study linking Howard's understanding of clouds and the poetry of the Romantic period, see Marjorie Levinson, "Of Being Numerous," *Studies in Romanticism* 49, no. 4 (Winter 2010): 633–657.

28 Robertson, *The Weather*, 2.

29 Lisa Robertson, *Occasional Work and Seven Walks from the Office for Soft Architecture* (Astoria: Clear Cut Press, 2003), 15.

30 Neeraj Bhatia and Lola Sheppard, "Going Soft," in *Bracket 2: Goes Soft*, ed. Neeraj Bhatia and Lola Sheppard (Barcelona and New York: Actar, 2012), 8.

31 In part, this adaptable contact between the Blur Building and its surrounding environment is facilitated by an inbuilt weather station, which "reads the changing weather conditions and electronically adjusts water pressure in response to shifting temperature, humidity, wind direction, and wind speed." Diller and Scofidio, *Blur*, 44.

32 However, an inverse mapping of temporal qualities is also necessary, so that the durational dynamics of human-made materials and anthropogenic effects, such as radioactive and plastic waste, need to be infused with the due stiffness of their actual inflexibility and long-term effects.

33 The movement between materiality and metaphor that I am elaborating here is complex and requires further development, which cannot occur within the scope of this paper. In short, my perspective is invested in generating affinities with Donna Haraway's category of the material-semiotic or Karen Barad's understanding of the simultaneous co-arising of the material-discursive, in which the two are co-emergent and neither precedes the other. In other words, the kind of material-semiotic intertwining that I am developing here suggests that there is no choice to be made between materiality and semiosis.

34 Lisa Robertson, *Nilling* (Toronto: Bookthug, 2012), 44.

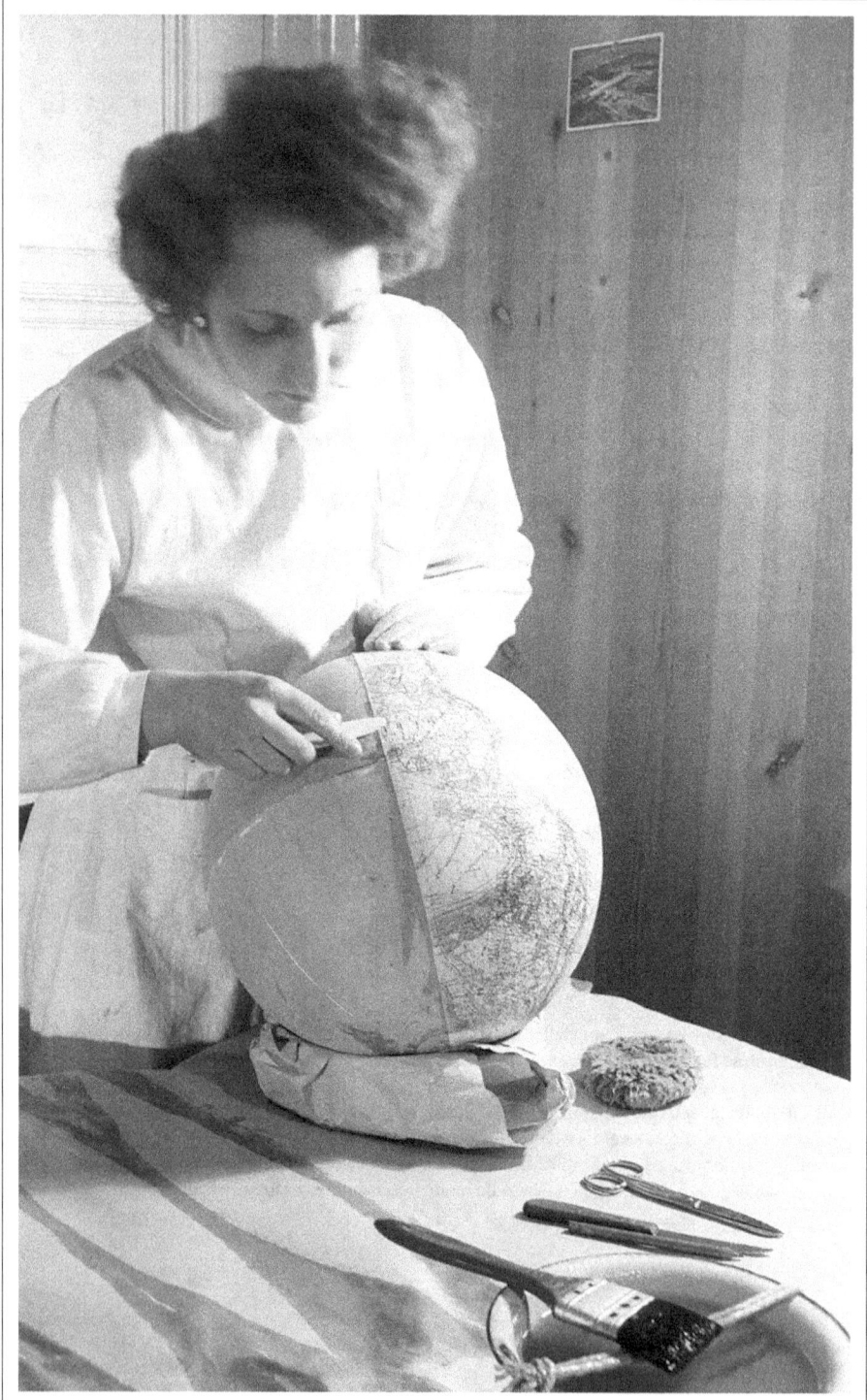

The Cerumen Strata:
From Figures to Configurations

Richard Streitmatter-Tran & Vi Le

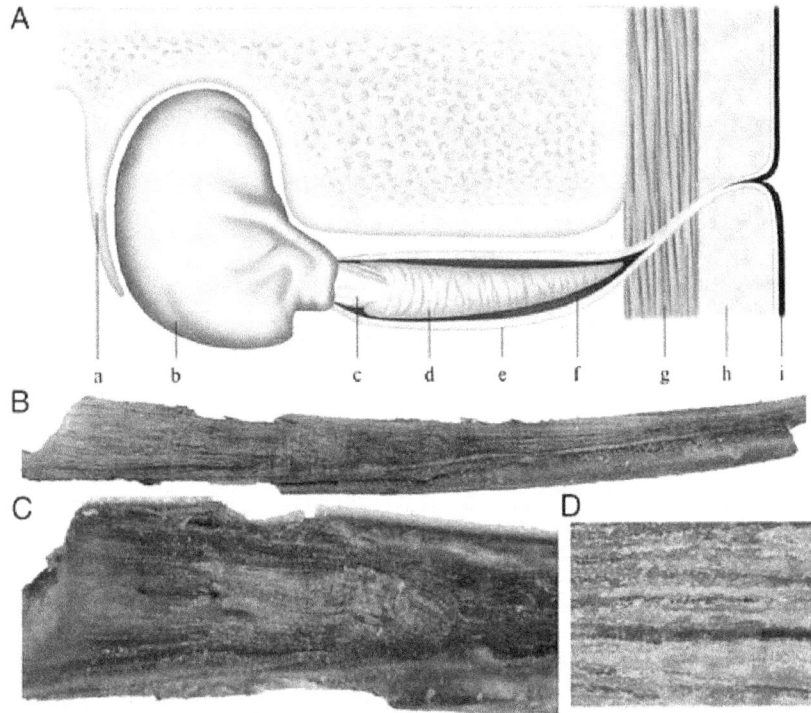

Illustration of a blue whale earplug.[1]   Fig. 01

In 2013, a group of scientists published a detailed account of their attempt to reconstruct a lifetime chemical profile of an individual blue whale through examining its cerumen, or what we commonly call earwax. It was discovered that the lipophilic compounds preserved in the earwax can reveal not only the biogenic physiological changes in the whale, but also the anthropogenic contaminants it was exposed to throughout its life. In blue whales, earwax accumulates continuously from birth and forms alternating dark and light layers correlated to periods of feeding or migration. This enables scientists to estimate the age of the whale in a manner that greatly resembles dendrochronology, the science of dating based on counting growth rings in trees.

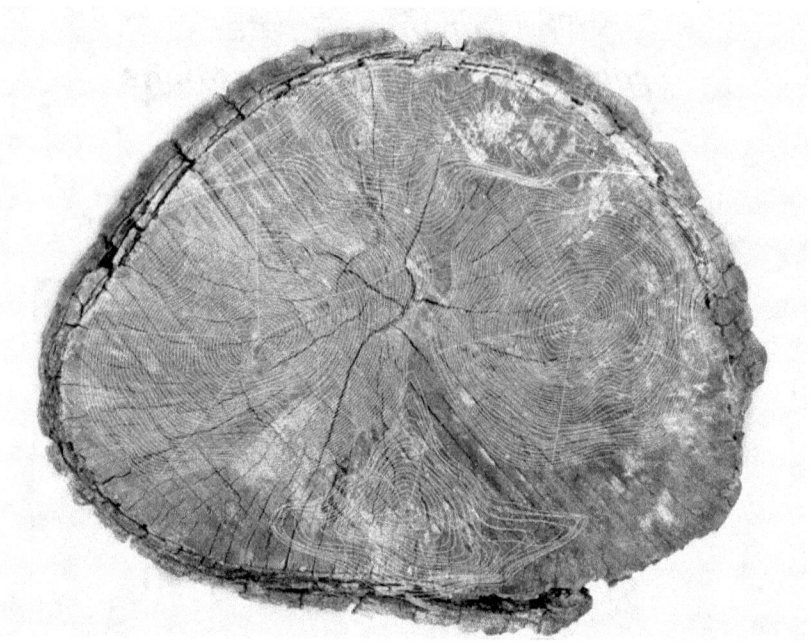

Fig. 02   Using biological growth to record time: Cross section of a tree. Superimposed ring lines resemble elevation contours in space; courtesy of the artist.

Like tree rings, which not only reveal to us the age of the tree, but also changes in climatic conditions during its lifetime, the chemical profiles uncovered through an analysis of the whale's earwax display a much more complex picture in which changes brought about by internal hormonal fluctuations intermingle with those induced by human activities. A geometrical cross section projects a three-dimensional object onto a two-dimensional plane, whereas a cross section of tree or earwax, with its temporal layers neatly stacking up next to each other, comes uncannily close to being a visualization of Einstein's spacetime.

It is becoming increasingly fashionable for historians to eschew the anthropocentric view and espouse a more non-human, object-oriented historiographical approach. This trend was initiated through material consciousness that has now reached the intensity of material conscientiousness. The vilification of anthropocentrism is manifest in the emergence and proliferation of philosophical movements such as object-oriented ontology and speculative realism. The influence of these movements appears to be, understandably, most evident in the arts, where objects increasingly occupy a central role in dictating the rhetoric of the field. In the discipline of history, the object-oriented current has also brought to the scene a new operational logic, guided by a certain wariness towards textual evidence

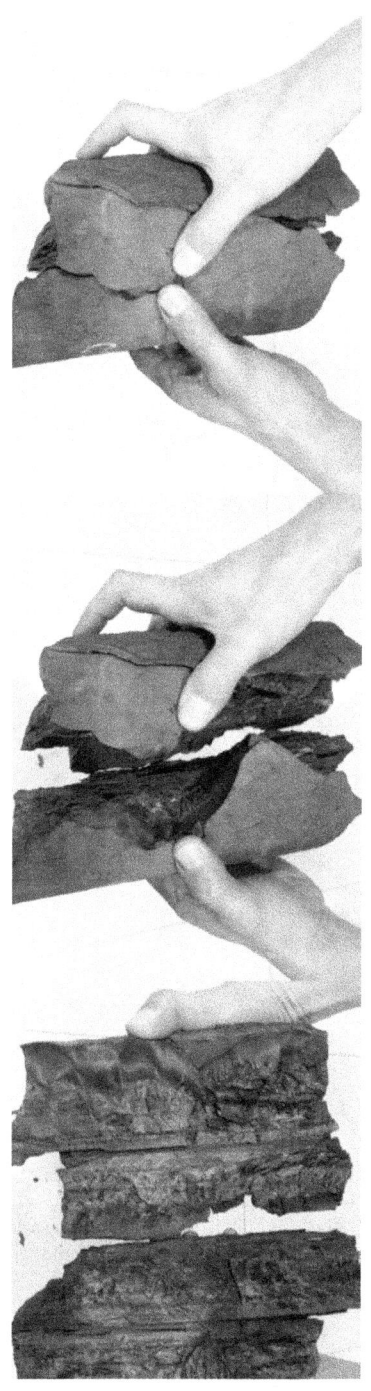

The fracturing of a carbonized log. Examining the interior lengthwise reveals a landscape, whereas the tree rings record time; courtesy of the artist.

Fig. 03

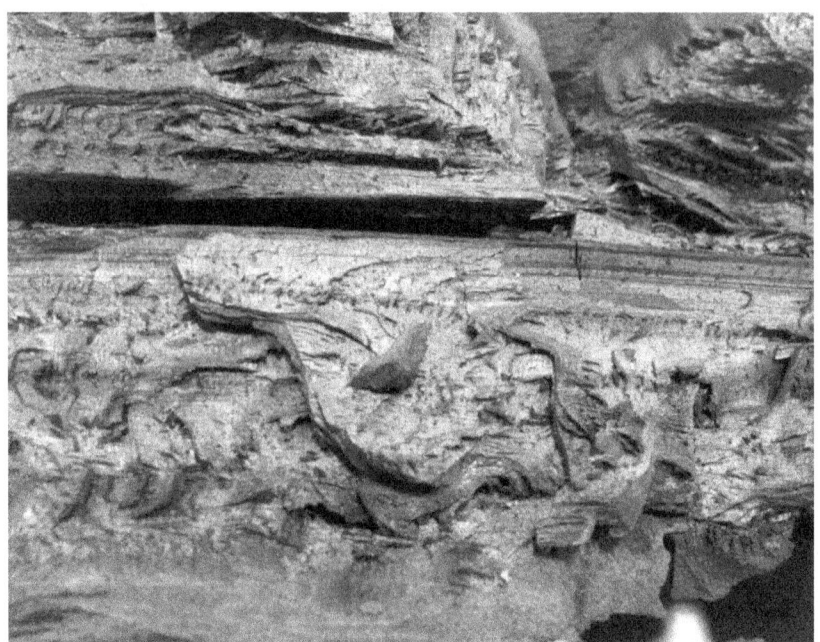

Fig. 04 Detail of log interior; courtesy of the artist.

and coupled with a dilating margin of approbation towards objects and materials. Not only are objects being studied as though they were vague texts, some historians are now calling for texts to be treated as vague objects.

Because of these trends, it is not a particularly novel or enlightening procedure to suggest that tree rings and earwax laminae can be read as texts that reveal to us their own biographical details. Any object, in the life bestowed by object-oriented enthusiasts, is to be treated and read as an embodiment not only of its own history, but also of the social and political histories that form the parameters of their existence. By laying tree rings and earwax on the table and claiming that these are exceptionally interesting objects which can provide an impetus for further theoretical discussion, what needs to be attended to—with a great amount of precision in the case of the earwax—is their capacity to invoke questions especially pertinent to the practice of historical periodization.

Besides being a relatively reliable tool for measuring the length of a distant time period, the major aesthetic appeal of tree rings or earwax laminae lies in their capacity to exhibit temporality spatially. Not only do they inform us of the cumulative length of time, the data we derive from them can be neatly divided into annual or semi-annual growth. For this very reason, tree rings are commonly marvelled at for being "natural clocks." Beyond their scientific

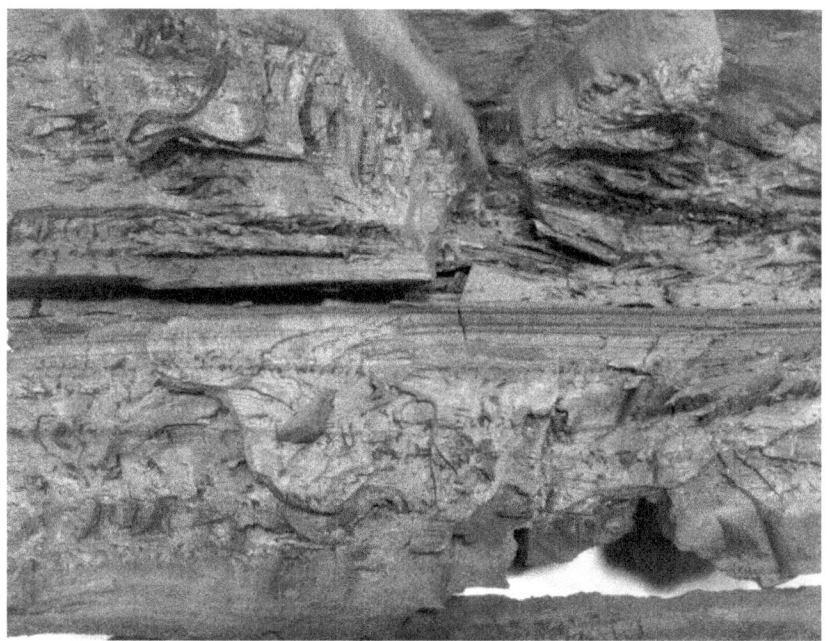

Detail of log interior; courtesy of the artist. Fig. 05

efficacy and, to some extent, accuracy, they correlate with and thereby reconfirm our choices of temporal division. History and philosophy routinely problematize things that are all too familiar to us, including our practice of giving specific units to certain groups of time. While tree rings and earwax record their history following an organic system of division, human history is written with punctuation drawn at the occurrences of epoch-making events. Such phrases as "history-changing" or "history-making" demonstrate the decisive role of these epoch-makers in historical periodization.

The placement of punctuation affects not only how historians apportion history into digestible sizes suitable for academic research, but also how we position ourselves as artists in the course of human development. The academic discipline of history cannot be conceived without epoch-makers, since they are precisely what gives epistemic value to historical studies. Epoch-makers add the weight that prevents history from drifting away into a monotonous course of events. However, as the historian Ulrich Raulff has contended, historical periodization is often characterized by the political allegiances of historians. This raises a question concerning objectivity in temporal division in historical studies. Since epoch-makers define what can properly be assembled under the sign of the epoch, assigning an epoch-making role to a certain event also inevitably leads to the elimination of anomalies that fall outside the extension and consequence of the epoch-maker.

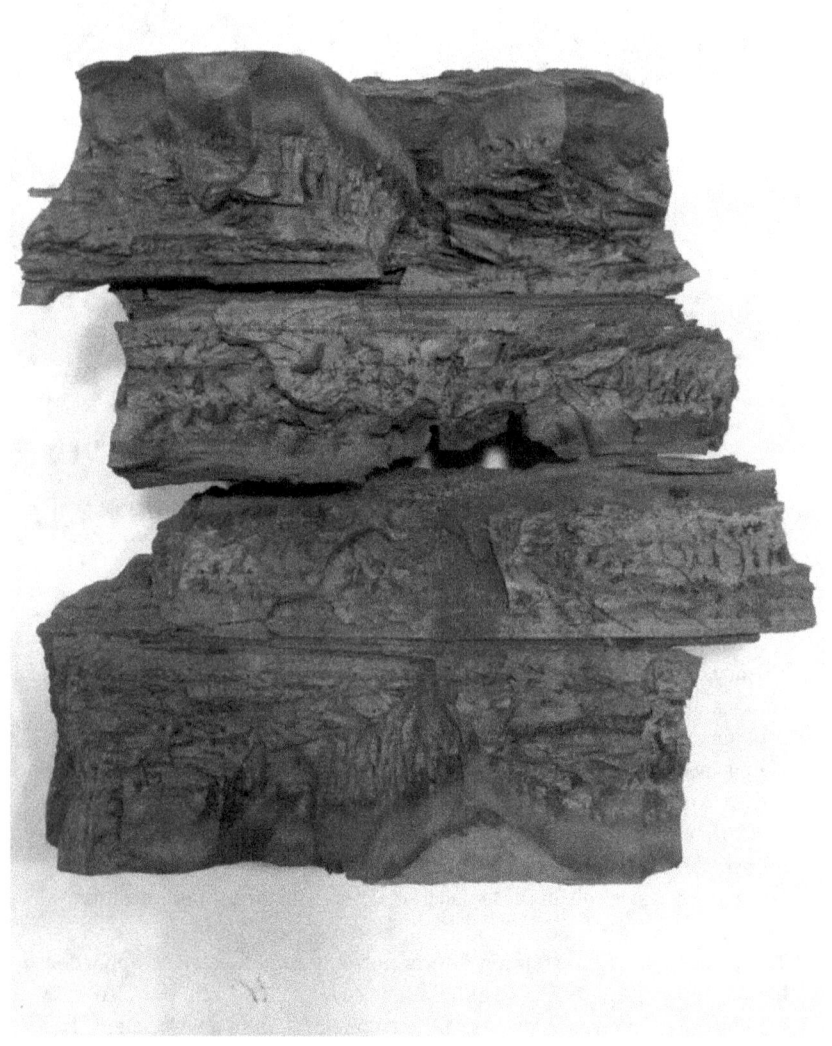

Fig. 05　Interior of a carbonized tree split lengthwise, mirroring the humanized landscape of the strip mine; courtesy of the artist.

This is particularly significant when one considers the implications of the Anthropocene, the new epoch of geological time currently being debated. In this case, the epoch-makers are no longer individual actors or discrete events; humans in general, and human impact in aggregate, has become the epoch-maker of our own human geological time.

As we noted above, the traces of epoch-makers are sometimes found in the organic temporal markers of trees and earwax. Missing tree rings in the year 1816 coincides with severe climatic abnormalities during what was later referred to as "The Year Without a Summer." Variations in the levels of mercury detected in layers of the whale's earwax also correlate with the exceptionally high level of regional anthropogenic contamination along the coast of California. The natural and spontaneous process of growth or accumulation are not exempted from the impact of our epoch-makers. Yet, we also rely on them for their ability to provide us with unadulterated access to the unfolding of human history and the cascading of human impacts over time.

The entanglements of natural temporal marking and artificial historical periodization become even more pronounced when we consider the process of calibration required for such scientifically advanced practices as radiocarbon dating. Calibration was implemented for radiocarbon dating after scientists realized that the ratio of carbon-14 to carbon-12 does not remain constant (as they initially assumed). Different types of records are taken into account to calibrate the carbon-14 ratio, many of which are related to the human impact on the atmosphere. Most notably, nuclear weapons testing almost doubled the amount of carbon-14, and has now been suggested as the Golden Spike marking a potential beginning of the Anthropocene. In fact, the acceptance of radiocarbon dating as a reliable method for calculating ages in the 1950s is itself an epoch-making event; it led to the creation of a new designation in time measurement: "Before Present" (BP). The phrase "Before Present" eerily suggests that since the first days of nuclear testing, humans have become suspended in a temporality identified by an epoch-maker of such great magnitude that all subsequent events cannot escape the shadow of its prefiguration. Calibration is a process of interweaving natural marking with artificial periodization to reveal points of intersection.

In establishing the Anthropocene as a new geological epoch, humans are asked to shoulder the weight of being our own epoch-makers. This weight is not just to be measured; it must also be felt, and endured. Artistic and historical research, contextualized within the Anthropocene epoch, faces the challenge of addressing how we are to live with our own impact. As the epoch-making weight becomes too great to be quantified, we also need to move beyond collecting figures of rings in trees, and layers in earwax, and begin constructing configurations that might escape the prefiguration of our own actions and impact.

Notes

1 (A) Schematic diagram showing the location of the earplug within the ear canal. Details for illustration: (a) whale skull, (b) tympanic bulla, (c) pars flaccida/tympanic membrane ("glove finger"), (d) cerumen (earplug), (e) external auditory meatus, (f) auditory canal, (g) muscle tissue, (h) blubber tissue, and (i) epidermis; (B) extracted blue whale earplug, total length 25.4 cm; (C) earplug longitudinal cross-section; (D) view (20x) of earplug cross-section showing discrete laminae; source: www.pnas.org/content/early/2013/09/10/1311418110.

Geochemistry & Other Planetary Perspectives

Ursula Biemann

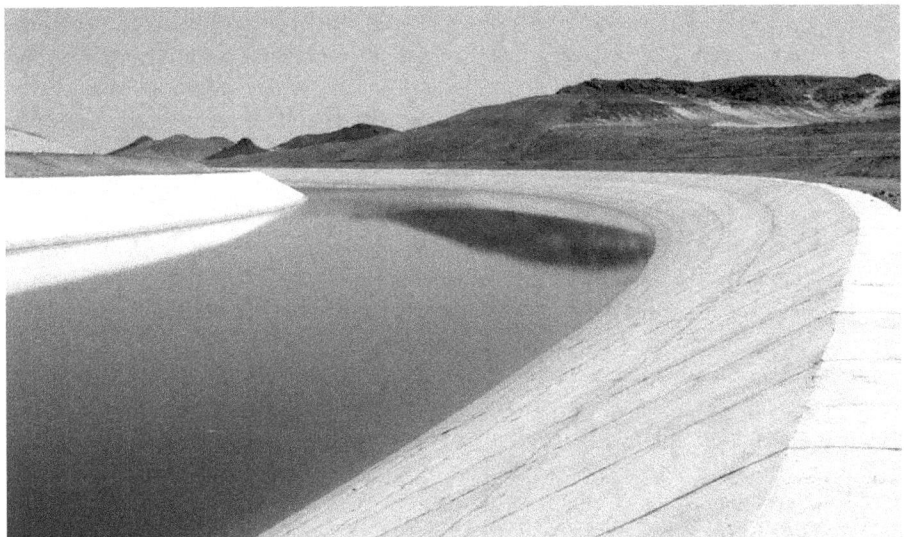

Main irrigation canal of Toshka, the giant land reclamation project on the Upper Nile, video still from *Egyptian Chemistry*; courtesy of the artist.

Fig. 01

In the summer of 2010, Egyptian farmers took to the streets in large numbers to protest against the lack of water for their land. Scarce irrigation had made vast surfaces of farmland around the country barren. The exorbitant water demands of large agro-industries coinciding with rising temperatures had taken their toll on peasant farming, and Egypt had dropped below the globally recognized "water poverty" line.[1] The insurgency of the farmers and the subsequent revolution amplified the dramatic physical transformations the country had undergone in the previous decades and made them internationally audible. Egypt is one giant chemical experiment catalyzed by water engineering, where water is a coalescing agent for land-use politics, crop cycles, nitrate industries, soil composition, farmers' collectives, oxidants, irrigation technologies, and hydropower. Comprising a significant part of Egyptian reality, these entities are the main protagonists in *Egyptian Chemistry* (2012), my artistic exploration of the water ecologies of the Nile Valley. In this essay, I will also discuss *Deep Weather* (2013), my short video essay that draws a connection between two remote settings: the reach for the heavy tar sands in Northern Canada and the efforts made by indigenous populations in the Bengal Delta to protect themselves from rising sea levels. The profound ecological changes currently underway have made it crucial to think with geological time scales and to link seemingly disparate events across the globe. Both of these projects explicitly engage with the physical and chemical composition of the Earth. They focus on oil and water as two primordial liquids that form the undercurrents of contemporary narration, animating profound changes in the planetary ecology. Considering minute but consistent material transformations a driving force in the reconfiguration of our terrestrial reality—including politics—these video works position scientific attention, fieldwork, and videography as reality-producing practices in this process.

Let me begin with *Egyptian Chemistry*, a multimedia art installation based on videographic field documents and actual water samples taken from numerous sites along the Nile. It examines water engineering and desert development projects, and inquires more generally into the hydraulic, social, and chemical conditions of soil and water in Egypt. Given Egypt's extreme hydrography, which is entirely dependent on the Nile, it is easy to make out the political potential of water to materialize national and societal visions. Indeed, *al-khemia*, the contemporary Arabic term for "chemistry," is based on the ancient word for the place we call Egypt; it means "the Black Land," possibly due to the muddy Nile floods which used to seasonally overflow the river banks and fertilize the entire valley. The term also alludes to a vision of an earth, which is above all a mighty chemical body where the crackling noise of forming and breaking molecular bonds can be sensed at all times. The three-part video unfolds this idea in relation to modern and contemporary Egypt, asking what kind of bio-political-chemical compositions are currently in formation, and what effects they will have on future constellations of biological, chemical, and political life.

Since Gamal Abdel Nasser's presidency (1956–1970), it has been clear to every Egyptian leader that to be in power in Egypt, you must have control of the water. In this hydraulic civilization, water could easily be examined through the lens of water governance, as the different regimes articulate a history of taming the forces of water and turning it into a resource. However, my artistic research work in the field, coupled with my own reading, led the film in a different direction. As my research on water systems entangled my thinking with the metaphysics of Bruno Latour and Graham Harman, the quantum physics of Karen Barad, and other chemical and ecological theories, my original point of departure from critical social theory mutated into a study of Egypt at the molecular level, organized into hybrid ecologies of social, technological, and natural interactions.[2]

Preamble to Revolution

There is no precise beginning for the current geochemical state of Egypt; the contemporary paradoxes of the Earth cannot be resolved by recovering or inventing hypothetical origins. As a primal cipher, the Nile has always meddled powerfully with other forms of life, including humans and their attendant patterns of settlement. The hydraulic ambitions of successive regimes have overlaid their conduits in a complex, improbable palimpsest, constituting the invisible substructure of the Nile Valley. If the origins of these configurations are all but impossible to

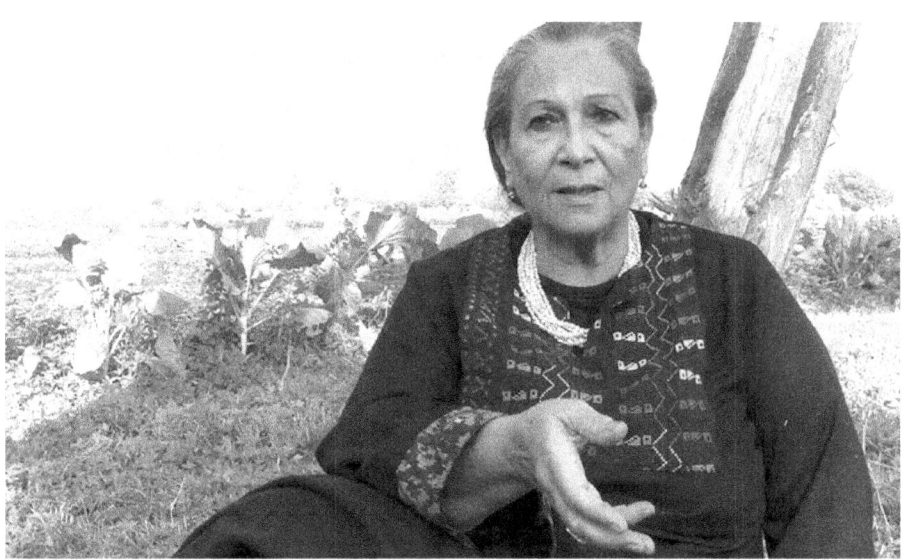

Shahinda Ma'al, peasant activist, video still from *Egyptian Chemistry*; courtesy of the artist. Fig. 02

trace, two more recent models of water governance stand out for their exemplary relation to, and explication of, hydro-political power. To grasp the scope of these two particular modes of civil engineering—capable of simultaneously mastering the course of water and of civil society—one must first envision water as a vehicle for epic narratives. The first such epic manifestation is the Aswan High Dam, a bombastic example of state infrastructure conceived by the socialist President Nasser, engineered by the Soviet Union (at the height of the Cold War), and built in the 1960s, predominantly by Nubian labour.[3] At the time of construction, the massive hydropower project united the Soviet vision of a progressive labour force with the modernizing Egyptian scheme to transport water and electricity to cities and villages. The project perfectly embodied socialist principles because it provided a means of rationing available resources into economically viable portions dealt out equitably to all citizens. The monolithic construction functions further as a mediating, centralizing force for technocratic state power. To this day, the dam is a symbol of a mass, collective achievement, and retains its role in fomenting national pride. The high degree of militarization of the Aswan area speaks of its utmost strategic importance for the country, reminding us that if the dam should ever become fatally damaged—by whatever natural or otherwise hostile forces—Egypt as a whole will be gone.

The second epic exemplar of civil engineering is the Toshka Project, a new Nile Valley irrigation scheme of Pharaonic proportions that enacts an entirely different vision of the relation between water and the nation-state. Organized through a system of canals, it aims to reclaim desert land for industrial agribusinesses growing cash crops for export.[4] Built in the late 1990s, this surface-consuming machine is driven by the Mubarak Pumping Station, which gushes Nile water into a vast land depression reasonably assumed to be one of the driest places on the planet. The ground there does not support or incubate anything; it is practically sterile, and hard as rock. Artificially producing wet fields by spraying water onto desert sand results in massive vapourization. Thus, in contrast to the conservation of the dam, the pumps and conduits of Toshka suggest a carefree, if not exceedingly wasteful, use of water in the desert. The facility is characteristic of Hosni Mubarak's neoliberal privatization of public land and water, which well served foreign princes and other murky, semi-private operators who bypassed normal state taxation.[5] Looking back from 2014, it seems inevitable that such a well-known yet sinister plot would surely help erode belief in state politics.

When farmers took to the streets in 2010, it was because the water-intensive export crops had dehydrated the valley and triggered a food and water crisis. The large-scale agribusinesses in the desert were competing for water that traditionally flowed to villages throughout the valley and the delta. Old villages at the end of the stream had to make do with the leftover water, yet because such massive volumes were diverted for new export crops, what little was left could not relieve the parched soil of smaller farms. Without enough water to grow their own food, Egyptians watched as food supplies dwindled and local food prices inflated. The urban centres, where the revolution sparked in 2011, were full of young people from the villages who had experienced a continuous assault on their livelihood.

Research Methods and Aesthetic Practice

Egyptian Chemistry does not directly address the power brokers behind Egypt's uneasy move from the old hydraulic state model to a neoliberal market model of water management because this style of critique limits generative thinking by reproducing state narratives. Instead, the project relays the itinerary of coincidences that constitutes fieldwork, focusing on the recordings from meetings with water and desert experts reporting on the chemical immanence of Egypt's territory. The fieldwork included taking water samples along the Nile and in the Delta wetlands. In artistic research, it is often more rewarding to direct only partial attention to the explicit object of analysis and to leave ample space to roam into the wider field, to encounter and examine the surprising juxtapositions and coincidences that all fieldwork generates. This open methodology favours a state of divided attention, granting the freedom to relax in all directions. In this mode of open research, one is disposed to not merely define the findings, but to create new and unlikely coalescences with semi-conscious affects and ideas, and with other material and immaterial surroundings, which all converge in a shared narrative matrix. The simple analysis of water chemistry thus expanded the inquiry through chain reactions, merging the sticky saturated air hovering above the reddish salt fields, the humming emitted by the high-voltage power lines in the sky, the oil-soaked sands swelling up to the ankles in the nocturnal refineries in the Delta Lakes, the

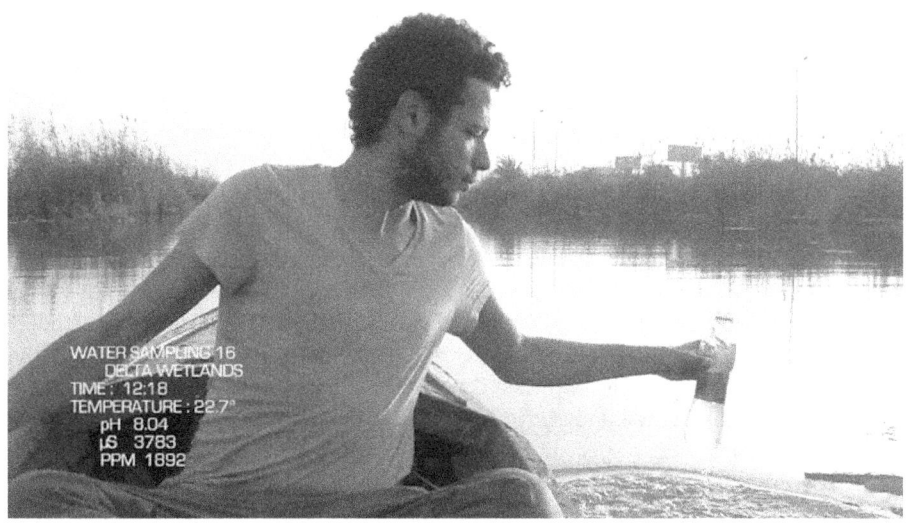

Water sampling in the Nile Delta, video still from *Egyptian Chemistry*; courtesy of the artist. Fig. 03

foul smell of the nitrate factory draining into the crystal-clear upper Nile, and the chanting of the crowds crossing the Qasr al-Nil Bridge to Tahrir Square—all scenes that are further complicated by countless conversations and social interactions in the field. The water samples are momentary cuts in a social ecology, temporary expressions of this specific material-mental configuration. Within *Egyptian Chemistry*, such moments are recorded on video as raw data; it was important not to format this loose cognitive fabric too quickly by immediately assigning it a structural form. The methodology and aesthetic of *Egyptian Chemistry* sets out to unhinge patterns of thought rather than affirm them. To encounter the meta-chemistry at the heart of the project, it was necessary to generate thought forms conducive to the perception of immaterial, energetic, and fluid phenomena, as well as their mutations and transactions.

By complementing the video recordings with material probes, my work aims to both intensify and complicate the performative notion of reality expressed in my artistic practice. It elicits a shift from epistemological questions about how things are known toward an ontological inquiry regarding how reality is characterized as coming into existence. For such an endeavour, I required a new set of analytical tools. Drawing on quantum physics, I could no longer assume a pre-existing and static world whose observable features possessed *a priori* values that could readily be recorded and interpreted. As Barad has convincingly argued in *Meeting the Universe Halfway*, it is the questions, choices, movements, equipment, and directed observations that generate a specific material reality which the artist-scientist co-produces, and of which she is a part. Before encountering these theories, I assumed space was produced through human practices that eventually inscribed themselves into topographies and materialized in all sorts of co-formations, such as migration networks and border fences. I understood reality to be constituted by discursive practices that gradually consolidate and materialize, and I was exploring how I contributed to this process of discursive materialization through my visual practice. The fact that I entered a scene when activity was already underway implied that I was deeply implicated in the process of representation. However, quantum physics suggests a far more radical ontological scenario where matter and meaning are mutually articulated; the two processes productively collapse into one. According to Barad, practices of knowing and forms of being cannot be isolated from one another; the entangled state of material-discursive practices is, in fact, what generates matter.[6] In this framework, there is no outside and no standing by; this suggests that the contingent and open-ended mattering process can and must be continuously reworked, and that this process will inevitably affect the object or institution under investigation. It also makes for a remarkably unstable materiality. With respect to image-making, Barad's account suggests that video recording does not *represent* but *generates* reality. The agency of image-making is not located within the assumed intentionality of the filmmaker who wants to represent a situation, but is found instead in a filmmaker's process and her direct contribution to changing configurations of materials, politics, and knowledges.

Fieldwork is central to this ontological orientation because it locates the research within time, space, and the obstinacies of physical existence. Fieldwork takes place in a series of present moments. There is something absurd in trying to locate and define the qualities of a particular place based on flowing water; one can only hope to get an approximate test result, and the researcher and artist both know that even when the results are returned from the lab, the water will have already changed. However, the classical scientific method is still the most attentive form of observation we have, the most focused advertence one can grant any object under investigation. As a gesture of earnest civil concern for water quality, there is certainly some merit in this acute, focused attention. For me, the purpose of measuring and obtaining quantifiable water data was less about determining the variable degree of water pollution than it was about the care brought to learning about it.

Egyptian Chemistry does not explicitly engage with the political upheavals of 2011, nor the street battles or the heated debates. After a single shot of a political manifestation on the bridge, the video turns to a scene of water sampling occurring further downstream. Only once does the revolution dramatically intrude the scene: a tear gas attack interrupted my interview with Graham Harman at the old campus of the American University in Cairo, which is located directly behind Tahrir Square. This happened just after I asked my last question, in which I expressed my hesitations about the political consequences of an object-oriented ontology; Harman asserted that we should free our minds from the omnipotence of the political just as the attack broke out. With this juxtaposition, the scene dramatizes the significance of politics in relation to both knowledge production and emergent reality; as Harman disavows the potency of political life, the backformation of revolutionary street fighting interrupts the calm of his allegedly neutral ontology.

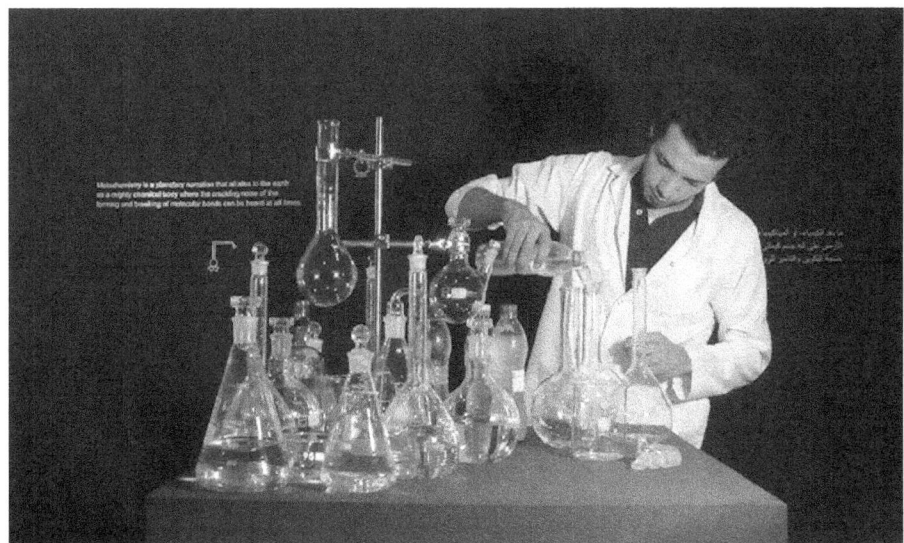

Video performance of trans-bottling Nile samples into lab flasks, video still from *Egyptian Chemistry*; courtesy of the artist.

Fig. 04

Apart from this disruption, the video acquiesces to the harmless. It turns to less forceful but equally transformative developments, namely the plurality of dynamic processes of water and soil chemistry that have been dramatically recomposing the physical territory from within. In T.J. Demos's words, the project "delivers an archeology of the revolution."[7] It inserts an imaginary tube camera into the subsoil, interrogating the microsystems and macrophenomenal force fields that actuate them. The project engages Egypt at this micro level, provoking, capturing, and sampling instances of materialization that register global forces. *Egyptian Chemistry* is an expression of the disrupted and re-emerging material bonds that form non-verbal narrative configurations. I wanted the project to move the boundary inside, toward the innermost dimensions of a composite reality.

Egypt's Chemical Transformation

Giant water tanks, parallel valleys, desert colonies, and food laboratories have manufactured a world in which science is programmed to overcome nature and its limits. The agro-industries located in this remote, arid land, miles away from the lush and sociable Nile Valley, grow seedless grapes and other delicacies to satisfy the European appetite for off-season foods. At Toshka, as with the other colossal land reclamation projects throughout Egypt, sterile lands are turned into field labs for testing new forms of human life. How is desert dust converted into soggy fertility? Bacteria are cultivated in chicken excrement on military-owned poultry mega-farms to make the aseptic desert terrain an altruistic host for germination. According to agro-scientific experts—mostly military officers educated

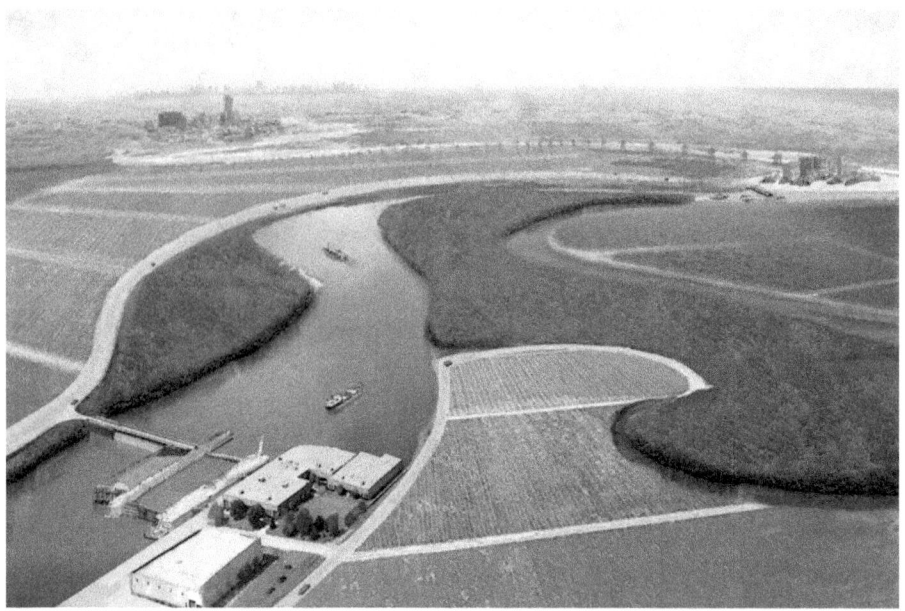

Fig. 05   Design for planned Integrated Seawater Agriculture at Red Sea; courtesy of Gensler.

in agricultural science—the bacteria, thriving on the organic residues of barley harvests, unfold their liveliness with every shower from the circular water sprinklers. It will still be years until wheat can grow in this hostile ground, but wheat is what matters most for feeding Egypt.

Egypt's topography is changing as a result of its strategic expansion of arable land, but so too are the strata deeper underground. Extended irrigation draws heavily on the subterranean aquifers causing the Nile Delta to subside at a rate of one centimetre per year.[8] Rising sea levels will predictably aggravate this hazardous development. One of the more futuristic land reclamation ventures, still in its planning phase, is integrated seawater agriculture. The New Nile Co. manufactures seawater landscapes near desert coasts for salt harvesting, fish and seafood aquacultures, and algae plantations for cattle feed and biofuel. Set up near El Gouna on the Red Sea, the project was conceived by atmospheric physicist Carl Hodges, whom I interviewed for the project. His acclaimed research integrates surface dynamics and their interaction with vegetation cycles. Besides enabling versatile food production from halophytes (salt-tolerant plants), the project proactively builds up biomass with fast growing mangroves to compensate for dwindling ground. For centuries, the runoff from intense agriculture has drained valuable nutrients into canals down the rivers and into the Red Sea. The Integrated Saltwater Agricultural System proposed by Hodges reverses this process by redirecting nutrients from the sea back into the soil, reintroducing sustainable cycles for recovery of water, energy, and materials.[9] Considering the dwindling world phosphate reserves, which have driven the exponential growth of agricultural productivity in the last few decades, sustaining fertile soil is a critical domain of research related to feeding the world's population in the future. Before it was tamed by engineers, the Nile was more generous and democratic: with every high flood, it evenly spread its fertilizing mud over the entire valley. After hydraulic structures were introduced, chemical fertilizers began to be used and market dynamics were established through the political mechanisms of agricultural subsidies. The seasonal occurrence thus became a matter of the social sphere. It is in pivotal sites like these where geophysical and social processes most dramatically intertwine.

With the infrastructural intervention of the Aswan High Dam in the watercourse, the ecology of the Nile inevitably changed. The fish that migrated from Ethiopia through the Mediterranean to the Atlantic and back were interrupted by this monumental architecture. It is important to remember, however, that the hydraulic regime of the Nile was already altered a century before by the construction of a series of barrages designed to raise the water line on the upstream side in order to feed irrigation canals without the use of pumping, but they had unintended consequences. The barrages reduced the velocity of flow, which diminished the supply of oxygen. This process facilitated the anaerobic decay of organic pollutants, infecting pools and, eventually, the land through the millions of irrigation canals. The result was an insurgency of tiny pollutants that reconfigured Egypt on a molecular level. While environmental engineers had a tremendous impact on the hydraulics of the Nile by regulating its velocity, gauge, and seasonal flows, the variations of water quality—based on its salinity, acidity, oxygen content, mineral composition, nutrient systems, organic pollutants, suspended particles, and silt—largely escaped human control. Although the hydraulic regime of the Nile was deliberately changed, the biological and chemical composition of the water was inadvertently though equally affected.

These water transformations in Egypt allow for the detection of emergent forces as various combinations of natural, technological, and social processes alter realities. Such modified water chemistry transforms soil quality, interferes with land management, drives urbanization processes, and disrupts food supply chains, infiltrating the human sphere through multiple venues and illicit channels. These components do not line up as a simple causal chain of reactions, as they constantly shift and create strange feedback loops—nor are they solely the result of specific economic policies. Each element interacts to create hybrid ecologies in which global organizations, desert developers, and tiny pollutants all forcefully affect the water and topography of Egypt.

Explanations of current events in Egypt overemphasize political forces, effecting a disregard for the multiple components that shape the complexity of the contemporary situation. Instead, *Egyptian Chemistry* attends to slower and more continuous transformations of geochemistry whose physical manifestations are not always relayed into political consequences. This geopoetic approach rather uses metachemistry as a link between the life worlds of chemical and human agents.

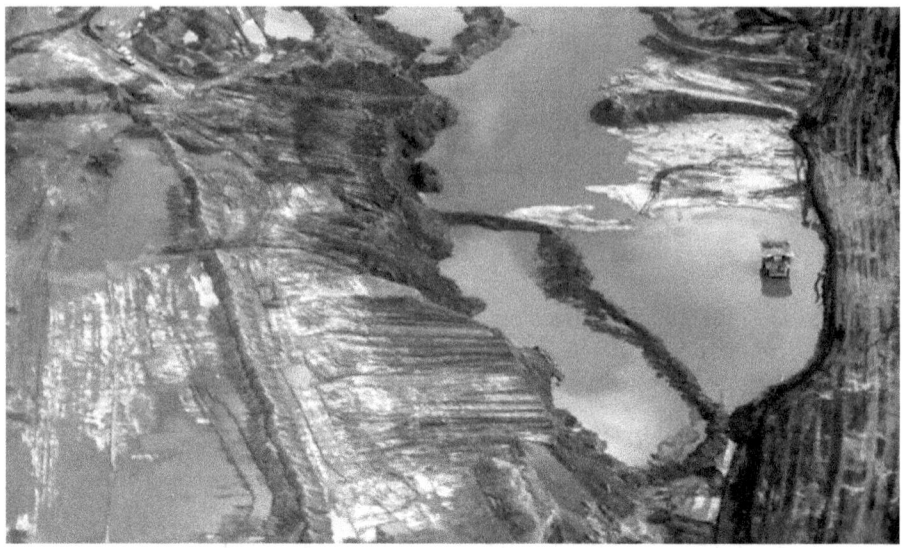

Fig. 06   Alberta tar sands, video still from *Deep Weather*; courtesy of the artist.

Weather's Deep Time

Deep Weather (2013) pursues a different strategy as it addresses the complex entanglements of water, chemistry, and politics by engaging the Earth as a closed system. This short, single-channel video essay draws the connection between the relentless unearthing of fossil fuels in Northern Canada and the protective measures undertaken by Bangladeshi communities on the other side of the world—two remote and simultaneously occurring scenes connected through their atmospheric chemistry. *Deep Weather* thickens the understanding of these geographies by reaching into the interior of the Earth and extending a hundred miles into the atmosphere, as fossil fuel extraction is not merely a geopolitical concern but also a bio-planetary reality tied to recombinant chemical life-worlds.

The opening shot of the film looks down from a helicopter on the huge open-pit extraction zone of the tar sands in the midst of the vast Canadian boreal forest, establishing a zone of dark, lubricant geology. After oil production peaked, ever dirtier, more remote, and deeper layers of carbon resources started being exploited in Alberta. In the tar sands, fresh water from the Athabasca River is used to boil the black sediment until the oil separates from the clay.[10] The toxic waste, a necessary by-product of bitumen processing, is stored in open tailings lakes that spread over large areas which until recently were covered by ancient spruce forests and spongy wet soil. Aggressive mining, steam processing, and the trucking around of the tar sands and equipment all impinge on environmental and human rights as energy companies devastate the living space and hunting territories of First Nations communities. Remote areas in the heart of the boreal forest, traversed

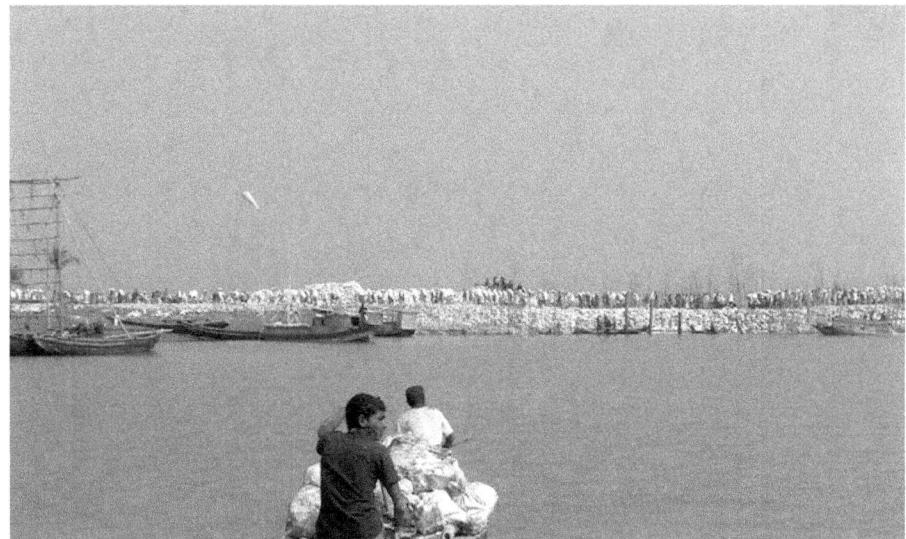

Bangladeshi communities building an earth embankment against rising water levels in the Ganges Delta, video still from *Deep Weather*; courtesy of the artist.   Fig. 07

primarily by Mikisew Cree and Athabasca Chipewyan hunters on foot, are being successively opened by the Canadian government for exploratory testing and oil mining. Pushing extraction frontiers far into pristine areas also necessitates the construction of extensive infrastructure projects, including roads, heliports, seismic lines, settlements, and communication networks reaching into these remote habitats. All of this drastically changes the living and migrating space of hundreds of species, including humans; native communities now travel several days before reaching their hunting grounds because their traditional territory has been rapidly overtaken by resource extraction.

The Athabasca River, which is used to power the extraction of the tar sands, flows north into the Arctic Ocean. It is the backbone of human existence in Northern Alberta. In the last few years, due to massive industrial use, the water level of the river is sinking to the point where far away settlements can no longer be reached by boat. But for Aboriginal folks, the damage reaches beyond blocking traditional knowledge and hunting practices. Local mythologies and divinities animate their land.[11] The landscape contains both worlds; it is a psychosocial habitat. The noise, subterranean sonar waves and vibrations, and the invisible toxic juices seeping into lakes and rivers affect not only the biological but also the psychic ecology through contamination. The legendary quality of this collective space teetering on the brink of disaster is evoked in *Deep Weather* in the whispered voice-over: "The wildlife has retreated / The traplines are empty, / The elders call the spirits, / The young ones sing rap songs, / And the acid wind's hissing. / Evolution isn't fast enough. Mutate!" The whisper, which resonates with the aerial video footage, activates a time-space beyond the immediate physical and political reality. Set in times of epic

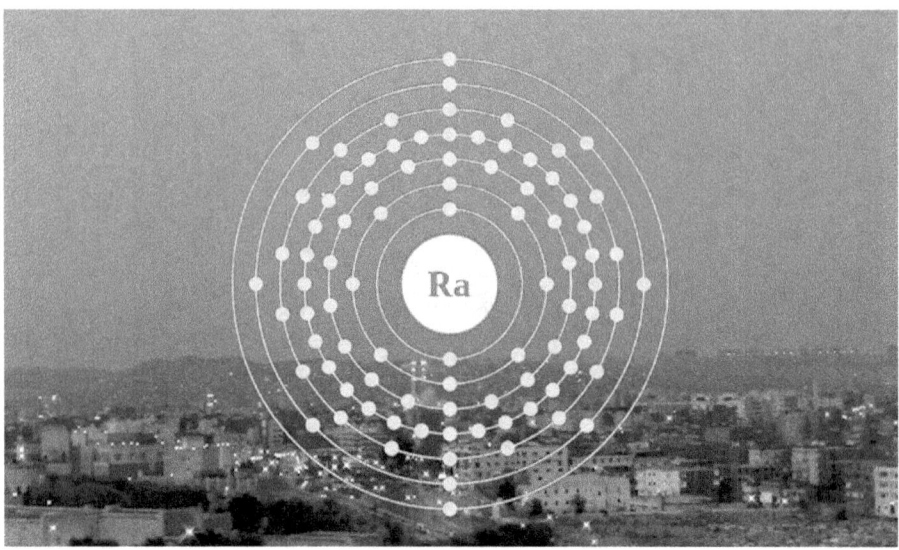

Fig. 08   Animated periodic table, video still from *Egyptian Chemistry*; courtesy of the artist.

geological, chemical, and hydrological disorder, the voice-over invokes a science-fictional narrative. The video attempts to offer an "evolutionary leap in the spatio-temporal horizons of human consciousness itself that would overcome the short-term, self-interested pursuit of material gratification characteristic of industrial civilization," as critic Yates McKee writes in relation to René Dubos.[12]

Every globally operating oil company has licensed parcels of land in the Alberta Tar Sands; an area the size of England has been partitioned and extractive activities have begun simultaneously in multiple sites.[13] Companies can acquire the license for any of the layers assumed to contain carbon deposits. A particular lot of surface land may actually have numerous owners beneath it, among the deeper layers of the Earth. Hence the disaster spreads into deep time as extraction practices reach down to the Triassic and Cambrian layers of the planet's formation. By now we are perfectly aware that the boreal forest—currently under extreme threat because of these practices—is of vital importance for carbon absorption generated by petro-capitalism.[14] At the same time, the dirty fuel being extracted from the tar sands requires not only a lot of energy for its own processing, but it is a lot heavier in carbon emissions than we have consumed so far. Local interventions are impacting the entire planetary life system, as oil extraction is forming legacies for the next 100,000 years, leaving residues for which we lack the proper cognizance and timeframe to comprehend.[15]

The second part of *Deep Weather* turns to Bangladesh, where the consequences of melting Himalayan ice fields, rising planetary sea levels, and extreme weather events largely define living conditions, particularly in the Delta. The fieldtrip to

Bangladesh in early 2011—eighteen months before the one to Alberta—originally aimed at exploring the country's multifarious water problems, and eventually zoomed in on the admirable ability of Bangladeshi communities to adopt an amphibian lifestyle, devising convertible houses, floating agricultures, hospitals, and schools. The video documents only one of these adaptations, but one that is particularly emblematic for an age of global warming: the tremendous community effort made to build protective mud embankments. This measure is undertaken by people who have to find ways of living on the water as large parts of Bangladesh gradually submerge. While climate change will mean hands-on labour for thousands of people in the deltas of the global south, there is a planetary distance between the sites of cause and effect. In Canada: the aggressive extraction of heavy fuel, major investment, large machinery, and the vertical desire of extraction into the depths of time; in Bangladesh: the drowning of delta communities, the manual labour of millions, and the submerged expansion into the horizontality of the rising oceans. As Canada strives for exhaustive accumulation, there is a sense in Bangladesh of an investment in a future, however precarious it may be. These different political economic realities ultimately express radically divergent attitudes toward the Earth.

The resonances between image-making, organisms, and topographies have produced new forms of awareness and knowledge. But if we are to speak about the non-human world—weather patterns, organic pollutants, copper atoms—it will not suffice to deploy an anthropocentric discourse. We need to examine the ways in which human and non-human realities emerge together in and through a variety of co-productions and surprising interplays. This can begin to happen by cultivating the hybrid attention required to navigate the manifold assemblages of social, technological, biological, hydrological, and geological matters. Metachemistry thus propels us into an altered dimension that can only be invoked mythically, as Egyptian Chemistry does, through space travel, time barriers, and the inter-biospheric mobility of species.

Notes

1   Karen Piper, "Revolution of the Thirsty," The Designer Observer Group, 7 December 2012, http://places.designobserver.com/feature/egypt-revolution-of-the-thirsty/34318.

2   See Karen Barad, *Meeting the Universe Halfway: Quantum Physics and the Entanglement of Matter and Meaning* (Durham and London: Duke University Press, 2007); Graham Harman, *Prince of Networks: Bruno Latour and Metaphysics* (re.press: Melbourne, 2009); James Lovelock, *The Revenge of Gaia: Earth's Climate Crisis and the Fate of Humanity* (New York: Basic Books, 2006); and Yates McKee, "The End of Environmentalism: From Biosphere to the Right to Survival," in *Non-Governmental Politics*, ed. Michael Feher (New York: Zone Books, 2007).

3   The Nubians, an ethnic group inhabiting the cross-border region of Southern Egypt and Northern Sudan, were forcefully displaced by the construction of the Aswan High Dam and constituted the majority of a cheap local labour force.

4 From video interviews with anthropologists Richard Tutwiler, Desert Development Center, American University Cairo; Philip Rizk, Cairo; and peasant activist Shahinda Ma'al, Kamshish, Nile Delta, April 2012.

5 A publicly much-discussed case, Saudi prince and business tycoon Al-Waleed Bin Talal had to return 75 percent of his Toshka property to the Egyptian state after the revolution. See Ahram Online, "Egyptian Government and Saudi Prince Reach Agreement on Toshka," 20 April 2011, http://english.ahram.org.eg/NewsContent/3/12/10457/Business/Economy/Egyptian-government-and-Saudi-prince-reach-agreeme.aspx.

6 Barad, *Meeting the Universe Halfway*, 235–240.

7 T.J. Demos presenting at a panel with Ursula Biemann and Irit Rogoff, *On the Aesthetics and Politics of Ecology*, Neuer Berliner Kunstverein, Berlin, April 16, 2013.

8 Interview with Carl Hodges at his New Nile Co research centre and test ground in El Gouna, Red Sea, April 2012. *Egyptian Chemistry*, Part 1: Agro-Sciences.

9 Ibid.

10 Based on information provided during a tour offered by Suncor Energy of their extraction and tar sand processing facilities in Fort McMurray, Alberta, September 2012.

11 During my field trip to Northern Alberta, I spent three days with a Cree elder, visiting community members and listening to the myths and politics of this landscape.

12 René Dubos, quoted in McKee, "Art and the End of Environmentalism," 544.

13 My knowledge of tar-sand extraction derives from a wide array of papers presented at the international three-day conference *Petrocultures* at the University of Alberta in Edmonton, September 2012, and a field trip to Fort McMurray, an extraction frontier town in Northern Alberta.

14 Petro-capitalism is a term that designates the particular capitalist logic of the global oil market. See Gavin Bridge, "The Hole World: Scales and Spaces of Extraction," in *New Geographies 2: Landscapes of Energy*, ed. Rania Ghosn (Harvard Graduate School of Design, 2010), and Timothy Mitchell, *Carbon Democracy: Political Power in the Age of Oil* (London: Verso, 2011).

15 Dipesh Chakrabarty, lecture given at The Anthropocene Project, Haus der Kulturen der Welt, January 2013. See also, David Archer, *The Long Thaw: How Humans Are Changing the Next 100,000 Years of Earth's Climate* (Princeton: Princeton University Press, 2009).

Images Do Not Show:
The Desire to See in the Anthropocene

Irmgard Emmelheinz

> There is no harmony in the universe. We have to get acquainted to this idea that there is no real harmony as we have conceived it.
>
> —Werner Herzog

> In the experience of deep sadness, the world itself seems altered in some way: colored by sadness, or disfigured [... this originates] in desolation, in the sense that the world is frozen and that nothing new is possible. This can lead to terrible paroxysms of destruction, attempts to shatter the carapace of reality and release the authentic self trapped within; but it can also lead away from the self altogether, towards new worldly commitments that recognize the urgent need to develop another logic of existence, another way of going on.
>
> —Dominic Fox

The Anthropocene is said to be the era in which human impact on the earth has become so forceful that we are seeing shifting seas, changes in climate, and the disappearance of innumerable species—as well as placing humanity itself at the brink of extinction. The Anthropocene thus announces the collapse of the future through "slow fragmentation towards primitivism, perpetual crisis and planetary ecological collapse."[1] Instead of being conceived as a speculative image of the future political economic system, the Anthropocene has been reduced to an apocalyptic fantasy of both human and world finitude. In the last decade, films like Lars von Trier's *Melancholia* (2011) and *World War Z* (2013) depict the end of the world as apocalyptic and doomsday narratives that may or may not end with some moral redemption. In parallel, the mass media narrative presents climate change as a "fixable" catastrophe, just like any other, comparable perhaps to the 2008 financial crisis or the 2010 British Petroleum oil spill in the Gulf of Mexico. In sum, neither our condition of finitude nor the world after the human has been imagined, and the massive human impact on the Earth, with its long-term geomorphic implications, has become unintelligible.

As I will argue in this essay, the Anthropocene has not meant a new image of the world; instead, it has meant, first, a radical change in the conditions of visuality; and second, the transformation of the world into images. These developments have phenomenological as well as epistemological consequences: while images now participate in the forming of worlds, they have also become forms of thought constituting a new kind knowledge. This form of knowledge is grounded in visual communication and thus depends on perception, thereby demanding the attendant development of an optical mind.[2] The radical change in the conditions of visuality under the Anthropocene has brought about a new subject position, or point of view, announced by the trajectories of impressionism and cubism (anti-humanism), and subsequently between cubism and experimental film (post-humanism), and then from experimental film to digital media (a non-grounded form of vision). As we will see, images have acquired status as "the extant," while becoming part of the fabric of daily life (via digital media). Such changes in the regime of visuality in the Anthropocene imply automatization, tautological vision, and signs leading to other signs, which has resulted in a proliferation of images—while also implying the cancellation of vision.

While cubism culminated in the anti-humanist rupture of the picture plane and converted the visual object, with support from surrealist devices, into "manifestation," "event," "symptom," and "hallucination," experimental film brought about a mechanical, posthuman eye that conveys images at the sensorimotor level of perception. The consequence of these changes is transformative: images, no longer relaying the subject of "beliefs" or the objects of contemplation and beauty, come to be perceived as "the extant." This involves a passage from representation to presentation; that is, instead of showing a perpetual present in a parallel temporality in order to make partially present what is absent, the image has become sheer presence, or pure immediacy: the here and now in real time. Made up of particles of time, wrested out of sensation and turned into cognition, the image deals more with concepts and enunciations than with intuition and showing.

Cubism decomposed anthropomorphism through its break with Renaissance point of view. Based on linearity, Renaissance perspective had normalized a viewing position as a centred, one-eyed, static entity within a mathematical and homogenous space. Creating the illusion of a view to the outside world, Renaissance perspective made the pictorial plane analogous to a window. Images constructed with this traditional perspective bestow identities and subjects *a priori*, configured by the point of view provided by the picture plane. Cubism, in contrast, turned space, time, and the subject upside down, redefining spatial experience and rupturing the picture plane.[3] If classical representation conveys a continuous space, cubism invented discontinuous space by subverting the relations between subject and object, making identity and difference relative, and necessarily questioning classical metaphysics. The cubist image renewed the image of the world by dissociating gaze, subject, and space, but without estranging them from each other; this brought about a new, anti-humanist subject position.[4] Moreover, with cubism, both duration and a perspectival multiplicity became embedded in the picture plane.

Influenced by Andy Warhol's filmic work, North American experimental (or Structural) film of the 1960s and 1970s allowed duration to become a key component of the aesthetic experience unfolding from an exploration of the filmic apparatus, seeking to make it analogous to human consciousness. By creating cinematic equivalents, or metaphors of consciousness, experimental film brought about a prosthetic vision giving way to solipsistic visual experiences.[5] A futuristic technoscape, Michael Snow's experimental film *La Région centrale* (1971) is exemplary in this regard. In the film, as in nearly all of his work, Snow explores the generic properties of the filmic apparatus by using it to intensify and diminish aspects of normal vision. *La Région centrale* shows images from the wilderness collected by a machine called "De La" specifically designed to shoot the film. The machine was able to move in all directions, turn around 360 degrees, and zoom in and out, reaching places no human eye could perceive before. The footage shot by "De La" was independent of any human decision or framing vision, aside from its initial parameters, and the action was shot at different times of the day and in various weather conditions. The result is a three-and-a-half-hour topological exploration of the wilderness, a "gigantic landscape."[6]

Because "De La" extracts gravity from the visual situation as much as human (pre-constructed or given) referential points of view, *La Région* hypostazises the cubist relativization of identity and difference, as well as its rejection of *a priori* space. Furthermore, the film puts on offer an experience of matter within itself, de-centring the subject, which is constituted by the experience of the work itself. To paraphrase Rosalind Krauss on minimalism, the film subverts the notion of a stable structure that could mirror the viewer's own self, a self that is completely constituted prior to experience. That is to say, the film formulates a notion of self that exists only at the moment of externality of that particular experience.[7] While someone views the film, the present is experienced as immediacy, a pure phenomenological consciousness without the contamination of historical or *a priori* meaning; the world is thus experienced as a self-sufficient, pure presence, thus foregrounding an awareness of the presence of the viewer's own perceptual processes. As Snow states: "My films are experiences: real experiences. [...] The structure is obviously important, and one describes it because it's more easily describable than other aspects, but the shape, with all the other elements, adds up to something which can't be said verbally and that's why the work *is*, why it exists."[8] By presenting every possible position of the framing-camera in relationship to itself, *La Región* releases the subject from its human coordinates, creating a "space without reference points where the ground and the sky, the horizontal and the vertical inter-exchange."[9] The references to human coordinates are the screen's rectangular frame and the breaks made by the intermittent appearance of big, glowing, yellow "X's" against a black screen. Every time the X comes up, it fixes the screen to transfer the movement in a different way or direction; the X's are the point of view *embodying* the *apprehension of the passage from chaos to form*. And, while there is something in the image delivered by *La Región* shared with the condition of thought beyond auditory or optical perceptions, it also delivers motor-sensory perceptions.[10] The machine thus delivers a posthuman, prosthetic enhancement of vision, which announces, first, the incipient normalization of perception as augmented reality and data visualization. Second, with *La Región*, machinic vision becomes an epistemological

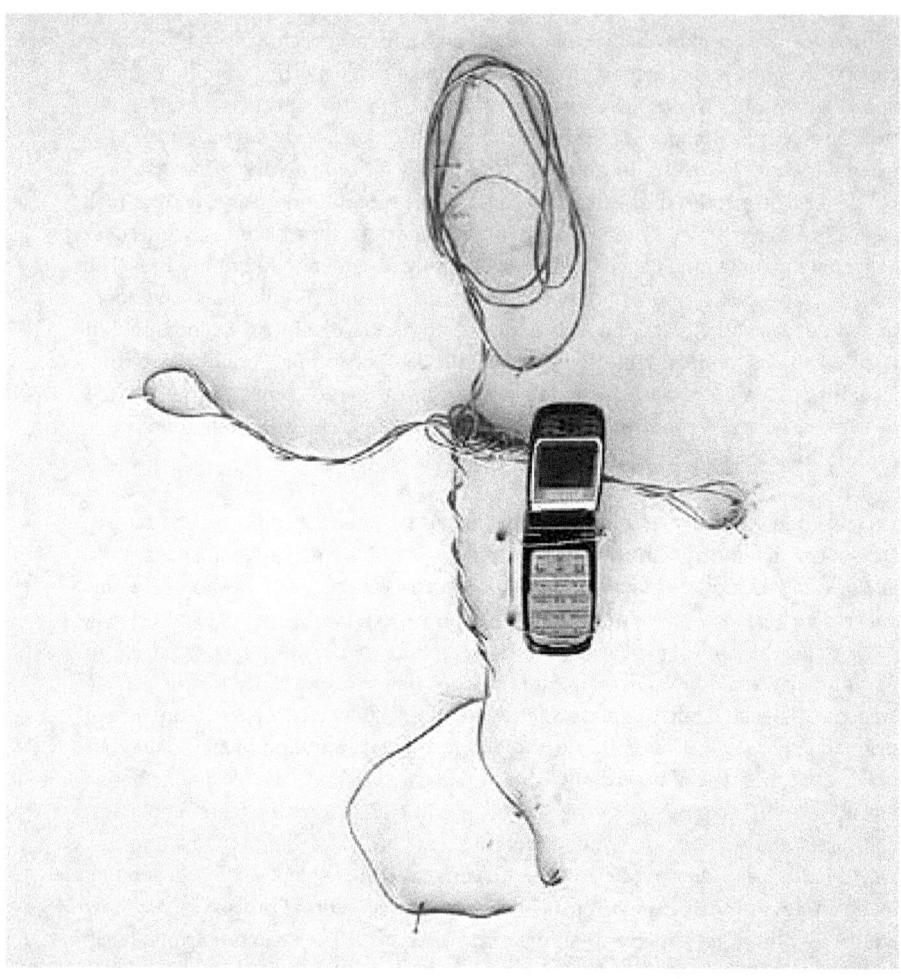

Fig. 01   From Jean-Luc Godard's exhibition *Voyage(s) en utopie* at the Centre Georges Pompidou, Paris, 2006; courtesy of Michael Witt.

product of a human-centred point of view without stable reference points, foregrounding the conditions of contemporary visuality, as I will further elucidate below.

While cubism embodies the anti-humanist scission of the subject and the possibility of the construction of many psychical planes, *La Région* embodies the displacement of the human agent from the subjective centre of operations.[11] Both epitomize modernity's fragmentation brought about by mechanization, its alienating character, and its impossibility to give back an image or serve as a reflective mirror because it is *indifferent to me*.[12] And yet, this was the fate of the image, and of art based on contemplation. These works also attest to the fact that the grounding experience of modernity is to refuse things as "given" in advance as the ground for thought.[13]

As I stated above, the Anthropocene era implies not a new image of the world, but the transformation of the world into images. Humanity's alteration of the biophysical systems of earth has occurred in parallel with the rapid modifications of the receptive fields of the human visual cortex announced by cubism and experimental film, as well as the unprecedented explosion of circulating visibilities, which are actually rendering the outcome of these alterations opaque.[14] For instance, the exhaustive visualization and documentation of wildlife is effectively concealing its ongoing extinction. In addition to acting as shields against reality, images have also become its mode of certification. In discussing the democratization of tourism in the 1970s, Susan Sontag described tourists' dependence on photography for making real their experiences abroad:

> Taking photographs [...] is a way of certifying experience, [but] also a way of refusing it – by limiting experience to a search for the photogenic, by converting experience into an image, a souvenir. [...] The very activity of taking pictures is soothing, and assuages general feelings of disorientation that are likely to be exacerbated by travel.[15]

Almost forty years later, posing, taking, sharing, and looking at images are actions ("liking," "tweeting," "forwarding") that have become integral to the tourist experience, though they also *shape* contemporary experience. This can be seen in the British TV series *Black Mirror*, the darkly humorous sci-fi drama written by Charlie Brooker, which explores the implications of images as an intrinsic part not only of our empirical experience, as Sontag pointed out, but of our cognitive apparatus as well. The "black mirror" is nothing other than the LCD screen through which we give shape to reality.

One of the episodes of the series, "The Entire History of You" (2011), depicts a world in which almost everyone has a "grain" implanted behind their ear. The "grain" has the capacity to transform their eyes into cameras that record reality and into projectors that can reproduce it, amalgamating lived experience, memory, and image with cognitive experience. In another episode, "Be Right Back" (2013), the main character is able to revive her dead partner through a program that builds his posthumous avatar with the prolific information he uploaded onto the Internet when he was alive. The deathless and bodiless information, these images and signs—the inert map of a life—become embodied by an avatar that exists in actual reality, albeit with a limited capacity to interact directly with other living humans. In the episode, the fabrication of subjectivity with data—which implies its automatization—foreshadows the core of the relationship between determinist automatism and cognitive activity. According to Franco Berardi, at the core of the Google Empire is the capture of user attention in order to translate cognitive acts into automatic sequences. The consequence of this translation is the replacement of cognition with a chain of automated connections, effectively automatizing the subjectivities of users.[16]

Aside from the fact that images and data are taking the place of or giving form to experience, they are also transforming things into signs; welding together image and discourse, images have inaugurated a tautological form of vision. With the widespread use of photography and digital imaging, all signs begin to lead to other signs, prompted by the desire to see and to know, to document, and to archive information. This is related to the actual form of the contemporary political economy: communicative capitalism (semiocapitalism, cognitive capitalism) derives surplus value from the volume and velocity of signs and data circulating in the *infosphere*—a new modality of quasi-public space that encompasses interrelated and attendant platforms of communication and their devices, such as touch-screens—and assumes a form of power related to the proliferation of signs and communication through technologies of publicity. In other words, power solicits communication, but what is seen, said, or shown is irrelevant; what matters is the sheer volume of content circulating around intensive global networks of communication. In the first episode of *Black Mirror*, "The National Anthem" (2011), an alleged terrorist group kidnaps the British princess and heir to the throne. In order to free her, they demand that the Prime Minister have sex with a pig on live television at 4:00 pm that same day. As the video containing the princess's description of this heinous ransom goes viral, the whole of Britain begins to pressure the Prime Minister to fulfill the demands of the kidnapers, and he eventually gives in to public pressure and performs the act. At the end of the episode, we realize that the kidnapping was the gesture of an artist critically pointing to the role the media have in shaping public opinion. Although the princess is liberated from her captors well before the 4:00 pm deadline, the artist's gesture sheds light on the shift in power brought about by the circulation of the video in the infosphere. The episode highlights how connective interfaces actually govern through their capacity to direct behaviour in a coordinated way, as the whole country is watching television at four o'clock.[17]

In communicative capitalism, images and signs acquire value and/or power by means of being seen, through dissemination structures such as "likes," "shares," and "retweets." The fact that sign-value has replaced exchange-value means, moreover, that material things are no longer consumed directly, but operate instead as cognitive signs embedded in and around viewers. Aside from consuming "experiences" or "moods," consumers of images purchase immaterial commodities (towards lifestyle and branding) and signs for "equality," "happiness," "wellness," and "fulfillment." In the following passage from Don Delillo's novel *White Noise* (1985), Jack Gladney, the main character, describes a trip to the supermarket, noting how the signs in the brands and labels of the things he and his wife buy have the power to assuage them of the mysteries and anxieties brought about by everyday life:

> It seemed to me that Babette and I, in the mass and variety of our purchases, in the sheer plenitude those crowded bags suggested, the weight and size and number, the familiar package designs and vivid lettering, the giant sizes, the family bargain packs with Day-Glo sale stickers, in the sense of replenishment we felt, the sense of well-being, the security and contentment

these products brought to some snug home in our souls—it seemed we had achieved a fullness of being that is not known to people who need less, expect less, who plan their lives around lonely walks in the evening.[18]

The acceleration and proliferation of cognitive signs is another feature of communicative capitalism's subjugation—submitting the mind to an ever-increasing pace of perceptual stimuli, not only generating panic and anxiety, but also destroying all possible forms of autonomous subjectivation.[19] Under the regime of communicative capitalism, images transformed into signs embody the current concatenation of knowledge and machines, that is to say, the technological organization of capitalism to produce value. With the enabling of data visualization by machines, images have become scientific, managerial, and military instruments of knowledge, and thus of capital and power.[20] In this context, *seeing* means accelerating perception in the fields of everyday experience, or rather, the field of trivial visual analogies of experience: a kind of groundless, *accelerated tautological vision* derived from constant passive observation. This, for Berardi, is another of communicative capitalism's forms of governance, as this kind of vision generates techno-linguistic automatisms by carrying information without meaning, and automating thought and volition.[21]

Images circulating in the infosphere are also charged with affect, exposing the viewer to sensations that go beyond everyday perception. Hollywood cinema, for instance, delivers pure sensation and intensities that have no meaning. In Alfonso Cuarón's *Gravity* (2013), the main characters try to survive in outer space by solving practical and technical matters. The movie repudiates a point of view and a ground for vision in favour of immersion: transforming images into physical sensations mobilized by the visual and auditory (especially in its 3D version)—and thus into affect. The affective quality of images derives from the ruthless cognition of sensation and aesthetic experiences by communicative capitalism: its transformation into information, sensations, and intensities without meaning is precisely what enables them to be exploited as forms of work, and sold as new experiences and exciting lifestyle choices.[22] One of the problems that arises is that affect cannot be linked to a larger network of identity and meaning. The movie is also a symptom of the normalization of a groundless seeing brought about by modernity's de-centring of the subject, which parallels our increasing exposure to aerial images (for example, through Google Earth). The hegemonic sight convention of visuality is an empowered but unstable, free-falling, and floating bird's-eye view that mirrors the present moment's ubiquitous condition of groundlessness. According to many contemporary thinkers, such as Hito Steyerl and Claire Colebrook, this groundlessness characterizes the Anthropocene, as we lack any ground on which to found politics, social lives, or a meaningful relationship to the environment. As Colebrook has suggested, with the Anthropocene we are facing human extinction: we are the cause of numerous extinctions as we also extinguish that which makes us, and supports us, as human. We are thus all thrown into a situation of urgent interconnectedness in which a complex multiplicity of diverging forces and timelines that exceed any manageable point of view converge.[23] In this context, criticality is troubled as it spins on its head. The questions that arise from such a scene include: How can we redefine the ground of deterritorialized subjectivation beyond the subsumption of subjectivity to the modes of governance of accelerated tautological forms of vision and communicative capitalism? And how can we transform our relationship to the indeterminant and deterritorialized multiplicity of diverging points of view to provide a heightened sense of place and thus allow for the possibility of collective autonomous subjectivation, and a new sense of politics, and of the image?

In an era of ubiquitous, synthetic digital images dissociated from human vision and directly tied to power and capital, when images and aesthetic experience have been turned into cognition and thus into empty sensations or tautological truths about reality, the image of the Anthropocene is still to come. The Anthropocene is the "Age of Man" that announces its own extinction. In other words, the Anthropocene thesis posits the human as the end of its own destiny. Therefore, while the Anthropocene narrative keeps the human as its centre, it simultaneously marks the death of posthumanism and anti-humanism, because there can be no redeeming critical anti-humanist or posthuman figure in which either metaphysics or technological and scientific advances would find a way to reconcile human life with ecology. In short, *images* of the Anthropocene are missing; thus, it is first necessary to transcend our incapacity to imagine an alternative or something better by drawing a distinction between images and imagery, or pictures. Although it is relayed by the optic nerve, the picture does not make an image.[24] In order to make images, it is necessary to make vision assassinate perception; to ground vision, and then to perform (as in artistic activity) and think vision as a critical activity.[25] Following Jean-Luc Godard, whose work operates between the registers of the real, the imaginary, and art, only cinema is capable of delivering images as opposed to imagery, conveying not a subject but the supposition of the subject and thus substance.[26] Alterity is absolutely necessary for the image, as the image is an *intensification of presence;* this is why it is able to hold out against all experiences of vision.[27]

In this light, Godard's cinematic project can be interpreted as a conception of the image as a promise of flesh. For Godard, the image is incertitude; it is "trying to see" and give "voices back to their bodies." For the filmmaker, images do not show; rather, they are a matter of belief and a *desire to see* (which is different from the desire to know or possess). *The Old Place* (2000), an essay-film Godard made with Anne-Marie Miéville and commissioned by the MoMA, addresses Anthropocenic concerns of life after the extinction of man. While we see images from outer space and a sci-fi spaceship, in the voice-over Miéville and Godard discuss "CLIO," the archaeological bird of the future, a microsatellite shaped like a bird sent to space in 2001. The satellite is supposed to come back to earth in 5,000 years to inform its future inhabitants about the Earth's past. In addition to carrying traditional subjects such as geography, philosophy, and history, among others, the bird will also deliver messages written by the residents of the Earth addressed to its future inhabitants. Miéville and Godard ponder whether humanist messages such as "Love each other,"

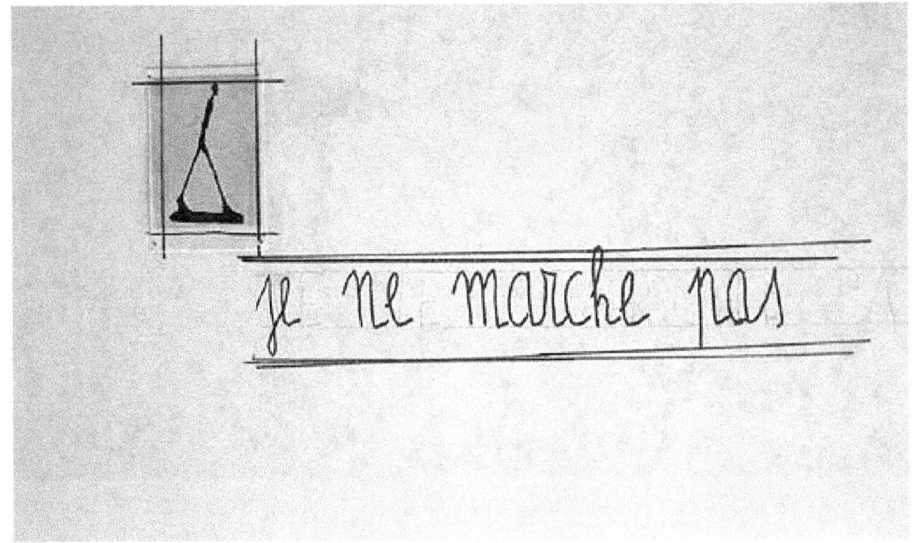

From Jean-Luc Godard's exhibition *Voyage(s) en utopie* at the Centre Georges Pompidou, Paris, 2006; courtesy of Michael Witt.

Fig. 02

or "Eliminate discrimination against women," would be included in the satellite (they doubt it). Later on, they state in the voice-over:

> We are all lost in the immensity of the universe and in the depth of our own spirit. There is no way back home, there is no home. The human species has blown up and dispersed in the stars. We can neither deal with the past nor with the present, and the future takes us more and more away from the concept of home. We are not free, as we like to think, but lost.[28]

Here Godard and Miéville describe the contours of the termination of a world, its exhaustion and estrangement from its conditions of possibility. As they underscore the lack of a home for the spirit, they highlight the loss of a sense of origin and destination, implying that the active principle of the world has ceased to function.[29] The last line of the film is spoken while we see an image of a dead bear cub being stared at by its mother, followed by an image of Alberto Giacometti's sculpture *L'homme qui marche* (*Walking Man*, 1961): life persists irrationally, not given form by imagination, ceasing to cohere into a higher truth.[30]

In *The Old Place*, Godard and Miéville explore the image of humanity throughout the Western history of art, underscoring the 2,000 or so Euro-centric Christian years of sacred images that constitute this history, and highlighting how misery, beauty, nature, the sacred, and capitalism are intrinsic to this formation of the image. We also see images of violence, torture, and death juxtaposed with beautifully sculpted and painted figures and faces, created throughout all the ages of humanity, smiling, screaming, or crying.

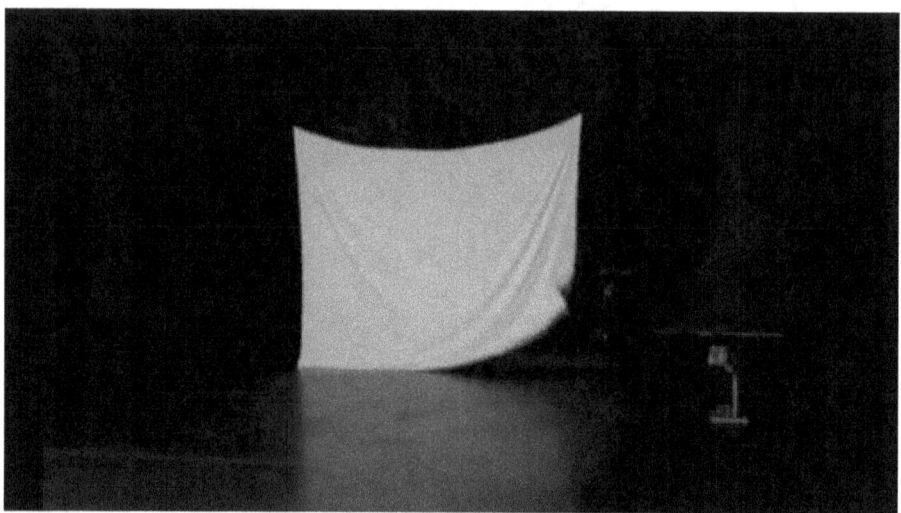

Fig. 03   Screen shot from *The Old Place*; courtesy of the author.

Furthermore, Godard and Miéville create a constellation of things and thoughts that are brought together to form images and explore what happens between them, a method of montage that delivers an image of thought. Positing the film as an exercise in artistic thought, they frame the image as art, and the work of art like a star: a unique appearance from afar, although it is also near. The image is also related to the origin that reveals itself as the new, but which has also been present all along—an originary landscape inextricable from history.

Marking the passage to the current regime of communicative capitalism, where images are permeated by discourse and tautological claims about reality, they state: "The image today is not what we see, but what the caption states." This is the definition of publicity, which they connect to the transformation of art into market and marketing, represented by both Andy Warhol and by the fact that "the last Citroën will be named Picasso," which entails that "the spaces of publicity now occupy the spaces of hope." Yet, despite the total ubiquity of communicative capitalism, for Godard and Miéville there is something that resists, and that remains, in the art of the image. While Miéville makes this claim, we see a blank canvas held by four mechanical legs that move furiously. The scene evokes an image to come, a purity of the image in a post-Christian secular sense, of the sacred and the redemptive, of an ambivalent relationship between image and text, foreign to knowledge and intrinsically tied to belief. At the end of *The Old Place*, the filmmakers posit the Malay legend of A Bao A Qu as the paradigmatic image of these times in which "we are lost without a home." As they state: "The text of A Bao A Qu is the illustration of this film," continuing:

> To see the most lovely landscape in the world, a traveler must climb the Tower of Victory in Chitor. A winding staircase gives access to the circular terrace on top, but only those who do not believe in the legend dare climb

the tower. On the stairway there has lived since the beginning of time a being sensitive to the many shades of the human soul known as A Bao A Qu. It sleeps until the approach of a traveler and some secret life within it begins to glow and its translucent body begins to stir. As the traveler climbs the stairs, the being regains consciousness and follows at the traveler's heels, becoming more intense in bluish color and coming closer to perfection. But it achieves its ultimate form only at the topmost step, and only when the traveler is one who has already attained Nirvana, whose acts cast no shadows. Otherwise, the being hesitates at the final step and suffers at its inability to achieve perfection [*"Its moan is a barely audible sound, something like the rustling of silk."*] As the traveler climbs back down, it tumbles back to the first step and collapses weary and shapeless, awaiting the approach of the next traveler. It is only possible to see it properly when it has climbed half the steps, as it takes a clear shape when its body stretches out in order to help itself climb up. Those who have seen it say that it can look with all of its body and that at the touch, it reminds one of a peach's skin. In the course of the centuries, A Bao A Qu has reached the terrace only once.[31]

In *The Old Place*, Godard and Miéville explore the imprint of the quest of what it means to be human throughout the history of images. Humanity transpires as a mark that is perpetually reinscribed in a form of address. A Bao A Qu is an inhuman thing activated by the passage of humans wishing to see the most beautiful landscape in the world; the act of vision is a unique event, and what delivers the vision of the landscape and of the creature are the purity and desire of the viewer. A Bao A Qu is an image of alterity; it stares back with all of its body. Indeed, A Bao A Qu is an antidote to the lack of imagination in our times: an inhuman image that undermines the narrative that centres the human as its ultimate form of vision and destruction.

Notes

1 Nick Srnieck and Alex Williams, "#ACCELERATE MANIFESTO for an Accelerationist Politics," 14 May 2013, www.criticallegalthinking.com/2013/05/14/accelerate-manifesto-for-an-accelerationist-politics.
2 Stan Brakhage, "From 'Metaphors on Vision,'" in *The Avant-Garde Film: A Reader of Theory and Criticism*, ed. P. Adams Sitney (New York: Anthology Film Archives, 1978), 120.
3 Georges-Didi Huberman, "Picture = Rupture: Visual Experience, Form and Symptom According to Carl Einstein," *Papers of Surrealism* 7 (2007): 5.
4 Ibid., 6.
5 The Anthology Film Archives is a film theatre in New York where during the late 1960s and early 1970s filmmakers and artists, including Michael Snow, would gather to watch films. At that time, the theatre had wing-like chairs that isolated the viewer sensorially in order to "equate" her vision to the screen and thus deliver a solipsistic experience.
6 Michael Snow, *The Michael Snow Project: The Collected Writings of Michael Snow* (Waterloo: Wilfrid Laurier University Press, 1994), 56.

7 Rosalind Krauss, *Passages in Modern Sculpture* (New York: The Viking Press, 1977), 87.

8 Snow, *The Michael Snow Project*, 44.

9 Gilles Deleuze, *The Movement-image: Cinema I*, trans. Hugh Tomlinson and Robert Galeta (Minneapolis: University of Minnesota Press, 1986), 84.

10 Ibid., 85.

11 Georges-Didi Huberman, "The Supposition of the Aura: The Now, the Then, and Modernity," in *Walter Benjamin and History*, ed. Andrew Benjamin (New York and London: Continuum, 2005), 34.

12 Melissa McMahon, "Beauty: Machinic Repetition in the Age of Art," in *A Shock to Thought: Expression After Deleuze and Guattari*, ed. Brian Massumi (London and New York: Routledge, 2002), 4.

13 Ibid., 8.

14 Rob Nixon, *Slow Violence and the Environmentalism of the Poor* (Cambridge: Harvard University Press, 2011), 12.

15 Susan Sontag, *On Photography* (New York: Farrar, Straus & Giroux, 1977), 177.

16 Franco Berardi (Bifo), "The Neuroplastic Dilemma: Consciousness and Evolution," *e-flux journal* 60, December 2014, www.e-flux.com/journal/the-neuroplastic-dilemma-consciousness-and-evolution.

17 Franco Berardi (Bifo), *The Uprising: On Poetry and Finance* (New York: Semiotext(e), 2012).

18 Don Delillo, *White Noise* (New York: Picador, 2002), 20.

19 Franco Berardi (Bifo), "Accelerationism Questioned from the Point of View of the Body," *e-flux journal* 46, June 2013, www.e-flux.com/journal/accelerationism-questioned-from-the-point-of-view-of-the-body.

20 Benjamin Bratton, "Some Trace Effects of the Post-Anthropocene: On Accelerationist Geopolitical Aesthetics," *e-flux* 46, June 2013, www.e-flux.com/journal/some-trace-effects-of-the-post-anthropocene-on-accelerationist-geopolitical-aesthetics.

21 Berardi, *The Uprising*.

22 Stephen Shaviro, "Accelerationist Aesthetics: Necessary Inefficiency in Times of Real Subsumption" *e-flux journal* 46, June 2013, www.e-flux.com/journal/accelerationist-aesthetics-necessary-inefficiency-in-times-of-real-subsumption.

23 Claire Colebrook and Cary Wolfe, "Dialogue on the Anthropocene," Haus der Kulturen der Welt Berlin, 23 January 2013, www.youtube.com/watch?v=YLTCzth8H1M.

24 Serge Daney, "Before and After the Image," *Revue des* Études *Palestiniennes* 40 (Summer 1991): www.home.earthlink.net/~steevee/Daney_before.html.

25 Didi-Huberman, "Picture = Rupture," 17.

26 Didi-Huberman, "The Supposition of the Aura," 8.

27 Daney, "Before and After the Image."

28 *The Old Place*, directed by Jean-Luc Godard and Anne-Marie Miéville (2000, Paris).

29 Dominic Fox, *Cold World: The Aesthetics of Dejection and the Politics of Militant Dysphoria* (Winchester: Zero Books, 2009), 7.

30 Fox, *Cold World*, 70.

31 The legend was recomposed by Borges from Malay sources. See Jorge Luis Borges, *The Book of Imaginary Beings,* trans. Andrew Hurley (New York: Viking, 1967), 2.

The Fates of Negativity

Anselm Franke in conversation with Etienne Turpin

Among the trajectories evident in recent exhibitions, biennales, and art fairs, one can easily discern the consistent murmur of a new thematic figure emerging from the noise. Indeed, the discourse of the Anthropocene has already framed major curatorial endeavours, including the ambitious exhibition cycle for Das Anthropozän-Projekt at the Haus der Kulturen der Welt (HKW) in Berlin. This cycle included a series of major exhibitions such as *The Whole Earth*, *After Year Zero*, *Forensis*, and *The Anthropocene Project: A Report*, as well as various episodes of the Anthropocene Observatory, and related projects, seminars, and workshops, as well as public and educational programming. The difficulty of maintaining precision in the formation of exhibitions while avoiding the closures, obstacles, and diversions of "semio-capitalist frontiers of interest" has been critical to the success of the exhibition cycle. As a curator, writer, and Head of the Department of Visual Arts and Film at the HKW, Anselm Franke's independent, institutional, and collaborative work has navigated the Anthropocene discourse and its various potential blockages to construct a series of exhibitions that challenge the universalizing tendency of planetary positions. His enduring work to avoid the exhibition becoming a mere appendix to the themes of semiocapitalism has forced him to become, in his words, "protective of the imagination of exhibitions." I interviewed Anselm during the HKW's *A Matter Theatre* conference in October 2014; what follows is an edited transcript of our conversation.

Etienne Turpin I'd like to begin with *The Whole Earth* because, as you know from our conversations during the SYNAPSE workshops, I thought it was quite an impressive intellectual manoeuver to situate the Anthropocene Project in this historical context.[1] It seems that the Anthropocene appears, in relation to the exhibition of *The Whole Earth*, as a second moment already anticipated by the universality of the "Blue Marble" image that frames the exhibition.

Anselm Franke Well, it so happened that *The Whole Earth* hit the nerve of what I didn't manage to reach with *Animism*.[2] It was just a coincidence that, after *Animism*, the Anthropocene Project came up. I'm not sure I'd have done it otherwise. Let's say that, within the Anthropocene Project, the frame was apt. I'd wanted to include something, somehow, on cybernetics and psychedelia already in *Animism*, but the matrix of the exhibition just couldn't accommodate it. There was too much of a tendency, whenever this material came up in *Animism*, toward New Age associations. I don't really know why; perhaps it was just because of the weight of these concepts. To actually come to terms with both 1990s globalism as a horizon of expectations, and then to include the 1980s New Age as well—these things were unapproachable through ideological critique within the matrix of *Animism*. There was a blockage, or, let's say a meagre approximation, because of the collapse of dialectics and the small differences that we hoped to uphold as a dramatic scenography in *The Whole Earth*. These concerns couldn't be upheld in *Animism*. Do you know what I mean?

ET Yes, and I recall that some people in attendance were critical that *The Whole Earth* was too didactic in its staging. But I was excited about this as a strategy because I understood that you were making an argument. So, bracketing the relation to the ideology of cybernetics that was held over from *Animism*, was there ever any question, within the institution, about beginning The Anthropocene Project with *The Whole Earth* exhibition?

AF I am fixed on a set of paradoxes surrounding genre; these questions are accelerated in the context of the Anthropocene. I'd started thinking about these things before we established the Anthropocene concept at the HKW as something that pertains to the institution as such. What kind of exhibitions can you actually do in a place like this, which is not automatically in the hygienic, purified regime of art? That is an important question because of the weight, power, and mysterious forms of authority that accompany the concepts in the Anthropocene discourse, or, more accurately, the fragments of discourse that compose this non-whole whole of the Anthropocene. They are capable of eradicating everything that is interesting in art. I was thinking: how can we actually relate to this thesis? How can we create a space that puts genealogies of art and their relation to larger imaginaries at risk, but simultaneously protects them, at least to a degree? Where do art and aesthetics end up? I was concerned with ontological transformations.

ET How do you prevent art from becoming a mere epiphenomenon of massive global processes comprising the Anthropocene?

AF Exactly. In a way, I've been trying to figure out this spectrum—it was more unclear to me before *The Whole Earth*—that goes from boundary practices with strong negativity toward the Anthropocene condition, where you no longer know how to circumscribe, address, or even deal with negativity, and hence with processes of ontological transformation. On the latter end, it leads to a tendency to re-inscribe things in strange new forms of positivity, but I don't have a really a good term for this process yet. I tend to call it "clinical positivism." It shifts the way that Deleuze and Guattari use the term "clinical," which still comes from a transformative investment in psychoanalysis and its offshoots. I think of the clinical more as an emergency room in which life movements have to be surveyed and life systems need to be maintained in a critical condition; at the same time, this condition seems to reduce or remove spaces from criticality or critique. I thought it might be necessary, within a larger sequence, to link that strong negativity to the rise of systems thinking and new reality principles based on information, which was simultaneously the idea of a global order coinciding with the end of colonial objectivism.

ET So you are attempting to review the consequences of the subsumption of conflict and enmity, formerly the basis of historical transformation, under clinical positivism?

AF The goal is always to be able to speak of things as symptoms, at least in the regime of aesthetics, because otherwise aesthetics become—even if you may claim otherwise—an appendix of these new forms of positivist knowledge. The sequence that interests us most, both Diedrich Diederichsen and myself, was very much the movement from accepting the unity of humankind in terms of a single nation or voice, etc., and then, in the 1970s, the move toward the majority of minorities. This constructivist imaginary was like a late echo of the modernist dream of social engineering and mastering the process of subjectification. Then, in the 1990s, we find this globalist imaginary and clinical notion of dialogue. What is this engagement, really? It is an order: you will participate.

ET You brought back some residual antagonism in *The Whole Earth*, not least by way of the punk culture of the 1970s, the Dead Kennedys, *California Uber Alles*, etc. How do these cultural skirmishes fit into the bigger picture of clinical positivism?

AF Diedrich would have his own vocabulary that would be very different from my stuttering or wayward terms here, but I guess we could agree that the narrative challenge is to find ways to reconstruct historical processes from the perspectives of the various fates of negation, or of different modalities of negation, and then consider the political spaces and forms of organization to which they were attached. 1968 was naturally a point of reference because it was the last moment of discernible momentum where there was a very modernist belief in ontological alterity and the ability to engineer (or return to, as some would have it) other ontologies. The negativity that was traced from that starting point—I think I said this back then—can be organized around various shifts or inversions, and so on.

The joy that I've had as a curator working with images—and this just as a working hypothesis, not unlike that of Aby Warburg—is the intimacy that these political histories have with inversions, intensities, the coining of margins, and also the genealogy of psychic intensities toward this equation of globalism and depression as a loss of psychic intensity, as a kind of deflation of ontological mobilities. This was the kind of discussion that Diedrich and I had before we got into *The Whole Earth* project, but they also relate to *Animism*. The animist desire of capitalism—its image products—ought to be diagnosed in relation to the clinical condition of depression. It is definitely not a new thing, but it has shifted to the foreground; capitalism compensates for the lack of psychic energies of transformation and the loss of the temporalities of psychic life. When you read through clinical studies of depression, they are full of interesting attempts to define it. It is very difficult to define depression; the more interesting descriptions deal with "illnesses of time," the loss of psychic temporality, the nervous shift between omnipotence and impotence that is already characteristic of paranoia and these more dramatic, established symptomatic psychic illnesses. The image of the washing machine globe of the 1990s, an oceanic washing machine, and the condition of hyper-visibility, which affects our discourses enormously, becomes our milieu. We do not really know how to *exit*, other than by calling upon older moments, from our phantom limb pain, when there was still some form of awe or some outside.

ET So how do you diagnose the phantom limb of negativity?

AF This was the challenge: how can you actually deal with these big questions in a non-depressive, but also non-affirmative way, at the same time? It's great to deal with pop culture; it's almost the only way of maintaining this balancing act. There is a very interesting *in-between-ness* of pop music, between consequentiality and inconsequentiality, if one can say that. The modern regime of the art exhibition is very closely tied to a specific bracketing off of consequentiality, which allows all kinds of other forms of literacy to emerge; but it also permits this shameful acceptance of the inferiority of art, which the avant-garde has always railed against. In an interesting way, pop culture sets up the subject, or the design of the subject, in a field permanently oscillating between consequentiality and inconsequentiality, where liberating oneself from certain vectors of subjectification becomes entangled in interesting dialectics: the gesture of posing, or suggesting how a certain attitude produces something. I always found the whole realm of where attitude becomes form much more interesting in music culture.

ET But at the opening of the Olympic Games in London we heard them play the Sex Pistols.[3] From the point of view of full subsumption, the fates of negativity can be quite depressing. In this depression, I'm unsure whether to find fault with the consequential or inconsequential.

AF To have regimes of inconsequentiality has great benefits. But the political question is always: where do you demand consequentiality? Quite honestly, this is the only line of argument anyone could have made against bourgeois culture. What is its version of consequentiality?

ET Does this relate to the idea for geographies of collaboration?[4] What is the political inheritance operative in *After Year Zero*?

AF It probably comes down to this question of what gets discussed in ontological theory, perhaps not always very satisfactorily. It's definitely inspiring to think through the questions that this discourse raises for aesthetics and the scaling of its consequentialities and institutional design. When you read something like, say, a collection of essays by Hal Foster—*The Anti-Aesthetic* was published in the mid-1990s—you realize that it is probably the last interesting moment around the *October* group.

ET   The final farewell to a militant posture?

AF   Militant, maybe, but it had a diagnostic sharpness as well. They managed to address the vacuum of identity politics and its failure to address *a priori* choices in ontological design. One of the great articles is Craig Owens's text on feminism.[5] That was really the apex; nothing that came after that was serious. Of course, there are the other threats discussed in *October*, of which *Animism* is one. I never had the patience to really work that out because it would be extremely laborious to do so. But, we could say that the whole Marxist psychoanalytic trajectory of *October* hits a dead end, as it does in Foster's writings in the mid-1990s. He would again and again arrive at animism, where the subject is pretty much just stabbed to death. That's it. Finished. End of analysis! It is very interesting that exactly where his thinking approaches the danger of ontological anarchy, and the sorts of questions raised by this anarchy, he recoils.

ET   Perhaps this is a point of exhaustion that was also confronted by Gilles Deleuze, albeit from a more properly philosophical angle. With the completion of *Difference and Repetition*, Deleuze had undermined the image of thought that propped up Western metaphysics and European philosophy since Plato.[6] It was the end of analysis, so to speak, and Deleuze was depressed. As you know, that's when Félix Guattari shows up, and they begin to create philosophy through a new mode of construction. I wonder if there is something similar in these two moments, between Deleuze and Foster, in that when thought can push itself no further, it still tends to shy away from clichés. Faced with the choice between precision or cliché, Deleuze had to reinvent philosophy with Guattari; in contrast, it seems Foster could not find a way to take perspectivism or animism seriously.

AF   This whole set of concerns is like a permanent construction site for me. What does each of these strange moments of recognition produce, which are built into the various anti-Cartesian genealogies—what are they and what do they produce? What do they do? It's still an open question for me. In this vein, I am doing a more or less "fun" project, one that should have been part of the Anthropocene Project, on "ape culture." In no way is it controversy mapping; there is the objectivist tradition, the Great Ape Project, the same kind of grand lines that intersect interestingly with the cultural industry of the animal metaphor, Donna Haraway's *Primal Visions*, and so on.[7] But there is a very strange sense that the kinds of recognition that are meant here—both as theoretical or epistemological insights, and as political recognition in the other sense of recognition with actors, agents, and subjects, etc.—intersect. This is exactly where the question of consequentiality is important to us.

So, yes, there may be trials that consider whether or not great apes should have subject status (which I do take seriously to some extent as a question), but I'm also trying to keep a critical distance from any of these lines of inquiry because what constitutes the "now of recognizability" is quite mixed up with regimes of inconsequentiality. That is, the "now of recognizability" in the Benjaminian sense of historical collapse, of always looking at the historical efficacy of positions, at what constitutes an out-lift position, and then how this is reflected in the elusive categories of dialectic images, and so on.[8] The "now of recognizability" in this grand anti-Cartesian consensus is very caught up with the regimes of inconsequentiality in the Straubian sense of "too early is too late."[9] I am just trying to keep these questions of consequence and consequentiality alive, not to close them, not to pacify them, because they are very relevant. When primatologists tell you that for decades now we have been realizing, step by step, that there are *cultural* properties in ape populations, they will say, in the same breath, "but it's too late." This is what I think is really important to listen to and to understand when considering the characterization of the "now of recognizability." To be attuned to its possibilities and negativities, to this *too-late-ness*, is very practical; of course, they know as scientists and activists that the ape habitats will be destroyed. Barring some revolution or catastrophe that they cannot even believe in, and given the expert calculations, it's impossible to save the apes' forests. So they operate in this strange double register of knowledge; it brings to mind this old anthropologist figure, who feverishly records as much as he can before it all goes away, as it is going away.

ET The great archival impulse! And, what an archive the Anthropocene deserves; already we are obsessed to collect every detail of our global exterminations. The terrifying effort of acquiring knowledge about the planetary human exterminations now extends to every facet of the sensorium. Surely, these collections will be part of a curatorial trope that gets played out again and again. But, I think you would agree, there's a fundamental difference between the vague imperatives mobilized around ecological collapse and the production of aesthetic evidentiaries as in, say, the *Forensis* project by Eyal Weizman.[10]

AF It is, of course, very connected to the different forms for mobilizing resources. In the case of *The Whole Earth* and *Forensis*, this mobilization was totally different, and not just of physical, but also mental resources, and literacies of different kinds. For me, it is always important to think between these registers: on the one hand, ideological critique or the semiotic turn, and then, on the other hand, with Eyal, as a kind of frontier studies, I would say.

ET Frontier studies? I would characterize Eyal Weizman's thinking as more of a kind of species antenna. In *Forensis*, I thought he was developing a new materialism that examined the world as a stratigraphic series, as infinite surfaces for the registration of violence. If I understand the work of the *Forensis* project—this is just my reading of it, of course—it's an attempt to move the sensorium from its place within the limited bourgeois franchise of aesthetics into a different, public register of sensing practices related to the politics and law of violence, accountability, etc.

AF Yes, but I'm trying to be very differentiated about all of this. I was trying to keep different spheres or genres of consequentiality apart. That's a general problem that I'm thinking about right now—how to keep the kind of ontological designations, or the footnote systems for these ontological designations, productively stable and differentiated. Only then, I think, should you risk their stability in such a way that the outcome is not necessarily their negation, or even transformation, but an increase of literacy. I was always saying that the *Forensis* project was wilfully oblivious of anything that had to do with art so that it could think about consequentiality in different ways. But that means that you don't ever think about tracing the fates of negativity in imagery, or even psychic realities, as evidenced in the *Forensis* forum. Sorry, but there just isn't a forum for that! But you might also call it a different genealogy of exhibitions, one that has always also existed in the history of exhibitions: the architecture exhibition is all about scaling, modeling, figuring out fields of action; there is a different ontological status of the image within that genealogy. But I don't think that message came across very well because *Forensis* scared away a lot of "art-minded" people who were asking: where is the art? Why is there no art in their art gallery?

Ten years ago, when I did the first exhibition with Eyal, there were different subtitles for different locations.[11] This was meant as a productive provocation, and it was received as such, but the *consequentiality* was not invoked as directly as I would have liked. There were clear legal implications: Eyal was saying that he was making maps because he wanted to sue architects for breaching international law. The idea and intent was there, but at the same time this project was bridging all sorts of questions of ontological statecraft and modernity and art, from the formative years of the state of Israel, to the geopolitical, colonial, and biblical imaginaries and what these may or may not have to do with Pier Paolo Pasolini. These things were still speaking to each other in *Territories*. With *Forensis*, I started to have a different feeling; I felt that I hadn't solved the problem of what speaks to what in terms of consequentiality and inconsequentiality within various image genealogies. I didn't make the registers clear or position that project in such a way that the issue of register was front and centre. So this has now become a key construction site for me—how to deal with the interrelation of registers.

In *Animism*, it was easy because you always had the refuge of coming back to the simple moment, the degree-zero moment, of modernist aesthetics in animation. It was like going back to the social drawing board; with ontological anarchy, you can do anything. You could always have a clear relation between aesthetics and its ontological boundaries. We could say that *Animism* was comfortable in its dialectics. *Forensis* left this comfort zone behind. The kind of conflict that I would have with Eyal and Tom Keenan over the years stemmed from my view that the claim toward a "forensic aesthetics" was insufficiently diagnosed, or established too early as a paradigm. I think that *The Whole Earth* analysis could only begin with the symptoms; this means admitting histories of defeat, including those of forensic aesthetics. So, this was our little quarrel. Eyal tends to just see the potential in forensics, which is great, because he motivates people. But it is not entirely realistic because the dialectics are extremely asymmetrical between technological appropriations and state powers.

ET He made precisely this point during our workshop at The Bartlett last week with some of the people from Forensic Architecture.[12] Addressing this problem of extreme asymmetry, he said that it's not an accident that the drone missiles are smaller than a single pixel in the satellite imagery that civilians can access. I understand his example as a provocation: of course, the tools of forensic architecture, or forensics, are intentionally limited, but that is the parameter for the research. How to get around the limit of the pixel size, for example, is an important problem for researching spatial politics.

But, I am interested in your remark that the forensic aesthetic paradigm comes too early. How can we characterize our horizon of intelligibility? In my recent conversation with Peter Galison, he suggests that "probable cause" is a critical threshold in this regard. In his forthcoming book *Building Crashing Thinking*, he is addressing the construction of the self through technological systems; I believe he is trying to develop a philosophical approach to technology outside or beyond Heidegger's dismissal of technology as a foreclosure of dwelling.[13]

AF Do you think he'll answer the question? It is a very important project.

ET It's a really critical question, especially when we are trying to develop practices in the Anthropocene. If we think of the missing MH370 flight, it becomes clear that the psychotechnical aspect of the search is as important as the establishment of probable cause; or, maybe more correctly—but here I'm digressing from Peter's own comments—probable cause has a fundamental role to play in the psychotechnical imaginary for beings living among large technical systems of overlapping infrastructure and information communication technologies. We saw that money was no concern if it meant that experts could locate the missing Malaysian flight; this is sold as a humanitarian concern, but one that is never extended to melting icebergs or collapsing ecosystems. The missing MH370 seems to manifest a more fundamental epistemological problem, which Lindsay Bremner discusses in remarkable detail.[14] Through its absence, the plane undermines the aesthetic of a controlled system. This is my take, not necessarily Peter's or Lindsay's, but we have to wonder about the mental collateral damage—here I mean the psychotechnical vulnerability—of not being able to provide a probable cause for a missing airplane that is so closely and carefully monitored and tracked.

AF [*Laughs*] Do you remember the George Clooney movie *Gravity*? The terminology I would use to construct the matrix of co-exhibitions is *groundlessness*;

that we ideally create, in exhibitions of art, a controlled crisis in order to understand *a priori* choices of ontology and how they are linked to subject formation, materiality, apparati, etc. There is an essay by Heidegger, "Cause and Ground"—cause and ground have the same word in German, *Grund*—but I like to think in terms of figure and ground.[15] You are in this Clooney movie as the hovering figure; the dream of the BBC or CNN post-Cold War globalism becomes a phantasm of visibility in which the GPS is a clinical surveillance tool, a systemic border controlled dynamically through permanent feedback and constant modulation. The pacifying power of that psychotechnical vulnerability was most powerful in the heyday of the Clinton years; it crashed with the Twin Towers into something rather undefined. Of course, it still remains, over-determined perhaps, in this postmodern language of hypervisibility. This Malaysian flight is the inversion of this, in a way, its opposite. We hear the sound of *BBC World*, of the signal trying to connect, but something is broken. "Major Tom to ground control," but wait, there's no ground! There is no ground without the language of space. Anyway, they're probably never going to find the airplane, are they?

ET The plane is gone. Oceanographers have now explained that due to the complexity of the ocean currents in this zone, finding meaningful evidence seems quite improbable.[16] I don't want to be too flippant about it—and I actually feel quite strange about this impulse—but I had an odd, momentary sense of relief while watching some of the coverage about the search for MH370. I thought, just for a moment, well, at least we can still lose an airplane; this is some fuzzy, psychotechnical interference, even for just a minute or two.

AF I agree, the disappearance of the outside means precisely this: there are no gaps in the map. But there are still gaps in the map, although a certain universal border condition has now spatialized and become infrastructure. So, I also share this thought, but I also try to repress it! [*Laughter*] I really don't want to become another crazy person praying to lost negativity. But, really, this is no anti-image of hope.

ET No, certainly not; but it's also not a dialectical image. It is more like a glitch at the scale of a large technical system. Maybe we could call it a superglitch. But, if we can't find the plane, at least the experts must figure out why they can't find it! This is the epistemological-aesthetic imperative of the superglitch.

AF Yes, precisely—a superglitch! But, one can also not deny—not that I'm supportive of or in any way romantically invested in its alternatives—that this is a very Anglo-American obsession, this idea of the probable cause. This is not necessarily shared with other cultures. Anyway, this last year has made a pretty good argument, as a series of events, that this psychotechnical apparatus of control is very fragile, but also somehow incredibly detached from the actual resources of psychosocial engineering. But, especially when reading Chinese newspapers, it's the relationship between the current technosocial apparati and the new imperialisms that troubles me the most at the moment.

ET What about the role of institutions? How does the Anthropocene thesis affect the institution? How has it moved through this one [the HKW] as it is being studied, especially though the *Anthropocene Observatory* and the exhibition cycle?[17]

AF I have a positive overall impression of the institution's ability to cope with insecurities on all levels. It is increasing, and I think that's great. But I answered your question about *Forensis* with some hesitancy because I'm always a bit worried about the acceleration of discourse formations in the sense that things tend to return very quickly as reified versions of themselves.

ET First as tragedy, then as farce? The problem for us, as curators now, is that the joke is collateral of the tragedy. There's barely a discernable pause between tragedy and farce in the world of exhibitions.

AF Yes, and in the aesthetic field this has specific consequences and yields particular effects that aren't exactly supporting any increase in literacy. The quick return of things as *genre*—I'm slightly paranoid and protective of the imagination of exhibitions in relation to this pattern. The infrastructure of genre ideas and how they articulate themselves makes me uncomfortable because I think that exhibitions are rarely capable of actually somehow acting upon these genres. This is also connected to an urgent need I have to tie things back into institutional and art historical genealogies. You cannot allow them to part ways just because you're a victim of discursive fashions! Not that I want to denounce things just because they're fashions; but I want to stay skeptical of the workings of what we might call *semio-capitalist frontiers of interest*. If you allow a hermetic medium, such as the exhibition, to become a mere appendix to that apparatus, the nervous system of this accelerated frontier of interest just kills the "fragile garden of semiotic difference." That is a joke, sure, but it is also really dangerous. So, that's why I'm always thinking of how to fortify the realm of the exhibition and, at the same time, sharpen the weapons.

Notes

1. The Anthropocene Project [Das Anthropozän-Projekt] was a two-year endeavour undertaken by the Haus der Kulturen der Welt in Berlin, which included a series of cultural events and conferences, various workshops, a large multidisciplinary curriculum project, a gathering of the HKW's SYNAPSE International Curators' Network, a group of publications including *Grain Vapor Ray: Textures of the Anthropocene* and the *intercalations: paginated exhibition* series, and a sequence of exhibitions, including multiple iterations of the Anthropocene Observatory, by Anselm Franke, Armin Linke and Territorial Agency; as well as *The Whole Earth: California and the Disappearance of the Outside* (26 April–7 July 2013), curated by Diedrich Diederichsen and Anselm Franke.
2. Anselm Franke, ed., *Animism: Volume 1* (Berlin: Sternberg Press, 2010).
3. Although the band declined to play live during the Closing Ceremony of the London 2012 Olympics, the infamous, anti-monarchist punk classic "God Save the Queen," originally released as the second single on the album *Never Mind the Bollocks, Here's the Sex Pistols* in 1971, was sampled during Danny Boyle's British musical history compilation during the Opening Ceremony.
4. The exhibition *After Year Zero: Geographies of Collaboration since 1945* (19 September–24 November 2013), curated by Anselm Franke, was the second exhibition within the framework of The Anthropocene Project at the HKW.
5. Hal Foster, ed., *The Anti-Aesthetic: Essays on Postmodern Culture* (Port Townsend, WA: Bay Press, 1983); see especially Craig Owens, "The Discourse of Others: Feminists and Postmodernism," 57–82.
6. Gilles Deleuze, *Difference and Repetition*, trans. Paul Patton (New York: Columbia University Press, 1994).
7. Donna Haraway, *Primate Visions: Gender, Race, and Nature in the World of Modern Science* (New York and London: Routledge, 1990).
8. On Walter Benjamin's dialectic image, see AK Thompson, "Matter's Most Modern Configurations: Rivera, Picasso, and Benjamin's Dialectical Image," *Scapegoat: Architecture/Landscape/Political Economy* 02—Materialism (Winter 2011): 2–5.
9. "Jean-Marie Straub (born 8 January 1933 in Metz, France) and Danièle Huillet (1 May 1936 in Paris – 9 October 2006 in Cholet) were a duo of filmmakers who made two dozen films between 1963 and 2006. Their films are noted for their rigorous, intellectually stimulating style. Though both were French, they worked mostly in Germany and Italy." Source: en.wikipedia.org/wiki/Straub-Huillet.
10. See Eyal Weizman, S. Schuppli, S. Sheikh, F. Sebregondi, T. Keenan, A. Franke, eds., *Forensis: The Architecture of Public Truth* (Berlin: Forensic Architecture and Sternberg Press, 2014).
11. *Territories*, curated by Anselm Franke, Eyal Weizman, Rafi Segal and Stefano Boeri, KW – Institute for Contemporary Art, Berlin, Germany, 2–7 September 2003.
12. The workshop "Contested Territories: Design and Spatial Politics" was hosted by Adrian Lahoud and Godofredo Periera at The Barlett in October 2014.
13. See the conversation with Peter Galison in this volume.
14. For a comprehensive reading of the search for MH370, see Lindsay Bremner in this volume.
15. Martin Heidegger, "On the Essence of Ground," in *Pathmarks*, ed. William McNeill (Cambridge: Cambridge University Press, 1998), 97–135.

16 Again, see Lindsay Bremner in this volume.
17 *The Anthropocene Observatory* is a project by photographer and filmmaker Armin Linke, architects and urbanists John Palmesino and Ann-Sofi Rönnskog (Territorial Agency), and curator Anselm Franke; it was commissioned by Haus der Kulturen der Welt for the Anthropocene Project, www.anthropoceneobservatory.net.

Design Specs in the Anthropocene: Imagining the Force of 30,000 Years of Geologic Change

Jamie Kruse & Elizabeth Ellsworth (smudge studio)

> Under the cloak of an intellectual aim, the materials have been completely murdered and can no longer speak to us. If one leaves the material as it is, presenting it just as material, then it starts to tell us something and speaks with a mighty voice.
>
> —Jiro Yoshihara, "Gutai Manifesto" (1956)

Now and then, the pace of geological change quickens, allowing human and geological time to intersect through events such as floods, landslides, sinkholes, and earthquakes. At these moments, the geologic erupts into human cognition and becomes palpable as a contemporary material force. In less eventful space-time, people tend to experience the geologic only peripherally, even though its force and attendant material realities are persistently and continuously shaping human experiences, dwelling habits, and productive activities. Whether or not we are attuned to this reality, the geologic delimits some of the fundamental dynamics that shape daily life.

The ability to sense and respond to the deep tellurian forces of monumental geological change inflecting daily life is a matter of urgency. "Design Specs in the Anthropocene" invites publics, designers, engineers, and architects to approach their work with a palpable sense of the power, scale, and dynamism of the geological forces that precede and exceed our human agency.

In what follows, our concern is in making the "slow," "deep" time of the Great Lakes region both visible and sense-able as our contemporary time. Through a photographic tale and speculative narration, we document a research trip to the eastern edge of the Great Lakes region; we wanted to feel for ourselves the geological forces presently shaping the contemporary Great Lakes. Our investigation was keyed to a practice that addresses designers, architects, and regional planners: the production of a series of design specifications. While in the field, we sought out sites where we could witness specific geological forces. We documented the material traces of the forces we experienced, and used this documentary material to stage an encounter between design specifications and the forces of geological change. What new ways of designing and planning in relation to the forces that compose the Great Lakes region might such an encounter elicit?

Our research took us to a peripheral space-time where the Wisconsin glaciation occurred 10,000 to 70,000 years ago, and to the ancient shores of Pleistocene Champlain Sea. The Champlain Sea (which existed between 10,000 and 13,000 years ago) is the Pleistocene predecessor of its more contemporary remnant, Lake Champlain, which lies between New York, Quebec, and Vermont. In 1998, the US Congress declared Lake Champlain to be the sixth Great Lake—a status it enjoyed for only 18 days before it was revoked.

During the late Pleistocene, the Champlain Sea existed as a vast inlet of the Atlantic Ocean, and its ancient shorelines are visible today in the surrounding hills. Fossils of sea life and skeletons of beluga whales greet visitors at museums in the area. The Great Lakes of today—Superior, Michigan, Huron, Ontario, and Erie—and Lake Champlain are deeply connected by their common origin. Each was created by the meltwaters from the Wisconsin glacier's retreat at the close of the last glacial period.

Here and now, the earth continues to rebound from the weight of the last ice age, a relay from the Pleistocene into the Anthropocene. Here and now, the remnant of a continental rift accommodates Lake Superior, which contains ten percent of the Earth's fresh water. Here and now, geological forces, many of them catalyzed by human action such as regional planning projects, assemble with planetary dynamics set into motion long ago, transforming regions such as the Great Lakes into worlds to come. The Anthropocene is a moment in the history of our species when the fabric of human life depends on extractions of rapidly depleting geological materials that took millennia to form. This is also a moment when anthropogenic activities have produced waste materials whose recognizable geological stratification will outlast the survival of the human species.

Our photographic tale attempts to evolve new capacities for imagining the material reality of the Great Lakes' geological forces. It presents these forces not as static, but instead as active, ongoing processes that directly shape daily life in the Anthropocene and beyond. Each image is annotated by a pair of terms, coupling a sensation, process, or force with a geological materiality shaping the Great Lakes region.

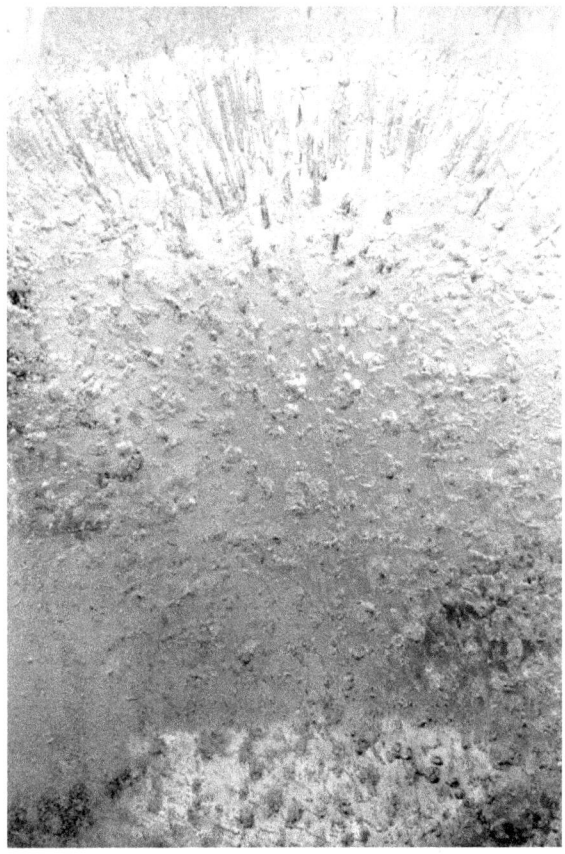

Fig. 01 MASS/ICE
Solid ice extends across the Great Lakes region

Go back 30,000 years. Immense downward pressure. During the Pleistocene, over 1.5 kilometers of ice (and at certain times and places almost 3 km), depressed what is now the Great Lakes region. During the Wisconsin glaciation, ice extended from the Pacific Ocean to the Atlantic Ocean. Pleistocene ice, a great scouring and scraping machine, was a primary shaper of today's Great Lakes.

Design Specifications: Ice-as-shaper is a geological force that underlies all design specifications that address the Great Lakes as a unified region (watershed, ecologies, natural resources).

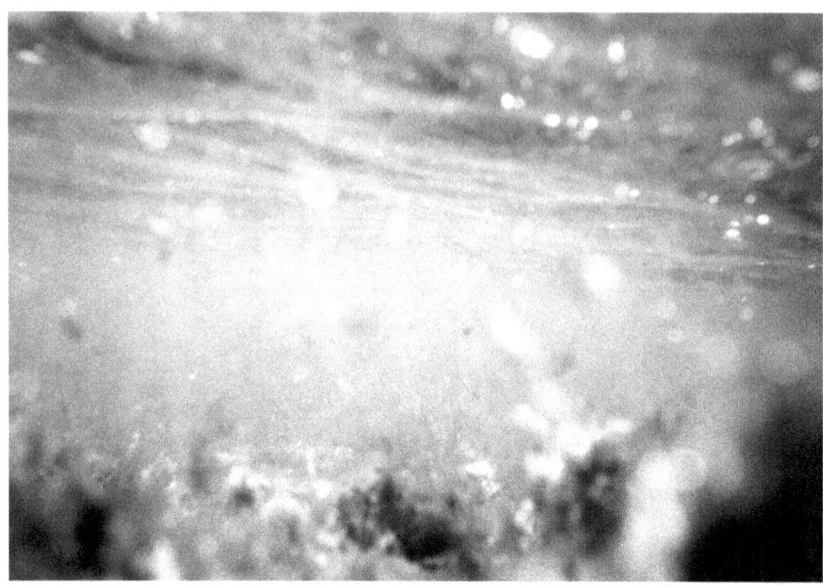

Fig. 02 EVENT/FLOOD
Under the Champlain Sea
44°28'35.63"N 73°13'17.63"W

Submerged. Catastrophic events (sudden instances of monumental change) are part of the region's geological history. Throughout the Pleistocene, glacial dams burst and dry land became inundated with water, or existing water levels in lakes dropped by hundreds of feet in days. The Great Lakes became lakes when their basins were flooded with glacial meltwater.

Design Specifications: Flooding is a geological event. It underlies all design specifications that respond to the Great Lakes as a region continuously shaped and reshaped by overflow events that submerge land: seiches, edge waves, derechos, storm surges.

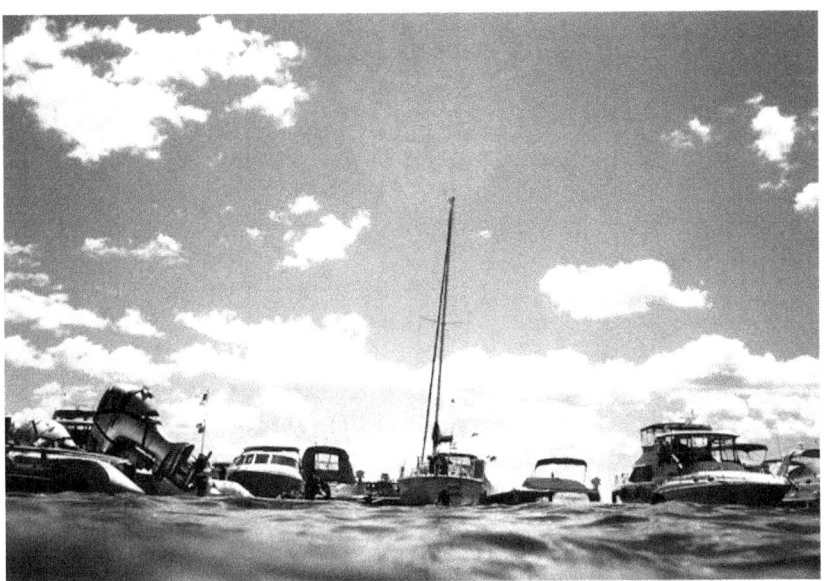

Fig. 03 IMPACT/ISOSTATIC REBOUND
Shore of Lake Champlain
44°28'35.63"N 73°13'17.63"W

As the ice of the last ice age retreated, vast expanses of land under the Champlain Sea, for millennia depressed under the weight of glaciers, began to seek equilibrium. The earth's crust rebounded, raising this inland sea's salty waters to above sea level. Isostatic rebound is the term used to describe the rise of land masses after they have been depressed by the weight of ice sheets. Over thousands of years, relentless increments amassed the power to reverse the direction in which the Sea drained—from south into the Hudson to north into the St. Lawrence River.[1] The reversal of its flow and a climate of ample rainfall transformed the Champlain Sea into a lake. The force of isostatic rebound is still in play throughout the Great Lakes region today and is expected to continue for at least the next 10,000 years.[2]

Design Specifications: Isostatic rebound is a geological force currently changing the elevations of entire regions, typically by one centimetre or less per year. The elevations for all construction sites in the Great Lakes region are rising with a force and power that in the past reversed the drainage patterns of the entire inland sea.

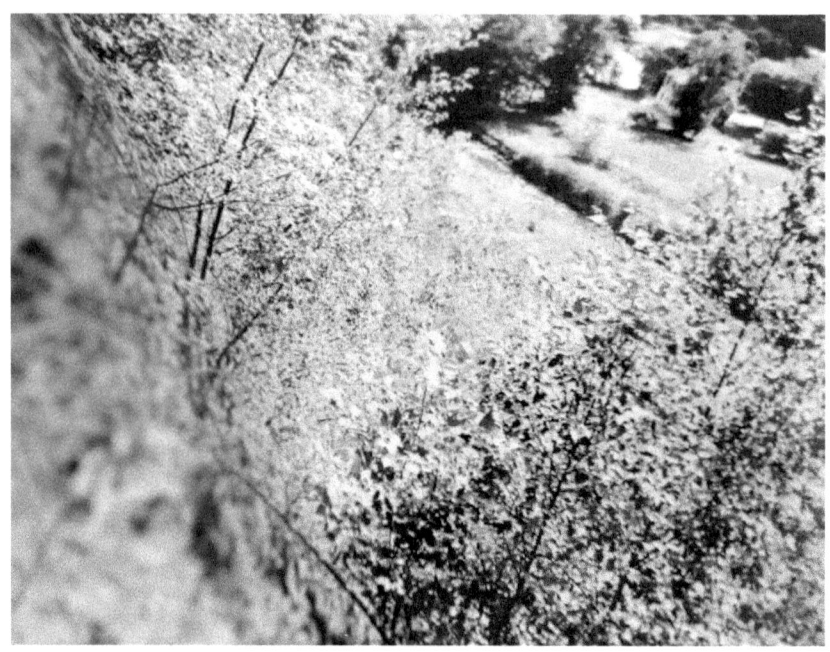

Fig. 04 DISCONTINUITY/UNSTABLE MATERIAL
Deer Run Heights, site of 1999 Jeffersonville landslide
44°38'45.54"N 72°49'27.53"W

Slippage. In its wake the Champlain Sea left Leda clay. This "quick clay" is known for its unpredictable geological make-up, including its ability to liquefy instantaneously. When it does, the human and the geologic dramatically converge in the present day basin of the ancient Champlain Sea. More than 250 Leda clay landslides are on record within sixty kilometres of Ottawa. According to a report by Natural Resources Canada, "Trigger disturbances include river erosion, increases in pore-water pressure (especially during periods of high rainfall or rapid snowmelt), earthquakes, and human activities such as excavation and construction."[3] And one professor of geology has also noted that "even a fly landing on the surface can set it off."[4] In 1999, a series of landslides occurred in Jeffersonville, Vermont, where 27,000 cubic metres of material tumbled downward.[5] Glacial sediments left by the Champlain Sea were the primary catalyst for the slide.[6] Today the site is closely monitored because it poses an ongoing risk to a nearby elementary school.

Design Specifications: Glaciation left landforms and construction sites in the Great Lakes region in a precarious state, requiring that design specifications take instability into account.

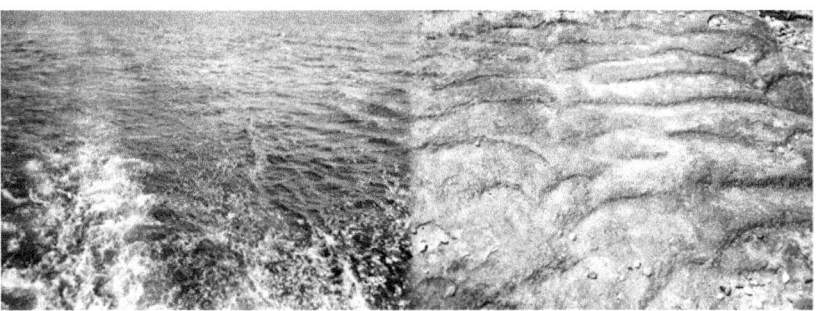

Fig. 05 FLUCTUATION/DURATION
Wake of Lake Champlain, fossilized Iapetus Ocean
(Burlington, VT)
44°27'38.51"N 73°12'18.87"W

Reach back in time 500 million years. Before the Champlain Sea and the Atlantic Ocean, there was the Iapetus Ocean.[7] It existed in the southern hemisphere. Today, incredibly, fossilized waves of this ancient ocean lap at the end of a dead end street in Burlington, Vermont. Seas, dry land, ice. All have come and gone, advanced and retreated here and throughout the region. We tend to perceive rocks and lakes as permanent givens of the landscape. But even when they endure as mountains or oceans for millennia, the force of their eventual fluctuations has material consequences. Here, waves that are 500 million years old remain fossilized in stone, the salty sea is now fresh, and water that once flowed south now flows north.

Design Specifications: Perpetual change is a sign of geological force. It underlies design specifications that anticipate and address the future (longevity of materials, trends, patterns of change).

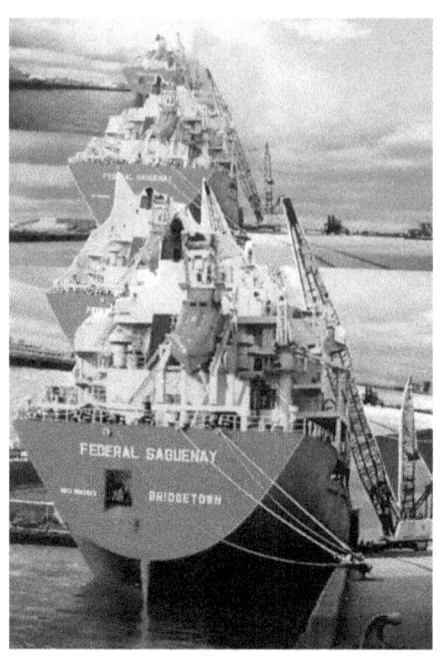

Fig. 06 FLOW/GEOMORPHOLOGY
Great Lakes Freighter, Jones Island, Port of Milwaukee
43°1'13.28"N 87°53'45.90"W

Through streams of transport the Great Lakes cross-contaminate. They channel flows of a globalized world. All six lakes empty into the Atlantic Ocean via the St. Lawrence River and Seaway. Economies, cultures, hydrologies, and biologies flow into, through, and out of these lakes, and around the globe. Materials are relocated. Locks raise and lower, interconnecting human and geological design.

Design Specifications: Geomorphology—the shapes and configurations of the land—provides the contemporary trace of geological forces that have unfolded through deep time. The geomorphology of the Great Lakes basin facilitates flow; as one of the region's most powerful forces, such flow underlies all design specifications for urban and regional planning.

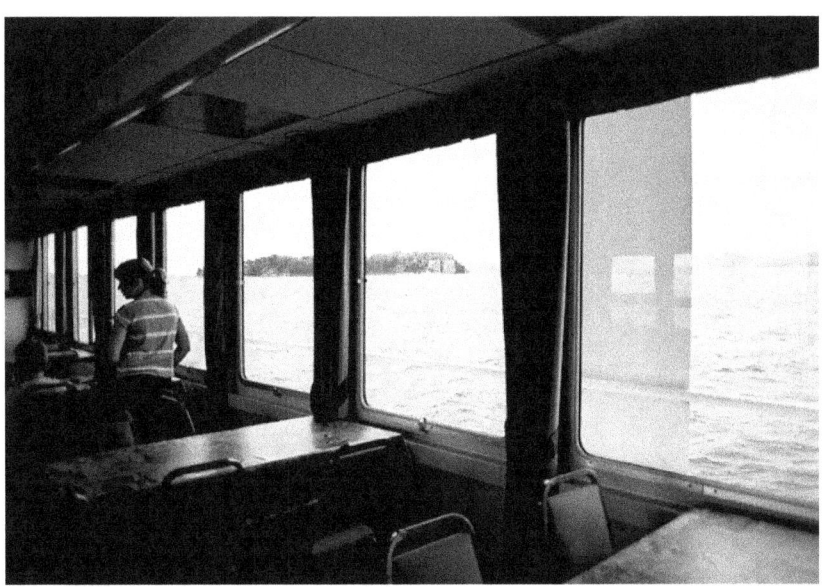

Fig. 07 LAND USE/HUMANS
Scenic boat tour, Lake Champlain
44°31'47.77"N 73°21'31.79"W

Ongoing evolution. Humans evolved during (some would even say *because of*) the Pleistocene. Today it is not only hydrology or geology that connects the lakes to one another; human activities do so as well. Human land use, recreation, development, trade, and transport introduce pollution, invasive species, and contamination, altering ecosystems throughout the region. Contemporary anthropogenic change is now comparable in scale to various geologic events of the past. This has prompted some geologists to declare that a new era has now begun, and that it should be named after the species that has become a powerful agent of contemporary geologic change. Hence, "The Anthropocene." Within the Anthropocene, humans are now required to navigate the material consequences of our land-use practices to date. These consequences act back upon us and other species, with ramifying and unpredictable consequences. [8]

Design Specifications: Human land use is a geological force that underlies design specifications for all projects sited in the Great Lakes region.

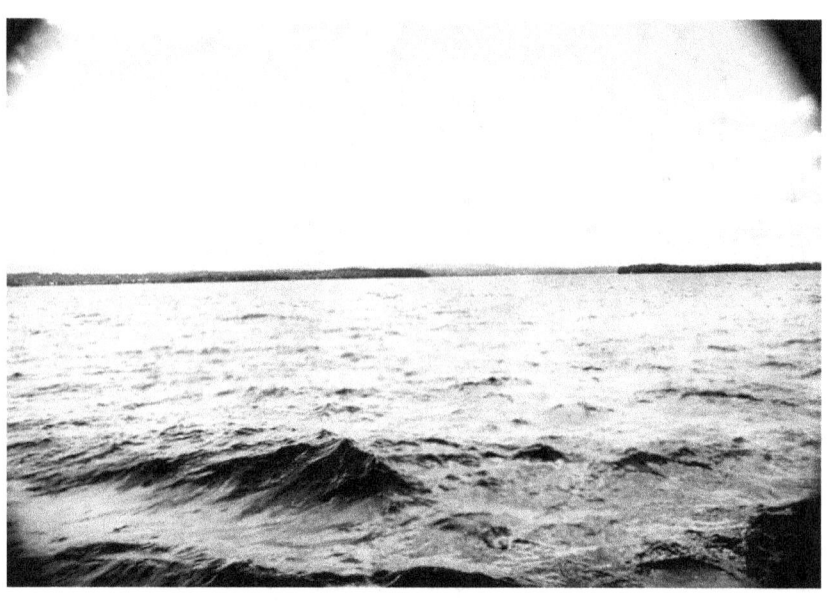

Fig. 08 ETERNAL RETURN/ADVANCE
Wave, Champlain Sea
44°26'43.58"N 73°18'6.79"W

Go back 30,000 years. The past inflects the present and the future. Many geologists agree that the Pleistocene is not over. We exist in an inter-glacial period. The eleven major glaciation events that occurred in the past 2.6 million years make up the most recent "ice age." There have been five major ice ages in the Earth's history. Waters will continue to rise and fall. Ice will continue to advance and retreat. Now, between the last and the next events of major glaciation, and in a volatile mix with planetary forces, human actions have ushered in the Anthropocene. The intersection of the human and the geologic will continue to play out into, and perhaps beyond, the next glacial advance. This return is expected 6,000 to 30,000 years from now.

Design Specifications: All design specifications that account for and respond to the ongoing forces of deep time must accommodate the geological force of the next ice age.[9]

Notes

1. "The Basin," *Lake Champlain Basin Program, Fact Sheet Series* 3, 1999, www.lcbp.org/factsht/Basinfs.pdf

2. *Apparent Vertical Movement Over the Great Lakes - Revisited,* Report prepared by The Coordinating Committee On Great Lakes Basic Hydraulic and Hydrologic Data, Geodetic Survey Division of Natural Resources Canada, November 2001, www.geod.nrcan.gc.ca/pdf/pgrreportnov2001.pdf.

3. "Geoscape Ottawa-Gatineau, Landslides," Natural Resources Canada, http://geoscape.nrcan.gc.ca/ottawa/landslides_e.php.

4. Ian Austen, "Quebec Family Dies as Home Vanishes Into Crater," 12 May 2010, *New York Times*, www.nytimes.com/2010/05/13/world/americas/13canada.html.

5. Laurence Becker, George Springston, and Leslie Kanat, *Progress Report for Geotechnical Study of the Jeffersonville Landslide, Northwestern Vermont, 2009*, 24 September 2009, www.anr.state.vt.us/dec/geo/pdfdocs/ProgressJeff.pdf.

6. *Jeffersonville Landslide, Vermont Geological Survey*, 2000, www.anr.state.vt.us/dec/geo/jeffland.htm.

7. "Nature of the Basin, Lake Champlain Basin Atlas," *Geology of the Basin*, www.lcbp.org/Atlas/HTML/nat_geology.htm.

8. The Anthropocene was coined by Paul Crutzen and Eugene Stoermer in 2000 as our most recent geologic era, marked primarily by the impact of humans upon the planet's ecological systems. See www.mpch-mainz.mpg.de/~air/anthropocene and the "New World of the Anthropocene," *Environmental Science and Technology* 44, no. 7 (2010): 2228–2231, pubs.acs.org/doi/abs/10.1021/es903118j.

9. Onkalo, in Olkiluoto, Finland, is the world's first geological repository for the storage of nuclear waste. The facility's design specifications require it to withstand the pressure and impact of returning ice and rising sea levels equal to that of the Pleistocene. See www.posiva.fi.

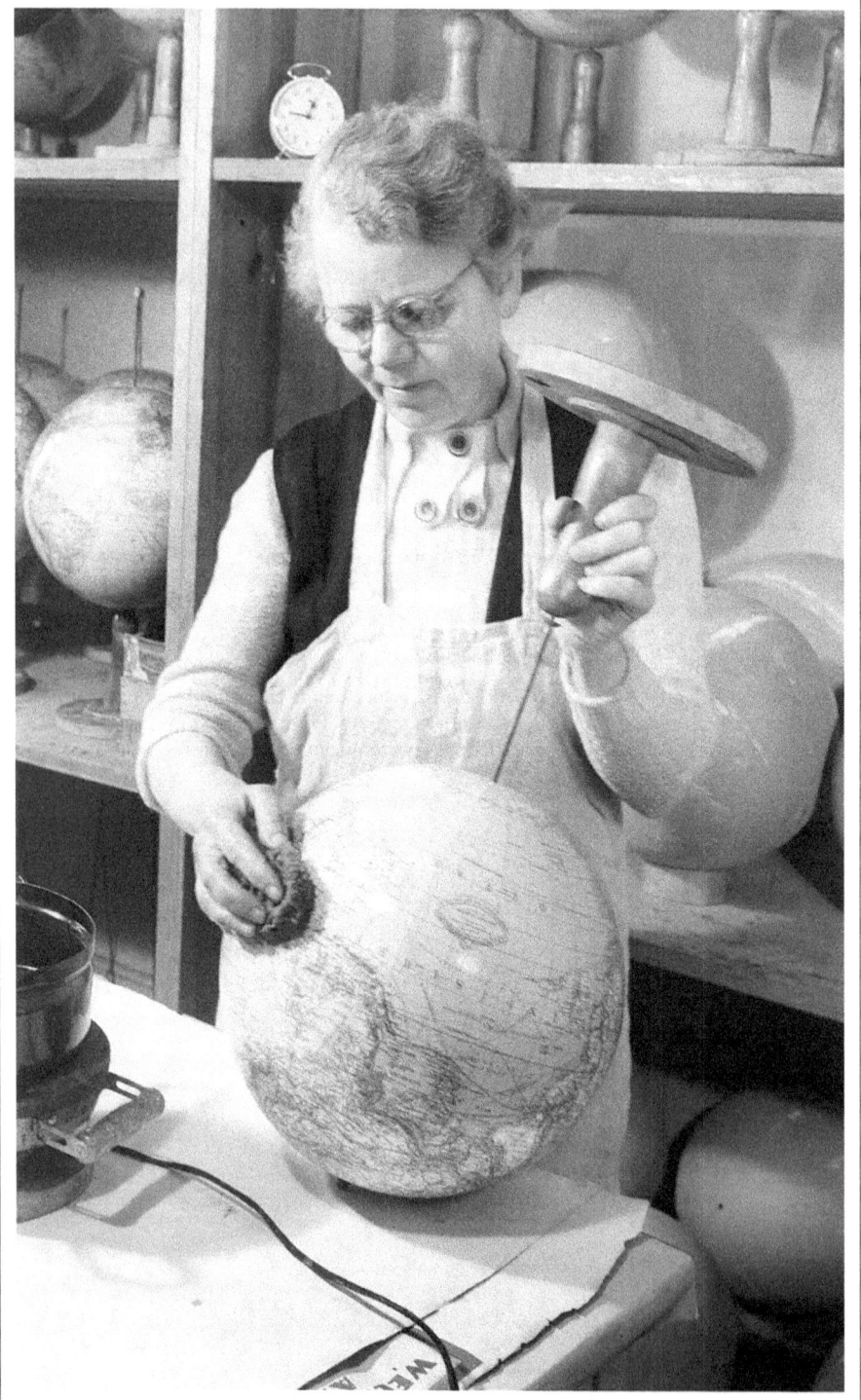

The Marfa Stratum:
Contribution to a Theory of Sites[1]

Fabien Giraud & Ida Soulard

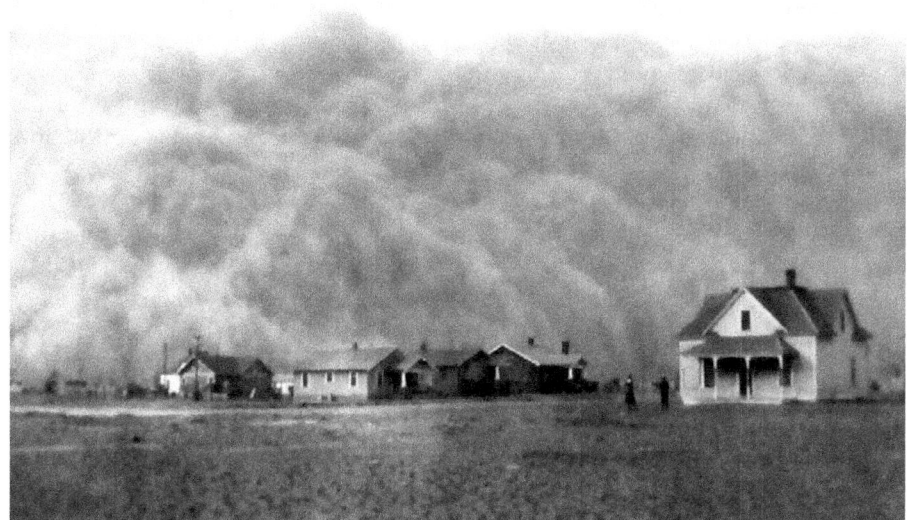

Dust storm approaching Stratford, Texas, 18 April 1935; photo courtesy of NOAA, George E. Marsh Album.   Fig. 01

REASON

In what follows, we wish to argue that one of the great benefits of the recent import of the Anthropocene concept into artistic discourses and practices pertains to the reevaluation of art's relation to rationality.[2]

Our contention here is that far from simply strengthening or rehabilitating an all too familiar romantic trope, the incursion of dwarfing geological time scales and magnitudes within our present should have the reinvigorating effect of questioning yet again art's potency for knowledge and rational explorations.

To do so first involves firmly contesting the common use of the concept of the Anthropocene as that which, by bringing into the scale of our experience the otherwise unbounded movements of Earth formation, conveniently allows the suturing of old epistemological partitions. In such a case, any clear distinction between what we can *feel* of the world's movements and what we can *know* of them—any characteristically modern divides between the sensible and the intelligible—come to be fused and erased.

It is notable that this dismissal of classical epistemological categories in favour of a flattened net of "hybrids" and "actants" is nevertheless often accompanied by a reinforcement of one of its categories, namely: art. Granting the Anthropocene with intensive power for reconfiguration, this conceptual line of flight paradoxically leaves "art" untroubled by its movements. "Art" in the Anthropocene thus remains intact as the exceptional and foreclosed pacification zone where "things are made public," where concerns are revealed, and invisibles are made visible. Against such an impoverished and paradoxically traditional conception of art's capacity, the concern here is obviously not to salvage the historically constituted partitions from which it has emerged, nor to further fuse their distinctions. Instead, what we hope to do is consider the Anthropocene not simply as a way to abolish or comfort these epistemic divisions, but as an opportunity for a revision of their constitutive dynamics.

The fact that tectonic activities have infiltrated our gestures, that wide scales and vast processes collide with the locality of our human actions, should in no way legitimate new forms of irrationalism evinced by the conception outlined above. Art need not remain the safe and reinsuring place where our limited capacity to reason within this turmoiled world is vibrantly exposed to our senses; nor does it need to be delegated as the *panic room* of a supposed unthinkable and viscous Outside. Quite on the contrary, positioning ourselves within this turbulent landscape requires a taking hold, again, of epistemological questions; surely such a grasping of the conditions of knowledge is not meant to erase or dismiss them. To address these epistemological loci implies wider theoretical movements, of which this short text can only operate as a rough and partial attempt.

First, investigating rational epistemologies calls for a revised account of what rationality is, and consequently, of the type of agency art can be said to have within it. This implies a consideration of art not as the "other" of reason, but as a set of fully efficient rational operations in their own right. Such a task begins by severing rationality from its historical instantiation and approaching reason in its most general definition as a "conceptual conduct," not inherently or necessarily bound to economical violence and colonial subjugation. In addition, it demands an embrace of a fully pragmatist perspective, where rationality is not considered as a monolithic institution of overarching judgments and divisions, but instead as an intrinsic and collective practice open to revision and continuous self-correction. In this pragmatist and mobile approach, thinking is also indistinguishable from a kind of *doing*. Reasoning, for pragmatists such as Charles Pierce, Wilfrid Sellars, or Robert Brandom, is not merely the discursive activity of a subject *about* the world, but a transformative engagement of this subject *with* the world. Far from any ruthless simplification that considers rationality as unilateral coercion, reasoning should be understood as a truly dynamic and plastic relation between what we do with concepts and what concepts do to us in return.

Secondly, this revised understanding of rationality has to be complemented with an approach to the Anthropocene as precisely that which *ungrounds* the very concept of nature. The Anthropocene can be said to have prolonged the historical transitions of modernity's approach to nature: it has concluded the progressive shift from a view of natural movements as driven by necessity and governed by static principles to the full-blown contingency of their drifting dynamics. Positing that one process among others (i.e. humans) can come to influence and determine the becoming of all processes should have strong conceptual consequences: it should open onto a groundless world without any proper identity or essence; it should beckon a conception of Earth as that which is constantly *unearthing* itself and thus produce a fully and continuously revisable concept of nature.

We think it is only on the condition of a particular re-alignment of these two revised conceptions—of a *morphing reason* and of an *ungrounded nature*—that an account of art in the Anthropocene can be meaningfully attempted. It is by engaging with the dynamic intricacy of these realms that epistemological questions can be effectively put back to work.

The way we can operate practically in between these levels can be best described in terms of a navigational process. Navigation, as we understand it here, is twofold: it is that which functions through a constant reevaluation of path and adaptation to the moving ground, while at the same time transforming the very ground on which it operates. As such, navigation is the most adequate mode of comportment with the revised notions we have just exposed. It is a type of conceptual and practical conduct which forbids any overdetermination by concepts (as in the standard conception of rationality), while avoiding any overgrounding of thought (as in an essentializing account of nature).

Navigation starts by recognizing that any concrete engagement with the world necessarily entails an engagement with the abstract. Or, to put it in our terms, that any orientation at the level of *unearthing contingencies* must be correlated to an orientation at the level of *morphing rationalities*.

In this text, we would like to take on the historical notions of *site* and *site-specificity* in art as precisely those which, in the context of the Anthropocene, permit a navigational binding of a concrete and abstract Earth. More precisely, we hope to rescue these notions from the pitfalls of postmodern and contemporary skepticism about rationality and to show how, from a pragmatist perspective, they can bring forward a definition of art as the practice of reasoning gestures.

To detach the notion of *site* from its misconstrued interpretations, we will start by presenting two different orientations in the space opened to us by the Anthropocene. We will then move to a presentation of the figure of Donald Judd and the locality of Marfa as exemplary of this revised pragmatist history and its rationalist perspectives.

ORIENTATION

The Plough That Broke the Plain[3]

The Dust Bowl of the 1930s in the Great Plains of North America is said to be the first "man-made" ecological disaster. Based on a nineteenth-century belief that "the rain follows the plough," and after a prolonged drought, many settler farmers of the Plains thought that by tilling the earth, they would eventually succeed in permanently transforming the climate of the region; they believed these rough-hewn lands could be transformed into a new agricultural Eden. However, by deeply ploughing the delicate and unstable topsoil, they accelerated large-scale processes of erosion and uprooted the native plants that fix moisture in the soil. When the drought started, it not only destroyed the harvest, but also turned the topsoil to dust.

The combination of several severe droughts and the use of inadequate and intensive agricultural techniques led to the "Black Sunday" of 14 April 1935, when a gigantic storm stirred and raised the dust on a scale previously unseen and covered the Great Plains with a thick dark haze. In some regions, the Dust Bowl lasted nearly a decade. Confronted by a radically new and unexpected situation, farmers tried to create shields against the dust and wait for the storm to pass. A survivor from the Dust Bowl described: "We live with the dust, eat it, sleep with it, watch it strip us of possessions and the hope of possessions. It is becoming Real."[4] Many of the survivors, pushed further west by misery and hunger, believed California and its mild climate was their last chance to start over.

The Cognitive Dust Bowl

The Dust Bowl of the 1930s provides us with a striking analogy for our contemporary situation. As a giant cloud of dust rising from the ground and infiltrating all dimensions of human life, the emergence of Earth formations into thought processes constitutes the irrespirable atmosphere of the Anthropocene. This is as much a material process as a mental one; the Great Plains of North America seem to fuse with our cognitive landscapes. In this "cognitive Dust Bowl," the horizon line dividing the ground from the sky is blurred as the human figure seems to slowly melt into the background. The landscape becomes a massive, opaque, and grounded sky, an all-over horizon of earth-infused thoughts or a thought-infused Earth.

Looking for an escape route from this epochal panic leads to fierce confusion: routes seem to have disappeared, observation tools are no longer efficient, and vehicles are inadequate. But the difference between the Dust Bowl of the 1930s and our present "cognitive dust bowl" is that there isn't even any "California" to flee to anymore.

What kind of orientation is required by such a situation? What kind of position should one take in order to decide on a possible path? In the wide range of contemporary discourses, it seems that two key critical orientations and positions within the storm can be traced. The first focuses on the blade of the plough and criticizes its inadequacy to the specific kind of soil it encountered. The second proposes to rebuild the blade, but at a greater scale, in order to exit the storm. As the first retroactively attempts to deconstruct the blade and invent new tools, the second commits to the blade while trying to reorient its furrows. We want to consider these two orientations as opposed strategies, and, despite the risk of caricature, as two schematic figures in the diagram of our present.

The Blade From Nowhere: Locationism

For what we will call "locationism" in this cognitive Dust Bowl another kind of plough broke the plain. It is a conceptual plough which by certain means of cutting, categorizing, and distributing our knowledge of the world provoked the conceptual and material panic we have inherited. This position envisages the causes and consequences of the Dust Bowl as already present in the birthing of modern rational tools. Such would be the position of Bruno Latour: understanding the Dust Bowl as one of those entities created by and despite the Moderns' will for purification and separation between humans and nonhumans. In this view, the blade of reason, "this eye [that] fucks the world to create technomonsters,"[5] raped the Great Plains and helped to complete a world defined by violence, expropriation, and domination. As such, this position proposes an account of reason as strongly entangled with colonialism.

For Donna Haraway, the inadequacy of the blade to its terrain is first and foremost a problem of vision and perspective. Most notably, in her critique of modern rationality, she names and attacks the "conquering view from nowhere" as an inadequate technique of vision that lead to an "unregulated gluttony."[6] The *blade from nowhere* is inadequate both because the earth is envisaged solely as a resource and because its abstract position cannot question itself: it implies neither commitment nor responsibility. For Haraway, feminism provides an inverse framework "about limited location and situated knowledge,"[7] allowing us to become "answerable for what we learn to see."[8]

In such a view, to orientate oneself within the storm requires a radical change in the tools of vision we have inherited from the Moderns. It requires that we abandon any attempt at generality or invariance in favour of an embedded practice of composition among irreducible, and thus necessarily singular, "situations." What such a view requires is a type of tool and operation capable of "re-stitching" and "reassembling"[9] what the blade of reason has violated and ploughed aside.

The Blade to Nowhere: Extensionism

According to the position we will call "extensionism," the plough should not be abandoned, but instead prolonged and repurposed. The only way out of the storm is a deepened engagement with the blade, not a retreat from its implications. The extensionist landscape is one of a planetary dust bowl where cattle and crops are slowly dying and the human species risks its own extinction by asphyxiation. This position is made popular at the beginning of the recent Hollywood film *Interstellar*: "We were born on earth but we were never meant to die here." Once the earth has become inhabitable, what is required is a dismantling of the blade and a remodelling of its metal in the form of a space rocket. To escape the dust bowl, the extensionists strive for the production of literal escape routes and the enhancement of all technologies as the only path to salvation. Contrary to its locationist counterpart, the Anthropocene works here as a trigger towards a radical autonomization from the ground.

The terraforming of other planets is an exemplary image of this extensionist strategy. It demands an overcoming of tellurian boundaries and the extension of the sphere of the human to other planets. To terraform a planet such as Mars would require warming its climate by means of polluting its atmosphere in order to melt its ice caps and develop the conditions for a suitable human habitat. What is a local problem on Earth becomes the solution on Mars. The extensionist route perpetuates a colonial movement: the infinitely ambitious replication of the same violent imperialism.

A Revised Reason

We would like to show that these common contemporary orientations are unsatisfactory to us for two main reasons: first, because their definition of what reason *is* insufficiently attends to its intrinsic revisability both as discursive and non-discursive conceptual practice, and second, because they precisely do not take fully into account what the Anthropocene as a concept *does* to reason itself.

What is at play in both cases—whether to withdraw *from* reason or to escape *by* reason—is a particular estimation of the relation between rationality and spatiality. While both trajectories recognize the transformative action of reason (the blade) on its spatial environment (the Great Plains) they seemingly endorse opposed strategies. The *locationist* can be said to be reactionary in so far as she not only reacts and questions but negates the bounded relation between rational movements and spatial production. The *extensionist* can be said to be conservative in so far as she tries not only to prolong but to preserve this very relation. As opposed as they may seem, both orientations embrace the same kind of positioning with regard to conceptual activity, and reasoning more generally. That is, they both posit a limit to what is eligible to conceptuality, or rational movements, and unfold their strategies from this very limit.

While the locationist critique of reason is performed by instantiating "locations" as bearers of some kind of non-conceptual truth, its extensionist endorsement excludes the possibility of questioning and revising the very relation of the blade to its terrain. This reason closed to any meaningful revision egregiously replicates its major blind spot. By establishing the irreducible kernel of locations or the imperialist dynamics of extensions at the heart of their respective accounts of reason, both seem to block the possibility of its reformatting.

Contrary to these positions, the type of rationality we are enquiring about here is not something one chooses to engage with or to dissociate from, but, we argue, the very process which makes us human. According to Robert Brandom, what conclusively sets us apart from other animals is our capacity not only to follow and adapt to rules, but also to transform and produce new rules.[10] Rationality is simply the name of this highly normative and properly human operation. It defines our ability to think as an embedded practice of moving through and adapting to conceptual norms—as a process of *inferring* and *navigating* through the space of reason.

For any critique or endorsement of reason to have any value, one must first account for the type of rational operativity these very gestures assume.[11] One must realize that they are in themselves specific engagements with conceptual norms, not some kind of non-conceptual exterior force or action. In other words, to be able to transform the game of reason one needs to enter the game in the first place, or to recognize that one has always been part of it. To assume otherwise is to fall victim to a kind of irrationalism and thus to abandon any attempt at transforming space or reorienting the blade.

We want to argue here that art, contrary to its historically constituted position of extraterritoriality, can claim a particular type of agency within the game of reason and its possible transformations. To reaffirm art as a conceptual practice requires that we revise the "representationalist" account of meaning in favour of an "inferentialist" one. For the pragmatists, meaning production is not solely the result of a direct relation between an idea and an object, but the product of an articulation between these relations.[12] As such, instead of the dialectical play of correspondence between subjects and objects, names and things, words and worlds, meaning is deduced through the comparison and evaluation of these assertions. This shift from meaning understood as "adequation to reference" to "production through inference" constitutes the operative ground of a truly pragmatist form of art.

If philosophy is a type of formalization making explicit what is implicit in our rational behaviours and thus allowing for their manipulations and transformations, it typically remains bounded to its discursivity as a linguistic practice. In what follows, we draft a definition of art as the proper formalization of the non-linguistic dimension of this conceptual practice.

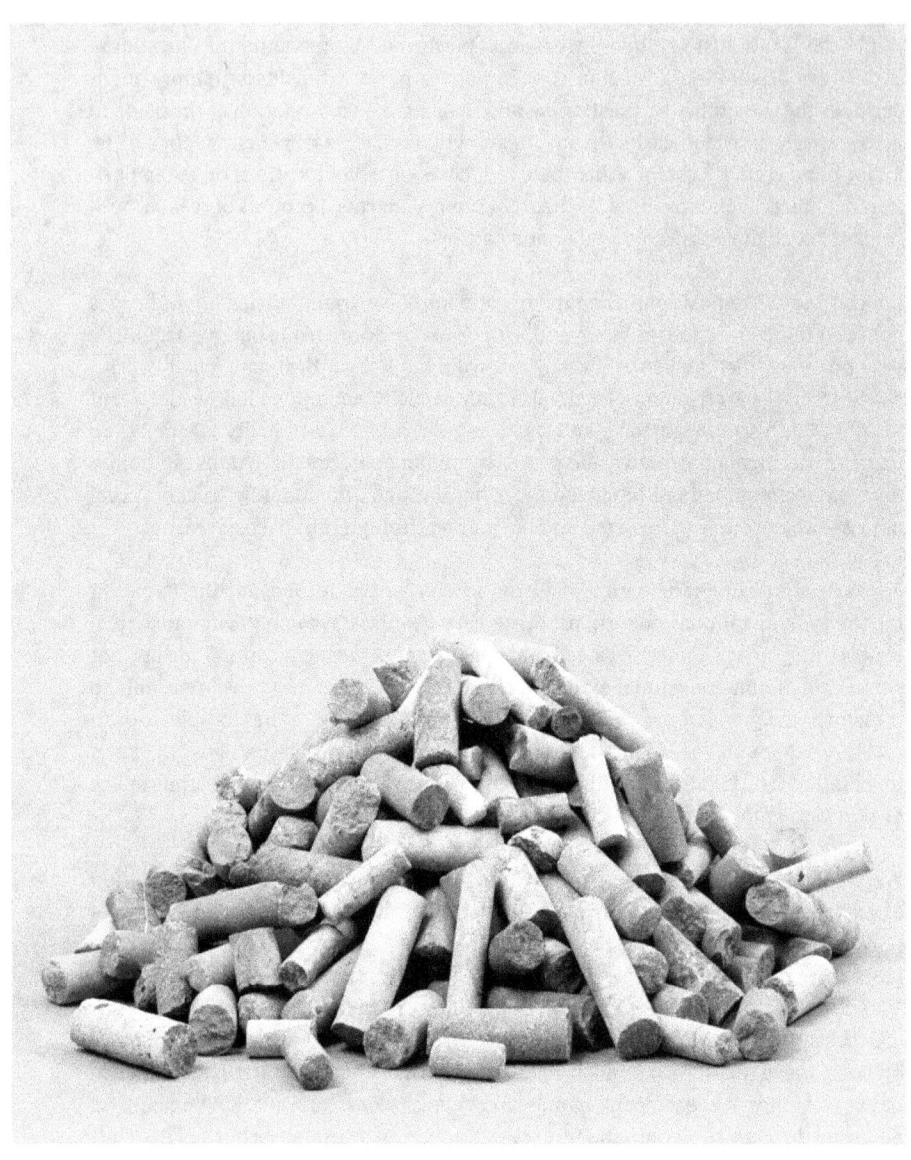

Fig. 02   Fabien Giraud, The Marfa Stratum, 2013; photograph by Alex Marks.

NAVIGATION

To address these notions does not only mean calling for a future kind of art; it requires us to enact an operative revision of our own history. It implies that we crawl back through the current of history, identify points of inflexion, and operate a reoriention of their becomings. It demands we take hold of untravelled paths or blocked routes and open them to bifurcations and reworkings; such notions include those of *site* and *site-specificity*.

Since their historical emergence in the 1960s, site-specific practices and discourses have become a normative framework and a standard of evaluation for any artistic gesture. Schematically, we can argue that the short history of site-specificity has had three phases. By binding the work of art to a complex set of material conditions, the first construction phase in the 1960s opened new relations to the notion of artistic experience and its constitutive gestures. In the 1970s, dynamic engagements such as institutional critique (Michael Asher, Daniel Buren, Hans Haacke, Mierle Laderman Ukeles) opened the site to the social, political, racial, and economic context of the aesthetic experience, thus highlighting the hidden power relations at play in art institutions. In the 1980s, these concerns were further extended by their encounters with feminism and postcolonial theories, as well as a systematic questioning of modes of coercion, racism, patriarchy, and other embedded systems of privilege (Andrea Fraser, Fred Wilson). The third phase started in the wider context of a liberalized economy and completely diluted the notion of site in the newly grounded mobilities best exemplified by the triadic circulation within the "art world" between art residencies, art biennials, and art fairs.

If the notion of site was constructed as a practical and conceptual tool that once aspired to artistic and political emancipation, it now seems to work effectively toward further alienation. Even though it has now become common to denounce the contemporary effects of this paradigmatic shift and the failure of its promises, instead of abandoning the notion of site to its critics, we would like to rescue its inaugural movement and emancipatory virtue through an in-depth reevaluation of its terms and potentialities. Furthermore, we wish to use this notion of site as a hinge in a revised history of the relations between art and rationality.

Marfa as a Site

To proceed to this revision, we wish to address the work of Donald Judd, as someone who opened the way for the notion of site to be developed through a practice of conceptual formalization. Although Judd himself never mentioned the concept of site as such, the array of concepts and practices he used clearly constitute a transitional phase in the overall epochal dynamics that led to its emergence. A specific is what relates dynamically to a generic. There is no specificity without its generic counterpart, and any practice of thought, any "meaningful act," as defined by Peirce's pragmatism, is always an articulation between these two polarities.[13]

For Peirce, "The idea of a general involves the idea of possible variations which no multitude of existent things could exhaust but would leave between not two, not merely *many* possibilities, but possibilities absolutely beyond any multitude."[14] In such a view, a generic does not designate a space, a particular entity or a set of elements but a truly indeterminate realm of pure possibility. A specific is nothing but the material and temporal instantiation of this generic, as Donald Judd elaborates in relation to his own work:

> Three-dimensionality is not as near being simply a container as painting and sculpture have seemed to be (...). Much of the motivation in the new work is to get clear of these forms. The use of three dimensions is an obvious alternative. It opens to anything.[15]

In his foundational text "Specific Objects,"[16] Judd attempts to think through the movements that occurred in art after 1946, with Newman, Rothko, and others, and tries to define a general form of art that would be "neither painting nor sculpture"[17] but a three-dimensional realm of possibilities. He defines the "old works" as those which instantiated the limit within which the relationship of colours and forms occur. In those works, the painting was conceived as a bounded form, an enclosed space of possibility founded on a fixed spatial identity. On the contrary, for Judd, the identity of an art object is never something in and of itself, but the result of a specific operation within a truly indeterminate and generic space: a painting is a rectangular volume on a wall, a wall is a folded plane in a room, and a room a volume nested in a building. The new works he calls for do not allude or refer to a space outside of themselves but—through a series of material inferences—construct and unfold their specific and continuous spatiality. As such, the Juddian notion of specificity allows one to depart from any standard representationalist account of a disjunctive relation between space and reason and opens to a concept of site as the formalization of their possible continuity.

How does such a formalization occur? In the *15 untitled works in concrete (1980–1984)*, as well as in the *100 works in mill aluminium (1982–1986)*, exhibited in Marfa, each individual work resembles the next one with slight variations as the viewer moves from one piece to the next. The serial nature of the work allows for the global to exist as a reflection into each of its local elements. Its completeness can only thus be fully grasped through the association of a careful wandering among the local elements and a mental projection into their possible globality. Each work functions as a navigational marker, a material hypothesis of what the global may be. The continuity of the work is more than the mere sum of its parts and can only be reached through a constant relaunching of local *abductive gestures*.

An abduction is a mode of inference employed both as a keystone for the scientific method and in everyday reasoning. In Peircian terms, an "abduction is the process of *inferring* certain facts and/or laws and hypotheses that render some sentences plausible, that *explain* (and also sometimes *discover*) some (eventually new) phenomenon or observation."[18] In the case of Judd, an abduction occurs when the globality of the sculpture is inferred in each of its local constituents. As such, for Judd, any attempt to reach out for what he calls the "wholeness"[19] of space can only be successful if the local—apprehended through direct and physical experience—and the global—seized through conceptual projections—achieve a sense of continuity. He writes:

> I've always considered the distinction between thought and feeling as, at the least, exaggerated (…). Emotion or feeling is simply a quick summation of experience, some of which is thought, necessarily quick so that we can act quickly (…). Otherwise we could never get from A to Z, barely to C, since B would have to be always rechecked. It's a short life and a little speed is necessary.[20]

Here, Judd introduces the notion of speed into the thinking process. "Fast-thinking" is for Judd the necessary condition for the production of new hypotheses that will then relaunch the thinking process. Meaning is nothing but a movement of temporary capture that allows one "to catch a gesture and to be able to continue."[21] Fast-thinking is the multiplication of material inferences in order to catalyze spaces of navigation. Abduction as an orientation tool, and fast-thinking as a constant retriggering of its movements, constitute the woven dynamics of Judd's formalizations. As we hope is evident from this brief account of Judd's work, the notion of site that it opens has little to do with the way "site" came to be understood in its later art historical stages.

This distinction should be stressed for two reasons; first, for Judd, the *specific* is not to be misconstrued with the "situated" and the *generic* is not to be confused with the "nowhere." These terms do not entail a kind of irreducible and local concreteness or embodiment that one could oppose to abstract generalities. On the contrary, what Judd proposes with his practice of specificity is a new distribution and material constructive binding of what we traditionally deemed as abstract and concrete. Second, the abductive logic at the core of Judd's work radically opposes our standard conception of experience as non-conceptual "presentification." The experience of continuity, especially in his large-scale installations, is not "revealed" or "given" by the work but inferentially and materially constructed through a navigation within the work. Experience is a rational process through and through.

Marfa as a Stratum

If a site has been defined as the formalization of continuity, we wish to prolong and conclude this investigation by asking: what does such a site become once confronted by the concept of the Anthropocene?

From Judd's arrival in the early 1970s until his death in 1994, the small town of Marfa in far West Texas was for him an ideal laboratory for the production of material navigations. For him, Marfa might have appeared as a specific fold in a generic desert, a site for the continuous extension of his rational formalizations.

In a hundred million years, if living entities were to drill core samples at the exact location of Marfa, what would they uncover in the fossil imprint that documents the human passage in the region? Among the inert and indifferent residues, they would find flattened remnants of navigation: Donald Judd's aluminium sculptures crushed and reduced as the compressed aggregates of old navigations.

Imagining a world where humans have disappeared constitutes a common grand narrative of the Anthropocene.[22] This tale of extinction of humans by humans tends to become a naturalized eschatology, a theory of the *ends* of which we would be both the trigger and the victim. Far from endorsing this falsely humbling and disabling new myth, the import of this image into our conception of sites nonetheless provides us with a necessary shift of perspective: it binds our account of rationality as horizontal and continuous navigation to the vertical intrusion of geological contingencies. As such, it introduces entirely new parameters in the game of reason and demands that we revise and reorient our abductive operations.

Classically, for geologists, a core sample works as a vertical cartography of natural processes and their evolution over time. It offers an image of history as a stacked up succession of fossilized movements. The thin line of compressed sediments testifying to Marfa's existence is one of them. It is the "human event stratum"[23] in so far as it holds the material traces of human activity in the region (from the first indigenous settlements to today's oil-infused art institutions) and, more importantly so, because it registers a unique correlation between two very different types of processes: those of *formations* (understood as the full range of geo- and bio-morphological movements) and those of *formalizations* (understood as rational constructions within these movements). The intricacy of their respective dynamics is what distinguishes Marfa as a stratum from all other strata in the core sample. Among the full genericity of stratified processes, the Marfa Stratum is the specific site of the human.

What is the nature of this site? How can we describe its distinctive constitutive movements and the kind of spatiality they open to? That formalizations have emerged from a cascade of natural formations is a well established fact. That formations themselves have come to be irreversibly altered by human formalizations is now widely accepted as well. What is much less frequently taken into account is the retroactive effect these movements have on reason itself. We contend that this dynamic feedback between human reason and natural causes constitutes the true conceptual import of the Anthropocene. As such, it can help us to shed an entirely new light on the tale of the cognitive dust bowl and serve to unlock orientations within it.

The dominant modes of problematizing of the relation of the blade of reason to its terrain had left us with only two possible alternatives: either to heal the wounded Gaia (*locationism*) or further prolong our geological humiliations (*extensionism*). While both recognize the transformative effect of reason within its environment, they fail to account for its inevitable reverse: the transformation of reason by its environment. In this view, the plough does not only irreversibly alter the Great Plains, but alters itself in the same movement. It opens to a space of reason as that which is constantly deracinating and reforming itself by the very gestures it triggers in the world.

To navigate within this space, to select orientations, and decide on rational conduct is to engage in the constant reconstruction of the vehicle that serves to enable these movements. From such a vehicle, to make an abduction on a possible route demands that one reconstruct the vehicle itself. In other words, if reasoning within a site, as we have argued above, is an inferential process of abducting possible routes of navigation, to reason within a stratum requires doubling this movement with an abduction of reason itself. As a particular binding of continuity and contingency, a site in the Anthropocene is such a vehicle: the deracinated morphing nexus of formations and formalizations.

We contend that the truly emancipatory aspect of the Anthropocene for art pertains to such a revised conception of sites and the type of rational practice to which it testifies. Art in this context cannot be reduced to representation. Art is not merely a conservation of *what we were* or a reaction to *what we are*, but a proper commitment to *what we could be*; it is the material formalization of the possible.

Notes

1. *The Marfa Stratum* is a book co-written by Fabien Giraud and Ida Soulard; divided into six chapters, or vehicles, departing from the historical concept of "site-specificity," and strongly influenced by the American pragmatist tradition in philosophy, the book attempts to define a contemporary theory of sites. This essay constitutes an introduction to this on-going research.
2. In this text, we are tremendously indebted to the work of Ray Brassier and Reza Negarestani for having introduced us to the renewal of rationalism in contemporary philosophy, and opening our cognitive horizon to the works of Wilfrid Sellars and Robert Brandom, as well as the use of a navigational paradigm. Most particularly, we draw on Brassier's lecture, "How to Train an Animal that Makes Inferences: Sellars on Rule and Regularities," presented at the *The Human Animal in Politics, Science, and Psychoanalysis* Conference, KW Institute for Contemporary Art, organised by Lorenzo Chiesa and Mladen Dolar (16–17 December 2011), vimeo.com/35371780; also, Ray Brassier, "Nominalism, Naturalism and Materialism," lecture at *The Matter of Contradiction - War against the Sun* Conference, Limehouse Town Hall, London (1–3 March 2013), vimeo.com/66702489. Additionally, from Reza Negarestani, "Where Is the Concept," a transcription of a lecture given at "When Site Lost the Plot," a conference organized by Robin Mackay at Goldsmiths College, University of London, 2013, blog.urbanomic.com/cyclon/Navigation-2013.pdf; and, Reza Negarestani, "Navigating with Extreme Prejudice (Definitions and Ramifications)," published on the Urbanomic blog, 25 January 2014, blog.urbanomic.com/cyclon/What-Is-Philosophy.pdf.
3. *The plow that broke the plain* (25 min.; 1936) was poet Pare Lorentz's first feature film, written in free verse, and the first educational feature movie commissioned by the US government for commercial distribution. The idea was to document the Dust Bowl and educate the population regarding the danger of using inadequate agricultural techniques. The film was premiered at the Mayflower Hotel in Washington, D.C., during an event sponsored by the Museum of Modern Art.
4. Avis D. Carlson, "Dust," *New Republic* 82 (1 May 1935): 332–333.
5. Donna Haraway, "Situated Knowledges: The Science Question in Feminism and the Privilege of Partial Perspective," *Feminist Studies* 14, no. 3 (Autumn 1988): 581.
6. Ibid., 581.

7   Ibid., 583.
8   Ibid.
9   We are thinking here mostly of Bruno Latour, "An Attempt at a 'Compositionist Manifesto,'" *New Literary History* 41 (2010): 471–490. According to Latour, "It is really a mundane question of having the right tools for the right job. With a hammer (or a sledge hammer) in hand you can do a lot of things: break down walls, destroy idols, ridicule prejudices, but you cannot repair, take care, assemble, reassemble, stitch together," 475.
10 According to Robert Brandom, "I think of us as essentially normative beings, that what sets us apart from the other animals is our capacity to commit ourselves, our worrying about whether we are entitled to those commitments, whether it's a cognitive commitment as to how things are or a practical commitment as to how things shall be. I think of us as discursive beings and that means that our normativity is inferentially articulated. We're beings who engage in practices of giving and asking for reasons. And I think these two dimensions—the normative dimension and the rational dimension—are what set us apart from beings that can feel but can't think." From transcription of the interview with Robert Brandom (Interviewer: G. Seddone, Leipzig, 30 June 2008), edited by Aaron Luke Shoichet, www.filosofia.it/images/download/multimedia/08_Brandom%20Interview_transcription.pdf.
11 "There can be no such thing as an extraterritorial or transcendent critique of reason, since critique is a normative term whose ultimate warrant derives from reason itself." Ray Brassier, "That Which is Not: Philosophy as Entwinement of Truth and Negativity," *Stasis* 1 (2013): 185, stasisjournal.net/images/brassier1_eng.pdf.
12 On the distinction between representational and referential reasonings, see Robert Brandom, *Articulating Reasons: An Introduction to Inferentialism* (Cambridge and London: Harvard University Press, 2001), especially Chapter 1, "Representationalism and Inferentialism," 45–47, bibliotecamathom.files.wordpress.com/2012/09/articulating-reasons.pdf.
13 Our approach to the philosophy of Charles Sanders Peirce is highly indebted to Fernando Zalamea's brilliant take on the Peircean continuity; see Fernando Zalamea, *Peirce's Logic of Continuity: A Conceptual and Mathematical Approach* (Docent Press, 2012).
14 Charles Sanders Peirce, "Lectures on Pragmatism," in *Collected Papers of Charles Sanders Peirce Vol. 5*, "Pragmatism and Pragmaticism," edited by Hartshorne, Weiss & Burks, Bristol (Thoemmes Press, 1998 [1903]; new reprint of Harvard University Press original edition, 1931–1958), 103.
15 Donald Judd, "Specific Objects," *Arts Yearbook* 8 (1965): 94; reprinted in Thomas Kellein, *Donald Judd: Early Works 1955–1968* (New York: D.A.P., 2002).
16 Ibid.
17 Ibid.
18 Lorenzo Magnani, *Abductive Cognition: The Epistemological and Eco-Cognitive Dimensions of Hypothetical Reasoning* (Berlin and Heidelberg: Springer, 2010), 8.
19 "A person thinking, feeling and perceiving, which occurs all at once, is whole." Donald Judd, quoted by Richard Shiff, "Donald Judd Fast Thinking," in *Donald Judd: Late Work* (New York: PaceWildenstein, 2000), 5.
20 Richard Shiff, "Donald Judd, Safe From Birds," in *Donald Judd*, exhibition catalog, ed. Nicholas Serota (London: Tate Publishing, 2004), 28–61.
21 Jean Cavaillès, "Méthode axiomatique et formalisme," in *Oeuvres complète de philosophie des sciences* (Paris: Hermann, 1994), 178.
22 See, for example, Jan Zalasiewicz, *The Earth After Us: What Legacy Will Humans Leave in the Rocks?* (Oxford: Oxford University Press, 2009).
23 The "human event stratum" is a term used by Jan Zalasiewicz; see Zalasiewicz, *The Earth After Us: What Legacy Will Humans Leave in the Rocks?*

On the Building, Crashing, and Thinking of Technologies & Selfhood

Peter Galison in conversation with Etienne Turpin

As the discourse of the Anthropocene solicits increasing reflection from a variety of disciplines and through a multitude of practices, the relationship between philosophy, technology, and science also beckons further scrutiny; such attention cannot recoil from the imperilling realities of human civilization, but must instead attend to the various obligations produced within the techno-scientific milieu as they modulate the expansion and expression of globalized human societies. Peter Galison has carefully attended to the entangled historical and philosophical stakes in the culture of scientific experimentation by diligently investigating the formation of scientific minorities, interlanguages, theory, and materiality as they produce our contemporary world. Investigating the complex interdependencies and interactions among experimentation, instrumentation, and conceptual abstraction, Galison's work has profoundly enriched our understanding of scientific inquiry, objectivity, and the role of design and aesthetics within the articulation of scientific knowledge. His previous monographs on experimentation, *How Experiments End* and *Image and Logic*, will be completed by a much-anticipated third volume, *Building Crashing Thinking*. Following a workshop at Harvard University's Graduate School of Design, I had the opportunity to interview Peter about the role of the accident in science, technology, and the discourse of the Anthropocene; what follows is an edited transcript of our conversation.

Etienne Turpin I would like to begin by asking about the accident as a framework for knowledge. In your lecture for *The Geologic Turn* symposium, you described the research for your forthcoming book, *Building Crashing Thinking*, as engaging the accident as a framework in relation to technologies of the self.[1] I am curious how you engage contingency as an organizing component within the production of both knowledge and selfhood.

Peter Galison Maybe I should first step back and just say a little about the Foucauldian idea of a technological self and the sense in which I want to use this idea. There's a tradition going back to Nietzsche and Heidegger that treats the self not as a fixed, transhistorical, or transcendental category, but rather as something that changes over time. For Heidegger, the self is very schematic; there are these blocks that correspond to the self in antiquity, the self in the early modern period, and so on. And Foucault follows a similar trajectory, although he is interested in giving the self a more materialized historicity by saying that certain practices represent a certain cultivation of the self, such as the way that religious practices are embodied in spiritual exercises that cultivate the self in a particular way. So, for example, Foucault is interested in the keeping of a diary as a mnemo-technic that establishes the continuity of the self in certain ways and produces a self as a result of these practices. But the technology he considers isn't very technological in the everyday sense that we mean it, and the technology, in some ways, comes first. For Foucault, technological actions cultivate the self; the self doesn't act on the technologies. I am interested in opening up this framework by looking at the relationship between the self and technologies as a reciprocal one. I want to know, first, what kinds of technologies are opened up by a regime of self. And then, once a certain form of technology is in action, almost ubiquitously, how does it train us to act or be a certain way?

I have written, for example, about the Rorschach test, which illustrates both sides of this back-and-forth action.[2] The idea of finding patterns or representations of objects—animals, people, plants—in what used to be called "random images" of clouds, of embers, of cracks in the wall, was for centuries (in a neoclassical picture) a way of encouraging the faculty of imagination. The self was organized into these different faculties, like memory, common sense, imagination, but this specific faculty of imagination was a thing that could be encouraged. So, when Leonardo Da Vinci writes about how important it is to stare at cracks in the wall and imagine figures, he was trying to offer training for the imagination. Now, when Rorschach comes along, he is not interested in imagination at all, or at least the imagination is a very secondary interest. He is interested, by contrast, in this procedure as a test of perception. I want to know what has changed. How did it come to pass that the primary thing—namely, the faculty of imagination—has its place taken by this other thing, namely, the characteristic forms of perception? What has changed is the introduction of the unconscious; a very different concept or theory of the self has entered into a long history, which culminates in Charcot and Freud and others in the mid- to late-nineteenth century.

So, a new form of self becomes the precondition for the establishment of this technology, this cardboard technology. But it is a technology: there are rules that govern its administration, scoring, interpretation, etc.; it is a real technology. But, when it becomes widespread, the Rorschach test becomes a kind of master metaphor for our time. It teaches us how to think about the self. It teaches us, even people that have no primary interest in Freud or the topography of the mind, that we are like magic lanterns projecting inner unconscious anxieties onto the outside world and seeing patterns there. And so, eventually, President Barack Obama can stand up and say: "I am a Rorschach," and expect 340 million Americans to understand, roughly speaking, what he means.

ET Obama referred to himself as a Rorschach test?

PG Yes, he's said it many times. If you look up Rorschach on Google you will get hundreds of returns. Andy Warhol makes it into giant paintings. It is the subject of fiction and graphic novels. It has become something much broader than a test. It becomes a technology infused with a cultural vector that teaches us to think of ourselves—about our "self"—in a certain way. So that's an example of this reciprocal action: what starts out as a precondition for the emergence of this technology—there's an actual technology with cardboard plates and rigorous methods of reproduction, of scoring and interpreting—becomes very widespread and starts teaching us how to be, in a way.

The book that I'm finishing, *Building Crashing Thinking*, looks at a series of technologies in this reciprocal back and forth between a self *a priori* (what has to be presupposed about the self for certain technologies) and a technological *a priori* (about how the technology acts on the self). So, there is a constant back and forth. Neither is taken to be the *ursprung* of the process. It bootstraps its way forward, or in some direction—I'm not sure it's always forward…

ET For anyone with a background in European philosophy, it's an especially provocative title for a book. Seeing the "dwelling" of Martin Heidegger's essay "Building Dwelling Thinking" replaced with "crashing," I am inclined to believe you are proposing a radical reorganization of the place and propriety of human thought with regards to technology.[3]

PG I have a very complex relationship to Heidegger. On the one side, I think of Heidegger as a transformative figure in helping to establish the idea of the historicity of self, and that this is quite essential in understanding the background against which Foucault (another reference for me) is writing. Heidegger is very concerned with technology, but in a very different way than I am. There are ways in which he dismisses a large part of the kinds of technology crucial in the formation of the contemporary self, of who we are, as not "things" at all. So when he talks about *das Ding*, it's in contrast to, say, nuclear weapons, or an airport hangar. For him, those technologies spell the end of the thing, and the end of thinking, because they are an enframing, or the lapsarian moment in our relationship with things as such.

ET It is all quite fatalist for Heidegger on this point; technology is reducible to the foreclosure of dwelling as such. This is precisely why Heidegger makes technology an essence by contending that "the essence of technology is nothing technological."[4]

PG Right, so I'm interested in airplane crashes and nuclear weapons. I'm interested in all the things Heidegger despises. These are, for me, fundamental technologies that we exist in relation to, but, in the Husserlian tradition, out of which Heidegger comes, once you get to Galileo, it's all just downhill. In their tradition, modern science is just the working out of the imposition of number on the world. As you might expect, I don't think that at all. In fact, I've devoted my life to understanding the way science unfolds and, in particular, to asking the kinds of questions that were posed by philosophy. But, instead of just damning the post-1610 moment, or the post-Cartesian, post-Galilean, post-whatever moment, as being merely enframing or instrumentalizing, I want to see how things actually unfold as they do.

ET This is clearly something of a departure from your previous books as here you're taking on a much broader philosophical tradition. While you have, in the past, been extremely precise in moving from concrete practices to the abstractions implicated by and explicated through these practices—as well as the contingencies entangled in such movements—it seems that now you have a broader agenda with respect to philosophy and science.

PG For a long time, as you say, I have been interested in contingency without debunking; that is to say, not a hermeneutics of suspicion, but not one of celebration either. It is not some great triumphalist march, nor does it mean that just because there's contingency in the construction of science and the reciprocal action against who we are, we can say "Gotcha! Science is valueless and we can dismiss it." In my work—from *How Experiments End* and *Image and Logic*, to my Einstein book and my work on objectivity—there is tremendous contingency. In the book I co-authored with Loraine Daston, *Objectivity*, we argue that objectivity is not co-terminous with science as such; objectivity is an epistemic virtue that enters in the first third of the nineteenth century. It's not the same thing as truth, pedagogical utility, or quantification; it's a *specific* virtue in the epistemic sphere, and we can see how it formed and what its relationship was to image-making and other technologies. And, as the concept is developed, what happens is that objectivity and subjectivity in a way enter together. For me, to say that objectivity and subjectivity form at the same time is like saying up and down or left and right enter together. Of course, you can't one day establish the convention of leftness without rightness, and so the self-abnegation that is a change in the scientific self is actually, in a certain sense, the same moment as the creation of scientific objectivity. As soon as you start to say that the *Hierzeit* of the line is me and the *Endzeit* is the thing, you're creating both an objective world and a subjective one. This is something I have been interested in, perhaps in a more restrictive way, since the beginning. In *How Experiments End* and *Image and Logic*, I was interested in what counts as an experiment and who counts as an experimenter. So they enter together.

ET I agree. And, although the philosophical implications of your earlier works are quite substantial, you've tended to emphasize the precision of the case in question over the speculative implications of such cases. It seems as though there's more consideration given to the speculative and philosophical implications in your current research. I'm curious about why that is.

PG I think that it's true. In this work, I want to put front and centre changing ideas and changing scales of selfhood. So, it starts with this idea of personality, of what perception is, and the magic lantern and iceberg conceptions of self. But by the end of the book, there's a chapter on wastelands and wilderness, where it's exactly the detritus of nuclear weapons (from producing and exploding them) that creates a new kind of space, a forbidden zone of the quasi-infinite future that puts us in a different relationship to land: we can only make short visits. It first seems like an odd or paradoxical relationship to the way we have described "wilderness," for example, in the Wilderness Act, according to which wilderness was the land of such purity that we would only be visitors there. I'm making a film called *Containment* about this sort of thing. When you go to visit the towns around Fukushima, you'll find them marked as "zones of limited habitation." The experience of these places, phenomenologically, is that you can't live there. You can't stay. You're a visitor. So this relationship, which I think of as—perhaps harshly—a kind of touristic relation to a space, joins the relationship of humans to places that are either too pure or too defiled. I've started to think of this land as "waste wilderness." The Savannah River site is 314 square miles, a contaminated zone where they made about a third of the material used for the 80,000 or so nuclear weapons made in the United States. And it's considered by the biological laboratory there to be the most biodiverse area east of the Mississippi, maybe in the entire United States. So this land, which we have a touristic relationship to, is in some ways both wasteland and wilderness at the same time. And our relationship is no longer a kind of supplicant theodicy. Thoreau says, "out of the swamp comes the redeemer." For us, it's more like nuclear tourism; there's a museum in Chernobyl now. It's a new kind of relationship between the human self and the land. The classic form of this relationship is something else. There was the Abrahamic, in which the land was given to us by God and we controlled and disposed of it, and in the Christian tradition it was our obligation to use it up before the Apocalypse. Or you have the Romantic view: we humans are the servants of the land; we are its eyes; we are its expression. What I am talking about is neither of those; we have become tourists in waste wilderness, and this land becomes the exemplar of the most natural and unnatural land, simultaneously. It's different.

ET   Michel Serres asks a similar question in *Malfeasance*, when he questions if we, as humans, are owners or renters of the land we inhabit.[5] There is, we might say, an ontological corrective at play in these discussions of tenancy.

PG   Well, you can come to this in different ways. The Wilderness Act came to this visitor relationship on other grounds, namely, as a reaction against the National Park. This might be expressed as something like: "Wilderness is not just for our entertainment or for the peace of mind of the busy urban dweller; it's something else." Anyway, I think we register this in different ways. In the book, I am looking at technologies—although I'm not saying this is the only way to read this material—of the 1920s, the technologies of WWII, cybernetics, then up to the present with surveillance, mining, and data, among other technologies.

ET   I'm curious about your method of selection, since there are so many ways to develop this argument of the co-constitutive relation between technologies and selfhood. How do you go about selecting your exemplary cases?

PG At some very deep level, I'm amused, entertained, and seduced by the relationship of very abstract and very concrete things when they enter together. Everything I do is about that. Not every concrete thing is attached to abstract thoughts, and not all abstractions correspond to materiality, but when they do coincide it's not always some kind of Platonic ascension. What interests me is not that we start with an iron triangle and then draw it with a pencil, and draw it with a finer and finer line until it becomes a Platonic idea in our minds. Or the reverse, where you start with a Platonic entity in your mind and then you apply it to modern physics and bring it down to the factory floor. To me, this is deeply related to an almost philosophical joke. If you look at Freud's theory of jokes, the sudden debasement of very abstract or grand things into material ones is the predicate for a lot of our humour. I find it very funny that, for instance, when Einstein talks about trains and clocks that he might actually be talking about... trains and clocks, and that his central abstraction and the most important move in physics of the last 150 years actually might have had to do with, you know, *stuff*—with clocks and wires going from Berne to one of its aristocratic suburbs. Or, Poincaré talking about telegraphers sending signals to measure longitude. This is not a "brain in a vat" or "philosophy in the suburbs." In fact, this was worldly work. Poincaré was in charge of the Bureau of Longitude along with friends, some of whom were dying on the mosquito-infested shores, dragging cables off of boats and up into wooden shacks and looking at little beams of light bouncing off of mirrors. So, Poincaré and Einstein were talking about something very material, very consequential, and using it to reform the most basic, transformative part of physics: saying that simultaneity and time were not the eternal verities that Newton thought they were, although these were the foundations of physics from the 1680s to 1905.

ET And, as you've explained, these concrecsences have serious political consequences, not least of which is the attempt by anarchists to bomb Greenwich in order to destroy the homogeneous imposition of Greenwich Mean Time.[6]

PG These things that begin in this sudden juxtaposition of materiality and abstraction can work their way into something that becomes a matter of concern for us in a deep, general way. In *Building Crashing Thinking*, I'm interested in, first, this juxtaposition, and then, choosing technologies that enter into our very concept of who we are. Not every technology does that. The interior mechanism on the forward landing gear of a transport plane isn't something that particularly shapes the self, although it is important in moving goods and people around the world. I have chosen things like the Rorschach test; or, this piece I did, "Aufbau/Bauhaus," about the relationship between architecture, cybernetics, and the "new man" through this idea that [Norbert] Weiner had that the self was actually nothing other than the working out of these electromechanical systems; all the way up through airplane accidents, nuclear wastelands, surveillance, and archiving and mining technologies.[7] These are things that do get at us; I'm interested in how they come about, become ubiquitous, and then train us up, collectively.

ET The Anthropocene itself seems like an especially compelling case of an extremely abstract idea—of the overall aggregate of human impact on the earth system—and extremely concrete realities, such as CO_2 in the atmosphere. The scale and consequence of this abstraction is currently under debate by philosophers as well, so that the work of the International Commission on Stratigraphy, on the stratigraphic importance of human impact, has migrated into the humanities as a means to ask very abstract questions about human activity, impact, and the meaning of human endeavours. Of course, if this is a joke on human hubris, it is worth remembering that not all jokes end well! Returning to the abstract-concrete tension, I'm curious if this plays out in the various media you work with as well?

PG Certainly, my interests in film and materiality are very connected. Film has been a way for me to make visible things that are thought to be invisible, which lines up with taking abstractions and connecting them to the material conditions in which they play out. My film *Secrecy* with Robb Moss takes on a subject you couldn't possibly talk about.[8] Obviously! Not only is there nothing to see, but how do you make a movie about it? How do you make a film about secrecy? That's part of what entranced me about the subject and why I began working on it. The first piece I did on it was for *Critical Inquiry* ten years ago, called "Removing Knowledge."[9] In a way, typical of the kinds of things that interest me, the mandate of the larger *Critical Inquiry* program was the transmission of knowledge. In order to explore what the transmission of knowledge looks like, I thought, let's look at how it's stopped. If you flip a question upside down you can often see its dynamics; if you want to know how a car works, you can learn a lot by looking at what stops it from working. I wanted to see the theory of how they believed they could stop the transmission of knowledge. What was the imputed theory telling them—that if they remove a topic or a name or place or a theory that they could stop knowledge from moving? I became interested in the materiality of how secrecy worked. And that became part of the work I did, for instance, on the redacted spaces in Freud's thought.[10] Freud's ideas of psychic censorship and the newspaper go back and forth as he theorizes the state and war using psychoanalysis; but, psychoanalysis is also reformed in light of the censorship of the war. It is exactly this kind of back and forth.

So, film for me has been a way to explore ways of making. The first film I made, *Ultimate Weapon*, was about the moral arguments regarding the use of the hydrogen bomb.[11] Or similarly, with my new film (also with Robb Moss), called *Containment*, the first thing I want to show you is what nuclear waste is like: here is where it's stored, this is how much it weighs, this is a picture of it.[12] Even though you can't go near it, this is what it does to the land, this is what it looks like when we come in contact with the stuff, this is what it looks like when your house has nuclear waste in it, and so on... There's a way in which understanding and historicity and materiality become part of advocacy. In a way, we can't come to a position on things that we can't yet imagine. So bringing things into the realm of the visible, or rather the *sensible* (surely senses other than sight play a part in our discourse), is very connected to the things I'm interested in. For example, how you actually go about determining the cause of a 747 falling out of the sky?

ET Do you mean that, as this type of large technological accident becomes ubiquitous, it reframes our sense of the event because it changes or challenges the modern episteme?

PG I'll give you another example. I think that what began as the specialized project of investigating train accidents (and later plane accidents) has become, in recent decades, the exemplar of public understanding of the techno-scientific sphere. We want to ask why the Deep Water Horizon blew up off the coast of Louisiana or why the space shuttle Challenger crashed. What happens in a presidential assassination investigation? We model all of these investigations on the best public dissection and account of causal processes that we have—those of airplane accidents. When we actually talk about why something happens, the most detailed kinds of inquiries that they get into are typically about airplane accidents. Why did MH370 crash? And, why does it create such a generalized panic if they can't figure out the cause?

ET But if the experts cannot reverse engineer the cause of the accident from its debris, for example, then we cannot specify any cause; this would mean, I suppose, that without cause we cannot call the incident an accident.

PG In Europe and the United States, roughly speaking, every accident report has to end with a probable cause; and, probable cause has a dual and contradictory meaning. On the one side, it means the kind of proximate thing, for example, the crack in the internal rotor that then separated out and sliced the hydraulic line, which caused the plane to lose control and crash. But, at the same time, it also means all of the necessary causes, all of the things that needed to happen in order for the accident to occur. These meanings pull in opposite directions—the sufficient cause, that is, the local, little thing that caused the accident looks for something proximate. In the ideal case, you get it down to the one-cubic-millimetre fault in the titanium alloy that was processed on such-and-such date in this or that location. Then, on the other side, it's all the things lawyers call the "but for" clauses (all these necessary causes), and those ramify exponentially. So, we have each of these accident reports holding a tremendous contradiction in that, on the one side, it looks for the local proximate entity and, on the other, it looks for *everything*: if the pilot got up on the wrong side of the bed; or what if her mother called her back that day; or, what if the safety regulations had been different, etc. The cause becomes "us," in the most general sense, and this back and forth between maximal and minimal accounts, necessary and sufficient causes, lies at the anxious epistemic core of our account of why things happen. We wrote this into the technology itself; we train people and devote many billions of dollars to these procedures, despite this core contradiction. This feeling of the search for control—this search for control over noise and signal, or cybernetics, or about causal ideology and accidents—becomes a deeper and deeper anxiety as our technologies gain in scale and impact. If we go from the Rorschach test, and even the Bauhaus, to the weapons systems of WWII, to these all-encompassing infrastructure systems of transportation, surveillance, and secrecy in large terms—as we centralize and organize the flows of energy, information, movement, and so on—then accounting for these large technological systems has a different scale of impact on our lives.

ET As the scale of our technological dependency increases, so does the magnitude of human impact; but, as Bruno Latour has noted, our agency to act or change these systems appears to be inversely proportional to their impact. Perhaps the disappearance of MH370, and the subsequent search, is an exemplary moment highlighting the contours of this epistemic horizon?

PG Control, explanation, and causal ideology. We could also look at other technologies, like nuclear reactors, but I don't think nuclear plants are more likely to blow up than petrochemical plants. Petrochemical plants blow up all the time. But, the scale of Chernobyl or Fukushima—to make a large part of the country uninhabitable for the indefinite future—that is different. You can get pretty bad with petrochemical spills, but Louisiana isn't being abandoned. When the Fukushima accident happened, it could have been much worse. If one of those fuel pools had caught fire, the Japanese prime minister and his advisors were considering the possibility of evacuating modern Japan. That is a different scale and, in a way, it is kind of a model system when we consider global warming. We find ourselves considering the consequences for major features of the earth, and that is something new. Scientists who have no explicit interest in epistemology will talk about the Anthropocene and say, "Of course I have to study global warming," because the object of inquiry for planetary science has changed. The atmosphere is not the same. Now, if you study electron-neutrino attractions, you can leave humanity aside, but not here: the object of inquiry has changed because we've changed it.

Notes

1   *The Geologic Turn: Architecture's New Alliance* was a symposium curated by Etienne Turpin at the University of Michigan, January–February 2012; some proceedings were published in *Architecture in the Anthropocene: Encounters Among Design, Deep Time, Science and Philosophy*, ed. Etienne Turpin (Ann Arbor: Open Humanities Press, 2013). I would like to thank Peter for his remarkable keynote presentation during the original symposium, as well as his compelling remarks during our follow-up interview for the present volume.

2   *X-Rays of the Soul: Rorschach & the Projective Test*, Special Exhibitions Gallery, Science Center, Harvard University, 2012; Peter Galison, "Image of Self," in *Things That Talk: Object Lessons from Art and Science*, ed. Lorraine Daston (New York: Zone Books, 2004), 257–298.

3   Martin Heidegger, "Building Dwelling Thinking" in *Basic Writings*, ed. David Farrell Krell (New York: Harper Collins, 1993), 343–364.

4   Martin Heidegger, "The Question Concerning Technology," in *The Question Concerning Technology and Other Essays,* trans. William Lovitt (New York and London: Garland, 1977), 3–35.

5   Michel Serres, *Malfeasance: Appropriation Through Pollution?* trans. Anne-Marie Feenberg-Dibon (Stanford: Stanford University Press, 2011).

6   Peter Galison, *Einstein's Clocks, Poincaré's Maps* (New York: W. W. Norton & Company, 2003).

7   Peter Galison, "Aufbau/Bauhaus: Logical Positivism and Architectural Modernism," *Critical Inquiry* 16, no. 4 (Summer 1990): 709–752.

8   Peter Galison and Robb Moss, *Secrecy* (Redacted Pictures: 2008), DVD.

9   Peter Galison, "Removing Knowledge," *Critical Inquiry* 31 (Autumn 2004): 229–243.

10 Peter Galison, "Blacked-out Spaces: Freud, Censorship and the Re-territorialization of Mind," *The British Journal for the History of Science* 45 (2012): 235–266.

11 Peter Galison, *The Ultimate Weapon: The H-Bomb Dilemma* (History Channel: 2000), DVD.

12 Peter Galison and Robb Moss, *Containment* (forthcoming), DVD.

We're Tigers

Ho Tzu Nyen

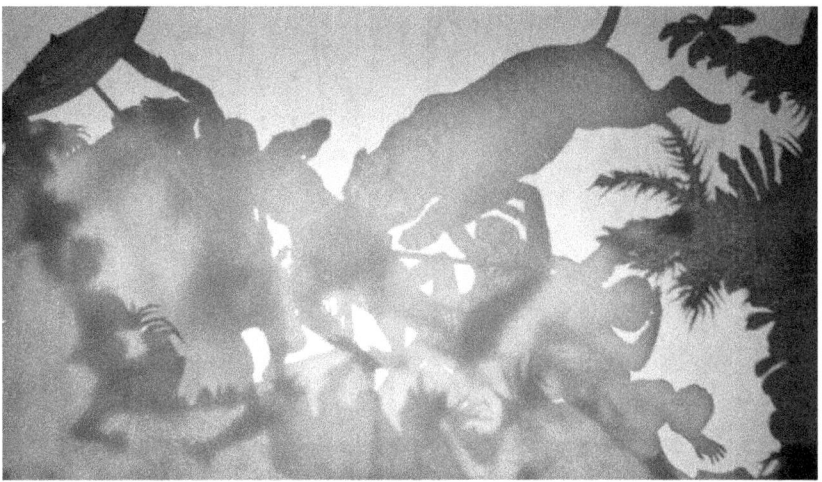

A play of shadows from *Ten Thousand Tigers*, 2014; courtesy of the artist.   Fig. 01

Speech is a spell, and words, once ejected into the air, warp the weave of worlds. This is why, as Robert Wessing tells us, the Javanese do not, after sundown, utter the word *macan* (tiger) for fear of invoking its presence. Instead, they refer to him as *guda*, from the Sanskrit word *gudha*, which means hidden, or secret.

The dispersal of tigers across the Malay world occurred more than a million years ago, long before the emergence of *Homo sapiens*. Their story precedes ours. And they have always been there at the origin of our histories.

What one cannot know, or does not wish to know, one passes in silence. This is why certain tribal groups in Malaya refer to the tiger only by stretching out their right hands in the shape of a claw. The Gayo of Sumatra call him *Mpu uton* (grandfather of the forest) or *Mpu tempat* (grandfather of the place), while the Acehnese refer to him as *datok* (grandfather or ancestor) or *gop* (other person, someone; used also for people from another village or place).[1] Yet these aliases tell us something of the tiger's secret: it is a creature of the forest, it is a being of nature, and it is other to humans—though never completely or radically so. For it is also kin, bound by blood to humans in the distant horizon of an ancestral time. To speak of this zoophilia is not to think *of* the tiger, but *with* the tiger, where thought can be propelled into a realm anterior to the formation of the human mind.

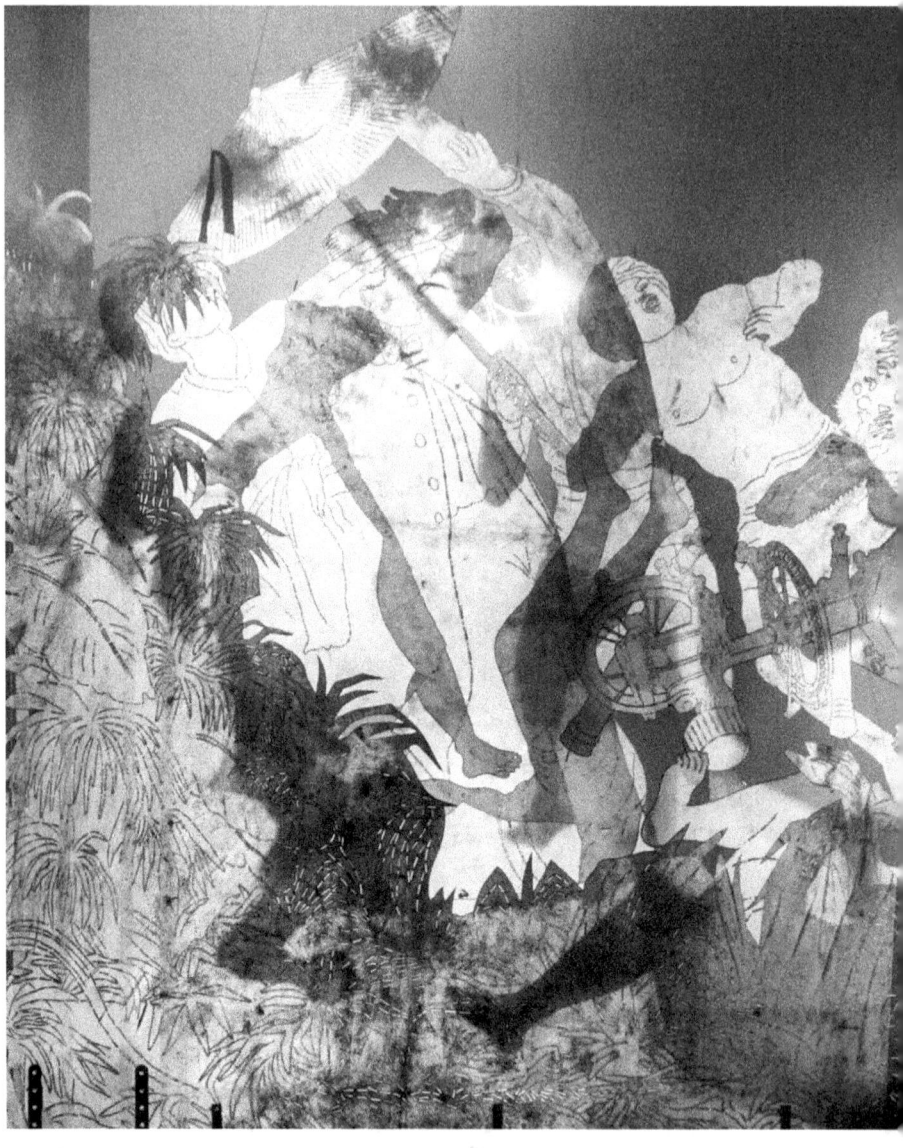

Fig. 02   Puppets made of buffalo hide from *Ten Thousand Tigers*, 2014; courtesy of the artist.

When early human settlers arrived in the region, they favoured as their habitat the transitory zones between the forest and the waters, an ecotone already occupied by other large, ground-dwelling mammals like the deer and the boar—and the tiger that preyed on them. Humans did not yet have the capacity to dominate this savannah-like landscape, for which the tiger was majestically adapted. With its paws masterfully designed for stealth, and its eyes attuned to darkness, the tiger, with its striped coat of yellow and black could melt into the golden brown fields of the tall lalang grasses.

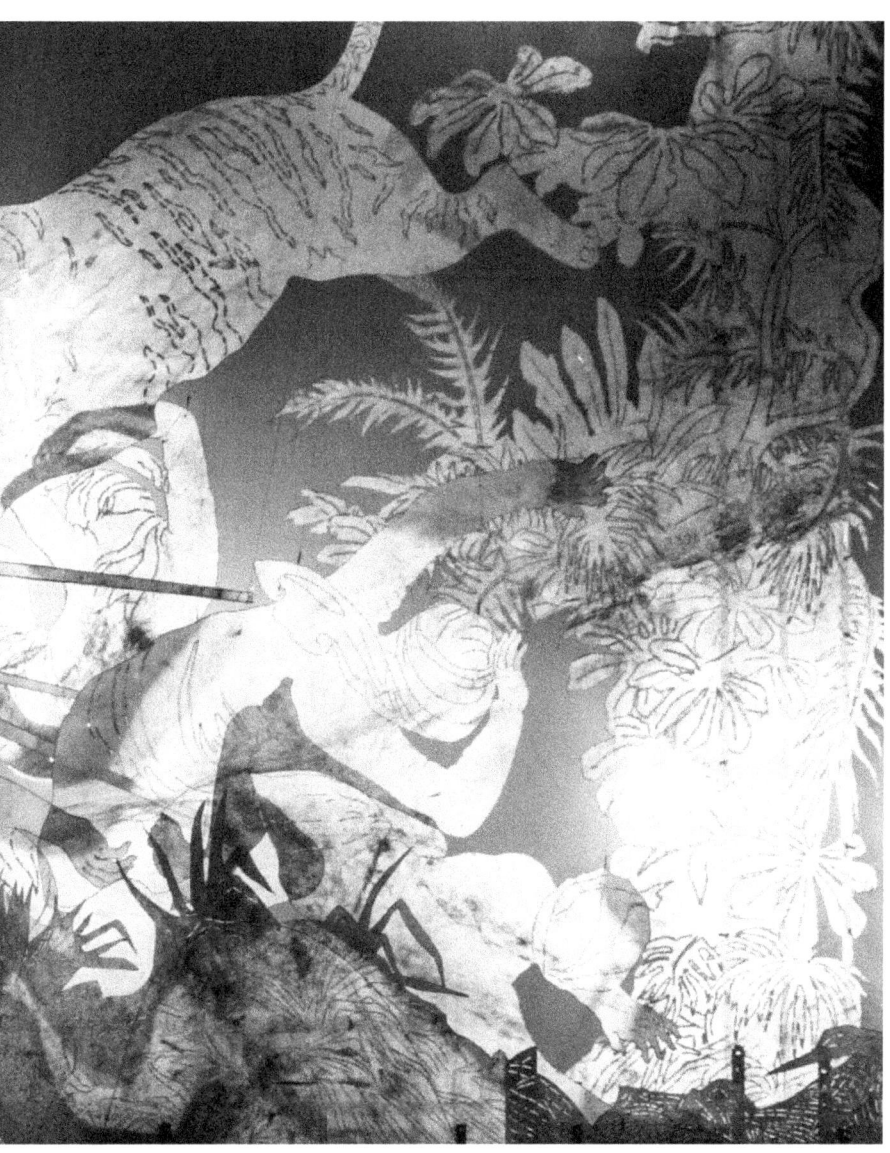

And in its midst, the tiger silently stalked its prey from behind, awaited the perfect moment before uncoiling and seizing its prey by the throat.

The proximity of these two species, which occupied the same niche in the food chain led to occasional conflicts, but the story as a whole, was one of co-evolution. Tigers avoided bipedal man as part of their adaptive behavioural strategy, while humans attuned themselves to the ways of the tiger, and the border between the two species became fuzzy. This is why in

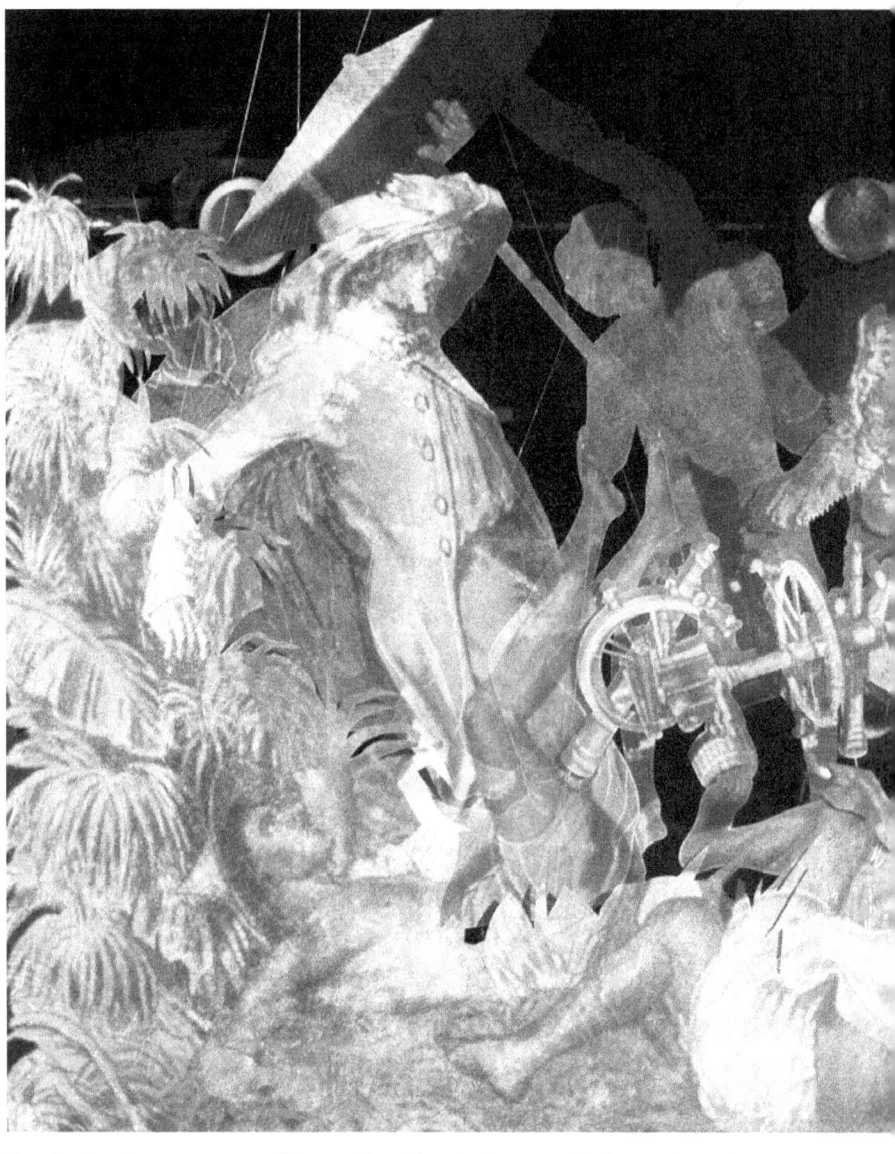

Fig. 03   *Unterbrochene Strassenmessung auf Singapore* (Road Surveying Interrupted in Singapore), wood engraving after Heinrich Leutemann (1824–1905), c. 1885; projected upon the puppets in *Ten Thousand Tigers*, 2014; collection of the artist.

the Malay world, the tiger was believed to live in villages, where the houses have walls of human skin, and the roofs are thatched with human hair. And when crossing lakes and rivers, the tiger can dissolve into the shape of man.

The first written record of the Malayan "weretiger" comes from an early fifteenth-century Chinese source, *The Triumphant Visions of the Shores of*

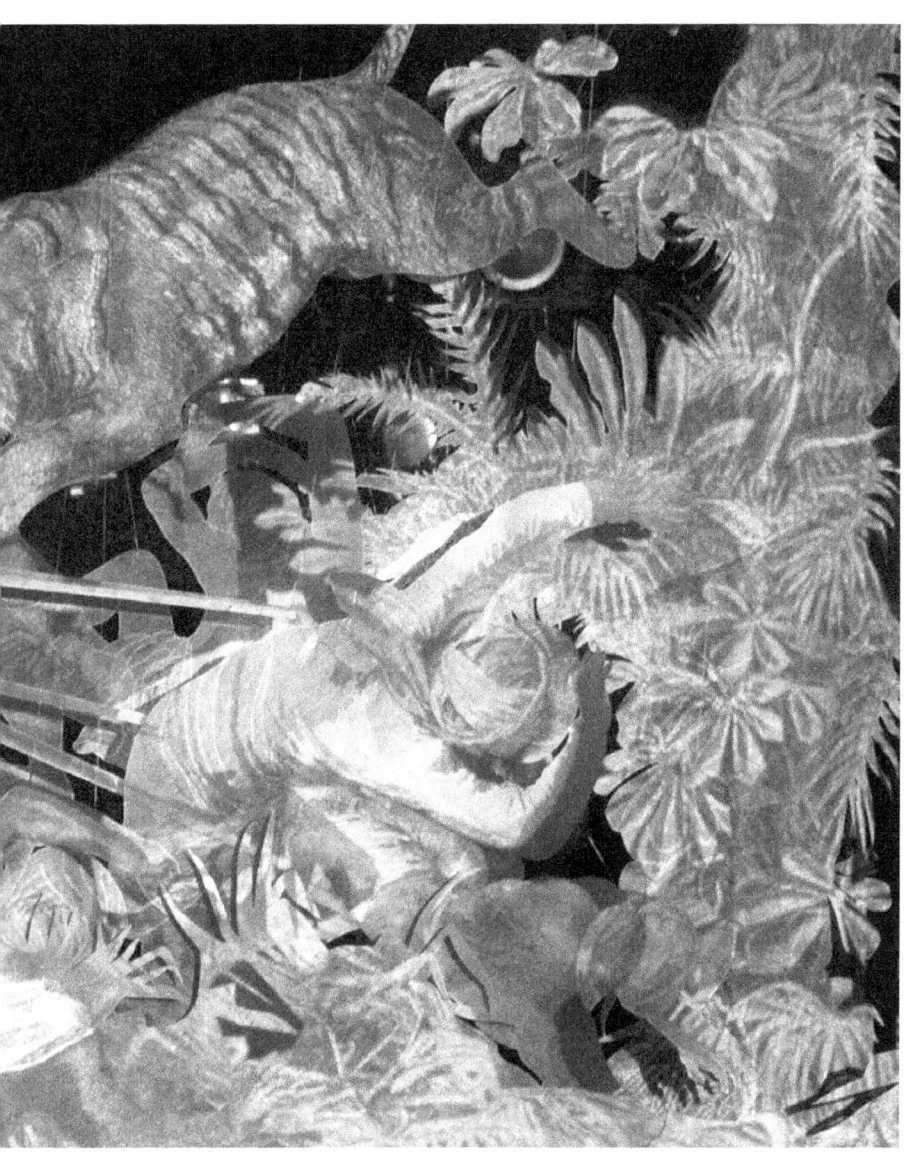

the Ocean, by Ma Huan, who served as an interpreter to Admiral Zheng He, the great navigator-eunuch of Ming Dynasty China. Of his visit to Malacca, he wrote: "In the town there are tigers which can assume human form; they enter the markets, and walk about, mixing with the populace. If anyone recognized one of these creatures, he would seize it and kill it." There were ways by which one could discern a weretiger. In its human form, it

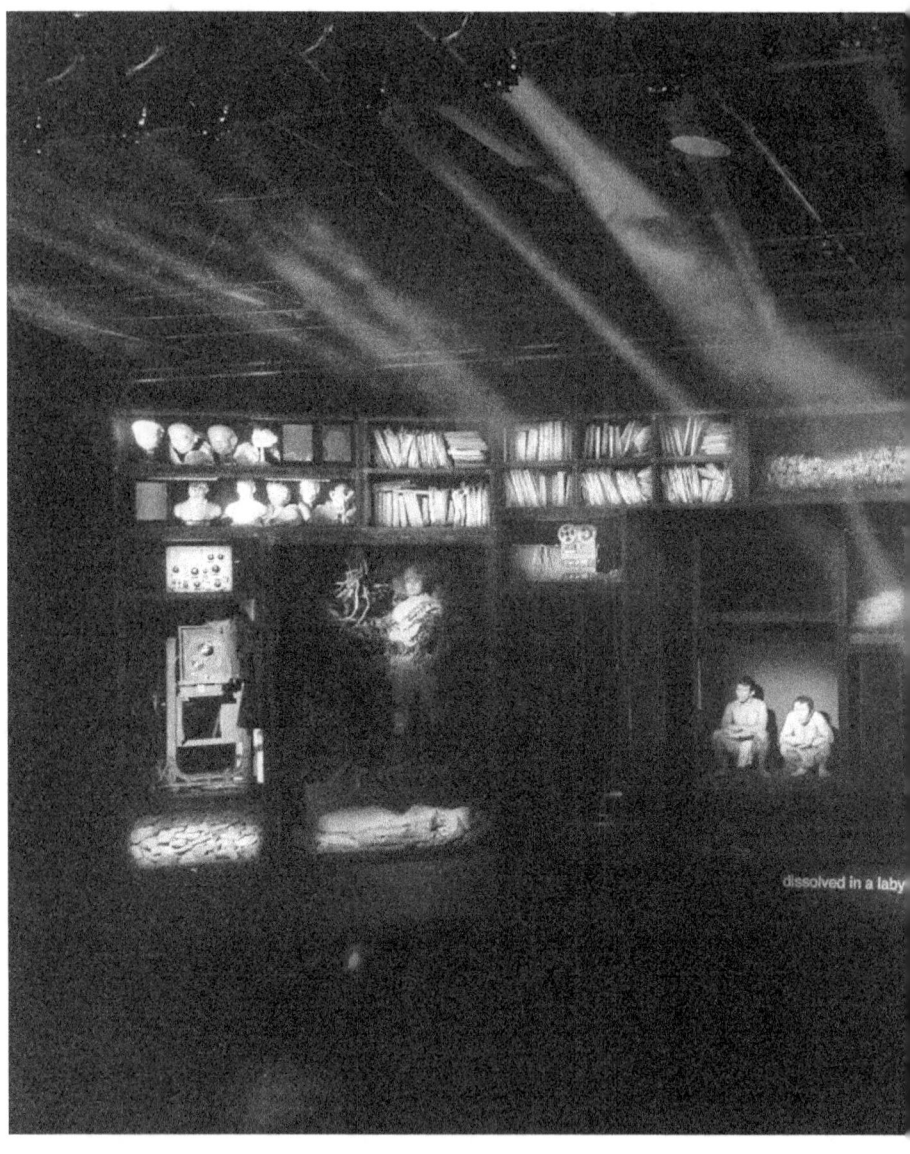

Fig. 04 *Ten Thousand Tigers*, documentation of performance, 2014; collection of the artist.

is believed to lack the philtrum, the cleft on the upper lip, and is a being without a fixed abode: a vagrant, a beggar, or a shaman who traverses the liminal space between nature and civilization.

The British colonial rule of Malaya brought about an unprecedented disruption that was at once ecological and cosmological. Tigers were massacred, and weretigers exiled to the realm of folklore.

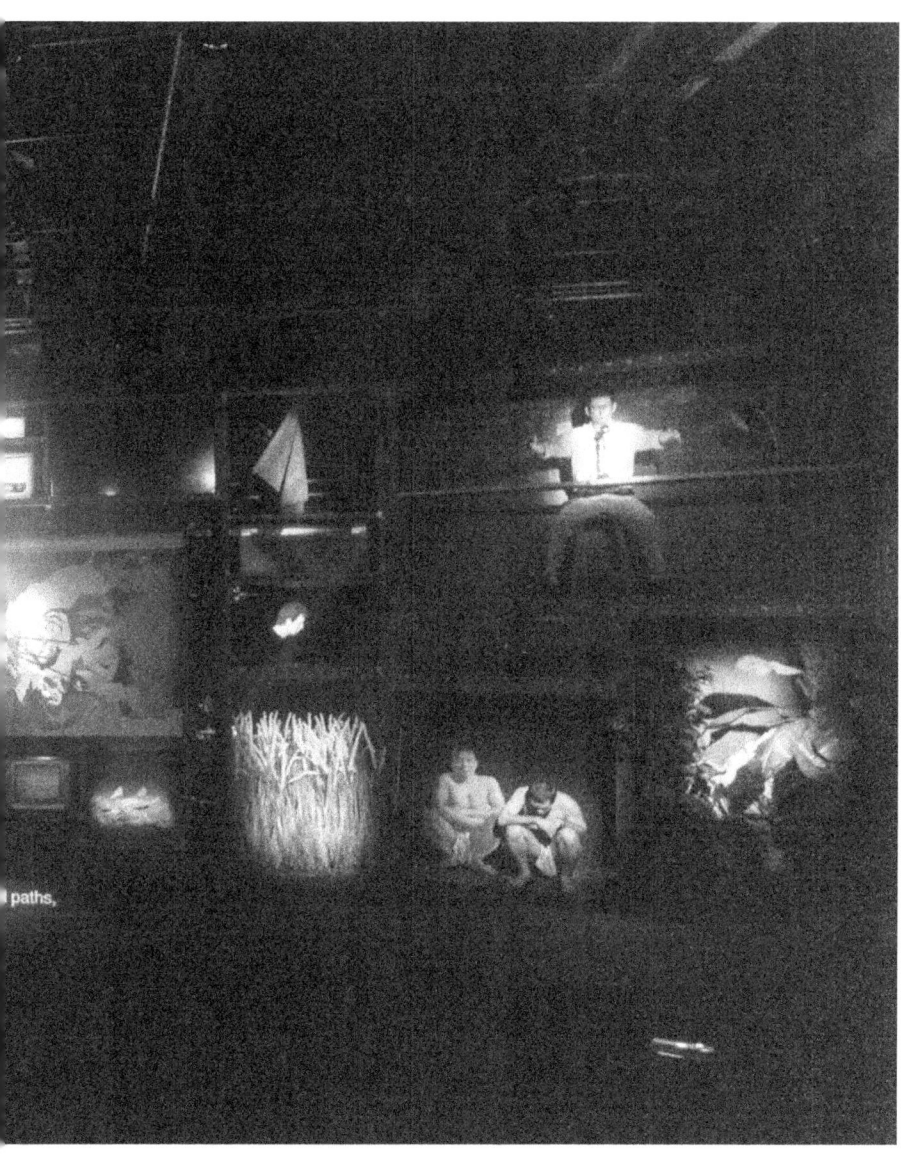

But they keep coming back in different forms. In 1942, the Japanese 25th Army led by Japanese General Tomoyuki Yamashita, known also as the "Tiger of Malaya," exacted revenge upon the British forces in Malaya. Moving swiftly through the forest—savage, amphibious, and full of guile in battle—the Japanese forces seem to embody the very qualities that had made the tiger such a feared adversary of the early British settlers.

The principal resistance in Malaya against the Japanese occupation was the Malayan Peoples' Anti-Japanese Army, a guerilla organization under the leadership of the Malayan Communist Party. When the Japanese forces surrendered in 1945, the epithet of "tiger" gradually transferred to the Communists, who now constituted a very real threat to the returning British forces which were deflated and weakened by the war. The British eventually responded by intensifying their regulation of forested zones, offering cash bounties, organizing hunts and ambushes—similar strategies previously employed to annihilate the Malayan tigers. And in the shadows of the dense tropical forest, the British hunters of Communist guerillas sometimes found themselves coming face to face with tigers instead.

To embark upon the trail of the weretiger is to follow through with its line of perpetual metamorphosis and seek in the entanglements of this anthropomorphic but not anthropocentric line, the shape of a Malayan world.

Notes

1 Robert Wessing, *The Soul of Ambiguity: The Tiger in Southeast Asia* (DeKalb: Center for Southeast Asian Studies, Northern Illinois University, 1986). See also Peter Boomgaard's *Frontiers of Fear: Tigers and People in the Malay World*, 1600–1950 (New Haven: Yale University Press, 2001), as well as Kevin Chua's "The Tiger and the Theodolite: George Coleman's Dream of Extinction," *FOCAS: Forum on Contemporary Art and Society 6* (Singapore, 2007).

Technologies of Uncertainty in the Search for MH370

Lindsay Bremner

It is very rare, if ever, that the Southern Indian Ocean has come into view with the intensity that it did than during the search for missing Malaysian Airways Flight MH370 in March and April 2014. In what follows, I will recount the futile search to locate the airplane in this remote and inhospitable part of the ocean and argue that its continued invisibility reveals that the ocean remains a limit condition to contemporary human knowledge—its validity, methods, technologies, and scope.

Other than for those present on search vessels or aircraft, the search unfolded as what Karin Knorr Cetina calls a "synthetic situation."[1] It was a distant and invisible operation made situationally present around the globe through an extended sensorium of remote-sensing and screen-based technologies, the self-same infrastructure through which global climate change is modelled, global financial markets driven, anthropogenic changes to Arctic ice tracked, and oil and gas exploration carried out, among other operations. As the search continued, the data produced by this scopic system did not merely presence the search: it propelled it forward. Measurements, statistics, and simulations served in lieu of evidence and as the basis of authoritative political pronouncements. At the same time, they were shown to be wired with uncertainty and failure, thwarted by the ocean's unassailable materiality and indifference not only to forms of life, but human ways of knowing.

The airplane cockpit is the quintessential scoped, synthetic situation, where all transactions take place with a future goal in mind—typically, a safe landing at a projected destination.[2] Pilots are continuously bombarded with and respond to streamed data leading them toward this predetermined goal. This makes a synthetic situation "fateful,"[3] as it is charged with significance and directed at an anticipated but uncertain future. An airplane flight is an "engine of fatefulness,"[4] thrusting pilots and passengers into a temporally organized, synthetic engagement within a vast scopic system—air traffic control towers, satellites, data link systems, data feeds, radio, radar, etc.—that articulates their developing fate. Knorr Cetina suggests that this fatefulness is inherent to all scopic systems because of their enhanced informational content: "They make visible, project, and record things that cannot be seen in a physical situation, [...] casually implicating themselves in the progress of the situation and its outcomes."[5] It is this scopic fatefulness that was scrolled through, replayed, modelled, and mobilized as evidence in the search for MH370.

The Aircraft Communications Addressing and Reporting System (ACARS) is a digital data link system used to transmit messages between aircraft and ground stations via radio or satellite. It is turned on and off manually by a switch on the ceiling of the cockpit or behind the throttles between the pilot and co-pilot, but it has a second terminal that operates independently and cannot be switched off while the aircraft still has power. After MH370's ACARS data transmission link ceased operating (or was shut down), this second terminal continued to respond automatically to seven hourly pings from Inmarsat-3 F1,[6] a geostationary satellite hovering 35,800 kilometres above the equator, over the Indian Ocean.[7] The last of the seven pings from MH370 was received by Inmarsat's satellite ground station in Perth, Australia at 08:19 on 9 March 2014.

This little batch of seven pings between MH370 and Inmarsat-3 F1 is, as yet, the only confirmed evidence of the airplane's existence after it disappeared from radar screens. They were extracted from deep inside the architecture of the scopic system that fed the airplane and were enhanced and "fatefully modelled," to use Knorr Cetina's terminology, to determine the airplane's likely destination.[8] Pings themselves do not specify a plane's location or the direction it is heading, but they provide two kinds of data that are useful for this purpose. The first is the time it takes for the ping to travel between satellite and aircraft, from which the distance between the two can be calculated; the second is the radio frequency at which the response is received by the satellite (the pitch of its voice), from which it can be calculated whether the plane was moving towards or away from the satellite when it was transmitted, using the so-called Doppler effect, which we commonly experience as the modulating sound of a train approaching and leaving a platform.[9] Inmarsat engineers took the data provided by the seven pings and modelled possible flight paths to fit them, one following a northbound trajectory, one a southbound. Ping frequency data closely matched the southbound path.[10] This is the basis on which engineers and officials have been so confident that the plane went south.

If one examines the ping data and their ongoing interpretation by investigators, it becomes clear that the judgments made about them were intricate, inductive arguments, not verifiable truths. They were mathematical models or simulations, on the basis of which decisions were made and actions followed. Models, however, cannot be verified; they can only be validated, i.e. be shown to have internal consistency. At best, they can be confirmed if their results agree with observation, but they can never be proven correct.[11] The ping data were subjected to mathematical and computational techniques for drawing information out of them to model likely flight paths and predict where the plane went down. This involved a raft of assumptions, algorithms, judgments and approximations, theories about airplane speed and height, satellite position and movement, atmospheric conditions, etc.—all of which produced different results. Modelling is only ever an "inexact science."[12] Even most data themselves depend on modelling and are inherently uncertain. Joseph Dumit reminds us that in all communication systems, every transponding event, such as a satellite ping, is cause for existential doubt.[13] Each interface a ping passes through generates a new ping; it does not just pass the ping received along. Pings are like whispered messages in a game of broken telephone. Participants (interfaces) can never be certain about what they have heard; they compile data from fuzzy audio sensoria and make judgments about them before relaying them on. "Each interface, gap, and infinitesimal delay," Dumit tells us, "poses the question of truth."[14] How much more so in the case of remote sensing systems, where interfaces are required to aggregate uncertain signals transmitted across vast distances through a changing atmosphere distorted by Doppler and other effects, and sort and rank them for truth before emitting them again. They are, says Dumit, "structurally and logically paranoid,"[15] wired with uncertainty, anxiety, and neuroses.

The Inmarsat data, once released, coursed through the media as maps, charts, diagrams, and pronouncements, and was mobilized in the service of socio-political priorities and agendas. The official map shared by Malaysian authorities with families of victims and the public on 15 March and sent around the world on Reuter's twitter feed showed a series of concentric circles radiating out from the Inmarsat F3-1 satellite.[16] On one of them, the two arcs are outlined in red, indicated the "last known possible position" of MH370, based on "satellite data."[17] Stamped with the seal of authority, this map ascribed to the data a regime of truth, anchoring its analyses with scientific and graphic certainty. On 24 March 2014, Malaysian Prime Minister Najib Razak announced that the airplane had crashed in the southern Indian Ocean "beyond reasonable doubt," and was lost with no survivors—thus attributing agency to the Inmarsat data.[18]

This directed the search to a vast, unbounded, deep, cold, turbulent ocean region subject to some of the most dynamic weather conditions on the planet. It is swept by unrelenting westerly winds *driving cold fronts ahead of them;* during the search, a typhoon swirled across the sea, cancelling search operations for two days. The waves in this part of the ocean are monstrous, dwarfing the ships sent out to search it; it is whipped up into storms by the bands of low-pressure sweeping eastwards across it. Powerful undercurrents run below its surface: the Antarctic Circumpolar Current, which transports 130 billion cubic metres of water per second eastwards around the southern part of the planet, and the Indian Ocean Gyre swirling counter-clockwise up the west coast of Australia. Moulded by little-known trenches and mountains on the seafloor, these currents connect deep, cold, abyssal waters with the surface and, influenced by differences in speed, temperature, salinity and pressure, they collide, swirling, eddying and transmitting energy in complicated, turbulent, non-linear ways. The crash site was located in the boundary between these two currents, in a "sea of uncertainty,"[19] where eddies are about sixty miles wide and debris can travel up to thirty miles a day. Oceanographic and meteorological experts expressed doubts of finding any plane debris at all; even if it was spotted, it could have drifted hundreds of miles before being verified.[20]

Looking for plane debris in the ocean began in outer space. It mobilized a vast array of satellites, floats, drifting buoys, data collection systems on ships, computer screens, imaging techniques, UN agencies and protocols, national agencies, and private companies. On 11 March, China's Meteorological Administration requested activation of the "Charter On Cooperation To Achieve The Coordinated Use Of Space

Facilities In The Event Of Natural Or Technological Disasters" (2000) to gain access to global satellite imagery. The fifteen national and international organizations signatory to the charter were required to supply space-based remote-sensing data free of charge in support of the search effort. DigitalGlobe, the commercial US satellite operator, expanded its Tomnod crowdsourcing platform to engage the public in the search for the missing plane.[21] Satellite imagery of the ocean's surface was uploaded to the Tomnod site; alerted on Facebook when new imagery was available, amateur data analysts were able to view it and tag potential signs of wreckage by dropping a pin onto a satellite map. A crowd-rank algorithm then identified overlaps in tagged locations before they were investigated by DigitalGlobe analysts.[22] On 16 March, images of two large objects floating in the Indian Ocean 2,400 kilometres southwest of Perth were sent to the Australian Maritime Safety Authority.[23]

The two DigitalGlobe images were assessed by the Australian Geospatial-Intelligence Organisation as "credible."[24] Two days later, Chinese news agency *Xinhua* published images of two more large objects, spotted close to the DigitalGlobe sightings by one of its satellites. A third set of satellite data, released on 23 March by French satellite sources indicated a possible debris field of 122 objects of varying sizes 2,600 kilometres southwest of Perth. At this point, Malaysia's acting transport minister Hishammuddin Hussein confidently said the find was "the most credible lead we have" and "consistent with a plane having struck the sea nearby."[25] A day later, Thailand's Earth Observation Satellite, Thaichote, spotted over 300 new objects 170 kilometres outside the international search area, and a report from Tokyo announced that a Japanese satellite had also spotted about ten objects possibly related to the missing airplane.[26] With this mounting evidence of possible plane debris, Australia set up a Joint Agency Co-ordination Centre (JACC), required of it by Section 2.2 of the International Convention on Maritime Search and Rescue, to co-ordinate the search operation. Each morning it issued a media release about the search to be conducted that day, including maps showing the current location of search vessels, grey patches indicating areas of the ocean already searched and the search area planned for the day, as measured from the land mass of Western Australia.[27]

While graphically appearing to represent the progress being made in the search, these maps failed to take into account the ocean's constitutive mobility. Static representations of ocean space are false representations of geophysical processes.[28] Put simply, an expanse of ocean water, designated as having been searched by a patch of grey on a map, would not be the same ocean from one day to the next. Knowledge of the ocean is not situated knowledge. One simply cannot plot the ocean through stable co-ordinates. To map it, one has to follow its vectors of movement. This Langrangian perspective[29] is beautifully illustrated in an animation released by Australia's Commonwealth Scientific and Industrial Research Organization (CSIRO) of part of the ocean off the west coast of Australia between latitudes 24°S and 47°S.[30] [Fig. 01] Ocean temperature is shown as a colour gradient, from blue (6°C) to red (27°C). Two strands of debris in the form of black particles are released into

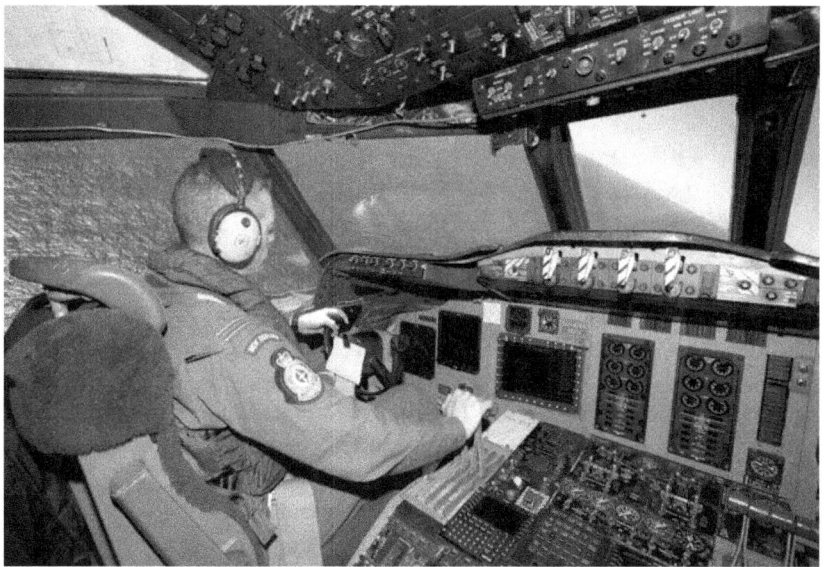

Debris Scattering in the Southern Ocean. From Carol Saab, "What's Our Role in the Search for Missing Flight MH370?" *news@CSIRO*, 28 March 2014, www.csironewsblog.com/2014/03/28/whats-our-role-in-the-search-for-missing-flight-mh370.

Fig. 01

this swirling mass of colour from the bottom left-hand corner. They are caught up in eddies and swirls and pushed in complex, non-linear ways northeastwards, dispersing laterally as they move. They are ultimately caught in a temperature gradient at around 30°S and spun around and around in swirling eddies and dispersed into a vast debris field. This was a far more truthful, but disorientating, portrayal of the ocean than the static grey patches released by the JACC. By alerting us to the incessantly mobile territoriality of the ocean, it radically un-grounded fixed notions of place, as well as the standpoint of authority over the ocean projected by the JACC.

The remoteness of the search location was barely comprehensible. Aircraft flew from Pearce Air Force Base on ten-hour missions each day searching for debris: three hours heading out to sea, three-to-four hours searching (depending on weather conditions), and three hours heading back to base. Searches were divided into legs, straight lines of flying lasting for thirty to forty minutes, clearly visible strips on the maps of areas searched. At this point, the vast scopic system mobilized by the search came down to the human eye. Each plane carried five observers, one resting while two peered through its windows in each direction. Most of the people doing this were among the 200 Australian State Emergency Service volunteers from Western Australia, New South Wales, and Victoria who signed up for it, indicating the extent to which Australians subscribed to the search-and-rescue narrative.[31] Searching required saccading, a particular way of looking that involved moving the head up and down in a fixed position to scan foreground, middle ground, background with pin point accuracy, while talking to keep the concentration going. Once a piece of potential debris was spotted, ships in the vicinity were alerted and divers were sent to investigate it further.[32] On 6 April, the Australian Defence Force released a video of a group of divers investigating a piece of ocean debris.[33] A diver surfaces from the water with a small item held between thumb and forefinger. He swims to the side of a dinghy where he hands it to a member of the Australian Navy. This person takes it between thumb and forefinger of both hands, inspects it briefly, and then tosses it contemptuously into the bottom of the dinghy. There is something enormously incongruous, funny even, about a search for a missing airplane that began in outer space, mobilized a vast scopic system, was modelled and simulated by countless agencies, and flowed across millions of computer screens coming down to this minute, intimate conclusion—a second or two of a tiny piece of marine trash held between eye, thumb, and forefinger being casually inspected and then tossed aside. Sightings of objects became more sporadic and none were linked to the disappeared plane. They turned out to be abandoned fishing equipment, the carcass of a dead whale, or other pieces of marine trash.[34]

As the surface-water search for debris went on, the underwater search for the airplane's black boxes began. This brought into play the agency of the oceanic volume, with its multi-layered spatiality, unassailable opacity, unreadability, and more-than-human cunning to thwart surveillance technology. The ocean volume is what Gastón Gordillo calls a "liquid vortex," a "pure multiplicity of intensities in motion."[35] It owes its materiality to the anomalous physical properties of water, kept in permanent motion because its molecules are constantly making, breaking, and reforming bonds with one another, and, in the ocean, adapting to the shape of the earth's surface and being mobilized by the forces of the planet and its atmosphere. The surface of the ocean is not level; it follows gravity, pushed up by underwater ridges and slumping down into underwater troughs. Its water mass is not homogeneous, but a multi-layered spatiality, defined by permanently changing differences in temperature, salinity, and pressure. These differences divide the ocean into layers through which huge volumes of water circulate as currents and underwater rivers, mobilized by the rotation of the earth around its own axis and around the sun, by exposure to the atmosphere, and the gravity of the moon. Sound waves move through water more than four times faster than they do through air, but in the ocean, their movement is affected by differences in temperature, pressure, and salinity. In the thermocline, the middle layer of the ocean, temperature and density change very quickly.[36] This can have the effect of warping sound waves, sometimes by 90 degrees.[37] Sound waves can take squiggly, unpredictable paths through this layer, bouncing back and forth and becoming caught up in sound channels that carry them sideways for long distances. The retired French naval officer Paul-Henry Nargeolet, who led the searches for the Titanic and AF447, said that because of this he did not put much faith in acoustic findings and would not believe MH370's whereabouts had been found until wreckage was seen.[38]

All commercial airplanes are required to carry underwater locator beacons, otherwise known as "pingers," to locate their black boxes should they crash into water. These emit ultrasonic pings at 37.5 kHz (the human ear hears sounds up to about 2 kHz) once per second for approximately thirty days after an aircraft goes missing, when their batteries die. In the search for MH370's black box, three types of devices were deployed. The Australian naval vessel *Ocean Shield* towed a one-metre-wide, thirty-two-kilogram underwater "trailed pinger locator" (TPL-25) on loan from the US Navy, built and operated by the US company Phoenix International. We saw a great deal of TPL-25 in the media; it looked like a yellow stingray and was equipped with a sensor that could recognize flight recorder signals up to 6,000 metres below the ocean's surface while towed at speeds of up to 3 knots. At this speed and because turning around was a long process given the huge lengths of cable involved, it was only able to scan a 4.8-square-kilometre area per day in seven-to-eight hour stretches. In addition, the Chinese patrol ship *Haixun 01* used hand-held devices lowered over the side of small open boats, and Royal Australian Aircraft dropped sonobuoy listening devices—small, portable sonar units—into the ocean. On 6 April 2014, the Australian Defence Force released two short videos of the pings picked up by TPL-25.[39] In the first video,[40] the yellow towed pinger locator is lowered into the water from the deck of *Ocean Shield*. It then cuts to an operator in front of a computer screen, the bottom half of which is covered with flickering horizontal yellow lines on a dark background, the upper half with a corresponding vertical graph; the visual display is accompanied by an acoustic hum. The video then cuts to full screen, where we see that this is a screen shot of data visualized by Spectrum Lab V2.79b11, freely downloadable spectrum analysis software. It displays the frequency of signals being picked up on the horizontal axis and amplitude on the vertical axis as a colour spectrum. The towed pinger locator appears as a red dot moving slowly across the lower part of the screen where a point is marked and labelled as 33.20271 kHz, -66.98 db. Slowly, a distinctive acoustic beat emerges from the low-level humming noise at approximately one-second intervals, corresponding with a spike on the vertical axis of the graph at the top of the screen. The display then changes to a three-dimensional sweep across a topography of sound waves visualized as a colourful, undulating surface, the distinctive signal puncturing upwards into the red colour spectrum at regular intervals. The second video repeats similar footage.[41] This imaging of the acoustic signal was an enormously powerful one. The signal was made available to experience through scopic media as rhythmic waveforms resembling those of heartbeats displayed by electrocardiograph machines. The missing airplane was made situationally present through what looked and sounded like tenuous, fragile, yet still living heartbeats.

This anthropomorphic association made the revelation on 30 May 2014, after weeks of fruitless underwater scanning for the missing airplane, that these signals were not from the aircraft's black boxes after all, doubly hard to bear. The pinger sounds, it was suggested, could have come from the search boat, the pinger-detector itself, or from other sources such as tagged sea creatures.[42] MH370's pulses could also have been drowned out by many other sounds in an increasingly industrialized marine environment of shipping traffic, oil and gas exploration and production, recreational activity, and so on, which scientists refer to as "ocean smog."[43] The ocean, they say, is "full of pings."[44] Not only had the ocean been shown to be capable of lying and the instruments used to listen to it faulty and prone to error, the screen-based media that filtered and translated their data had been shown to be cruelly deceptive. Its affect was not a reduction of uncertainty in the face of disaster, but its magnification, increasing feelings of anger and helplessness in families of the crash victims and affirming, more generally, the "dangerous threshold of existence" in a contemporary world where the human sensorium is increasingly dependent on such remote sensing technologies.[45] However, scientists and political authorities continued to lay claim to the ping data as incontestable evidence of the airplane's whereabouts. "There is no other noise like this," said oceanographer Chari Pattiaratchi, "I have absolute confidence that the airplane will be found."[46]

This data resulted in the deployment of *Ocean Shield* to scan the ocean floor within a twelve-kilometre radius of the strongest pings, while the surface hunt for debris continued. Another instrument on loan from the US Navy, Phoenix International's Autonomous Underwater Bluefin-21 "Artemis," was deployed for this task, a yellow, 5.3-metre-long, 725-kilogram remotely operated vehicle. The depth it could operate at was upgraded from 1,500 to 4,500 metres only in July 2013, so this was likely one of its first deployments at deeper depths.[47] It worked by sweeping sonar pulses underneath its chassis in two arcs, producing acoustic reflections of objects on the seabed, while also collecting high-resolution black-and-white imagery at up to three frames per second. Hopes of finding the plane were pinned on this single piece of equipment diving to unprecedented depths. After some initial programming glitches, it was deployed on eighteen twenty-four-hour missions, taking four hours to dive and resurface, sixteen hours to scan, and four hours to download the recorded data each time. Significantly, none of this data has ever been publicly released. In its absence, however, some extraordinary and somewhat comical depictions of the oceanic volume appeared in the media, attempts at visualizing the ocean's depth and make it more humanly comprehensible.

The *Washington Post Online* published a scroll-down visualization of ocean depth titled "The Depth of the Problem."[48] [Fig. 02] At the top of the drawing are vector shapes of a Boeing 777-200 and the Australian naval vessel *Ocean Shield*, with their dimensions annotated (18-metres-wide for the airplane, 106-metres-long for the vessel, with a draft of 7 metres). Beneath this, a number of buildings are overlaid, floating upside down, with their heights annotated: the Washington Monument (-170 metres), the Empire State Building (-381 metres) and the Burj Khalifa (-828 metres). As one scrolls down, one passes lines annotated with water depth and pressure and the colour of the ocean gets gradually darker. After the Burj Khalifa, sea creatures, underwater submersibles or previous disasters are used to give a sense of scale: the test depth of the American Seawolf-class submarine (-515 metres); the maximum known depth at which giant squid swim (-792 metres); the maximum depth sperm whales are known to dive (-1000 metres); the depth at which the towed pinger locater detected ping signals (-1403 metres); the depth the pinger locater would probably have to reach to hear a ping on the ocean floor, depending on oceanic conditions (-1829 metres); the maximum known depth

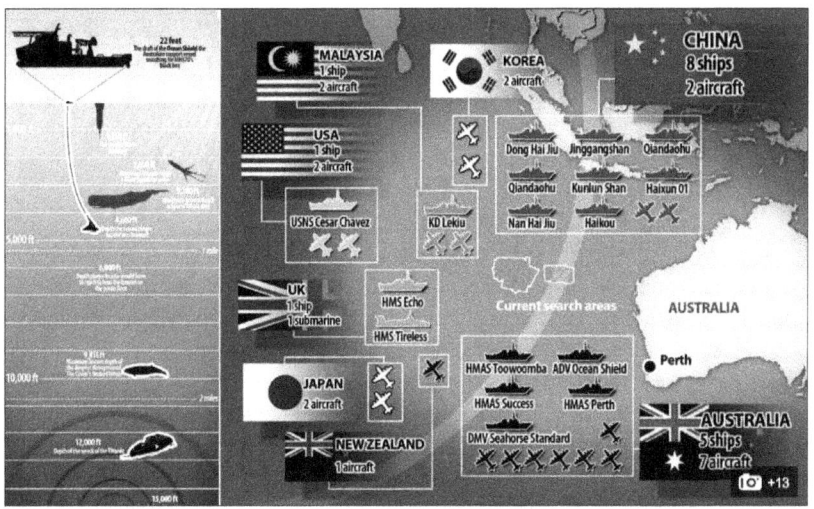

Richard Johnson and Ben Chartoff, "The Depth of the Problem," *Washington Post*, apps.washingtonpost.com/g/page/world/the-depth-of-the-problem/931. Fig. 02

reached by a Cuvier's beaked whale (-2992 metres); the depth at which the wreck of the Titanic was found (-3810 metres); the depth at which flight data recorders from Air France Flight 447 were found (-3993 metres); the depth Alvin, the first deep-sea submersible able to carry passengers dived (-4500 metres); and, the depth the signal from MH370 was thought to have been detected (-4572 metres).

This graphic is a patchwork of data drawn from multiple sources: the Australian Maritime Authority, *Hydro International* magazine, NOAA Fisheries, the BBC, and Plos One. It reveals its own institutional address, *The Washington Post*, through the selection of objects it uses to scale the ocean. These lay claim to the ocean as a cultural artifact by comparing it with objects whose dimensions are likely to be familiar to a US audience. A similar graphic on the UK's *The Guardian* website does so through a different set of cultural co-ordinates, more familiar to a British or European audience: the wreck of the Russian submarine Kursk (-108 metres); an inverted London Shard (-306 metres) and 1 World Trade Centre (-541 metres); the depth light can penetrate the ocean (-1000 metres); the average depth of the Mediterranean (-1494 metres); and the deepest living octopus (-3962 metres).[49] Making the ocean comprehensible in this way uses familiarity to appropriate and colonize it; it is represented as a US ocean or a UK ocean by way of the things that inhabit it in media space.

These diagrams reduce oceanic volume to a two-dimensional swatch of graded turquoise colour overlaid with a rhetorically selected collection of textual information and icons. These incorporate an eclectic mix of land- and sea-based images, buildings, mountains, bits of technology, sea creatures, past disasters at sea, current events, and straightforward empirical measurements such as ocean depth and pressure. They get us no further in imaging the ocean than the medieval Catalan Atlas (1375) or Cantabrian sailor and cartographer Juan de la Cosa's *Mappa Mundi* (1500), which depicted the ocean as a two-dimensional surface crossed by rhumb lines and illustrated with astronomical, astrological, and religious references and images from travel literature. Sense is made by constructing the ocean as a mythological space, in which multiple places and times overlap, and multiple representations are conjoined. These diagrams are not so much diagrams of the ocean as diagrams of ways of navigating the assemblage of technologies and institutions that make ocean space visible today. To quote from Stephan Helmreich, in his discussion of Google Ocean, they are diagrams of "the ways that many of us image now, layering icons, indexes, and symbols on top of a world of previous infrastructures, transparent and opaque, taken for granted and found as well as forgotten."[50] But this eclectic collection of icons and measurements only really makes sense relative to the objects chosen; and in fact, they render the entity they are supposed to give scale to even more vast and incomprehensible. Beyond a certain depth, there are no measures of ocean depth left, and uncertainty prevails; the depth a pinger locater *would probably* have to reach, the depth the signal *was thought to have been* detected, etc., are the only clues given. Thus the ocean ultimately evades attempts to codify and scale it against objects or events whose dimensions are strictly terrestrial or a part of human history.

After it disappeared on 8 March 2014, the on-going invisibility of Malaysian Airlines flight MH370 opened a window onto the forceful, turbulent materiality of the southern Indian Ocean and brought it into contact with humans with an intensity and at a scale never experienced before. This made a remote oceanic region and hidden information worlds situationally present via the global media, the internet, blogs, social media, through reports and official statements, videos, diagrams, and images. An extensive scopic system transformed the ocean's surface, waves, currents, and depths into what Heller and Pezzani call "a vast and extended sensorium, a sort of digital archive,"[51] which could then be interrogated and cross-examined as a witness to the airplane's disappearance. As we have seen, however, the ocean is not a very reliable witness, and the very instruments and techniques used to probe, calibrate, and digitize it are easily outwitted by its materiality—its fluidity, turbulence, crushing water pressure, impenetrable depths, and seawater's capacity to "suck up"[52] the electromagnetic radiation most modern communication technology relies on. The ocean was shown to be an unassailably opaque, more-than-human vortex, whose materiality and agency unhinged the global panopticon and thwarted all human attempts to probe it. This provided a privileged, if tragic, moment to get a little closer to understanding the properties of the ocean itself, "a vast liquid space whose ambient thickness and intensity is in a permanent state of becoming: folding, shifting, arching, twisting; always in motion, always displacing its volume across vast distances, always indifferent to the life forms enveloped by its mobile flows."[53]

Notes

1   Karin Knorr Cetina, "The Synthetic Situation: Interactionism for a Global World," *Symbolic Interaction* 32, no. 1 (2009): 61–87.

2   Ibid.

3   Ibid, 81.

4   Ibid.

5   Ibid, 82.

6   "Ping" is a common term in IT networking vocabulary. It refers to the utility used to test the reachability of a host on an IP network and measure the round-trip time of a signal. In an ACARS network, a satellite sends a signal about once an hour to a receiver on an aircraft, which sends back a response signal, or handshake, thus confirming that it is still on the network. See David Cenciotti, "What SATCOM, ACARS and Pings Tell Us about the Missing Malaysia Airlines MH370," *The Aviationist*, 16 March 2014, www.theaviationist.com/2014/03/16/satcom-acars-explained.

7   A geostationary satellite is one that moves around the earth at the earth's own angular velocity and thus appears not to move. Because Inmarsat-3 F1 was launched in 1996 and has deteriorated, it is no longer absolutely geostationary, but moves from a height of 35,793 to 35,806 kilometres above the earth's surface, from 1.539N to 1.539S and 64.471E to 64.594 E. Taking into account these slight movements in relation to the earth adjusted the analysis of where the airplane had come down. See Duncan Steel, "The Locations of Inmarsat-3F1 when Pinging MH370," 24 March 2014, www.duncansteel.com/the-locations-of-inmarsat-3f1-when-pinging-mh370.

8   Alan Schuster-Bruce, "Where is Flight MH370?" *BBC Two, Horizon*, 17 June 2014.

9   Ari N. Schulman, "Why the Official Explanation of MH370's Demise Doesn't Hold Up," *The Atlantic, Technology*, 8 May 2014, www.theatlantic.com/technology/archive/2014/05/why-the-official-explanation-of-mh370s-demise-doesnt-hold-up/361826.

10 Ibid.

11 Paul Edwards, "Global Climate Science, Uncertainty and Politics: Data-laden Models, Model-filtered Data," *Science as Culture* 8, no. 4 (1999): 437–472.

12 Ibid.; see also Gordon Rayner and Nick Collins, "MH370: Britain Finds Itself at Centre of Blame Game Over Crucial Delays," *The Telegraph*, 24 March 2014, www.telegraph.co.uk/news/worldnews/asia/malaysia/10722009/MH370-Britain-finds-itself-at-centre-of-blame-game-over-crucial-delays.html.

13 Joseph Dumit, "Neuroexistentialism," in *Sensorium: Embodied Experience, Technology and Contemporary Art*, ed. Caroline Jones (Cambridge, MA.: MIT Press, 2006), 182–189.

14 Ibid., 184.

15 Ibid., 185.

16 Reuters Aerospace News, "Two red arcs pinned up in media centre describe possible position of #MH370," *AerospaceNews@ReutersAero*, 15 March 2014, twitter.com/ReutersAero/status/444870615330078720.

17 Ibid.

18 "Malaysia Plane: Families Told Missing Flight Lost," *BBC News*, 24 March 2014, www.bbc.co.uk/news/world-asia-26718462.

19 Jonathan Amos, "Malaysian Airlines MH370: Searching in an Ocean of Uncertainty," *BBC News*, 9 April 2014, www.bbc.co.uk/news/science-environment-26956798.

20 Paul Farrell, "Flight MH370: Indian Ocean Objects Might Have Drifted Hundreds of Miles," *The Guardian*, 1 March 2014, www.theguardian.com/world/2014/mar/21/flight-mh370-indian-ocean-objects.

21 "Missing Airplane: Malaysian Airlines MH370," *Tomnod*, 18 March 2014, www.tomnod.com/nod/challenge/malaysiaairsar2014.

22 Dave Lee, "Malaysia Missing Plane: Armchair Aeroplane Hunters Head online," *BBC News*, 18 March 2014, www.bbc.co.uk/news/technology-25051663; Amy Svitak, "Digital Globe Supplies Images to MH370 Search," *Aviation Week*, 20 March, 2014, www.aviationweek.com/space/digitalglobe-supplies-images-mh370-search; also, Germany's commercial remote-sensing service provider, BlackBridge, offers a similar crowdsourcing capability, with images from its satellites loaded onto a MapBox platform: "Search for Flight MH 370," *BlackBridge*, www.mapbox.com/labs/blackbridge/flight-mh370/#4/-25.44/105.73.

23 It was not revealed whether Tomnod played a role in identifying the data sent by Digital Globe to the Australian authorities. What was released, though, was that before its use in the MH370 search, Tomnod had 10,000 users. After the flight went missing, the platform was visited by 3.6 million participants, who generated more than 385 million map views and tagged 4.7 million objects.

24 Svitak, "Digital Globe Supplies Images to MH370 Search."

25 Adam Withnall, "Missing Malaysian Flight MH370: Satellite Images Show 122 Objects in Indian Ocean 'Debris Field'," *The Independent*, 26 March 2014, www.independent.co.uk/news/world/asia/missing-malaysia-flight-mh370-french-satellite-images-show-possible-debris-field-of-122-objects-in-search-area-9216139.html.

26 "Malaysian Plane Search: Thai, Japan Satellites Detect over 300 Objects in Indian Ocean," *Zee News, World*, 28 March 2014, www.zeenews.india.com/news/world/malaysian-plane-search-thai-japan-satellites-detect-over-300-objects-in-indian-ocean_920705.html.

27 See www.jacc.gov.au.

28 Philip E. Steinberg, "Forward: On Thalassography," in *Water Worlds: Human Geographies of the Ocean*, ed. Jon Anderson and Kimberly Peters (Farnsworth: Ashgate, 2014), xiii–xvii.

29 Philip E. Steinberg, "Free Sea," in *Spatiality, Sovereignty and Carl Schmitt*, ed. Stephen Legg (London: Routledge, 2011), 268–275.

30 Carol Saab, "What's Our Role in the Search for Missing Flight MH370?" *news@CSIRO*, 28 March 2014, www.csironewsblog.com/2014/03/28/whats-our-role-in-the-search-for-missing-flight-mh370.

31 Paul Farrell, "SES Volunteers the Eagle Eyes of the MH370 Search," *The Guardian*, 19 April 2014, www.theguardian.com/world/2014/apr/19/ses-volunteers-eagle-eyes-mh370-search.

32 Ibid.

33 Australian Government, Department of Defence, "Divers Checking Debris, DDM Video: V20140204," 6 April 2014, www.video.defence.gov.au/#searchterm,0,OP Southern Indian Ocean ADV Ocea,All.

34 "MH370: Chinese and Australian Ships Draw Blank," *BBC News*, 29 March 2014, www.bbc.co.uk/news/world-asia-26797866.

35 Gastón Gordillo, "The Oceanic Void," *Space and Politics*, 3 April 2014, spaceandpolitics.blogspot.co.uk/2014/04/the-oceanic-void.html.

36 John Roach, "Ocean 'Conveyor Belt' Sustains Sea Life, Study Says," *National Geographic*, 15 June 2004, www.news.nationalgeographic.com/news/2004/06/0615_040614_SouthernOcean.html.

37 Tania Branigan, "MH370: Australia 'Very Confident' Pings Are from Black Box, Says Prime Minister," *The Guardian*, 11 April 2014, www.theguardian.com/world/2014/apr/11/mh370-australia-very-confident-pings-are-from-black-box-says-prime-minister.

38 Ibid.

39 Australian Government, Department of Defence, "Waveforms of Possible Black Box Signal, DDM Video: V20140203," 6 April 2014, www.video.defence.gov.au/#searchterm,0,OP Southern Indian Ocean ADV Ocea,All; Australian Government, Department of Defence, "Second Ping Waveform, DDM Video: V20140224," 6 April 2014, www.video.defence.gov.au/#searchterm,0,OP Southern Indian Ocean ADV Ocea,All.

40 Australian Government, Department of Defence, "Waveforms of Possible Black Box Signal."

41 Australian Government, Department of Defence, "Second Ping Waveform."

42 Chris Richards, "MH370: Black Box 'Pings' May Actually Have Come from Satellite Tracking Devices Tagged to Marine Animals," *Daily Record*, 8 May 2014, www.dailyrecord.co.uk/news/uk-world-news/mh370-black-box-pings-actually-3511000.

43 Ben Brumfield, "Listen for a Ping, and the Water May Play Tricks on You," *CNN*, 13 April 2014, edition.cnn.com/2014/04/11/tech/innovation/mh-370-underwater-sound/index.html.

44 Richards, "MH370: Black Box 'Pings'."

45 Brad Evans and Julian Reid, *Resilient Life: The Art of Living Dangerously* (London: Polity Press, 2014), 13.

46 "Malaysia Airlines Flight MH370 Will Be Found, Expert Says," *CBC News*, 19 April 2014, www.cbc.ca/news/technology/malaysia-airlines-flight-mh370-will-be-found-expert-says-1.2615099.

47 Phoenix International, "Phoenix AUV Now Capable of Diving to 4,500 Meters," 9 July 2013, www.phnx-international.com/news/Phoenix_4500%20meter_AUV_Upgrade.pdf.

48 Richard Johnson and Ben Chartoff, "The Depth of the Problem," *Washington Post*, apps.washingtonpost.com/g/page/world/the-depth-of-the-problem/931.

49 Branigan, "MH370."

50 Stephan Helmreich, "From Spaceship Earth to Google Ocean: Planetary Icons, Indexes and Infrastructures," *Social Research* 78, no. 4 (2011): 1236, web.mit.edu/anthropology/pdf/articles/helmreich/helmreich_spaceship_earth.pdf.

51 Charles Heller and Lorenzo Pezzani, "Liquid Traces: Investigating the Deaths of Migrants at the EU's Maritime Frontier," *Forensis: The Architecture of Public Truth*, ed. Forensic Architecture (Berlin: Sternberg, 2014), 674.

52 Charlie Campbell, "The Reason We Can't Find MH370 Is Because We Are Basically Blind," *Time*, 18 April 2014, www.time.com/67705/mh370-ocean-oceanography-sonar-exploration.

53 Gordillo, "The Oceanic Void."

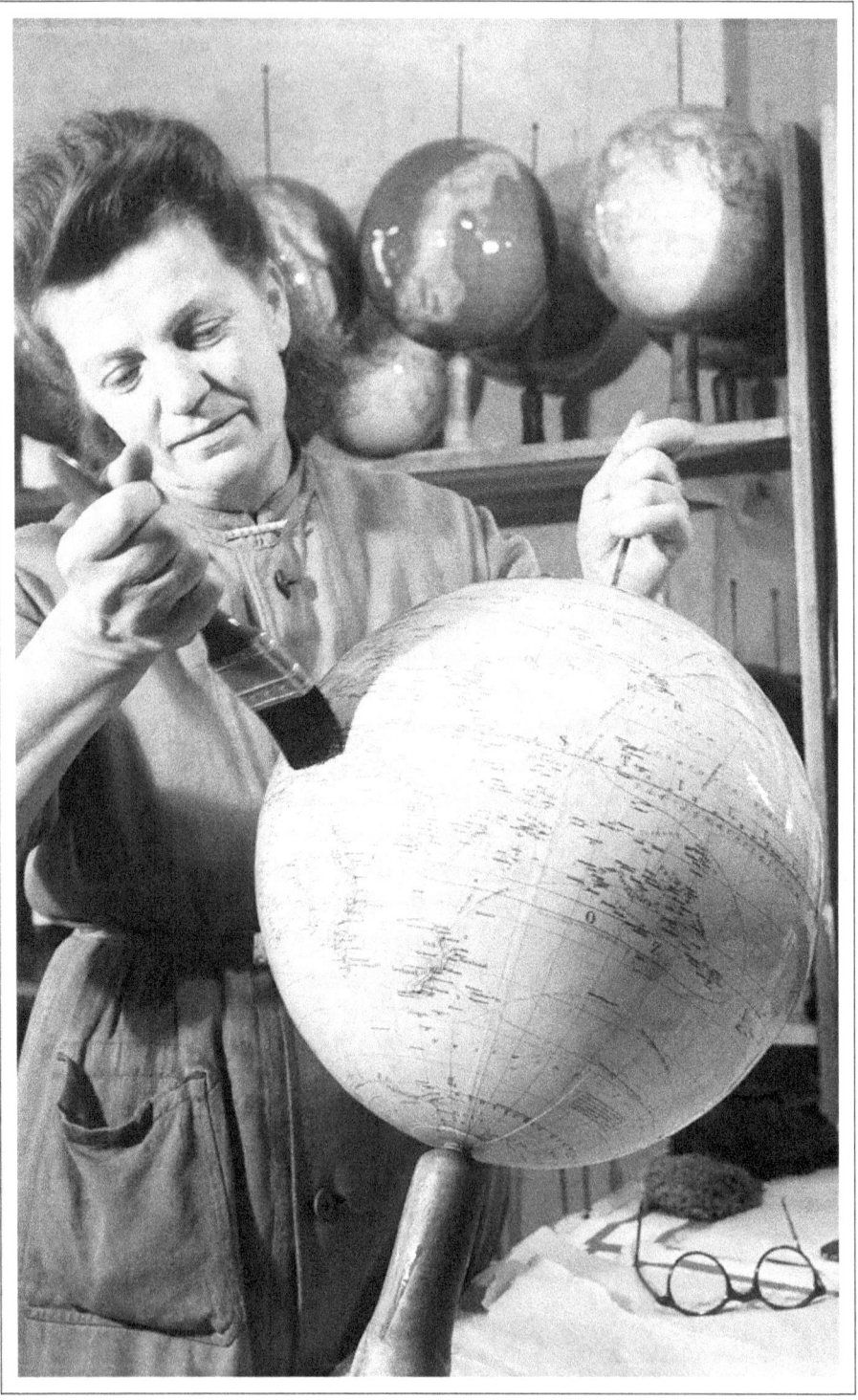

Last Clouds
Karolina Sobecka

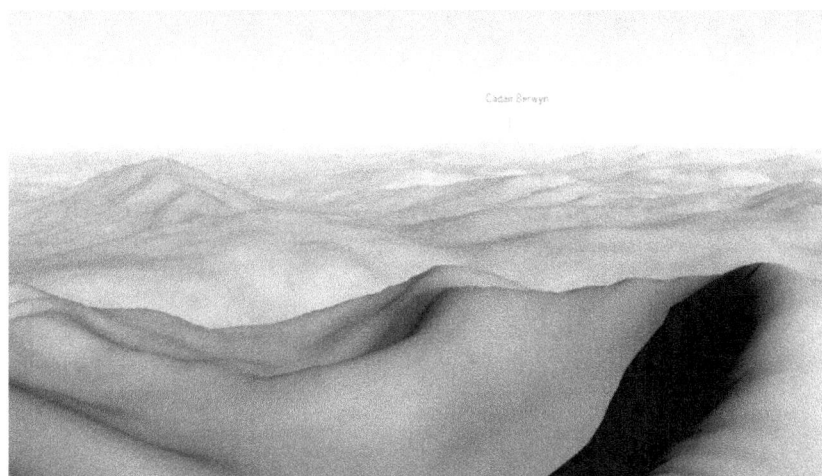

Cadair Berwyn obscures any view of Wrekin. Fig. 01

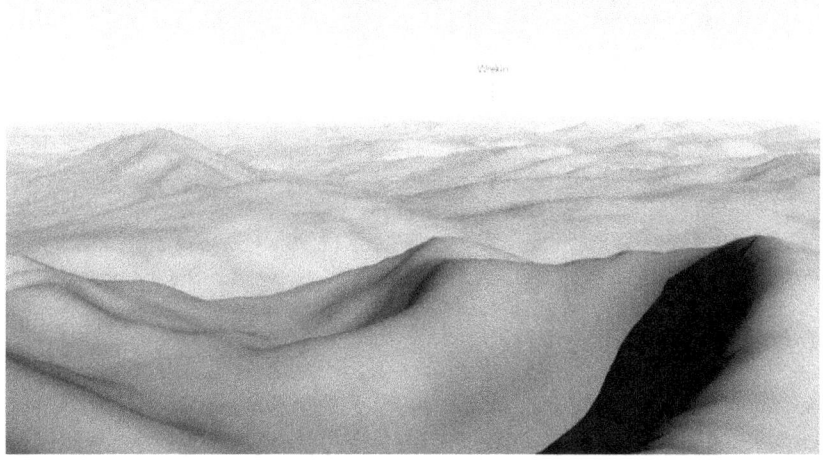

Wrekin is visible on the horizon, peaking from behind Cadair Berwyn. Fig. 02

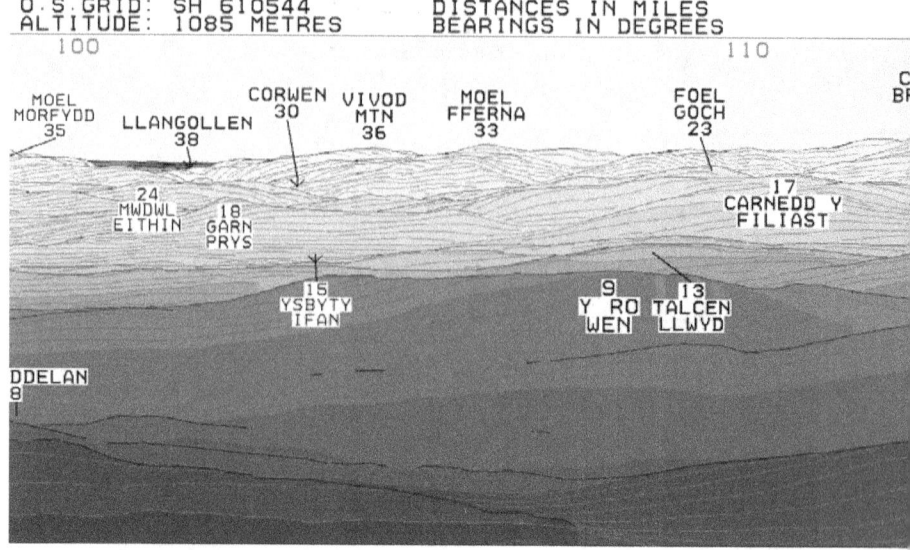

A heated debate has been raging in East Shropshire, England for generations: Can Wrekin mountain be seen from the peak of Snowdon? This question, originally rooted in the experience of standing on a mountaintop and gazing towards the horizon, was eventually settled using digital technologies and remote data sets. Contrary to popular belief, there is no line of sight between these two mountains, according to the topographic data.

Where did this belief come from? It is not based in experience—nobody claims to have actually seen Wrekin from Snowdon. David Squires has tracked the origin of this belief to a suggestion in an poem from 1833, but its subsequent persistence might stem from the fact that the abstract line between Wrekin and Snowdon is much more vivid in our imagination than the hazy view towards the horizon. We know Wrekin is there, so we believe it can be seen: imagination and knowledge extend human vision at its limit.

The more hazy the view towards Wrekin is, the more we rely on our mental model to infer what we see. In this project, I'm interested in how data modelling juts through the experienced world, and how models influence the object being modelled. Scientific models, in a mathematical form, are not mere representations: they generate predictions that shape our actions. Climate models, for example, are used to determine environmental policy decisions in regards to climate change. Moreover, climate models form an epistemological basis for climate engineering, argues philosopher Clive Hamilton: a conception of the Earth as a digital system projected back on Earth makes geo-engineering conceivable. Snowdon-Wrekin

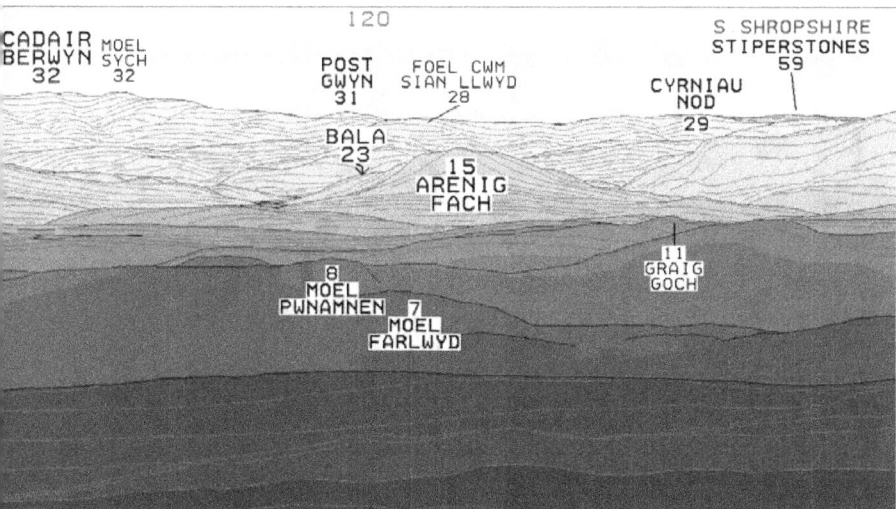

Part of panorama view from Snowdon, looking towards Wrekin. Fig. 03

case is an innocuous example for mapping out the epistemological investments of data modelling in the contemporary world.

In 2000 the Shuttle Radar Topography Mission (SRTM) onboard the Space Shuttle *Endeavour* obtained the elevation data of earth to generate a nearly seamless digital elevation model (DEM). For this project I use SRTM data to reconstruct the geography between Wrekin and Snowdon, and to place the imaginary line connecting the two mountains back in the experience of an eye looking over a landscape. Each of these three proposals accounts for a different notion of what the world is like to reconstruct geography in such a way that the line of sight between Snowdon and Wrekin is uninterrupted. The truisms accounted for are:

1. IMPOSING MOUNTAINS ARE IMPOSING
2. THINGS ON THE HORIZON ARE MYSTERIOUS
3. THE UNKNOWN IS INVISIBLE

The history of the Snowdon-Wrekin sightline is recounted in detail by David Squires in "Can Snowdon Be Seen from Wrekin? A Topographic Detective Story."[1] I was fascinated by this story, as well as by the work of Jonathan de Ferranti, whose website linked to Squires's story and is dedicated to accuracy in geographical representation.[2] His work includes filling in the voids in SRTM data and creating digitally derived panoramas in order to identify geographic features seen from mountain summits.

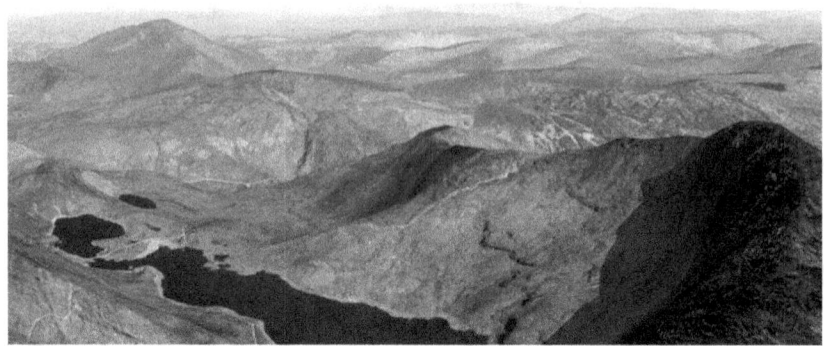

Fig. 04 This is a view from Snowdon after adjustment for our perceptual inflation of isolated peaks.

His panorama from Snowdon [Fig. 03] is the definitive word on whether the line of sight to Wrekin is interrupted or not. Had Wrekin been visible, it would appear in the centre, beyond Cadair Berwyn.

I used SRTM[3] data to reconstruct the region between Snowdon and Wrekin in Vue,[4] a 3D application that is a recent addition to terrain-generation tools.[5]

1. IMPOSING MOUNTAINS ARE IMPOSING

"In the field," writes de Ferranti, "the eye tends to magnify the vertical scale on the horizon."[7] In this proposal, a cartographic projection is created to simulate this effect of our perception on tall mountains. In keeping with the human perception of contrast, the effect is that of a slight inflation of the isolated peaks.[8]

Thus, the magnifying aspect of the eye might be responsible for errors in mountain peak height measurements, as they are frequently inflated compared with topographic data measurements.

Such distortions in our geographical representations are not only frequent, but also necessary for us to be able to categorize the things we encounter. "Not only is it easy to lie with maps, it's essential," writes Mark Monmonier in *How to Lie with Maps*. "To portray meaningful relationships for a complex, three-dimensional world on a flat sheet of paper or a video screen, a map must distort reality."[9]

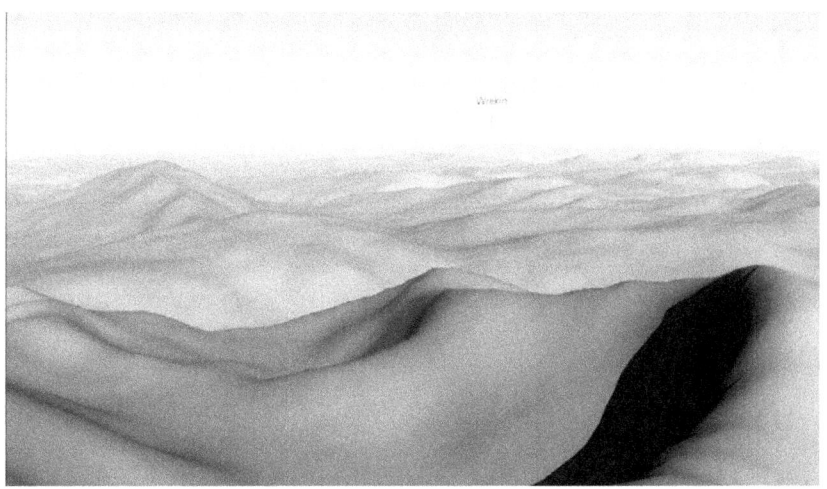

Wrekin is visible on the horizon. Fig. 05

2. THINGS ON THE HORIZON ARE MYSTERIOUS

Things close to the horizon don't always appear as they are. David Squires considers atmospheric refraction in his story, noting that "atmospheric refraction, i.e. the bending of light rays as they pass from lighter, high-altitude air to denser low-altitude air can account for features of the landscape becoming visible or invisible under special atmospheric conditions (e.g. temperature inversions)."[10]

For this proposal, conditions of extreme refraction are created in the simulated atmosphere (equivalent to a refraction coefficient of 0.75). Wrekin is now visible from Snowdon as one looks through such a highly refractive atmosphere.

These graphs [Figs. 07-09] (generated at www.heywhatsthat.com) demonstrate the line of sight: the path of light travelling through the atmosphere at different refraction conditions.

After examining the possibility that special atmospheric conditions might *sometimes* make Wrekin visible, Squires decides it would be very unlikely, as the refraction coefficient would have to be far higher than has ever been recorded in the UK. Squires writes:

> What would be needed for the summit of Snowdon to come into view is for the curvature of the light ray to be greater than the curvature of the earth. This unusual situation, in which flat terrain appears to rise around the viewer like a saucer, has been observed for rays near the ground in certain parts of the world. Such conditions were encountered on occasion [...]. But have they ever been encountered in Britain for long rays such as Wrekin-Snowdon?[11]

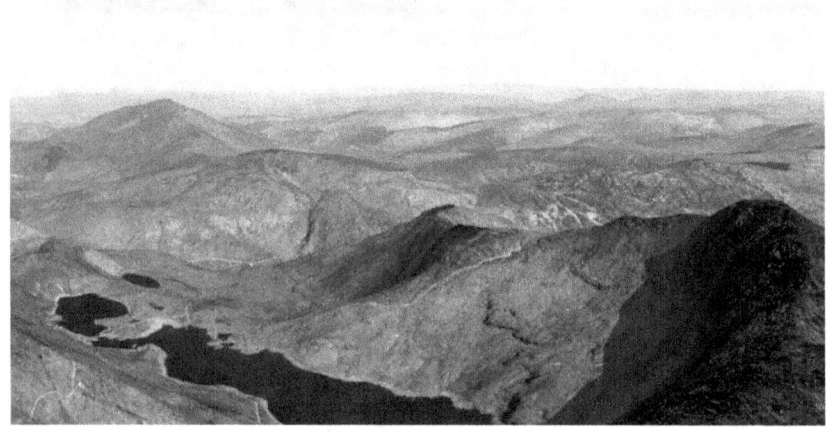

Fig. 06   This is a view from Snowdon after adjustment for allowing that horizon presents mysterious things to us.

Squires references measurements of refraction taken in the UK by Ordnance Survey, which are well below 0.5, and concludes: "It is reasonable to suppose that hills which would be brought into view by a refraction coefficient within the range measured by the Ordnance Survey will from time to time be visible."[12] Thus, however unlikely, it is possible.

3. THE UNKNOWN IS INVISIBLE

In this proposal, the terrain suggests that we only see what we pay attention to: all the mountains in between Snowdon and Wrekin are reduced, rendering them invisible when one's eye searches out Wrekin on the horizon. Cadair Berwyn, the peak that blocks the direct sightline between the two mountains, is not considered in the question, and so goes unnoticed.

In psychology, inattentional blindness is the failure to notice something when we are paying attention to something else: "Failure to notice an unexpected stimulus that is in one's field of vision when other attention-demanding tasks are being performed."[13]

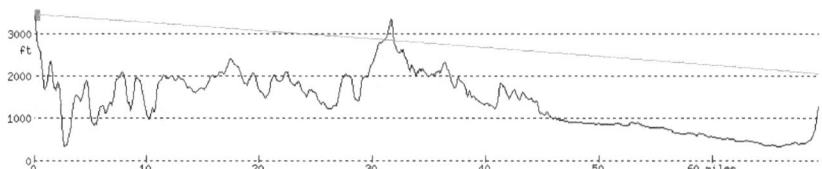

Sightline from Snowdon to Wrekin, with a refraction coefficient of .03 (normal conditions). Fig. 07

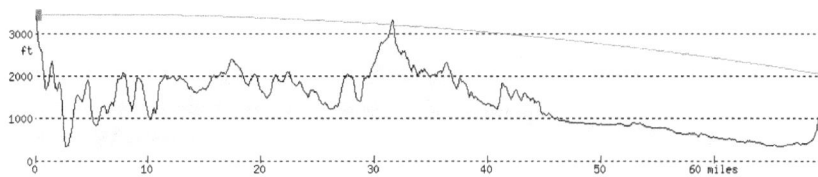

Refraction coefficient of 0.5. Fig. 08

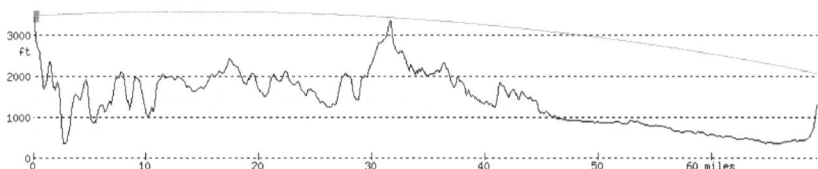

Refraction coefficient of 0.75; in this case, the sightline would clear the peak of Cadair Berwyn, which obstructs the view in the two other cases. Fig. 09

While inattentional blindness has been demonstrated subsequently in a variety of different experiments, Squires traces the beginnings of the Snowdon-Wrekin line-of-sight belief to a poem by Reverend Corfield, rector of Pitchford and vicar of Waters Upton in Shropshire, published in 1833:

> From WREKIN's summit cast the eye around,
> To view the objects which th' Horizon bound;
> O'er Salop's plains with beauteous verdure drest,
> The Cambrian Mountains stretch along the West,
> And though Snowdonia's cloud-capt tops are hid,
> Yet, through the vast expanse the eye is bid...

"Corfield's comment on Snowdonia is dangerously ambiguous," writes Squires. "Are Snowdonia's tops hidden by intervening hills or are they hidden by clouds?"[14] This question makes it clear that mountains can be like clouds when they obscure a peak which we know is there, even though we can't confirm it with our sight. Represented as data, the mountains are as ephemeral as the clouds, and the imaginary line of sight can become more real than the surrounding landscape.

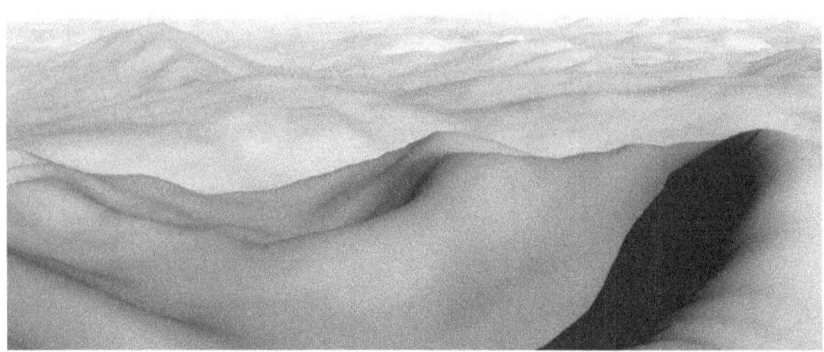

Fig. 10   Wrekin visible on the horizon.

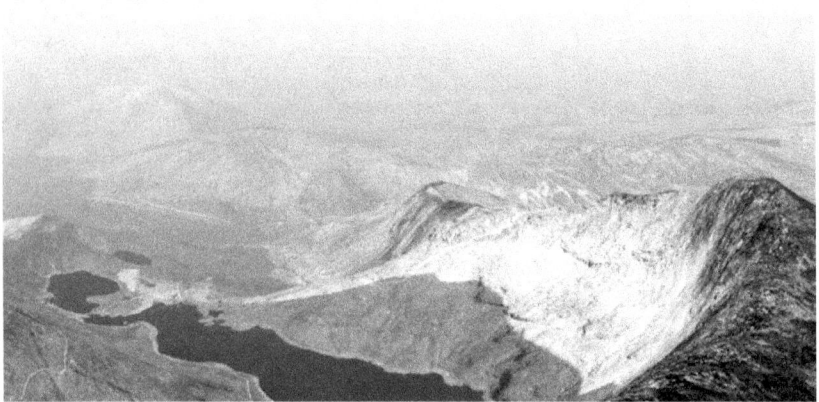

Fig. 11   On most days the atmosphere will obscure the view to the horizon from Snowdon's top. These images are two digital atmospheric variations.

On most days the view from Snowdon wouldn't be very far reaching. The atmosphere would obscure the landscape near the horizon, as it does in the following images [Figs. 12-14].

Immersed in data realities we dismiss the experiences conveyed to us by our bodies. But data representations of reality are still confirmed by "ground truth": the mass of human judgments collected and fed to the data analysis systems. This

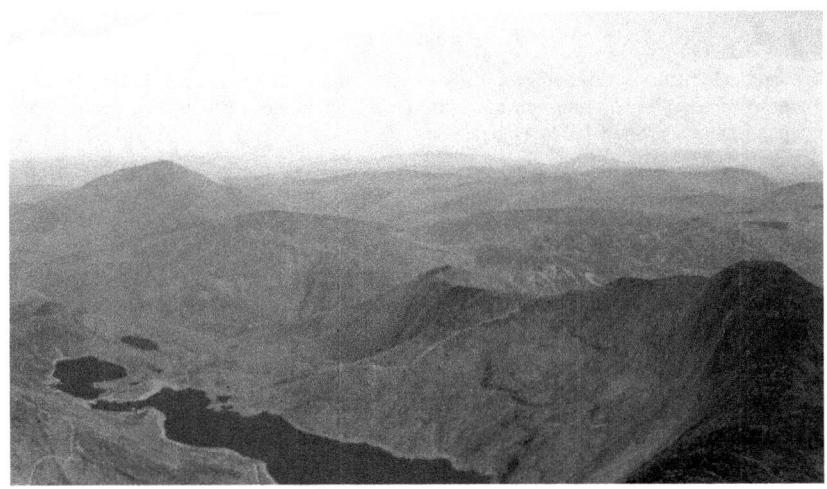

On most days the atmosphere will obscure the view to the horizon from Snowdon's top. These are two digital atmospheric variations.

Fig. 13

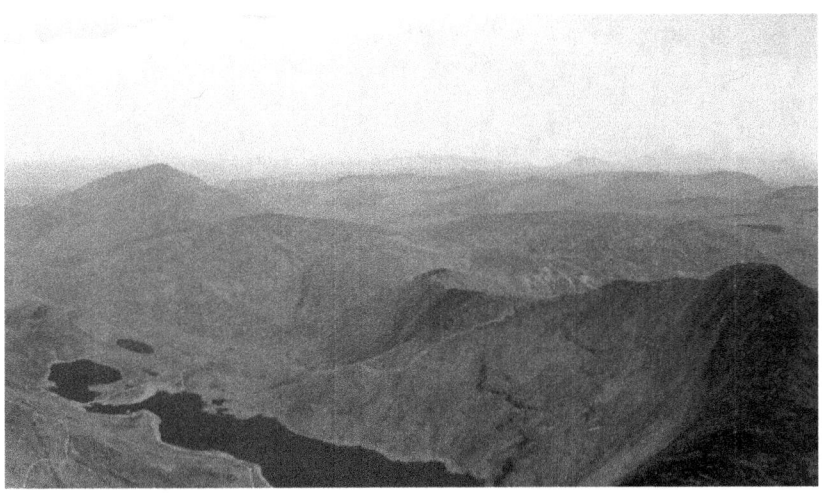

On most days the atmosphere will obscure the view to the horizon from Snowdon's top.

Fig. 12

makes the practice of "ground truthing" an opportunity for creative intervention. Through it, a single model of reality might instead be replaced by many co-existing, contradictory and incomplete models that ground us again in a limit-ful existence, with a horizon and a beyond.

Notes

1. See David Squires, "Can Snowdon Be Seen from Wrekin? A Topographic Detective Story," *Proceedings of the Cotteswold Naturalists' Field Club* 45, no. 1 (2010), www.viewfinderpanoramas.org/Snowdon-Wrekin.pdf.
2. See www.viewfinderpanoramas.org.
3. See www.amateurhuman.org/instruments/elevation-data.
4. See www.amateurhuman.org/module/last-clouds.
5. The progenitor of these application is Bryce, a software program that arose from the fractal geometry of Benoît Mandelbrot and his student Ken Musgrave; Mandelbrot first used the term "fractals" to describe mathematically modelling natural patterns.
6. See www.e-onsoftware.com/products.
7. Squires, "Can Snowdon Be Seen from Wrekin?"
8. Contrast is one of the fundamental features of perception. A contrast effect is defined as perceiving a quality of an object as enhanced or diminished compared to its context and exaggerating the difference between the two. This is illustrated in our very definition of a mountain: "A natural elevation of the earth surface rising more or less abruptly from the surrounding level and attaining an altitude which, relatively to the adjacent elevation, is impressive or notable." See en.wikipedia.org/wiki/Mountain.
9. Mark Monmonier, *How to Lie with Maps* (Chicago: University of Chicago Press, 1996), 9.
10. Squires, "Can Snowdon Be Seen from Wrekin?"
11. Ibid.
12. Ibid.
13. See en.wikipedia.org/wiki/Inattentional_blindness.
14. Squires, "Can Snowdon Be Seen from Wrekin?"

Islands & Other Invisible Territories
Laurent Gutierrez & Valérie Portefaix (MAP Office)

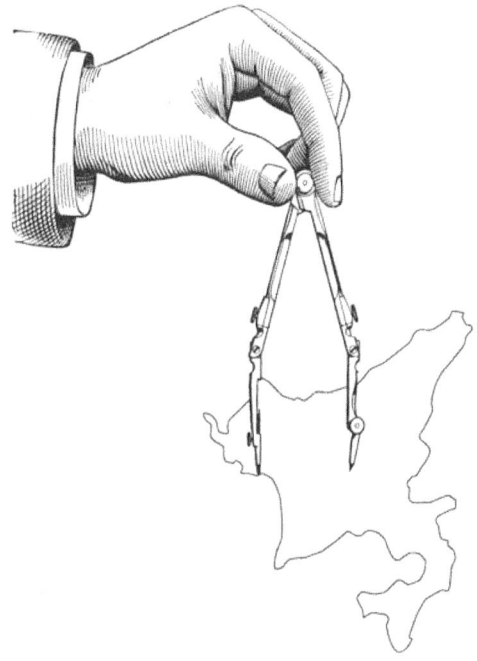

The Invisible Islands, research project, 2013   Fig. 01

The Invisible Islands (2013) details the specific position of thirty-three islands disseminated throughout Hong Kong's territorial waters—a configuration that impacted the making of the city, from surveillance and port defense (from China to the UK), storage of all sorts (opium, guns, and gold), aqua- and agriculture, refugee communities (drugs addicts, escapees), etc. Hong Kong is in essence a plurality, and its history is contained in those islands as an archipelago of multiple possibilities. Many were occupied long before 1850 as families migrated from Guangdong to begin farming and fishing. The archipelago also played an important role during the opium wars. Other islands have served as important landing bases for waves of migrants from China or Vietnam. Between 1949 and 1951, for example, Hong Kong received 670,000 refugees, who frequently arrived from the sea using fragile vessels or simply by swimming. The figure of the swimmer, escaping the nearby coastline in China— and at high risk in a shark-infested sea—is firmly anchored in the memory of the archipelagic territory.

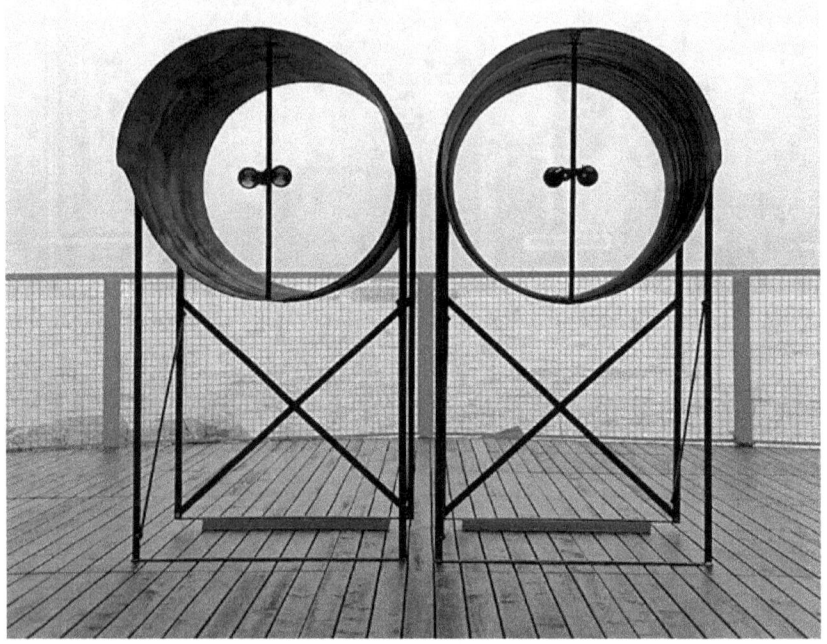

Fig. 02 *Bloody Haze*, 2009; steel structure, binoculars

"As far as I am concerned, I try to direct my telescope through the bloody haze upon a mirage of the nineteenth century, which I seek to depict according to those features that it will show in a future state of the world liberated from magic." Walter Benjamin, *Briefe*, Vol. II, Letter to Werner Kraft, 28 October 1935.

Notions of visibility and invisibility are central to *Bloody Haze* (2011). The predetermined intensification of the magnifier allows for the construction of a new reality. The distortion by means of an optical instrument, the double binocular, creates an illusion of an object being close or far, while always at the same position. The distorted distance is here reinforced by the instrument itself—the two lenses—and multiplied by two in order to experience the two opposite options: so far... so close... The skyline of Hong Kong, the subject of this optical experience, is the mere illustration of capitalistic development and has become its best representation. Here, the celebration takes the shape of a fragmented city. Each of its components disappears for the construction of singular masses that aim to become a mediated image, acquiring the status of "skyline" and becoming hyper-visible (when the weather allows it).

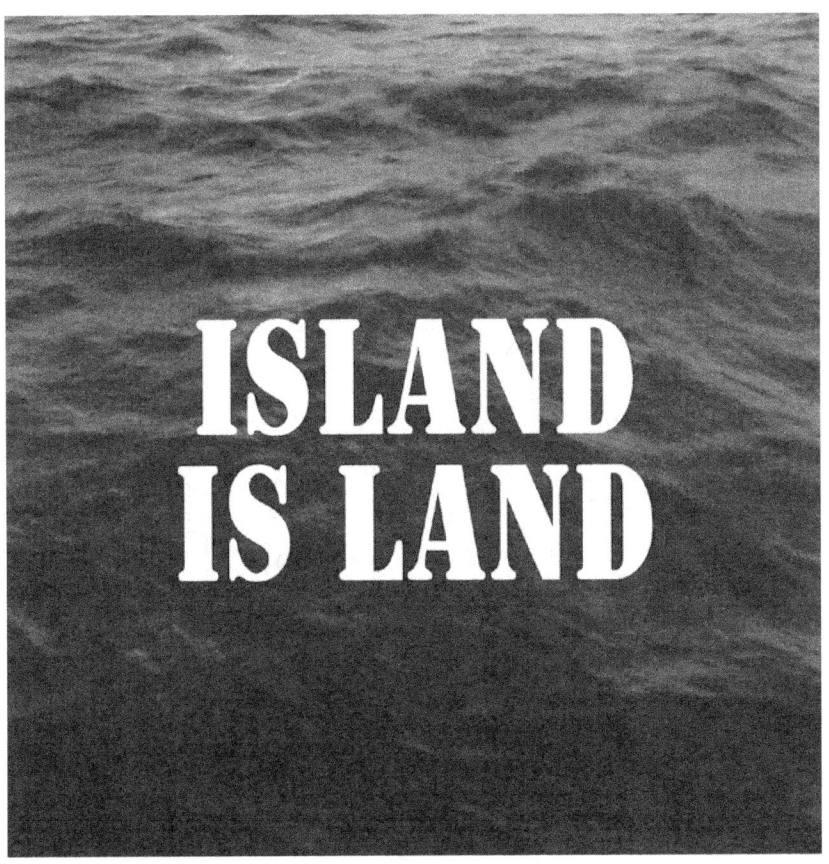

Island Is Land, 2009; photograph mounted on dibond, styrofoam letters   Fig. 03

"To dream of islands—whether with joy or in fear—is to dream of pulling away, of being already separate, far from any continent, of being lost and alone—or to dream of starting from scratch, recreating, beginning anew." Gilles Deleuze, *Desert Islands*, 1953.

Following a Deleuzian logic, a desert island is the possibility of the re-, the return to the origin. The re- is embedded in the figure of the castaway unfolding two kinds of dimensions. The first one is spatial. Through his involuntarily discovery, the castaway appears as an original figure taking possession of a new land, later his home and prison for the duration of his unfortunate exile. For this particular purpose, the castaway is forced to domesticate the island. Re-constructing his original place or developing a utopian place, he remains with no choice than to dominate the new domain or otherwise perish. *Island Is Land* (2009) recalls this simple statement. Floating on the background of a black, agitated sea, the fourteen letters perform the motion of continental detachment or an oceanic emergence, emphasizing new land formed by tons of plastic garbage.

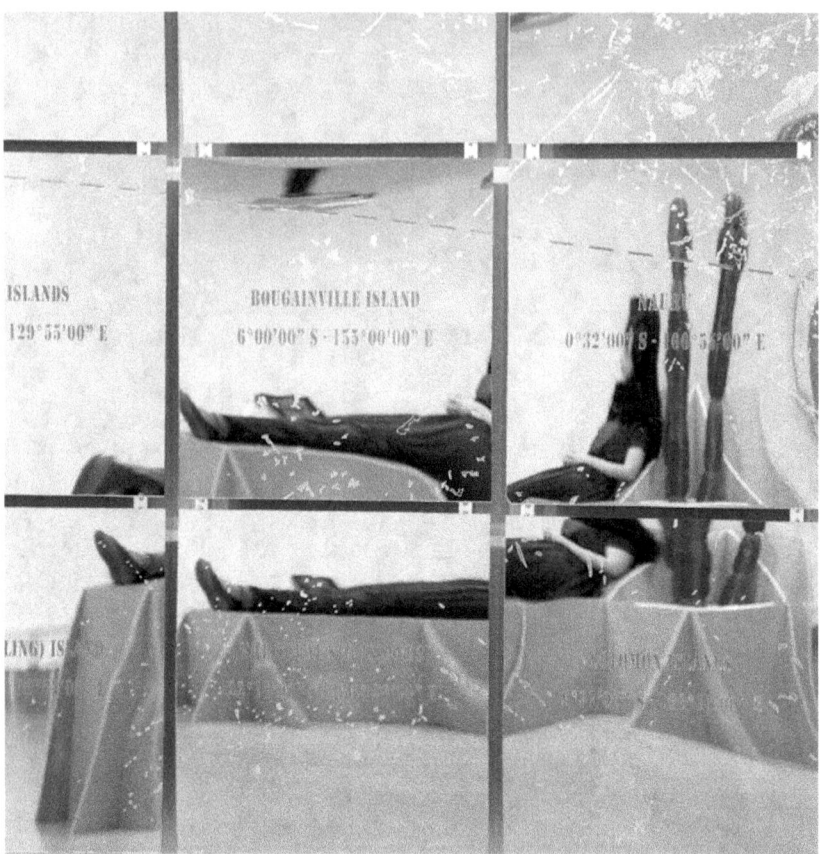

Fig. 04 *Desert Islands*, 2009; 100 engraved mirrors, MDF, cardboard, plant, video

"The history of the twenty-first-century will be written on water. When sea levels are certainly on the rise, the sea becomes our new desert." Paul Virilio, *The Original Accident*, 2007.

Paul Virilio announced the "end of geography," meaning that time (history) had won over space. Time now lies on top of space, as the sea sits on the surface of the earth. For the exhibition *Desert Islands* (2009), the surface of the sea is translated to a fractured surface of 100 mirrors. Each mirror frames one island, as well as its geographical position to the others. Assembled into a new world map, the meticulous selection of 100 islands presents a multifaceted laboratory of major human actions and experimentations on these islands—utopian communities, fiscal paradises, military spheres, clandestine migration zones, drug exchange points, prostitution hubs, and exclusive leisure areas. The 100 islands serve as a new reference, to not only feed the desires but also the fears and secrets of our time.

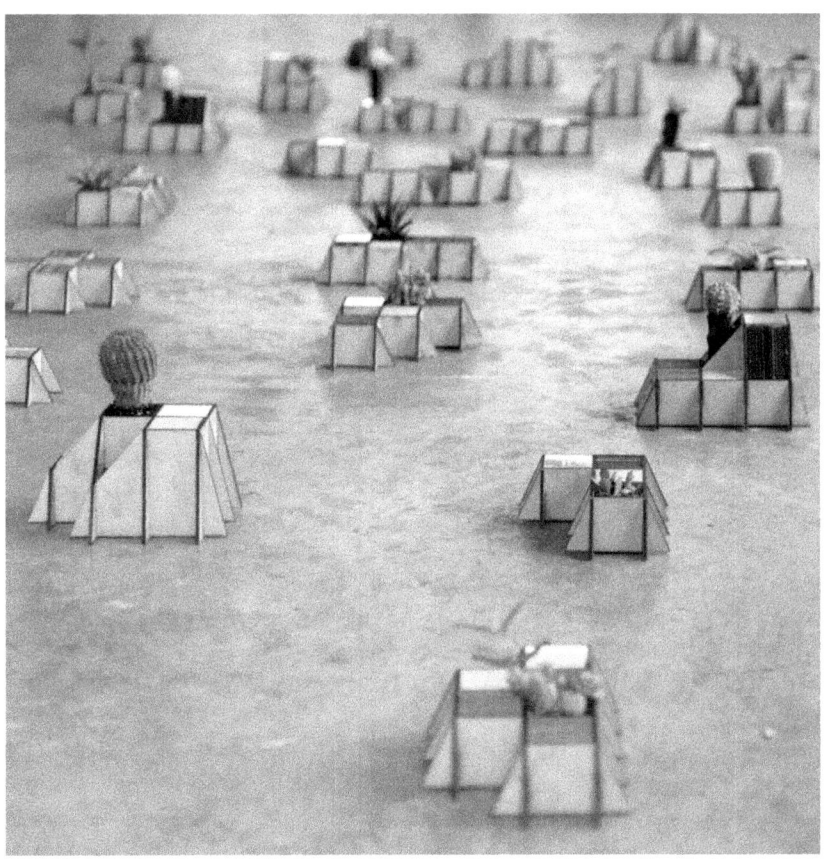

Simply Enjoy the Scenery, 2011; MDF, cardboard, foam, acrylic mirror, plants Fig. 03

"Koh Tapu, aka James Bond Island, co-starred in the 1974 James Bond movie, *The Man with the Golden Gun*. Although the island itself is just a limestone karst in the middle of Phang Nga Bay, it doesn't stop a seemingly steady stream of tourists taking boat trips to the location." Tourist brochure, Phuket

For most of us, the island is an ideal temporary escape from our everyday lives. Feeding our imagination with images of unaltered beaches and pristine wilderness, the island is an accessible therapeutic refuge. Yet, the level of expectation is often matched by an equivalent level of frustration. *Simply Enjoy The Scenery* (2011) anticipates the bulimic demand from the public to be continuously entertained. Famously featured in *The Man with the Golden Gun* (1974), Koh Tapu disappoints visitors because of its small size. In the James Bond movie, the island served as a base where the villain Scaramanga hid his laser weapon, eliciting a sense of déjà-vu as you set eyes on the famous mushroom-shaped rock. For this exhibition, we played around with the viewers' possible disappointment when approaching the 100 + 1 islands at one-tenth of their original size. Here, exhibition and landscape share a similar power of attraction with an infinite set of ways of perceiving a projected reality.

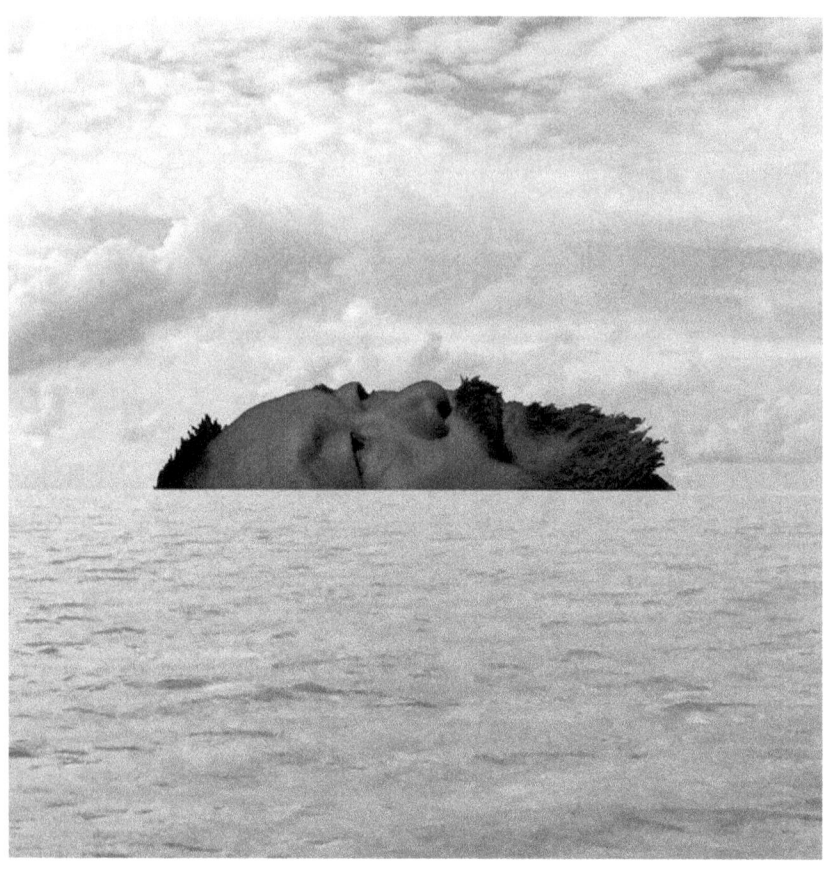

Fig. 06   *Island Profile*, 2013; C-print on Hahnemühle FineArt paper, burnt wood, acrylic paint

Island Profile (2014) draws on multiple geographical considerations by exposing the isolation of an island remotely located in the middle of the Ocean. This unique piece of land stands against the flow of natural calamities. Viewed from an anthropomorphic perspective, the island strengthens the link between characteristics of human nature and its geological setting. *Island Profile* confirms this landform's imposing stature as it resists the elements, surrounded on every side. A refuge for the castaway, in this case the Chinese artist and activist Ai Wei Wei, it is a prominent sanctuary defending its right to exist for what it believes in.

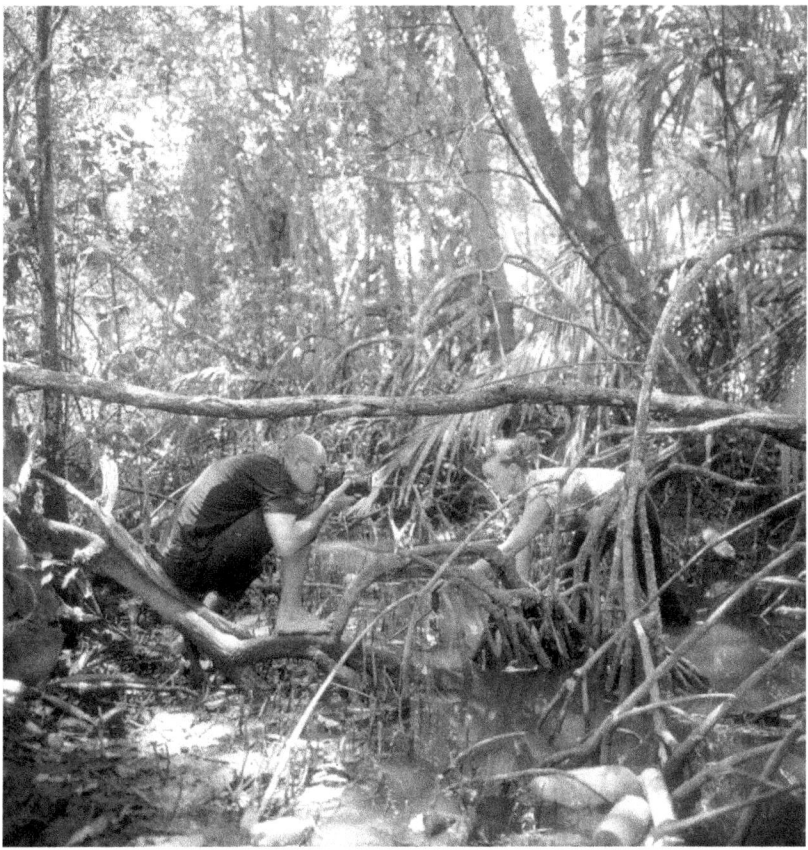

Intruders, no.3, 2014; lenticular print, light box

Fig. 07

A recent opportunity has taken MAP Office from Hong Kong to Singapore, a laboratory of a very different kind. Over the last forty years, Singapore has created the conditions to radically experiment with new strategies, beginning with a tabula rasa of its natural and built order. Recently, it has proven its capacity to plan long-term, taking up the challenge to become a well-planned city in the tropics, or, to paraphrase the Singaporean government, the "Tropical City of Excellence." Singapore is an island of a special kind, an island where you could barely see any bordering water, until the last urban development of Marina Park. The photographic series *Intruders* (2014) is formalized in a series of lenticular prints staging two characters photographing the pristine mangroves at Pulau Ubin. Playing with the layers of invisibility/visibility offered by this type of multi-layered printing format, intrusion takes the form of a portrait at work.

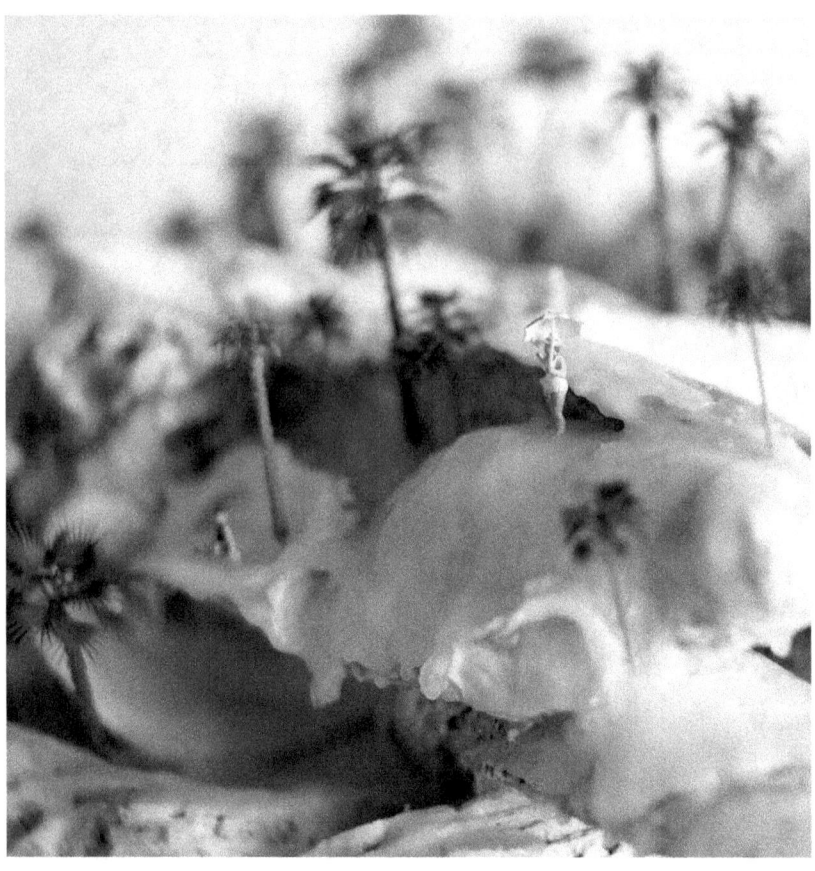

Fig. 08   *PRD Colony: From Hong Kong to Macau*, no.1, 2014; oyster-shells, wax, hand painted copper trees, plastic figurines, wooden base, glass box

MAP Office's territories of production, or its production of territories, are an extension of a compulsive search for what is called "Island." Beyond Hong Kong Island, we have traveled from China to Venice, from Lau Fau Shan to Israel, from New Orleans to Tenerife, following the thread of various opportunities in the construction of Island. With *PRD Colonies* (2014), a new archipelagic network of islands was created at the centre of gravity of the Pearl River Delta River. From Hong Kong to Macau, entertainment is taking over the new islands with a full ensemble of integrated attractions: Wedding Island, Water Park Island, etc. From Hong Kong to Shenzhen, another set of islands is being configured as new residential developments, adding up an alternative dual-property market: Golf Island, Work Island.

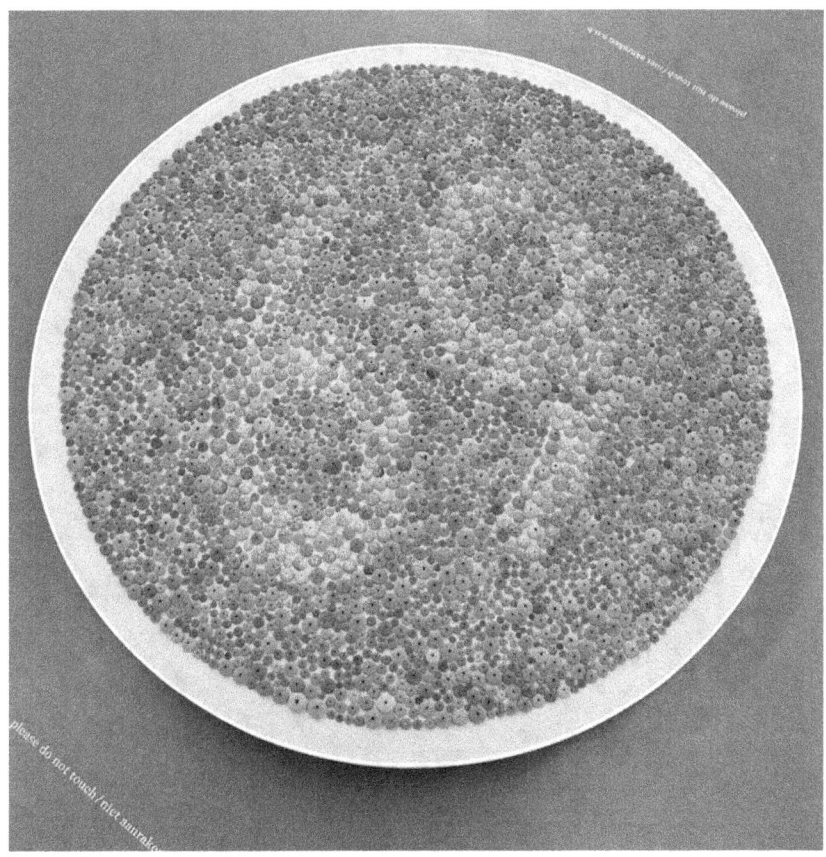

Island for Colorblind, 2014; urchins shells (3,200 greens and pink), sand, wooden base Fig. 09

"But if they were impulsive and unsystematic, my island experiences were intense and rich, and ramified in all sorts of directions which continually surprised me." Oliver Sacks, *The Island of the Colorblind*, 1997.

In 1997, neurologist Oliver Sacks wrote *The Island of the Colorblind* following the story of Pingelap, a tiny Micronesian atoll where achromatopsia affects most of the population. *Island For Colorblind* (2014) is a territory that cannot be seen by everyone. Inspired by the Ishihara color test, the figure 69 is embedded in the landscape as a number of pink urchin shells among many green ones. In this particular installation, the island is exclusive and visible to only a few.

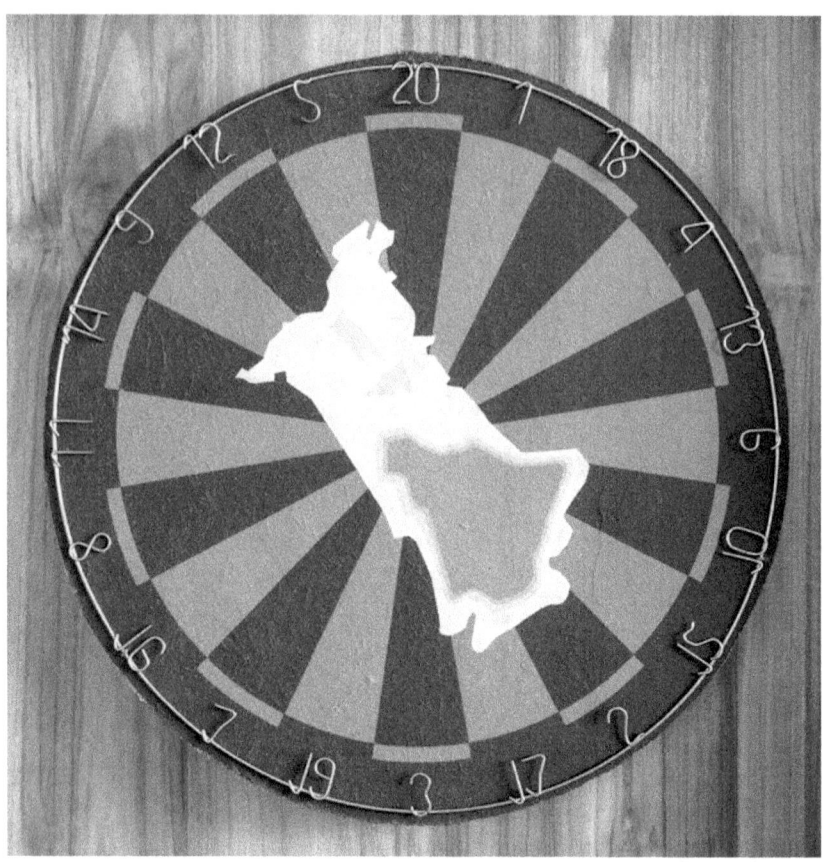

Fig. 10 *Disputed [Bei Xiaodao (China) - Kita-Kojima (Japan) - Bei Xiaodao (Taiwan)]*, 2014; wooden dart game, booklet

Disputed (2014) responds to recent escalations in island disputes around the world. These islands are much more than small, uninhabited rocks lost in the ocean. With the exhaustion of natural resources, territorial waters are becoming a precious extension of the land, explaining countries' often violent fights to claim them. With rich fisheries and natural oil contained in their seabed, these islands are huge attractions in crowded regions with competing interests. Geopolitical strategies over contested areas foster nationalist sentiments toward neighbouring countries. The role of militaries occupying the same strategic space and planting their countries' sovereign flags is a visible sign of these tensions. Borrowing elements from these ongoing fights, MAP Office has created a dart game designed to conquer those disputed territories according to the countries that claim them.

Plants that Evolve (in some way or another)

Mixrice (Cho Jieun & Yang Chulmo)

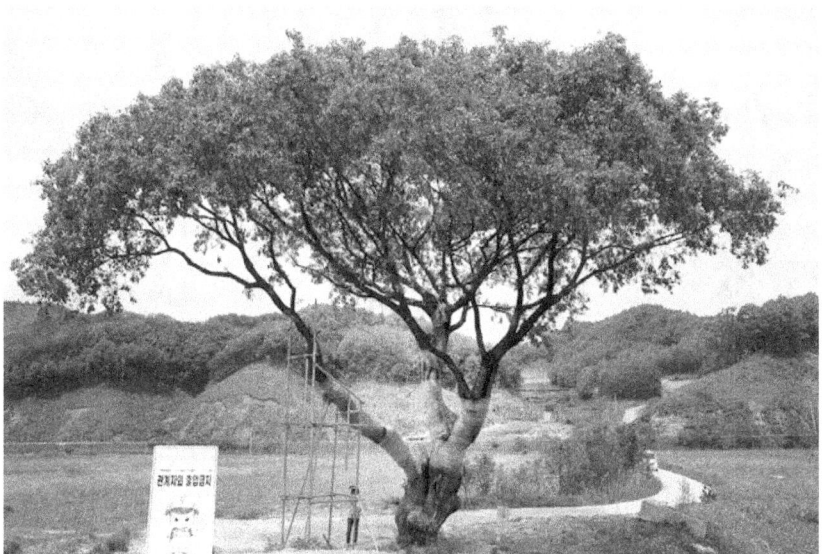

Protected tree in danger of being submerged – Trees for Public Services; a site where living rocks are placed, Naeseongcheon, 2013.   Fig. 01

In this work, various stories overlap, unfolding various episodes of plants that turn an abandoned city lot into a forest; unexpected landscapes are found in a thirty-year-old apartment complex; exotic vegetable gardens are tended by immigrants; a thousand-year-old tree is transplanted; and people guard forests and submerged landscapes. Traditionally, plant totems functioned as beings that people should believe in, in order to connect a community to the world. In the present day, when traditional communities have collapsed and new communities are still unstable, it is not unnatural that plant totems have lost their ground. However, while landscaping huge apartment complexes, those old myths were readopted through plants, and materialized. Deprived of their histories and stories, trees are transplanted elsewhere. Having observed these surreal situations, Mixrice visits sites where trees were originally located, tracing the process of immigration and evolution. What follows are some textual excerpts and film stills from the video *Plants That Evolve (in one way or another)*.[1]

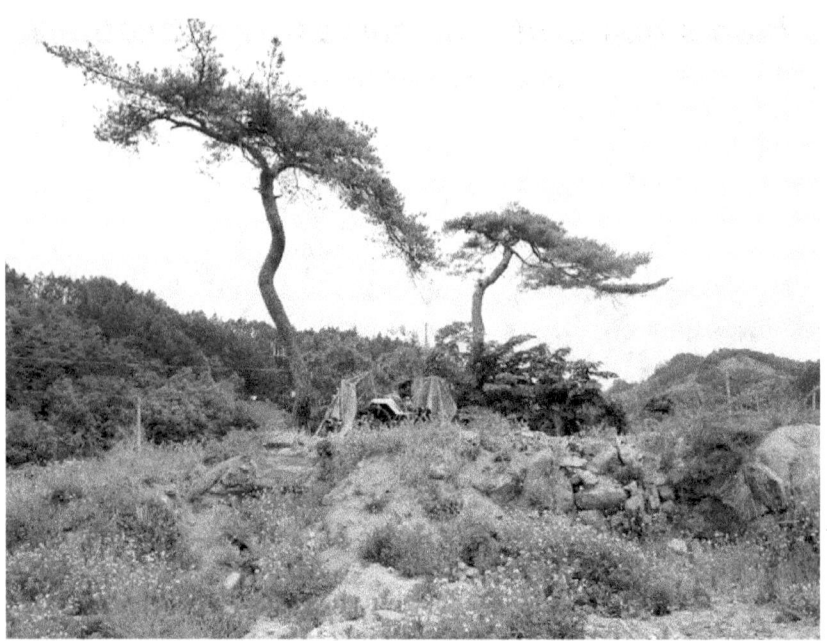

Fig. 02　A site where a 400-year-old Zelkova tree used to be, Gangdong-ri, Pyeongeun-myeon, 2013.

It is not a new story that your familiar landscapes have changed.

Too many things changed and you are lost in your memory.

As the feverish development of a new city or a new town continues, more and more trees are being planted every day.

The old trees are actually aged, but maintained to look old by constant trimming.

You search for trees with stories.

Well-preserved trees growing thick and free in their original place,
other trees were moved to somewhere else,
some trees were chopped down,
other trees were relocated to nowhere…

One day, upon hearing that there is a place with many nettle trees, you make a visit to Mok-dong, a big apartment complex.

There, the trees were planted in a designated lot in front of a building.

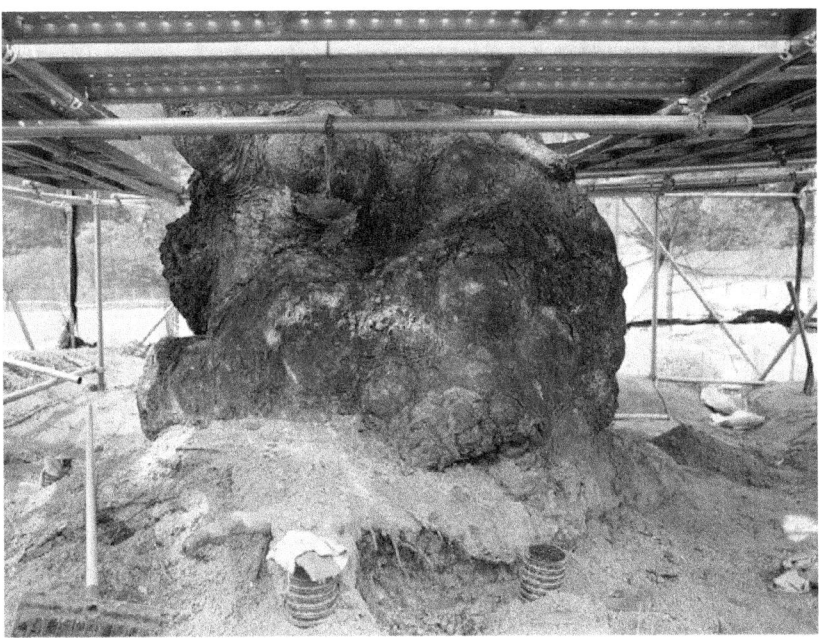

Replanted Zelkova tree from Gangdong-ri, K-water (Korea Water Resources Corporation) Yeongju Dam construction office in Yonghyeol-ri, 2013.   Fig. 03

They were transported from Jeju Island by jet.

You became curious about where the trees came from, what their original place looked like.

An ecologist on the island watched nettle trees dug out from the front of a house.

Rocks and nettle trees were transplanted from Jeju Island where the spring of gentrification has finally come.

You used to plant trees in Korea imaging a future view of the scenery in ten years' time.

But the apartment complex foresaw the scenery after ten years and represented the future scene in the present.

You find some traces left by a botanist.

You meet him in one of those books.

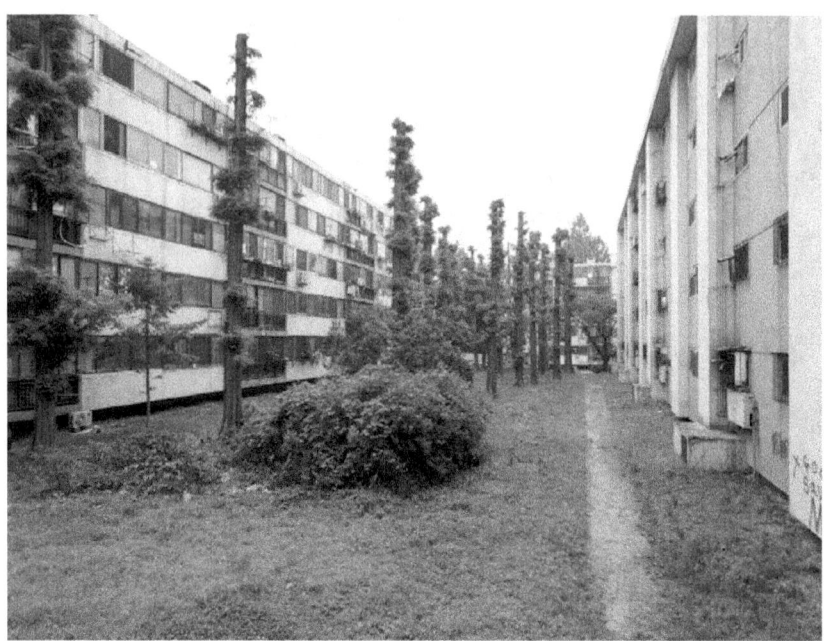

Fig. 04   Forest of Jugong, a planed site for housing redevelopment of Jugong Apt., Gaepo-dong, 2013.

He was wearing "Tanggeon" and "Got" and carrying a lunch box and a rifle.

In 1917, Wilson, the plant collector, took a sample of Korean fir tree seeds, researched them and presented a paper at the International Botanical Congress.

In rare materials left by Wilson and the Japanese botanist Nakai, the unfamiliar sceneries of Korea in the early 1900s were also represented.

Many Western plant collectors have collected numerous botanical species from colonies, in spite of their tough climates and environments.

You imagine the attraction, fascination and strong desire that they must have felt.

They came attracted and left fascinated.

In the middle of summer you see an exotic vegetable garden on a rooftop.

Naheed, the owner of this garden grows plants that he brings from his mother country each year.

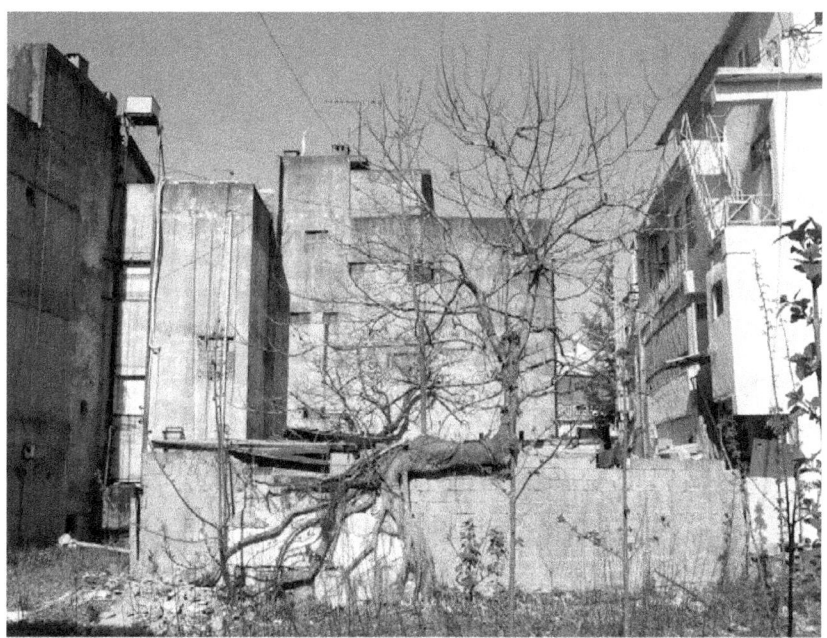

Plant at 84th Street, Jeonju, 2012.   Fig. 05

He collects discarded pieces of lumber and plywood from furniture factories to build frames for vegetable gardens and shabby pots.

His factory colleagues are unfamiliar with these plants but enjoy tasting Naheed's fruits. He gives out seeds to them.

You meet another thousand-year-old tree.

This tree was originally located in the water next to a huge block of concrete in Gunwi Dam, Gyeongsang Province.

These thousand-year-old trees were transplanted to the apartment complexes in Banpo and Dongcheon for landscaping purposes.

You thought of a span of a thousand years.

You try to think of this frame of time, almost intangible in its distance and weight.

A grandma remembers the exact shapes of the tree's leaves and branches, informs you of its original place.

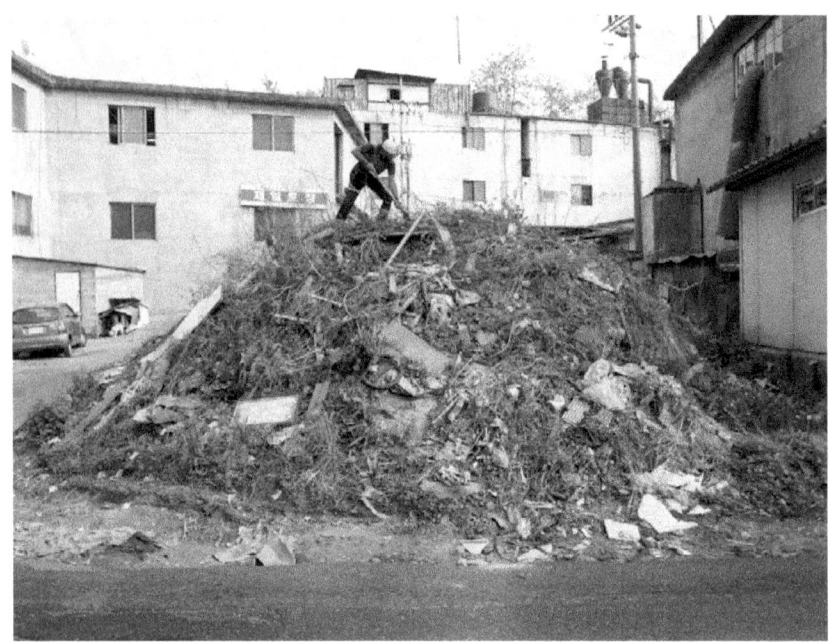

Fig. 06   Disappearing hills, Maseok, 2013.

You believe this tree, now deprived of its stories, has lost its ability for budding.

One of these trees died, unable to adapt to the new environment, and another put forth buds in spring at only two-thirds of its normal quantity.

There must be a number of villages submerged due to the dam.

There must be many trees in those villages.

The sound of these trees' weeping must be watery.

You meet a strange forest in the middle of an old apartment complex.

Contrary to contemporary landscaping, trees in these forests planted more than ten years ago create unexpected scenery.

This forest located in this redeveloped area will soon disappear and become something totally new.

What will happen to this great forest? Where will these trees go?

You meet old women who are struggling to guard trees.

They are fighting against Korea Electric Power Corporation's plan for building a transmission tower.

The true nature of their cheerfulness becomes a political movement in daily life.

You hope this story will become a myth or a legend in the future.

The power that keeps nuclear power plants and transmission towers away is none other than aged naked bodies armed with excrement and saliva.

This is what you have forgotten in this world overflowing with tools.

You encounter a tree that took root in a collapsed wall.

This plant is one of a few plants left in the world without ruins, the world where people who have never seen ruins are living.

In this world, only the present exists.

The first colony was a part of nature, and the last one will also be.

However, you hope there will be more strangeness in this flat and dull world.

There is a story about the settlement of the guard mountains and lands in Miryang, and another story about transplantation in Maseok. How are these two stories related to each other?

Those women in Miryang long for settlement and preserve time, whereas migrant workers in Maseok long for transplantation to fill up time in the state of drift.

Maybe settlement and migration will put down their roots like plants in a different position.

Korean society devours time.

It eliminates time by itself. And it erases time.

There was an unforgettable time once.

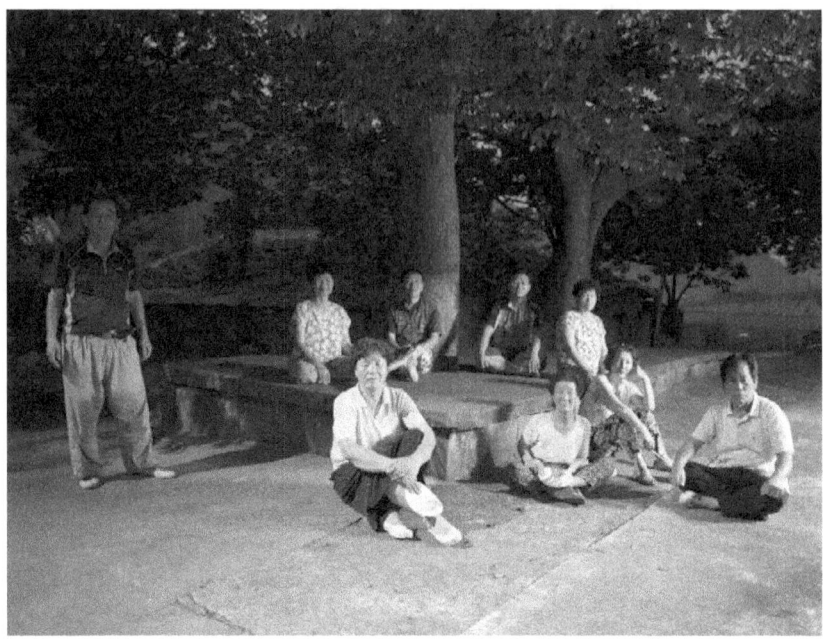

Fig. 07   People who protect mountain and Borra village, Miryang, 2013.

As moments accumulate, they become the power to endure pain.

Plants evolve in some way or other.

A story is meant to travel around, here and there.

There is an old saying that if a story does not circulate and stays stagnant, it becomes a ghost.

What you imagine is a world where stories are not yet formed or disappeared.

A real story is created where communication and relation disappears.

You may hope that such legendary stories will be passed down from generations to you.

Note

1   Excerpts below from Mixrice, *Plants that Evolve (in one way or another)*, two-channel video, 17 pigment prints, 10 min., 21 sec. (2013).

Indigenizing the Anthropocene
Zoe Todd

> The language of postmodernism is ethnocentric and insufficient.
>
> — Guillermo Gómez-Peña[1]

> Art is supposedly well within the digital age of fusion, beyond boundaries and anthropology.
>
> — Loretta Todd[2]

When I was a little girl in the 1990s, my dad, Métis artist Garry Todd, used to take my little sister and me to his painting studio in Edmonton. It was a basement warehouse space in the inner city, a dusty and creaky building used by artists and theatre troupes and photographers and others to *make things.* We had little easels on which to paint, and we used non-toxic acrylic paints my Dad bought for us. Early on, he taught me about cross-hatching and shading, dimensions and perspective, how to mix colours, and how to view the world as a series of pigments mixed together in shadow and light. While he painted landscapes and images of buildings slated for demolition in my hometown of Edmonton, Alberta, my sister and I painted flowers and cats and other things that struck our fancy. Once, he cut out wooden templates for us to try our hand at carving our own wooden spoons, and he supervised us as we worked with his chisels. My Dad says I was obsessed with coyotes (properly pronounced in central Alberta as *kai-oats*), and I drew them over and over and over again, referencing the haunting howls of packs of coyotes that would call over the water when we spent our summers at Baptiste Lake at my mom's family's summer cabin. There, I learned how to fish and pick berries, and to see the land with a painterly eye as my dad sketched out drawings of the landscape. My mom took me out in our little rowboat and I would cast a fishing rod into the water. She gutted and cleaned what we caught, cooking it in a hot frying pan. Land, art, animals, material, and space all intertwined in my understanding of myself as a Métis person from very early on.

Fifteen years later I walked into the warehouse where my Dad used to paint, only now it was a high-end condominium and I was there to attend a poetry reading in a private residence. The cognitive dissonance of entering space that I had known so intimately as a child, that had loomed so large in my *making* as an artist and as an urban Indigenous person, only to find it finished with ten-foot ceilings, burnished metal and tasteful art, was jarring. The space had literally been gentrified.

As I stood there in the condo listening to poetry being read, I was struck by how I had stopped making art; how I had stopped writing poetry and fiction; how I

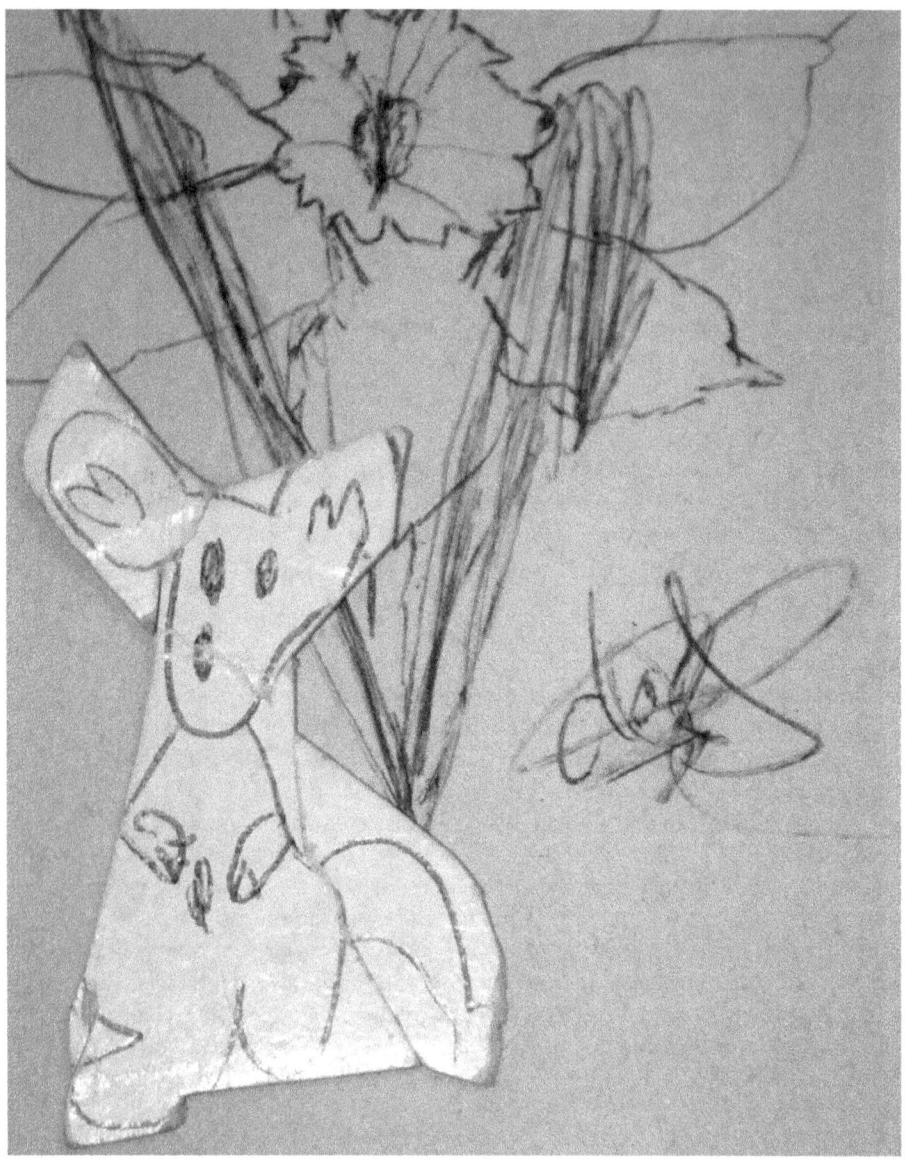

Fig. 01   Daffodil and coyote—an early work saved by my dad.

had stopped believing I could make a good life for myself as a "creative" person. I had watched my dad struggle to support himself as a Métis artist in Canada, and imperceptibly and slowly, I stopped making art because I did not feel welcome in the gentrified, *intensely white* spaces where I perceived "real art" and "real literature" were made. And, when I stepped out for a bit of fresh air that evening, I cried because I realized that I had lost a part of myself in the process of trying, and failing, to make my body and my practice fit into those spaces. When our gritty, dusty, poor lives were erased to make way for shiny condos, so too had my belief that I could participate in the world of *making* as it is defined by a persistently white, Eurocentric academy and art world.

To be at the margins, be they aesthetic, intellectual, or physical, is a shared experience for Indigenous people in Canada. What shape this marginalization takes is different for each person, and each Nation or People. But it occurs again and again, in slightly different forms: gentrification (or colonialism in the form of gentrification) appears as a shape-shifter.[3] When spaces are gentrified, which intellectual buildings are Indigenous and/or People of Colour allowed to occupy? I draw the building analogy from Sara Ahmed, who points out:

> To account for experiences of not being given residence (to be dislodged from a category is to be dislodged from a world) is not yet another sad political lesson, a lesson that we have had to give up in order to keep going. We learn from being dislodged about lodges. We come to know so much about institutional life because of these failures of residence: the categories in which we are immersed as forms of life become explicit when you do not quite inhabit them.[4]

Despite the shock of seeing my dad's former studio transformed into gleaming high-end downtown real estate, there was a part of me that I reclaimed that evening in the warehouse-condo. There was a part of me that suddenly stepped into the "explicitness of my category,"[5] as an Indigenous woman, as an outsider. Looking around at the crowd that night, I realized I *could* make things, that I *could* insert my Indigenous self into white spaces without apology or shame. Ever conscious of my complex position as a white-passing Métis woman and scholar, I insert here a note about the ways that my identity is contradictory, and acknowledge that the very act of occupying white spaces as someone who *looks white* courts the simultaneous familiarity and distance that comes with "passing" in non-Indigenous contexts. Everything I write in this essay is couched in the simultaneous belonging/not-belonging that I straddle as I study and work between Canada and Europe.

What follows is an examination of art and the Anthropocene as variations of "white public space"—space in which Indigenous ideas and experiences are appropriated, or obscured, by non-Indigenous practitioners. First, I offer a short exploration of how to use Indigenous philosophy and teachings from Indigenous legal orders, specifically the work of Papaschase Cree scholar Dr. Dwayne Donald, to decolonize and Indigenize the non-Indigenous intellectual contexts that currently shape public intellectual discourse, including that of the Anthropocene. Second, I explore how the Indigenization of the Anthropocene is taking place through Indigenous thought, praxis, and art. This decolonization/Indigenization is necessary in order to bring Indigenous epistemologies, ontologies, and practices to the fore in a meaningful and ethical way.

A Crisis in Search of a Name

In a time of anthropological engagement with diverse and urgent environmental crises, current academic discourses in the Euro-Western academy have coalesced around the notion of the Anthropocene as a narrative tool.[6] Popularized by Paul Crutzen in 2002, and subsequently taken up by the humanities, the Anthropocene references an epoch in which humans are the dominant drivers of geologic change on the globe today.[7] As a Métis scholar, I have an inherent distrust of this term, the Anthropocene, since terms and theories can act as gentrifiers in their own right, and I frequently have to force myself to engage in good faith with it as heuristic. While it may seem ridiculous to distrust a *word*, it is precisely because the term has colonized and infiltrated many intellectual contexts throughout the academy at the moment that I view it with caution. However, my distrust is well-founded: Swedish scholars Andreas Malm and Alf Hornborg, among others, highlight the manner in which the current framing of the Anthropocene blunts the distinctions between the people, nations, and collectives who drive the fossil-fuel economy and those who do not. The complex and paradoxical experiences of diverse people as humans-in-the-world, including the ongoing damage of colonial and imperialist agendas, can be lost when the narrative is collapsed to a universalizing species paradigm. As Malm and Hornborg state, "a clique of white British men literally pointed steam-power as a weapon—on sea and land, boats and rails—against the best part of humankind, from the Niger delta to the Yangzi delta, the Levant to Latin America."[8] Not all humans are equally implicated in the forces that created the disasters driving contemporary human-environmental crises, and I argue that not all humans are equally invited into the conceptual spaces where these disasters are theorized or responses to disaster formulated.

As an Indigenous scholar working both in Canada and the UK, I am intensely aware of how discourse is deployed within and between geographies, disciplines, and institutions. Whenever a term or trend is on everyone's lips, I ask myself: "What other story could be told here? What other language is not being heard? Whose space *is* this, and who is *not* here?" With the prevalence of the Anthropocene as a conceptual "building" within which stories are being told, it is important to query *which* humans or human systems are driving the environmental change the Anthropocene is meant to describe. What "modernist mess," as Fortun eloquently describes it,[9] characterizes this moment of "common cosmopolitical concern"—Latour's term to describe the fact that the climate is a shared heritage, cross-roads, site, or milieu that we all inhabit, and one which deserves our deep attention as a commons and context for engaged involvement in the crises of climate change[10]—that is the Anthropocene? And, finally, who is dominating the conversations about how to change the state of things?

I am not alone in questioning the Euro-Western academy's current approach to human-environmental relationships. A number of other scholars have critiqued current popular trends in the Euro-Western humanities: posthumanism and the ontological turn have all been queried and challenged as Eurocentric.[11] These critiques re-centre the *locus* of thought, offering a reconfiguration of understandings of human-environmental relations towards praxis that acknowledges the central importance of land, bodies, movement, race, colonialism and sexuality. Human geographer Juanita Sundberg, for example, takes posthumanism to task for its erasure of non-European ontologies. She writes, "the literature continuously refers to a foundational ontological split between nature and culture *as if it is universal*,"[12] and points out that posthumanist theories tend to erase both *location* and Indigenous epistemologies. Sundberg urges scholars to enact the "pluriverse" as a decolonial tool, in her case drawing on Zapatista principles of "walking the world into being," as one locus of thought and praxis to decolonize posthumanist scholarship and geographies.[13] As Sundberg notes, "the Zapatista movement theorizes walking as an important practice in building the pluriverse, a world in which many worlds fit."[14] For Sundberg, walking and movement are necessary to bring a decolonizing methodology to fruition because, "As we humans move, work, play, and narrate with a multiplicity of beings in place, we enact historically contingent and radically distinct worlds/ontologies."[15] This methodology of decolonization through walking worlds into being aligns very closely with geographer Sarah Hunt's (Kwakwaka'wakw, Kwagiulth) discussion of dance at a Potlatch as a mode through which Indigenous ontologies—she specifically describes her own experience of engaging with Kwakwaka'wakw ontology—are brought to life.[16] Hunt outlines the epistemic violence inherent in Euro-Western academic treatments of Indigenous knowledge, specifically by analyzing the ways that Indigenous ontologies are reified and distorted in the ongoing colonial structures of the European and North American academy. In fact, she notes that "the potential for Indigenous ontologies to unsettle dominant ontologies can be easily neutralized as a triviality, as a case study or a trinket, as powerful institutions work as self-legitimating systems that uphold broader dynamics of (neo)colonial power."[17] Hunt argues that the systems of knowledge production that we, as Indigenous scholars, engage with and legitimize through our presence in the academy, must be changed.[18] Hunt evokes dance as a way to negotiate the demands of colonial academic institutions and praxis, for it is through dance that Indigenous ontologies are brought to life.[19] Zakiyyah Jackson also problematizes the erasure of race from posthumanist philosophies, bringing the focus back to topics all too often sidestepped by posthumanism, including "race, colonialism, and slavery."[20] By returning to decolonial theorists overlooked and forgotten by dominant posthumanist discourses, such as Aimé Césaire, Jackson reminds scholars of the continuing need to decentre the Eurocentric, heteropatriarchal focus that posthumanist studies ironically perpetuates within the "order of rationality" that shapes Euro-Western institutions.

Haudenosaunee and Anishinaabe scholar Vanessa Watts operationalizes a principle of "Indigenous Place Thought,"[21] which can stand in place of, or alongside, discourses such as an "ontology of dwelling,"[22] the theoretical position advanced by British anthropologist Tim Ingold, based in part on his close reading of Irving Hallowell's ethnographic work with Anishinaabe people.[23] This Place-Thought "is based upon the premise that land is alive and thinking, and that humans and non-humans derive agency through the extensions of these thoughts."[24] Watts takes Euro-Western Science Studies theorists to task, including Latour and Haraway, for operationalizing non-human agency in Eurocentric, colonial ways.[25] For example, Watts points out that:

> Haraway resists essentialist notions of the earth as mother or matter and chooses instead to utilize products of localized knowledges (i.e. Coyote or the Trickster) as a process of boundary implosion: "I like to see feminist theory as a reinvented coyote discourse obligated to its sources in many heterogeneous accounts of the world" (Haraway, 1988, 594). This is a level of abstracted engagement once again. While it may serve to change the imperialistic tendencies in Euro-Western knowledge production, Indigenous histories are still regarded as story and process—an abstracted tool of the West.[26]

Watts also rejects the "hierarchies of agency"[27] imposed by common understandings of Actor Network Theory. She urges an understanding of non-human agency that integrates Indigenous Place-Thought and which implodes the mechanistic, hierarchical delineation made by some Euro-Western scholars between flesh and things. Rather than situate elements like soil as mere "actants,"[28] who can only have agency in relation to the interactions they have with humans and exist "where the plane of action is equalized amongst all elements,"[29] Watts suggests that "if we think of agency as being tied to spirit, and spirit exists in all things, then all things possess agency."[30]

In critiquing the locus of agency, and by re-centring motion, bodies, spirit, race, and sexuality within the frame of the posthuman, Sundberg, Hunt, Jackson, and Watts plainly demonstrate the dangers of a Eurocentric conception of ontology and posthumanism. What do these critiques of posthumanism have to do with the Anthropocene? Put simply: both threads of inquiry, posthumanism and the Anthropocene, share a terrain, even if they do not have in common the same central emphasis in their respective discourses.[31] Posthumanism (and, more specifically, its concurrent stream of work on multispecies ethnographies) "aims to decenter the human"[32] in Euro-Western scholarship, whereas the Anthropocene is *intensely pre-occupied with the human, the anthropos*. John Hartigan recently examined the prevalence of the terms "multispecies" and "Anthropocene" at the recent meeting of the American Anthropological Association in Washington, D.C. in December 2014. Noting the "overlapping concerns highlighted by these two keywords,"[33] Hartigan was struck by the dominance of the word Anthropocene, rather than the term multispecies, throughout the conference presentations. Hartigan deems the Anthropocene a "charismatic mega-category,"[34] which sweeps many competing narratives under its roof.

So, the Anthropocene narrative gathers discursive steam, dominating contexts where other discourses struggle to circulate. And, it dominates in what is an undeniably *white* intellectual space of the Euro-Western academy. It is perhaps unsurprising for popular thought to be Eurocentric when the institutions and structures within which it is generated continue to be largely heteropatriarchal, Eurocentric, and white. For example, Sara Ahmed takes the British academy directly to task for the whiteness and sexism of its praxis: she describes the problem of "white men" as an institution and code of conduct within the academy that reproduces whiteness and is inherent in what she calls the "citational relational" practice of citing white men generation after generation, reinforcing the white, patriarchal Eurocentrism of our disciplines.[35] To drive the point home in a quantitative manner, journalist Jack Grove reports on the under-representation of people of colour, and particularly women of colour, in *Times Higher Education*. There were only eighty-five black professors of a total of 18,500 professors in the United Kingdom in 2011.[36] And as philosopher Catherine Clune-Taylor points out, none of those professors were working in the discipline of philosophy. [37]

Anthropologists Karen Brodkin, Sandra Morgen, and Janis Hutchinson have studied the experience of people of colour in American anthropology departments, revealing widespread racism and discrimination within the discipline in North America,[38] and describing it as "white public space," a term they credit to a 1994 article by Page and Thomas.[39] For Brodkin, Morgen, and Hutchinson, anthropology in America is "white public space" because it operates both to: a) *physically* and *procedurally* discriminate against people of colour in anthropology departments; and, b) *conceptually* discriminate by minimizing or denying experiences of racism within departments. So, the "buildings," or "white men as buildings" that Ahmed describes,[40] within which ideologies are produced, serve to both literally and figuratively reinforce whiteness. If the academy's structures reproduce whiteness, what can we expect of the stories it is telling about the Anthropocene and our shared struggles to engage with dynamic environmental crises on the planet? Anthropologist Paul Stoller suggests that the current state of things—which has arguably arisen within a configuration of the "academy as white public space"—has not produced an engaged or *active* response to the challenges of the Anthropocene. As an anthropologist, Stoller suggests that "the politics of the Anthropocene is an anthropological challenge,"[41] which requires an *active* and *engaged* academic praxis as crucial to responding to the impacts of the Anthropocene. I argue that in order to enliven and enact *active* scholarship and praxis as responses to the Anthropocene, the academy must dismantle the underlying heteropatriarchal and white supremacist structures that shape its current configurations and conversations.

However, academia is not the only white public space; Guillermo Gómez-Peña describes the appropriation of the bodies/aesthetics/epistemologies of people of colour/Latinos, and the uncritical centralization of whiteness of the American art world. He claims:

> In the same way the US needs a cheap undocumented labor force to sustain its agricultural complex without having to suffer the Spanish language or

unemployed foreigners wandering their neighbourhoods, the contemporary art world needs and desires the spiritual and aesthetic models of Latino culture without having to experience our political outrage and cultural contradictions. What the art world wants is a "domesticated Latino" who can provide enlightenment without irritation, entertainment without confrontation.[42]

As Gómez-Peña demonstrates, the erasure of Latino/Latina bodies and the sanitization of rage or dispossession in contemporary art obscures the visceral, racialized, gendered, and geographically distinct experiences of socio-political and environmental crises in the world today. His critiques resonate with my aunt Loretta Todd's critical analysis of the North American art world and its treatment of Indigenous people, bodies, and ideas today. She says: "Our 'past' was once the preoccupation of the colonizers, and we developed codes to negotiate the performative nature of being the Aboriginal of an imagined past. Now our future is the growing preoccupation *but the power dynamics seem to remain the same.*"[43]

In a special issue of the journal *Decolonization: Indigeneity, Education, and Society* on Indigenous art, Jarrett Martineau and Eric Ritskes emphasize critiques resonant with that of Gómez-Peña. Martineau and Ritskes both highlight the ongoing whiteness of mainstream art praxis, positing Indigenous art as a counter-narrative to the heteropatriarchy and white supremacy that informs artistic discourses. They argue that "the task of decolonial artists, scholars and activists is not simply to offer amendments or edits to the current world, but to display the mutual sacrifice and relationality needed to sabotage colonial systems of thought and power for the purpose of liberatory alternatives."[44] I would add that the non-human must also be incorporated into this equation. The "sacrifice and relationality" asserted by Martineau and Ritskes evoke the analysis of contemporary Indigenous materialist art by art historians Jessica Horton and Janet Berlo. Horton and Berlo suggest that in works by Indigenous artists like Rebecca Belmore and Jolene Rickard, which engage with materials (water, pollutants, corn) and urgent politics, "material might act as a bridge, instead of a mirror"[45] to Euro-Western scholars, artists, and ideologies. Material as bridge—between people and non-human agents—can allow a different understanding of the Anthropocene to emerge. In other words, the materials as conceptualized and enacted in the work of the Indigenous artists that Horton and Berlo review are no mere actants. They are, rather, as Watts proclaims in her intervention into Euro-Western materialist thinking, enlivened with spirit.[46] With relationship. With sentience, will, and knowing. They thus bind whomever they encounter to the relationality that Martineau and Ritskes evoke. This understanding of material-as-bridge is therefore one site where Martineau and Ritskes's "mutual sacrifice and relationality" is possible.

There is no way to get around the fact that the business of making knowledge and making art in the European and North American academies is still very much a Eurocentric endeavour. But I would offer: *An effective art of the Anthropocene is one that directly engages with the structural violences of heteropatriarchy and white supremacy as they shape discourse and praxis.* This is where the work of Indigenous scholars and artists promises to speak back, reshape, and change the direction of current human-centric and Eurocentric framings of the Anthropocene. I now attend to the promise of Indigenous praxis and thought as decolonizing tools in the Anthropocene.

Indigenizing the Anthropocene: Dwayne Donald's "Ethical Relationality" and Indigenous Métissage

Thankfully, there are ways to counter the Eurocentrism of the academy and the art world and its discourses about global environmental crises. I investigate here how Indigenous scholarship can accomplish what anthropological and arts discourses struggle to do: decolonize the academy and its contemporary concerns, including the Anthropocene. As discourses of the Anthropocene heat up across and within various disciplines, Papaschase Cree scholar Dwayne Donald, who teaches and writes about education in Canada, has called for an "ethical relationality."[47] Though his work originates in education and curriculum discourses, his thinking serves as a powerful tool with which to examine underlying assumptions about, and responses to, human and non-human relationships in the Anthropocene. He advances two related ideas that can serve as strong responses to the current structures and frameworks that shape discussions about the Anthropocene, and indeed our complex existence on the planet. The first idea is "ethical relationality," which in a 2010 talk he defined as:

> an enactment of ecological imagination. Ethical relationality doesn't deny that we're different, so it's not a way to say we're all the same. But it seeks to understand more deeply how our different histories and experiences position us in relation to each other. It puts those at the forefront: who you are, where you come from, what your commitments are, what your experiences have been. So, it's a desire to acknowledge and honour the significance of the relationships we have with others, how our histories and experiences position us in relation to each other, and how our futures as people in the world are similarly tied together. *It is an ethical imperative to see that despite our varied place-based cultures and knowledge systems, we live in the world together and must constantly think and act with reference to those relationships.*[48]

Donald envisions ethical relationality as rooted in what he defines as our "ecological imagination."[49] At its core, Donald's approach to our position as humans on this fraught planet is rooted in balance and reciprocity:

> I use that term "ecology," and this comes from, I guess, the little bit I know about Cree and Blackfoot philosophies, which I know are connected in this

way. And of course I use ecology not in the sense I use it, typically, in Science. I don't mean "ecology" in that you study the environment separate from where we live or who we are as people. Actually, ecology, the way I think of it—the way I've been taught to think about it—is: paying attention to the webs of relationships that you are enmeshed in, depending on where you live. So, those are all the things that give us life, all the things that we depend on, as well as all the other entities that we relate to, including human beings.[50]

In turn, his notion of "ethical relationality" also "seeks to understand more deeply how our different histories and experiences position us in relation to each other,"[51] and provides an Indigenous framework through which to read the discourses of the Anthropocene. Donald unambiguously emphasizes the relationality between *all* things, all relationships. Though humans may drive some changes on the planet, Donald's framework re-centres how these connections are enmeshed in "webs of relationships."

The second idea that Donald advances is that of Indigenous Métissage, which he defines as "a place-based approach to curriculum informed by an ecological and relational understanding of the world,"[52] one that fosters reciprocal discourse between colonizer and colonized. In outlining the logics and praxis of Indigenous Métissage, Donald reminds readers that in order to mobilize Indigenous Métissage, there must be an "ethic of historical consciousness":

This ethic holds that the past occurs simultaneously in the present and influences how we conceptualize the future. It requires that we see ourselves related to, and implicated in, the lives of those yet to come. It is an ethical imperative to recognize the significance of the relationships we have with others, how our histories and experiences are layered and position us in relation to each other, and how our futures as people similarly are tied together. It is also an ethical imperative to see that, despite our varied place-based cultures and knowledge systems, we live in the world together with others and must constantly think and act with reference to these relationships. Any knowledge we gain about the world interweaves us more deeply with these relationships, and gives us life.[53]

An orientation towards Donald's philosophical framework helps to address the shortcomings that Malm and Hornborg[54] identify in the current framings of the Anthropocene, which currently acts as white public space and erases the differential histories and relationships that have led to current environmental crises. Historical consciousness, ethical relationality, and Indigenous Métissage—rooted in reciprocity, relationships, and responsibility—are among many principles the Eurocentric academy struggles to address in current framings and responses to the Anthropocene. Donald offers a philosophy rooted in the things he has learned from Cree and Blackfoot legal orders and his experiences in the world. His ethical relationality and Indigenous Métissage are processes through which to move away from human-centric discourses about the Anthropocene, and to envisage ourselves as rooted in reciprocal, ongoing, and dynamic relationships that are informed by Indigenous legal orders and our embeddedness in the meshworks that connect us through an "ecological imagination."[55] Such relationality can inform decolonizing approaches to both art and anthropology in the Anthropocene.

In the brief space remaining, I attend to ways of "Indigenizing the Anthropocene," or at least providing Indigenous responses to the notion *of* the Anthropocene, in order to mitigate the gentrifying forces it is embedded in.

Conclusion

When discourses and responses to the Anthropocene are being generated within institutions and disciplines which are embedded in broader systems that act as *de facto* "white public space," the academy and its power dynamics must be challenged. Eduardo Viveiros de Castro's call for the "permanent decolonization of thought"[56] must be coupled with a radically decolonizing praxis: a praxis that dismantles and re-orients not only the academy's and the art world's presuppositions about themselves, but also dismantles the heteropatriarchy, racism, and whiteness that continue to permeate political and intellectual systems in North America and Europe. It is important that the academy's current push to challenge the Euro-Western ontological split between nature and culture not obscure the concurrent, ongoing radical questioning and disruption of racism and colonialism that permeate academic institutions. Decolonization requires that we change not only who is spoken about and how, but also *who is present* in intellectual and artistic "buildings." This is because there are so few of us, so few Indigenous bodies, within the European academy. Even when we *are* present, we are often dismissed as biased, overly emotional, or unable to maintain objectivity over the issues we present.

Ultimately, what I am contesting are the ways in which well-meaning contemporary artists and academics recreate exploitative patterns from the past. The Anthropocene, like any theoretical category at play in Euro-Western contexts, is not innocent of such violence. Exploitative patterns, when they manifest, in turn concentrate the *voice* of Indigenous issues in white hands. It is precisely these power dynamics that must be questioned and challenged. Gómez-Peña puts it beautifully: "'We want understanding, not publicity.' We want to be considered intellectuals, not entertainers; partners, not clients; collaborators, not competitors; holders of strong spiritual vision, not emerging voices; and, above all, full citizens, not exotic minorities."[57]

As Indigenous actors, we do not need anyone to speak *for* us. And, all of us involved in the business of art and academia need to question existing relationships in intellectual and/or art contexts that privilege white voices speaking Indigenous stories. In order to engage in global conversations about the state of the world, such as the current discourse of the Anthropocene, there must be a concomitant examination of where such discourses are situated, who is defining the problems, and who decides the players involved. Rather than engage with the Anthropocene as a teleological fact implicating all humans as equally culpable for the current socio-economic, ecological, and political state of the world, I argue that we should turn to examining how other peoples are describing our "ecological imagination." To tackle the intertwined and complex environmental crises in which the world finds itself, a turn towards the reciprocity and relationships that Donald addresses in his writings and talks must be seriously considered, as locally informed responses to *in situ* challenges around the globe cannot be constructed using one philosophical, epistemological, or ontological lens. Art, as one mode of thought and praxis, can play a role in dismantling the condos of the art and academic world and help us build something different in their stead. The Anthropocene, after all, need not gentrify our discourses of outrage at the state of things when there are so many other ways to engage with our shared plight as beings on this planet. In order to resist the hegemonic tendencies of a universalizing paradigm like the Anthropocene, we need joyful and critical engagement through many forms of praxis. I see Indigenous thought and practice—including art—as critical sites of refraction of the current whiteness of Anthropocene discourses.

In recent years, my dad has engaged with the complexities of space and place, environmental degradation, and Indigeneity in his own work. In one series, he painted landscapes in diptych—one half presenting a landscape as it was pictured a hundred years ago, and the other half presenting how a landscape appears in his *pleine air* bicycle painting trips today. He also painted a series of ships, capturing their economic, political, and environmental presence in Vancouver harbours today, juxtaposed against the sea, mountains, and sky. The incursion of capitalist, resource-hungry interventions in the land is perhaps unavoidable at this point in time; however, Indigenous artists offer an important perspective on the intertwined and relational connections between people and land, and through their art can craft concrete responses to the mess and violence of the economies operating in the Anthropocene. Ironically, when my dad tries to show this new work, he is told it is not "Indigenous enough" by non-Indigenous curators and gallery owners, and so he continues to quietly paint on his own terms, radically questioning the landscapes and materials around him. Maybe someday this type of work will be seen as an "authentically Indigenous" response to the Anthropocene, too. This will only happen, though, if we manage to shift the ethical relationality of the academy and the art world, and the understandings of the Anthropocene produced within these "white public spaces." I know that I am already doing everything that I can to make that change possible. And I know there are many others involved in the same gleeful disruption.

Notes

An earlier version of this piece, exploring voice and appropriation, appeared on my blog *Urbane Adventurer* in 2014. See www.zoeandthecity.wordpress.com/2012/09/25/art-and-solidarity.

1. Guillermo Gómez-Peña, "The Multicultural Paradigm: An Open Letter to the National Arts Community," in *Negotiating Performance: Gender, Sexuality and Theatricality in Latin/o America*, ed. Diana Taylor and Juan Villegas (Durham: Duke University Press, 1994), 183–193.
2. Loretta Todd, "Close Encounters: The Next 500 Years," curated by Candice Hopkins, Steve Loft, Lee-Ann Martin, Jenny Western (Plug In Institute of Contemporary Art, 2011).
3. Taiaiake Alfred and Jeff Corntassel, "Being Indigenous: Resurgences against Contemporary Colonialism," *Government and Opposition: An International Journal of Comparative Politics* 40, no. 4 (2005): 597–614.
4. Sara Ahmed, "White Men," Feminist Killjoys Blog, 4 November 2014, www.feministkilljoys.com/2014/11/04/white-men.
5. Ibid.
6. Understandings of the Anthropocene as a narrative are articulated in John Hartigan, "Multispecies vs Anthropocene," *Somatosphere*, 13 December 2014, www.somatosphere.net/2014/12/multispecies-vs-anthropocene.html, and Andreas Malm and Alf Hornborg, "The Geology of Mankind? A Critique of the Anthropocene Narrative," *Anthropocene Review* 1, no. 1 (2014): 62–69.
7. Ibid.
8. Ibid., 64.
9. Kim Fortun, "From Latour to Late Industrialism," *HAU: Journal of Ethnographic Theory* 4, no. 1 (2014): 309–329.
10. Bruno Latour, "A Shift in Agency—with Apologies to David Hume," Gifford Lecture, University of Edinburgh, 19 February 2013, www.youtube.com/watch?v=w7s44BEDaCw.
11. See, for example, work by Sarah Hunt, Zakiyyah Jackson, Juanita Sundberg, and Vanessa Watts.
12. Juanita Sundberg, "Decolonizing Posthumanist Geographies," *Cultural Geographies* 21, no. 1 (2013): 35.
13. Ibid., 39.
14. Ibid.
15. Ibid.
16. Sarah Hunt, "Ontologies of Indigeneity: The Politics of Embodying a Concept," *Cultural Geographies* 21, no. 1 (2014): 27–32.
17. Ibid., 30.
18. Ibid., 29.
19. Ibid., 31.
20. Zakiyyah Jackson, "Animal: New Directions in the Theorization of Race and Posthumanism," *Feminist Studies* 39, no. 3 (2013): 671.
21. Vanessa Watts, "Indigenous Place-Thought and Agency amongst Humans and Non-humans (First Woman and Sky Woman go on a European Tour!)," *DIES: Decolonization, Indigeneity, Education and Society* 2, no. 1 (2013): 20–34.
22. Tim Ingold, "Hunting and Gathering as Ways of Perceiving the Environment," in *Redefining Nature: Ecology Culture and Domestication*, ed. Katsuyoshi Fukui and Roy Ellen (Oxford: Berg, 1996), 121. Ingold expands on his ideas of dwelling in *The Perception of the Environment: Essays in Livelihood, Dwelling and Skill* (London: Routledge, 2000).
23. A. Irving Hallowell, "Ojibwa Ontology, Behaviour and Worldview," in *Culture and History: Essays in Honour of Paul Radin*, ed. Stanley Diamond (New York: University of Columbia Press, 1960).
24. Watts, "Indigenous Place Thought," 21.
25. Ibid.
26. Ibid., 28.

27 Ibid.
28 Ibid., 29.
29 Ibid., 30.
30 Ibid.
31 Hartigan, "Multispecies vs Anthropocene."
32 Ibid.
33 Ibid.
34 Ibid.
35 Ahmed, "White Men."
36 Jack Grove, "Black Academics Still Experience Racism on Campus," *Times Higher Education*, 20 March 2014, www.timeshighereducation.co.uk/news/black-scholars-still-experience-racism-on-campus/2012154.article.
37 Karen Campos, "Cato Was Here," HeartBeats Blog, 13 December 2014, www.heart-beats.ca/HDB/exhibit/catotaylor.
38 Karen Brodkin, Sandra Morgen and Janis Hutchinson, "Anthropology as White Public Space?" *American Anthropologist* 113, no. 4 (2011): 545–556.
39 Helán E. Page, and R. Brooke Thomas, "White Public Space and the Construction of White Privilege in U.S. Healthcare: Fresh Concepts and a New Model of Analysis," *Medical Anthropology Quarterly* 8, no. 1 (1994): 109–116.
40 Ahmed, "White Men."
41 Paul Stoller, "Welcome to the Anthropocene: Anthropology and the Political Moment," *Huffington Post*, 29 November 2014, www.huffingtonpost.com/paul-stoller/welcome-to-the-anthropocene_b_6240786.html.
42 Gómez-Peña, "The Multicultural Paradigm," 24.
43 Todd, "Close Encounters," 128.
44 Martineau, J. and E. Ritskes, "Fugitive Indigeneity: Reclaiming the Terrain of Decolonial Struggle through Indigenous Art," *DIES: Decolonization, Indigeneity, Education and Society* 3, no. 1 (2014): ii.
45 Jessica Horton and Janet Catherine Berlo, "Beyond the Mirror: Indigenous Ecologies and 'New Materialisms' in Contemporary Art," *Third Text* 27, no. 1 (2013): 20.
46 Watts, "Indigenous Place-Thought and Agency amongst Humans and Non-humans," 20–34.
47 Dwayne Donald, "On What Terms Can We Speak? Lecture at the University of Lethbridge," 2010, www.vimeo.com/15264558.
48 Ibid., emphasis added.
49 Ibid.
50 Ibid.
51 Dwayne Donald, "Forts, Curriculum and Indigenous Métissage: Imagining Decolonization of Aboriginal-Canadian Relations in Educational Contexts," *First Nations Perspectives* 2, no. 1 (2009): 6.
52 Ibid., 1.
53 Ibid., 7.
54 Malm and Hornborg, "The Geology of Mankind?"
55 Tim Ingold (2008) advances the idea of "meshworks" in place of networks, which he contrasts quite pointedly in his critique of Latour. Tim Ingold, "When ANT Meets SPIDER: Social Theory for Arthropods," in *Material Agency: Towards a Non-Anthropocentric Approach*, ed. Carl Knapett and Lambros Malafouris (New York: Springer, 2008).
56 Eduardo Viveiros de Castro, *Metaphysiques cannibales* (Paris: Presses Universitaires de France, 2009), cited in Martin Holbraad, Morten Pedersen and Eduardo Viveiros de Castro, "The Politics of Ontology: Anthropological Positions," *Cultural Anthropology*, 13 January 2014, www.culanth.org/fieldsights/462-the-politics-of-ontology-anthropological-positions.
57 Gómez-Peña, "The Multicultural Paradigm," 26.

Anthropocene, Capitalocene, Chthulhucene
Donna Haraway in conversation with Martha Kenney

Since long before the recent interest in the Anthropocene, Donna Haraway has been concerned with the question of how to live well "on a vulnerable planet that is not yet murdered."[1] One of our most vital thinkers on the politics of nature and culture (which she believes cannot and should not be separated), Haraway's writing bristles with generosity, outrage, wit, and fierce intelligence. She has inspired generations of readers to think critically and creatively about how to live and work inside the difficult legacies of settler colonialism, industrial capitalism, and militarized technoscience.

This work of inheriting violent pasts and presents in the process of building more liveable worlds, Haraway argues, must be understood as a collective project composed of connections that are only partial, fraught with contradictions, disagreements, and refusals—and made up of mundane practices that are nevertheless consequential. She models this approach in her own writing, where she thinks with and through the work of fellow feminists, artists, activists, science-fiction writers, biologists, and critters of all kinds. As this interview demonstrates, Haraway's citation practice is interdisciplinary, multi-generational, and exuberant. She cites her own PhD advisor, ecologist G. Evelyn Hutchinson, as well as her former students Astrid Schrader, Eva Hayward, and Natalie Loveless. For Haraway, thinking, writing, and world-making are always the work of *sym-poiesis*, of making together.

These days, Haraway is committed to "staying with the trouble" in multispecies worlds where suffering and flourishing are unevenly distributed and always at stake. Worlds at stake—whether the decolonizing lands, animals, and peoples in the US Southwest, or the vulnerable multicritter webs of coral reefs—are messy and always unfinished; but the necessary work of *sym-poiesis* promises new ways of going-on together.

I spoke with her at her home in Santa Cruz, California, in December 2013; what follows is an edited transcription of our conversation.

Martha Kenney Your work has always been concerned with the possibilities for living and dying well on this planet, for humans and other earth-bound critters. What are some of the most urgent questions informing your current scholarship in the context of increasingly visible anthropogenic devastation?

Donna Haraway Well that's a big question. I think that I could do this by listing certain kinds of urgencies that I feel in my bones. We live in a time of mass extinctions and exterminations, including the genocides of other critters and of people.[2] We live and die in a time of permanent war, multi-species surplus killings, and genocides. Coupled to that, but distinct from it, is the urgency of climate change. We inhabit a planet that is undergoing systemic transformations, including the already-experienced ones and the anticipated flips of set points in geosystems, such that complex, biodiverse assemblages like coral reefs can undergo rapid and irreversible changes of state. Rich worlds crucial to human and nonhuman flourishing can and do disappear. Things can be very gradual, and then boom—systems changes mutate life and death radically and suddenly. Understanding that in the tissues of our flesh seems to me really urgent.

Related to this is the question of a human population of seven billion and counting; it is anticipated to be eleven billion by the end of this century. Eleven billion! The sheer number of people and the demands they/we make on the earth matter hugely. We need to be committed to radically reducing this obscene weight of reproduction, consumption, and production while helping to craft the will, imagination, and apparatuses for people and other critters to be better off as both a means and an end. Reducing human numbers must involve more social justice, more wealth, not less, the kinds of wealth that make for good living for billions of human beings in a living, diverse world; this commitment must be intrinsic to reducing human demands on the earth. Addressing the question of human beings within manufactured scarcity apparatuses, including the particular ones we are experiencing now in the so-called economic crisis with its various unjust austerity measures, is necessary. We are living in a period of intolerable extraction, unequal human deprivation, multispecies extinctions, and blasted ecosystems. Even so, it is also true that for the great bulk of people on this planet now hunger is actually less, disease is in retreat in many areas, and acute global poverty is reduced—which is unbelievable given the intensities of exploitation. How do you get back to two billion, which is about where the human population was shortly before I was born, and how do you do that while increasing justice and well-being in a multi-species way? I think that question gathers together most of the problems for me.

MK In your recent writing, you have used the term "response-ability" as one of the virtues that we need to cultivate in the context of these felt urgencies. Could you tell us what you mean by response-ability?

DH Like all of the words that feel vital in me now, these are words that come out of communities of practice; they are *sym-poietic* terminologies (made-together-with: *poiesis* as making, *sym* as together-with). These terms and ideas are made together with many other people. When I speak about response-ability, I feel Astrid Schrader, Karen Barad, and Vinciane Despret emerging to the foreground.[3] I feel like I'm channelling as well as weaving, knotting, crocheting. Response-ability is that cultivation through which we render each other capable, that cultivation of the capacity to respond. Response-ability is not something you have toward some kind of demand made on you by the world or by an ethical system or by a political commitment. Response-ability is not something that you just respond to, as if it's there already. Rather, it's the cultivation of the capacity of response in the context of living and dying in worlds for which one is for, with others. So I think of response-ability as irreducibly collective and to-be-made. In some really deep ways, that which is not yet, but may yet be. It is a kind of luring, desiring, making-with.

MK You have described your scholarship as an ongoing process of refiguring what counts as nature. What do you mean by figuration? And how do you feel that attention to the liveliness and deadliness of figures might help strengthen ecological response-ability?

DH I love words that just won't sit still, and once you think you've defined them it turns out they are like ship hulls full of barnacles. You scrape them off, but the larvae re-settle and spring up again. Figuring is a way of thinking or cogitating or meditating or hanging out with ideas. I'm interested in how figures help us avoid the deadly fantasy of the literal. Of course, the literal is another trope, but we're going to hold the literal still for a minute, as the trope of no trope. Figures help us avoid the fantasy of "the one true meaning." They are simultaneously visual and narrative as well as mathematical. They are very sensual.

I am interested particularly in string figures, in string games like cat's cradle—a game played on tentacles or digits of many kinds, like fingers and toes. Cat's cradle, as Isabelle Stengers pointed out, involves one set of digits or tentacles holding still long enough to receive a pattern passed by another set and then passing a mutated pattern back, so there is stillness and motion, giving and receiving, staying and moving. String figures are also old games; they show up all over the world. So they are an obvious figure for me in thinking about response-ability, feminist environmentalism, and science studies. String figures are SF games. SF games are science fiction, science fact, speculative fabulation, speculative feminism, *soin de ficelle*, so far (in that these games are ongoing and not finished). Connected to this is Ursula K. Le Guin's carrier bag theory of fiction, where storytelling is about collecting things up into a net, a bag, a shell, a recipient, or a hollow, for sharing. SF is full of old, important feminist figures.

There's another set of figures that I want to bring up here that are in a kind of Venn diagram relationship with string figures. They partly intersect, but they also pull against and are different. And that is tentacular figures. The tentacular ones, the tentacled ones, like jellyfish, extravagant marine worms, the Hawaiian bobtail squid, like the Ood in *Doctor Who*, like the Cthulhu in H.P. Lovecraft, like many things. I'm working a lot these days with the tentacular ones and with the face as a feeling, entwining, tentacular, negatively curving/waving hyperbolic surface. Medusa is my friend these days.

MK Why do you find yourself drawn to these tentacular figures?

DH Well, part of it has to do with what Eva Hayward gave us when she was paying attention to coral reefs.[4] She thinks about the haptic visual. She's interested in the way human beings studying coral reefs often work through visual technologies, visual apparatuses. She shows that visuality is also haptic; her term for this is "fingeryeyes." There is an incredible array of sensory apparatuses in the critters of the sea that Eva's interested in and that are especially important in global warming. So they are more than a metaphor for thinking about the way that human beings, while we are hugely visual, are visual in a haptic modality; vision can be figured as touch, not distance, as entwined with, or negatively curving in loops and frills, not surveying from above. For a long time, since before I wrote "The Cyborg Manifesto" and certainly in "Situated Knowledges," I was interested in reclaiming visuality as a becoming-with or being-with, as opposed to surveying-from. You can't walk away from important things like vision, you can't give them away; you must refigure, and then you discover that they are already deeply refigured and all you really have to do is re-inhabit.

MK I also love the word "feelers" for the tentacles, because none of our other organs say what they do... we don't have "seers" or "smellers."

DH Feelers are actually an action name. Think of Medusa. The snakes, of course, freeze the man who looks directly at them, but they are also feelers, the snakes are sensory apparatuses. Rusten Hogness pointed this out to me. They swirl...

MK ...and also that wonderful word that I learned from Eva—*tentacularity*—the ways that figures, stories, multi-sensory apparatuses reach out to their audience and enrol them...

DH ...and engulf them and sometimes sting them [*laughter*] because a lot of these tentacles have little poison sacks and darts on them; they are apparatuses of predation as well. These are not innocent figures; these are figures of living and dying, of risk and entanglement. These are figures for inhabiting attentively with response-ability.

MK There is always the question of who is enrolled by figures, who is enticed, who is scared. I am curious about the figure of the Anthropocene, how it reaches out and how it gathers. It has been very charismatic in enrolling people.

DH And fast!

MK What do you feel are the some of the possibilities and limitations of organizing our efforts around this figure of the Anthropocene?

DH Well, first, let me say something historical. The current use of the term Anthropocene dates to the year 2000, when it is used in a paper in a geology context. The term was coined by ecologist Eugene Stoermer and the Nobel-Prize-winning atmospheric chemist Paul Crutzen to refer to the influence of human behaviour on the earth's atmosphere, lithosphere, and hydrosphere in recent centuries, and has been proposed as a name for a geological epoch. But it has quickly become way bigger than that. It has been picked up by artists, humanists, politicians, scientists, and the popular press. The charismatic quality of the figure is worth staying-still with. There's a need for a word to highlight the urgency of human impact on this planet, such that the effects of our species are literally written into the rocks. In the evidence for the current mass extinction "event," any geologist of the future will find the synthetic chemistry of DuPont in the composition of the rocks, will find in the hydrosphere the synthetic chemistry of multinational pharmaceutical and petrochemical corporations. The hydrosphere, lithosphere, atmosphere, everythingsphere, the multiple worldings of the earth will show the effect of the activities of industrial human beings. The need for a word for that, I think, is obvious, and accounts for a huge amount of popularity of the term.

I also think the term feeds into some extremely conventional and ready-to-the-tongue stories that need far more critical inquiry. The figure of the *anthropos* itself is a species term. The *anthropos*—what is that? *All* of *Homo sapiens sapiens*? *All* of mankind? Well, *who exactly*? Fossil-fuel-burning humanity is the first short answer to that. Industrial humanity, however, is still a kind of a species-being; it doesn't even speak to all of industrial humanity, but specifically the formations of global capital and global state socialisms. Very much a part of that are the exchange networks, the financial networks, extraction practices, wealth creations, and (mal)distributions in relation to both people and other critters. It would probably be better named the Capitalocene, if one wanted a single word. The mass extinction events are related to the resourcing of the earth for commodity production, the resourcing of everything on the earth, most certainly including people, and everything that lives and crawls and dies and everything that is in the rocks and under the rocks. We live in the third great age of carbon, in which we are witnessing the extraction of the last possible calorie of carbon out of the deep earth by the most destructive technologies imaginable, of which fracking is only the tip of the (melting) iceberg. Watch what's going on in the Arctic as the sea ice melts and the nations line up their war and mining ships for the extraction of the last calorie of carbon-based fuels from under the northern oceans. To call it the Anthropocene misses all of that; it treats it as if it's a species act. Well, it isn't a species act. So, if I had to have a single word I would call it the Capitalocene.

I'm not exactly against the figure of the Anthropocene, partly because it's already focusing people on something that needs urgent attention. Besides, the term can't be dislodged now, I don't think, even though it's recent. So I'm not against it, but I really want to complicate it.

The Anthropocene has had a conflicted etymological history. A number of experts think of *anthropos* as "the one who looks up from the earth," the one who is earth-bound, of the earth, but looking up, fleeing the elemental and abyssal forces, "astralized." "Human" is a better figure for our species, if we want a species word, because of its tie to humus, compost. Unlike *anthropos*, humus is not about looking up; it's about being hot. [*Laughter*] Beth Stephens and Annie Sprinkle have this little bumper sticker "compost is so hot," for one of their feminist ecosexual slogans. It's not post-human, but *com-post*. Katie King has been playing with the term "composting humanities," and Rusten Hogness came up with "humusities" to replace "humanities." "Homo" needs to re-root in *humus*, not bliss out into an apocalyptic *anthropos*. Compost provides the figures for making multispecies public cultures, sciences, and politics now.

MK Maria Puig de la Bellacasa's work on soil and the permaculture movement is really wonderful for thinking about compost and the Anthropocene.[5] She critiques the figure of "crisis" and articulates the important difference between reacting to a crisis and creating sustainable relations across generations.

DH I think this is so deep in feminist environmentalism. The word "urgency," rather than crisis, is an energetic term for me. Urgency is energizing, but it's not about apocalypse or crisis. It's about inhabiting; it's about cultivating response-ability.

MK Since *The Companion Species Manifesto*, your own storytelling practice has been concerned with vital and deadly relations among organisms. You write about laboratory animals, agility sports, critter cams, sites where multi-species-becoming-with is the name of the game. How can telling these kinds of stories help us to learn how to *respond*, as Karen Barad puts it, within and as part of our more-than-human world?[6]

DH Multi-species-becoming-with, multi-species co-making, making-together, *sym-poiesis* rather than auto-poiesis. *Sym-poiesis* was coined originally in the late 1990s by Beth Dempster—a Canadian systems thinker—in her master's thesis about landscape design and environmentalism.[7] I keep having the need to cite; part of it is the need to not pose as original, but to remember the collective, the compost pile that makes heat.

MK You're performing *sym-poiesis*.

DH For me performing *sym-poiesis* or performing storying is also about constantly looping back and interrupting. I work to tell stories *sym-poietically* out of those things I really care about. And those things almost always involve non-human critters. They almost always involve scenes where biologies are intimately part of worlding, where naturecultures can't be separated. So, it's no surprise that I tell stories about the working and playing critters and got really, really interested in the becoming-with a dog who is my sports partner and the dog of my heart.

The training practices helped me rethink the evolutionary roots of the capacity for ethical reasoning. How do we think of evolutionary stories of our response-abilities, of our capacities to respond? Biologist Marc Bekoff developed this really wonderful theory that the roots of ethical possibilities, ethical response-ability, are in play.[8] Critters respond to the meta-communicative apparatuses of play signalling, so that play can go on and remain inventive rather than turn into aggression or something else boringly functional. Because play is one of those activities through which critters make with each other that which didn't exist before, it's never merely functional; it's propositional. Play makes possible futures out of joyful but dangerous presents. Think of the way Stengers theorizes Whitehead's propositions.[9]

Play proposes new abstractions, new lures. Marc didn't quite say all that, but I took what he gave me and told my stories with his; we played with each other. This is a *sym-poietic* telling of propositional stories about the origin of ethics—a string-figuring. It figures response-ability as becoming-with, and it's rooted in the riskiness of play. It's rooted in taking chances with one another, not in prohibition. Ethics is not primarily a rule-based activity, but a propositional, worlding activity.

If people start telling these kinds of stories around things that they care about—dogs, coral reefs, immigration, the problems of Israel-Palestine, the questions of permanent war in the Democratic Republic of Congo, or of desalination in Santa Cruz—if we really engage in storytelling as a *sym-poietic* practice, which is propositional and invitational, then we have a chance for re-worlding. Play always involves the invitation that asks "are we a 'we'"? A "we" that doesn't pre-exist the propositional risk and testing. I think all the important problems involve this propositional, questioning, interrogative "we."

MK There's also a pragmatics of storytelling and figuration at play: "Does *this* story work *here*"? What might be a wonderful figure in one context might not work, might not enrol, it might not have tentacularity, might not create the "we" in another. I think playfulness in this context is also an aesthetic playfulness, a playfulness of form, of genre, of style, a willingness to see what these things can *do*.

DH Yes! And let's face it: I love ideas. I think intellectual play is a blast, and I want to invite people into intellectual play rather than dump on it.

MK And to work against an understanding of scholarship as self-serious and final, rather than as a collective compost heap...

DH ...that generates heat and might get too hot. [*Laughter*] There is also another issue here about this mode of storytelling that has to do with history. You're never starting from scratch; the questions of how to inherit are always there. I'm consumed by the question of how to live with our inheritances, how not to disown them. We have many inheritances, so we need that kind of humility, the humility of never starting from scratch and never starting clean, as well as inheriting obligations we did not and cannot choose, but which we must respond to.

MK What kinds of figures and stories and propositions from others, from biologists, writers, and scholars, have you recently found promising around these questions of inheritance and response-ability?

DH Let's begin from within biology and consider ecological-evolutionary-developmental biology: eco-evo-devo. I've ended up making that into "eco-evo-devo-techno-histo-psycho," ending with psycho to please my friends who need to think about subjectivity more than I do. I'm being facetious; adding "psycho" signals that I've gone off the deep-end, necessarily. Ecological-evolutionary-developmental biology stresses the symbiogenetic quality of all becoming-with that makes critters. I'm avoiding the word organism, because it has the appearance of being closed off at the boundaries. Biologist Scott Gilbert and colleagues have started using "holobiont" and "holobiome" rather than "organism" and "environment" to signal the webbed multiplicities that make up any "one" in time and space.[10]

MK Could you define symbiogenesis for us?

DH Lynn Margulis took it from a Russian biologist who studied lichens, Konstantin Sergeyevich Merezhkovsky, who coined the term in 1910. Margulis was, among other things, a scholar who actually read German. She then re-introduced symbiogenesis to refer to the origin of complex cellularity through which the prokaryotes in the world of bacteria—who need to eat in order to live—eat each other but get indigestion, that kind of partial eating but not digesting, that kind of coming together but not fully assimilating, whereby two become less than two but more than one, where number gets troubled and the complex modern cell originates through indigestion—or, in Marilyn Strathern's term, "partial connections."[11] It happens when things eat each other but are not fully assimilated. Sym: together-with; bio: the way living critters do it; and, genesis: this is the way the beginnings worked. These are connections that make cobbled-together, still-hungry-for-affiliation beings that can never be wholes. The origin of the modern cell is a symbiogenetic event.

Contemporary biologists are saying this isn't just the origin of the modern cell, but that animal multi-cellularity is probably a symbiogenetic event. Take, for example, these single-celled critters with flagella that swim around in the water, choanoflagellates. One kind clumps when they're infected with a certain strain of bacteria and when they clump they look and act like a sponge. If you take sponges apart, it turns out they have included bacteria that are absolutely fundamental to their being a sponge at all. It begins to look like the earliest moves of animal multi-cellularity were symbiogenetic events involving bacteria in and among nucleated cells. This is a terrible over-simplification of Nicole King's elegant, experimental work at UC Berkeley, but you get a sense of how exciting these results are.[12]

How about developmental programs? The Hawaiian bobtail squid, which hunts at night, have bacteria associated with them that make light at night, so they look like starry skies from below. They crust sand over themselves on their backsides, so they look like a sandy bottom from above and like a starlit sky from below, so they're really incredibly well camouflaged as they squirt their way around and capture their prey. It turns out their light organ, without which they couldn't exist, is made not just from their genetic action, but requires the action of associated bacteria at a particular point in the development of the squid, so that to be a squid at all requires another set of organisms. So to be a one takes much more than one.

There are also entities that nest their genomes. For example, to make a protein it might take three separate species of critters that are nested inside of each other, partially assimilated and partly not, each having DNA that codes for different parts of the protein which they all need. You outsource part of your own genetic apparatus or you insource these multiple collaborations of entities in order to make things what they are. Call that symbiogenesis, origins of the cells, origins

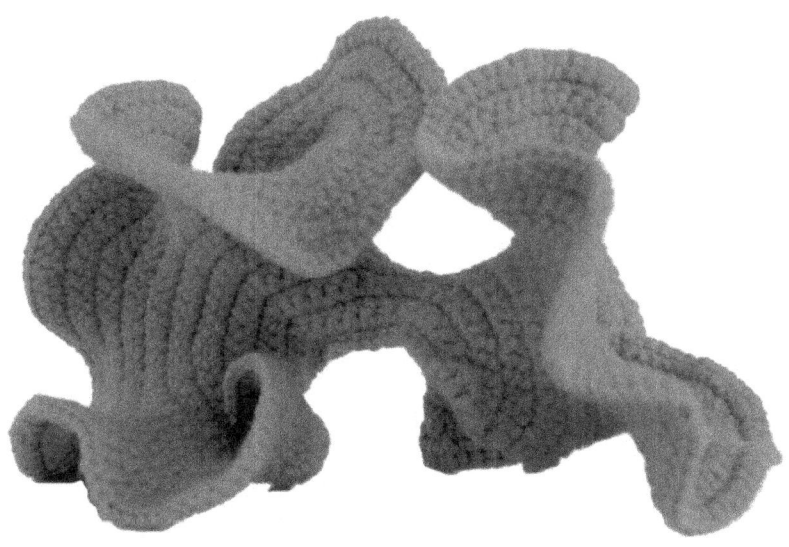

Crocheted hyperbolic plane by Dr. Daina Taimina; photo courtesy of the Institute For Figuring. Fig. 01

of multi-cellularity, developmental programs, nested genomes, all of this and more. Holobionts are entities appropriate to symbiogenesis and appropriate to the worlding not well named by the figures of the Anthropocene.

MK Along with the biologists and feminists that we have been talking about, how do you see artists participating in what Anna Tsing calls "the arts of living on a damaged planet"?[13]

DH My own practice for a long time has involved thinking with artists in the tissue of their work—artists like Kathy High, Beatriz Da Costa, or Natalie Jeremijenko. I'm extremely interested in the artists who work in multi-species complexities, and who work with them propositionally, in collective practice, in performance art. Natalie Loveless taught me so much about performance and performativity, and about thinking and making together.[14] Working with artists has become more and more essential to my material practice, and clearly included among artists are writers. I think the first artists I worked with in intimate detail were writers, primarily science-fiction writers. When I was a graduate student studying with Evelyn Hutchinson—who wrote that beautiful book *Kindly Fruits of the Earth, An Introduction to Population Ecology*, as well as "Circular Causal Systems in Ecology," "Homage to Santa Rosalia," and so many other things—he had us reading C. H. Waddington and pondering the importance of painting in his thinking about genetic assimilation and developmental plateaus.[15] Our thinking about ecology, evolution, and genetics in the 1960s, when I was a graduate student, already involved some serious consideration of modernist painting, as well as modernist poetry. We talked about all this in our biology tea groups; our lab group meetings involved thinking about philosophy, biology, art. I was really lucky to be part of an educational scene that took for granted that artistic practice is intrinsic and necessary to good thinking and to good science. Most biology research groups at Yale, then and now, were not like that, but my favourite biologists, like Scott Gilbert and Mike Hadfield, are like that.

So, our example—the one that you and I wanted to talk about, because it ties up so closely with both string figuring and tentacularity—is the Hyperbolic Crochet Coral Reef Project at the Institute for Figuring (IFF) in Los Angeles, where they have play tanks rather than work tanks. Margaret and Christine Wertheim are deliberately setting themselves off in a serious, joking relation to the Rand Corporation and their think tanks. Evelyn Hutchinson would have loved the IFF!

One of the streams of inspiration for the project comes from Margaret Wertheim's training in mathematics. She became interested in the ideas of mathematician Daina Taimina, who proposed the crocheted figure as a model for hyperbolic space. Mathematicians had material models for studying Euclidean spatialities, but hyperbolic, non-Euclidean space didn't have good material models until Taimina proposed crocheting. Margaret wrote a book called *A Field Guide to Hyperbolic Space*, in which she details the mathematical history.[16] By the way, if you buy red leaf lettuce or if you look at the structure of a coral reef: hyperbolic forms. They are everywhere. Remember, too, "A Non-Euclidean View of California as a Cold Place to Be," Ursula Le Guin's instructions for reading her looped and frilled novel, *Always Coming Home*.[17]

MK In the early twentieth century, non-Euclidean geometry was so unimaginable that H. P. Lovecraft used "non-Euclidean" alongside a host of other terrifying adjectives to describe the ancient and horrible realm of Cthulhu, yet here we're finding these forms in crochet. So, the other-worldly, even the terrifyingly other-worldly, turns out to be mundane.

DH And mundane in a very particular way, namely, as part of women's fibre arts. This is important to Margaret and Christine Wertheim, who foreground the feminist aspects of women's fibre arts, the collective and *sym-poetic* aspects of fibre arts, the mathematics, the ecological activism of bringing more than 7,000 people together in 25 globally distributed locations to crochet a coral reef to think with, become with, work with in a time of extinctions and exterminations. They explore the facts of the already-in-place inevitability of some extinctions, but also the opening to prevent at least some damage and to restore and rehabilitate partially. This is not a project of melancholy and mourning. Theirs are figures of response-ability. The crochet coral reef project is a materialization of response-ability, of cultivating, of caring with and for coral reefs and their situated critters, including people. So, thousands of women, as well as children and men, old and young, are participating in crocheting these reefs that are then produced as installations in all sorts of places. By proposing fundamental questions about extinction and survival and response through material figuring, both the crocheting and the installations create publics that learn to care, to make a difference.

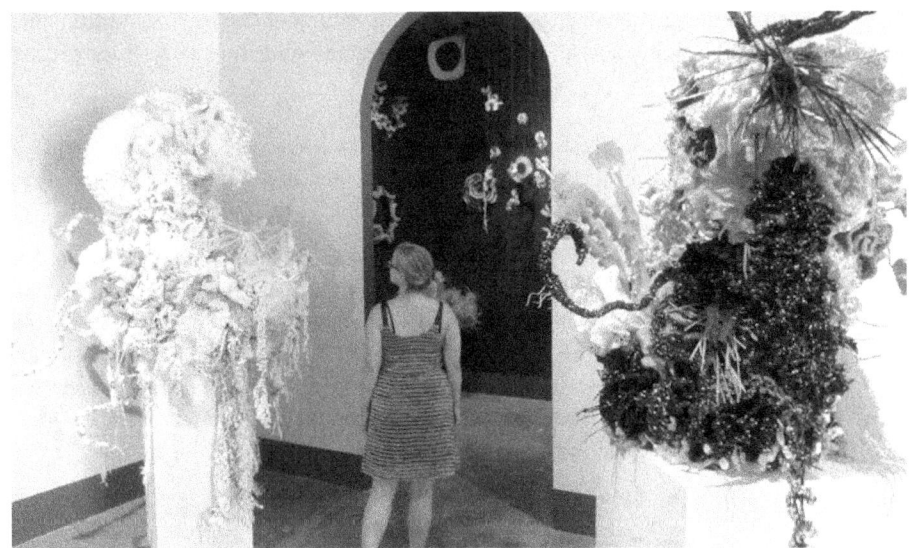

Coral Forest - Plastic. Coral sculptures crocheted from plastic bags and other plastic detritus. Constructed by Christine Wertheim. Photo by Margaret Werthein; courtesy of IFF Archive.

Fig. 02

They also crochet these reefs from trash. The reef that is especially affectively and politically powerful for me is the toxic coral reef, which is made out of thrown-away plastic trash. The Wertheims are interested in the Pacific gyre—the great plastic garbage patch in the ocean—and the excess death caused by plastic pollution.[18] So the only reefs that they allow to grow indefinitely are those that are made of trash; other reefs have limits, even the two heart-rending bleached reefs delicately crocheted from mostly white yarns by some of their most skilled collaborators. The Wertheims have a fantasy/nightmare project going now where some of the crocheting is done with old reel-to-reel tape and all kinds of industrial cast-offs that get crocheted into critters made of the trash that chokes the earth. There is amazing beauty to these pieces, a kind of inhabiting the possibility of a future out of a haunted past. It's beautiful and ugly; I think they are deliberately working with these multiple modalities.

MK Do the crocheted coral reefs mimic natural forms or are these fantasy organisms?

DH In the case of the "Coral Fantasies" work, these are fantasy organisms. In their Hawaiian Coral Reef Project, there are certain rules for people who want to play in this play tank. One of the rules is that you need to be crocheting or stitching together or making with fibre. There is some appliqué as well as crochet, but crocheting is the main thing. The crocheted critters have to be endemic Hawaiian species, so the Hawaiian coral reef is all critters who belong there. Hawaii, an island ecosystem at the heart of the history of colonialism and empire, has vast numbers of introduced species and many extinctions of endemics. So, with the Hawaiian coral reef, you are crocheting an imagined world full only of natural belonging, itself a troubling colonial fantasy, but also an indictment of extreme—and undeniable—destruction and dislocations.

MK That's what's interesting about it; it's not that the real reefs and the fantasy reefs are different projects, but the real and the fantasy exist in different measures in different exhibitions.

DH And then there's just the sheer beauty. The Wertheims are very careful about attribution, and I was surprised and delighted to find out that the science-fiction writer Vonda McIntyre was one of the early and ongoing contributors of crocheted coral figures. McIntyre's SF worlds figure the atmosphere and the oceans as fluids; her entities inhabit the watery seas and rivers of airs, so no wonder she was drawn to the crochet coral reef project. She's also very much part of feminism, environmentalism, and the narrating practices of feminist SF.[19]

MK Which is another traditionally feminine handicraft.

DH Exactly right. One of the practices of feminists across the generations is to always remember what we've inherited from those who went before, so that those who come after, can, in Deborah Bird Rose's thinking about country in an Australian context, inherit more quiet country.[20] So that those who come after can live in less blasted country.

MK One of the threads that has gone through our discussion so far is the question of making practices: crocheting, storytelling, figuration...

DH ...remembering that *poiesis* itself translates into making...

MK ...and the Latin for making is *fingere*. Fingers and figures and fiction come from *fingere*, so these fictions, these makings, are both real and consequential.

DH Fact is a past participle of *facere*, another Latin word for making. A fact is that which has been made, and they are precious.

MK ...but they are not uncontestable, they've been stabilized...

DH ...and they can be destabilized. Some of our facts need protection, nurture, and care; other facts should be undone. But facts do not, and should not, exit the zone of care. Facts require response-abilities.

MK What are some of the figures that you've been working with in your own play tank in this context of the Anthropocene?

DH I'm not sure that I myself have drawn original figures; I've adopted figures.

MK I think we always adopt figures.

DH We always adopt figures; besides, I am into adoption, not reproduction. I'm into poly-parenting and adoption rather than generating one's own offspring. The many-fingered ones capture me; I am consumed, partially digested, remade within tentacularities. I have been working extensively with the tentacularities of coral reefs. I've also been figuring with spiders, like *Pimoa cthulhu*. "Pimoa" is a Utah Gosiute word for long legs. I like the worldliness of the leggy Greek-Native American Gosiute chimera, which captures its prey in Sonoma and Mendocino County redwood forests far from Utah or the Mediterranean. This is not the Navajo's Spider Old-Woman, but her spinnerets extrude a non-innocent welcome, too. The naturalist who named this California spider chose "Cthulhu" for H. P. Lovecraft's monster deity who terrified men. I want this spider renamed, instead, for "chthonic" ones, a litter of the tentacular dreadful without gender. *Pimona chthulhu*, not *Pimona cthulhu*. I've been co-habiting with the chthonic ones, the sym-chthonic ones, who become with each other in and from the slimy mud and brine, in tangled temporalities that evade binaries like modern and traditional. I'm working with string figures a lot, for example, with the convergence and divergence of Navajo/Diné string figures called Na'at'lo and Euro-American cat's cradle, the ways that both tell the same stories and also tell very different stories. I'm intrigued by the question of who owns stories. Some peoples don't get to own their stories; the question of sovereignties comes up. In my lectures and in my work in general, I try hard to have a thread of vexed questions of indigeneity in play—thinkers like Kim TallBear and James Clifford help me do that.

MK So let's talk about the chthonic ones, specifically Medusa.

DH The reason the Ood of *Doctor Who* have been figuring for me is because their faces are tentacular. Since human beings are often proposed as facial because of the eyes, what happens when the faciality is tentacular, not ocular? Then there is Medusa, whose head is tentacular and snaky. Medusa is a Gorgon, of whom there are three and only one is mortal—Medusa. And she is killed in a murder-for-hire instigated by Athena. Medusa's body is decapitated, her head drips blood, and out of that blood sprang the coral gorgone reefs of the Western Sea, onto which the ships of the hero-explorers are dashed. So, her blood generates the coral reef—Eva Hayward pointed that out to me. From her decapitated body springs Pegasus, the winged horse, and of course feminists have big stakes in horses. So I'm interested in the figure of Medusa as a tentacular, Gorgonic figure full of feely snakes, who threatens the children of Zeus, most certainly including the head-born daughter of Zeus, Athena. The head-born daughter is not a feminist—quite the opposite.

The Gorgons are also ambiguous about gender. They are earlier than, or other than, Chaos. Gaia/Terra are offspring of Chaos, and they don't really have a gender, despite their iconography as goddesses; Bruno Latour emphasizes this. Gaia is not he or she, but *it*. They are forces of generativity, vitality, and destruction. But the dreadful ones are even more powerful. The Gorgons are dreadful—the word *gorgones* translates as dreadful. I think the abyssal and elemental dreadful ones are the figures that we need to inhabit in these moments of urgency which we tried to sketch at the beginning of our conversation, this living in a time of excess mass death, much of it human-induced.

MK It strikes me that outside the frontier epistemologies of discovery and conquest, Medusa and Cthulhu and the Ood aren't so terrible or terrifying. The non-Euclidean horrors that Lovecraft feared lurked beneath the sea—they were there. And they were these (potentially) solar-powered sea slugs that fascinated Margulis, and these mucous-secreting corals that are now at risk of extinction, and they are not horrible, although they are definitely slimy. So outside the hero story…

DH …they are not terrible, they are not so dreadful—except to "those who (only) look up."[21]

MK What narrative work do you hope that these chthonic figures will do when enrolled to remediate the fallout of techno-scientific progress—remediate as both remedy and to re-mediate?

DH I like that. They're medicine, they're *curare*, they are poison and cure. Outside the techno-hero story, inside the carrier-bag story, they are not so terribly dreadful, but they also aren't safe; they are not "us." So we're no longer looking at the apocalyptic, dreadful other that Athena fears and needs to slay; we're looking at the earth that's made of concatenated differences. We are looking at the holobiont that is Gaia, Terra, Medusa; and, of course, we're just doing Western stories here; there are many other stories, like those of the now world-famous Incan Pachamama—sisters and *not* sisters of Egyptian Gorgones, Greek Gaia, Wiccan Terra, Yoruban Oya, or Navajo Spider Old-Woman, much less the leggy Pimoa. The remediation I lust for is about re-inhabiting the ordinary and re-inhabiting it with response-ability. When we tell the parabolic and spiked tales of tragic detumescence, tales of the Modern and the Traditional, we get off easy. We don't have to do a thing. We are not urged to action, we aren't urged to caring, we aren't urged to decomposition and recomposition. I want non-Euclidean ruffled tales, studded with tentacles for risky tangling. Ongoing caring requires that we work with figures of re-mediation that are risky and also fun, that we work, play, live, die, that we are at risk *with* and *as* mortal critters, that we don't give in to the techno-tragic story of self-made final death of the Anthropocene, but that we do inhabit the realities of excess mass death so as to learn to repair, and maybe even flourish without denial.

MK To return to play, I was playing around with the figure of the Ood, because *Doctor Who* is fun and it's good to think with. The Ood are particularly good figures for the Anthropocene because of their biological vulnerability. They have these hind-brains that are outside of their bodies, attached by a kind of umbilical cord. In addition to the hind-brain, they are connected telepathically to a collective brain. This is what makes them vulnerable to colonization and enslavement by the humans who lobotomize them; when they cut off their hind-brains, they cut them off psychologically from their collective consciousness. In fields like epigenetics and microbiome research, we are hearing new stories about the human body, not as a citadel, but as something porous and vulnerable to exposures. The world passes through us and we are not unchanged. I was wondering what the Ood, who are born with their brains in their hands, can teach us about these sorts of uneven landscapes of exposure that cut us off from what sustains us, and also what practices of resilience…

DH ...and how dangerous they become when they are enslaved.

MK It's the opposite of the Lovecraft story: they're not the horrible monster lying in wait.

DH They are made the enemy when they're enslaved.

MK It's our exploration and exploitation that's the horrible thing.

DH You could say that about techno-humanism: that we make ourselves the enemy when we enslave ourselves to the heroic-tragic man-makes-himself story. When we cut ourselves off from our collective, our becoming-with, including dying and becoming compost again. When we cut ourselves off from mortality and fear death, we become our own worst enemy in this relentless story of making ourselves in the image of death. These are the lived stories of the Anthropocene as Capitalocene. But there's a third story, or actually myriad stories. The *Chthulhucene* probably won't catch on because not enough people know the word. But the Chthulhucene would be truer. I am resigned to the term Anthropocene; I'm not going to be abstemious, and I'm not going to play purity games here. But, if only we had not started with that term... What if we had started instead by renaming our epoch, even—especially—in the Geophyiscal Union, with *sym-poietic* power, to signal the ongoing and non-Euclidean net bag of the Chthulhucene, a story of SF, speculative fabulation, speculative feminism, scientific fact, string figures, so far? This unfinished Chthulhocene must collect up the trash of the Anthropocene, the exterminism of the Capitalocene, and make a much hotter compost pile for still possible pasts, presents, and futures.

Notes

1 Donna Haraway, "Sowing Worlds: A Seed Bag for Terraforming with Earth Others," in *Beyond the Cyborg: Adventures with Donna Haraway*, ed. Margaret Grebowicz and Helen Merrick (New York: Columbia University Press, 2013), 137.

2 Ed. note: for an especially compelling discussion of mass extinction, see Elizabeth Kolbert, *The Sixth Extinction: An Unnatural History* (New York: Henry Holt and Company, 2014).

3 See, for example: Astrid Schrader, "Responding to *Pfiesteria piscicida* (the Fish Killer): Phantomatic Ontologies, Indeterminacy, and Responsibility in Toxic Microbiology," *Social Studies of Science* 40, no. 2 (April 2010): 275–306; Vinciane Despret, "The Body We Care For: Figures of Anthropo-zoo-genesis," *Body & Society* 10, no. 2–3 (2004): 111–134; and Karen Barad, "On Touching—The Inhuman that Therefore I Am," *differences* 23, no. 3 (2012): 206–223.

4 Eva Hayward, "Fingeryeyes: Impressions of Cup Corals," *Cultural Anthropology* 25, no. 4 (November 2010): 577–599.

5 Maria Puig de la Bellacasa, "Soil Times: Notes on Caring Temporalities," Unpublished Manuscript.

6 Karen Barad, *Meeting the Universe Halfway: Quantum Physics and the Entanglement of Matter and Meaning* (Durham: Duke University Press, 2007), 37.

7   Beth Dempster, "A Self-Organizing Systems Perspective on Planning for Sustainability," (master's thesis, University of Waterloo, 1998).

8   Marc Bekoff, *The Emotional Lives of Animals* (Novato, California: New World Library, 2007).

9   Isabelle Stengers, *Thinking with Whitehead: A Free and Wild Creation of Concepts*, trans. Michael Chase (Cambridge: Harvard University Press, 2011).

10 See, for example, Scott Gilbert, Jan Sapp, and Alfred I. Tauber, "A Symbiotic View of Life: We Have Never Been Individuals," *The Quarterly Review of Biology* 87, no. 4 (December 2012): 325–341.

11 See, for example, Lynn Margulis, *Symbiotic Planet: A New Look at Evolution* (Amherst: Sciencewriters, 1998); Marilyn Strathern, *Partial Connections* (Walnut Creek, California: AltaMira Press, 2004).

12 Rosanna Alegado, Laura Brown, Shugeng Cao, Renee Dermenjian, Richard Zuzow, Stephen Fairclough, Jon Clardy and Nicole King, "Bacterial Regulation of Colony Development in the Closest Living Relatives of Animals," *eLife* 1, no. e00013 (2012): elifesciences.org/content/1/e00013.

13 This is a reference to Anna Tsing's conference at UCSC in May 2014, Anthropocene: Arts of Living on a Damaged Planet.

14 Natalie Loveless, "Acts of Pedagogy: Feminism, Psychoanalysis, Art and Ethics" (PhD diss., University of California Santa Cruz, 2010).

15 See Evelyn Hutchinson, *An Introduction to Population Ecology* (New Haven: Yale University Press, 1978), and C. H. Waddington, *Principles of Development and Differentiation* (New York: Macmillan, 1966).

16 Margaret Wertheim, *A Field Guide to Hyperbolic Space: An Exploration of the Intersection of Higher Geometry and Feminine Handicraft* (Los Angeles: Institute for Figuring, 2007).

17 Ursula K. Le Guin, *Always Coming Home* (Oakland: University of California Press, 2011).

18 See: en.wikipedia.org/wiki/Great_Pacific_garbage_patch.

19 Vonda N. McIntyre, *Superluminal* (New York: Houghton Mifflin, 1983).

20 Deborah Bird Rose, *Reports from a Wild Country: Ethics for Decolonization* (Kensington: University of New South Wales Press, 2004).

21 As one of its many possibilities, the Greek word *Anthropos* means "the upward looking one" (www.wordnik.com/words/Anthropos).

Ecologicity, Vision, and the Neurological System

Amanda Boetzkes

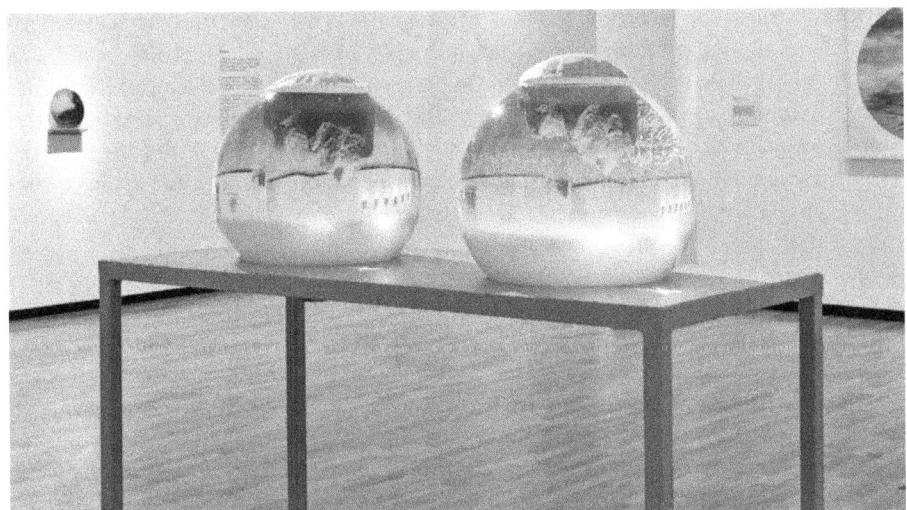

Mariele Neudecker, *400 Thousand Generations*, 2009; photo by Ware, courtesy of Mariele Neudecker.   Fig. 01

Introduction: The World Tilts on its Axis

In the documentary *Inuit Knowledge and Climate Change*, directed by Zacharias Kunuk and Ian Mauro, members of Inuit communities in Nunavut describe the dramatic transformations of the Arctic landscape due to global warming.[1] Strikingly, the changes they identify have instigated fundamental reorientations of bodily perception. Hunters observe that the sun sits in the sky at an unusual angle and that it sets in a different place than it did several decades ago. It casts a different light in the atmosphere, which complicates the practice of spearing fish and seals in the water, a skill that requires a grasp of the relationship between the ray of light and its refraction from the surface of the water. Those experienced at night-hunting note that the stars appear in new positions, and that the tips of snow drifts (tongue drifts) that they have been accustomed to following like points on a compass cannot be trusted. The winds are not as predictable as they were a generation ago. Communities have seen a rise in floods, and on occasion blankets of acid rain. "The world has tilted on its axis," one elder summarizes.

To a culture accustomed to carefully reading the environment—the sky, the movement of clouds, the direction of the wind, the position of stars, the thickness of ice, the rays of the sun, subtle animal behaviors—the signs of the Anthropocene are manifold. In this new geological epoch, the environment has become illegible. It appears that Husserl's idea of the earth as "original ark" is now obsolete; we now have to recalibrate our sensorial systems to adjust to contradiction, catastrophe, and ecological volatility born of human activities that override and neutralize long-standing histories of local knowledge.

What is of interest about the Inuit's testimonies is the extent to which they experience signs of the Anthropocene to which many of us are still blind. How many of us can see climate change in the sky? On the ground? In the air? Their experiences are not simply a matter of documenting the glaring effects of global warming perpetrated by "Qalunaat" [white people] or "Southerners," but of recognizing the transformation of the visible world as a phenomenological reality. The Anthropocene has changed the way they see; it has altered the terms and parameters of perception itself.

How might we conceptualize a politics of ecological being in conjunction with the new terms of vision and visibility precipitated by the Anthropocene? If this new epoch calls us to imagine the impact of modern human life beyond the parameters of individual phenomenology, to account for systemic activity on micro and macro scales, and in relation to geological time, then there is equally a desire on the part of artists to redefine the limits of vision in order to incorporate and represent new orientations. I would suggest that the Anthropocene cannot simply be represented in art (as in, for example, images of anthropogenic landscapes), but that art is the means by which this ecological perspective is incorporated into vision and becomes a visuality. That is to say, art does not simply make ecological information and scale available to the eye, but, more forcefully, it consolidates a cultural orientation—a way of seeing. I call this mobilization of visuality "ecologicity." In the essay that follows, I outline the terms by which we might understand our ecologicity by charting three critical trajectories of inquiry: ecological perception, neuroaesthetics, and the visualization of their convergence in and through art.

Visualizing Ecological Perception

A theory of visuality in the Anthropocene would have to account both for the fact of ecological perception as such, and for the ways in which ecological change registers in vision. Consider the work *400 Thousand Generations* by German artist Mariele Neudecker. [Fig. 01] Inspired by a study that showed how the microfibers of the retina have taken four-hundred thousand generations of environmental adaptation, Neudecker constructed a set of glass spheres that resemble a pair of eyes. Curiously, the fibrous tissue of the retina doubles as a microcosm of a cloudy mountain range. Filled with a white solution that simulates a thick layer of mist surrounding a fibreglass mold of blue mountain peaks, the work visualizes the complex sensorial capacities of the eye as a sublime landscape. The work is one of a series of "tank projects" in which Neudecker recreates ecosystems in glass vitrines that appear as different geological eras, from Precambrian rock shields to Mesozoic fern forests.

400 Thousand Generations situates human vision in the midst of and in response to earthly evolutions, a move that coincides with the rise of geo-aesthetics. That is to say, her work does not simply visualize geologic transformation, but advances a visuality as such—a circuit between ecosystemic activity, the morphology of the human visual organs, and practices of representation. I am working here from Whitney Davis's definition of visuality as a way of seeing shaped through interaction with items of visual culture, and his call for an account of the recursions of visuality in natural vision.[2]

To better understand how this recursion takes place, we might consider some foundational ideas from the cognitive psychologist James J. Gibson, who developed a theory of ecological perception between the 1950s and 1970s.[3] Gibson bridged ethology, the study of animal behaviour, with traditional cognitivist models of consciousness, conceiving of a perceiving subject whose actions and interpretations are interwoven with the environment. Which is to say that "exteroception is accompanied by proprioception—that to perceive the world is to co-perceive oneself."[4] While this statement is entirely consonant with the phenomenological tradition, and particularly the writings of Maurice Merleau-Ponty from a few decades earlier, what is significant about Gibson's work is his way of overcoming the dichotomy between a physical reality and a phenomenal one. While phenomenologists focused on embodied perceptions of the world, Gibson advances the possibility that there is an objective reality nested in perception.

Gibson's perceiving subject is decidedly active; it continuously samples the ambient surroundings, obtains information from the optic array, and separates changes in the environment from its invariant structure. But the activity of perception does not limit or distort the objectivity of the world. While perception involves the extraction of information from a stream of stimulation, this is not to say that the information obtained is finite, distilled, or altered upon being perceived. In Gibson's assessment: "Information is not specific to the banks of photoreceptors, mechanoreceptors, and chemoreceptors that lie within the sense organs. Sensations are specific to receptors and thus, normally, to the kinds of stimulus energy that touch them off. But information is not energy-specific. Stimuli are not always imposed on a passive subject. In life, one obtains stimulation in order to extract the information. The information can be the same, despite a radical change in the stimulation obtained."[5]

Another way to explain the process of information pick-up at the threshold between the sense-system of the organism and the invariance of the environment is the concept of "affordance." As Gibson developed a definition of affordance, it came to refer to the limitless information that an environment yields, the possible meanings this information may have to the perceiver, and the full range of actions the perceiver may choose to respond with. In other words, affordance cuts across the subjective-objective distinction and stands as both "a fact of the environment and a fact of behavior."[6] For example, the edge of a knife might afford cutting, or it might afford being cut: use or harm; a bush full of berries might afford nourishment for one creature and poison for another; a fence may afford imprisonment from one perspective and freedom from another. Affordance accounts for the experiences of the observer, but is not a property of the observer, and is therefore not merely an added subjective feeling.[7] It is both invariant *and* relational.

There are two important concerns to be found in Gibson's model of ecological perception. First, while behaviours may appear to respond purely to the needs and intentions of an actor, that actor nevertheless perceives a full range of environmental affordance. Affordance acknowledges any potential behaviour, or what he terms "action-possibility." One may or may not attend to an affordance according to one's needs, but whether or not one does, the affordance remains: "[T]he object affords what it does because it is what it is." Second, the specifically ecological approach of Gibson's theory of perception comes from the way in which it accounts for an exchange between a mobile perceiver and an environment that is perceived for its invariant structure, despite the fact that it appears through a flux of stimulation.[8] That is, it acknowledges that objective information about an environmental system can be obtained both in spite and because of perceptual change. In this respect, the kinds of observations the Inuit describe in *Inuit Knowledge and Climate Change* are not simply of the order of a "cultural perspective." They are, rather, a form of objective testimony, derived from the appraisal of discrepancies in the environment, made by people who are keenly attuned to its invariant structure. The perceptions they describe are of the order of information and not simply a traditional or local "point of view."

Information Pick-Up, Skill, and Recognition

Affordance is a primary relation between a perceiver and the environment that describes the limits and possibilities of both, as these become visible in the moment of perception. There is perhaps a temptation to understand the objective dimension of affordance as a condition that predetermines the possibilities of behaviour, and how we might interpret that behaviour.[9] However, the complexity of the concept lies precisely in its refusal to reduce environments, objects, and actions to the basic function they may have to the perceiver in her/his or its world, or to mechanistic causes and effects. It permits a level of consciousness of the world beyond function. We can see an example of this horizon of consciousness in an essay by Francisco Varela and his team of researchers about colour vision in birds.[10] The essay outlines the enormous range of perceptual capabilities of the bird eye—which, in terms of colour and subtlety, exceeds the primate eye—due to its finely honed cones, rods, UV sensitivity, and the cells of the optic tectum. Varela and his co-authors consider the role of colour vision, most naturally turning to its "functional significance." But they indulge a compelling speculation that it may also have "cognitive significance" for birds.[11] Certainly, the sophistication of colour vision is relevant to feeding, for example, in the identification of fruits and coloured insects, but also for other

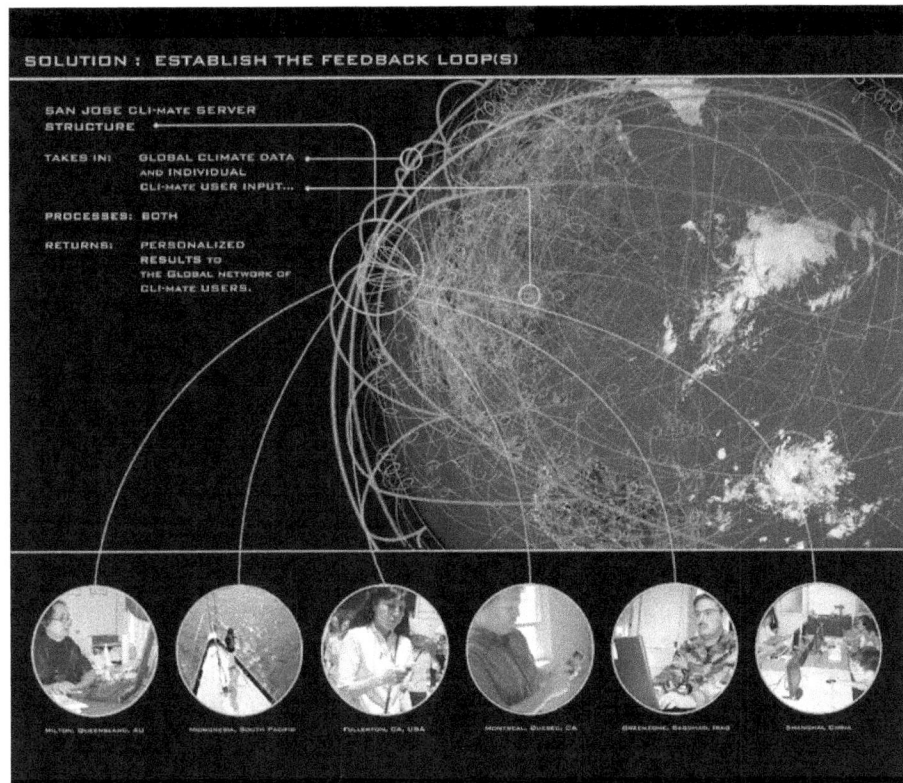

Mel Chin, *CLI-mate*, 2008; image courtesy of the artist.

Fig. 02

behaviours such as mating rituals. The essay concludes with the suggestion that colour may have an affective dimension that cannot be explained simply in terms of the discrimination of objects. One might think of the mating ritual of the Australian bowerbird in which the male builds an elaborate nest to attract a female. The sheer diversity of configurations and colours have tempted ornithologists to consider that the nest has an aesthetic dimension, that it is an expression of the male, and that the female makes a choice, not simply in terms of the brightest or the most colourful—what best captures the eye—but as an aesthetic judgment with criteria that are unknown to us, but deciding factors for the bird.

So, on the one hand, there is a disconcerting facet of affordance insofar as it situates the possibilities of behaviour and its meaning within the parameters of an ecological mesh. At least, it would certainly be disconcerting for a beetle to know that its shiny carapace had caught the perfectly attuned eye of a bluebird, and that its image came to rest on the bird's retina like two pieces of a puzzle fitting together. On the other hand, the intertwining of facts of environment with facts of behaviour throws into relief a new way of thinking about the "cognitive significance" of an environmental situation. Through the concept of affordance, a behaviour may bloom and yield excessive meanings beyond the mechanistic balance of an ecosystem, and thus new ways of thinking about ecological being become possible.

The question is, to what extent are affordances visualizable, which is to say, to what extent can an ecological perception become virtualized, represented, and returned to vision as a condition, or style of being? After all, if there is any project at hand (one that is indeed already being taken up), it is that of how to take consciousness of the ecological beings that we are. This does not simply mean representing a new worldview, but rather, attuning vision to an ecological reality. It is here that art enters the equation.

The difference between simply restating the fact of ecological perception, as Gibson defines it, and assessing the terms of a perceptual system conditioned by the age of the Anthropocene can be understood as identifying a new attentiveness to the vast perspective from which systemic activity is gauged—for example, through global warming, or the oil economy and its attendant carbon footprint, which spans geological time. This attentiveness appears in the cultural field in two ways. First, there is a palpable attempt to rethink the relationship between individual behaviour and its systemic effects. On this point, we can consider the conceptual artist Mel Chin's *CLI-Mate* (2008), a proposal for a widget that would create a "personal to global feedback loop" in such a way as to personalize one's individual connection to climate change. [Fig. 02] The user would input daily choices and receive data about the impact of those choices combined with the sum of actions of other users of the software. The widget would take in global climate data and individual user input, process these together, and return personalized results to the global network of users.

Whereas NASA's climate change report gives continuous information regarding key indicators of climate change as factual data, *CLI-Mate* would incorporate individual behaviour into this data and vice versa, making the systemic activities of global climate accessible through a form of information pick-up throughout the day. While Chin's work assumes, perhaps, that behavior modification will ensue in response to this information in ways that distract from, or compensate for, the systemic impact of government policies, free trade agreements, and corporate profit structures that generated the Anthropocene, it also shows the extent to which an ecological reality is being conceived as perceptual information to be responded to, acted upon and accounted for by a being that is integrated within that reality.

The second way in which we can register a consciousness of the Anthropocene is in the persistent re-figuration of our perceptual and representational capacities as neurological shaping. Gibson's model of ecological perception has had a profound impact on the domains of design, ergonomics and human-computer interaction (HCI), psychology, phenomenology, eco-criticism, art history, and beyond. It could also be positioned as a central concern for a genealogy of neurovisuality that includes a range of approaches to the interpretation of art by way of cognition, affect, mirror-neurons, attention, developmental biology, and evolution.

A key highlight of this lineage pertinent to the question of art is Gibson's exchange with the art historian E. H. Gombrich in the 1960s and early 1970s, which was essential for Gombrich's formulation of the relationships between perception, illusion, recognition, and artistic style.[12] For his part, Gombrich's understanding of how we view art took an ethological turn, whereby one's interpretation of art—its cognitive significance—was defined by "perceptual readiness."[13] Of importance here is the fact that Gombrich understood the perception of art as a process of cultivating the visual skills of recognition in the eye itself. He identified a reciprocal relationship between vision as such and visuality, a term that is more commonly associated with style, but which implies, more profoundly, both individual and historical ways of seeing. For Gombrich, art operates from visual schema that are geared to trigger pattern recognition, a skill we have in spite of environmental variances. He uses the example of recognizing a face in a crowd—despite the fact that that face is situated in the midst of fluctuating perceptual variables, and despite the fact that physiognomies are themselves entirely mobile due to their expressive variability, the perceiver nevertheless has a framework of identity that enables recognition. Here one can see the notion of affordance as both an objective and subjective property.

Gombrich goes on to elaborate what he calls the "plasticity of vision," namely the fact that our codes of recognition can also be altered by representation.[14] For example, a caricaturist captures the invariants of a character's features that are commonly recognizable (the visual code), but also picks out and magnifies other invariants that are not used for recognition; by focusing attention on these features, one can no longer see without also attributing to the subject these caricatured elements. For example, we can think of how Charlie Chaplin's imitation of Hitler in "The Great Dictator" stretched and distorted the code of recognition of the latter, by exaggerating the pinched mouth, imperious chin and eye-whites, while bringing his gestures to the point of spastic hysteria. Chaplin's caricature demystifies the spectacle of the dictator's political speech through these comedic distortions. The caricaturist does not teach us how to see, but rather instantiates a new code of recognition. A visuality is nested into vision; vision is reciprocally primed to recognize a visuality.

Neurovisuality-Ecologicity: The Eye of the Anthropocene

In its fullest implications, then, visuality involves more than pattern recognition; it is the calibration of perceptual equipment. This re-focalization of visual studies has led to the rise of scholarship on neuroaesthetics, neuroarthistory, and neurovisuality. Whitney Davis's claim that there are recursions between vision and visuality suggests that there is a level of consciousness within the workings of vision that is integral to the formation of an artwork, and definitive of its historicity, even as works of art and culture give definition to our neuro-psychological activity. Michael Baxandall's concept of the "period eye," which elaborates Gombrich's approach to art through recognition and visual plasticity, is especially relevant in this regard. Baxandall draws an analogy between the visual skills of a fifteenth-century merchant to judge the size, weight, and mass of objects in order to determine their value and cost by sight, and the coextensive emphasis on simulations of volume and shape in the period painters' perspectives.[15] In his reading, a painting both deploys a specialized visual skill and depicts it for a culture that is oriented to see that skill in action. John Onians further underscores the neurological dimension of Baxandall's analysis of Georges Braque's *Violin and Pitcher* (1910) by highlighting the link the artist draws between the attention-grabbing power of the ambiguous forms on the left flank and the specific strength of peripheral vision to recognize solid shapes, so that the composition is clearly shown to appeal to different parts of the eye, thus generating a saccade across the retina from the fovea to the periphery.[16] For Onians, Baxandall's achievement lies in the way he integrates knowledge about the neurological functions of the eye with a reading of Cubism's broader critical and formal project to create a perceptual "lock" that carries the eye over and across the canvas. Perception is not the tool by which we experience art, but its very content and substance. Onians concludes that "each painting forms its own 'eye.'"[17]

What kind of eye, then, does art of the Anthropocene cultivate? With this cursory sketch of the neuroaesthetic eye, I am suggesting it is not simply descriptive of the ways we see historically or even evolutionarily, but actually part and parcel of the visuality of the Anthropocene. This visuality can be characterized as a heightened consciousness of our ecologicity. Our neurological transactions with the environment—mediated through what Gibson calls "the optic array"—are increasingly becoming integrated into the form and content of art. To say that art cultivates and develops an ecologicity is to do more than make a claim about how our perception is grounded in a bodily-environmental experience, as we process the perceptual basics of shape, depth, shadow, and texture in a formal or phenomenological sense. The ecologicity of art is both a call to "read" environments in terms of information pick-up and to accommodate that information; which is to say, not simply to perceive as we do, but to parlay our perceptual system into a modality of processing, response, and responsiveness. The neurology of the visual brain is precisely the mediation of this contact between the individual and the ecosystem. Neurovisuality is therefore a condition of the attentiveness to, and elaboration of, ecologicity.

To return to Neudecker's work, what is so striking is not merely the staging of either the neurological function of the eye, or its ecological imbrication through an analogy between nerves and landscape, though this is indeed impressive; what matters most is the way this work coordinates the neurological/ecological scenario into an ocular sensitivity. The concepts on which ecology is founded— such as diversity, complexity, climactic conditions, receptivity, and change (as well

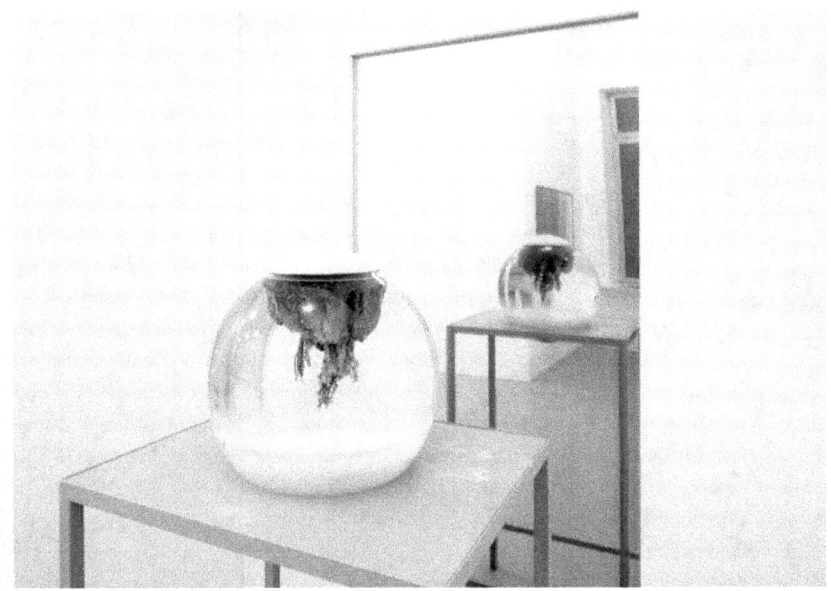

Mariele Neudecker, *24 hours/48 hours (1) + (2)*, 2011. Photo: Simon Vogel; courtesy of Mariele Neudecker.   Fig. 03

as the various threats to all of these processes)—have an aesthetic realization as geological time, atmosphere, and the modulation of ethos in landscapes that are also "inscapes," to borrow a term from Alfred North Whitehead. Ecological affordance becomes more than the perceptual scenario of oneself in an environmental niche; it coincides with a neurological extension into a planetary consciousness. *400 Thousand Generations* asserts an awareness of geological time, precisely as the idea of the Anthropocene is beginning to gain currency, and it brings this awareness to bear on visuality—now represented and "felt" as a longstanding process of coextensive neural shaping. In a similar work, *24 Hours/48 Hours (1) + (2)* (2011), one "ocular" bowl stands in front of its mirror reflection to constitute a pair of eyes in which the retinal tissue and nerves are likened to old growth forest and the earth positioned as a fibrous, feeling tissue. [Fig. 03] In *Parhelion* (2012), three bowls filled with puffy, gold clouds over a shadowy horizon line are arranged to simulate the arc of a sun dog in the sky.[18] In these works, Neudecker presents the neurology of the eye as, alternately, glacial and layered like geological strata, rooted and dense with life, climactic and atmospheric.

Insofar as Neudecker's work visualizes perception in tandem with a planetary consciousness shaped by geological time, the aesthetic recalibration she undertakes is not simply a representation of ecology. Rather, the embodied awareness of the ecological predicament is positioned as a sensible capability. Along with the science of ecology, we have generated a great deal of information and knowledge that has transformed our understanding of ourselves, including epigenetics, climate change, and geologically scaled reconfigurations of the planet. For the most part, this knowledge is based on a worldview almost entirely imperceptible to the naked eye, but which is, at times, technologically accessible. As Mark Hansen has pointed out, visual media can overcome, bridge, and integrate these discrepancies in perception. He uses the example of Bill Viola's videos, which make "machine time"—in which a second of digital capture is replete with far more information than one could ever process—available to the bodily time of an average range of perception.[19] Certainly, the technological capacities of new media are part and parcel of ecologicity; but I also want to suggest that these capacities are mobilized in and as a new visual capacity, or, as Gombrich puts it, a new code of recognition. Moreover, this way of sensing does not necessarily have to be advanced in the vernacular of new media, though the technologies associated with it are certainly shaping the visual field. But, if ecologicity is born of recognition, attunement, attention, and behaviour, as much as by extending the perceptual field beyond its average range, then relatively low-tech works like those of Neudecker can be considered as much a part of an ecological turn as the bioart of Eduardo Kac or the "tactical media" of Critical Art Ensemble. In fact, low-tech works may be critical for developing a visuality that is not yet integral to or explicit within new media, visualizing the specifically neurological dimension of ecologicity and mobilizing vision as a perceiving organ to cultivate this self-awareness.

The work of Levi van Veluw gives an inverse view of this convergence, especially in his *Landscape* series. [Fig. 04] Instead of positioning the eye as simultaneous inscape and landscape, the artist distributes the landscape onto the body in such a way as to turn it inside-out, as its neurological circuitry and reaching dendrites double as trees, soil, and foliage. Van Veluw made these portraits by actually applying props and photographing himself, so they cohere as both a portrait and an externalization of the subject. More than a visual analogy between neurons and ecological phenomena, he mobilizes the portrait to demonstrate a particular awareness of a mode of their co-extensiveness. I cannot but see this body as neurologically primed. Moreover, this recognition is encapsulated by the consistency and intensity of the artist's own expressionless stare from one portrait to the next, as the series proceeds through different conditions: snow-covered, parched and deserted, lush and green. The eye's ecologicity is provoked as the viewer grapples with the uncanny textures, growth, and substances of the landscapes that appear as bodily surfaces.

Conclusion

The constellation that I have outlined here between neurology, ecology, and visuality attempts to formulate an emergent cognitive process that is enacted and elaborated through art. I call this increased awareness—which is also a honing of optical experience—ecologicity. It emerges in and through the existential net of affordance, the coexistent facts of environment and facts of behaviour that constitute perception. The Anthropocene, as both a geological age and a cultural

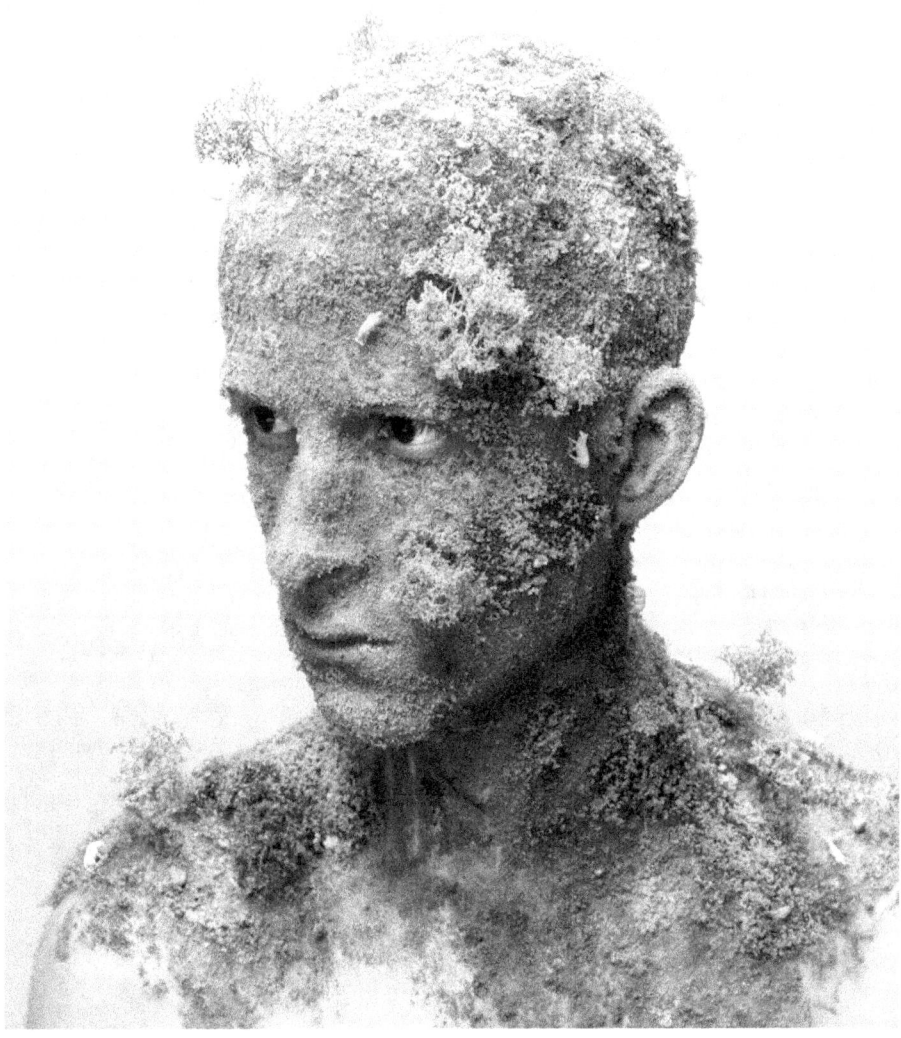

Levi van Veluw, *Landscape I*, 2008; courtesy of the artist.

Fig. 04

phenomenon, has introduced new terms of interpretation that affect ecological activities. This interpretation is not simply a matter of applying a scientific framework to the perception of the environment, nor of extending vision so that it aligns with that framework; it is a matter of living and seeing through new forms of information pick-up, attention, recognition, and interaction. The affordance of environments is therefore newly discovered in artworks that both position the eye in relation to the planetary condition and figure this ecologicity as incorporated into vision.

Notes

1. *Inuit Knowledge and Climate Change,* directed Zacharias Kunuk and Ian Mauro (Igloolik Isuma Productions Inc., 2010), www.isuma.tv/inuit-knowledge-and-climate-change.
2. Whitney Davis, "Neurovisuality," nonsite.org, no. 2 (June 2011), nonsite.org/issues/issue-2/neurovisuality.
3. It would be more precise to characterize his scholarship as an ecological approach to visual perception (as per his 1979 book of that name) rather than a theory of ecological perception. However, if we are to consider the philosophical impact of this scholarship, what is most striking is its insistence on the co-perception of the perceiver and the environment, a move which raises the possibility that the environment equally "perceives" the subject and that perception as such is not uni-directional. To entertain this thought would be to come to a more encompassing theory of ecological perception and not just an ecological approach to human visual perception.
4. James, J. Gibson, *The Ecological Approach to Visual Perception* (New York: Taylor & Francis Group, 1979), 141.
5. Ibid., 243.
6. Ibid., 129.
7. Ibid., 137.
8. Ibid., 247.
9. This temptation found its way into the work of Gibson's student, design theorist Donald Norman's approach to human-centred technologies. In integrating the notion of affordance into design, Norman subtly shifts the concept from possible to probable actions.
10. Francisco Varela, Adrian G. Palacios, and Timothy H. Goldsmith, "Color Vision of Birds," in *Vision, Brain and Behavior in Birds,* ed. Harry Philip Zeigler and Ians Joachim Bischof (Cambridge, MA: MIT Press, 1993), 77.
11. Ibid., 92.
12. For the basic terms of this conversation, see Gombrich and Gibson, "Exchange of Letters," *Leonardo* 4 (1971): 195–203.
13. Davis, "Neurovisuality," 3.
14. E. H. Gombrich, *The Image and the Eye: Further Studies in the Psychology of Pictorial Perception* (Oxford: Phaidon Press, 1982), 28.
15. Davis cites this example, but foregrounds the fact that Baxandall's approach is more a sociological than ethological account of visuality; see Davis, "Neurovisuality," 3.
16. Michael Baxandall, *Painting and Experience in Fifteenth-Century Italy: A Primer in the Social History of Pictorial Style* (Oxford: Oxford University Press, 1988), 401.
17. John Onians, N*euroarthistory: From Aristotle and Pliny to Baxandall and Zeki* (New Haven: Yale University Press, 2007), 184. See also Michael Baxandall, "Fixation and Distraction: The Nail in Braque's Violin and Pitcher," in *Sight and Insight: Essays on Art and Culture in Honour of E. H. Gombrich at 85,* ed. John Onians (London: Phaidon Press, 1994), 399–415.
18. A sun dog is an atmospheric formation in which ice crystals in the sky create the effect of patches of light on either side of the sun. Sometimes these are joined by a halo-like line.
19. Mark B. Hansen, *New Philosophy for New Media* (Cambridge, MA: MIT Press, 2006), 236.

My Mother's Garden: Aesthetics, Indigenous Renewal, and Creativity

Laura Hall

Indigenous aesthetics are rooted in culture and community, with the enmeshed responsibilities of living well in the ecologies of our ancestors. Utilizing Native American arts and media scholar Steven Leuthold's broad take on Indigenous aesthetics, the Indigenous artistic practice outlined here is rooted in community responsibility, accountability "in religion, myths, and relations to nature."[1] Challenging Western dichotomies between art and craft, aesthetics and spiritual practice, I am naming the garden I've inherited from my mother as the core of my own aesthetic practice. My mother's garden is both the garden around the home where my Haudenosaunee-French mother raised my brothers and me, but it can also be considered in a wider sense—the garden as a creation within Creation—evoking not only cultural lineage but territorial histories and stories that can serve to renew fractured cultural and ecological connectivity.

My mother's garden was a space where we could talk; planting, tending to, and caring for the garden and its medicines were topics that my mother and I discussed without tension. When my mother passed into the spirit world, and my grieving hit so hard that I could barely breathe—not just because she was gone (though that was enough to floor me) but because her own life had been so pressured by the impacts of colonialism—the garden was and is a place to continue these conversations with her, albeit on a very different level. These conversations now appear as tending to tobacco plants, or cultivating the perennials favoured by the Monarch butterflies she once insisted we see in their annual migration from the Lake Erie shoreline.

There is a daily and material quality to the work of making, appreciating, giving thanks to, and finally letting go of, the beauty in the world's cycles in Indigenous aesthetics. The garden is daily life—daily conversation—in a family life made tense and raw by the scars of my mother's residential school experiences and her father's before her. My mother's garden is embodied thought and thanksgiving, where I plant seeds, watch them grow, come to fruition, and die, and where I plant roots in this place and commit to working toward and helping with the renewal of the people's rights and environmental responsibilities. This embodied and creative project—with tobacco, the Three Sisters (corn, beans, and squash), heirloom potatoes, and local species of flowers and plant medicines—is my reminder that we have a distance to travel in healing journeys. If an Indigenous aesthetic practice is one that is embodied and rooted in spirit, then burying my hands and feet in soil and breathing the air is how I express and recreate beauty in the blooming of flowers from seeds sung to.

My mother's garden is not the possessive singular; the garden is part of Anishinaabe territory, as is the house within its boundaries. And the garden is not singular. Soil, water, and air stream toward the same Great Lakes that continue to nourish both Anishinaabe and Haudenosaunee nations, and indeed an entire continent, moved as they are by Grandmother Moon, warmed by Elder Brother Sun, resting and dancing and breathing on the back of Grandfather Turtle.

The garden enfolds not just daily aesthetic and spiritual practice, but can be seen as a microcosm of Mother Earth as rooted in Haudenosaunee Creation. In this teaching, Mother Earth was the daughter of Sky Woman, who lived and then died during childbirth, and was buried in the earth to continuously nourish life forever.[2] As Barbara Alice Mann writes, Sky Woman, so long after her descent from Sky World into the world we know, created the Milky Way, reaching into her "to show her grandchildren the way home. She also lifted up the Moon, so that her grandchildren might never be lost in time."[3] An important element of an Indigenous worldview, which maintains an understanding of our interconnections and dependency upon the rest of Creation, comes in the form of women's teachings about new life and singing life out the doorway through which it came, when the time comes. Anishinaabe scholar and writer Leanne Simpson describes the significance of sacred stories: "Creation stories in several different cultures speak to the ability of Indigenous women to give new life to beings, to transform, and to vitalize."[4] Gendering Indigenist thought doesn't just highlight the exclusions of women and LGBT/2Spirited peoples, but this approach also deepens our understanding of the profundity and potentiality of learning and working within an Indigenous worldview, and supports those who do.

In an age of colonial violence, the creative resistance of Indigenous Peoples is inherently rooted in the work of healing within Creation. Indigenous aesthetics are rooted in the original ecologies and lifeways of traditional territory, and of the responsibilities that come from Creation. Creation stories are truths of origin, of responsibility, and of wholeness in worldview and in being. Learning about these interconnections—between our human ancestors, and spirits, animals, and the cosmos—further actualizes our own creative endeavours. Our ancestors who have communicated with their ancestors, have co-created, learned, and furthered a reflexive and rigorous epistemology, rooted in experiential and Elder-led learning. Indigenous creative expression occurs in daily engagement with the territory I find myself on within Turtle Island. As Joe Sheridan and Dan Longboat describe it, "The ecology of traditional Haudenosaunee territory possesses sentience that is manifest in the consciousness of that territory, and that same consciousness is formalized in and as Haudenosaunee consciousness."[5] This general understanding is part of the complex web-work of Indigenous knowledge, within which I have my own responsibilities and understandings. At the same time, the pressures of colonization have demanded that we interrogate false and simplistic interpretations of tradition, while renewing the voices of those most specifically targeted by the colonial system.

Gardens of Knowledge

My mother's garden carries the seeds that were planted far before her generation. Those seeds come in the form of stories, providing direction for my generation to continue to swim, while "unpacking the keeper current" that Marie Battiste describes: "The keeper current drags a person to the bottom and then to the top, but if one fights against the current one usually drowns. Decolonizing then is a process of unpacking the keeper current."[6] A decolonizing framework is one that assumes that complex Indigenous knowledge systems are capable of renewal despite centuries of oppression. Indigenous renewal is inherently about renewing human connections with all of life. As No One Is Illegal activist and writer Harsha Walia highlights, decolonization is a "prefiguring framework" that "grounds us in an understanding that we have already inherited generations of evolving wisdom."[7] Decolonization is not about undoing alone, but about creating the space and time necessary for Indigenous nations to flourish and renew themselves and their land against the toxins of colonization. Indigenous renewal is also inherently responsible for thanksgiving and honouring the laws and governance systems gifted by Creation.

Suppressing the voices of Indigenous women and indeed a diversity of voices within Indigenous nations—along lines imposed by a colonial system based on hierarchies of race, class, ability, sexual orientation, and gender—has served to obscure the real meanings of traditional knowledge. As seminal Indigenous scholar Vine Deloria Jr.'s work attests, the loss of traditional knowledge is about a loss of understanding of our immense responsibilities to the spirit world that has been damaged by the material, anthropocentric paradigms taught in Canada's Residential Schooling system.[8] This has lead our people:

> [T]o discredit or discard facts that call into question the socially acceptable explanations of phenomena [...]. This uncritical acceptance of modernism has prevented us from seeing that higher spiritual powers are still active in the world. We cannot, for the most part, believe that a firm relationship with them can be cultivated today. We need to glimpse the old spiritual world that helped, healed and honored us with its presence and companionship.[9]

Returning to the land is the return that actualizes these rememberings and reconnections. However, if Indigenous nations remain forcibly removed from their traditional territories, memory and belief will continue to be severed, for it is primarily in connection to the land that the stories and healing practices come.

So forceful was the interference of European newcomers and their systems of power and control that stories of "contact" include the undermining of some

Indigenous nations by others. Haudenosaunee scholar Barbara Alice Mann writes about the Clan Mothers who unwisely sold Lenâpé nation land holdings. This story makes an historical point about the ways that colonization contextualizes Indigenous disconnections from land and culture; it is also about what comes next, about what we have to heal, and heal from, in order to move forward. For women's leadership to be revitalized and renewed in Haudenosaunee contexts, the interferences and damages of colonial systems have to be pushed back. And crucially, the power plays of the colonial system have direct ecological effects, severing ties to the land until such time as they are renewed and restored.

The massive gardens of the Haudenosaunee inspired Euro-settler society to better understand that the world they had arrived in was rich in beauty and what now might be understood as a material and spiritual abundance nearly unimaginable in a context of escalating environmental destruction. Mann describes the abundance of Haudenosaunee cultivations, inclusive of diverse crops (of which the Three Sisters are perhaps the most well known) and governed by female leadership to whom the land holdings were entrusted and by whom their harvests were distributed fairly to each family.[10] Haudenosaunee gardens were at the edge of treelines of "old growth engaged in a cultural relationship with the minds and spirits of everything that once existed and still exists in the spirit world."[11] Elder Jan Longboat teaches that Indigenous natural sovereignty has never been surrendered. She calls for Indigenous Peoples to strengthen spiritual ties to "our place" and recover the "richness" existing within traditional worldviews and lifeways.[12] Battiste and Henderson reinforce these connections, telling us, "Ecological teachings have defined for Indigenous Peoples the meaning of life, our responsibilities, our duties. They have also developed our consciousnesses, our languages, and what others have categorized as our 'cultures.'"[13] Environmental, ecological, or natural world-based knowledge is embedded in Indigenous worldviews in such a way that arguing for their inclusion becomes almost unnecessary when those worldviews are actually centred in methodological assumptions. As Lynn Jacobs contends: "The concept of planning for the Seventh Generation, or the faces yet to come, was an integral part of indigenous decision-making long before the Brundtland Report. Through the intimate knowledge of our traditional territories upon which we survived, Indigenous Peoples have been living this concept since time immemorial."[14] When my mother passed away, I was astounded at all of the seeds and medicines she had left behind. I felt as though she had thrown these medicines ahead of her on the path when it was time for her to take another, parallel journey.

That our responsibility as Indigenous people is to renew the beautiful lifeways of our ancestors both past and future seems clear at times, but how do we think our way through to the necessary reconnections? When my mother was alive, she started tobacco seeds that grew into massive plants. When she passed away, I couldn't get the seeds to grow the way she could. I am still working through the grief of the generations in my family whose cultural connections were interrupted, and this has had a direct effect on the garden, and the land on which I live. Indeed,

Elders and Knowledge Keepers instruct us to understand our interconnections. Carol Hopkins and Jim Dumont describe this process, writing: "All of us are responsible for being related *in a good and caring way* within the family of creation. The Earth herself is a living, breathing, conscious Being, complete with heart/feeling, soul/spirit, and physical/organic life, as it is with all the relatives of creation."[15] Using Hendry and Fitznor's concept of "storying" as a practice, I see storytelling as a sacred way of renewing relationships and well-being.[16] Storying is how we speak truths back to life and how we bring to light the continuity of culture and worldview. Similarly, describing the worldview of the Haudenosaunee, Sheridan and Longboat write that "the encounter with Creation's authentic qualities embodies what is and was and what can be in a cycle that is always returning to sacred time's forever."[17]

Working for the "Good Life," or *Mino Biimaadziwin* in Anishinaabe thought, or working for the "Good Mind" in Haudenosaunee thought, means honouring life's cycles and the raw beauty of our relationships with Creation. Indigenous movements toward independence and the recovery of culture are as much about environmental restoration and sustainability as they are about human health. In order to better understand the impacts that colonization has had on the environments of Turtle Island, it is vital to understand the colonial movement as rooting, justifying, and furthering those violations, especially in their gendered realities, where women have been displaced from central and powerful roles and are now, all too often, the recipients of colonial violence. It is equally important to understand the need for critique amongst ourselves. Indigenous traditions are reflexive and flexible, and require a deeper sense of multi-layered renewal.[18] The layers of this approach strike me as being similar to that of a garden. It isn't just the success (or lack thereof) that I find in growing the original seeds I've been given, though this is part of that reflexive and reflective process—failing and learning from those mistakes; it's also about understanding the depths of the garden and the interconnections of lifeforms. The garden is connected to the woods, to the responsibilities that I have to my clan, to the name I was given, and to the animal, plant, and spirit helpers of the whole of Creation. So it isn't just a matter of growing a family garden for sustenance; it is also about learning how deeply the work of giving away, and giving thanks for the gifts of the garden, has changed and shaped my understanding of these interconnections. Renewing sustainable lifeways is about also renewing Indigenous knowledge of interconnection and responsibility.

Ongoing colonization compounds the environmental impacts that lead to Indigenous displacement. The colonial system in Canada is one of "internal colonialism, the biopolitical and geopolitical management of people, land, flora and fauna within the 'domestic' borders of the imperial nation [...] to ensure the ascendancy of a nation and its white elite."[19] Mohawk scholar and activist Taiaiake Alfred laments that, "For a long time now, we have been on a quest for governmental power and money; somewhere along the journey from the past to the future, we forgot that our goal was to reconnect with our lands and to preserve our harmonious cultures and respectful ways of life."[20] This is a result of internalized colonization, being forced to live in a society not of our choosing which has committed untold violence upon Indigenous Peoples.

Ongoing colonization is reinforced through storytelling that privileges a Eurocentric worldview.[21] Take, for example, the words of Dr. Ulrich Loening of the Centre for Human Ecology. He writes, in the introduction to *Indigenous Knowledge and Human Ecology*: "People have always *exterminated* whatever was eatable wherever they migrated, over thousands of years."[22] Here, the assumptions of a colonial mindset sneak in through one brief statement. For the Haudenosaunee, the "extermination" of food and medicine (and food *as* medicine) was not part of a vibrant and abundant approach to either agriculture or sustainable forest management. Instead, animal and spirit relations are understood as helpers, as the source of ancient and new knowledges.[23] As vitally important as it is to take on the human and ecological challenges facing our species as a result of environmental degradation, perspectives that do not seek to understand the Creation stories and truths of Indigenous Peoples globally—and which pin evolutionary nihilism equally on all groups involved throughout time and history—exacerbate existing ecologically damaging colonial relationships.

The divide between humans and the "natural" world cannot be understood in the Americas without contextualizing its origins in the Eurocentric project of genocide, ecocide, and control over Indigenous Peoples and Indigenous lands. Well-being diminishes in relation to environmental destruction, as "diminishing biodiversity augers against the continued capacity to know how to think with everything."[24] My mother's garden is where I find my own healing, where I create a home for the Indigenous woman with whom I share my life, and for our future child or children.

Deloria Jr. remarks, in relation to James Lovelock's Gaia hypothesis and the ensuing debate over whether or not Earth can be considered one sentient system, that it "has often centered on false arguments, with both the advocates and the opponents of the theory restricting the definition of 'life' to reactive organic phenomenon that are observed primarily in the higher organisms."[25] Deloria Jr.'s words resonate, as does his quip that traditional Indigenous thinkers "are quite amused to see this revival of the debate over whether the planet is alive."[26] Healing from colonization has meant reconnecting to the whole web of life on Turtle Island and to the understanding of living histories and roots in each territory. Colonization reduced land bases, stole sacred foods and medicines, and attacked the very belief in the Good Life; the responsibility for individual wellness is a responsibility for the wellness of relationships with more-than-human beings. For example, diabetes rates in Indigenous communities, and subsequent prevention efforts, have raised discussions about "food sovereignty,"[27] while evoking far deeper issues related to Indigenous land-based practices of food gathering.[28] At the same time, and deeper still, is the knowledge shared by Elders and Knowledge Keepers who remind us that our relationships with the land, territory, and space were first nurtured in seeds planted all the way back at the beginning. For my mother's nation, some of those sacred seeds—corn, tobacco, strawberry—came first with Sky Woman. The sacred foods, which are also sacred medicines, are part of Sky Woman's arrival, so they are Sky World foods; in coming to understand how important their growth and sharing are for the Haudenosaunee, it is as important to link back to that story and to the teachings of the first sacred women, to walk and sing and think a good path on Turtle Island. This is no less significant than understanding the physical and physiological benefits of those foods. To talk about food security and food sustainability in a culturally and spiritually rooted manner changes the terrain of the discussion, moving from utility to relationality, expressed through love and gratitude. Discussing the Canoe Journeys undertaken by Coast Salish peoples, Dian Million points to the ways that the community asserts "their responsibility to articulate sustainable practice in the bioregion, in sustaining interdependent life without an anthropomorphic focus,"[29] while linking their wellness to ancient responsibilities to care for their territory—a responsibility protected through treaty rights.[30]

Knowing Our Beauty Again

Remembering the origins of Indigenous nations in the sacred stories of the spirit beings who first sang life-forms into the world means remembering and knowing the beauty of our ancestors and families again. Leanne Simpson draws on the words of Anishinaabe Elder and Knowledge Keeper Edna Manitowabi: "Our culture is beautiful and loving, and it nurtures our hearts and minds in a way that enables us to not just cope, but to live."[31] This is the beauty that is nurtured every day in our thanksgivings, in our thought, in our stories, and in our gardens. Importantly, rather than romanticizing a construct of past traditional thought, an Indigenist-feminist approach treats the process *as* a process—a methodology for adding and uncovering and renewing missing and lost pieces of our collective cultural traditions. This is a process of renewing deeper understanding of "true sovereignty" and freedom from the enforcement of heteropatriarchal family structures and limitations on the rights of Indigenous women to lead in governments, practices established by the US and Canadian nation-states.[32] It is a process of healing from the horrific, genocidal acts of physical, psychological, and spiritual violence enacted against Indigenous Peoples, especially women, and Indigenous lands in the name of claiming "fertile" and "productive" areas.[33] This violence has also manifested as intellectual thievery, whereby Indigenous communities are handcuffed into negotiations with non-Indigenous scientific and environmental interests for the purposes of freeing up Traditional Ecological Knowledge for all to use.[34] When we sing to the sacred foods and seed flowers and life into our gardens, it is a reminder of the beauty of the life gifted to us.

We care for one another when we share the original stories of Indigenous lifeways. In Anishinaabe culture, this gifting is described by Jill Doerfler, Niigaanwewidam James Sinclair, and Heidi Kiiwetinepinesiik Stark "as a relationship between people, animals, spirits, and other entities in the universe, given in the interests of creating ties, honoring them, or asking for assistance and direction." The authors continue: "[O]fferings are acts of responsibility. Making one includes acknowledging value, promising respect, and affirming the presence of another, [...] forming what is hoped to be a mutually beneficial partnership, not only for participants, but for the universe around them."[35]

My mother used to tell me absolute horror stories about the school she went to and the acts of priests in that place. She said that the children called each other *sauvages*, and that this was her story to carry and hers to tell. I remember being young myself, imagining my mother as a young person, surrounded by other Indigenous children, all of them speaking such hateful words about themselves. I remember thinking "no, you're beautiful, you're beautiful," like a chant in my mind. I wanted to go back in time and think it into reality. When I last saw my mother in this life, I remember thinking that she was somehow experiencing peace—more than I could recall in all the time I'd known her. When I met with her again it was in my dreams and in ceremony, and she told me to take care of myself; we walked together in an empty field and she told me: "I have work to do and so do you, so get to it... but don't work too hard." She made me sit by a fire in one of my dreams, the very night she passed into the spirit world; in another dream, she made me laugh out loud about the rush I was in to get things perfect. When I told an Elder about this, he also laughed; when I asked him about the ultimate meaning of time and environmental sustainability in Anishinaabe thought, he put me out to fast and told me to sit on Mother Earth for a few days. I don't think that I am accomplishing anything all that profound in my mother's garden, but I do think that she found a way to seed and deeply root peace in this place. I think this is the accomplishment of the women in our communities; they are planting peace and life for all the generations, and they are making the way beautiful.

Notes

1. Steven Leuthold, *Indigenous Aesthetics: Native Art, Media and Identity* (Austin: University of Texas Press, 1998), 1.
2. See Barbara Alice Mann, *Iroquoian Women: The Gantowisas* (New York: Peter Lang, 2000).
3. Ibid., 34.
4. Leanne Simpson, "Birthing an Indigenous Resurgence: Decolonizing our Pregnancy and Birthing Ceremonies," in *Until Our Hearts Are On the Ground: Aboriginal Mothering, Oppression, Resistance and Rebirth*, ed. Memee Lavell-Harvard and Jeannette Corbiere Lavell (Bradford, ON: Demeter Press, 2006), 27.
5. Joe Sheridan and Roronhiakewen Dan Longboat, "The Haudenosaunee Imagination and the Ecology of the Sacred," *Space and Culture* 9, no. 4 (2006): 366.
6. Marie Battiste, *Decolonizing Education: Nourishing the Learning Spirit* (Saskatoon: Purich Publishing, 2013), 107.
7. Harsha Walia, *Undoing Border Imperialism* (Oakland: AK Press, 2013), 11.
8. The residential school system, which ran from the 1870s until 1996, was an assimilationist program within which Indigenous children in Canada were subjected to Eurocentric education models, physical, sexual, and emotional abuse, and the violent denial of their cultures and languages. See *The Royal Commission on Aboriginal Peoples* (1996).
9. Vine Deloria, Jr., *The World We Used to Live In* (Golden, CO: Fulcrum Press, 2006), xviii–xix.
10. Mann, *Iroquoian Women*.
11. Sheridan and Longboat, "The Haudenosaunee Imagination and the Ecology of the Sacred," 366.
12. Jan Longboat, quoted in Steven W. Koptie, "Inferiorizing Indigenous Communities and Intentional Colonial Poverty," *The First Peoples Child and Family Review* 5, no. 2 (2010): 101.
13. Marie Battiste and James Youngblood Henderson, *Protecting Indigenous Knowledge and Heritage: A Global Challenge* (Saskatoon: Purich Publishing, 2000), 9.
14. Lynn Katsitsaronkwas Jacobs, "A Commentary on Sustainable Development," *The Journal of Aboriginal Economic Development* 3, no. 1 (2002): 4. In 1987, the United Nations World Commission on Environment and Development published *Our Common Future*, also known as "The Brundtland Report," declaring a new international approach to sustainable economic development.
15. Carol Hopkins and James Dumont, Cultural Healing Practice within National Native Alcohol and Drug Abuse Program/Youth Solvent Addiction Program Services," (National Native Alcohol and Drug Abuse Program, First Nations and Inuit Health Branch, Health Canada, 2010), 9.
16. Joy Hendry and Laara Fitznor, *Anthropologists, Indigenous Scholars and the Research Endeavour: Seeking Bridges Toward Mutual Respect* (New York: Routledge, 2012), 281.
17. Ibid., 369.
18. Leanne Simpson, *Dancing on Our Turtle's Back: Stories of Nishnaabeg Re-Creation, Resurgence, and a New Emergence* (Winnipeg: ARP Books, 2011), 31.
19. Eve Tuck and K. Wayne Yang, "Decolonization Is Not a Metaphor," *Decolonization: Indigeneity, Education & Society* 1, no. 1 (2012): 5.
20. Gerald Taiaiake Alfred, "Colonialism and State Dependency," *Journal of Aboriginal Health* 5, no. 2 (2009): 2.

21 James Youngblood Henderson, "Postcolonial Ghost Dancing: Diagnosing European Colonialism," in *Reclaiming Indigenous Voice and Vision*, ed. Marie Battiste (Vancouver: University of British Columbia Press, 2000).

22 Ulrich Loening, "The Attitude of Human Ecology," in *Radical Human Ecology: Intercultural and Indigenous Approaches*, ed. Lewis Williams, Rose Roberts and Alastair McIntosh (London: Ashgate, 2012), 19, emphasis added.

23 Sheridan and Longboat, "The Haudenosaunee Imagination and the Ecology of the Sacred."

24 Ibid., 369.

25 Vine Deloria Jr., *Spirit and Reason: The Vine Deloria Jr. Reader* (Golden, CO: Fulcrum Publishing, 1999), 49.

26 Ibid.

27 Dian Million, *Therapeutic Nations: Healing in an Age of Indigenous Human Rights* (Tucson: The University of Arizona Press, 2013), 171.

28 Ibid.

29 Ibid., 169.

30 Ibid.

31 Simpson, *Dancing on Our Turtle's Back*, 13.

32 Jennifer Nez Denetdale, "Chairmen, Presidents, and Princesses: The Navajo Nation, Gender, and the Politics of Tradition," *Wicazo Sa Review* 21, no. 1 (2006): 9–28.

33 Mann, *Iroquoian Women*.

34 Leanne Simpson, "Traditional Ecological Knowledge: Marginalization, Appropriation and Continued Disillusion," lecture at the Traditional Knowledge Conference, 2001.

35 Jill Doerfler, Niigaanwewidam James Sinclair, and Heidi Kiiwetinepinesiik Stark, eds., *Centering Anishinaabeg Studies: Understanding the World through Stories* (East Lansing: Michigan State University Press, 2013), xv.

A History According to Cattle

Terike Haapoja & Laura Gustafsson

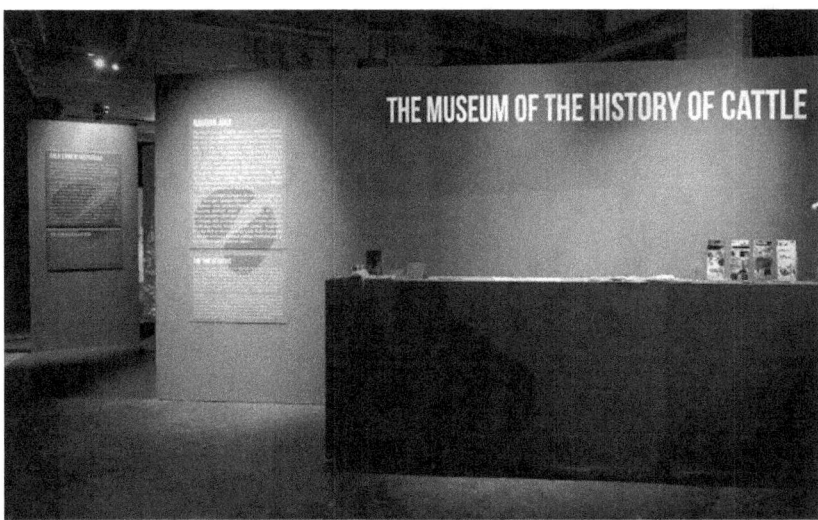

Entrance to the Museum. The Museum of the History of Cattle is the world's first ethnographic museum portraying the history of a non-human species. All photos by Noora Geagea and Terike Haapoja.

Fig. 01

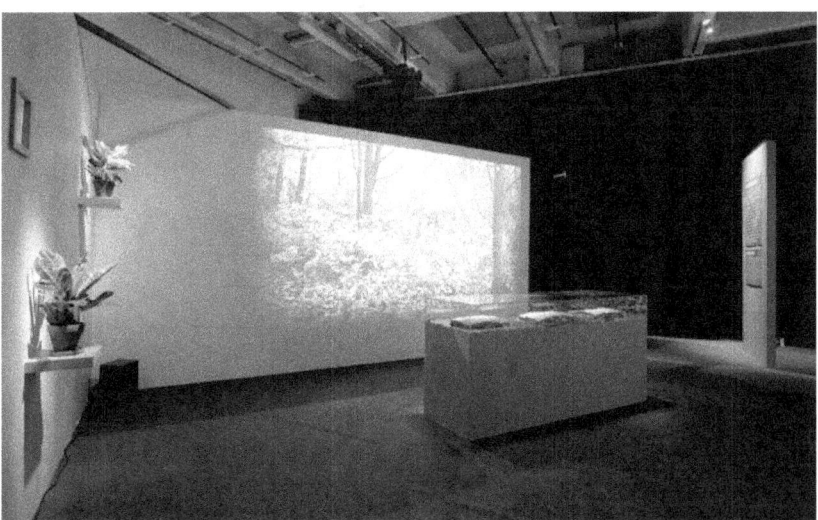

The Hall of Indigenous Cultures. On the left: edible vegetation from the grazing lands of the indigenous Banteng populations. In the glass case: replicas of ancient Aurorch hoof prints (1 million - 627 years, human time).

Fig. 02

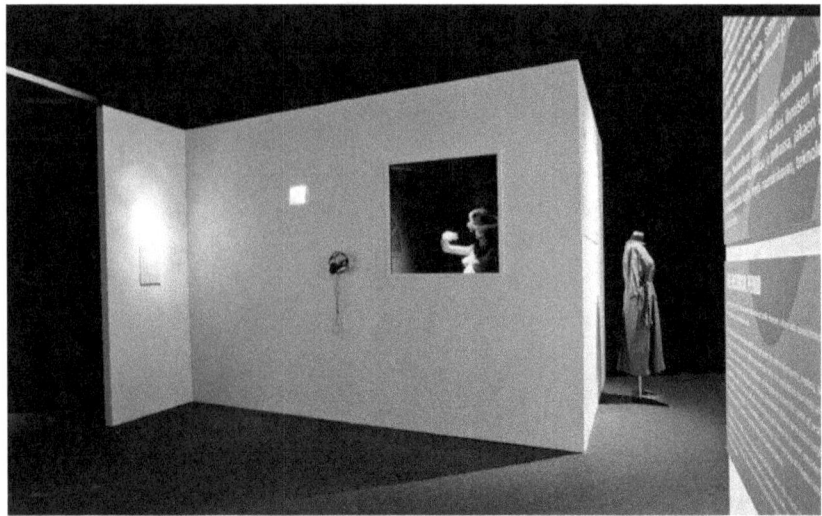

Fig. 03   *The Diorama of Companion Species*. The Housefly (*Musca Domestica*) and the Human (*Homo Sapiens Sapiens*) are the most important companion species of cattle. Though different in size, both are invasive species that can live in harsh conditions and populate most of the earth.

In the beginning there's a void. A void between us and history, between words and our muted existence. How to cross this void when language is by definition something we don't possess? You think that because of your writing you are the author of the world, but you're wrong. You were just an accident like the rest of us, floating in the sea of time. Everybody tries to explain the world. Even the stone, with its stony reasoning, finds order in its rocky little world. You are nothing special. There's an inside to everything.

But here I am, with my horns and tail and compartmented stomachs and a line of ancestors queuing and pushing behind me as if trying to enter the spring field. Why? When history itself has rejected us and rendered us invisible, with language as its weapon? The answer is, simply: because we were there. We saw it all. But to break my silence, or what you take as silence, I must enter your language and domesticate you, just like a cow whisperer tames a wild bull by talking to him using words he knows. So I borrow your words and carve myself into them, make a hole in the shape of a cow. You might not see me, but you'll notice my absence. This is where my story begins.

The history of cattle is divided into three eras. The Time Before History emerges gradually from the cooling climates of the Pliocene Epoch more than two million years ago. There in the grasslands of India, our ancestors,

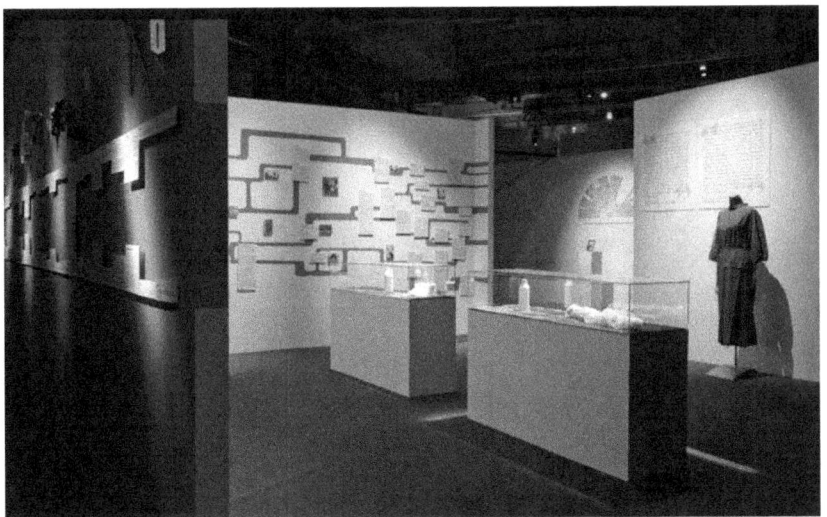

The Hall of The Time of History. On the right: the inseminator. In the glass case: the inseminator's hand, lubricant, scissors, semen straws, tissue. On the left wall: the historical continuum of the science of the improvement of human and cattle bodies.

Fig. 04

the great aurochs, came to life. Tall and heavy, they grazed in groups of twenty or thirty, changing location when in need of water or fresh edible grass. Their life was peaceful as they did not practice war, and the power relations in the community were tested in display fights, which both females and males participated in. The young ones were born in the spring, staying at their mothers' side until strong enough to join the community on its endless travel. Beasts of the era, saber-toothed cats, hyenas, and Hominini, hunted them down when they could, but the aurochs could not be conquered—there were too many. Roaming in the millions, they gradually expanded their presence eastward and westward as far as the great grasslands extended. Over a million years later they inhabited most of the world, from Asia and North Africa all the way to the western coasts of Europe.

With the emergence of the common ape and its culture, we entered Historical Time. At the beginning of the Holocene more than 10,000 years ago, the great aurochs started to live side by side with the ape, gradually forgetting its traditional customs, and learning a new way of life. Why this anomaly in history, this exchange, took place, we don't know. The last free aurochs who could have passed down this knowledge died alone in the remote forests of Jaktórow in 1627, taking the secret with her. We have only guesses and interpretations, unreliable traces of evidence. What we do know is that we—all 1.3 billion of us living today—are the descendants of approximately

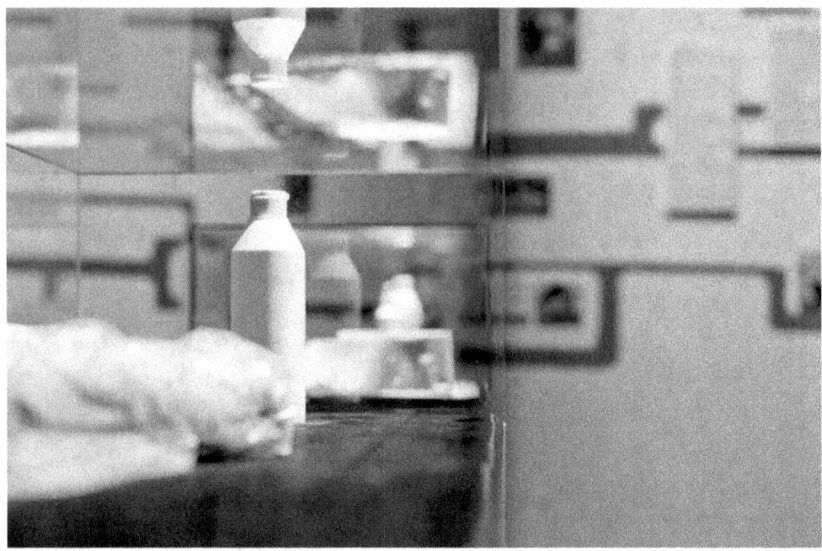

Fig. 05   The inseminator's hand and lubricant are used during insemination.

eighty individuals living with the Mesopotamian common ape 8,000 years ago. From that moment on our species' destinies have been intertwined. The great aurochs became cattle, and the ape, humans.

If the time of the aurochs had been cyclical, determined by subtle changes in the weather and by the signs and traces of its companions, this new era was moving forward like a bull. From our manure, milk, and flesh human history rose like a wave, generating wealth and prosperity beyond imagination. Cultures emerged; wars were fought. New lands were conquered and more and more of our kind were needed to support the lives of humans. Technology and writing and rituals of the afterlife were invented. Richness emerged, and so did theft. Corn, potatoes, antelope skins, pearls, rubber, children, woman, men of all sizes were exchanged as commodities. Animals crossed oceans along with parasites and diseases. Populations collapsed as new ones emerged. Kings were crowned and then beheaded. The generation and distribution of wealth knew no balance but determined destinies, fortunes, and misery randomly.

Meanwhile, unaware of our role as the source of this wealth, we lived a modest life. We lived in the world knowing it was only for us on loan. Everything passed, and we accepted it. The great tides of history arrived to us as streams so small they were hardly noticed. Wars killed us, but so too

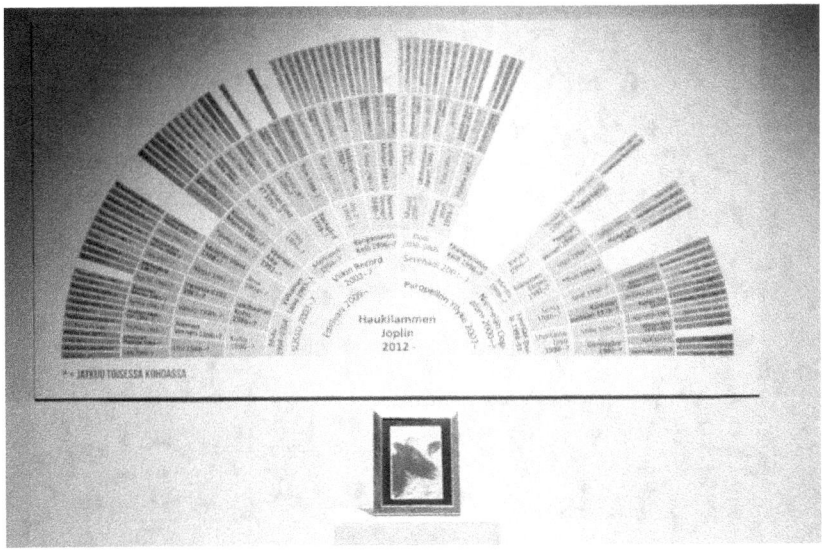

The Pedigree of Haukilammen Joplin (2012–unknown). The blank areas mark family lines that are represented two or more times. Most cattle parents are related.

Fig. 06

did peace. Food was the same, century after century. Barns were smaller or wider, our companions fewer or more numerous, but the daily routine remained. Birth, grazing, feeding, sleeping. Our centuries were defined by the hot breath of a companion in the silence of the shelter, the return to the fields in the day, and by the absence or weight of the plough, sledge, or carriage. We were poor in words for things: our vocabulary was verb-based, built from our doings and those of our companion beings. Our name was given to us by humans. That name rendered us objects. We were so deep inside history that we did not see ourselves within it, nor did we notice when it abandoned us altogether.

Ahistorical Time, the third era we unwittingly entered, is neither linear nor cyclical. We no longer went outside, nor did we sleep with our companions. Now we live inside the factory. It has become impossible to pass on any heritage. Calves are taken from us immediately after being born, and family lines are scattered out of our sight. We do so little that all our culture and habits have faded to nothing. We no longer learn from our mothers, but from the machine that tells our bodies how to stand and how to eat. Stuck in the industrial process we live in collective isolation, cut off from all relations that could anchor us to time, history, or culture. For how could we have culture, if culture was the transformation of things into objects? How could we have history, if history was the weaving together of times from the present

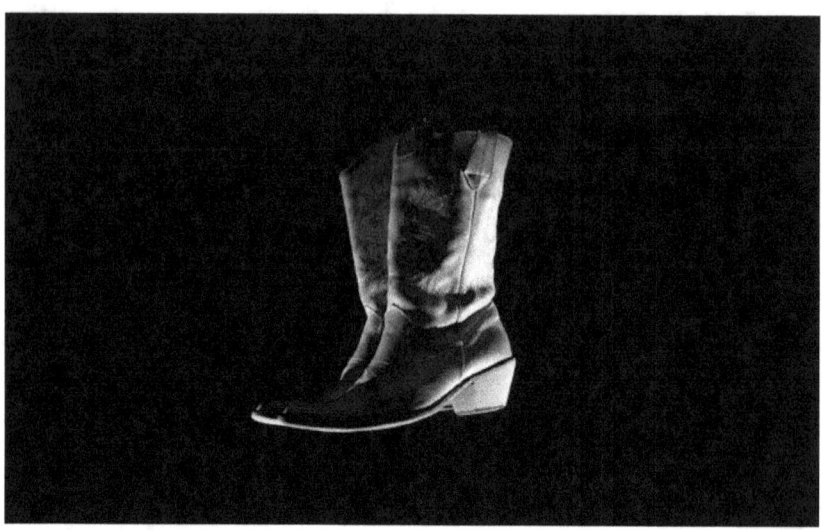

Fig. 07   Artificial human hoofs, made of cattle skin.

moment into the past? We did not even have time, just the monotonous ticking of the clock, the parcelling of hours, minutes, and repetitions.

So here I am, claiming what is mine and my ancestors' by law: the history that we so generously gave to you. By incorporating your tongue, we—the foundation, the mute—are pulled into existence, into human thought. But as we approach the threshold of history, we realize that outside language we are still nothing. I can only point to my absence, hoping that in this failure, a hole would emerge though which a cow could enter. But as I leave you now I do not evaporate into the realm of ideas and imagination. Instead I melt, I dissolve into your body, as my bovine colleagues have dissolved into the bodies of your family and friends. I remain close, hidden between your concepts, curled into your muscles, waiting to be noticed. And, some day, I will enter.

The History of Others *is a large-scale art and research project by visual artist Terike Haapoja and writer Laura Gustafsson. The project investigates cultural histories from non-human perspectives through exhibitions, publications, performances, and writings.* The Museum of the History of Cattle *is the first part of the ongoing project, which had its premier in November 2013 in Helsinki, Finland. www.historyofothers.org.*

PostNatural Histories

Richard W. Pell in conversation with Emily Kutil & Etienne Turpin

> Welcome to the Center for PostNatural History. More than 10,000 years ago, humankind first succeeded at raising wild plants and animals in captivity. By breeding plants and animals for traits that we desire, humans have also influenced their evolutionary path, altering the form and function of the living world in surprising ways. The word "postnatural" refers to the living things that have been intentionally altered by human beings, through domestication, selective breeding, induced mutation, and genetic engineering. These include familiar entities such as farm animals, pets, food crops, racehorses, decorative flowers, and laboratory organisms. Unlike the life forms on display in a natural history museum, postnatural organisms can also be viewed as instruments of culture. They are living embodiments of human desire, hunger, power, and fear. Please continue on the self-guided tour. Questions and suggestions may be addressed on the blue cards available near the exit.
>
> — Description at the entrance of the Center for PostNatural History

Emily Kutil First, could you describe "postnatural" history? How does it differ from natural history?[1]

Richard Pell The postnatural includes all the living things that were intentionally shaped by people in some heritable way. We have defined this idea not so much as a geological period, or anything that has a hard dividing line; the postnatural goes back all the way to the dawn of domestication and selective breeding, and continues through to contemporary genetic engineering and synthetic biology.

An organism crosses over from the natural to the postnatural at the moment it begins to share its habitat with us—when we move in together. For example, when dogs stopped living out on the prairie and started living in town. The other, more extreme component of this transformation is when we take responsibility for the sex life of that organism. This is where selective breeding comes into play. When we begin to decide who gets paired off, who is included and who is not, these organisms begin to change dramatically. And, those changes are quite often a reflection of human desires. They're cultural choices, based on aesthetics and taste, and even sport, entertainment, or religion. This extends to industrialized animals. In the US, we breed our chickens for uniformity. We also breed them for fat content and things like that, but above all else, they have to be virtually identical so that they fit into the machines we've built to process them.

As the Center for PostNatural History, we look at the postnatural world similarly to how one might look at the architecture of a civilization, and then try to infer things about the values of that civilization. We're looking at how that civilization has shaped their world.

EK It's an investigative process, then, in a sense?

RP It is. We put things under the microscope; we research the context, the circumstances that created what we're seeing. We are always reverse-engineering the things that we're looking at. We start off with something that seems incredibly boring on the surface, and it often leads to really extraordinary stories.

EK One of the most striking things that I saw in the museum was the collection of books of standards of different species. You talked a bit about industrialization, the desire to standardize things. But some of the books were for show animals. It seems that there is almost a desire to fix the animal in a certain moment of development.

RP Absolutely. This is a very Western way of looking at things, to create hard and sharp categories that separate, for example, five different kinds of "poodle." We codify exactly what the traits are that define each of those different kinds.

At one point we had an exhibit of publications such as *The American Standard of Perfection*, which the poultry industry has used for 100 years, and *Variations in Dog Breeds,* which the American Kennel Society put out in the 1960s. For almost every breed, there is some kind of publication that tries to be the standard-bearer of what is and is not good within that breed. This crosses over into laboratory science as well. We have quite a lot of publications, including the *Mouse News Letter*, which goes back to the 1950s. Mouse researchers all over the world used this to compare notes, describing the mice that they had in their collection, and the sorts of mutations that were arising. This is how standardized names started to appear for laboratory animals.

Etienne Turpin Is standardization a critical part of the story of the postnatural? How do you characterize the role of standardization with respect to animals used in the context of scientific experimentation?

RP Well, it's kind of a twentieth-century concept; it's post-industrial. The first place it appears, to my knowledge, is in science; in the very basic definition of science, you have repeatability. If you're going to make a scientifically valid statement about the biology of an organism, you're going to have to ask: what organism? And in order to answer that, you have to have a standardized platform. The first place I see this is in the breeding of mice. C.C. Little, in the Jackson Laboratory, tries to create a reproducible line of mice so that everybody can be talking about the same thing despite being in very different places.[2] And that same concept is repeated in all subsequent model organisms. So when we're talking about *C. elegans* worms or *Arabidopsis* plants or fruit flies, all of these are in part an attempt to create an identical "chassis." And then, from that standardized model, scientists create all kinds of standardized variations—the standard "hairless" model, for example—and it goes on and on from there. So, that is the postnatural at the level of science, imbedded in our very definition of science.

The other place that you see standardization is at the industrial level, where the animal is the component of a machine. We see this in slaughterhouses; in particular, in the whole way we raise chickens and cattle. They have to fit the machine, therefore they have to be the same size; they have to be an identical, repeatable product. The imperatives of capital are such that everything that comes off the assembly line has to be identical. The fact that we're dealing with *meat* makes no difference.

ET It is quite provocative to describe biological life as a mere platform. Did the development of standardization in science and industry explicitly reduce biological life on those terms?

RP Well, as a scientist, you are supposed to be controlling for variables: so, if you control variables as I've done, and you follow this recipe, then you should get these results. That's the idea at least. This kind of control attempts to create *terra firma* in the biological landscape, and then it assumes that we have done so; of course, we never have. Organisms all over the world are constantly mutating in different ways. Scientists are always going back to the Jackson Lab to the founding stock to refresh the gene pool. But, of course, the models at the Lab are increasingly adapting to the weird habitat created for them over the last hundred years or so in Bar Harbor, Maine. There is no *terra firma*, but whenever I talk to biologists, they describe this struggle to keep something the same to maintain a point of reference; at the same time, there's a secret acknowledgement that it's all just a moving target, a weird flow of mutation and selection, whether we like it or not.

ET Can scientists foresee the consequences of all these attempts at control?

RP There are many unknowns, and a tendency to attribute unknowns as "dangerous." I would caution against that. I'm not so worried about glowing genes getting out. Laboratory organisms don't generally do well in the wild. Take Starlight Avatar,[3] one of the famous glowing tobacco plants; the Center has two of them. One of them died immediately after we tried to move it to a larger container. Moreover, if you want to see the glowing tobacco actually produce light, you have to lock yourself in the darkest closet possible for twenty minutes in order to discern even the faintest photon. In terms of spectacle and expectation, it's a bit disappointing.

ET So how are you approaching these developments critically?

RP The danger really has more to do with these larger historical trends, like industrialization, rather than these relative new-comers trying to master gene-swapping and single-trait swapping. It has to do with industrializing a massive food chain and making monocultures in increasingly high density. Then, when problems inevitably occur, we patch them and continue and patch them and continue until we have a very fragile machine. You cannot let the pigs out of their airtight containers anymore because they no longer have immune systems. Of course, genetic engineering plays a supporting role in this, but the larger threat to security and sustainability is still this larger, 150-year trend to industrialize food production.

ET And that trend is connected to homogenization and standardization?

RP Yes, it's like the guiding hand of capital. It doesn't have a brain attached to it. It gives you what you want as long as you're paying. If you want ubiquitous bacon—just bacon across the board, on everything—capital will provide that whether it kills you or everyone else. Disease is just another future market. I have a *New York Times* article about this pig virus that is just incredible.[4] The virus has taken out five percent of the pig population in the US, just in the last six months, and when the farms get this disease the pigs get quarantined. They can't leave the site, and they are buried on site, so these farms have these enormous mass graves. But the graves are not contained; there's nothing under them...

ET How are these decisions made? How much do we really know about the management of these outbreaks?

RP There is no single intelligence that is in charge of the whole thing. That's not a vantage point available to us as a narrative. It's really just a cluster of various, contingent interests. So, when incidents like these are covered in the media, there is generally a simplified narrative and a privileged subject—from the farmer or the CEO or an advocacy group. We look at all of those agents, remove them, and see what's left. The whole system is still very complicated and there are many viewpoints that are never presented in the media. We start from the assumption that nobody understands how this enormous system works, and our strategy is to further complicate that with things that people don't know. As an advocacy strategy, this may not be the best, but we're not advocating anything in particular, other than... knowing more. We want everyone to know how little they know—this makes us want to know more.

EK Is the postnatural being discussed in contemporary zoos and museums of natural history? How do organisms like this fit within the taxonomic systems used by these kinds of institutions?

RP A lot of people haven't noticed this absence, but natural history museums tend to avoid or downplay domesticated animals. If they're there at all, they're a kind of footnote or sideshow. Museums almost entirely ignore twentieth-century laboratory organisms. There are a few reasons for this. One of them was exemplified in an exhibit at the Carnegie Museum of Natural History, which describes what an "artifact" is. The exhibition said that an artifact is a man-made object; they showed an iPod: "Is this an artifact? Yes." And, next to it they showed a raccoon skull: "This is not an artifact." That's where our view differs from traditional natural history. Actually, I'm willing to go along with the raccoon skull, but I would put that alongside a Chihuahua skull and say: "This is an artifact." Prior to human intervention, there was nothing in the wild that looked like a Chihuahua. A Chihuahua is a long way from a grey wolf. This layer of human intervention is what defines the postnatural for us.

There is also the issue that natural historians are asking a different set of questions. They want to know about ecology, evolutionary history, perhaps climate. Animals that were raised in captivity, from their perspective, are *bad data*. Also, on an intuitive level, natural historians find animals raised in captivity to be incredibly boring. I found this attitude across the board—whether I was talking to reptile people, mammal people, bird people, or plant people. The kinds of organisms I was researching were beyond their frame of reference. "How could you... why would you...?" When I asked people who spent their whole lives studying squirrels about laboratory rats, they would just shake their head in disbelief.

But, you asked about taxonomy. The whole project of the Center for PostNatural History started from a taxonomic perspective. Initially, I was reading a lot of evolutionary history at the same time as I was reading about synthetic biology. I was reading about how we map out the evolutionary tree by looking at genes, and I was learning about how we take genes and add them to different species where they haven't originated. I started to wonder how that would affect the shape of the tree. Is there a way that we could map out these changes? We're taking a leaf of the evolutionary tree over here and duct-taping it to a branch over there—so, what does that look like? I found that there really isn't a vocabulary for doing that. Even among scientists, each lab has a different system for describing organisms. There was no system that could put them within a larger evolutionary tree, so our first project was to try to fill in that space.

It proved to be a much larger project than we expected. There are hundreds of thousands, if not millions, of new, genetically modified varieties all over the world—far too many to track. I was intrigued by the near impossibility of creating such a system. Various proposals have been made along the way to try to classify these transgenic organisms as sub-species; people have developed acronyms, so you would have genus, species, and then a long hyphenated tag after that, but these names are cumbersome so no one really uses them. There is also the issue of visualizing this tree. What shape does the tree take? Our logo is a binary tree (an evolutionary tree is almost always described as a "binary tree") with an arrow going from one branch to another, representing transgenic gene flow and sort of... completing the tree.

EK So is there a taxonomic ambition for the Center?

RP We're open to a taxonomy emerging from the bottom up, and from our collection. We're continually discovering the postnatural to be larger and more complicated than we had anticipated. If we came up with an overarching scheme of representation, it would constantly be broken. At the same time, we are surprised by the common threads we find in the collection. One of the first things we did was build a database of genetically modified organisms, the genes that had been added to them, and where those genes came from. Just by entering maybe fifty organisms into the database, we realized that the genes were actually coming from a very small subset of organisms. They were coming from E. coli, the plant *Arabidopsis thaliana*, on occasion from mice, from the *C. elegans* worm, from *Drosophila* (fruit fly), from zebrafish. These are all considered model organisms. They're what we use in the lab, so they're the organisms that we know the most about. And as a result, they're the organisms that we take our genetic "parts" from. We found an unexpected taxonomic order already in place because of the relationships to these organisms that humans had already established over the last fifty years or so in the lab. And the reason we had each of these organisms in the lab in the first place was a result of relationships humans developed with them for maybe the previous 100 years. Hobbyist breeders were breeding lab mice and lab rats for different coat colours before anyone even understood how Mendelian genetics worked. The tobacco plant is also a standard model organism because humans have been breeding it for so long; we've been breeding it for so long because we like using tobacco.

Every time we tried to map out an overall taxonomy, it started to look like culture more than the natural world. If we were to map out where these organisms live, they all, not surprisingly perhaps, would map out primarily to urban areas, and also to ports. Frequently, they map on to universities. Almost any angle we take leads us to a cultural frame. Our taxonomy is still in process and probably always will be. We're using a system now where we just give objects numbers based on the day they were added to the collection. We'll probably revisit that at some point, when we have a large enough collection to come up with a more general picture.

EK Could you give an example of how the process of genetic research works?

RP We have an exhibit of fruit flies that were engineered in a lab in upstate New York. Fruit flies are important for genetic research because they have a short life cycle. Scientists can tweak a gene and fairly quickly have a full-grown adult animal that will express that gene. These fruit flies were all bred just to figure out what a single gene does. The scientists micro-injected a bunch of fruit fly embryos with a certain muscle gene, raised them to adults, and then dissected them for that muscle gene. It's a mechanical, reductive approach to looking at genetics. Those tiny flies are dissected under the microscope just to get one muscle fibre out. As a result of this experiment, we discovered that the muscle gene controls their wing muscles and makes them really weak. They never develop into the adult stage, so their wings fall off.

EK What is the motivation behind discovering what this one muscle gene does?

RP It's really just about understanding gene function, understanding how this one part works. It's impossible to study that one part by itself—it's like trying to study what a car part does without knowing anything about the rest of the car. So maybe we'd make a car that doesn't have that part, and then maybe we'd make a car that has too many of that part, and then we would use the results to infer what the part might be doing. This is how a lot of genetics works. It's reductive. We make a million of something in order to guess.

But it's a very noisy, random process. With bacteria, it's very easy to use something like electroporation to try to get a gene into a million cells at once. We know that one of them will work, even if we're only interested in that one. But with something like a goat or a sheep the process is long and expensive, and it takes a lot of damaged goat embryos before there's one that works. In this case, we're adding a part, but we don't have a lot of control as to where it goes in the machine. We're adding a carburetor, and most of the time it ends up on the backseat. Sometimes it's hooked up to the horn, and sometimes it's in backwards…

EK We're trying to work on it like it's a machine, but it's not actually a machine.

RP The whole idea behind synthetic biology is that we look at living things through the eyes of an engineer. Synthetic biology uses all kinds of machine metaphors—for example, the host organism will often be referred to as a chassis. But biological things don't always work the way we expect them to.

EK So we have to work at massive scales in order to get the results that we're looking for.

RP More and more now, we're able to do these things with some care. We're not just adding one gene; we're adding a kind of constellation, a program of genes that turn each other on and off. These genes are substantially different from how they exist in nature. They're created by a DNA printer, a big machine that has four jars, literally labeled A, G, T, and C. The machine just squirts out different gene sequences.

EK So in order to make a GloFish® we wouldn't have to borrow a gene from coral; we could make our own glowing gene?

RP Exactly. Then we might make different versions of that gene to see which ones are the brightest. Then we might add them to bacteria, and then we might expose the bacteria to radiation to create mutations in the gene, such that every now and then the colour changes a little bit. Eventually what was green is now blue.

ET What motivates these modifications? It seems like there is a tremendous effort on the part of humans to appropriate every trick, skill, or otherwise useful capacity of non-human creatures. Is this primarily why these gene experiments are so prevalent?

RP So, starting from the organism itself, we [biologists] looked for traits. We didn't know what made traits. Is it genes? How do genes work? We don't really know. We were always trying to reduce life down to the smallest discrete unit, and for the longest time we thought that genes were it. But, of course, it's much more complicated than that: there are little fragments of DNA that are controlling complex constellations of genes. But worse, where we still see that reductive language is when engineering gets involved, when biology becomes *synthetic* biology, and those genes are understood as parts or abstractions, when organisms are merely chassis or devices. Using this cold engineering language allows us to plough ahead with the assumption that we can mechanize operations and guarantee repeatability. They're always looking for the smallest possible genome. Again, this is mainly just controlling for variables. They want to be able to completely rationalize how an organism works. They're all still heavily invested in the language of reductionism in the world of synthetic biology.

When biologists reduce organisms down to parts by separating them out as discrete units, what we're doing is preparing them for circulation as capital. You have to be able to extradite the thing from the gooey organism so that it can be sold, patented, or downloaded. What you see in the GloFish®, for example, is that it glows; there is a single gene doing that. It was a triumph of reductionism: they said, "Look, we have a single part and you can see how that part works. Boom!" But GloFish® is a unique case; it's the exception. It is like the LED in the world of electrical engineering; it's the part of this complicated circuit that we know how to install and it creates the signal that everyone can see. So we can use that to stall everybody for a while. GloFish® is used as a proof of concept, but in my opinion they're not being very honest about the limitations of that proof. GloFish® was a lab organism; it was used to visualize steady development. A lot of important research came out of these studies; we could see, at critical points, when certain developmental genes turned on. But GloFish® really found its home in American pet stores, at least in forty-nine states—not California. So genetic engineering hasn't really crossed into pop culture. You know, if only we can just make things glow... we're just starting to see the first products that have this signifier of genetic engineering—glowing—which is weird because glowing used to signify radioactivity! Now we're supposed to think this is cool, not terrifying.

EK Your exhibit about lab rats is really amazing, and I was wondering if you could talk a little bit about the ways that lab rats and mice are used to stand in for humans, both genetically and behaviourally.

RP Lab rats have a really interesting history. As I mentioned, they were raised for fancy coat colours in the nineteenth century. Prior to that, they were raised as a part of a blood sport called rat-baiting, where you'd have 100 rats against one dog, and people would bet on how long it would take the dog to kill all the rats. But when we use them in the lab, we're basically using them as miniature people, as stand-ins for humans. In terms of behaviour studies, we put them in situations where they're either being denied food or something else that they want, and we study how they respond to it. We change their genetics to map human genetic conditions so that they develop human diseases: cancers, obesity, etc. Researchers use these animals as the model stand-ins for people to develop treatments that are subsequently used on people. We also engineer lab rats and mice to develop human conditions like baldness—things that aren't necessarily a health problem but that are considered a cultural problem for some people.

EK Did the use of rodents emerge because there was a need to avoid using human test subjects?

RP Yes, using human subjects gradually became unacceptable, and for related reasons, after dropping the atomic bomb in the Second World War, we needed to know how dangerous radiation was, and what it was good for.

ET It all sounds exceptionally violent, despite the small scale of the specific experiments. Without becoming victims of the good vs bad Anthropocene "debate," I'm curious if you try, in the Center, to emphasize the positive outcomes as well as the dystopian characteristics?

RP Well, if there's one term we don't use around here, it's good; or, for that matter, evil. In one Anthropocene narrative, there's this system that humans can influence, but it's not necessarily one that we have control over. When we talk about the post-natural, we're focusing intensely on things that we do have control over. That's why intention is so important in our definition. What you start to see—when you gather all these narratives together like we do—is how little we know, relative to what we can do. We thought we knew what we were doing by breeding bulldogs, but over a period of fifty years, we've lost the dog's face. We've literally lost the dog's face... so that's how much we understand all of this! And, *we did that on purpose*. We actually circulated how-to manuals on what the bulldog is, and therefore what we want to preserve—and we still lost its face. So, for us, squeezing the issue down to those things we do on purpose, with clear intention, further highlights what we don't know. And that's not something we say explicitly in our exhibitions, although I am being explicit it in this interview. It's something that's latent in what we present.

ET So it's not unintended consequences of things we didn't intend, it's unintended consequences of things we did intend…

RP Yes, and that makes a big difference in terms of what you do with all this information—and what you go on to question. The latter makes you question what you plan to do; the former just makes you want to prepare for imminent disaster, or worse.

EK Locality is a recurring theme in the museum. Many of the exhibits tell you how far away the organism is from Pittsburgh, and you have also done some locally focused exhibits. There was one about New York State, and one about Southern California. I'm interested in the interplay between this idea of locality and the massive scales of production of some the corporations that develop genetically modified organisms. What role does locality play in the postnatural?

RP Particularly when we are talking about genetically engineered organisms, habitat is defined in a really interesting way. It has nothing to do with ecology, or with any of the ways that one would typically define a habitat for an organism. It's defined by policy. It's defined by where the organism is legally allowed to live. This differs from country to country, and even from state to state—in the US, you have to get permits if you're going to move an organism that's genetically engineered across a state line. So when we do an exhibit like "Genetically Modified Organisms of New York State," that state border isn't just an arbitrary designation of place, it's a specific definition of habitat.[5] Similarly, the European Union has its own mechanisms of control. There are organisms there that don't exist here; there are organisms here that can't be taken there in their living form. As a function of our collection, for the most part we deal in dead organisms, because they're not controlled in the same way. Once it's dead, it's not able to reproduce—that's the main concern.

You asked about the interplay between large corporations and place. When corporations like Monsanto or DuPont come up with a new variety of genetically modified corn, they apply for a federal permit, which is issued on a state-by-state basis. Initially they'll file for a permit only in Iowa and possibly Hawaii, where they've got their two experimental stations. Maybe a few years later, if this particular variety is successful, they'll apply for a general release permit so that they can take the corn to market in whichever state they want.

At the Center, this phenomenon becomes a useful vista, a way of looking at the world of genetically modified organisms that are otherwise fairly indistinguishable. They often look exactly like their un-engineered counterparts, which is why genetic engineering remains largely invisible. But, looking through the federal permit databases, we start to see unexpected places appear. For example, Hawaii and Puerto Rico are really important sites for corn and soy beans. Hawaii is not normally considered part of the Corn Belt, but it absolutely is if you look at it over the course of the last ten years. It plays a role in containing the upstream experimental parent seed of genetically modified corn. So, we have containment in a biological sense, where a small patch of corn is surrounded by almost a kilometre of dirt so that it can't cross-breed with any other plants, but also containment in a cultural sense, in terms of keeping out people that might want to sabotage those fields for political, economic, or ecological reasons. Again, cultural factors define postnatural places. In this sense, islands serve as a bunker of protection for industrial crops.

Farmers sign license agreements, like the Monsanto Technology Stewardship Agreement in our current exhibit. In that case, the technology is the seed and the farmers are stewards, meaning they don't own it; legally, they're just taking care of it for Monsanto. So, Monsanto owns the technology, but the farmers assume all the responsibilities. It's kind of like a software license agreement. You agree to those terms by opening the bag of seed.

One of our exhibits is a little plot of Monsanto corn that we managed to acquire without opening the bag of seed. We wanted to have specimens of the corn for our collection, but how would we get them without violating these terms and inviting their attorneys' wrath? We went to the pet store, bought pet food that had corn in it, like bird seed and squirrel food, and sprouted the corn seed in the front window for a couple of months. Then we sprayed it with Round-Up. About a third of the plants died immediately, and the rest of the plants were fine. Those were obviously owned by Monsanto.

EK Monsanto is the only company that has plants that are...

RP "Round-Up Ready," yes. In these federal permit databases, there is often a designation for species and for genes called "C.B.I.," which stands for "confidential business information." This is a way that a company can protect its proprietary information. It is the black marker that people are not supposed to know about. Presumably the federal government knows about it, but the information is redacted for the public. The government allows for a certain degree of anonymizing the nature of the organisms that are being engineered in order to protect the intellectual property of the companies. In the database, C.B.I. shows up as a species in the list of all the different varieties: corn, potatoes, C.B.I.... It's also a gene. It starts to take on the quality of a character, the unknown organism. That's why we gave C.B.I. its own exhibit here at the museum. Its specimen is a little sign that says "specimen not available." It's a species of conjecture.

EK In that vein, you must have some interesting stories about obtaining specimens for the museum. What are some of the complications of collecting postnatural objects?

RP There are a number of typical complications. Genetically engineered organisms are not allowed to leave the lab alive. There are a lot of containment policies in place to prevent that from happening. As a function of collecting, these organisms have to be killed before they leave the lab. That job sometimes falls to me. I'm not an expert in killing; actually, I'm not an expert in virtually any aspect of this—it's all on-the-job training. I collected mosquitoes from a lab at UC Irvine that was trying to genetically engineer them so they couldn't carry malaria or dengue fever, with the hopes that the natural world could be repopulated with these mosquitoes. In that case, I was left with a collection of living mosquitoes in ice cream containers, and some tools including a bucket of ice and a tank of carbon dioxide. I had no idea how all of these things worked together, so I ended up with dead mosquitoes and then pinned them to a block of Styrofoam. Later I learned that no entomologist would pin mosquitoes. They're far too tiny, and the pin is almost exactly the same size as they are, so it rips them apart. You're actually supposed to glue them to a tiny slip of paper and then pin the paper.

In maintaining the collection over time, the goal is to remove a living thing from the economy of food. Every living thing is also food for some other living thing. In a natural history museum they try to keep dead things dead forever, which ends up being a lot harder than you might think. The Smithsonian has elaborately sealed rooms and white steel cabinets, so they can very quickly see if there's any kind of infestation going on. If an insect got in and ate some of their collection, that animal, that specimen, would be returned to the economy of food, which is also intimately connected to the economy of shit. You know you have an infestation when you see tiny piles of poop near your specimens.

I became aware of this when I left to work as a fellow at the Smithsonian for almost a year, and then came home and checked on my mosquito specimens. Half of the pins were bare. At the base of each pin were tiny specks—little poops. I eventually found the culprit: a little worm curled up in the corner of the lid. I put it under the microscope and found out that it was a *Dermestid* beetle. The natural history museum keeps a living colony of these—they are used to clean the flesh off of bones for their collections. Natural history museums have a love-hate relationship with this particular bug. My mosquitoes were eaten by a *Dermestid* beetle, but it actually felt good in a way, like my collection was worth eating, just like the Smithsonian's! So it wasn't all a loss. We kept that *Dermestid* beetle as a mascot for a few months; I named him Ringo.

EK You explained how the territories of postnatural organisms are controlled with permits and licenses, and how the term "C.B.I." is used to protect intellectual property pertaining to genetically modified organisms. Are there any other ways that the postnatural world is regulated and controlled?

RP We haven't even talked about patents! Our first major publication, *Biological Properties: U.S. Patents on Living Organisms, 1873-1981*,[6] documents every patented living organism, from Louis Pasteur's beer yeast all the way through to General Electric's bacteria for breaking down oil.

EK This is every patent for every living organism?

RP We accessed the list from the G.E. archives. When they tried to patent a species of bacteria they made that was supposed to break down oil, the patent office denied them on the grounds that they couldn't patent a living thing. G.E. took the case to the Supreme Court. There are two important things to point out here: one is that their bacteria didn't actually work. They were more interested in expanding the idea of what commercial ownership could involve. In their argument to the Supreme Court, G.E. presented a list of patent numbers that they claimed were patents for living things, going all the way back to Pasteur. We took that list of patents, found all of the actual patent documents that go along with them, and put them in a book together. This is Volume 1. Volume 2 would be the collection of patents that came after the Supreme Court decision [in favour of General Electric], which was really the moment the biotech industry was invented. Many companies were poised to profit from biology prior to 1980, but there was a fundamental problem of ownership. When your product makes copies of itself for free, how do you keep selling it? This Supreme Court decision was very significant: it ruled that companies could not only own an organism but could also own its entire offspring, an entire branch of the evolutionary tree.

EK And that's when the experiments limiting reproduction in different ways come into play?

RP Exactly. This led to our second publication, *Strategies in Genetic Copy Prevention*,[7] which is a collection of different techniques, contemporary and historical, that people have developed to stop life from doing the thing that actually defines it: making copies of itself. The book includes spaying and neutering; castration of pets, farm animals, and people; cross-breeding; and hybridizing. The book also includes the famous terminator gene, which companies like Monsanto use to keep their crops from producing a second generation. This gene is not actually on the market, because it has drawn a lot of resistance. It will probably be approved eventually, but it hasn't at this point.

EK The illustration for the terminator gene looks a lot like your logo.

RP One of the things that we're trying to show with the terminator gene is that it is not a single gene; it is more like a genetic machine. It is made of many different genes taken from many different parts of the evolutionary tree. So we depict them in that way. Some of the genes come from bacteria and viruses, some come from *Arabidopsis*, and they're all used to produce a feedback loop. This feedback loop essentially kills all reproductive abilities when the plant reaches puberty, unless it's bathed in an antibiotic called tetracycline. The tetracycline bath would allow Monsanto to keep propagating its seed internally. But, like I said, this gene is not actually on the market yet. It's in the lab, but there has been too much resistance for its use to be approved.

EK Legal resistance?

RP Yes, largely from agricultural and ecological activists concerned that this would be a tool for very rapidly creating a monopoly. Imagine you are a developing nation. Your crops fail, or for whatever reason you need help, and the US gives you a bunch of seed. Imagine the US gives you Monsanto seed, and imagine those seeds have the terminator gene such that the next season, you won't be able to plant that crop again. You will now be dependent. There has been a lot of resistance for reasons like this. But it's interesting to note that historically, environmental activists often lobbied for the development of the terminator gene, arguing that if we were going to be developing genetically modified organisms, there had to be a mechanism...

EK ...to stop them.

RP Yes. It's important to see the ways these technologies operate in relation to power. Technology doesn't have a built-in moral or ethical "thumbs up" or "thumbs down." Its uses are very situational. And, they're very difficult to predict. What makes sense in one context might have wildly unpredictable consequences in a different one.

EK The design of the museum seems to take cues from early cabinets of curiosity; there's a sense of wonder and mystery about the place. How does that relate to the tone the museum is trying to create, and to the imagined audience of the museum?

RP We're trying to get at a lot of things, not any one thing. Aesthetically, we do reference the nineteenth-century cabinets of wonder and the traditional natural history museum, in part because it's a familiar way for people to look at dead animals. It's a familiar frame, and one in which people don't expect things to move very quickly. We want time to slow down here in the museum—not television speed, not internet speed—so that we can tell stories that sometimes take a while to unfold.

But we also take aesthetic cues from the biotech industry—from twentieth-century science, as opposed to nineteenth-century science. Another frame at work is that of the hobbyist. We often conduct our own experiments when we're trying to figure out how to preserve a certain kind of organism: how to preserve flowers, for example, such that we can keep their colour and their shape. But we keep those experiments where people can see them. We're very open about the fact that we're not experts, so we invite experts to come talk with us, work with us, and share their knowledge.

The other aspect of the cabinet of wonders idea is related to your previous question about taxonomy. Cabinets of curiosity, in the seventeenth and eighteenth centuries in particular, before Linnaeus created the biological taxonomy that we use today, were organized by free association. Things were put together because they had the same colour, or the same shape, or were from the same place. Or, maybe they were put next to each other because they were remarkably different. It was wide open—a curator would visually craft a narrative by putting constellations of objects together. That idea is really important to us because we don't have a hard and fast taxonomy. We're not illustrating an evolution of complexity, or anything with an obvious beginning and end. We rely on each exhibit being different from the ones that are right next to it, so that the concept of what is postnatural is constantly being challenged and expanded. I think that's actually what wonder is: the feeling that the world is a little bit larger than it was just a moment ago. We're not trying to convince people of anything; we're just trying to open up the realm of possibility a little bit further.

ET In the natural history museum, humans appear near the end, usually in caves and with clubs. You have included an exhibition about Henrietta Lacks; are there other places where you think humans should be appearing in the postnatural constellation?

RP Henrietta Lacks is there. We also exhibit vaccines; these are very specific attempts to modify our immune systems to allow us to live in circumstances and places that are challenging. We also have this very accepted practice of sterilizing our pets; we used to do that with poor people and anyone we thought was "funny"—that was totally normal. I have a lot of books from the 1920s, from my home state of Delaware, wherein the authors are presenting to their stockholders all the testicles they cut off poor kids. And, this was celebrated as a liberal cause! It sneaks in in that way. A friend of ours got her cat neutered; we have the remains of her cat's castration on exhibit. The narrative starts out about the cat and ends with the definition of an imbecile. Being an imbecile—that would get you castrated during the 1920s in the United States. Humans are constantly in our exhibits. Even though they may be players behind the scenes, but they're often the subject, the body, or the meta-platform. That is only going to increase. What I really want is a hall—a hall of people.

ET We've been talking about eugenics historically, but in 2014, what is our contemporary equivalent of early- to mid-twentieth century eugenics?

RP We still do it. It's still present in our fertility clinics and the various DARPA-funded initiatives to improve the soldier. The person is always the weak link in the loop. No matter where that person is, if they're at a joystick or they're on the ground, they need enhancing—fixing the sleep problem, bettering our reaction times, speeding up decision-making… if only we could fix that with electrical brain stimulation. That's where the positive side of eugenics is going. The negative side—the sterilization and culling of the past—all this genetic information that we're getting about hypothetical people, or foetuses, is being used in decision-making earlier and earlier in the developmental chain, and it's becoming a function of wealth and excess. Upper- and middle-class people are making informed eugenic decisions about their children. That has been going on for about ten years now. It is easy to imagine that, as this gets cheaper, it may become a compulsory or expected trend. It might become more expensive in the long run *not* to have eugenic procedures done—for example, your insurance may not cover you for certain illnesses if you forego early eugenics. So, where is eugenics now? Eugenics is just a function of the marketplace, and it's just a matter of how expensive those choices are going to be. Capital has a way of making things really cheap and ubiquitous. Jello Biafra sums it up really well: "The convenience you demanded is now mandatory."

ET What was an ideological principle at the beginning of the twentieth century has become an investment principle at the start of the twenty-first?

RP Yes. And, at a certain point in our library at the Center, the insurance industry appears, around the 1940s—not surprisingly, right after WWII. That's when a lot of the same people championing the cause of eugenics in the US became involved in starting the first US insurance companies. It's not a conspiracy. It's what we do in the US; it's what money does.

ET To come back to Emily's question, I'm interested in how you are currently building the collection. With so many strands of research and areas of concern, how do you choose what's next for your collection?

RP We build the collection one thing at a time. Usually I read something or somehow become aware of an organism—we always focus on the organism—and then it's just a matter of contacting people and cold-calling. Where we fall short is private companies. We don't have a whole lot from them. Sometimes we can get into their records and tell their stories that way, but usually it is public researchers who are interested in helping out. They help us and we always represent them fairly. We're ultimately concerned with the artifact; we're not interested in the advertising picture on the web; we're interested in the organism being made or modified. The point is, when I think about the Anthropocene, there is so much fuzzy rhetoric around it; it very quickly became a metaphor for a million different things. I'm interested in thinking about it in terms of core samples. If we took a core sample at Wendover, that top layer would be full of bullets and mustard gas—that's the Anthropocene.[8]

EK The museums of natural history share a certain mood. What's your museological mission in relation to this inherited solemnity? Does the relationship between humans and the postnatural necessitate other strategies?

RP Our mission certainly does include us humans. We're part of the picture. One of things I like to do is to document, within a natural history museum, where people finally appear. Sometimes as far as they get is a gorilla skull next to a human skull. The American one, in New York City, just seamlessly becomes an ethnographic museum, and that just makes you feel awkward. We're still trying to figure out exactly how to represent the postnatural. There are these narratives that are not very flattering, particularly to the West, about our various attempts to breed people in the same way we've done with other organisms—to genetically engineer them like any other organism. There's an enormous amount of literature from the US, from about 1880 up to WWII (a lot of which became popular), about the wonders of eugenics and breeding people, and about how awesome blond, blue-eyed white people are; these publications suggest that because of how hard they had it in the cold north, these white people are just better suited to running the show. These are exactly the books that were blowing Hitler's mind as a young man, and they were incredibly popular right up until WWII. I have a few years of eugenics journals from the late 1920s that feature Charles Davenport, a major writer on eugenics. He's the founder of Cold Spring Harbor Laboratory—what is to this day the major genetics research site in the US and was founded with money by Andrew Carnegie as one of his first philanthropic gestures. So, there's this whole undisclosed wing in any enthnographic museum, which is really the ethnography of white people, and what it is that we have imagined in the past as our role in shaping humanity as a whole. So, this is all in our museum, but it's upstairs. How exactly you start telling this story without waving some sort of advocacy flag is very tricky.

Notes

1. An abridged version of this interview appeared as "Welcome to the Center for PostNatural History: Richard W. Pell in Conversation with Emily Kutil," *Scapegoat: Architecture | Landscape | Political Economy* 05 – Excess, ed. Etienne Turpin (Summer/Fall 2013): 328–344.

2. Karen Rader, *Making Mice: Standardizing Animals for American Biomedical Research, 1900–1955* (Princeton: Princeton University Press, 2004).

3. "Starlight Avatar," BioGlow, bioglowtech.com/glowingplant.html.

4. Stephanie Strom, "Virus Plagues the Pork Industry, and Environmentalists," *New York Times*, 4 July 2014, www.nytimes.com/2014/07/05/business/PEDv-plagues-the-pork-industry-and-environmentalists.html.

5. On "The Genetically Modified Organisms of New York State," visit www.postnatural.org/Exhibits/Transgenic-Organisms-of-New-York-State.

6. Center for PostNatural History, *Biological Properties: U.S. Patents on Living Organisms, 1873–1981* (Pittsburgh: Center for PostNatural History, 2013).

7. Center for PostNatural History, *Strategies in Genetic Copy Prevention* (Pittsburgh: Center for PostNatural History, 2013).

8. Richard W. Pell and Lauren B. Allen, "Preface to a Genealogy of the Postnatural," in *Land & Animal & Nonanimal*, ed. Anna-Sophie Springer and Etienne Turpin (Berlin: K. Verlag & Haus der Kulturen der Welt, 2015), 75–101.

Dear Climate

Una Chaudhuri, Fritz Ertl, Oliver Kellhammer & Marina Zurkow

Dear Climate,

We really blew it. We're sorry. We had other ideas and forgot about finitude.

But we're trying.

These broadsheets, really just bits of paper, are our missives, our small odes of affection and awe, and our helpful hints that have been scattered by your whirlwinds. They are our apologies, our jests and protests, our bright ideas, bad ideas, and mental quick fixes. We'd like to make amends, to start by shifting relations: with you, with other species, and with our own tempestuous, impetuous inner climates, too.

We hope you're still listening, and that you'll appreciate that we're trying to cultivate a new imagination.

If you'll accept them, dear Climate, these offerings will seal our promise to meet the terrors ahead and build the tolerances they will demand.

Love,
Una, Fritz, Oliver, and Marina

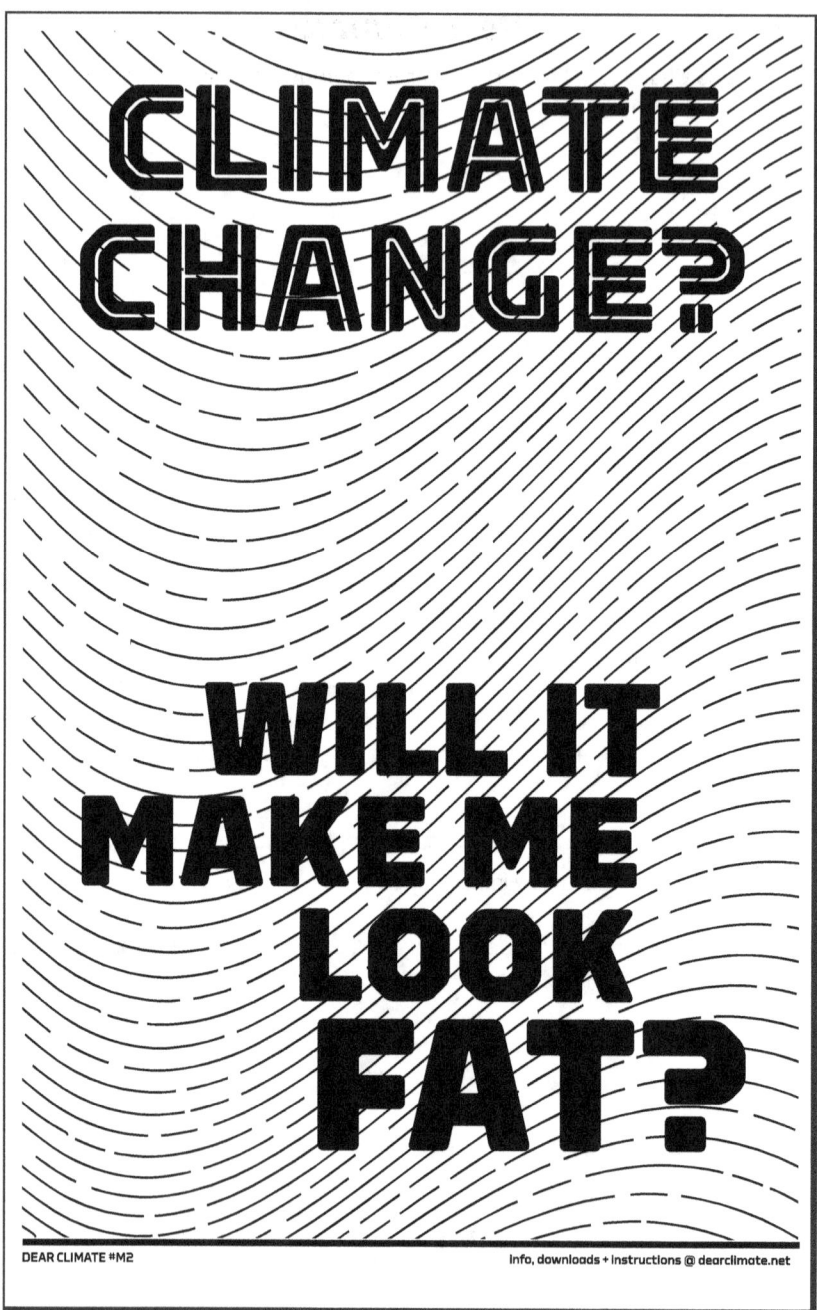

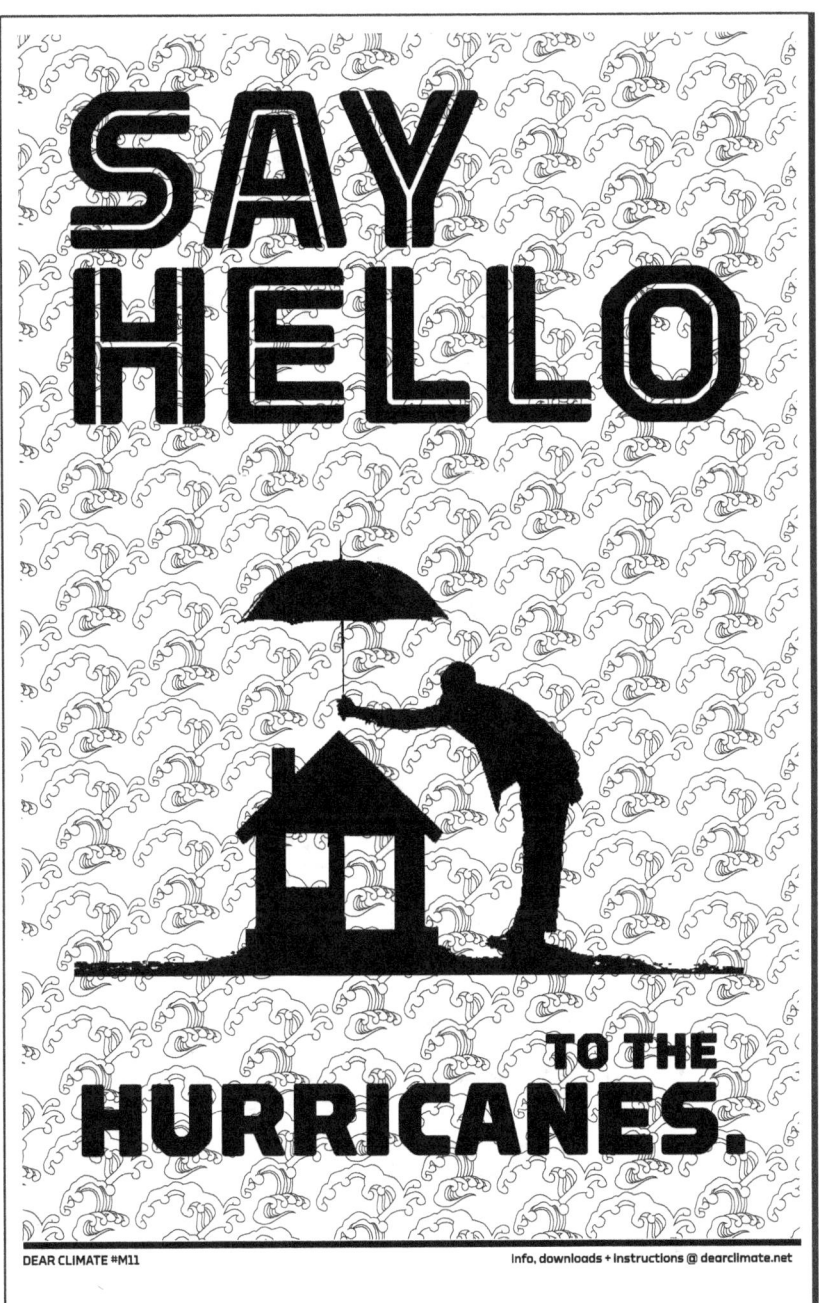

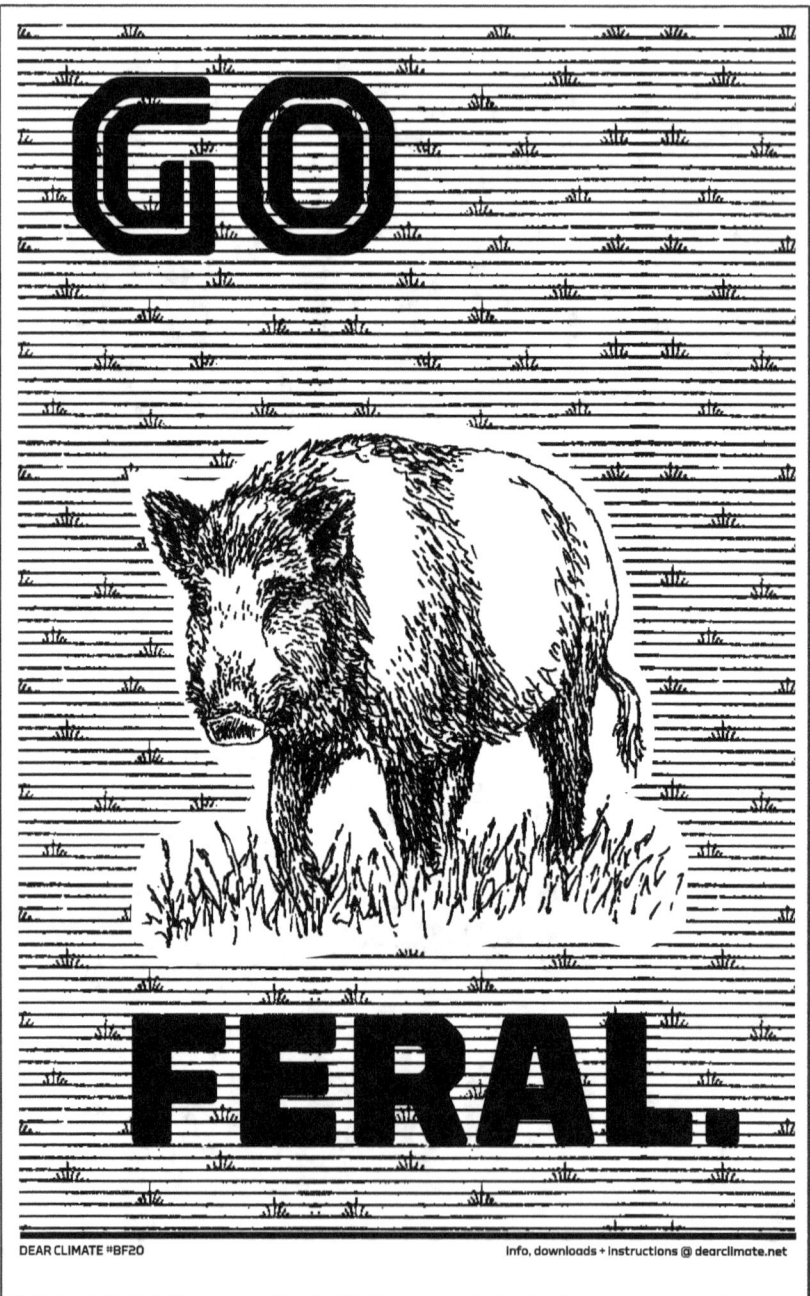

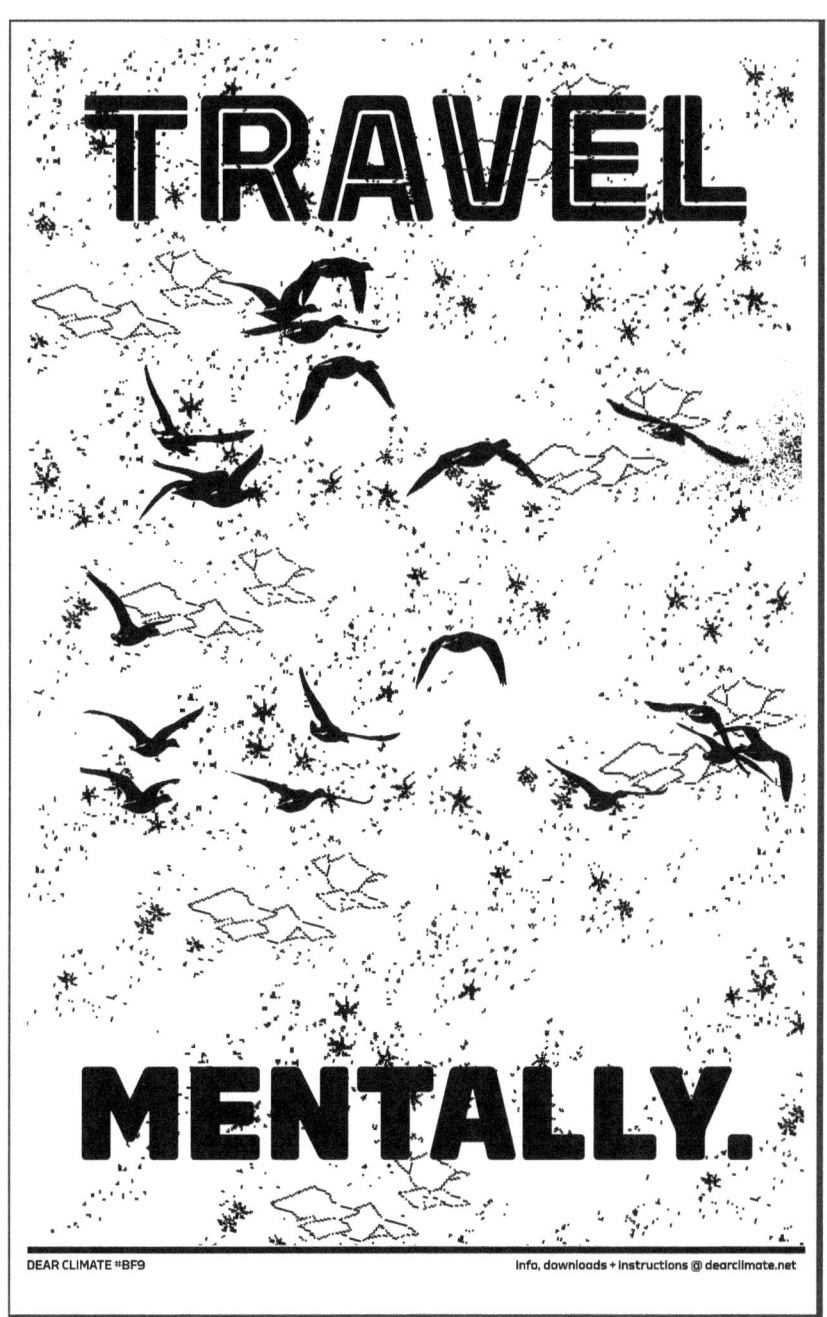

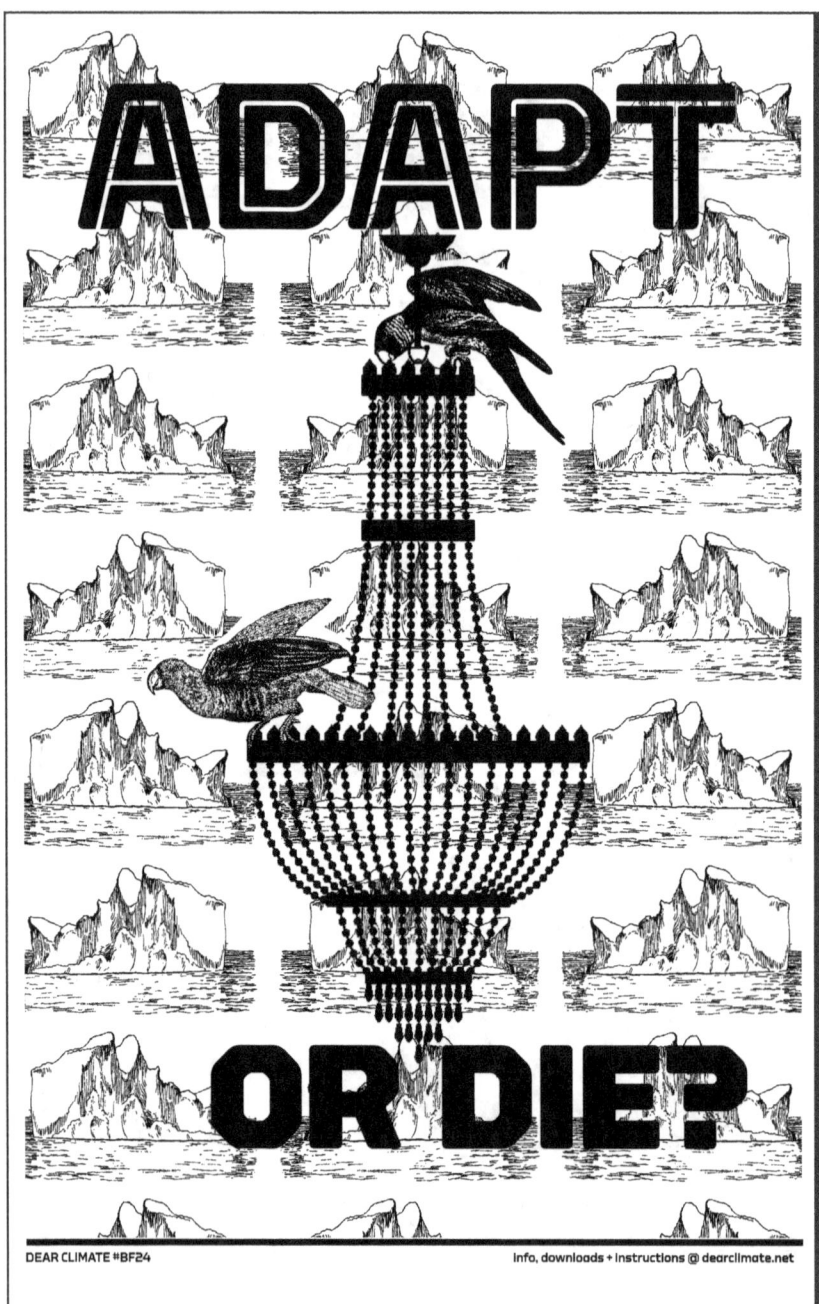

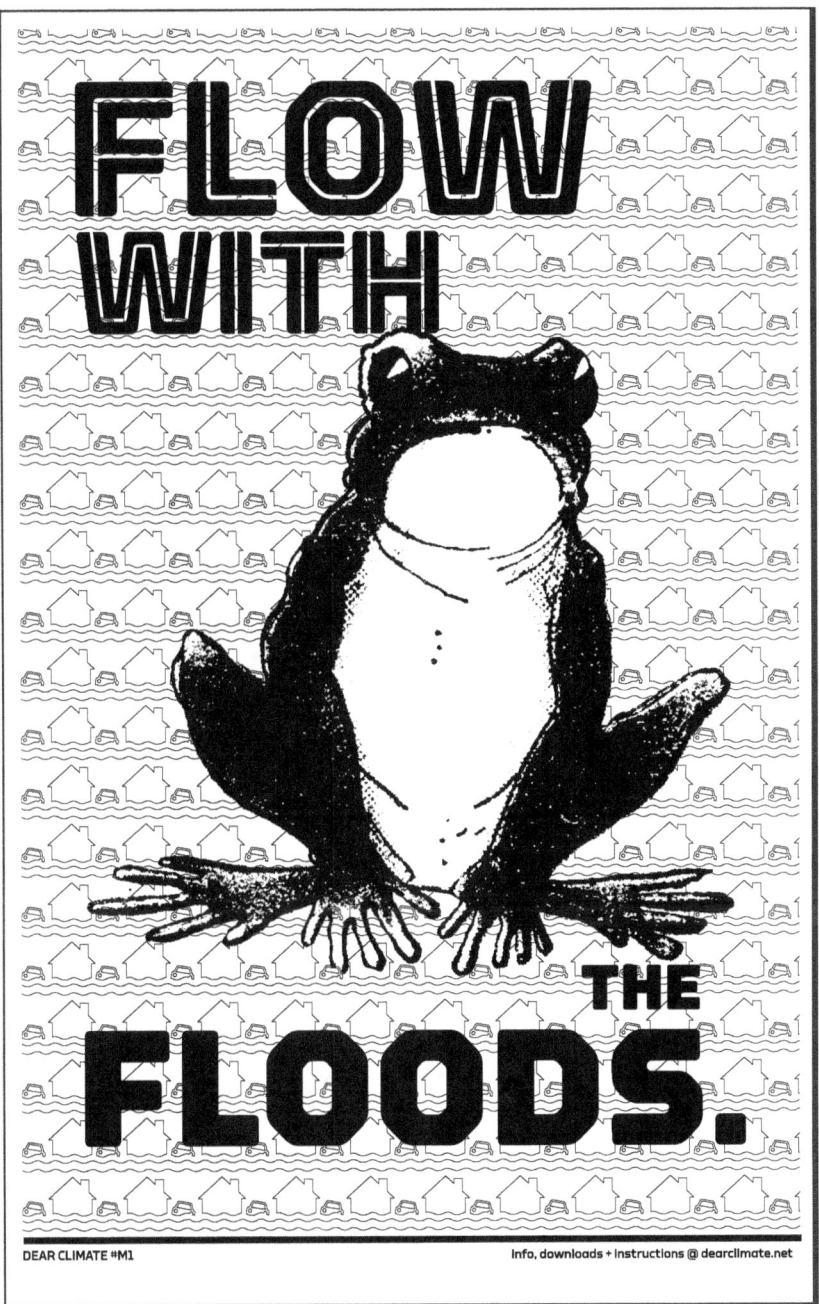

"Dear Climate" responds to the psychic dimensions of climate change and global "weirding." It is a training program for the spirit and the imagination, using a tone, aesthetic, and vocabulary that's the opposite of the prevailing ones: instead of crisis and catastrophe, "Dear Climate" animates the familiar and ordinary; instead of desperation and heroism, it fosters playfulness and friendliness. Dear Climate is after a conceptual nudge rather than a paradigm shift.

"Dear Climate"'s training tools come in the form of posters, podcasts, a website, and installations. Its media are images and texts—both written and spoken—and sound. Its venues are home screens and walls, streets, and galleries. Its form is open-ended: more to come.

Underneath the training program lie three "movements of mind": Meeting Climate Change, Befriending Climate Change, and Becoming Climate Change. When you make acquaintance with something, you invite it into your mental world. Then it's only a matter of time before you get to know it better. The imagination gets seriously involved now, the conversation deepens, the plot thickens. Being hospitable—truly hospitable—involves opening oneself to the unknown, and the gifts of the guest can change the host profoundly. Becoming follows. Becoming disturbs the existing set-up, crosses "clear" boundaries, confuses convenient categories. Becoming is about mixing, spilling, leaking, seeping, suffusing, pervading. It's about sleeping around, telling strange tales, making nonsense: it's about weathering the weather, claiming the climate, taking the temperature of our times.

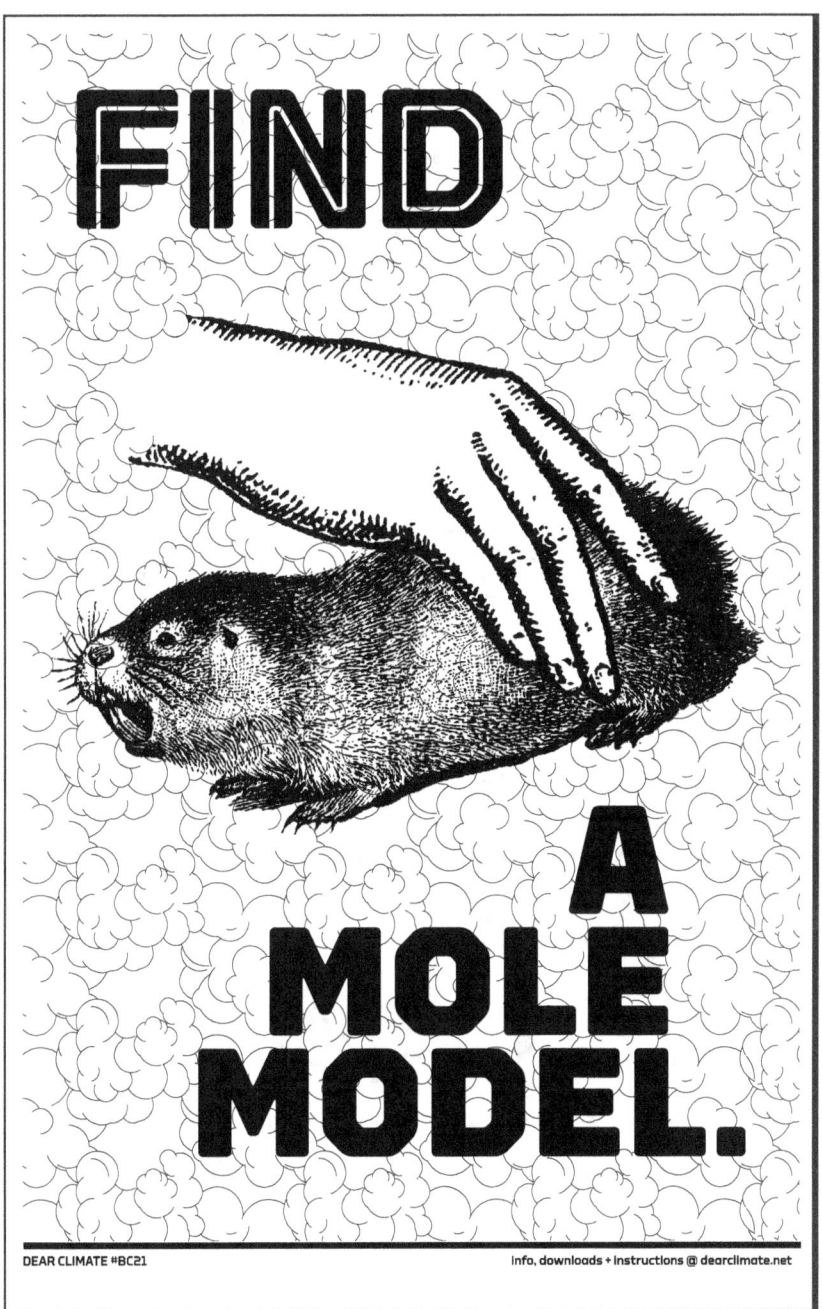

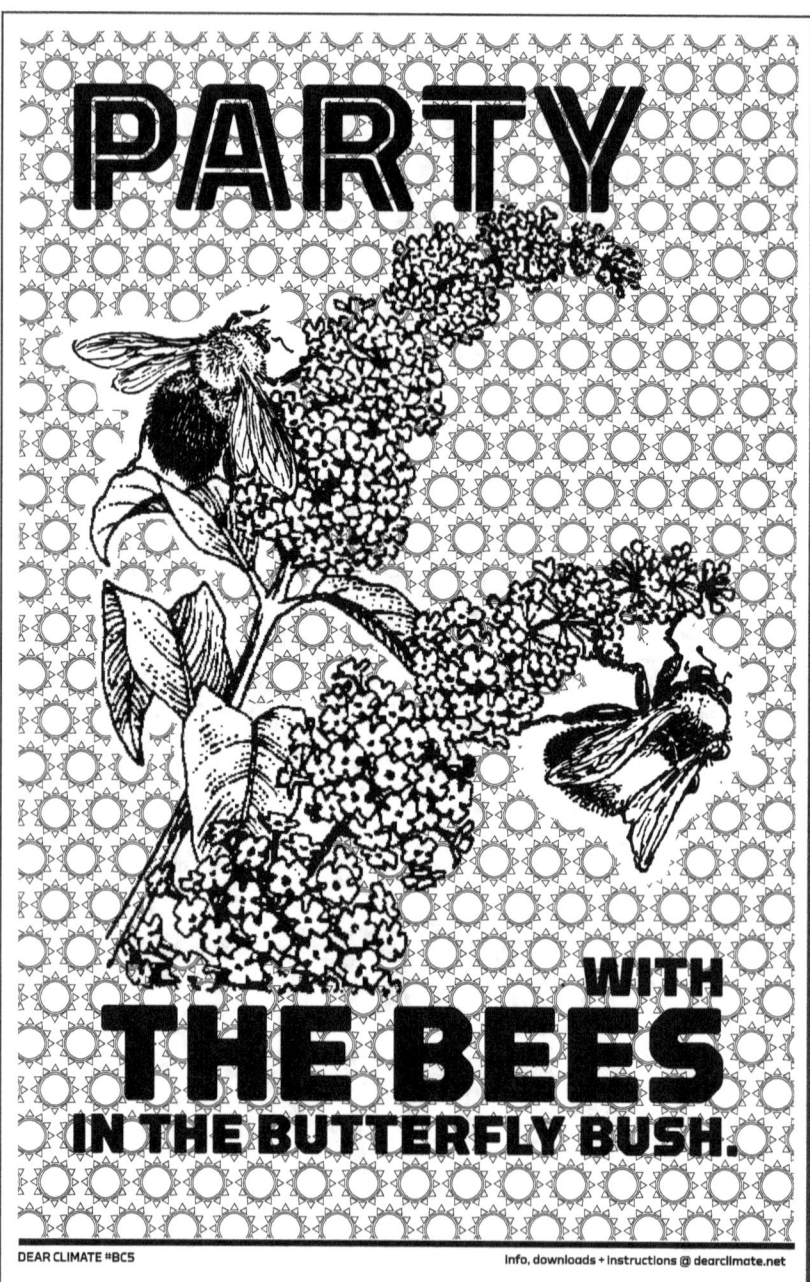

The Anthropocene:
A Process-State at the Edge of Geohistory?

Peter Sloterdijk
translated by Anna-Sophie Springer

§ 1 Weightless Humanity

When the Dutch atmospheric chemist Paul J. Crutzen proposed the term "Anthropocene" in the year 2000—appropriating an analogous concept introduced by Italian geologist Antonio Stoppani in 1873—in order to mark the current age from a natural historical point of view, it seemed probable that this term would only remain part of a hermetic discourse taking place behind the closed doors of institutes analyzing gases and geophysics.

Through an unknown series of coincidences, however, the synthetic-semantic virus must have managed to pass through the well-isolated doors of the laboratories and spread into the general life world—indeed, one gets the impression that it reproduces particularly well in the context of the *feuilleton*, the museum, macro-sociology, and recent religious movements, as well as within alarmist ecological literature.

It seems that the proliferation of this new term can be explained above all by the fact that, in the guise of scientific neutrality, it transmits a message of nearly unsurpassable moralist-political urgency; a message which, in explicit language, reads: Humans have become responsible for the inhabitation and business administration of the earth as a whole ever since their presence on it stopped unfolding in the mode of more or less traceless integration.

Seemingly of geologic relevance, the term "Anthropocene" contains a gesture, which, if it were in the context of law, would be characterized as the designation of a responsible agent. The attribution of responsibility establishes an address for possible accusations. This is precisely what we are dealing with today when we attribute to "the human"—without any specifying epithet—an ability to perpetrate crimes of geo-historical dimensions. Whenever we say "Anthropocene" we find ourselves only seemingly in a geo-scientific seminar. In reality, we are participating in a court case; more precisely, in a pre-trial negotiation in which the legal culpability of the accused first needs to be clarified.

Because the perpetrator is below the age of majority, this pre-trial negotiation must address the question of whether it even makes sense to begin criminal proceedings. In such hearings the author Stanisław Lem would be among those raising the word, seemingly exonerating humans by ascribing to them the status of a *quantité négligeable* with respect to the terrene context. This is what he says: "If all humanity—those five billion bodies—were cast into the ocean, the water level would rise less than a hundredth of a millimeter. A single splash, and Earth would be forever unpopulated."[1]

For quantities such as these it does not matter if we replaced Lem's assumed image of a five-billion-strong humanity with today's number of seven billion, or with the eight or nine billion that could be reached after the year 2050. In terms of biomass even a humanity multiplying at any arbitrarily chosen speed will remain infinitesimal—as if submerging humanity *toto genere* into the ocean were possible. Why, then, lead a trial against a species, which represents a near-nothing in relation to the main material body of the Gaia system, the world's water? Incidentally, Lem's position is very close to the position of those who classically depreciated the human—one is reminded of Schopenhauer's contemptuous remark about the human race as a fleeting cover of mould on the surface of Planet Earth.

The prosecutor will counter these objections by saying that aggregated humanity in its current evolutionary state is by no means merely reducible to biomass. If humanity ought to be put in the dock, then it is precisely because it embodies a meta-biological agent whose agency is capable of exerting much more impact on the environment than its relative physical weightlessness would make it seem.

Of course, one immediately conjures up the technological revolutions of the modern age and their side effects, which are billed not without reason to the account of human collectivity. In truth, and for the time being, one here only speaks of the European civilization and its technocratic elite. It is the latter which, ever since the seventeenth and eighteenth centuries, has introduced a new player into the game of global forces—first through the use of coal and later through petroleum and power engines of all kinds. On top of that, both the discovery and representation of electricity shortly before the year 1800, as well as its technological mastery in the nineteenth century, produced a new universal within the discourse on energy without which it is now impossible to conceive the metabolic interaction between human beings and nature—to evoke Marx's definition of "labour." The collective that today is characterized with terms such as "humanity," and whose influence on Earth is described as "anthropogenic," consists mainly of agents who have, in less than one century, appropriated the technologies developed in Europe. When Crutzen talks about the "Anthropocene," one is confronted with a gesture of Dutch politeness—or fear of conflict. In this case one should rather speak of a "Eurocene" or a "Technocene" initiated by Europeans.

That human agents affect nature is not an entirely new observation. Already in antiquity deforestations were noted in Hellas and Italy, which were attributed to the demand for wood used to build ships. Also, the development of European cultivated landscapes would be unthinkable without the influence of agriculture and animal husbandry. The latter in particular continues to be an explosive item on the bill that the ecosystem "Earth" is going to present to humanity. It was only recently that the correlation between human pastoral power and political expansionism has been exposed.[2] From a macro-historical perspective, a relatively recent causal nexus is evident, that is, one spanning 3,000 years, between cattle breeding and imperial politics: ultimately, more than a few historical empires—such as the Romans, the British, the Habsburgs, and the Americans—were based on the cultivation of large cattle herds, providing their herdsmen with a significant surplus of labour power, mobility, protein, and leather—not to mention the nexus between a daily assurance of calories and political expansionism. We have also recently discovered that cattle herds have a notable impact on the environment due to their metabolism.

There are currently approximately 1.5 billion cattle on Earth; if one submerged all of them in the ocean it would rise by about five times as much as from submerging humanity—bringing us at least into the dimension of a tenth of a millimetre, albeit still not exiting the range of quasi-weightlessness. Nonetheless, the indirect anthropogenic strain on the environment through cattle breeding is impressive: over a three-year lifespan and due to digestive flatulence, each cow that a human keeps produces an amount of greenhouse gases equal to a 90,000-kilometre voyage in a car with a medium-sized engine.

Having referred to human pastoral power in the current dimensions of its application, we are now leaving the realm of negligible magnitudes. As producer of enormous, indirect emissions, "humanity" of the industrial age might indeed—and regardless of its biomass weightlessness—play a geologically relevant role, specifically by operating gigantic fleets of automobiles, airplanes, and ships with combustion engines; but also regarding its thermal efficiency in those regions of the world where extreme winters occasion a compensation through pyrotechnics. The litigation of the "Anthropocene" may be admitted to the main trial.

§ 2 Doctrines of Ages

When geologists use the term "Anthropocene," they adopt the nineteenth-century epistemological habitus of historicizing any arbitrary object and of classifying all historicized fields into eons, ages, and epochs. The triumph of historicism was fuelled in particular by the idea of evolution, which could be attributed to every realm of reality—from minerals to those large assembled bodies we call human "societies."

This is why Marx and Engels could assert, in harmony with the spirit of their time: "We know only a single science: the science of history."[3] In their eyes, human history thus merely marks an exceptional case of natural history, provided that the human naturally be the animal that has to secure its own existence through production.

The history of the "relations of production" would thus be nothing other than the continuation of natural history in another register, and human meta-naturalism merely a technologically distorted natural history. What we call human's inner "nature" would be what Spinoza identified as the impulse (*conatus*) of self-sustainability at any price, impressing upon every life the form of a forward flight.

The Marxist worldview temporarily popularized the saga of the "relations of production"—including its great stages of the era of hunter and gatherers, slave-keeping societies, feudalism, capitalism, through to communism. It was the merit of this myth to replace the ancient doctrine of the eons—descending from the Golden Age to the Iron Age—as well as the doctrine of world empires according to the biblical Book of Daniel—with a pragmatic theory of the epochs. It contended that the epochs differed from each other through the ways in which humans organized their "metabolic engagement with nature."

The logical grammar of the "Anthropocene" belongs to the group of pragmatic epochal theories, of which Marx's grand narrative delivered a prototype. It makes a case for a state of terrene metabolism, in which human-made emissions have begun to influence the course of "planetary history." The term "emission" makes apparent that so far this influence has occurred in the mode of a side effect—for otherwise one would be speaking of a "mission" or a "project." The "e" in "emission" betrays the involuntary character of the anthropogenic impact on the exo-human dimension. The term "Anthropocene" thus contains nothing less than the task of verifying whether the agency of "humanity" is capable of making an "eject" into a project, or of transforming an emission into a mission.

Thus, "Anthropocene" is appealing to a "critique of narrative reason" that does not yet exist. Since effective narratives can only be organized in terms of their ending, the standpoint of the Anthropocene is identical to a powerfully moralistic narrative. In the narrative cultures of the West, this position was hitherto reserved exclusively for apocalyptic literature, which attempts to evaluate the world from the perspective of its end. It implies a cosmic-moralistic sorting process in which the good are separated from the evil. To separate the good from the evil means nothing other than sorting those worthy of survival from those unworthy: what has been called eternal life is a metaphysically overheated expression for being allowed to continue; whereas eternal perdition means that a certain *modus vivendi* has no future, and will therefore be retired from the series of forms of life that are worth carrying on.

This is to say that everything suggests we ought to understand the term "Anthropocene" as an expression that only makes sense within an apocalyptic logical framework. Apocalypse means: evidence comes from the end. However, since as a collective we cannot yet fully be at the end, but instead and until further notice, we do always somehow continue, the human intellect cannot effectively adopt a retrospective view onto its history. It can only test it in diverse forms of anticipation—substantiated through an illustrious series of both eminent and profane simulations: from the Egyptian book of the dead to the first report of the Club of Rome.

Humanity's current interference in natural history proves that Heidegger's original insight of grasping being as time was fundamentally correct. Yet, this intuition certainly lacked one essential element: namely, that time becomes conspicuous only as its even passage is disturbed. The disruption of which the ancients were the most conscious was *delay*, which provided one of the bases of tragedy. Humanity is also currently threatened by delays—notably with regards to the apprehension of "eco-political" action. In general, however, the Moderns notice time *per se*, especially through acceleration, the utmost limit of which provides the trajectory, the *movens*, of the apocalyptic as a figure of temporal logic. It was through this that Heidegger derived the concept of "being-towards-death"—by accepting, in the anticipation of the end, an existentialist shortening. Already in his time, the actual mental task would have consisted of exploring why modernity, for immanent reasons, has been laid out in anticipation of a total ending. This would have required an investigation into the motives of the general acceleration of processes that had imposed the form of an absolute forward on the *modus vivendi* of the Moderns.

§ 3 Virtuous Circles of Modernity

Whoever inquires into the forces of the acceleration typical for the modern age must attend to the mechanisms of positive feedback, for which the American sociologist Robert K. Merton suggested the term "Matthew Effect" in reference to the well-known passage in the New Testament. In the words of Jesus, "For whosoever hath, to him shall be given, and he shall have more abundance: but whosoever hath not, from him shall be taken away even that he hath," the logic of a self-amplifying feedback loop effect is anticipated in an intuitively complete way. It is effects of this kind that impress the form of the *circulus virtuosus*—the virtuous circle—upon the Moderns. Although the modern age is marked also by the occurrence of the fearful *circuli vitiosi*, its overall development nevertheless forms a nexus of virtuous circles whose impacts add up to a new perception of time.

Here, six such self-reinforcing circular processes shall be named that are mutually interwoven with each other in multiple forms of interaction: the visual arts, the credit system, mechanical engineering, the state system, scientific research, and the legal system.

Since the fourteenth century, the visual arts in Europe have featured an entirely new historical organization. What we call the Renaissance is the consequence of a centuries-long continuous self-intensification of artistic capability in the workshops of Northern Italy, Flanders, and Germany—until, thanks to continuous positive feedback, in the sixteenth and seventeenth centuries, a high level of unsurpassable mastery was finally reached—further increased by competition and mutual spying. It suffices to mention names such as Titian, Caravaggio, and Rembrandt to suggest how artistic skill advanced into the stratospheric. In the studios of the fourteenth-century masters a virtuous circle established itself, allowing modern art to move upward as long as, in its essence, it was the art of virtuosos. In contrast, the emergence of modern art and its transfer into the Global Art Age have established the standards of a world market for post-virtuoso productions.

Analogous processes can be observed with regards to the field of positive feedback commonly known as the economy. Here too a powerful *circulus virtuosus* was activated in the fourteenth and fifteenth centuries—which, by connecting credit and talent, catered to the emergence of large fortunes and the transformation of modest seed capital into companies striking out worldwide. Here it would be appropriate to include a digression about interest, which is the tool (alongside real saving) *par excellence* for generating more from less.

Certainly, the self-reinforcing dynamic of the art of economic company management would have come to a halt at the level of a nascent manufacturing economy—as had been the case in classical China—had there not been, in the seventeenth and eighteenth centuries, an alliance with another advancing dimension of self-reinforcing processes. We are used to referring to this sphere with summarizing names such as "mechanical engineering," but whoever might like to remain entirely unreflective could simply say "technology." The close alliance between the second and third virtuous circles, that is, interest-driven economy and innovation-driven machine engineering, produced that dynamic ogre we still identify by the clumsy term "capitalism," due to an intellectual inertia learned in the nineteenth century—though had it been identified in more accurate terms, it would have been called "creditism" or "inventionism" from the very beginning. Schumpeter refers to this self-reproducing ogre when he notes in this harmless-sounding—in truth, however, abysmal—sentence from 1912: "Development always generates more development."

This statement could just as well refer to the circle of self-intensification that has unfolded throughout the course of the modern state. Ever since its troublesome beginnings during the age of the Wars of Religion, the modern state of administration, care, and taxation has generated a Matthew Effect of its own by continuously generating—while obeying a logic of happily expansive independence—new competencies, more administrative areas, and penetrative authorities of encroachment for itself. Here it is worth remembering Wagner's Law, also known as the "law of expanding state activity," two observations their author Adolph Wagner (deceased in 1917), a spry development optimist and Berlin professor, still judged entirely positively. Wagner, a prototype of the subsequently heavily scolded "lectern socialists," had the gift of still being able to see the autogenous expansion of state activity entirely within the framework of the fulfillment of community needs; today we regard the complex of statism, fiscalism, and interventionism rather sceptically, sensing in it more and more the absurd theatre of a self-serving and counterproductive large-scale institution.

In addition, the self-reinforcing circle of the contemporary knowledge industry deserves mention. Every European schoolchild today knows that modern times are times of research. This has been so ever since Bacon wrote his *Novum Organon*, pleading to the Goddess of Experience, in order to multiply humanity's *no-nonsense* knowledge and its proven expertise. It has been so since Leibniz sought to inaugurate the academies so as to grant research a shelter in buildings solely dedicated to the search for new truths. Indeed, the world in which we live is defined by nothing more than the way we "let in" knowledge, similar to how a state with a labour shortage admits migrant workers. One has to express it in this unusual manner because modern-style research by no means signifies the idyllic multiplication of knowledge kept in separate repositories for the delight of the contemplatively minded. Research *per se* means that more knowledge is generated through knowledge. Moreover, most typical modern knowledge, which runs through cognitive *circuli virtuosi* in order to constantly multiply itself, is practical knowledge—thus, it is truth in search of an application. It waits for the next opportunity to infiltrate the life worlds of modern populations. We live in a type of reality defined by a constant, barely controlled immigration of epistemic and technological aliens; we can only hope that these new cohabitants of our cognitive environments will, in the long run, prove themselves to be civilized neighbours.

We arrive at the last *circulus virtuosus* on our list, though not the weakest in terms of impact. What we are talking about here is the judicial system as we encounter it in its current systemic constitution. Only in a Europe already excited by the modern age, and already gripped by various kinds of self-reinforcing games, did it become possible for the seemingly trivial, yet in truth audacious, idea to emerge that human beings by their nature possess inalienable rights. Indeed, only here could the idea appear that life was nothing but the successful exercise of rights by their holders. Certainly, humans have sought shelter in local constructions of justice—but only in Europe, the motherland of the Matthew Effect, could the circle arise which emerged from the mother of all metarights, the "right to have rights," to quote Hannah Arendt. This takes us to the heart of the expansion of jurisdiction. Only in a civilization where the right to have rights had become both a core attitude and an institution supported by the organs of the state could the spiral of continuously expanding juridification, which has become typical for European social dynamics over the last few decades, get off the ground. This expansion of the field of entitlement to rights casts an increasingly problematic shadow. In our times, the intense interaction between overarching lawmaking and the gargantuan self-reinforcing system of the state is creating a monster of national and supranational legal regulation unprecedented in history.

All the aforementioned mechanisms contribute their own specific part to the new conspicuousness of time by placing the anticipating intelligence before the task of being-towards-the-end, although no longer with its own mortal existence in mind, but rather the entire ensemble of relations and situations that we call "modern society."

§ 4 Crisis of Strong Externalization

The coining of the term "Anthropocene" thus inevitably obeys an apocalyptic logic: it indicates the end of any peace of mind in the cosmos, on which historical forms of human being-in-the-world rested. Remembering Max Scheler's treatise, we could translate the conventional "human place in the cosmos" as a kind of backdrop ontology. In this ontology, the human being plays the dramatic animal on stage before the backdrop of a mountain of nature, which can never be anything other than the inoperative scenery behind human operations. The thinking anchored in this backdrop ontology remains virulent long after the Industrial Revolution, even though it is now seen as an integrated depot of resources and a universal dump.

The possibility of resource exhaustion was not considered until later. In his book *The Energetic Imperative*, published in 1912, the German chemist Wilhelm Ostwald gives the first explicit rendition of finite terrestrial resources. He also critiques industry and the state, arguing that since it is not possible to construct an infinite superstructure on a finite base, humanity is summoned to immediately adopt an alternative ethos for natural consumption. The energetic imperative he proposes is one of frugality: "Don't waste energy, use it!" Because warfare is the worst waste of energy, Ostwald suggests that it should be eliminated from humanity's behavioural repertoire—an argument that two years before the eruption of World War One was not entirely without substance. Ostwald's text marks the beginning of the "analytics of finitude" that Heidegger would translate from the sphere of science into an existential context. Max Weber's best-known phrase, which appears at the end of his essay *The Protestant Ethic and the "Spirit" of Capitalism*, published in 1920, also contains a hidden response to Ostwald's ethic of economy for finite beings in a finite world. Weber notes that the current economic order is banishing human beings inside a "shell as hard as steel with overwhelming coercion [...] and may well do so until the day that the last ton of fossil fuel has been consumed."[4] An even more dramatic version of the same idea is offered by Werner Sombart. According to Sombart, Weber had on occasion said to him that capitalism would not end until "the last ton of ore has been smelted with the last ton of coal."[5] Just how dated this statement is—and not only due to the inner dialogue with Ostwald—is revealed by Weber's equation of capitalism with old, heavy industry. He does not mention the new actors who began appearing on the industrial and social stage around 1920: oil, chemicals, financial capital, solar technology, and telecommunications. The reference to "last tons" clearly reveals the apocalyptic logic of Weber's reasoning. Thanks to a rapid being-toward-death of the system, this melancholic sociology gains a synoptic perspective on "capitalism" as a global fatality.

The replacement of the traditional backdrop ontology by an ecological logic reaches back into the nineteenth century. In *The German Ideology*, written in 1845/1847, Marx and Engels had already summarily postulated a joint history of nature and humanity, although they went on to exclude natural history in order to focus on the historical formation of the "conditions of production." This omission is characteristic of a time in which the difference between intended products and unintended side effects was not yet the yawning gap it became in the late twentieth century. In their cheerful productivism, Marx and Engels (as well as their successors) rely on the basic assumption of a backdrop ontology, according to which nature reinterpreted as resource will continue in the future to absorb more or less unperturbed the externalized effects of industrial production. The assumption of a limitlessly acquiescent external nature granted a cosmic peace of mind to humans after the Industrial Revolution longer than it would have been entitled to, given the dawning environmental problematic. With this peace of mind coming to an end, the backdrop ontology and the longstanding background/foreground distinction on which it relied reached the limits of their plausibility.

§ 5 Managing Ignorance

When R. Buckminster Fuller published his *Operating Manual for Spaceship Earth* in 1969, he made the bold assumption that the time was right in social systems for politicians and financiers to hand over managerial responsibilities to designers, engineers, and artists. This assumption was based on the diagnosis that the members of the first group—like all "specialists"—only ever view reality through a small hole that allows them to see no more than a small segment. The second group, by nature of their professions, rather develops a more holistic view based on the panorama of reality as a whole. Fuller's argument sounded as if the romantic slogan "All power to the imagination!" had crossed the Atlantic and was decoded as "All power to design!" The audacity of Fuller's publication, which quickly became a "countercultural" bible, and thereafter one for alternative culture, lay not in his disdain for the world's seemingly great and powerful, whom he believed to be "now only ghostly."[6] It consisted in the truly outrageous redefinition of our native planet. From this critical moment on, good old Earth could no longer be thought of as a natural force, but was to be regarded as a gigantic artifact. It was no longer a base; it was a vehicle. It was no longer the epitome of material; it was the sensitive system of all systems.

It is a testament to the outrageousness and irresistibility of Buckminster Fuller's metaphor that it seeped into the collective consciousness within less than half a century. We have since understood that the talk of Spaceship Earth is not an evasive move into poetic vagueness for a lack of more precise terminology. The metaphor embodies the higher form of the term. Its truth is revealed in the adequacy of the term's implications regarding the real situation. If Earth is a "spaceship," or perhaps more precisely an interconnected structure full of delicate sensors and integrated intelligences, then its crew must indeed show a primary care for maintaining liveable conditions within the vehicle—space scientists describe "Life Support Systems" that mimic the constraints of our biosphere aboard space stations. Atmosphere management thus becomes the first criterion for the artful steering of this craft. Here we must remember that on this vessel no oxygen masks will automatically drop from the cabin roof in the "unlikely event" of a shortage of air. And it would also be absurd to claim that any fluorescent strips on the floor will lead to any emergency exists—Spaceship Earth has no exits, neither for emergencies nor ordinary situations. And regarding those illuminated strips on the plane floor, what are they other than a mild sedative for those passengers with a fear of flying? The anxiety of the guests onboard Spaceship Earth must be assuaged using more concrete means; its treatment requires revolutionary cognitive and technological procedures.

Fuller stated precisely the hitherto most important condition for human residence onboard Spaceship Earth. The passengers have not been provided with an instruction manual, presumably because they were supposed to unravel the secret of their situation by themselves. Indeed, as far as we know, humans and their predecessors have inhabited Earth for almost two million years "hardly knowing that they were onboard a ship."[7] Put another way: in the past, humans were granted a large measure of ignorance in their navigations because the system was designed to tolerate high degrees of human uncertainty. But, to the extent that the passengers begin to uncover the secret of their situation and seize power over their environment by means of "technology," the initial tolerance of the system for their ignorance decreases, until a point is reached at which certain forms of ignorant behaviour are no longer compatible with the passengers concerned about remaining onboard. The human being-in-the-world addressed by twentieth-century philosophy thus reveals itself as a being on board a cosmic vehicle—call it Gaia or Terra or Sphaira or whatever else—that is susceptible to malfunctions. Some time ago I suggested the term "monogeism" to describe the appropriate cognitive relationship of human beings to this entity—a term that designates, as it were, the minimum contemporary, non-ignorant relationship to Earth's pre-eminence. At the same time, it forms the basic axiom for a political ontology of nature.

Seen from today's perspective, the history of thinking on this planet turns out to be a finalized cognitive and pragmatic experiment over the course of which the truth about the global situation has been brought to light. Anyone on the spaceship who has the courage to use their own reason will sooner or later account for the fact that we are also autodidacts of space travel. The right term for the *conditio humana* is therefore: autodidact of life and death. An autodidact is someone who must learn decisive lessons without a teacher. I may add that for this reason a merely restorationist recourse to religious traditions is of no help in these things, because the so-called world religions without exception are based on a pre-astronautical worldview. Even by ascending to heaven, Jesus was unable to contribute anything worth mentioning to the manual for Spaceship Earth.

These ideas also imply something about the relationship between being and knowing. Traditional knowledge by its nature must lag behind reality—indeed, we could even say that it always arrives late. This prompts the question of whether the habitual delay of knowledge necessarily means that it will also arrive too late with regard to problems in the future. Fortunately, we are able to answer this question in the negative. There is a kind of prognostic intelligence which asserts itself precisely in the gap between "late" and "too late." This intelligence is what should articulate itself more vigorously in the future. Whereas for a large part of human education to date people have had to "learn from their mistakes," the prognostic intelligence must become prudent before misfortune occurs—an innovation in the history of learning. To penetrate the logic of such learning we require a critique of prophetic reason. Those performing such a critique should not be deterred by the basic paradox of the prophecy of disaster, according to which such a warning, after the fact, will appear superfluous if it was successful, because due to its very intervention, the misfortune did not occur. A critique of this kind has been outlined by Jean-Pierre Dupuy in his study *Pour un catastrophisme éclairé*. According to Dupuy, only experienced apocalyptics can perform reasonable future policy-making because only they are courageous enough to consider the worst as a real possibility.

§ 6 A Politics for the Earth

The subtitle to this essay refers to the concept of the "Anthropocene" as a "state" at the edge of geo-history. Now we see how the expression "state" is undermined by a radical irony. Because it is determined by an apocalyptic logic (according to which being-towards-the-end remains connected to a return to the present moment), the situation of the Anthropocene is contrary to everything that humans have historically related to any kind of settled state—whether it be the state as body politic, the status quo, "all that is solid," the institution, or as "*Ge-stell*." At a decisive moment in his fifth *Gifford Lecture* in February 2013, Bruno Latour pointed out that Thomas Hobbes's legendary pair of concepts—the "state of nature" and its overcoming by the "State"—is currently undergoing a change in meaning. A new "state-of-nature" has opened up that no Leviathan is capable of taming, a new "war of all against all" has been unleashed where not only wolves and sheep, but armed people and ideologues willing to kill, face off against each other. The collisions taking place along fronts that are highly blurred and involve an extremely diverse ensemble of actors (for the time being without a constitution) who, together with human "societies," populate the field of events and the field of battle that is Earth. These include: CO_2, the sea level, algae, computers, microbes, tuna fish, meteorites, antibiotics, algorithms, methane, human rights, wind turbines, GMO-corn, and transplanted kidneys. The ironically renewed "state-of-nature" is neither identical to the chaos of creation, nor is it able to provide what until now people had associated with the modern concept of state: a constitution. It follows from this that the Anthropocene situation requires a new constitutional debate, which in the best-case scenario will result in a non-Leviathan regulatory process—or better, a network of such processes. Within this, not only would the constitutional organs and legal subjects of a yet-to-be-established political arrangement with the name of "Earth Citizenship" be defined. The process or network of processes would also reconstitute the collective of Earth Citizens as a collective subjective in various arrangements—within and beyond the *Universal Declaration of Human Rights*. These processes will resemble a Titanomachy. Here the Earth Citizens would likely gather under the battle cry launched by poet Friedrich Grabbe in 1836: "Nothing but despair can yet rescue us!"

Just how desperate the Anthropocene climate really is can be seen from the fact that by reminding people in our contemporary civilization of religious movements, some of the Anthropocene's most important commentators are trying to motivate a necessary change of attitude through paradigms from the history of mentality. Authors such as Ivan Illich, Rudolf Bahro, Hans Jonas, Carl Friedrich von Weizsäcker, René Girard, and Carl Amery were arguing along these lines in the 1970s and 1980s. More recently, they have been joined by the voices of Robert N. Bellah, Bruno Latour, Pope Francis, and others.

The tone of eschatological despair is heard most clearly in the publisher and novelist Carl Amery, the Catholic leftist who was among the intellectual founders of the German Green Party, before he turned his back on the party because of its disappointing course of pragmatic conformism. Amery predicted genocidal competition and resource wars arising in the twenty-first century, which led him to postulate a mobilization of forces to found religious movements on a scale beyond all previous religious practices. In his view—as developed in the text *Die Botschaft des Jahrtausends: Von Leben, Tod und Würde* ["The Message of the Millennium: On Life, Death, and Dignity"] from 1994—it is paramount that the technologically highly developed faction of humanity should grow out of its biologically determined, earthly—all too earthly—sense of panic over survival. It faces the task, so he claimed, of developing a new, religious (meaning meta-biologically founded) *ars moriendi*, which at the same time would work towards an ethos of a more just distribution of life chances among peoples and the species.

As desperate as such ideas might sound, Amery's intervention did clarify this much: the political ontology of Earth Citizenship entails the demand for a political anthropology in which humans would once again regard themselves as rooted in mortality, as they did in the days of the Hellenic epic and the Attic tragedy. Their common point of reference would no longer be an Olympus populated by gods removed from the world. It would be an Earth that the mortals themselves share, in all its diverse regions, an Earth too real to perform the role of conventional transcendence, yet also too transcendent to ever become the possession of a single imperial power. In this view, Friedrich Hölderlin's vision of humans dwelling upon the Earth poetically remains compelling. The concept of the Anthropocene includes the spontaneous *minima moralia* of the current age. It implies concern regarding the cohabitation of the citizens of Earth in human and nonhuman forms. It prompts us to cooperate in the network of simple and higher-level life cycles, in which the actors of today's world generate their existence in the mode of a co-immunity.

Notes

A previous translation of this essay appeared as Peter Sloterdijk, "The Anthropocene: A Process-State on the Edge of Geohistory?" trans. John D. Cochrane, *Grain Vapor Ray: Textures of the Anthropocene*, ed. Katrin Klingan, Ashkan Sepahvand, Christoph Rosol and Bernd M. Scherer (Berlin: Haus der Kulturen der Welt, 2014): 257–271.

1 Stanisław Lem, *One Human Minute*, trans. Catherine S. Leach (San Diego: Harcourt Brace Jovanovich, 1986), 13.
2 Jeremy Rifkin, *Beyond Beef: The Rise and Fall of Cattle Culture* (London: Thorsons, 1994).
3 Karl Marx and Friedrich Engels, *The German Ideology: I. Ideology in General, and Especially German Philosophy*.
4 Max Weber, *The Protestant Ethic and the Spirit of Capitalism and Other Writings*, ed. and trans. Peter Baehr and Gordon C. Wells (New York: Penguin Books, 2002), 120–21.
5 Werner Sombart, *Das Wirtschaftsleben im Zeitalter des Hochkapitalismus* (Leipzig and München: Duncker & Humblot, 1927), 1010.
6 Buckminster Fuller, *Operating Manual for Spaceship Earth* (Zurich: Lars Müller Publishers, 2008), 67.
7 Ibid., 58.

Public Smog

Amy Balkin

As a citizen of _____, "The Nation," I urge you to act now to initiate an extraordinary nomination process to inscribe Earth's Atmosphere on the UNESCO World Heritage List on an emergency basis, consistent with the aims and goals of the World Heritage Convention, and lead a coalition effort to that end,

Recognizing the outstanding universal value of Earth's Atmosphere, and responding to the formidable threats and risks to its integrity from greenhouse gases, including a forecast global temperature rise of 3 to 6 degrees Celsius by 2100,

Finding it in the common interest to protect the Atmosphere for present and future generations, and acknowledging that its preservation is the duty of the international community,

Further recognizing the impacts of climate change on sites of tangible and intangible natural and cultural heritage currently inscribed on the World Heritage List,

The Nation should undertake and faithfully carry out a coalition-led effort for inscription of Earth's Atmosphere on the World Heritage List, consistent with the aims and goals of the World Heritage Convention.

Willing governments should 1) Immediately notify the World Heritage Committee and relevant Advisory Bodies of the decision to present a nomination with the request for processing on an emergency basis, and 2) Register at *d13.publicsmog.org/initiate* to announce the nomination plan publicly via dOCUMENTA (13), the German cultural initiative (Attn: Carolyn Christov-Bakargiev/ Amy Balkin).

UNTERSCHRIFT / SIGNATURE   DATUM / DATE

Public Smog: Earth's Atmosphere as UNESCO World Heritage Preserve, Postcard, 2012.   Fig. 01

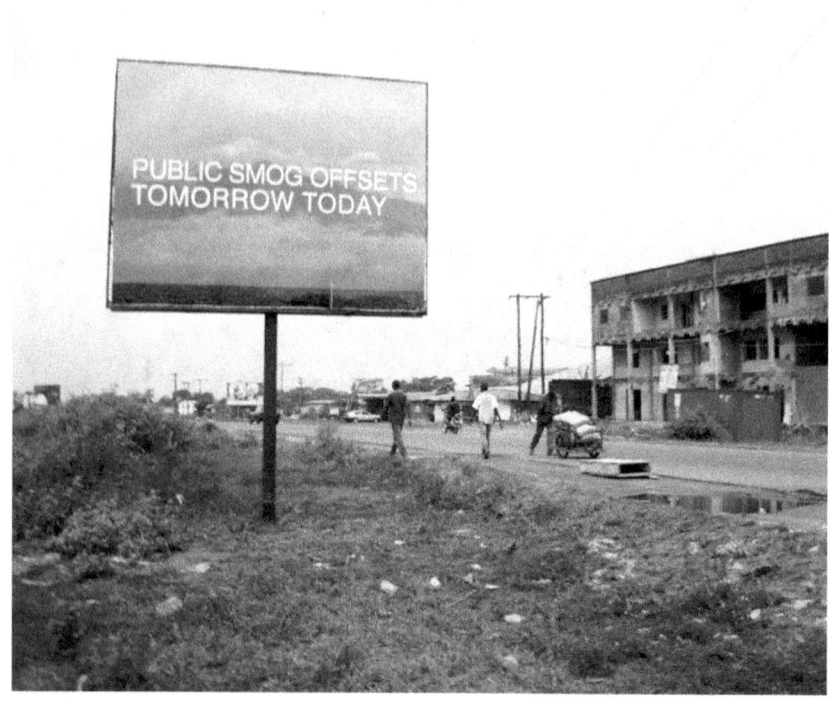

Fig. 02   PUBLIC SMOG OFFSETS TOMORROW TODAY, Billboard, Isenbeck, Douala, Cameroon, 2009; photo by Benoît Mangin.

Public Smog is a "clean-air" park in the atmosphere that fluctuates in location and scale, subject to prevailing winds and the long-range transit of gases. The park is constructed through economic, political, and legal activities that open it for public use. The Lower Park, when open, features particulate-free breathing, and lower-risk athletic activity. Upper Park activities include the ongoing terrestrial enjoyment of familiar birds and plants, glaciers, islands, and coastal areas. Activities to create the park have included purchasing and retiring emission offsets in regulated emissions markets, making them inaccessible to polluting industries. When *Public Smog* is built through this process, it exists in the unfixed public airspace above the region where offsets are withheld from use. The park's size varies, reflecting the amount of emissions allowances purchased and the length of the contract, compounded by seasonal fluctuations in air quality. Between 2004 and 2014, the park opened three times through actions to purchase and withhold emissions credits in greenhouse gas markets.

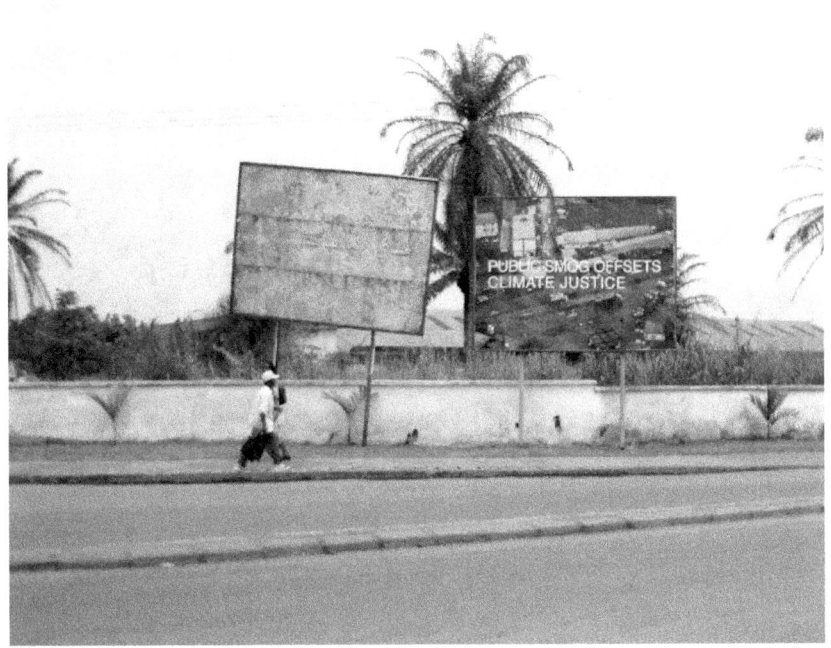

PUBLIC SMOG OFFSETS CLIMATE JUSTICE, Billboard, Ndokoti, Douala, Cameroon, 2009; photo by Benoît Mangin.   Fig. 03

The Lower Park first opened for two weeks in the summer of 2004 in the troposphere over Los Angeles, Orange, Riverside, and San Bernardino counties in California, through the purchase and withholding of the "right to emit" twenty-four pounds of nitrogen oxide (NO_x) in the South Coast Air Quality Management District. The Upper Park then opened in 2006–2007 in the stratosphere above the European Union through the purchase of EU CO_2 Allowances (EUA) on the European Union Emissions Trading Scheme (EU ETS) with the assistance of anonymous Hungarian brokers, who transferred the right to emit fifty-one tons of carbon dioxide to Public Co. Trading. The park closed when these allowances expired.

In 2010, the Upper Park opened over the United States with the purchase of the right to emit 500 tons of CO_2 through the climate charity Carbonfund. Carbon offsets in the form of Chicago Climate Exchange (CCX) Carbon Financial Instruments (CFIs) were purchased as the price of offsets were

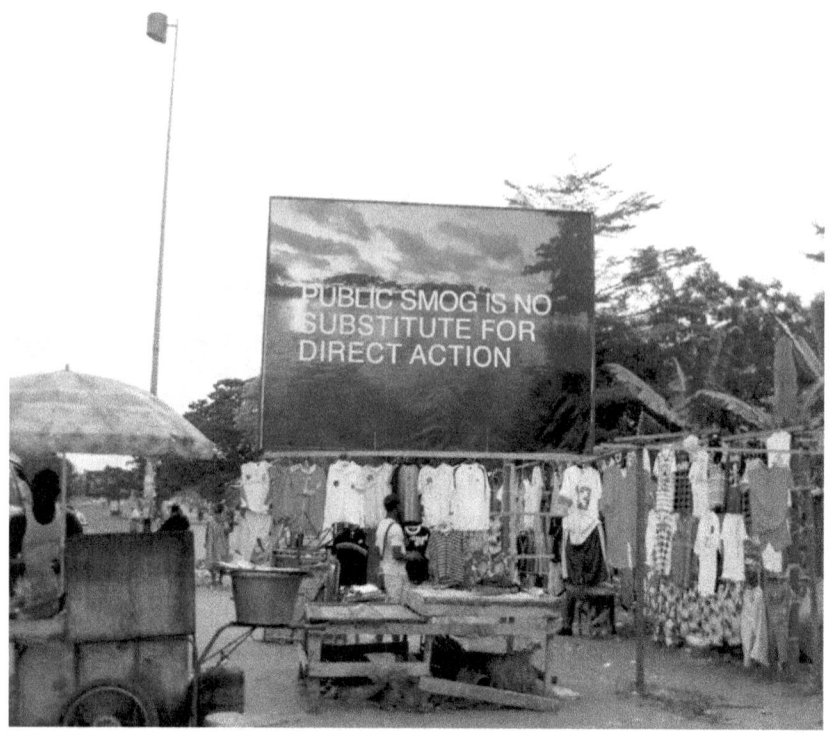

Fig. 04   PUBLIC SMOG IS NO SUBSTITUTE FOR DIRECT ACTION, Billboard, Bonamoussadi, Douala, Cameroon, 2009; photo by Benoît Mangin.

crashing to ten cents a ton amidst low-volume trading in April 2010. From 2003 to 2010, the CCX was North America's sole voluntary and legally binding greenhouse gas emissions trading scheme. Five CFIs, "exchange allowances" equal to 100 metric tons of CO_2-equivalent, were purchased from Carbonfund's inventory at twenty-five cents per ton. As the market collapsed, few entities were selling CFIs, but a deal was arranged through Carbonfund, and the Upper Park opened over the United States on April 7, 2010. Soon after, a ruling by the US Commodity Futures Trading Commission found CFI contracts illiquid. On August 31, 2010, the CCX shut down at market close, and the Upper Park with it.

Other activities that create *Public Smog* impact the size, location, and duration of the park. These activities include an attempt begun in 2006 to submit the Earth's atmosphere, from sea level to the Kármán Line (100 kilometres above sea level), for inscription on UNESCO's World Heritage List. In 2010, with support from German art exhibition dOCUMENTA (13), Professor Gerd Weiß (who has been in charge of the application for

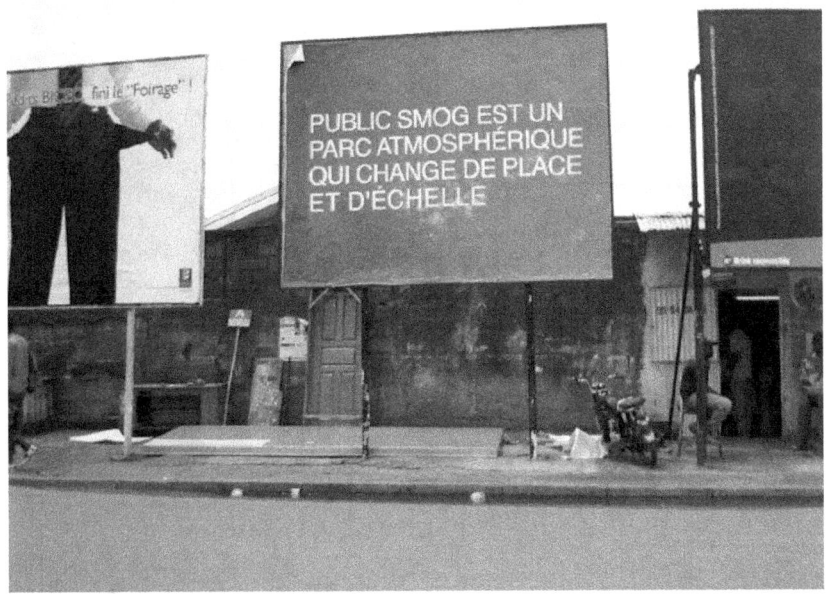

PUBLIC SMOG EST UN PARC ATMOSPHÉRIQUE QUI CHANGE DE PLACE ET D'ÉCHELLE, Billboard, Cetic, Douala, Cameroon, 2009; photo by Benoît Mangin.

Fig. 05

Bergpark as a World Heritage Site in Hessia, Germany) recommended the initiation of an extraordinary process for inscription, as the atmosphere impacts all UNESCO States Parties. The process requires a UNESCO State Party to lead a coalition for ratification, and all States Parties must sign on for the inscription effort to succeed. Germany, as host to dOCUMENTA (13), was first invited to lead a coalition. The invitation was rejected in 2010 by Norbert Röttgen, Germany's Federal Minister for the Environment, Nature Conservation, and Nuclear Safety. The invitation was then extended to all UNESCO States Parties, with 186 invitation letters mailed and thirteen replies received. Dr. 'Ana Maui Taufe'ulungaki, Minister of Education, Women's Affairs, and Culture for the Kingdom of Tonga was the sole r espondent to express interest, but she said the country lacked the resources to initiate and lead a nomination process.

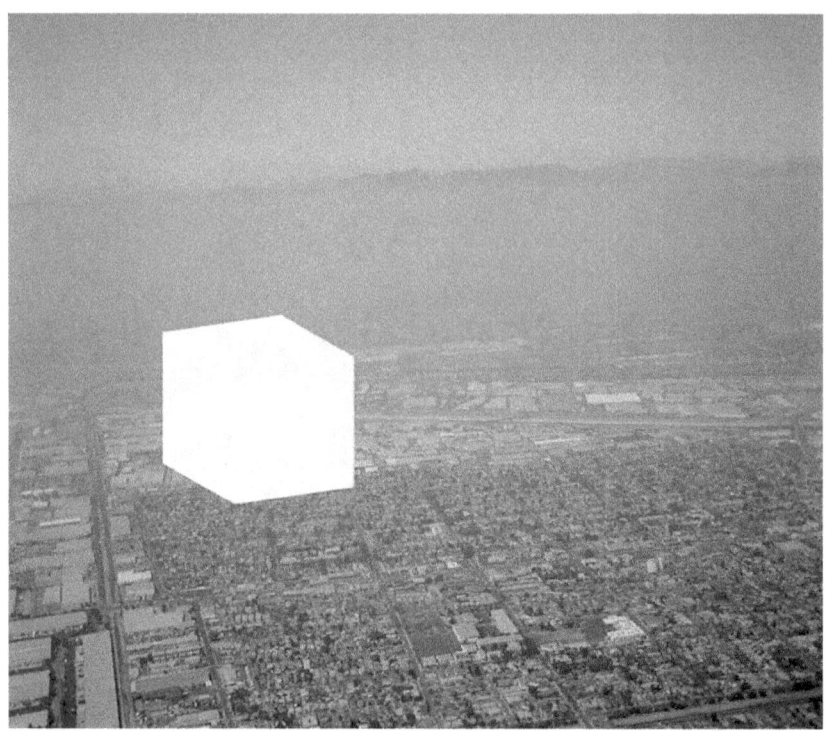

Fig. 06   *Public Smog* over Los Angeles in 2004. *Public Smog* first opened during the 2004 summer smog season over California's South Coast Air Quality Management District, which includes urban Los Angeles and Orange County.

After the effort to find a State Party stalled, the expected 800,000 visitors to the exhibition were asked to petition their respective governments by postcard from within the exhibition, urging the initiation of a coalition process to inscribe the Earth's atmosphere on the UNESCO World Heritage List on an emergency basis. In August 2012, 50,000 signed postcards were shipped to Peter Altmaier, Germany's new Federal Environment Minister, followed by 40,000 more in September, when the exhibition closed. In November 2012, a letter of reply was received from Altmaier's office in response to the postcard petition, reconfirming that Germany would not lead a coalition for inscription. A State Party is still sought, and as of September 2014, *Public Smog* is closed.

Life & Death in the Anthropocene:
A Short History of Plastic

Heather Davis

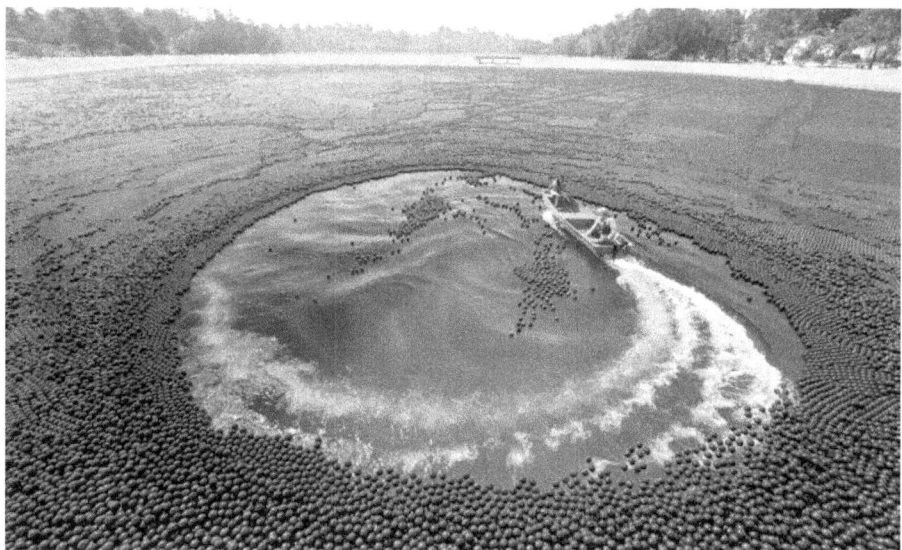

Ivanhoe Reservoir, photo by, G L, courtesy of National Geographic Creative.   Fig. 01

> The present is conditioned by the accumulated traces of the past, and the future of the earth will bear the marks of our present. While the manufacture of plastics destroys the archives of life on the earth, its waste will constitute the archives of the twentieth century and beyond.
>
> —Bernadette Bensaude-Vincent

In 2007, the Los Angeles Department of Water and Power (LADWP) detected high levels of bromate, a carcinogen, in Los Angeles's Silver Lake and Elysian Reservoirs. Bromide is found naturally in groundwater, and chlorine is added to drinking water in order to kill bacteria. But when exposed to sunlight, as was the case in these open-air reservoirs, the two chemicals react and carcinogenic bromate forms. The facilities serve about 600,000 people in downtown and South Los Angeles, and the city was forced to dump the water.[1] The municipal government began to build a new underground facility, but until its completion they needed a way to control this chemical reaction on the other major reservoir, Ivanhoe Reservoir. The temporary solution was to put 3.4 million black plastic balls onto the surface of the reservoir, with the idea that they would absorb sunlight, drastically reduce water evaporation, and also lessen algae growth, while stopping the chemical reaction and thus the formation of bromate.[2] The four-inch-diameter polyethylene balls covered the surface of the reservoir, sealing out the sunlight. The newspaper images associated with this event—thousands of plastic balls being poured down a cement embankment to re-surface the water—bore a striking resemblance to contemporary art, such as the earth works and land art of the 1960s and 1970s. Viewers could easily be forgiven if they accidentally thought the event was a new piece by a contemporary landscape or installation artist, such as Olafur Eliasson or Maya Lin. But, in this case, the relationship to contemporary art was entirely accidental, speaking both to the state of art practice today and to environmental aesthetics.[3] This phenomenon, of accidental or incidental aesthetics, is a hallmark of what is being called the Anthropocene—the era in which extractavist logic and capitalist economics have drastically reshaped the chemical, geological, and biospheric conditions of the earth. From the extraordinarily beautiful colours made from tar for the World Exhibition in 1862, to the London smog that inspired Monet and other impressionists, to the trash vortex, "the largest water architecture of the twenty-first century," the re-shaping of the earth by humans has also meant the birth of entirely new colours and aesthetics.[4] The aesthetic effects—as in *aisthesis*, or affects produced by our sensorial experience of the environment—have been entirely re-ordered by the presence of plastic. The use of the term "plastic arts" was first recorded in 1624.[5] Until the invention of the synthetic polymer that we have come to know as plastic; the arts held a virtually monopoly on artifice, now it is chemical engineers who re-make and re-fashion the earth.

The inadvertent aesthetics produced by the event of covering the Ivanhoe Reservoir in plastic balls draws attention to the larger ways in which aesthetics is shifting under the conditions of the Anthropocene. These "shade balls," as they are called, are typically used to keep birds out of water near industrial facilities and airports and to stop water evaporation in petroleum operations. The LADWP initially bought three million balls to cover the Ivanhoe Reservoir (after the initial phase of introducing 400,000 balls), then nine million more for two other reservoirs in the city, and is scheduled to blanket the L.A. Reservoir, which has a surface area of 176 acres, with eighty million balls, permanently.[6] These procedures reveal what plastic does best: it acts as a sealant, a barrier, both literally sealing something off from its surrounding environment—in this case, a reservoir—while also materializing the desire for impenetrability, for objects, bodies, and selves to be discrete, for categories not to mix, for a monadic identity separated from its environment.

Plastic: The Substrate of Advanced Capitalism

The first synthetic polymer, Bakelite, was created in 1907 and patented in 1909 by Leo Baekeland. It was invented to fill consumer demand for items that were becoming more difficult to get—such as ivory and silk—as anti-colonial resistance movements started simmering, and as the earlier pillaging of resources made these items increasingly unavailable and expensive.[7] Lauded as the material of a thousand uses, plastic became the cheap alternative, the perfect substance for a burgeoning commodity society that would emerge full force in the post-WWII era. Plastic has always been a thoroughly profit-driven material. Even when the category of what we now think of as plastics was still in formation, its nature was more "commercial than scientific," as Jeffrey Meikle argues in his illuminating and far-reaching cultural history, *American Plastic*.[8] In other words, the invention and proliferation of plastics was driven less by a need to develop new technologies, such as medical or warfare applications (although WWII boosted the use of plastics greatly), than to simply replace the objects we already had—but at a price and in a quantity that helped to instantiate a middle class defined by consumption.

Plastic created the conditions for global trade and consumerism, while these systems themselves became increasingly reliant upon various forms of plastic. As Andrea Westermann notes in her study of PVC (or vinyl) in Germany: "Plastic packaging, in particular, facilitated mass consumption […] The new ways of handling and distributing commodities in retail and wholesale were not only based on plastic containers and plastic bags, but also required an improved stackability of goods, achieved by material innovations like shrink-wrap."[9] Indeed, the infrastructure and speed of advanced capitalism, and the fantasy of unending economic growth fuelled by extractivist policies and mass consumerism depend upon plastic. This explains why 280 million tons of plastic was produced worldwide in 2012, with a projected increase to 33 billion tons annually by 2050.[10]

Plastic can be considered the substrata of advanced capitalism.[11] It reveals our utter dependency upon petrochemicals. But its role in our life, unlike the more abstract relationship that we have with other oil products, such as gasoline or electricity, is intimate. We use plastics to eat, clothe ourselves, as sex toys, as soothers for babies. Our computers and phones, those objects we seemingly can not do without, could not exist without plastics as the lightweight portable devices that they are. Nor could the Internet, with thousands of underwater and underground cables sealed from the elements with plastic coating.[12] Plastic is ubiquitous and infiltrates so many aspects of our daily lives that its presence is easy to take for granted and also hard to fathom. It has introduced entirely new sensorial regimes with its smooth surfaces and bright colours. It also implicates us: there is no way to extract one's life in the twentieth century from plastic. This is true for people across economic classes and geographies, even if the objects we interact with and the ways we do it remain stratified. Plastic is a problem that can not be externalized. However, the value attributed to plastic, as Gay Hawkins reminds us, is not intrinsic to the material, but rather is enacted.[13] It accumulates value precisely because of how it is used, what it enables, and how it circulates through the economy.[14]

Plastic represents the promises of modernity: the promise of sealed, perfected, clean, smooth abundance. It encapsulates the fantasy of ridding ourselves of the dirt of the world, of decay, of malfeasance. As Westermann argues, "vinyl's plasticity and its chemical creation captured what high modernity expected from technology at large: a world freed from the material restrictions that nature traditionally imposed on humanity. By implication, we would also have a world freed of scarcity, a world of plenty."[15] Plastic represents a shiny new world, one that removes people from the cycles of life and death, one that supersedes the troublesome, leaky, amorphous, and porous demands of our ancestors, our bodies, and the earth. Ridding ourselves of the demands of the earth seemed to promise a world of prosperity through scientific control. In 1941, chemist V.E. Yarsley and research manager of B.X. Plastics Ltd., E.G. Couzens, wrote that the plastic future would be shiny and bright:

> "Plastic Man," will come into a world of colour and bright shining surfaces [...] He is surrounded on every side by this tough, safe, clean material which human thought has created [...] [W]e shall see growing up around us a new, brighter cleaner and more beautiful world, an environment not subject to the haphazard distribution of nations' resources but built to order, the perfect expression of the new spirit of planned scientific control, the Plastics Age.[16]

This idealist dream, or dream of transcendental idealism, represents the apex of the Cartesian split, as matter itself is dictated and rearranged by the human mind. Planned scientific control envisions this clean, smooth world, sealed off from the outside—it is not just the barriers of a hazmat suit or the miracles of Tyvek house wrap, but the basic building blocks of matter that are manipulated and re-built. As Bernadette Bensaude-Vincent writes: "Matter came to be presented as a malleable and docile partner of creation—a kind of Play-Doh in the hands of the clever designer who informs matter with intelligence and intentionality. Just like the *demiurgos* in Plato's *Timaeus*, the material engineer can impose forms on a passive, malleable *chora*."[17] This dream of the ultimate passivity of nature, pliable to the wills and whims of the modern subject, has had horrifying implications. Plastic—in its production, distribution, and waste cycles—represents the inevitable corollary to unfettered economic growth: it is both intensely resource-depleting (eight percent of world oil production goes into the manufacture and production of plastics) and ecologically devastating. Indeed, plastic brings together some of the most abiding environmental concerns of our time because of its pervasiveness, banality, and longevity.

For although plastic maintains its identity under virtually all conditions, impervious to what surrounds it, all the matter that exists outside of the logic of chemical engineering (everything that existed prior to 1850, say) has been radically altered by the presence of plastic. At the present moment, nowhere on Earth can be considered free of plastic. And no one in Canada, the United States, and many other countries who has been tested has been found to be free of plastic chemicals.[18] Plastic not only spreads while maintaining its molecular form, but the plasticizers that are added to plastic (one or more of a possible 80,000 chemicals added to make plastic pliable or pink or heat-resistant) leach and off-gas; detached from the polymer bond, they are able to move into the surrounding environment and whatever bodies may be found there. These chemicals are having untold effects on the bodies and ecologies that they are now composing. In addition, "various plasticizers have been correlated with infertility, recurrent miscarriages, feminization of male fetuses, early-onset puberty, obesity, diabetes, reduced brain development, cancer and neurological disorders such as early onset senility in adults and reduced brain development in children."[19] This is only the list of possible effects on the human body, without even beginning to account for all the *other bodies* affected by plastic and their associated chemicals.

Plastics also accumulate. They gather in the environment in the forms of blighted landscapes, bags fluttering in the wind, or lighters and wrappers found in ditches, masses of untold plastic items piled in garbage dumps, and in the gyres of the ocean, where they swirl and are eaten by many forms of marine life, from bacteria to birds, tortoises to whales. Plastics also accumulate what is around them, particularly by adsorbing persistent organic pollutants, which due to a similar chemical structure, tend to latch on to oil-based plastics. Once this happens their toxicity grows, and the threat to anything that might mistakenly take it for food also amplifies, bioaccumulating up the food chain. As plastics gain in toxicity their value depletes, they are cast off, re-entering market chains for what little profit can be made from recycling, spreading their accumulated toxins wherever they go.

They are then sifted, filtered through, recognized for their worth by those who cannot afford to participate in this throw-away culture, for those who are also placed elsewhere, out of sight of the markets of capital that rely on invisible labour in order to perpetuate this system. Recycling—first-world atonement for single-use plastics and unfettered consumption—is, for the most part, a highly costly and dangerous process. As Gay Hawkins reminds us, "What makes recycling such a labour-intensive practice, and therefore often concentrated where labour is cheap, is the demands [...] plastic makes on the human, the ways in which it refuses to cooperate in processes of dematerialization and requalification."[20] The stubbornness of the material of plastic is worked through the body, and the poisons that it harbors are also transferred. It spreads its reign of death as it refuses to go away. These problems get shipped to places with fewer regulations, such as Wen'an, China, which, after twenty-five years of operating as a plastics recycling village, is effectively a dead zone with rampant and pervasive negative health effects for the population and local ecology.[21] This can be understood within the framework of what Rob Nixon calls "slow violence," the violence enacted by chemical industries, late capitalism, and paradigms of western economic growth on the rest of the planet. That is, a "violence that occurs gradually and out of sight, a violence of delayed destruction that is dispersed across time and space, an attritional violence that is typically not viewed as violence at all."[22]

Recalcitrant Matter

Plastic has an unfortunate metaphorical connotation. For although plastic is often thought of as a malleable material, as in the common use of the term "plasticity," or in the case of Catherine Malabou's conceptualization of the functioning of the brain, it is perhaps the hardest material there is.[23] It is hard, because it refuses its environment, creating a sealant or barrier that remains impermeable to what surrounds it. It influences its environment while remaining mute to that environment's influence. Instead, plastic serves as a container, both literally and metaphorically, as about thirty-five percent of plastic produced is for the purposes of packaging. These items are then cast off, placed elsewhere, re-appearing as unsightly objects of debris and refuse. As James Marriott and Mika Minio-Paluello from Platform London—a group of activists and artists who track the relationship of oil to violence and conflict—illustrate, in a typical bucket of ice cream, we can:

> recognize a remarkable lifespan: crude oil formed 3.4 million years ago in rocks under the Caspian comes to rest on the bed of the Atlantic [as a fragment of a plastic container] for the next 10,000 years. Between these two stretches is a tiny window of transformation. It might take just 22 days for Azeri oil to be transported from beneath the Caspian to the Munchmunster plastics factory. Then the container could be moulded, filled, sold and discarded in the span of the following 40 days. In the space of only two months, this oil is extracted, transported, traded, transformed and transformed again before it is sold and ultimately trashed.[24]

Not only are the lifespans of plastic products often extremely short, synthetic polymers, derived from oil, are a kind of living dead among us. After digging up the remains of ancient plants and animals, we are now stuck with the consequences of these undead molecules, the ones that refuse to interact with other carbon-dependent life forms. For although plastics photodegrade and break apart, they do not biodegrade. That is, the pieces may get smaller and smaller, but they do not turn into something else. They do not go away. The molecules themselves remain intact, holding onto their identity. In her excellent book on the relation of the chemical industry to our notions of art, artifice, and nature, Esther Leslie writes:

> What is revealed [...] is the drive of the chemical industry towards "the impersonation of life," "from death to death transfigured". Refuse turns into worth in an act worthy of alchemy, but rather than cracking the code of life itself, all that has been achieved [...] is the polymerization of a few dead molecules. [...] Death imitates life and reinforces its domain.[25]

And, in its proliferation and accumulation, it does indeed extend death outwards, transforming the ecologies that it now composes. Mimicking the properties of many substances that have a relation to the cycles of life and death, such as endocrines and POPs. Plastic survives, lives on, and accumulates for a projected 100,000 years.[26] This quality of the undead is what plastic is often used for: to package and preserve, to seal off bacteria and other organisms to prevent the decay of fruits, vegetables and other organic matter, and, of course, reservoirs.

This recalcitrance of matter, plastic's non-plasticity, is illustrated perfectly by an advertisement for Wemco, a laminating firm in Austin, Texas, used in July 1985:

"Plastic is forever [...] and a lot cheaper than diamonds."[27] Mike Michael reflects on the fact that plastic is an entirely industrial material, existing outside of craft or domestic circuits, and he also comments on the relationship between the metaphor and material of plastic. He writes, "In a word, there is little plasticity in plastic, especially if we take plasticity to connote the potential for new or renewed connections to be rendered domestically (i.e. outside of a professional or industrial setting) and thus for the functions of plastic to be recovered or altered or adapted or invented."[28] Plastic, once it has been formed through the miracles of the chemical industry, remains recalcitrant both to biological processes as well as to human creativity. It is the materialization of the horror of identity, of the stability of form, of a futurity without change. As Luce Irigaray writes in the *This Sex Which is Not One*, "Because you need/want to believe in 'objects' that are already solidly determined. That is, again, in yourself(-selves), accepting the silent work of death as a condition of remaining indefectibly 'subject'."[29] Here, the materiality of plastic takes this epistemological framing too seriously, the relationship between the solidity of the object accepts the silent work of death by existing outside of death and life. It seals off the cyclical mechanisms of circulating matter, clinging desperately to an identity that reaches far beyond biological time and into geologic time. Plastic suggests that we in the post-Kantian world have become voracious and solipsistic subjectivities driven by a dangerously self-interested will.

Finitude

Plastic, in this sense, represents the fundamental logic of finitude, carrying the horrifying implications of the inability to decompose, to enter back into systems of decay and regrowth. In our quest to escape death, we have created systems of real finitude that mean the extinguishment of many forms of life. I take the concepts of finitude and extinguishment from Elizabeth Povinelli's forthcoming book *Geontologies: A Requiem to Late Liberalism*.[30] Povinelli uses finitude to represent a Western metaphysics of understanding death as the end of a carbon-based life form. Finitude represents the drama of existence played out in relationship to the teleological orientation of time towards our own end: a one-way trajectory from birth to growth to death, focused on the individual. Jean Baudrillard also remarks that, as we are increasingly "[p]lunged by chance [or by a blind design] into an abnormal uncertainty, we have responded with an excess of causality and finality."[31] This drama of finitude is intimately tied to our notions of existence, as an individual and as a species, and is seen explicitly in some current narrations of apocalypse within the discourse of the Anthropocene.

The Anthropocene, by relying upon the oft-cited and problematic use of the *anthropos*, seems to fulfill this narrative teleology by advancing a notion of the human as the masculinist technological agent doomed to bring about humanity's own end. What is troubling in this scenario is both the logic of finitude that it proposes—that there will be a clear, clean and defined end, rather than the much more probable scenario of ongoing devastation, species extinction, and mutation towards a future that will become increasingly toxic but otherwise difficult to predict—and that Man will finally burn through his own glory.

This undifferentiated drama of the end is evidenced in Benjamin Bratton's explication of what he calls the "post-Anthropocenic"[32]; it is also seen in a more sinister form in those who embrace the current conditions as an opportunity to create more money and promote unfettered growth. And these are the kinds of politics associated with what Clive Hamilton has identified as the "good Anthropocene." He writes that,

> A new breed of ecopragmatists welcomed the epoch as an opportunity. They have gathered around the Breakthrough Institute, a "neogreen" think tank founded by Michael Shellenberger and Ted Nordhaus, the authors of a controversial 2004 paper, "The Death of Environmentalism." They do not deny global warming; instead they skate over the top of it, insisting that whatever limits and tipping points the Earth system might throw up, human technology and ingenuity will transcend them.[33]

This techno-utopianism is precisely the kind of logic deployed to divorce us from the conditions of being earth-bound creatures in the first place. It is interested only in the extension of a particular way of life, and the individuals who benefit from it, instead of understanding the cyclical, processual, and transformative nature of life itself.

The reign of death already spread through our naivety in believing that we could control and dominate earth systems should be enough to dissuade us from pursuing this path any further. Plastic materializes the desire to give complete freedom to the mind and to control our environment: "[P]lastic established unprecedented control over the material environment. Taken to extreme, such control implied the possibility of stifling humanity in a rigidly ordered artificial cocoon, or, in the event of a loss of control, the possibility, as a retired Du Pont chemist predicated in 1988, that humanity would 'perish by being smothered in plastic.'"[34] What we have seen is that it was exactly the rigidly ordered artificial cocoon of plastics, as well as other fallouts from chemical engineering, that are causing humanity to perish. This holding onto itself that most clearly and molecularly differentiates plastic—a materialized wish to exit the cyclical processes of becoming to which all matter is subject to—has inaugurated an era where "men shall seek death, but death shall flee from them," as Werner Herzog says at the end of *Lessons of Darkness*.[35] It is a form of nihilistic lust that pulls, like a black hole, so many of the biological organisms on earth, even as it differentially affects those who benefit from the uses of plastic and those who suffer its consequences.

Extinguishment

As an alternative framework to finitude, Povinelli asserts extinguishment, which recognizes that things live and die, re-composing in a different form, but without the drama of *the end*. Particular configurations of matter, politics, ideas, and organisms obviously cease to exist, while others come into being. However, extinguishment abandons the teleological impulse by recognizing the circularity and fecundity of living systems. *This* civilization may die, but within that death is the possibility for a reconfiguration with what may be left. Humanity will most certainly one day die off, and it wouldn't be a great surprise if that happened in the relatively near future, but that doesn't mean that species won't evolve or mutate, or that our descendants, even if primarily bacterial, won't inherit the world we leave behind. Apocalypse or the "end of Man" rids us of the questions of inheritance, of a sense of obligation and responsibility to a future, however bleak, too easily. With the concept of extinguishment comes both an acknowledgement of biological, technological, and social limits, but without the drama that would have those neatly encapsulated into a clean break. The framework of extinguishment then recognizes the fact that plastic is killing off *particular* worlds through its proliferation, even as plastic itself remains a materialization of the drama of finitude, refusing to participate in the cycles of extinguishment.

To return again to the black plastic balls in the Ivanhoe Reservoir, I want to think about the fact of their blackness, what their blackness might open up in parallel to the concept of extinguishment. Fred Moten, in a lecture titled "Black Kant (pronounced Chant)," discusses the regulatory framework that Kant applies to the aesthetic and moral regime.[36] He argues that the categories of moral and aesthetic judgment have been deployed to regulate the overabundance of the nonhuman world, the threatening fecundity that then gets displaced through racist logic onto the bodies of black people. In "Blackness and Nothingness," Moten elaborates on these themes; he writes "blackness is ontologically prior to the logistic and regulative power that is supposed to have brought it into existence but that blackness is prior to ontology."[37] Although Moten is writing specifically from the point of view of thinking about the unthinkable conditions of slavery and its continuation into contemporary black life, there seems to be a necessary reworking of the category of ontology, and the relationship to exhaustion, that bears on what it means to live with toxicity, to live in a time of mass extinctions, a time that arises precisely due to the same kinds of ontological positions that excluded blackness, and black people, from ontology to begin with. What would it mean, then, to return blackness to the black plastic balls? What new relations might we humans have to plastic if we thought of its emerging in blackness, from the black of oil, to the black of these balls? Certainly, if the fantasy of separation were abandoned, plastic might be seen as a powerful and in some respects ancient material that does not separate, but that connects us to an unforeseeable future. This future is not one that is then filled with optimism, but rather one that seeks to elide or overturn the comfort of transcendental subjectivity, and instead finds a way to live with "existence without standing."[38] It "is not only to *reside* in an unlivability, an exhaustion that is always already given as foreshadowing afterlife, as a life in some absolutely proximate and unbridgeable distance from the living death of subjection, but also to *discover and to enter* it."[39] We must learn to enter into an untenable world, instead of operating from the fantasy that it can be barricaded against.

If we simply give in to the drama of finitude then there is no point in fighting, in organizing, in creating new economic and political systems that will allow us, or allow other species, to continue. Extinguishment offers another narrative framework for recognizing the horrors of species death but without seeing this as a pre-ordained or necessary movement. It embraces both the fecundity of life as well as the complete randomness of its systems, while proposing a model within which humans can begin to take responsibility for what we have done—but without tying this to the destiny of humanity. Exhaustion is the understanding of the cyclical movement and transformation of life through death. Exhaustion is the way in which different beings come into the world and pass through it, transforming into something else. For although, as Peter Sloterdijk reminds us, we are "condemned to being-in, even if the containers and atmospheres in which we are forced to surround ourselves can no longer be taken for granted as being good in nature,"[40] we must find ways of living without the categories and fantasies of containment, either in relation to time or in relation to matter. We must recognize the porousness of our bodies and thoughts that leach into economics and materials, that transfer our wastes across the planet and into the deep future. We must allow for a certain doubt in our thought, one that eschews mastery in favour of the idiot, and insists on practices of slowing down, of hesitation, as Isabelle Stengers suggests in her cosmopolitical proposal.[41] It is not by neatly announcing the end of days that we can begin to change the path that we are on: and even in its inevitability, we have a responsibility to account for the slow violence enacted on the poorest in the world as well as other creatures. We must finally break free of the logic of plastic.

Notes

1. Duke Helfand, "L.A. Must Dump Water from Two Reservoirs," *Los Angeles Times*, 15 December 2007, www.latimes.com/local/la-me-water15dec15-story.html.
2. Francisco Vara-Orta, "A Reservoir Goes Undercover," *Los Angeles Times*, 10 June 2008, articles.latimes.com/2008/jun/10/local/me-balls10.
3. See the conversation with Sylvère Lotringer in this volume.
4. Beatriz Preciado, *Testo Junkie: Sex, Drugs, and Biopolitics in the Pharmacopornographic Era* (New York: Feminist Press, 2013), 33. See also Nicholas Mirzoeff, "Visualizing the Anthropocene," *Public Culture* 26, no. 2 (2014): 220–226, and Esther Leslie, *Synthetic Worlds: Nature, Art and the Chemical Industry* (London: Reaktion Books, 2005), 75–78.
5. "Plastic Art," *Oxford English Dictionary*.
6. Catherine Kavanaugh, "Plastic Balls Protect California Reservoirs" *Plastic News*, 3 January 2014, www.plasticsnews.com/article/20140103/NEWS/140109973/plastic-balls-protect-california-reservoirs.
7. Jeffrey L. Meikle, *American Plastic: A Cultural History* (New Brunswick, NJ: Rutgers University Press, 1995), 26.

8   Ibid., 5.

9   Andrea Westermann, "The Material Politics of Vinyl: How the State, Industry and Citizens Created and Transformed West Germany's Consumer Democracy," in *Accumulation: The Material Politics of Plastic*, ed. Jennifer Gabrys, Gay Hawkins and Mike Michael, (London: Routledge, 2013), 76-77.

10 Chelsea Rochman, Mark Anthony Browne, Benjamin S. Halpern, et al., "Policy: Classify Plastic Waste as Hazardous," *Nature* 494 (14 February 2013): 169-171.

11 My understanding of substrate is informed by Craig Dworkin's analysis, where no matter how mundane or "blank" an object may appear, it plays a crucial role in the complex articulation of communicative networks. See Craig Dworkin, *No Medium* (Cambridge, MA: MIT Press, 2013).

12 For a detailed examination of the historical, political, and environmental dimensions of underground cables, specifically those that traverse the oceans, see Nicole Starosielski, *The Undersea Network* (Durham: Duke University Press, forthcoming 2015).

13 Hawkins writes: "Plastic is represented as something that seems to have an unfolding logic already within it—it is an instrument for capital accumulation. The assumption is that plastic has intrinsic economic values that are realized in processes of industrial research or market application." Gay Hawkins, "Made to Be Wasted: PET and the Topologies of Disposability" in *Accumulation: The Material Politics of Plastic*, ed. Jennifer Gabrys, Gay Hawkins and Mike Michael (London: Routledge, 2013), 49.

14 For further reading on the importance of the cultures of circulation as the enabling matrix of social forms, see Dilip Parameshwar Gaonkar and Elizabeth A. Povinelli, "Technologies of Public Forms: Circulation, Transfiguration, Recognition," *Public Culture* 15, no. 3 (Fall 2003): 385-397; and for an analysis of the relationship of circulation to cities and infrastructure see Alexandra Boutros and Will Straw, eds., *Circulation and the City: Essays on Urban Culture* (Montreal: McGill-Queens University Press, 2010), especially Will Straw, "The Circulatory Turn."

15 Westermann, "The Material Politics of Vinyl," 69.

16 Victor Emmanuel Yarsley and Edward Gordon Couzens, *Plastics* (Harmondsworth Middelsex: Penguin, 1941), 149-52.

17 Bernadette Bensaude-Vincent, "Plastics, Materials and Dreams of Dematerialization," in *Accumulation: The Material Politics of Plastic*, ed. Jennifer Gabrys, Gay Hawkins and Mike Michael (London: Routledge, 2013), 22.

18 Max Liboiron, "Plasticizers: A Twenty-first-century Miasma," in *Accumulation: The Material Politics of Plastic*, ed. Jennifer Gabrys, Gay Hawkins and Mike Michael (London: Routledge, 2013), 134.

19 Ibid., 142.

20 Gay Hawkins, "Made to Be Wasted," 64.

21 Adam Minter, "Plastic, Poverty and Pollution in China's Recycling Dead Zone," 16 July 2014, www.theguardian.com/lifeandsytle/2014/jul/16/plastic-poverty-pollution-china-recycling-dead-zone.

22 Rob Nixon, *Slow Violence and the Environmentalism of the Poor* (Cambridge, MA: Harvard University Press, 2011), 2.

23 See Catherine Malabou, *What Should We Do With Our Brain?* (New York: Fordham University Press, 2008); Catherine Malabou, *Plasticity at the Dusk of Writing: Dialectic, Destruction, Deconstruction* (New York: Columbia University Press, 2010); and Catherine Malabou, *Ontology of the Accident: An Essay on Destructive Plasticity* (Cambridge, UK: Polity, 2012).

24 James Marriott and Mika Minio-Paluello, "Where Does This Stuff Come From?" in *Accumulation: The Material Politics of Plastic*, ed. Jennifer Gabrys, Gay Hawkins and Mike Michael, (London: Routledge, 2013), 180–181.

25 Leslie, *Synthetic Worlds*, 8.

26 This is the number given by Anthony Andrady, a chemical engineer and leading expert in plastics. See Alan Weisman, "Polymers Are Forever," *Orion* 26, no. 3 (May–June 2007): 16, www.orionmagazine.org/index.php/articles/article/270. However, one of the troubling things about plastic is that its lifespan is unknown.

27 Quoted in Meikle, *American Plastic*, 25.

28 Mike Michael, "Process and Plasticity: Printing, Prototyping and the Prospects of Plastic," in *Accumulation: The Material Politics of Plastic*, ed. Jennifer Gabrys, Gay Hawkins and Mike Michael (London: Routledge, 2013), 33.

29 Luce Irigaray, *This Sex Which is Not One* (Albany, NY: Cornell University Press, 1985), 115.

30 For notes and talks that relate to this argument in her upcoming book, see Elizabeth Povinelli, "Geontologies of the Otherwise," *Cultural Anthropology* (13 January 2014) culanth.org/fieldsights/465-geontologies-of-the-otherwise; Elizabeth Povinelli, "Keynote Speech" (presented at The Anthropocene Project: An Opening, Berlin, Germany, 20 January, 2013), youtu.be/W6TLlgTg3LQ; Elizabeth Povinelli, "Geontologies: Being, Belonging and Obligating as Forms of Truth" (talk presented at The Northern Institute, Charles Darwin University, Darwin, Australia, 1 October 2013), youtu.be/oRcEydtnM3w.

31 Jean Baudrillard, *Fatal Strategies: The Crystal Revenge* (New York: Semiotext(e), 1990), 12.

32 For an elaboration of Bratton's argument, and his particularly troubling assertion of accelerationism, see Benjamin Bratton, "Some Trace Effects of the Post-Anthropocene: On Accelerationist Geopolitical Aesthetics," *e-flux* 46 (June 2013), www.e-flux.com/journal/some-trace-effects-of-the-post-anthropocene-on-accelerationist-geopolitical-aesthetics.

33 Clive Hamilton, "The New Environmentalism Will Lead Us to Disaster," *Scientific American* (19 June 2014), www.scientificamerican.com/article/the-new-environmentalism-will-lead-us-to-disaster.

34 Meikle, *American Plastic*, 9.

35 *Lessons of Darkness*, directed by Werner Herzog (1992).

36 Fred Moten, "Black Kant (Pronounced Chant)," (paper presented at the California Institute of the Arts, Valencia, California, 18 March 2014).

37 Fred Moten, "Blackness and Nothingness (Mysticism in the Flesh)," *The South Atlantic Quarterly* 112, no. 4 (Fall 2013): 739.

38 Bryan Wagner, *Disturbing the Peace: Black Culture and the Police Power after Slavery* (Cambridge, MA: Harvard University Press), 1.

39 Moten, "Blackness and Nothingness," 746.

40 Peter Sloterdijk, *Terror from the Air* (Los Angeles: Semiotext(e), 2009), 108.

41 Stengers wrties: "It is a matter of imbuing political voices with the feeling that they do not master the situation they discuss, that the political arena is peopled with shadows of that which does not have a political voice, cannot have or does not want to have one. [...] The cosmopolitical proposal therefore has nothing to do with a program and far more to do with a passing fright that scares self-assurance, however justified." Isabelle Stengers, "The Cosmopolitical Proposal," in *Making Things Public: Atmospheres of Democracy*, ed. Bruno Latour and Peter Weibel (Cambridge, MA: MIT Press, 2005), 996.

Ecosystems of Excess

Pinar Yoldas

Earth is a misnomer, says oceanographer Sylvia Earle; the planet should in fact be called "Ocean."[1] For not only do oceans cover over seventy percent of the earth's surface, they are its life support system, its salty womb. The primordial soup of ancient oceans gave birth to the very first organic molecules and living organisms. That was four billion years ago. Today the composition of the oceans is undergoing a dramatic change in which synthetic molecules are taking over. Anthropogenic waste has noticeably begun to fill our oceans over the last two decades. A strikingly illustrative site is the Great Pacific Garbage Patch. Covering between 700,000 and 15 million square kilometres, it is a monument to plastic waste on a global scale, a horrifyingly sublime kinetic sculpture built by the nations that surround the Pacific Ocean through years of mindless, unsustainable consumption. As environmental activist and discoverer of this trash vortex Captain Charles Moore boldly claims, "the ocean has turned into a plastic soup."[2]

Tracing the lineage from primordial to plastic soup, *An Ecosystem of Excess* asks a very simple question: if life evolved from our current, plastic-debris-filled oceans, what would emerge? The project introduces pelagic insects, marine reptiles, fish, and birds endowed with organs to sense and metabolize plastics as a new Linnean order of post-human life forms. Inspired by the groundbreaking discovery of new bacteria that burrow into pelagic plastics, *An Ecosystem of Excess* envisions life forms of greater complexity, life forms that can thrive in extreme, man-made environments, life forms that can turn the toxic surplus of our capitalistic desire into eggs, vibrations, and joy.[3] Starting from excessive anthropocentrism, *An Ecosystem of Excess* reaches anthropo-de-centrism by offering life without humankind.

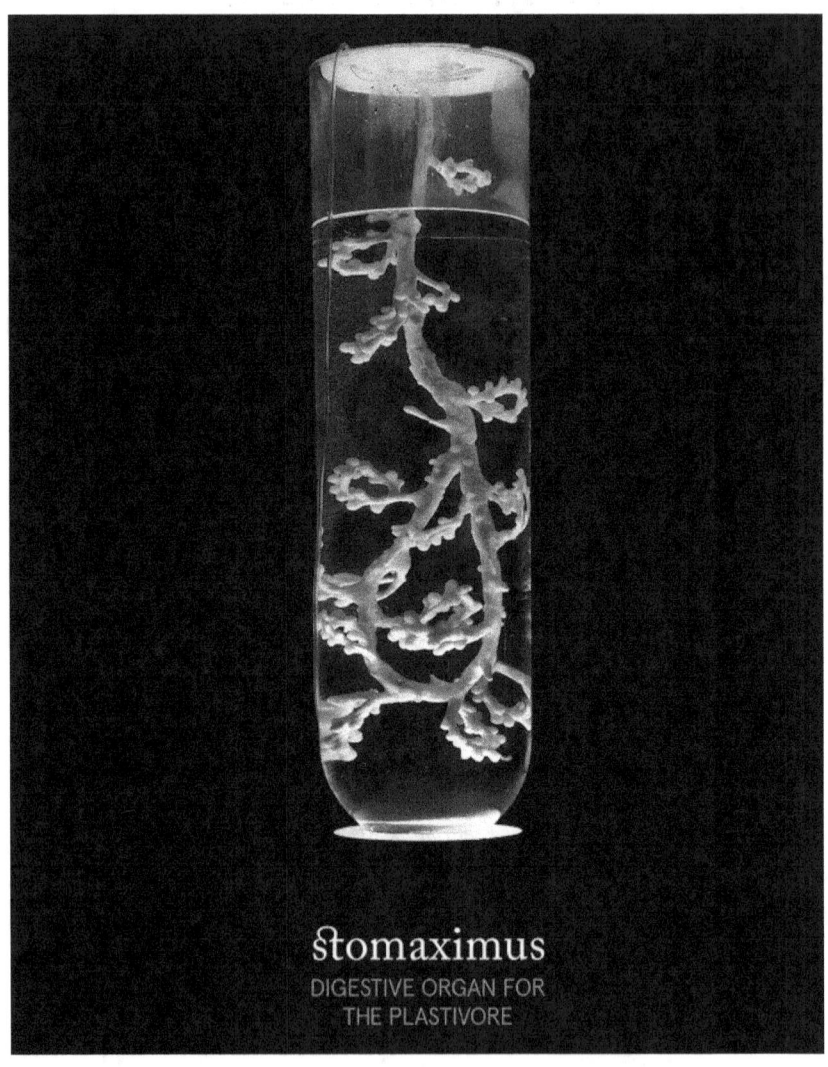

Fig. 01 STOMAXIMUS
Plastivore Digestive Organ

The evolutionary success of a plastivore is dependent on the ability to sense and metabolize plastics. Stomaximus is a maximized stomach. Each mini ventricle hosts bacteria specializing in breaking down a particular kind of plastic. This poly-chambered digestive organ is capable of metabolizing a variety of plastics, including high- and low-density polyethylene, polypropylene, polyvinyl chloride, polystyrene, polyurethane, polyethylene terephthalate, acrylonitrile butadiene styrene, phenolics, nylon, polycarbonate, and acrylic.

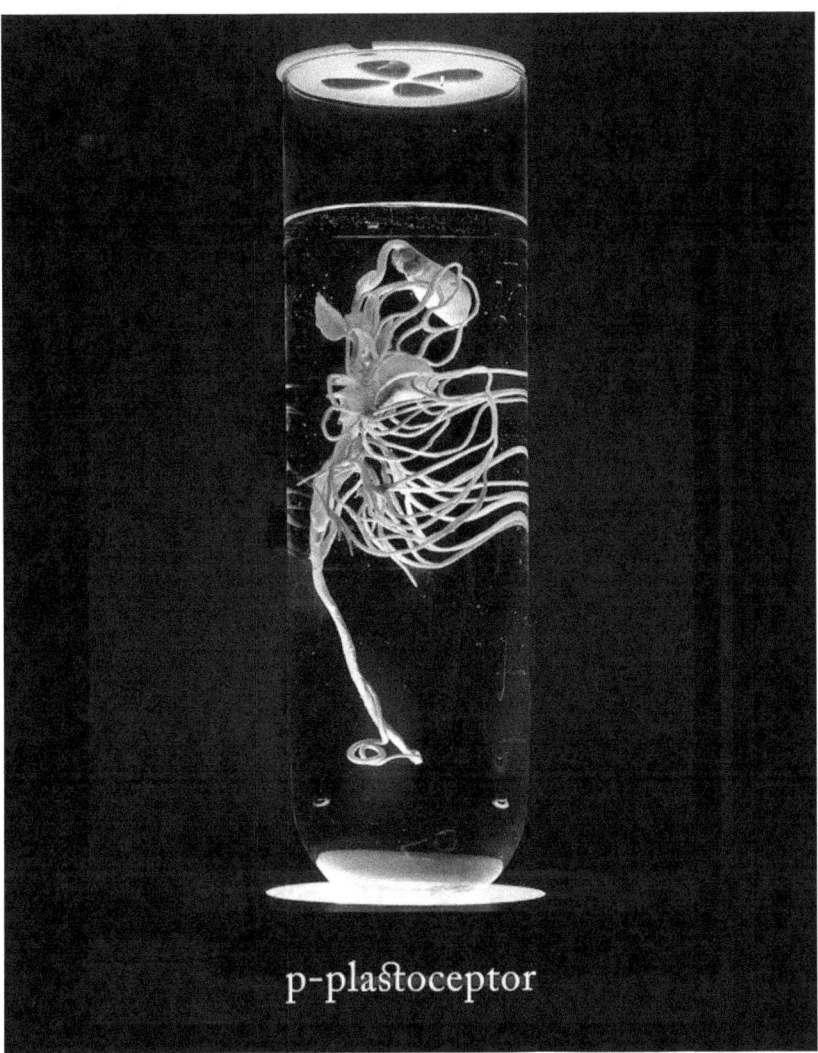

Fig. 02　P-PLASTOCEPTOR
　　　　　Plastosensory Organ

P-plastoceptors are named after their physical appearance, which resembles the letter P, as well as their superb performance in sensing the polypropylene family. The plastosensory organ works like a spectrograph, exemplifying quantum biology in action.

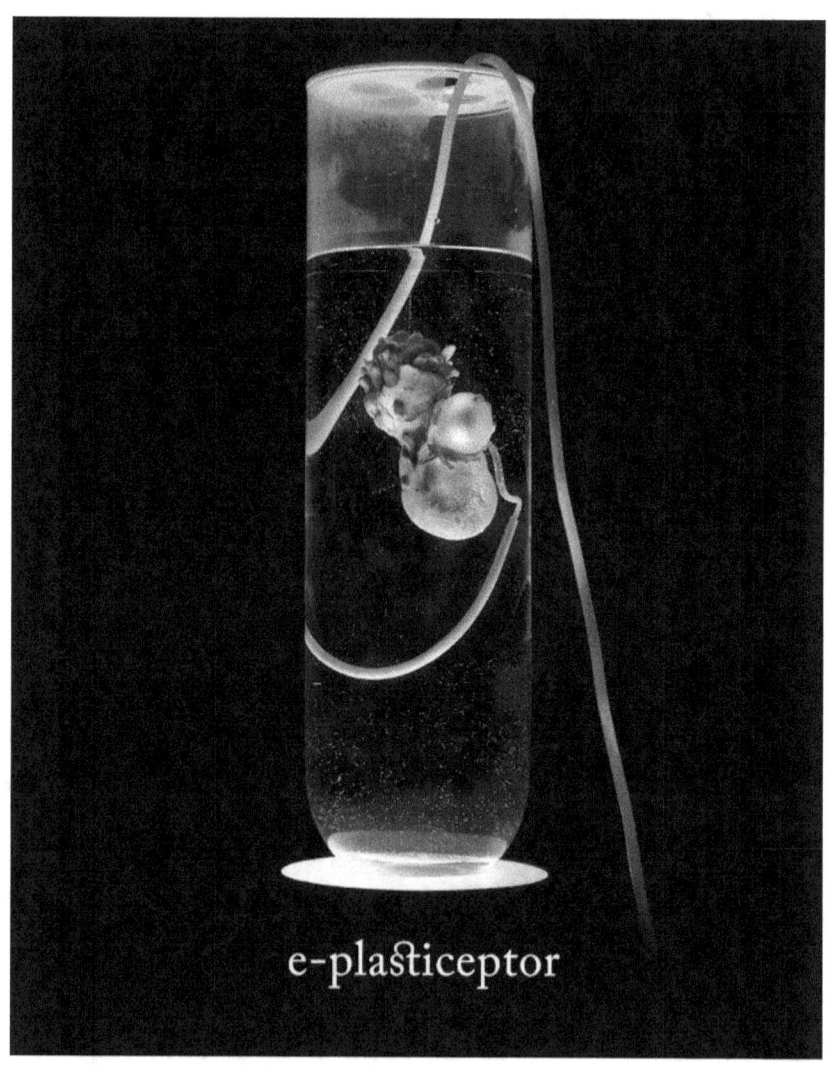

Fig. 03 E-PLASTOCEPTOR
Plastosensory Organ

Plastoception is the sense by which an organism perceives plastics in the environment. Neural encoding and processing of plastics are carried out by an array of plastosensory structures. E-plastoceptors are the most common organs in the plastisphere, possibly due to the abundance of anthropogenic polyethylene.

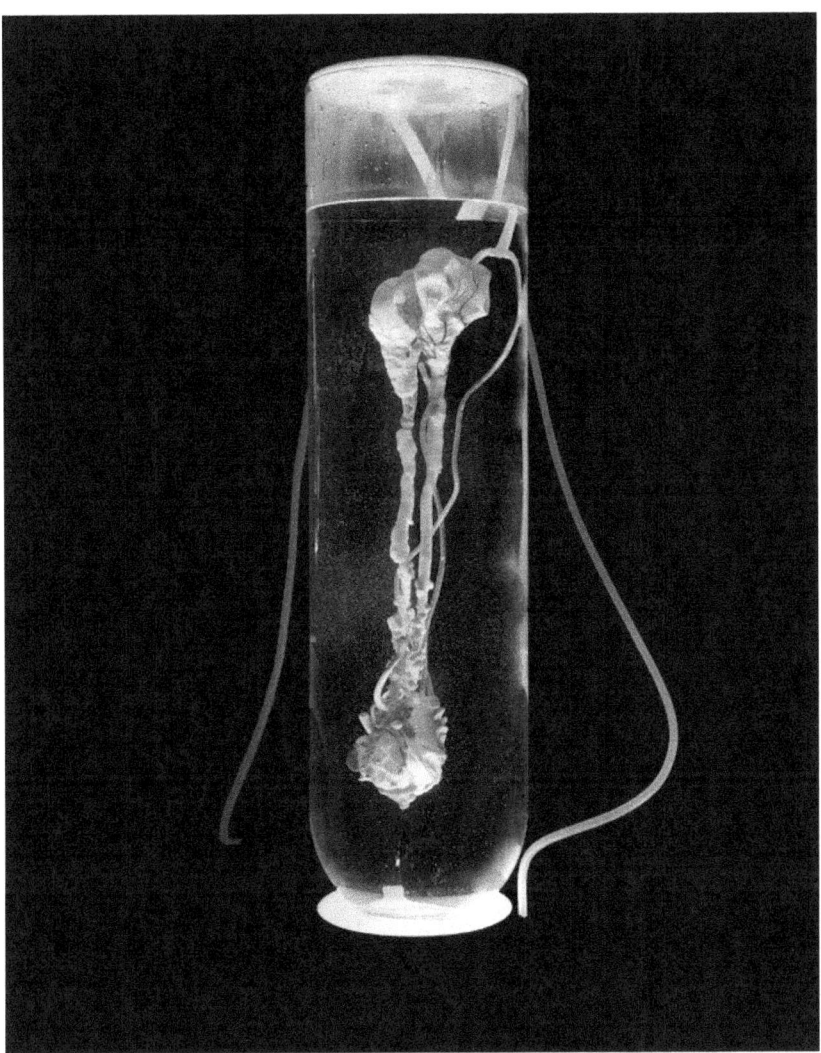

Fig. 04 PETRONEPHROS
Kidney For The Plastivore

Anthropogenic plastics are composed of plasticizers and accumulate additives such as persistent organic pollutants (POP), bisphenol (BPA), phtalates, and so on. Even the inhabitants of the plastisphere need a filtering system to remove these substances from their circulatory system. Petronephros is a kidney-like organ that serves homeostatic functions while keeping the organism free of endocrine disrupters, carcinogens, and other plastic-related obnoxiousness.

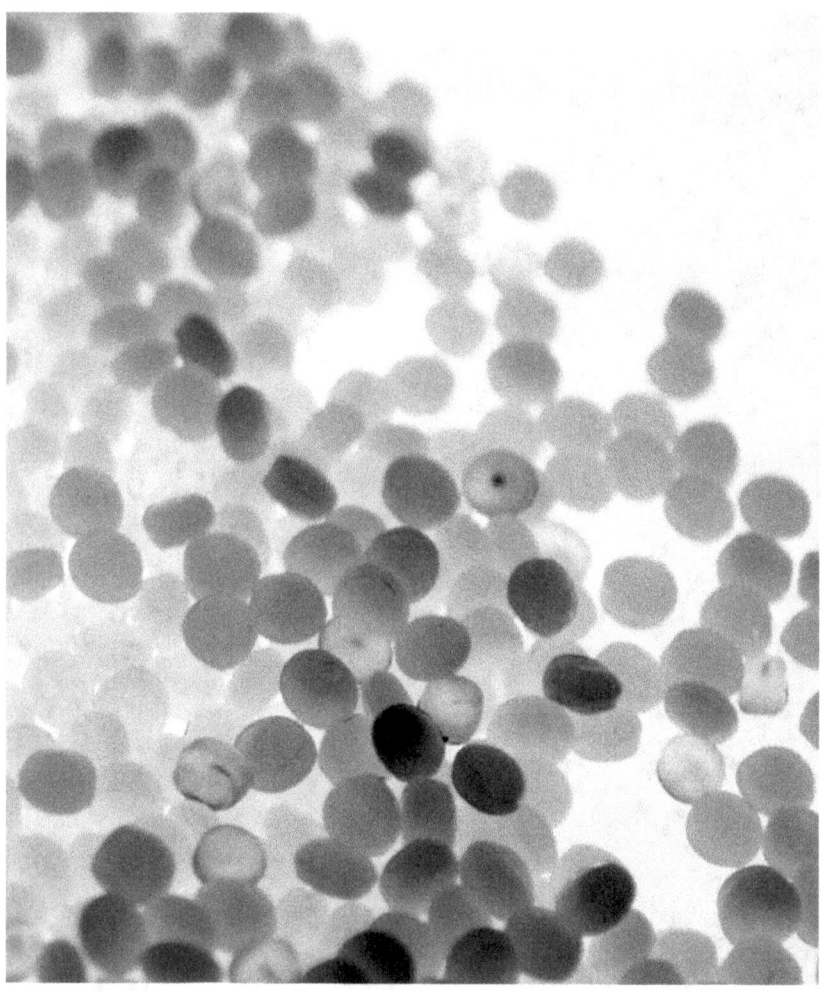

Fig. 05 THE NURDLE BEACH
Plastic Sand

Nurdles (pre-production plastic pellets) are the currency of the plastic industry. In 2013, it was estimated that over 113 billion kilograms of nurdles were manufactured and shipped globally.[4] Yet nurdles easily escape the corporate borders of the plastic empire: they are a major contributor to marine debris and one of the most common beach contaminants. Nurdles are also called "Mermaid's Tears" because of their diaphanous translucency and shape; but these tears last for eternity. In the vast beaches of *An Ecosystem of Excess*, nurdles are the grains of sand, where HDPE crabs crawl and the Garburator Turtle lays its eggs. Are the Mermaid's Tears, then, tears of sorrow or tears of joy?

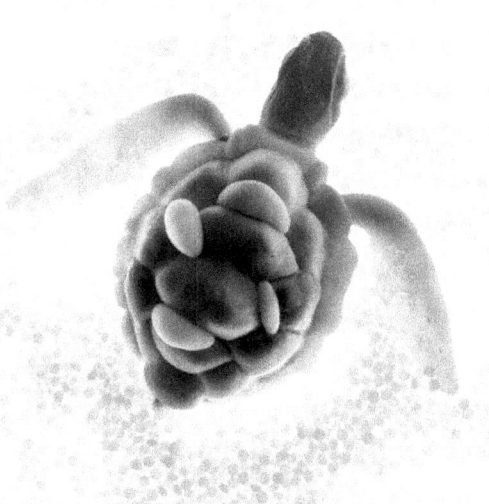

Fig. 06 CHELONIA GLOBUS AEROSTATICUS
Pacific Balloon Turtle

Synthetic rubber and boPET balloons are an important category of trash in the marine environment. Balloons—once released into the air as an embodiment of hope, dreams and joy—descend down into the ocean and, ultimately, into the digestive tracts of hungry marine turtles deprived of natural food. Studies show a preference for coloured latex over clear plastics among marine turtles, making this 250-million-year-old species highly susceptible to ingesting large amounts of balloons. In a Lamarckian twist, the shell of the Pacific Balloon Turtle demonstrates pneumatic qualities. The elastomer lining on top gives this nimble animal an edge by allowing it to float when it is exhausted. Also, the size of the balloon-like compartments is a fitness indicator for sexual selection.

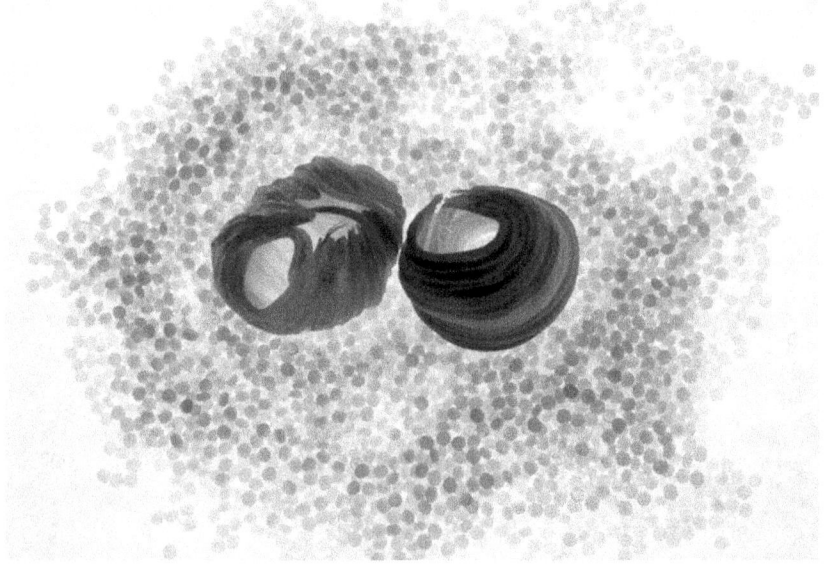

Fig. 07 ANNELIDA INCERTAE SEDIS
PV Sea Worm and Sea Snake Symbiosis

What looks like an exquisite polyvinyl chloride nest woven in the sand is in fact the abandoned shell of a family of sea worms. The sea worms are in a perfectly symbiotic relationship with an ovoviviparous sea snake. They are a very rare sight on the Nurdle Beach, and the details of the exchange between these two enigmatic taxa is undefined.

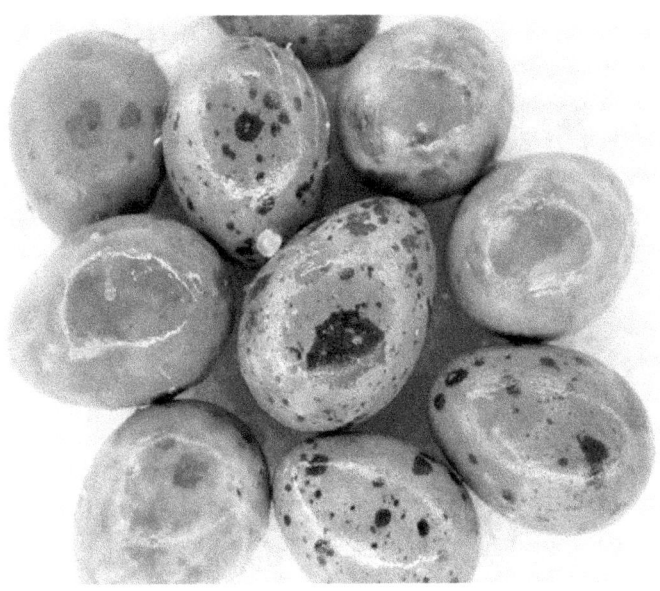

Fig. 08 TRANSCHROMATIC EGGS
An Example of Adaptation from a Benthic Reptile

The eggs of this exquisite plastivorous reptile have colour-changing properties. Plastivore eggs are a delicacy for their intensified plastic content. The benthic reptile lays its eggs at the bottom of the ocean, where there is little or no sun but lots of heavy plastic. At the bottom, the eggs are a bright plastic red. As the embryo matures, the eggs get lighter and start to float to their final destination, the Nurdle Beach. Eggs that make it to the beach turn white for camouflage.

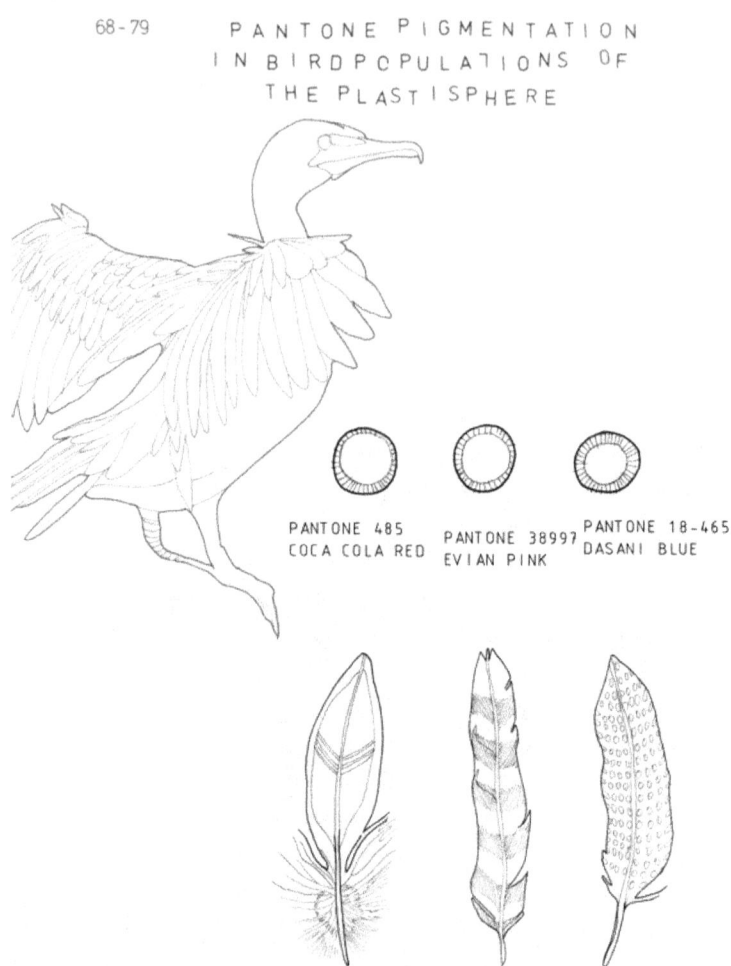

68-79 PANTONE PIGMENTATION
IN BIRD POPULATIONS OF
THE PLASTISPHERE

PANTONE 485
COCA COLA RED

PANTONE 38997
EVIAN PINK

PANTONE 18-465
DASANI BLUE

Fig. 09 PIGMENTATION IN THE PLASTISPHERE
"From Factory to Feather"

In the animal kingdom one finds many instances where a positive correlation between an organism's colour and its diet can be easily observed. Plastisphere birds are a perfect example. They obtain their beautiful colours from pigments in the plastivorous organisms they eat, while other plastivores get their colour directly from plastics themselves. Since it introduced a proprietary colour system, Pantone has become the industry leader in the standardization and commodification of the colours of the visible spectrum. As a result of metabolizing plastics that consist of colorants produced in the Pantone Universe, the feathers in this display exhibit "Pantone colours."

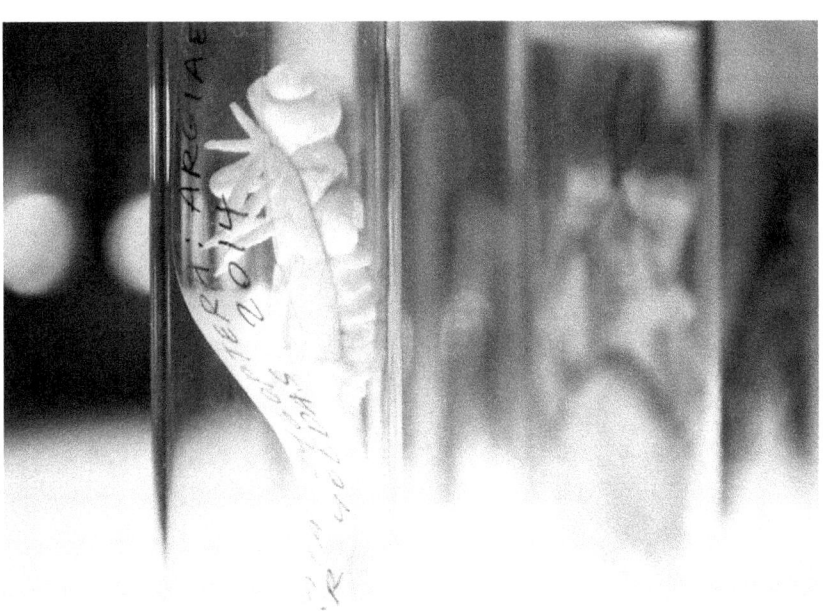

Fig. 10 MICROPLASTICS AND PLASTISPHERE INSECTS
Enhanced Oviposition

Pelagic insects require hard substrates upon which to lay eggs, and their reproduction is limited by the availability of floating materials. Microplastics—i.e., the main ingredients of the plastic ocean—are the perfect sites for the oviposition of aquatic insects. According to a 2012 scientific study, there is a positive correlation between increased levels of microplastics in the neuston (surface) layer and the reproductive success of pelagic insects.[5] As a consequence, the plastisphere opens a new chapter in the wondrous world of aquatic insects. With their state-of-the-art microplastic nests, their delicate and nutritious eggs, and their wildly coloured bodies, plastisphere insects are key players in our Ecosystem of Excess.

Notes

1 Sylvia A. Earle, *The World Is Blue: How Our Fate and the Ocean's Are One* (Washington, D.C.: National Geographic, 2009).

2 Source: news.nationalgeographic.com/news/2009/08/090820-plastic-decomposes-oceans-seas.html.

3 Erik R. Zettler, Tracy J. Mincer, and Linda A. Amaral-Zettler, "Life in the 'Plastisphere': Microbial Communities on Plastic Marine Debris," *Environmental Science & Technology* 47, no. 13 (2013): 7137–7146.

4 Charles Moore and Cassandra Philips, *Plastic Ocean: How a Sea Captain's Chance Discovery Launched a Determined Quest to Save the Oceans* (Avery, 2011).

5 M.C. Goldstein, M. Rosenberg, and L. Cheng, "Increased Oceanic Microplastic Debris Enhances Oviposition in an Endemic Pelagic Insect," *Biology Letters* 8, no. 5 (2012): 817–820.

The Last Political Scene

Sylvère Lotringer in conversation with Heather Davis & Etienne Turpin

As the general editor of Semiotext(e), Sylvère Lotringer has shaped several generations of thinkers and artists. The Semiotext(e) journal and its various book series' have brought to bear on an English-speaking audience critical concepts about the intersection of power and desire, from the work of Michel Foucault, Gilles Deleuze and Félix Guattari, Jean Baudrillard, Paul Virilio, and Lotringer himself, who entered an American scene dominated, at the time, by the Frankfurt school and deconstruction theory. His interests span a wide range of topics, but he has always been critically engaged in the struggle against capitalism, especially through books like *Italy: Autonomia – Post-Political Politics* which documented the post-Marxist Autonomia movement, and *Still Black, Still Strong* that he co-authored with former Black Panther Dhoruba Bin-Wahad. His monograph *Overexposed: Perverting Perversions* advanced the parallel struggle against the psycho-managerial containment of everyday life. He has been a key writer on contemporary art since the 1960s, publishing *The Accident of Art* and *The Conspiracy of Art*; his philosophical work has addressed the profound shift from the 1960s New York art scene—that was focused on building an alternative, collective culture—to the current domination of art by speculative finance.

On the occasion of a public talk, "Between Rock and Hard Plastic: Aesthetics of the Anthropocene," at Human Resources in Los Angeles, Sylvère generously agreed to engage in a conversation on the role of art between the Fifth Assessment of the IPCC and the sixth planetary extinction. Describing the Anthropocene as the "last political scene," he argued that art may no longer be capable of providing the kind of critical intervention that is desperately necessary. Instead, public works, such as the 3.4 million black polyurethane balls that were released into the Ivanhoe reservoir in 2008 by the Los Angeles Department of Water and Power, move beyond the realm of the symbolic, enacting instead a certain kind of meta-horror toward 'nature' and the 'panic' humans face with the onset of rapid climate change. What follows is an edited transcript of our conversation.

Etienne Turpin Since we are here at Human Resources, maybe we can start by asking if Los Angeles suggests a unique urban assemblage, or is it really just an apotheosis of the global aesthetic regime in the time of the Anthropocene? Can we talk about the Anthropocene in Los Angeles?

Sylvère Lotringer Well, let me say first of all that I have been struck by the surge of the Anthropocene onto the scene, onto the art scene. I have seen this kind of scene or theme repeated many times in the art world—from the Abject and the *Informe* to the commons, and now to the Anthropocene... It is as if these recurrences are the fuel that keeps the fire of the art world burning. I took a look at what you sent me this afternoon, and I have to say, we disagree, in a way...

Heather Davis Good!

SL All these themes—or these scenes—became obsolete and dated after a while. What characterizes the Anthropocene is that it is the last scene; it is like announcing our exit as a species. So this escalation to the extremes doesn't concern art primarily, although there is an *art* of disappearance and this would be our last chance to disappear gracefully from a scene that we have degraded and destroyed at an ever-accelerating pace over the last three centuries. Unfortunately everything indicates that the outcome won't be aesthetically pleasing, but will involve an inexorable breakdown of everything we need in order to survive on this planet. What is in the offing is so unprecedented that we are still struggling to acknowledge its existence, not just in the near future, but in the present time. And capitalism, with its blind thrust for profit and its mindless cynicism, doesn't seem to be the best system to deal with it even when the global panic will set in.

I'm very curious to see how art could respond to this state of emergency, and whether it may rejuvenate itself by engaging creatively this terminal scene. When I looked at the images that you sent me I thought it was a very promising idea not to make another artwork, which would add to the present art pollution, but indicating the possibility a kind of non-art art, an art that would be produced for reasons other than aesthetic. As we all know, nowadays art can be anything and could be found everywhere, but there's always someone to claim for it and it is always aimed at a specific audience. The Los Angeles Department of Water and Power project that you got me interested in was not made with art in mind.[1] So much of what we call art today is so inflated and replaceable that it might as well have no author. Maybe we finally are in a position to talk about famous "death of the author." By doing away with the artist, but not with the art, we would finally take this death seriously. Unlike ready-mades, un-made art wouldn't be displaced and recontextualized, but would remain in place to fulfill its function. It would have no name, and no pre-conceived intentions but exist in some kind of collective form. The first time I heard of it I felt that it was very poetic, celebrating what is instead of projecting into the future. It could be terminal art, the art of the Anthropocene. We are having a conversation about the Anthropocene right now, but this kind of conversation could be replicated around any other art theme or scene. What is really specific to the coming involvement of art with the Anthropocene? How does the Anthropocene change art, or the nature of art? We are powerless in front of what we are trying to confront. Anyway, this is the kind of reflection I had, but I am not sure it is exactly what you had in mind...

HD No, it is. Our impact on the planet has changed so much of the form and texture of our environment. So, our question is how do these transformations in scope and scale open to other ways to conceive of artistic practice and production?

SL The Anthropocene has to do with the willful destruction of our entire environment. It has to do with self-inflicted death. So, I wonder if one can understand anything about it without placing death squarely at the center. This would require a major shift in our thinking. We need to find a way a way to experience death in a different way. In Western countries, at least, we are not yet ready to enter the Anthropocene. It would involve reconnecting with death instead of pushing it away. As a culture we are not prepared for such an incredible experience. That's why I got interested in Antonin Artaud's first book, *Art and Death*.[2] To think of an art of the Anthropocene without raising the question of collective extinction and death doesn't make sense. I am afraid that we are going to get into another discussion that would merely paper over the grave…

As regards Los Angeles, there is something of a deadening effect in the city. Geographically speaking, it is a gorgeous city—surrounded by mountains, forests, the ocean, which everyone can take advantage of. There are one hundred faults which are, of course, uncontrollable. So our fate is pretty much dependent on nature. Whenever major quakes occur, they set up some waves of panic and many people leave the city. The specter of California breaking down and sent drifting into the ocean is not exactly comforting, but the threat doesn't last and is soon forgotten. Earthquakes remind us that life is fragile and that death is never too far. It could be a fitting place for the idea of the Anthropocene.

HD In what sense?

SL Reminding people that we dealt so many blows to our planet that it may not be here for us for much longer.

HD Isn't there also a question of how the body feels this geological time, how the body and geology are not separate, as we like to think, but indelibly interconnected?

SL This reminds me of the writing of Roger Caillois, a close friend of Georges Bataille. His book about the language of stones showed that the more abstract art tries to be, the closer it gets to natural forms. The juxtaposition the two was quite striking. The more we try to escape nature, the more we return to it. There is something to be said for the fact that man is steeped in geology.[3]

HD I am thinking, for example, of the work of Ilana Halperin, whose work disrupts the presumed linearity between geology and biology by eliciting the capacity of biological bodies to produce geological formations, or bodily, physical geologies.[4] These body geologies are a part of the archive produced by bodies.

SL You can also look at it the other way around—technology that invades the human biology, so that there is a struggle in our own bodies between nature and artifice with all the transplants that are invading us. This is some kind of endo-colonization of the body by technology, which is an active way of making the human body disappear. The most disturbing aspect of our present situation is the disappearance of history—not the history of the past, but of the future. It is impossible for us to imagine that our history will have happened for no one. The very idea throws up in a panic. But a panic of that sort has nothing irrational about it. Actually it reveals what our present is. In the absence of any religion capable of protecting us from it, losing one's head is an adequate reaction to the objective situation that we are now experiencing. "Since we cannot exclude the absence of a future that will remember us, panic, as an unavoidable feature, penetrates in the signature of the present. [...] It's as if a black hole was opening up in time and everything that was happening in time disappeared in it."[5]

I got interested very early on in thinkers and writers like Antonin Artaud, Simone Weil and Georges Bataille, Celine and Cioran, who were the yellow canaries of the horrors of WWII. They were putting scarecrows everywhere to alert us to ominous events that were still in the offing. But the A-Bomb and mass exterminations apparently weren't enough. Something less spectacular but even more all-encompassing now threatens the entire human environment. Thinkers were the first ones to analyze the phenomenon. Heidegger warned against the nihilist aspect of technology, the root of permanent change and of irreversible transformations that were engulfing the planet. Heidegger still believed that catastrophes could play a pedagogical role and reveal the magnitude of the threat, just as Paul Virilio, more recently, relied on the accident to render explicit the dark side of any technological invention.[6] Both wondered whether reason would prevail. But they already knew the answer: there is no example in history of a technological invention that renounced developing all its possibilities. And something that one cannot renounce is an addiction. The last two centuries have been totally destructive; nobody talks about progress anymore, yet progress is still in the order of the day. We have not reached a point where we can talk about the Anthropocene. How much time do we need to recognize the fact that the planet is at its end? How many catastrophes do we need before we start panicking? But there is panic and panic. In the early 1980s, Semiotext(e) started working on an issue on panic. And then AIDS came along and I thought it would not be right to make an issue on panic when everybody was panicked. But now we would need a certain dose of panic to force us to realize what is happening right now. We are confronted with something unprecedented, something that we are not cut out for, or trained to experience.

ET Was "critical theory" just a conceptual dress rehearsal, but one that was never prepared to take the political stage?

SL What we are beginning to experience does not fit into the idea of politics or critique. I have been talking against critique for a long time because critique is not an adequate response to the events. It is not an answer to capitalism. The whole intellectual apparatus that we have been furbishing for the last century or two is mostly solipsistic. It is meant to confirm one's position, not address an issue for what it is, let alone do something about it. Critique introduces a distance where there is none. Any counter-discourse plays into the hand of the institution, of what it is supposed to criticize. Occupy Wall Street was an intimation of what could be done, but it didn't go all the way. It stopped at the door of the institutions—not just the stock market, but the auction houses. It was effective in publicizing the idea of the 1%, but it didn't affect the way society is run. The revolt in Ferguson, hopefully, may do more to change the way Black Americans are treated in the United States than months of camping outside. But collective action is more than a critique; it anticipates the kind of response to the questions raised by the Anthropocene, which is a creature of savage industrialization and the cynical exploitation of natural resources by global capitalism. In 1970, at Aspen in Colorado, Baudrillard gave a paper for the French Utopie group where he likened revolution to an earthquake. His speech created a scandal, but he had a point—earthquakes, like revolutions, can be man-made, as is happening presently with fracking for oil in Arkansas. With the Anthropocene, humanity managed to replace nature and its disasters in the destruction of our planet. And nature itself seems to be taking sides as well, since southern countries, the poorest, are going to be hit harder by climatic changes than the richer Western or northern countries. In this respect one could say that the Anthropocene will be the last political scene.

ET I am not certain I believe panic is a productive affect in mass society; perhaps our paralysis in this moment is already a result of too much panic: panic in the city, panic in the workplace, panic about our sex. To come back to Deleuze and Guattari, I'm curious about this notion of panic in relation to the project of *Capitalism and Schizophrenia*. Was the schizoanalytic developed by Deleuze and Guattari not, at least in part, a way out of the panicked madness produced by planetary-scale networks of capital?

SL As Artaud said, we aren't panicked enough. That was the goal of the theatre of cruelty.

Shocking the audience into realizing that they were already dead. To panic is to lose one's head, but who can be sure that my head belongs to me, and not massively manufactured, just like the shallow notion of the individual, which is a creation of consumerism. There is no easy way out of the madness that capitalism is. But precisely, schizophrenics like Artaud go for broke, they challenge the flows of capital to reveal themselves for what they are, but they never do. During the financial crisis of 2008, the system could well have collapsed. Everyone believed that it was systemic, and that it would self-destruct, but no, it wasn't mad enough and hastened to reterritorialize at the expense of the whole society. Surfing with madness can bring huge profits, but becoming mad is something else. It remains a precarious model for subversion.

What could the expression "panic civilization" mean, Sloterdijk asked. Can the panic experience be turned into a civilization? It would require that "a warning pain be imprinted on our nervous system." But news of catastrophes circulate too fast to leave any trace behind. There is no civic mobilization possible because there are no civilians anymore; we have all been turned into warriors, part of a war because war and technology now mean the same thing. We are powerless because all the tools that we have—all the little trinkets given to us by the CIA and NASA, etc.—are there to turn us into the soldiers of the death of our civilization. That is what we are now. We can communicate, and they make sure that we isolate ourselves in our mental space in front of the computer, in front of the little gadgets that we fight for. Even when we have our social networks in hand we are being isolated. We cannot mobilize for anything. We do not have classes anymore. We have the poor, but no classes. Classes meant that there was at least an attempt to do something, but now everyone is poor and the poor are said to deserve it. Nobody is going to do anything about it, and that is where politics joins the Anthropocene. It joins through capitalism. We make sure people are dead before they are dead; we make people impotent before they are impotent. We are confronted now with phenomena beyond anything we have experienced in human history. And, we're not mobilizing. What is a culture that does not do anything to save itself?

HD Haven't we seen this same petrified passivity in previous epochal shifts where there is an irreversible collapse? And isn't the fantasy of THE END part of the problem, part of what makes us passive? The figure of apocalypse has long been a part of our culture. Of course humanity will die out, and the planet will go on without us, but this might not happen for a long time, despite all we are doing to bring about our own end.

SL Humanity was a good try. But we blew it. Your friend the priest, Antonio Stoppani, could very well see the end of man because man was not everything.[7] God could create something else. Man was just an experiment and God could take it back. But now, what kind of god is there to invoke?

ET Survival is an aesthetic practice; it is projecting into a future that we do not and cannot know. It is the act of preparing to live in an unknowable future.[8]

SL We are already preparing the planet for man after the Anthropocene. Man had fieldwork; he had to adapt to pure lightness, or speed, or circulatory power. We managed to get to the point where the machine is breaking down, but we are constantly inventing other machines. Maybe the fate of man is going to play out somewhere else and not in our own 'cene.

HD One reason the figure of the Anthropocene is so troubling is because of its alignment with the particular capitalist fantasy that the end of capitalism will mean the end of humanity. It is this fantasy that obscures the possibilities for the arts of survival.

ET But the arts of survival are eclipsed by the boredom of the 'cene, too! In *Overexposed,* you wrote: "[T]oday death has been forgotten, or rather, it has eclipsed itself from our memory. What we need is to bring it back, kicking and shouting, into everyday life. For without death there is no meaning. Yet is death's return still possible? Suffering has limits, whereas boredom has none. Boredom has become far more reliable, for it is worse than death. The death we are speaking of is neither sacrifice, nor sacred horror; it is dead death, surviving in a deep coma."

SL I have to say, boredom is a luxury.

ET *Laughing* And, it is a luxury that is running out.

SL A luxury that we cannot afford...

ET So how do we begin to narrate our species-death in the Anthropocene? It is remarkable that the most "boring" institutions—boring in the sense of attracting little media attention, and a minimum of spectacle, like the International Commission on Stratigraphy and the Union of Geological Sciences—have formulated the most important, the most profound speculative question for our species. They have asked the question of the meaning of the human by asking about the legacy of human action. Isn't this, finally, a suggestion that "science" is not the real problem? That, instead, art might have something to learn about speculation and survival from science.

SL Are we going to be closer to understanding the Anthropocene by turning ourselves into scientists? Will we be better equipped to do something with it? Should artists get into this becoming-scientist? As Sloterdijk said, it used to be that when people were afraid they would go to the priest, or they would deny that anything terrible was actually happening. Now, when we talk about catastrophe, people just say, "Well, there is a specialist for that." Dealing with disaster has become a highly specialized profession. Disasters are unavoidable, so we can specialize in them. We can see how art is already getting in on this too, can't we?

Notes

1. Los Angeles Department of Water and Power project for Ivanhoe reservoir; see Heather Davis in this volume.
2. See *"Art and Death* (1925-1927)," in *Antonin Artaud: Selected Writings*, ed. Susan Sontag (Berkeley and Los Angeles: University of California Press, 1988), 121–138.
3. For an excellent re-reading of Roger Caillois' geological scripts, see Marina Warner, "The Writing of Stones," *Cabinet* 29 – Sloth (Spring 2008).
4. See Ilana Halperin in this volume.
5. Peter Sloterdijk, *La Mobilisation infinie*, trans. by Hans Hildenbrand (Paris: Seuil, 2003).
6. Martin Heidegger, "The Age of the World Picture," in *The Question Concerning Technology*, ed. and trans. William Lovitt (Harper Torchbooks, 1977 [1938]), 115–154.
7. Antonio Stoppani, "The Anthropozoic Era: Excerpts from Corso di Geologia," ed. Valerian Federighi and Etienne Turpin, trans. Valeria Federighi, in *Scapegoat: Architecture | Landscape | Political Economy* 05 – Excess (Summer/Fall 2013): 346–355.
8. See Yates McKee, "Of Survival: Climate Change and Uncanny Landscape in the Photography of Subhankar Banerjee," in *Impasses of the Post-Global Impasses of the Post-Global: Theory in the Era of Climate Change, Vol. 2*, ed. Henry Sussman (Ann Arbor: Open Humanities Press, 2012), 76–105.

#MISANTHROPOCENE:
24 Theses

Joshua Clover & Juliana Spahr

First of all. Fuck all y'all.

Second of all. We would all like to be violet-haired pure honey-smiling Sappho hanging out at all hours of the day and night in the air-conditioned $83,200-a-night Royal Penthouse Suite at the Hotel President Wilson with twelve bedrooms and twelve marble bathrooms plus a wraparound terrace with views of the Alps singing the praises of Anaktoria. The misanthropocene has proven to be a time when this is possible for some and not for others.

Third of all. It keeps busy. It makes deserts bloom. It makes luxury towers just like it makes architects. It makes blockbusters and it makes producers to make them. It makes universities roads conceptual poets it makes oil-drum pyramids it makes ships of a size called Malaccamax. It makes endless small plastic representations of the African jungle or plains animals and fish ingest them and vomit them up or don't and there they sit in their stomachs and then they die.

Fourth of all. You know: it. The *it* that seems to be nothing but the doing of the world. As in *it's raining*. It's Raining Men is a moment of happiness within the misanthropocene.

Fifth of all. But then there is this other rain tilting in to soak vast acres of eurodollars and we call this west melancholy. West melancholy is related to but not the same as the misanthropocene.

Sixth of all. When we speak of time we speak of processes. Things going bad. We speak of entropy and the shedding of particles. A cold caesium fountain deep underground.

Seventh of all. The sheer scale of the misanthropocene. Our minds feel small and inert. Once every fragment seemed to bear within it the whole. Now the whole being too large for the mind to see stands before us always as a fragment.

Eighth of all. Fragments. The new Sapphic rage. Fuck Water Garden Condos Camel Garden Condos Royal Garden Sea Garden Garden City Beach and everyone who lives in condos named after gardens. One day gardens will come to get you. If they don't we will do it for them.

Ninth of all. Fuck the French Revolution the concept of the quintile Burning Man "England is a nation of shopkeepers" capital-L Literature and the citizens of Passy. Fuck Whole Foods sustainability the Piketty craze of 2014 Harvard University Press indie rock and *Fight Club*. Fuck community policing. Fuck poststructuralism The Universal Declaration of Human Rights the rock banjo. Fuck critiquing the rock banjo. Fuck self-reflexive meta-commentary about critiquing the rock banjo. Fuck cupcakes and/or Park Slope fuck the martini fuck your Noguchi Coffee table fuck the crisis in the humanities Jonathan Safran Foer's Chipotle-cup literature home ownership HBO and fuck pedantically explaining that "the bourgeoisie" doesn't really apply to any part of US class structure.

Tenth of all. Fuck the propelling of sand from the bottom of the ocean floor in a high arc so as to construct new islands. Fuck that this is called rainbowing. Fuck any sort of dredge. Fuck how racehorses don't get to fuck each other but instead the stallion is trained to mount a dummy mare made of plywood and fuck a heated plastic vagina. Fuck the prince of any country ever fuck Palm Jumeirah and Palm Jebel Ali and atrazine. Fuck everyone who has bought a big bag of ant poison because ants have a social stomach and you are one selfish motherfucker if you can't let them have the very small amounts of food they want to share equally among themselves. And fuck this list with its mixture of environmental destruction and popular culture smugness and fuck every one of you that laughed at that rock banjo joke and fuck us all for writing it. And fuck not just the Googlebus but the Googledoc this poem rode in on and fuck us for sitting here reading you a rock banjo joke while the New Mexico meadow jumping mouse went extinct. Fuck that this happened two days and twenty hours ago. And fuck that next up is the Sierra Nevada yellow legged frog because we've always liked frogs their vulnerable skin our vulnerable skin.

Eleventh of all. And fuck that self-insulating move where you call yourself on your own bullshit to prove you aren't self-righteous. Fuck it for just being a version of liberal "please don't hit me" politics. And srsly how did this poem come to revolve around the rock banjo?

Twelfth of all. The tempo of the misanthropocene has been measured precisely by the decay of the workers' movement. Zero o'clock came and went. More west melancholy.

Fuck Robert Berger Mounir Haidar and Scott Hutchinson. They are but bit players in this misanthropocene but fuck them and everyone who has ever been nice to them. That was thirteenth of all for those of you counting. And that list is just the beginning. It ends with the names of everyone at this reading Ben Furstenberg Natalie Cornflakes Andrew Kenower Juliana Spahr Brian Glasscock Happy Birthday but fuck you Wendy Trevino fuck Joshua Clover Jeune Fille and Ali Bektaş because those motherfuckers from the beginning of this section are still alive because we haven't killed them yet.

Fourteenth of all. Back to that banjo. If you've ever imitated that "Dueling Banjos" riff fuck you and your homophobia.

Fifteen. Unable to bear their loans the graduates and the dropouts drift off from the formal economy into student favelas cheek by jowl with the new poolings of the wage diaspora and we act as if this informalization has nothing to do with the misanthropocene but really that's just what it is.

Sixteen. And our nostalgia for when students were students and workers were workers is the formal rain in this poem. Fuck your west melancholy.

Seventeenth of all. That's what she saidn't.

Eighteenth of all. You know that moment when you realize there is nothing to be done and you just walk outside because you need to get away from the family form perhaps maybe from the home you own sort of or the bank does or maybe just the cat's constant mewling and yet whatever it is that family debt or cat stands in for comes with you and so you start to walk down the street to see if you can get away and you can't for whatever it is follows you as if it knows you in the way that your undergraduate institution knows you that always knows your address to send you requests for money even if you just moved last week sort of way and it's dark out and there's a small moon so not much light and even the street light doesn't work and the street is darker than usual and you sit down on the low concrete fence that surrounds the neighbour's house and you realize there is nothing that can be done to get rid of this thing that you need to get away from and so you just sit there staring out into space getting cold thinking about the short strong legs and small ears and eyes of the yelm pocket gopher how their lips close behind their front incisors how they use their front incisors for burrowing how as they burrow their soft loose pelts enable them to move backwards through their tunnels as easily as they move forwards how they have two oh-so-soft fur-lined cheek pouches extending from the lower portion of their face to their shoulders that they use to transport food and these can be turned completely inside out and how the UC Davis website notes that gophers are nongame mammals which means that anyone can control them at any time and in any legal manner and so they recommend trapping baiting with toxic baits fumigation exclusion dogs chewing gum laxatives vibrating snakes and gas explosive devices and you think about these things with despair and Sapphic rage because you can't bear to think about whatever it is that is only realizable as the family the debt the cat and thinking about the almost extinct soft fur-lined cheek pouches at least lets you feel. Fuck that moment most of all.

Fuck that moment most of all when you have to write an essay about the avant-garde and you begin filled with resentment for this essay filled with resentment for the people who asked you to write it filled with resentment for yourself filled with resentment for the idea of the avant-garde but you start writing because you exist only in the phrase *you start writing* and then halfway through you start to feel like maybe you do care about the avant-garde and would like to be part of the avant-garde and would like to arrive at a party wearing a caterpillar for a moustache and have parts of your life transpire in a subtly lit gallery in I don't know Zurich or something just a white room filled with a sweet feeling called west melancholy and you feel this even as you are completely aware that what you are writing is of the genre *studies in comparative whiteness* and the avant-garde is lower limit terrible idea upper limit totally unnecessary and even as you are aware of these things you are really moving in the essay you are listening to Pharrell and Shakira and Iggy Azalea who are not the avant-garde but you are moving you are making short paragraphs about the avant-garde and the short paragraphs make you feel empty and clean like you haven't eaten for a day or two the short paragraphs make you feel empty and clean not like you are a Zurich gallery with subtle lighting and almost nothing on the walls no you are not the gallery but you are filled with the same sort of sensation as the gallery with the melancholy of the text with text melancholy and the problem is this nineteenth of all the problem is this you have friends you like and friends you don't like and you can sort of imagine the friends you don't like milling around the gallery possibly exchanging that special kind of one-eyebrow-up glance that conveys your twitter handle directly to the minds of others but you cannot imagine the friends you like being in the gallery together and then you remember you can't imagine the friends you like being in the same room together in general and that the last year or two has been characterized by the impossibility of people being in the same room together whether you like them or not and this is so much the case that you are glad when one of your enemies moves away because fuck them but you are also glad when one of your friends moves away because even though you are in Oakland centre of the universe it seems like getting out and this is the truth of things not the avant-garde not the gallery not the caterpillar that is not your moustache not even the Miami blue butterfly caterpillar which is the next caterpillar to go extinct *Ohhhhh Miami* but the rifts that now make up roughly seventy percent of all social life and you feel the rifts as truth because the hatred is real the hatred is an objective force like debt is an objective force and the wage and the heat and the end of the world are objective forces and the rifts are in this sense objective and you call this objectivity the misanthropocene.

Twentieth of all. This is how the misanthropocene ends. We go to war against it. My friends go to war against it. They run howling with joy and terror against it. I go with them.

Twentyone. This is how to set an oil well on fire. Rub and lean against it. Spread your front legs and swing your neck at it. The power of a blow depends on the weight of your skull and the arc of your swing. Then sparks.

Twentytwo. Here is how to take out the electrical grid. Pierce the switching protection and control equipment and transformers with hypodermic genitalia and eject into the circuit breakers so as to short circuit or overload currents. Smaller distribution stations may use recloser circuit breakers or fuses for protection of distribution circuits. These too can be pierced by the introduction of a specialized intromittent organ through an external groove overlying the pleural membrane in the fuse wall.

Twentythree. Here is how to capsize a container ship. Swim along behind it in a train then grip with the teeth and continue to swim as you insert your claspers into the cloaca and pump.

Twentyfourth of all. Here is how to kill a policeman here is how to abolish culture here is how to knock down a Boeing AH-64D Apache Longbow here is how to loot a grocery store here is how to levitate the Pentagon. Sappho Sappho Sappho not by chanting.

Contributors

Amy Balkin's work involves land and the geopolitical relationships that frame it. Her solo and collaborative projects consider legal borders and systems, environmental justice, and the allocation of common-pool resources. These include *This Is the Public Domain*, an ongoing effort to open a permanent public commons, *A People's Archive of Sinking and Melting* (Balkin et al.), a collaborative archive of the future anterior, and *Public Smog*, a "clean-air" park in the atmosphere that fluctuates in location and scale. She has also collaborated on *Invisible-5*, an environmental-justice audio tour along California's I-5 freeway corridor. Recent exhibitions include *Rights of Nature-Art and Ecology in the Americas* at Nottingham Contemporary, *Anthropocène Monument* at les Abattoirs, Toulouse, and *dOCUMENTA (13)*, Germany. Her work will be included in the forthcoming book *Critical Landscapes* (Scott and Swenson, 2015). She lives in San Francisco.

Ursula Biemann is an artist, writer, and video essayist. Her practice is strongly research-based and involves fieldwork and video documentation in remote locations. Biemann investigates global relations under the impact of the accelerated mobility of people, resources, and information, working these materials into multi-layered videos by connecting a theoretical macro level with the micro-perspective on political and cultural practices on the ground. The videos are neither linear nor didactic, but reflexive explorations of planetary and videographic organization.

She has had retrospective exhibitions at the Bildmuseet Umea in Sweden, Nikolaj Contemporary Art in Copenhagen, Helmhaus Zurich, Lentos Museum Linz, and at film festivals FID Marseille and TEK Rome. Her work also contributed to major exhibitions at the Arnolfini, Bristol; Tapies Foundation, Barcelona; Museum of Fine Arts, Bern; LACE, Los Angeles; San Francisco Art Institute; Kunsthalle Brandt Odense; Kunstverein Hamburg; the Biennials in Gwangju, Shanghai, Liverpool, Bamako, Istanbul, and Sevilla; steirischer Herbst, Graz; Flaherty Film Seminars, NY, and many others. In March 2013, she had a solo show at Neue Berliner Kunstverein n.b.k. The Broad Art Museum of the Michigan State University has awarded Biemann with a Land Grant Commission that premiered in August 2014.

Biemann received her BFA from the School of Visual Arts (1986) and pursued post-graduate studies at the Whitney Independent Study Program (ISP) in New York, where she lived thoughout most of the 1980s. Today, she is a senior researcher at the Zurich University of the Arts. Biemann was appointed Doctor honoris causa in Humanities by the Swedish University, Umea (2008) and received the 2009 Prix Meret Oppenheim, the national art award of Switzerland.

Amanda Boetzkes is Associate Professor at the School of Fine Arts and Music at the University of Guelph. Her research and publications focus on contemporary art, theory and criticism, with an emphasis on the intersection of the biological sciences, visual technologies, and artistic practices of the late twentieth and early twenty-first centuries. Her first book, *The Ethics of Earth Art* (University of Minnesota Press, 2010), analyzes the development of the earth art movement, focusing on how ecology became a domain of ethical and aesthetic concern. She is co-editor, with Aron Vinegar, of *Heidegger and the Work of Art History* (Ashgate, 2014). She has published in the journals *Art History, Reconstruction: Studies in Contemporary Culture, RACAR, Antennae: The Journal of Nature and Visual Culture, nonsite.org,* and *E-Flux,* and has contributed book chapters to *Fueling Culture* (Fordham University Press, forthcoming); *West of Center: Art and the Countercultural Experiment in America, 1965-77* (University of Minnesota Press, 2011); and *Art History: Contemporary Perspectives on Method* (Wiley-Blackwell, 2010). She is currently writing a book entitled *Contemporary Art and the Drive to Waste*, which analyzes the use and representation of garbage in contemporary art, and more subtly, how waste as such is defined, narrativized, and aestheticized in the age of global capitalism.

Dr Lindsay Bremner is Director of Architectural Research in the Faculty of Architecture and the Built Environment at the University of Westminster and runs M Arch Design Studio 18 (Architecture, Energy, Matter) with Roberto Bottazzi. She was formerly Professor of Architecture in the Tyler School of Art at Temple University in Philadelphia (2006–2011) and Chair of Architecture at the University of the Witwatersrand in Johannesburg (1998–2004). She is an award-winning architect and writer and has published, lectured and exhibited widely on the transformation of Johannesburg after apartheid. This included *Writing the City into Being: Essays on Johannesburg 1998–2008* (Fourthwall Books, 2010), *Johannesburg: One City Colliding Worlds* (STE, 2004), and chapters in *Johannesburg: The Elusive Metropolis* (Duke University Press, 2008), *The Endless City* (Phaidon, 2008), *Desire Lines: Space, Memory and Identity in the Post-Apartheid City* (Routledge, 2007), *Future City* (Spon, 2005), *Under Siege: Four African Cities: Freetown, Johannesburg, Kinshasa, Lagos* (Documenta, 2002*), blank__architecture apartheid and after* (NAi, 1998), and contributions to *Domus, Public Culture, Social Identities* and *Cities*. Her design work includes a third-place entry for a Cyclone Shelter in Bangladesh (with Jeremy Voorhees, 2011), award winning Sans Souci Cinema project in Kliptown, Soweto (with 26'10 South Architects, 2004–2007), and a second-place entry in the Freedom Square Competition (with Mashabane Rose Architects, 2002). Bremner's work since leaving Johannesburg has taken a materialist turn. Her research project *Folded Ocean* investigates the transforming spatial and organizational logics of the Indian Ocean; this has been published in *Journal of the Indian Ocean Region, Social Dynamics, Bracket,* and the edited book *Design in the Terrain of Water* (Oro Editions, 2014); *Geoarchitecture* investigates intersections between architecture, geology and politics, and has been published in *Urban Forum* and the edited books *Ponte City* (Steidl Verlag, 2014), *Questions Concerning Health* (GSAPP, 2014) and *Architecture and the Paradox of Dissidence* (Routledge, 2013). Bremner holds a B.Arch from the University of Cape Town and an MArch and DScArch from the University of the Witwatersrand, Johannesburg.

Una Chaudhuri is Professor of English, Drama, and Environmental Studies at New York University. She is the author of *No Man's Stage: A Semiotic Study of Jean Genet's Plays*, and *Staging Place: The Geography of Modern Drama*, as well as numerous articles on theatre, performance, literature and the environment, and animal studies. She is the editor of *Rachel's Brain and Other Storms*, a book of scripts by performance artist Rachel Rosenthal, and co-editor, with Elinor Fuchs, of the award-winning critical anthology *Land/Scape/Theater*. She was guest editor of a special issue of *Yale Theater* on "Theater and Ecology," and of a special issue of *TDR: The Journal of Performance Studies* on "Animals and Performance." Her book *Animal Acts: Performing Species Today*, co-edited with Holly Hughes, will be published later this year, as will her book *Ecocide: A Research Theatre Casebook*, co-authored with Shonni Enelow.

Heather Davis is a researcher and writer from Montreal. She is currently a postdoctoral fellow at the Institute for Arts and Humanities at Pennsylvania State University where she is working on a project that traces the ethology of plastic as a materialization of the philosophic division between the subject and object. Previously, she was a FQRSC postdoctoral fellow in the Department of Women's Studies at Duke University. She completed her Ph.D. in the joint program in Communication at Concordia University in 2011 on the political potential of community-based art. She has been a visiting scholar in the program in Aesthetics and Politics at CalArts, the Experimental Critical Theory program at UCLA, the Hemispheric Institute of Performance and Politics at NYU, and the Department of Women's and Gender Studies at Rutgers University. She is the editor of *Desire/Change: Contemporary Feminist Art in Canada* (MAWA/McGill-Queen's UP, forthcoming 2016). She has written widely about the intersection of art, politics, and ecological disaster. Her writing can be found at heathermdavis.com.

Sara Dean is an architect and designer based in Berkeley, California. She is the Director of Research and Partnerships at Stamen Design in San Francisco, and co-director of the design research practice anexact office. She is also a Project Investigator for the crowd-sourced disaster response platform PetaJakarta.org. Her work considers the implications of emerging digital methodologies on public engagement, environmental justice, and related political practices. Dean is currently a Senior Lecturer in Graduate Design at the California College of Art, and has taught previously at UC Berkeley, the University of Michigan, and the College for Creative Studies. She is the designer of *Art in the Anthropocene* (Open Humanities Press, 2015) and *Architecture in the Anthropocene* (Open Humanities Press, 2013), as well as other artist books, printed works, and small-press publications. Sara has a Master of Architecture and Master of Science in Design Research, both from the University of Michigan. She is committed to open-access media and crowd-enabled platforms.

Irmgard Emmelhainz is an independent translator, writer, and researcher based in Mexico City. In 2012, she published a collection of essays about art, culture, cinema and geopolitics, *Alotropías en la trinchera evanescente: Estética y geopolítica en la era de la guerra total* (BUAP). She has collaborated with visual artist Miguel Ventura for his projects: *NILCSTAC,* Panajachel Biennial and MUACC.NILC.blogspot (2010), and *Oratorio de Arte Neoliberal* (2011). Her work about film, the Palestine Question, art, culture, and neoliberalism has been translated to French, English, Arabic, Turkish, Hebrew, and Serbian. She has presented it at an array of international venues: Casa Comal, Guatemala City (2010), York University, Toronto (2011), Facultad de Letras, Universidad de Salamanca, Spain (2011), Telecápita, Mexico City (2012), Americas Society, New York (2013), Universidad Distrital de Colombia, Bogotá (2013), Bureau Publik, Copenhagen (2013), KHIB, Bergen (2013), and The Fire Next Time (Ghent, 2014). In 2014, she co-edited an issue of the journal *Scapegoat* dedicated to Mexico City; she is teaching at the Esmeralda National School of Engraving and Painting in Mexico City.

Sasha Engelmann, a native of Los Angeles, holds degrees from Stanford University in Earth Systems and English and French Literatures. Sasha's academic work lies at the intersection of environmental science, art and spatial theory. Her recent writing concerns the political and aesthetic dimensions of air and atmosphere. In the past year, she has worked closely with the studio of Tomás Saraceno in Berlin, especially on a publication about solar, lighter-than-air vehicles for an exhibition curated by Bruno Latour, Bronislaw Szerszynski, and Olivier Michelon at Les Abattoirs, Toulouse. She is a co-lecturer at the New Art Institute directed by Saraceno at the Technical University of Braunschweig. Together with a group of seminar students, she is further developing the notion of "becoming aerosolar." Sasha is currently a Clarendon Scholar and a DPhil Candidate in the department of Geography and Environment at Oxford University.

Fritz Ertl is a theatre director and educator. He has produced and directed world premieres of plays by Steven Drukman, Erik Ehn, and Paula Vogel, and has worked at theatres such as Berkshire Theatre Festival, HERE, and Incubator Arts Project. At present he is the head of acting at the Playwrights Horizons Theater School at NYU; there he has directed *PENTECOST*, by David Edgar, *THE PAINS OF YOUTH*, by Ferdinand Brukner, and *MAD FOREST*, by Caryl Churchill. In collaboration with Una Chaudhuri, Fritz he has been working over the past ten years on a series of new plays exploring the catastrophic consequences of globalization: *YOUTH IN ASIA: A TECHNO FANTASIA* (aka the resistance project), written by Steven Drukman; *FOXHOLLOW* (aka the animal project), by Steven Drukman; *THERE WAS AND THERE WASN'T: AN OLD IRAQI FOLK TALE* (aka the queeraq project), written by Daniel Glen; and *CARLA AND LEWIS* (aka the ecocide project), by Shonni Enelow.

Anselm Franke is a curator and writer based in Berlin, Germany. He is head of the Department of Visual Arts and Film at the Haus der Kulturen der Welt. In 2012, he curated the Taipei Biennial, *Modern Monsters / Death and Life of Fiction*.

His project *Animism* was presented in Antwerp, Bern, Vienna, Berlin, New York, Shenzhen, Seoul, and Beirut in various collaborations from 2010 to 2014. At the Haus der Kulturen der Welt, he has co-curated *The Whole Earth: California and the Disappearance of the Outside* (with Diedrich Diederichsen), and *After Year Zero: Geographies of Collaboration* (both 2013).

Peter Galison is the Joseph Pellegrino University Professor of the History of Science and of Physics at Harvard University. His work explores the interaction between the subcultures of physics—experimentation, instrumentation, and theory—and their embedding in politics and materiality. Among his books are: *How Experiments End* (1987), *Image and Logic: A Material Culture of Microphysics* (1997), *Einstein's Clocks, Poincaré's Maps* (2003), *Objectivity* (with Lorraine Daston) (2007), and (among other co-edited volumes) *The Architecture of Science, Picturing Science; Producing Art, Scientific Authorship; Atmospheric Flight in the Twentieth Century*, and *Einstein for the 21st Century*. To explore the relation of scientific work with larger issues of politics, he has made three documentary films: *Ultimate Weapon: The H-bomb Dilemma* (2000), and, with Robb Moss, *Secrecy* (about national security secrecy and democracy), which premiered at the Sundance Film Festival in 2008. At present, he is completing a book, *Building Crashing Thinking* (on technologies that re-form the self), and a new documentary (also with Robb Moss) on the long-term storage of nuclear waste, *Containment*.

Fabien Giraud was born in 1980 and he presently lives and works in Paris, France. Since 2007, he has collaborated extensively with the artist and filmmaker Raphael Siboni, with whom he has exhibited internationally (Palais de Tokyo, 2008, Musée d'Art Moderne de la Ville de Paris, 2009, Santa Fe Biennial, 2008, and the Moscow Biennial 2009). In 2014, their new body of work entitled *The Unmanned* was presented in a series of monographic shows in Luxembourg (Casino du Luxembourg), Canada (Vox in Montreal), and France (Centre International d'Art et du Paysage de l'Ile de Vassiviere). Apart from this collaboration, he has developed a theoretical and sculptural practice through two long-term projects entitled *Du Mort qui Saisit Le Vif* and *The Marfa Stratum*. The latter will presented in the form of a book (in collaboration with art historian Ida Soulard) on the occasion of his show in Marfa, Texas, in 2015. In 2011, he co-founded a series of seminars and workshops, entitled *The Matter of Contradiction*, which addresses questions regarding the geological concept of the Anthropocene and its consequences for the theory of art. In 2013, he initiated *Glass Bead*, a research platform and a journal, to be launched in 2014 through a series of events in New York, Paris, and Istanbul.

Laura Gustafsson is a Helsinki-based author and theatre-maker. She has published two novels, *Huorasatu* ("Whore Story," 2011) and *Anomalia* ("Anomaly," 2013), and is currently working on her third. She is also the author of several plays, including a radio play series for Finnish public broadcasting company. In her works, Gustafsson has dealt with language, structural violence and the perspectives of the Other, as well as themes of motherhood and power. Her texts draw on everything from mythologies to contemporary media. Together with the artist Terike Haapoja, she established the History of Others project in 2012, which won the Kiila prize for cultural act of the year.

Terike Haapoja is a visual artist, based in Helsinki, Finland. Her work consists of installations and collaborative projects characterized by the use of new media and new technology. In her projects Haapoja investigates our relationship to the non-human world from scientific, existential, and political viewpoints. Her projects are mostly large-scale and built around a thematic framing, often including a working group and collaborations with professionals from other fields of research. Haapoja's work has been shown extensively in solo and group exhibitions and festivals both nationally and internationally. Haapoja is the recipient of numerous awards including the Finnish Art Association's Dukaatti-prize in 2008, Finland Festivals' Young Artist of the year prize in 2007, and the SÄDE prize for best visual design in theatre in 2010. Haapoja represented Finland in the 55th Venice Biennale in 2013. She is currently working on a practice-based PhD at the Academy of Fine Arts in Helsinki. Her research, titled "Technologies of Encounter," examines connections between the use of new technology in contemporary art with natural scientific worldviews and environmental ethics. Haapoja's articles and essays have been published in journals and anthologies in Finland and internationally. www.terikehaapoja.net

Laura Hall My mother (Mohawk/Haudenosaunee) and father (English/Scottish-Canadian) raised my siblings and I in Northern Ontario on Anishinaabe territory. My studies focus on Indigenous knowledge, environmental sustainability, and the gendered renewal of Indigenous worldviews. As a queer/two-spirited and mixed-descent Native woman, I have approached my scholarly work on sustainability and Indigenous renewal from a perspective that not only challenges heteronormative settler-colonialism, but visions alternatives rooted in the gender-fluid/gender-egalitarian concepts of Haudenosaunee governance, economy, and culture.

Donna Haraway is Distinguished Professor Emerita in the History of Consciousness Department at the University of California at Santa Cruz. Her work explores the string figures composed by speculative feminism, speculative fabulation, science and technology studies, and multispecies studies. She earned her PhD in Biology at Yale in 1972, and she taught biology at the University of Hawaii and the history of science at The Johns Hopkins University. Her books include *When Species Meet* (2008), *The Companion Species Manifesto* (2003), *The Haraway Reader* (2004), *Modest_Witness@Second_Millennium* (1997), *Simians, Cyborgs, and Women* (1991), *Primate Visions* (1989), and *Crystals, Fabrics, and Fields* (1976). Haraway's book-in-progress, *Staying with the Trouble*, weaves together human and non-human engagements in multispecies art activisms, histories, ethnographies, technologies, and sciences.

Ho Tzu Nyen makes films, video installations and theatrical performances that are related to his interests in philosophy and history. His works have been shown internationally in museums, galleries, film and performing arts festivals. Ho has had solo exhibitions in Singapore (Substation Gallery, 2003, Galerie Michael Janssen, 2013), Adelaide (Contemporary Art Centre of South Australia, 2007 and 2010), Sydney (Artspace, 2011) and Tokyo (Mori Art Museum, 2012). He represented Singapore at the 54th Venice Biennale (2011). Some group exhibitions he has taken part in include the 26th Bienal de São Paulo (Brazil, 2004), 3rd Fukuoka Asian Art Triennale (Japan, 2005), 1st Singapore Biennale (2006), Thermocline of Art: New Asian Waves (ZKM, Karlsruhe, Germany, 2007), 6th Asia Pacific Triennial (Queensland Art Gallery, Brisbane, Australia, 2009), No Soul for Sale (Tate Modern, London, 2010), 5th Auckland Triennial (Auckland Art Gallery, New Zealand, 2013), No Country (Guggenheim Museum, New York, 2013), 10th Shanghai Biennale (Shanghai Power Station of Art, China, 2014), and the 2nd Kochi-Kuziris Biennale (Kochi, India, 2014). Some of the film festivals that have presented his work include the 41st Director's Fortnight, Cannes International Film Festival (2009), 66th Venice International Film Festival (2009), 64th Locarno Film Festival (2011), Sundance Film Festival (2012) and the 42nd Rotterdam Film Festival (2013). He was also the subject of profile screenings at transmediale 09 (2009) and the 59th Oberhausen Short Film Festival (2013). His theatrical performances have been staged at the Singapore Arts Festival (2008), the Esplanade Theatre Studios (2007, 2012, 2014), KunstenFestivaldesArts in Brussels (2006 and 2008), the Theater der Welt in Mulheim, Germany (2009) and the Wiener Festwochen (2014). Ho Tzu Nyen is currently an artist-in-residence at the DAAD, Berlin.

Oliver Kellhammer is a Canadian land artist, permaculture teacher, activist, and writer. His botanical interventions and public art projects demonstrate nature's surprising ability to recover from damage. His work facilitates the processes of environmental regeneration by engaging the botanical and socio-political underpinnings of the landscape, taking such forms as small-scale urban eco-forestry, inner city community agriculture and the restoration of eroded railway ravines. His process is essentially anti-monumental; as his interventions integrate into the ecological and cultural communities that form around them, his role as artist becomes increasingly obscured. He describes what he does as a kind of catalytic model-making, which lives on as a vehicle for community empowerment while demonstrating methods of positive engagement with the global environmental crisis. Recent articles include: "Violent Reactions," an account of his father's life while working in a plastic factory and "Neo-Eocene" where he makes the case for the reintroduction of prehistoric ecosystems as a strategy for adapting to climate change. His short story "Crush," which explores such realms as bioluminescent deep sea fishes and Japanese model train porn, was nominated for the 2010 Canadian National Magazine Award.

Martha Kenney is Assistant Professor in Women's and Gender Studies at San Francisco State University. She completed her PhD in the History of Consciousness at UC Santa Cruz under the direction of Donna Haraway. Located in the tradition of feminist science studies, her work looks at the politics and possibilities of biological storytelling, both in the lab and in the world. She studies how stories open up and foreclose different *bio-political imaginaries*, how they enliven and inform our relationships with one another and our more-than-human world. Her current project examines and intervenes in the narratives emerging from the new field of environmental epigenetics.

Emily Kutil is a member of the Metabolic Studio and a recent graduate of the Master of Architecture program at the University of Michigan. She lives and works between Los Angeles and Detroit.

Bruno Latour is a professor at Sciences Po, Paris, and director of the Theory of Actor Network and Digital Environments (TARDE) program. He has written extensively on science studies. All references and most of his articles may be found on his website: www.bruno-latour.fr.

Sylvère Lotringer is the General Editor of Semiotext(e), Professor Emeritus in the Department of French and Romance Philology at Columbia University, and a Professor of Foreign Philosophy and Jean Baudrillard Chair at the European Graduate School. He is the author of *Overexposed: Perverting Perversions* (Semioxtext(e), 2013).

Vi Le is a researcher in History and Philosophy of Science. Vi previously completed her MSc degree in the department of Science and Technology Studies at University College London. Her research is broadly construed around the nature of scientific knowledge and the epistemology of secrecy. She is particularly interested in the mutually constitutive workings of science and politics during the Cold War. Her award-winning dissertation examined how Wittgenstein's *Tractatus* was deliberately misinterpreted by Bertrand Russell and the Vienna Circle in order to facilitate their own philosophical and political agenda. Much of her work has been guided by the methodological concern to integrate history and philosophy of science in a way that enables both accounts to illuminate and reinforce each other.

Jeffrey Malecki is an independent, wandering editor, translator, researcher, and chess teacher based in Montréal, Québec. He currently works with the *Scapegoat* architecture journal and the *intercalations* publication series from K. Verlag, as well as other fringe and/or engaged texts.

MAP Office is a multidisciplinary platform devised by Laurent Gutierrez (1966, Casablanca, Morocco) and Valérie Portefaix (1969, Saint-Étienne, France). This duo of artists/architects has been based in Hong Kong since 1996, working on physical and imaginary territories using varied means of expression including drawing, photography, video, installations, performance, and literary and theoretical texts. Their entire project forms a critique of spatio-temporal anomalies and documents how human beings subvert and appropriate space. Humour, games, and fiction are also part of their approach, in the form of small publications providing a further format for disseminating their work. Their cross-disciplinary practice has been the subject of a monograph, *MAP OFFICE – Where the Map is the Territory* (2011), edited by Robin Peckham and published by ODE (Beijing). Map Office was the recipient of the 2013 edition of the Sovereign Asian Art Prize.

Laurent Gutierrez is the co-founder of MAP Office. He is an Associate Professor at the School of Design, Hong Kong Polytechnic University, where he leads the following Master programs: Environment and Interior Design, Design Strategies, and Urban Environments. In addition to his professorial position and artistic practice, Gutierrez is also the co-director of SD SPACE LAB. Valérie Portefaix is the principal of MAP Office. After receiving a Bachelor in Fine Art, and a Master of Architecture degree, she earned a PhD in Urbanism.

Mary Mattingly is a sculptor and photographer based in New York. She creates sculptural ecosystems and interprets them through photography. She views the bureaucratic document as an art form. In 2014 Mattingly collaboratively launched WetLand, a floating ecosystem and artist residency on the Delaware River, and also completed the Flock House Project: three spherical living-systems that were choreographed through New York City's five boroughs. Triple Island was a home and community garden with livestock on the East River built in 2013. She also founded the Waterpod Project, a barge-based public space containing an autonomous habitat that migrated through New York's waterways. Her work has been featured in *Art in America*, *Artforum*, *Grey Room*, *Sculpture Magazine*, *China Business News*, *The New York Times*, *Financial Times*, *Le Monde*, *New Yorker*, *The Wall Street Journal*, on BBC News, MSNBC, Fox, NPR, WNBC, and Art21. Her work is currently part of the International Havana Biennial.

Natasha Myers is an Associate Professor in the Department of Anthropology and a member of the Institute for Science and Technology Studies at York University. She is an anthropologist of science and technology, and examines forms of life in the contemporary arts and biosciences. She completed her PhD in 2007 in the History | Anthropology | STS Program at MIT. Her forthcoming book, *Rendering Life Molecular*, is an ethnography of an interdisciplinary group of scientists who make living substance come to matter at the molecular scale. Her essays and collaborative works have been published in *differences*, *Social Studies of Science*, and *Science Studies*, as well as numerous edited volumes. Her new research project, "Sensing Botanical Sensoria," engages artists and scientists who conduct inquiry into plant sensation and perception. She is the founder of the Plant Studies Collaboratory and co-organizer of Toronto's Technoscience Salon. natashamyers.org.

Mixrice (Cho Jieun, Yang Chulmo) is duo team who explore various traces and processes, routes, results, and memories of circumstances caused by "immigration." Their current work illustrates transportation and evolution of plants, unexpected situations, and contexts around immigrants through photography, video and cartoons. Their work reminds us of an unnamed time between past and present, flattened spaces due to incomprehensible development plans and systematic construction, individuals who do not belong to any place, and moments of absence that we experience. As both artists and curators, Mixrice is capable of all kinds of practices including workshops, cartoons, video, photography, painting, drawing, design, action and writing. Their main exhibitions include: APT7_Asia Pacific Triennale (Gallery of Modern Art, Brisbane, 2012), The Antagonistic Link (Casco, Utrecht, 2009), Dish Antenna (Alternative Space Pool, Seoul, 2008), Activating Korea: Tides of Collective Action (Govett-Brewster Art Gallery, Plymouth, 2007), Bad Boys Here & Now (Gyeonggi Museum of Modern Art, Ansan, 2009), The 6th Gwangju Biennale (Biennale Hall, Gwangju, 2006). Following an artists residency in Cairo, 2010, they published two artists books, *Badly Flattened Land* (Forum A, 2011) and *Message to Dakar* (Sai Comics, 2013).

Jean-Luc Nancy—one of the leading philosophers working in the continental tradition today—is Distinguished Professor of Philosophy at the Université Marc Bloch, Strasbourg, and Georg Wilhelm Friedrich Hegel Chair at the European Graduate School. For the past four decades he has published numerous books on such thinkers as Descartes, Kant, Hegel and Blanchot, and on topics ranging from art and aesthetics; deconstruction and Christianity; to democracy, the political, and the experience of freedom. More than thirty of Nancy's books have been translated into English. Recent titles include: *What's These Worlds Coming To?* (with Aurélien Barrau); *After Fukushima: The Equivalence of Catastrophes*; *Identity: Fragments, Frankness*; *Being Nude: The Skin of Images* (with Federico Ferrari); and *The Pleasure in Drawing*.

Vincent Normand is an art historian, writer and curator living in Paris. His exhibitions projects include *Sinking Islands* (Labor, Mexico City, 2012), *Fun Palace* (Centre Pompidou, Paris, 2010), as well as the three-part project *The Sirens' Stage, Le Stade des Sirènes, Lo stato delle sirene* (David Roberts Art Foundation, Londres; Fondation Kadist, Paris; Fondazione Nomas, Rome, 2010). He is coauthor of the films *Metaxu* (with Fabien Giraud, 2011) and *Counter History of Separation* (with Etienne Chambaud, 2010). From 2010 to 2012 he co-directed the art space FORDE in Geneva, Switzerland, and he is currently MFA teacher in charge of theory and research at ECAL, Lausanne. He is co-director of *Glass Bead*, a journal and international research laboratory (www.glassbead.org). His texts have been published in various reviews and collective publications, and his research has been the object of lectures delivered at the Centre Pompidou (Paris), the Banff Center (Banff, Canada), the Artist's Institute (New York), and the Witte de With (Rotterdam). He is also a member of the SYNAPSE International Curators' Network at the Haus der Kulturen der Welt, Berlin.

Richard W. Pell works at the intersections of science, engineering, and culture. He is the founder of the Center for PostNatural History (CPNH), an outreach organization dedicated to the collection and exposition of lifeforms that have been intentionally altered through selective breeding or genetic engineering. The CPNH operates a permanent exhibition facility in Pittsburgh, Pennsylvania, and produces traveling exhibitions that have appeared in science and art museums throughout Europe and the United States. The CPNH has been awarded a Rockefeller New Media fellowship, a Creative Capital fellowship, a Smithsonian research fellowship, support from Waag Society, and ongoing support from the Kindle Project.

John Paul Ricco is the author of *The Logic of the Lure*, and *The Decision Between Us: Art and Ethics in the Time of Scenes* (both from the University of Chicago Press). He is currently completing a third book in this trilogy on "the intimacy of the outside," titled: *The Outside Not Beyond: Pornographic Faith and the Economy of the Eve*. Recent publications include: "Pornographic Faith: Two Sources of Naked Sense at the Limits of Belief and Humiliation," in *Porn Archives*, edited by Tim Dean, Steven Ruszczycky, and David Squires (Duke University Press); "Drool: Liquid Forespeech of the Fore-scene" in a special issue of the online journal *World Picture* on "Abandon" and "The Separated Gesture: Partaking in the Inoperative Praxis of the Already-Unmade," in *Jean-Luc Nancy and the Political*, edited by Sanja Dejanovic (Edinburgh University Press). Ricco is Associate Professor of Contemporary Art, Media Theory, and Culture in the Department of Visual Studies, and Graduate Professor in the Centre for Comparative Literature, at the University of Toronto. He is a 2015–16 Chancellor Jackman Faculty Research Fellow at the Jackman Humanities Institute, University of Toronto, where he will continue his research on "The Collective Afterlife of Things."

Tomás Saraceno studied art and architecture. He lives and works on this planet earth and beyond. His works have also been shown at a variety of museums and major installations including the Venice Biennale 2009, the São Paulo Biennial in 2006, Bonniers Konsthall in Stockholm in 2010, the Hamburger Bahnhof in Berlin in 2011, on the roof of the Metropolitan Museum in New York in 2012, the Hangar Bicocca in Milan 2012, and currently at K21 in Düsseldorf 2013. Saraceno was artist-in-residence at the International Space Studies Program of NASA in the summer of 2009. He was in residency at the MIT Center for Art, Science Technology (CAST) in 2012, and was visiting artist for the Paris Atelier program at Columbia University's Graduate School of Architecture 2013. He is currently participating in a residency at the Centre National D'Études Spatiales (CNES). He is the 2009/10 Winner of the Calder Price and Calder Residency. Tomás enjoys cooperation with other disciplines and is the co-author of several scientific papers. He is currently director of the New Art Institute at the Technical University of Braunschweig.

Ada Smailbegović is a PhD Candidate in the Department of English and American Literature at New York University. She is completing her dissertation, "Poetics of Liveliness: Literary Experiments in Natural Histories of Matter," in which she addresses the way that twentieth and twenty-first century writers, including Gertrude Stein, Francis Ponge, Christian Bök, and Lisa Robertson draw on history of science and philosophies of materiality to construct poems about natural phenomena that range from the molecular scale of DNA and proteins, to moss, snails, and clouds. She is currently at work on two publications: an article on the poetics of matter in the work of the physicist Karen Barad for the journal *Rhizomes*, and a poem "Of the Dense and Rare," based on the work of Francis Bacon, commissioned by the digital publishing platform Triple Canopy. In July 2015, she will take up the position of Assistant Professor of English at Brown University.

smudge studio Since 2005, smudge studio has pursued what we take to be our most urgent and meaningful task as artists and humans: to invent and enact practices capable of acknowledging and living in responsive relationship to forces of change that make the world. Through our current projects and performative research, we design and cultivate embodied practices that support us in paying nuanced attention to the fast and intense material realities that area now emerging on a planetary scale—without leaving us reeling in states of distraction or despair.

Elizabeth Ellsworth is Professor of Media Studies at the New School, New York. Elizabeth's research and teaching focus on media and change, the design of mediated learning environments, and documentary media forms. Her scholarship consists of projects and practices that fuse performative research with aesthetic experience and public pedagogy. She translates the results of her research into media forms and exhibitions. She is the author of *Places of Learning: Media, Architecture, Pedagogy* (Routledge, 2004) and T*eaching Positions: Difference, Pedagogy and the Power of Address* (Teachers College Press, 1997). She has served as a consultant on pedagogical design for museums and design schools. She is co-founder, with Jamie Kruse, of a nonprofit media arts collaboration: smudgestudio.org. smudge has received funding from a variety of international foundations to produce and exhibit work on the material conditions of life and learning in the Anthropocene. Elizabeth earned her PhD in Communication Arts from the University of Wisconsin-Madison.

Jamie Kruse is an artist, designer and part-time faculty at Parsons, The New School for Design (New York, NY). In 2005, she co-founded smudge studio, with Elizabeth Ellsworth, based in Brooklyn, NY. Her work has been supported by the Graham Foundation for Advanced Studies in the Fine Arts, The New School Green Fund (Office of Sustainability, The New School); New York State Council for the Arts (2010, 2011) and the Brooklyn Arts Council. She has exhibited and presented her work both nationally and internationally. In the spring of 2014 she was a guest researcher for Future North (AHO Oslo). She is the author of the Friends of the Pleistocene blog, (fopnews.wordpress.com) and has co-edited a collection of essays with Elizabeth Ellsworth entitled, *Making the Geologic Now: Responses to Material Conditions of Contemporary Life* (punctum books, 2012).

Peter Sloterdijk, philosopher, cultural theorist, essayist, has been a freelance writer since the 1980s, with publications on questions about time diagnostics, culture and the philosophy of religion, art theory and psychology. From 1989 to 2008, he was director of the Institute for Cultural Philosophy at the Academy of Fine Arts in Vienna. Since 1992, he has been Professor of Philosophy and Media Theory at the Karlsruhe University of Arts and Design, and since 2001, Rector of the Karlsruhe University of Arts and Design. His recent publications in English include: *Spheres Volume II. Globes: Macrospherology* (Semiotext(e), 2014); *In the World Interior of Capital* (Polity Press, 2013); *You Must Change Your Life: On Anthropotechnics* (Polity Press, 2013); *Spheres Volume I. Bubbles: Microspherology* (Semiotext(e), 2011); and, *Neither Sun Nor Death*, translated by Steve Corcoran (Los Angeles: Semiotext(e), 2011).

Karolina Sobecka works with animation, design, interactivity, computer games and other media and formats. Her work often engages public space and explores the ways we interact with the world we create. Karolina received her BFA from the School of the Art Institute of Chicago and her MFA from Calarts in Experimental Animation/Integrated Media. She has also studied and taught in the University of Washington's DXARTS PhD program. Karolina's work has been shown internationally, including at the V&A, MOMA Film, Science Gallery, Beall Center for Art and Technology, ISEA and Zero1. She has received awards from, among others, NYFA, Creative Capital, Princess Grace Foundation, Rhizome, Platform International Animation Festival, Vida Art and Artificial Life Awards, and the Japan Media Arts Festival.

Ida Soulard was born in 1985. She lives and works in Paris, France. Soulard is an art historian and writer. She currently works as the research program director for Fieldwork: Marfa, an international research program run by les beaux-arts de Nantes (France)/HEAD-Geneva (Switzerland). She worked as an assistant curator for the cultural department of La Monnaie de Paris and as a teaching assistant at Science Po Paris, and currently teaches at les beaux-arts de Nantes and the CAPC in Bordeaux. She co-founded the series of seminars and workshops entitled *The Matter of Contradiction* in 2011, and is currently working on a book co-written with artist Fabien Giraud, entitled *The Marfa Stratum*. She collaborates regularly with a diverse range of specialized magazines.

Anna-Sophie Springer is an independent curator, editor, and co-director of the art press K. Verlag, exploring the book as a site for exhibitions, based in Berlin. She has MAs in Contemporary Art Theory from Goldsmiths College, London, and in Curatorial Studies from the Hochschule für Grafik und Buchkunst, Leipzig. In 2014, she was Associate Editor of publications for the 8th Berlin Biennale as well as the Craig-Kade Visiting Scholar at Rutgers University, NJ; she has previously worked as Editor for the pioneering German theory publisher Merve Verlag, before launching K. in 2011. Anna-Sophie is a member of the HKW's SYNAPSE International Curators' Network at the Haus der Kulturen der Welt, Berlin, where she co-edits *intercalations*, a book-as-exhibition series co-published by K. in the framework of the HKW's "Anthropocene Project." Co-curated together with Etienne Turpin, the exhibition cycle *125,660 Specimens of Natural History* on the enduring legacy of Alfred R. Wallace's Malay expedition will premier at Komunitas Salihara, Jakarta, Indonesia in the summer of 2015 and travel to Berlin in 2016. She has translated books and essays by authors including Beatrice Preciado, Nina Power, Mark von Schlegell, and Reza Negarestani; her own writing was published in various publications, including *C Magazine*, *Rheinsprung*, *Fillip*, and *Scapegoat*.

Richard Streitmatter-Tran (b. 1972, Bien Hoa, Vietnam) is an artist and researcher based in Ho Chi Minh City where he directs the contemporary arts initiative Dia/projects. Working primarily in sculpture and drawing, his solo and collaborative work has been exhibited throughout Asia and Europe, including: the 52nd Venice Biennale; Asia Triennial Manchester 2011; 4th Guanghou Triennale; Shenzhen & Hong Kong Bi-city Biennale of Urbanism and Architecture; the Singapore Biennale 2006 and 2008; the 2004 Gwangju Biennale, 2005; ZKM/Karlsruhe, the Singapore Art Museum, and the Palais de Tokyo. Writing, education, criticism and curatorial projects include The Rotterdam Dialogues at Witte de With, the Para/Site curatorial programme in Hong Kong, The SYNAPSE Curators' Network at the Haus der Kulturen der Welt/Berlin, Times Museum in Guangzhou, China, The Asian Art Space Network (AASN) in Korea, and the co-curation of The Mekong platform for Sixth Asia Pacific Triennial (APT6) at the Queensland Art Gallery/GoMA in 2009. He was a Teaching Assistant at Harvard University (2000–2004), conducted media arts research at the MIT Media Lab (2000), and was Visiting Lecturer at the Ho Chi Minh Fine Arts University in 2003. He returned to Boston in 2012 to receive the Alumni Award from the Massachusetts College of Art. From 2006–2015 he was Senior Lecturer at RMIT University Vietnam. Working with Le Vi as the collaborative "Vile Rats," they investigate the interrelations between history, science and philosophy, often reframing their research through contemporary art.

Bronislaw Szerszynski is Senior Lecturer at the Department of Sociology, Lancaster University, UK, where he also works at the Centre for the Study of Environmental Change (CSEC). His highly interdisciplinary research crosses the social and natural sciences, arts and humanities, and situates the changing relationship between humans, environment and technology in the longer perspective of human and planetary history. His recent work, including both academic publications and multi-media performance pieces, explores themes such as the Anthropocene, geoengineering and the interplanetary. Szerszynski is the author of *Nature, Technology and the Sacred* (2005), and co-editor of *Risk, Environment and Modernity* (1996), *Re-Ordering Nature* (2003) and *Nature Performed* (2003). He has organized or co-organized a number of events with a major arts component, including *Between Nature: Explorations in Ecology and Performance* (Lancaster, 2000), *Experimentality*, a year-long collaborative research programme on experimentation in the sciences, arts and wider society (Lancaster/Manchester/London, 2009–10), and *Anthropocene Monument*, with Bruno Latour and Olivier Michelon (Les Abattoirs, Toulouse, 2014–2015).

Zoe Todd (Métis) is from Amiskwaciwâskahikan (Edmonton) in the Treaty Six Area of Alberta, Canada. She writes about Indigeneity, art, architecture, decolonization and healing in urban contexts. She also studies human-animal relations, colonialism and environmental change in northern Canada. Her art practice incorporates writing, spoken word, beading, drawing and film to tell stories about being Métis in the Prairies. She is a PhD Candidate in Social Anthropology at the University of Aberdeen and is a 2011 Pierre Elliott Trudeau Foundation Scholar. In July, she will be Assistant Professor of Sociology and Anthropology at Carleton University.

Etienne Turpin is a philosopher studying, curating, designing, and writing about complex urban systems, political economies of data and infrastructure, visual culture and aesthetic practices, and Southeast Asian colonial-scientific history. At the University of Wollongong, Australia, Etienne is a Vice-Chancellor's Postdoctoral Research Fellow with the SMART Infrastructure Facility, Faculty of Engineering & Information Sciences, and an Associate Research Fellow with the Australian Center for Cultural Environmental Research. In Jakarta, Indonesia, Etienne is the director of anexact office and co-principal investigator of PetaJakarta.org. Through strategic community organizing, institutional ethnography, and novel approaches to social media platforms, data-gathering, and designed engagement, Etienne's research develops new tools, techniques, and methods to democratize processes of urban transformation by meaningfully engaging the concerns and capacities of the urban poor. As a member of the SYNAPSE International Curators' Network of the Haus der Kulturen der Welt in Berlin, Germany, he is the co-editor of *intercalations: paginated exhibition* series as part of Das Anthropozän-Projekt. Etienne is the editor of *Architecture in the Anthropocene: Encounters Among Design, Deep Time, Science, and Philosophy* (Ann Arbor: Open Humanities Press, 2013), co-editor of *Fantasies of the Library* (Berlin: K. Verlag & Haus der Kulturen der Welt, 2015), *Land & Animal & Nonanimal* (Berlin: K. Verlag & Haus der Kulturen der Welt, 2015), and *Jakarta: Architecture + Adaptation* (Depok: Universitas Indonesia Press, 2013). He has taught visual culture, theory, and urban design at the University of California Berkeley, the University of Michigan, and the University of Toronto. http://anexact.org

Pinar Yoldas is a Turkish cross-disciplinary artist/researcher and a neuroenthusiast. Her research investigates the two-sided dynamics between cultural and biological systems. Based on her varied background in architecture, interface design, computing and neuroscience she seeks to enhance the transformative power of art through the creation of hybrid artforms. Pinar has been awarded fellowships in art and science venues including the MacDowell Colony, UCross Foundation , VCCA and National Evolutionary Synthesis Center. She was the recipient of the Transmediale Villem Flusser Art/Theory Award for her project "An Ecosystem of Excess," on the Pacific Trash Vortex and was awarded a Guggenheim Fellowship in 2015. Yoldas holds an MFA from University of California Los Angeles and is currently is a PhD student in Visual and Media Studies program at Duke University, as well as pursuing a certificate in the Center for Cognitive Neuroscience. Prior to her education in the United States, she received a BArch from Middle East Technical University, an MA from Istanbul Bilgi University and an MS from Istanbul Technical University. She holds a bronze medal in organic chemistry in the national science olympics and had her first solo painting exhibition when she was five.

Marina Zurkow builds animations and participatory environments that are centred on humans and their relationship to animals, plants and the weather, that engage audiences using video, software, sculpture, print graphics, food, and public interventions. Recent solo exhibitions of her work include bitforms gallery in New York; the Montclair Art Museum, New Jersey; Diverseworks, Houston; and she has also been featured at FACT, Liverpool; San Francisco Museum of Modern Art; Walker Art Center, Minneapolis; Smithsonian American Art Museum, Washington D.C.; Museum of Fine Arts, Houston; Wave Hill, New York; National Museum for Women in the Arts, Washington D.C.; Bennington College, Vermont; Borusan Collection, Istanbul; Pacific Northwest College of Art, Oregon; Marian Spore, New York; 01SJ Biennial, San Jose; Brooklyn Academy of Music; Museum of the Moving Image, New York; Creative Time, New York; The Kitchen, New York; Ars Electronica, Linz, Austria; Transmediale, Berlin; Eyebeam, New York; Sundance Film Festival, Utah; Rotterdam Film Festival, The Netherlands; and the Seoul Media City Biennial, Korea, among others. Zurkow is the recipient of a 2011 John Simon Guggenheim Memorial Fellowship, and has been granted awards from the New York Foundation for the Arts, New York State Council for the Arts, the Rockefeller Foundation, and Creative Capital. She is on faculty at NYU's Interactive Technology Program (ITP), and lives in Brooklyn, NY. She is represented by bitforms gallery.

Permissions

Photographs reproduced with permission on pages 30, 56, 108, 166 and 212 courtesy of SLUB Dresden / Deutsche Fotothek / Fritz Eschen.

Edenic Apocalypse: Singapore's End-of-Time Botanical Tourism,
by Natasha Myers
    Copyright retained by the author / artist.

Becoming Aerosolar: From Solar Sculptures to Cloud Cities,
by Tomas Saraceno, Sasha Engelmann, and Bruno Szerszyski
    Copyright retained by the author / artist.

In the Planetarium: The Modern Museum on the Anthropocenic Stage
by Vincent Normand
    Fig. 01 courtesy of the Los Angeles, California Historical Society Collection.
    Fig. 02 courtesy of the Bibliothèque nationale de France.
    Fig. 03 copyright retained by the author / artist.

Physical Geology / The Library
by Illana Halperin
    Copyright retained by the author / artist.

Cloud Writing: Soft Architectures in Lisa Robertson's Poetics
by Ada Smailbegovic
    Fig. 01 courtesy of Diller + Scofidio; copyright Diller + Scofidio.
    Fig. 02 from Luke Howard's *Essay on the Modifications of Clouds* (London: John Churchill & Sons, 1865).
    Fig. 03 from Luke Howard's *Essay on the Modifications of Clouds* (London: John Churchill & Sons, 1865).

The Cerumen Strata: From Figures to Configurations
by Richard Streitmatter-Tran & Vi Le
    Copyright retained by the author / artist.

Geochemistry and Other Planetary Perspectives
by Ursula Biemann
    Copyright retained by the author / artist.

Images do not show: The desire to see in the Anthropocene
by Irmgard Emmelheinz
    Fig. 01 courtesy of Michael Witt.
    Fig. 02 courtesy of Michael Witt.
    Fig. 03 from the collection of the author.

Design Specs in the Anthropocene
by smudge studio (Jamie Kruse & Elizabeth Ellsworth)
    Copyright retained by the author / artist.

The Marfa Stratification
by Ida Soulard & Fabien Giraud
    Copyright retained by the author / artist.

We're Tigers
by Ho Tzu Nyen,
    Copyright retained by the author / artist.

Technologies of Uncertainty in the Search for MH370
by Lindsay Bremner
    Fig. 01 courtesy of AFP/Getty Images.
    Fig. 02 courtesy of the *Washington Post*.

Last Clouds
by Karolina Sobecka
    Copyright retained by the author / artist.

Islands & Other Invisible Territories
by Laurent Gutierrez & Valérie Portefaix (MAP Office),
    Copyright retained by the author / artist.

Plants That Evolve (in some way or another)
by Mixrice (Cho Jieun & Yang Chulmo)
    Copyright retained by the author / artist.

Indigenizing the Anthropocene
by Zoe Todd
    Copyright retained by the author / artist.

Anthropocene, Capitalocene, Chthulhocene
by Donna Haraway & Martha Kenney
    Fig. 01 courtesy of the Institute for Figuring.
    Fig. 02 courtesy of the Institute for Figuring.

Ecologicity, Vision and the Neurological System
by Amanda Boetzkes
    Fig. 01 courtesy of Mariele Neudecker.
    Fig. 02 courtesy of Mel Chin.
    Fig. 03 courtesy of Mariele Neudecker.
    Fig. 04 courtesy of Levi van Veluw.

A History According to Cattle
by Terike Haapoja & Laura Gustafsson
    Copyright retained by the author / artist.

Dear Climate
by Marina Zurkow, Oliver Kellhammer, Fritz Ertl & Una Chaudhuri
    Copyright retained by the author / artist.

Public Smog
by Amy Balkin
    Copyright retained by the author / artist.

Life & Death in the Anthropocene: A Short History of Plastic
by Heather Davis
    Fig. 01 courtesy of Gerd Ludwig/National Geographic Creative.

Ecosystems of Excess
by Pinar Yoldas
    Copyright retained by the author / artist.

www.ingramcontent.com/pod-product-compliance
Lightning Source LLC
Chambersburg PA
CBHW051353220526
45469CB00001B/234